MAKING THE MODERN CRIMINAL LAW

Making the Modern Criminal Law

Criminalization and Civil Order

LINDSAY FARMER

Professor of Law, University of Glasgow

OXFORD

UNIVERSITY PRESS

OXFORD
UNIVERSITY PRESS

Great Clarendon Street, Oxford, OX2 6DP,
United Kingdom

Oxford University Press is a department of the University of Oxford.
It furthers the University's objective of excellence in research, scholarship,
and education by publishing worldwide. Oxford is a registered trade mark of
Oxford University Press in the UK and in certain other countries

First Edition published in 2016
Impression: 1

Published in the United States of America by Oxford University Press
198 Madison Avenue, New York, NY 10016, United States of America

British Library Cataloguing in Publication Data
Data available

Library of Congress Control Number: 2015956791

ISBN 978–0–19–956864–2

Printed and bound by
CPI Group (UK) Ltd, Croydon, CR0 4YY

Acknowledgements

This book has been a long time in the making. In some ways it is hard to remember a time when I didn't seem to be working on it, or at least on one of a number of different projects and studies that, in my own head, I saw as being linked to the bigger project that has finally come together in this book. Inevitably, then, I have incurred a large number of debts, both personal and institutional.

The immediate catalyst for writing the book was the AHRC funded project on Criminalization (Grant No.128737) which ran between 2008 and 2012. Although I was initially a little sceptical about the choice of criminalization as a topic, and whether I might have anything to contribute to criminal law theory in this area, I came to see that the theme of criminalization was a way of bringing together a number of my own interests in the area. I am immensely grateful to the AHRC for their financial support which made this possible and to the colleagues too numerous to mention who gave up their time to meet with us and contribute to our workshops and discussions. I owe a particular debt to the core team—Andrew Cornford, Antony Duff, Christine Kelly, Sandra Marshall, Massimo Renzo, and Victor Tadros.

The School of Law at the University of Glasgow has provided a supportive environment throughout this project. Long-suffering students have been patient as I tried out ill-formed ideas in my 'Criminal Law: History and Theory' seminar. And in recent years we have been lucky enough to have a growing group of enthusiastic postgraduate students in the area of criminal law who have contributed greatly to making the School a stimulating place to work. Amongst colleagues, I would like to thank James Chalmers and Fiona Leverick in particular. They have both read long sections of the manuscript, listened patiently while I tried to clarify what I was trying to do, and helped by providing thoughtful comments, support, and knowledge of criminal law. Antony Duff was kind enough to organize a workshop on the manuscript in Glasgow in November 2014. I am very grateful to those colleagues and students who gave up their time to participate in the workshop, and especially to the commentators on specific chapters: Andrew Cornford, Emilios Christodoulidis, Chloe Kennedy, Sarah Summers, Antony Duff, and Sandra Marshall. The contributions of all greatly stimulated, and challenged, my thinking. In addition to this, numerous colleagues and friends read and commented on sections of the manuscript in draft. Thanks in particular to Stuart Green, Jeremy Horder, Chloe Kennedy (again), Claes Lernestedt, Arlie Loughnan, Ngaire Naffine, Martino Mona, Peter Ramsay and Barry Wright. I would also like particularly to thank Scott Veitch, sadly no longer in Glasgow, who read several chapters and provided detailed and helpful comments on responsibility and civil order.

The University of Glasgow supported two periods of study leave connected with the project, the second of which enabled me to spend a year at the Faculty of Law at the University of Toronto. This was a tremendous place to work and I benefited greatly from the wider perspective on the development of the law that being in Canada offered. I was lucky enough to test some initial ideas in the hospitable environment of the Criminal Law Sciences Club. I would like to thank Alan Brudner, Vincent Chiao, David Dyzenhaus, Markus Dubber, Angela Fernandez, Marty Friedland, Karen Knop, Mayo Moran, Jim Phillips, Martha Shaffer, Hamish Stewart, Mariana Valverde, and Stephen Waddams, all of whom contributed in different ways to making my visit there a particularly enjoyable experience. I owe a particular debt to two colleagues at Toronto. Simon Stern was enthusiastic and knowledgeable about many diverse aspects of the history of the criminal law and assisted in particular with my reading of Blackstone. He also read and commented on substantial portions of the manuscript. And Markus Dubber's role as commentator, host, interlocutor, and friend has been immeasurable. Much of the book has emerged from the extended and wide-ranging conversation that I have been engaged in with him since our first meeting over 10 years ago. He has been an enthusiastic supporter of this project and has contributed in many different ways.

I have been extremely fortunate to have the support and encouragement of Niki Lacey who read most of the manuscript, sometimes more than once, and often at extremely short notice. She was talking about the importance of criminalization long before it became fashionable to do so, and has also long argued the need for forms of jurisprudence beyond philosophical jurisprudence. Her influence on my work has been profound, and her friendship over many years has meant a great deal to me.

I have already mentioned them, but must offer further thanks to Antony Duff, Sandra Marshall, and Victor Tadros. I have been very fortunate to work together closely with them for a period of over 10 years, surviving the move of Victor to Warwick and Antony and Sandra to Minnesota (for a time). This group has been the model of an academic community. They have individually and collectively been unfailingly supportive and encouraging, and their impact on the shape and argument of the book has been great.

Jose Manuel Fernandez gave invaluable support in preparing the bibliography and getting the manuscript ready for publication. Jenny Scott helped out by preparing the index. I am also extremely grateful to the staff at Oxford University Press, in particular to Natasha Flemming and Elinor Shields who waited patiently as deadlines were extended—and who have been professional in seeing the book through the production process.

Finally, my greatest debt, both intellectual and personal, is to Sarah Armstrong. I literally could not have written the book without her. She has contributed in many different ways: to the formation of the ideas; as a stern critic of my writing style; through endless encouragement and enthusiasm; and by keeping things together at home with the support of Thomas and Lucas. She is my best reader, and much much more. I am sorry that it took so long, and I hope that in the end it has been worth the wait.

Glasgow
July 2015

Table of Contents

'Who here can give reasons of any different kind for believing that half the criminal law does not do more harm than good?'

OW Holmes (*Collected Legal Papers*, p.139)

Introduction

This is a book about criminalization—what and who should be treated as criminal under the law and the ways that this can be justified. It is thus about making criminal law in the conventional sense. It aims to make a contribution to the vital and important contemporary debates about the proper scope of the criminal law and of the kind of principles that should guide legislatures, courts, and other law enforcement agencies in determining that scope. My starting point, though, is rather different from most of the contributions to the recent debate. Instead of beginning by asking what principle or principles should guide us in defining or limiting the scope of state action, I ask what I see as the prior question of how it is that the question of criminalization has come to be framed in these terms. And, going further, I want to look at the development of the institutional conditions that underpin and make possible our contemporary understanding of criminalization. This is a matter of placing the emergence of this question in an account of the development of the modern institution of criminal law. The book is thus about the making of the modern criminal law in this much broader sense.

It has become commonplace now to remark on the recent and rather sudden emergence of criminalization as a topic in criminal law theory. Writing in 1995, Niki Lacey noted the striking absence of questions of criminalization from academic discussion of criminal law theory, dominated at the time by discussions of theories of subjective liability and criminal responsibility, and remarked that many of the conceptual issues discussed in legal theory could, and perhaps should, be understood in terms of their implications for criminalization.[1] Some twenty years later it is equally striking that criminalization has now become one of the dominant themes of academic criminal law theory. There are a number of new monographs on the topic, which is also routinely addressed in textbooks; and the leading criminal law and theory journals have published special issues on aspects of criminalization.[2] Some

[1] N Lacey, 'Contingency and Criminalisation' in I Loveland, *Frontiers of Criminality* (London: Sweet & Maxwell, 1995).

[2] E.g. D Husak, *Overcriminalization* (Oxford: Oxford UP, 2008), AP Simester & A von Hirsch, *Crimes, Harms and Wrongs. On the Principles of Criminalisation* (Oxford: Hart Publishing, 2011); D Baker, *The Right Not to Be Criminalized* (Farnham: Ashgate, 2011). For textbooks, see AP Simester et al., *Simester and Sullivan's Criminal Law. Theory and Doctrine* (5th edn) (Oxford: Hart Publishing, 2013) Ch.16; J Herring, *Criminal Law. Text, Cases and Materials* (5th edn) (Oxford: Oxford UP, 2012) Ch.1. For special issues of journals, see e.g. Citizenship and Criminalization (2010) 13(2) *NCLR* 181; Overcriminalization (2011) 14(1) *NCLR* 1; Vice and the Criminal Law (2013) 7(1)

of this literature, taking its cue from the influential work of Husak, can be seen as responding to a process of 'over-criminalization'. For these writers, the question is framed in terms of the perceived recent growth in the criminal law, both in terms of legislation and enforcement, and asks the question of how this activity might be limited. Much of the literature takes a fundamental approach, arguing that in order to understand criminalization it is necessary to go back to basics: the approach is not to ask about how to limit state power, but more fundamentally how the relationship between state and citizen should be conceived, and about the proper place of the criminal law in this relationship.[3] What these approaches share is a common understanding of the problem of criminalization—as a problem of determining the proper scope of the criminal law—and of the kind of theoretical framework within which this topic should be addressed—that is, as a problem primarily of moral and political philosophy. As a general approach then, this places these approaches to theorizing criminalization firmly within a tradition of liberal theorizing about the role and limits of the state. This, however, is generally seen as an ahistorical question as neither approach demonstrates a particular awareness of its own history. There is a routine invocation of those theorists who are seen as predecessors—notably John Stuart Mill—with an acknowledgement that while Mill wrote on liberty and the limits of state action, he was not addressing the use of the criminal law specifically. That few other eighteenth- and nineteenth-century writers can readily be identified reflects the fact that 'criminalization', as we understand the term, was not an issue of concern. There was, it is true, a vast amount of contemporary discussion of the criminal law, but it did not discuss questions of criminalization as such. This, I shall show in this book, was for a reason, and if we are to understand the significance of contemporary debates, it is also important to understand why the 'criminalization question' was apparently neglected in earlier periods.

The contemporary understanding of criminalization as a problem of legal theory can more readily be traced to the revival of legal theory stimulated by the work of HLA Hart and others in the 1960s. In the United Kingdom, this was framed by the celebrated Hart-Devlin debate about the decriminalization of 'morals offences', principally the decriminalization of private homosexual conduct as recommended by the Wolfenden Committee in 1957. As is well known, Hart defended the idea, drawn from Mill, that the limits of the criminal law should be understood in terms of the 'harm principle': that the only reason the criminal law could intervene in private conduct was to prevent harm to others. He thus took the general Millian claim about the limits of state action and linked it specifically to a claim about the proper scope of the criminal law.[4] Lord Devlin, by contrast, adopted a position with its origins in a more traditional understanding of the

Criminal Law and Philosophy; Symposium on Law, Liberty and Morality (2013) 7(3) *Criminal Law and Philosophy*.

[3] For a review see RA Duff et al., 'Introduction' in RA Duff et al., *The Boundaries of the Criminal Law* (Oxford: Oxford UP, 2010); Duff et al., 'Introduction' in Duff et al., *Criminalization. The Political Morality of the Criminal Law* (Oxford: Oxford UP, 2014).

[4] HLA Hart, *Law, Liberty and Morality* (Oxford: Oxford UP, 1963).

common law. In his view, society was bound together by certain common moral understandings or standards. It was the function of the criminal law to reflect and preserve those understandings; and if the law failed to do so then there was a risk that society would disintegrate.[5] Whatever the rights and wrongs of these views, it is clear that Hart's views were more closely in tune with the emerging 'permissiveness' and modernizing ethos of the period and were drawn on in support of further liberalizing reforms, notably the decriminalization of some forms of homosexual conduct in 1967. However, whatever its significance at the time, the Hart-Devlin debate more generally could be packaged and taught to students in the ever-expanding number of university law degrees as a problem of jurisprudence that could be applied to a range of different areas and problems. Most importantly for our purposes, it came to be understood as framing the question of criminalization in terms of a debate between consequentialist conceptions of 'harm' and non-consequentialist theories of 'legal moralism'—even if, as we shall see, the content of these terms has shifted considerably in recent discussions.

Notwithstanding the attractions of Hart and Devlin as a simple framework for illustrating some conceptual issues, this story is plainly inadequate as an account of the origins of our modern understanding of criminalization. But this is not a minor issue for, as we shall see, it has significant implications for how we might go about theorizing criminalization. My first concern is that it finesses the gap between recent debates and the longer liberal tradition. The period between the 1860s, when Mill wrote, and the 1960s of Hart and Devlin is elided, with the writers treated as though they are addressing an identical set of issues. And this is then presented as part of a longer liberal tradition running from Hobbes and Locke to the present day. This allows the question of criminalization to be presented as an ahistorical question of the limits of state power. The kind of issues that this theory might apply to then appear as purely contingent—be it sedition and treason in the 1840s, 'morals' offences in the 1960s, or 'preventive' offences or over-legislation at the turn of the twenty-first century. The questions of how and why these topics get framed as problems for the criminal law is not addressed and, more importantly, the question of how the role or function of the criminal law is understood in particular periods—and hence how this might shape understandings of what is 'proper' for the criminal law—is passed over. Second, this understanding offers neither a particularly convincing explanation of its own contemporary significance nor of the place of criminalization within a broader tradition. Between the 1960s and the 1980s, theories of criminalization were concerned with the *de*-criminalization of morals offences. By contrast, much of the recent debate is about problems of 'over-legislation', with a theory of criminalization being understood in terms of how to limit the legislative capacities of the state or of how constitutional constraints or courts might restrain legislation. How should we understand these differences? Is criminalization just about limits and morals offences, or do these changes reflect more fundamental shifts in

[5] P Devlin, *The Enforcement of Morals* (Oxford: Oxford UP, 1965).

the function and scope of the criminal law? But to present the question in these terms is to raise a further set of questions about how criminal law relates to the modern state.[6] Finally, as I shall suggest below, the concept of criminalization is itself linked to the emergence of a certain modern understanding of the criminal law, and for this reason it cannot properly be understood except in this kind of historical perspective.

The *Oxford English Dictionary* gives two main meanings for the verb 'to criminalize'.[7] The first is, 'to turn a person into a criminal, esp. by making his or her activities criminal'. This draws a direct analogy with the French term '*criminaliser*', meaning to accuse, and most of the early usages listed relate to the accusing of particular individuals with having committed crimes. It is not until the middle of the nineteenth century, that it takes on a more modern (and sociological) sense of defining individuals or groups as criminal or deviant in some way.[8] The second meaning is more familiar from philosophical writings on the topic and is 'to turn (an activity) into a criminal offence by making it illegal'. However, this 'legislative' understanding is relatively recent in origin. The first recorded usage in this sense listed dates only from 1832 and is (not surprisingly) from Jeremy Bentham. What is surprising, though, is that in using the term he is not referring to a legislative process, or at least not directly: 'Asceticism has sought to brand and criminalize the desires to which nature has confided the perpetuity of the species'.[9] It is not until the end of the century that it is listed as being used to refer directly to a formal legislative process, in a statement taken from the *Columbia Law Review* in 1906: 'it may confiscate the goods... or criminalize the selling of them'.[10] What tentative conclusions can be drawn from this? The first is that to understand criminalization in this sense is connected to the emergence of a certain kind of modern legislative mentality. The world was seen in accordance with certain principles of order that could be known and manipulated if there were adequate knowledge and understanding.[11] The criminal law could thus be seen as a kind of instrument which might produce positive or negative social effects, and which should be used accordingly. Second, this understanding of the term does not pre-date the existence of modern legislative bodies that actively pass laws to make certain activities

[6] Cf A Ashworth & L Zedner, *Preventive Justice* (Oxford: Oxford UP, 2014) and P Ramsay, *The Insecurity State* (Oxford: Oxford UP, 2012) both of which analyse the contemporary criminal law in terms of changes in the form of the state. These are discussed further in Ch.3 Section V.

[7] 'criminalize, v.'. OED Online. December 2013 Oxford University Press, accessed 3 March 2014 http://www.oed.com.ezproxy.lib.gla.ac.uk/view/Entry/271579?redirectedFrom=criminalisation.

[8] Thus from the *Law Magazine* in 1854: 'Young offenders had better be reformed than criminalized' (1854) 20 (ns) *Law Magazine* at p.52.

[9] *Principles of Penal Law*, III, v, in (Bowring ed.), *Works* (Edinburgh: Wm Tait, 1838) I, 544/1.

[10] W Trickett, 'The Original Package Ineptitude' (1906) 6 *Columbia LR* 161 at p.169.

[11] Z Bauman, *Legislators and Interpreters. On Modernity, Post-Modernity and Intellectuals* (Cambridge: Polity, 1987). Bauman notes the emergence of other 'active' verbs in the same period: 'An action... turned upon an outside object; an action which aims at transforming the said object; and not just a random transformation, but one whose end result is known and approved in advance'. 'On the Origins of Civilisation: A Historical Note' (1985) 2 *Theory, Culture and Society*, 7 at p.7.

or conduct criminal, and indeed more positively can be associated with the emergence of modern parliaments. To be sure, conduct was made criminal by law prior to this, but the legislative sense implies some sort of choice about, and a certain kind of rational approach to, how or why this is done. Third, it seems clear that it implies the prior existence of an understanding of the criminal law as a distinct body of rules with a defined area of application—'crime' as a conceptually unified group of serious offences—such that to criminalize something is to bring that activity within the scope of what it means to be criminal.[12] Criminalization in this sense, and consequently a theory of criminalization, thus necessarily requires both a prior understanding of the existence of the criminal law as a distinct area of law with a discrete area of application (or jurisdiction) and an understanding of 'crime' as the object to be regulated. Since, as I shall argue, this did not exist in any meaningful sense before the end of the eighteenth or the beginning of the nineteenth centuries, criminalization (and theories of criminalization) must be understood as a distinctly modern phenomenon, linked to the emergence of this understanding of criminal law. It follows that being criminal in the modern sense is not, and cannot be, a quality of the conduct or activity itself, but must be understood as intrinsically linked to the emergence of the criminal law. Thus the meaning of any particular act of criminalization depends on our understanding of what the criminal law is and does. It is this question, of the emergence of an understanding of criminalization in this sense, which frames this work.

Central to this argument, then, is the claim that our understanding of criminalization is linked to the emergence of the modern criminal law, understood as a unified body of rules, organized according to a conceptual structure which is unique to itself, and which is understood as performing a distinctive social function. A substantial part of the argument of the book is thus focused on exploring the development of the legal concepts and the institutional structures that have allowed this understanding of criminal law to emerge and develop. Here I also argue that the emergence of the criminal law is linked to a more general aim of criminal law in securing civil order. This claim operates on two levels. First, it is part of an argument that the scope of the criminal law, and hence of criminalization, cannot be understood solely in terms of the interests which are to be protected, but also requires reflection on the purposes or aims of that protection, the kind of order that is being secured through law. And just as the criminal law in general is directed towards certain ends, so too particular areas of criminal law are shaped by the perception of the end that is to be secured by the protection of these goods or interests and their relation to the ends of the criminal law as a whole. In general, I shall argue that theories of criminalization have focused on goods or interests at the cost of considering the aims of the law and that a normative theory of criminalization needs to address the question of the ends that are to be secured by law.

[12] Just as family law applies to the family, contract law to contracts, or property law to property.

Second, this idea of securing civil order operates as a broad normative framework that allows us to understand how the modern law has developed. Civil order, I argue, represents a kind of ideal or social imaginary of modern law where self-governing individuals are guided by general rules and interact in civil society and the market. Law, and criminal law in particular, plays a key role in securing this civil order, as society is seen as rule-governed. This idea of civil order also has a certain content, whether it be in terms of ideas of civility, 'civilized' social conduct or the making of civil society: these institutions and the individuals and communities who populate them are made through law. And the fact that civil order is secured by law also means that it is subject to certain formal institutional constraints, that I shall refer to as the modality of law or legalism, which give further content to ideas of civility. Criminal law has not always taken this form, and the ideal expressions are not always matched by legal practice, but it aspires to these ideas of civil order and these, I shall argue, have shaped the development of the law. The importance of the idea of securing civil order then for a normative theory of criminalization, is not that it has particular consequences for the content of the criminal law, but that it places normative questions about the scope of the criminal law within the institutional framework of modern society.

These general ideas about criminalization are then explored in relation to particular crimes or areas of criminal law, to analyse patterns of criminalization in these areas. I look at the development of particular areas of criminal law to see how particular objects of criminal law have been conceptualized and at how interferences with these objects have come to be treated as criminal. I look, for instance, at how the idea of property or the person has been formulated in criminal law as something that is worthy of protection, and then at the types of interference with property that have been regarded as sufficiently serious to fall within the scope of the criminal law. The aim here is to show, first, how the objects of the law change over time and that our ideas of wrong or of harm are in many cases contingent, or linked to the aims of the particular area at particular periods. Second, I shall show how the patterns of criminalization in particular areas have developed in a way that is relatively autonomous from the development of the criminal law more generally, with the law in each area pursuing slightly different aims or ends, and operating according to different logics or principles. There has, to be sure, been a move towards increasing homogeneity in recent times, but I want to argue that we should be wary about the assumption that this kind of homogeneity is the natural end of the law, or that the aims, objects, or principles of criminalization are identical across the criminal law.

The overall aim is to suggest that our understanding of the object of criminalization (and thus of the criminal law) is closely related to our understanding of the aims or ends of the criminal law or particular parts of it. We cannot properly make sense of the wrong or its place in the law without an understanding of the purpose of criminalization; and this purpose must be understood as being linked to the broader aims and institutional form of the criminal law as a body of rules which aims both at the securing of civil order and at the prevention and punishment of crime. It is only with the creation of this modern understanding of criminal law as a (relatively) unified body of rules directed at this aim that the idea of criminalization emerges—and consequently that it becomes possible to consider the possibility of a theory of criminalization (or of the scope of the criminal law as something that is capable of being understood in terms of certain principles or concepts).

This is a book about criminalization, but it should now be apparent that it is also about a great deal more than criminalization. Or rather, it should be apparent that understanding criminalization entails nothing less than addressing the relationship between criminal law and civil order in modernity. This book, then, is about the making of the modern criminal law.

*

The book does not adopt the structure of other criminal law texts. While I have used the terminology of 'General' and 'Special' in Part II and III to distinguish between those parts of the law which relate to the development of the criminal law as a whole, and those which relate to bodies of rules governing specific areas, this should not be taken to imply any sort of logical or conceptual priority of the general over the special. In fact, I aim to show that the relationship between the two parts, as it is conceived in contemporary legal thought, is much more complex than is normally recognized and that thinking about general principles of liability can only really make sense if we recognize the different kinds of relationship that particular areas have with ideas of the criminal law as a whole. Thus, not only can there be no single principle of criminalization, but that a theory of criminalization should also attend to the institutional dimensions of the criminal law.

In Part I, I analyse contemporary discussions of criminalization and argue that these fail to take into account the aims and social functions of the criminal law. I argue that we can make good on this shortcoming if we understand criminal law as a particular type of social and legal institution directed at the general aim of securing civil order. Chapter 1 argues that criminalization must be understood as a legal question, and that this can best be understood in terms of an institutional theory of law. It uses MacCormick's institutional theory of law as a means of identifying the central features of the criminal law. The second chapter then discusses the idea of securing civil order as an aim of the criminal law. It looks specifically at themes of civil order, the civilizing process and conceptions of civility and civil society as key to the analysis of the emergence and development of the institution of criminal law.

Part II then goes on to develop this idea of securing civil order and to link it specifically to the modern understanding of the criminal law. This is then further developed by looking at certain key themes in the institutionalization of the criminal law—those of jurisdiction, codification, and responsibility. Chapter 3 is a long chapter which provides an overview of the development of the modern criminal law, looking in particular at the ways in which the scope and function of the criminal law have been understood in the modern period. This chapter looks at the changing scope of the different areas of social life that criminal law has been called on to regulate—how in different times and places these different areas have been understood as being central to the securing of social order. It is concerned with the questions of how certain areas have become understood to be fit (or unfit) for regulation by the criminal law; how these have been regulated; and the impact of these changes on the criminal law. It is also concerned with the understanding of the role of the criminal law as a governmental project. What is it understood that criminal law can achieve? And finally, it looks at how order was itself conceived within the criminal law, setting out the kinds of conceptual structures or ideas that allowed criminal lawyers and theorists to think of the criminal law as a distinct or coherent body of rules.

This is followed by three chapters which go back over some of the same ground to trace the development of specific dimensions of the institutionalization of modern criminal law: jurisdiction, codification and responsibility. Each chapter begins with a theoretical discussion of each of these terms as an institution before going into a more historical account. Chapter 4 looks at *jurisdiction*. Jurisdiction can be understood as a question of the proper scope of the application of the criminal law, encompassing a range of questions: from the spatial extent or ambit of the criminal law, to the persons to whom the law applies, and the kinds of conduct which are subject to criminal laws. In these terms it is easy to see that it is fundamentally related to questions of criminalization, and that questions of how the jurisdiction of the criminal law is conceived and organized must be central to our understanding of these issues. Chapter 5 looks at *codification*, in the sense of understanding how particular knowledge of criminal law and its proper scope was codified in the creation and organization of a specialized body of rules accessible to criminal lawyers. This chapter looks at different forms of literature, from treatises to textbooks to legislative codes, and at the changes in the form and content of these works over the modern period. The final chapter in this part, Chapter 6, looks at *responsibility*. If there has been one concept which has been central to the conceptual ordering and self-understanding of the criminal law in the modern period it has been that of responsibility. However, rather than seeking to define a normative concept of responsibility, this chapter traces the emergence of different conceptions of responsibility and the function that these play in co-ordinating and legitimating the criminal law.

In Part III, I move from the general, or the idea of the criminal law as a whole, to look at the law relating to certain distinct areas—namely property (Chapter 7), the person (Chapter 8), and sex (Chapter 9). These are areas of law that would now, on most accounts, be understood as belonging to the 'special part' of the law, and as accordingly somehow subordinate to, or governed by principles of the general part. They are also areas which are thought to contain core wrongs based on stable liberal values and so are often seen as marginal to questions of criminalization. Criminalization is about challenging and justifying 'peripheral' crimes which do not fit the paradigm of criminal wrongs. In part the aim here is to challenge this kind of thinking, to show that there are no core values, and that patterns of criminalization in these areas demonstrate that the law develops in response to specific social needs. I also aim to give equal weight to these areas: to understand their development, to identify the interests that they seek to protect, and the ends of this protection not just as illustration of general principles of criminal law or criminalization but as developing in distinct ways. I accordingly look at how the object of each of these areas is understood or has been constructed in the criminal law, at the kinds of infractions that are to be protected against, and the forms of liability associated with them. The aim is, in part, to demonstrate that each of these areas has its own pattern and logic of development and also, crucially, that they are not each based on a single understanding of a 'core' interest or wrong but that the understanding of wrongdoing has been shaped by the changing aims of the law in each area. This, however, also opens up a larger question of the relation between each of these areas and understandings of civil order. In abstract terms this can be framed as questions of the relations between persons and things, persons and others, persons and the self (particularly sexual identity), and consequently persons and civil order. There is also an important historical dimension to this: if security of property was originally understood as the foundation of modern civil order, we can see that civil order has broadened out to include the security of the person, and the regulation of conduct and civility. Moreover, I argue that in each of these areas it is possible to see how the content of property, person, sexual conduct, and identity has changed in ways which have an impact on our understanding of the proper scope of the criminal law. The aim is thus both to contribute to our understanding of the particular areas, but also to enable us to understand more clearly the relationship between general and special in the modern criminal law. This does not pretend to be a comprehensive account of all the features of the modern criminal law or to cover every doctrinal or institutional development that might be addressed. These areas have been chosen both because of their centrality to modern accounts of the criminal law and because the development of criminalization in this area can contribute substantially to our understanding of civil order. The aim, while still ambitious, is rather to set out a framework of analysis, and the themes are suggested as a way of capturing the main developments.

Finally, in the conclusion, I return to the question of the consequences of this argument for theories of criminalization. Without wishing to pre-empt the argument at this stage, in the conclusion I seek to draw out the normative implications of the institutional account of the criminal law that I have developed here, and conclude with some reflections, less on the question of what a normative theory of criminalization would look like, than on what is at stake in the enterprise of constructing a normative theory of criminalization.

*

One final introductory comment is necessary. Although the overall argument makes claims about the development of the modern criminal law, the focus throughout the book is primarily on the development of criminal law in England. However, the focus on English law should not be taken as any kind of assumption, implicit or otherwise, as to the superiority of English criminal law—and as a Scot writing in a Scotland which retains its distinctive system of criminal law in the shadow of English law, I am acutely aware of the sensitivities in this area. However there are good reasons, both historical and practical, for focusing on English criminal law in order to make this more general argument. In historical terms the English common law was the foundation of many Anglophone systems of criminal law, whether it was adopted voluntarily, used as a source for borrowings, or (more usually) imposed as part of the process of imperial government, so a study of the English law continues to offer insights into the foundations of many systems of criminal jurisprudence worldwide.[13] Conversely, the development of English criminal law cannot be seen in isolation from its own understanding of its imperial role, and I have tried to give proper weight to this throughout the book. In practical terms, in a book of this size it has proved necessary to be somewhat selective both in terms of the jurisdictions covered, and even in terms of the coverage of developments in the law within that jurisdiction. This does not aim to be a comprehensive history; rather I have tried to pick out themes or areas in the development of the law which exemplify and explain the more general trends in the development of the modern criminal law. Inevitably this has meant excluding some important areas of law, or excluding discussion of legal development in other jurisdictions. Overall it is clear that this focus thus introduces a degree of specificity into the argument. As a historian I have not wanted to bleach this specificity out for it gives us a richer understanding of the process of development; but nor do I want to obscure the general argument with a mass of detail. It will be for the reader to judge whether or not I have struck this balance in an appropriate way.

[13] Cf. P Cane, *Responsibility in Law and Morality* (Oxford: Hart Publishing, 2002) at p.7, referring to 'Anglian' systems where the conceptual structure derives from English law.

PART I

CRIMINAL LAW AS AN INSTITUTION

1

The Institution of Criminal Law

I. Introduction

Criminal law is usually seen as distinctive, and requiring a distinctive form of justification. It is uniquely coercive. A breach of the criminal law leads to state punishment, and punishment as the imposition of hard treatment requires it to be justified. Crimes violate the rights and subjective sense of security of individual victims, but they are not solely a matter of private right. They are usually seen as a form of public wrong, engaging a collective or community interest in condemning the wrong and calling the perpetrator to account. This kind of public response requires justification. Criminal law, moreover, establishes rules for the conduct of society: identifying prohibited actions and providing a backdrop to the regulation of activities from interpersonal sexual conduct to waste disposal. It is, to be sure, not the only social institution that does so, but it is an important one, and the decision to resort to criminal law should not be taken lightly. The use of the criminal law, moreover, is politically contentious. It is seen as vital in the protection of social institutions and values, but its overuse, or the discriminatory application of the law to certain sectors of society, can bring the legitimacy not only of the law but also of the other political institutions of the state into question.

All of these issues engage the question of criminalization in a more or less direct manner. The decision to charge and punish an individual for criminal conduct and the articulation of forms of criminal responsibility clearly require justification. But the prior questions of which conduct should be made criminal in law, or of which breaches of rights should be backed by criminal sanction are of equal importance. These are usually addressed by resort to theories of criminalization. The aim of this chapter is to give a brief introduction to some of the main theoretical approaches to the issue of criminalization and to raise some questions about these kinds of theoretical approach. Indeed I will argue here that while these theories offer highly sophisticated accounts of concepts such as harm and wrong, they frequently rely on surprisingly unsophisticated accounts of the criminal law, reducing the aims or function of a complex social institution to claims about the justification of punishment. I will argue in this chapter that theories of criminalization need to give greater attention to the distinctive character and aims of the criminal law.[1] If we are to have

[1] I am aware of the extensive literature on the definition of crime but, as I shall argue below, much of it reproduces the structure of the above argument. Cf. MD Dubber, 'Criminal Law

a normative theory of criminalization—what conduct is properly subject to regulation by the criminal law—it must surely be essential to have a richer account of what the criminal law is, what it is for, and what is sought to be achieved by resort to the criminal law. This, I will argue, should not be approached as a prima facie moral question, as something that can be defined a priori and independently of the legal institution. It is rather a question that, notwithstanding significant moral dimensions, must be understood primarily in terms of the development of the modern institution of criminal law.

The chapter is in three main parts. In the first part, there is a discussion of different theories of criminalization which will develop the claim made here that there has been a failure on the part of such theories to attend to the nature or purpose of the criminal law. In the second part, I go on to set out an understanding of criminal law as an institution, as a framework that can combine a normative perspective on issues of criminalization with a richer understanding of the nature and purpose of the criminal law.[2] In the concluding section, I then return to the question of how this account, which gives more weight to the nature and function of the modern criminal law, might contribute to normative theories of criminalization.

II. Criminalization and Criminal Law

In very general terms there are two main strands in liberal thought about criminalization: those which begin from questions of harm and harm reduction or prevention, and those theories, often called legal moralism, which are centred around questions of wrongdoing and retribution. The first is animated by John Stuart Mill's famous 'harm' principle: that 'the only purpose for which power can be rightfully exercised against any member of a civilised community, against his will, is to prevent harm to others'.[3] In this tradition, efforts have focused on attempting to define the concept of harm. What is it? Does it include forms of potential as well as actual harm? Are forms of paternalism to prevent self-harm justified? This has achieved perhaps its fullest contemporary expression in the four-volume work of Joel Feinberg, in which harm was defined as a 'setback to interests', and which took particular aim at what he saw as the illegitimate criminalization of various forms of non-harmful conduct simply on the basis that it was regarded as immoral or offensive.[4] The use of the criminal law was thus seen as justified

between Public and Private Law' in RA Duff et al. (eds), *The Boundaries of the Criminal Law* (Oxford: Oxford UP, 2010) p.191: 'This means that an account of criminalization needs an account not of crime *simpliciter*, but of law in general, and of criminal law within it.'

[2] See e.g. N MacCormick, *Institutions of Law. An Essay in Legal Theory* (Oxford: Oxford UP, 2007).

[3] *John Stuart Mill on Liberty and other Essays* (1859) (ed. John Gray) (Oxford: Oxford World Classics, 1991) p.14. For further discussion see Ch.2 at p.48.

[4] *The Moral Limits of the Criminal Law*, (4 vols) (Oxford: Oxford UP, 1984–8). He did allow that offensiveness could sometimes justify criminalization (vol.2), and that some non-harmful wrongs might be criminalized (vol.4). For discussion, see RA Duff, *Answering for Crime* (Oxford: Hart

primarily, though not exclusively, as a means of preventing serious setbacks to the interests of others. The alternative approach—legal moralism—argues that we should begin from the idea of wrongdoing, since it would be unjustifiable for the state to punish a person for conduct which is not morally wrong.[5] This approach begins with a more explicit link to the ends of punishment, since punishment is understood as being justified only when imposed for wrongful conduct. Moore, for example, asserts that the proper aim of the criminal law is to inflict deserved punishment on culpable wrongdoers—and thus that the wrongfulness of conduct provides prima facie positive reasons for criminalizing it.[6] From this perspective, then, it would be unjustifiable either to punish non-culpable actors or to criminalize conduct which was not wrongful.

While there are significant differences between these approaches, which have been discussed at length in criminal law theory, it is less often remarked that there are also striking similarities. This can be seen both in the concessions each make to the other's position, and in the acknowledgements of the limits of 'principle' in this area. Defenders of the harm principle, such as Feinberg, concede that a criminal law which punished all harmful conduct would be too broad, and therefore introduce a limiting principle, which is that only 'wrongful' harms should be subject to criminal punishment—with the measure of 'wrongfulness' depending on either the rights that are to be protected or the mode of infringement.[7] It is also acknowledged that the specification of 'harms', and thus the content of the law, will further depend on community values or standards as these are determined through the political and legislative process. Conversely, legal moralists concede that not all *prima facie* wrongful conduct (lying, cheating at games, sexual infidelity) should be the subject of the criminal law because, once again, the law would be too broad. They accordingly argue the need for a limiting principle, such as that the criminal law should be concerned only with 'harmful' wrongs—though this throws them back into acknowledging the unspecific or conventional nature of the concept of harm.[8] It is also worth noting that many legal moralists also concede that some conduct will be wrongful by virtue of having been made so by law, and so must either allow that the category of wrongs is broader than merely 'pre-legal' moral wrongs, or that the criminalization of non-wrongful conduct may in certain instances be justified.[9] In either case—wrongful harms or harmful wrongs—the language and the structure of the arguments have a great deal in

Publishing, 2007) Ch.6; H Stewart, 'The Limits of the Harm Principle' (2010) 4 *Criminal Law and Philosophy* 17; BE Harcourt, 'The Collapse of the Harm Principle' (1999) 90 *Jnl. of Criminal Law and Criminology* 109.

[5] See the illuminating discussion in RA Duff, 'Towards a Modest Legal Moralism' (2014) 8 *Criminal Law and Philosophy* p.217 distinguishing between different versions of legal moralism. See also e.g. D Husak, *Overcriminalization. The Limits of the Criminal Law* (Oxford: Oxford UP, 2008).

[6] M Moore, *Placing Blame* (Oxford: Oxford UP, 1997) Ch.1.

[7] J Feinberg, *Harm to Others* (Oxford: Oxford UP, 1984) pp.31–6.

[8] E.g. Moore, *Placing Blame*, n.6, Chs.1 & 16.

[9] See Duff, 'Modest Legal Moralism', n.5, pp.3–5; Duff, *Answering for Crime*, n.4, pp.89–93. Cf. Husak, *Overcriminalization*, n.5, pp.103–19 for a more sceptical account.

common. The initial category (harm or wrong) is defined independently of law and is thought to shape the proper scope of the law; the aim of criminalization is understood as an aim of punishment (deterrence or retribution); and in each case it is acknowledged that the initial organizing principle is too broad, and that the eventual content of the criminal law will depend on factors which have little to do with categories of moral thought. I shall say more about each of these points as a way of developing my central claim about the failure of these theories to address the nature of the criminal law.

Most contemporary theories understand the scope of the criminal law as being properly determined by some combination of the rights or interests which are to be protected and the identification of harms or wrongs—wrongful harms or harmful wrongs—to those rights or interests. Their starting point is that these interests or wrongs can, and should, be identified a priori and independently of law, and they are identified primarily in terms of individual rights or interests, the protection of which is seen as the foundation or core of the criminal law.[10] It is sometimes recognized that there are also common or public interests which must be protected, such as public order, state security, or the market, and that these are not simply reducible to private interests, but these are generally regarded as secondary to the individual interests.[11] And while there are some interests, such as property, which might appear to fall somewhere between public and private—they are directed either at the protection of individual interests in personal private property, or at the protection of the system of property rights or interests—it is, once again, the protection of the underlying private interest that is given priority.[12]

What these views share is an understanding of the scope of criminal law as being determined by private right, and of the purpose of criminal law as the protection of these rights. On this view, criminal law is something adjunct to private moral or legal rights: the role of the law is to protect the pre-existing rights.[13] Criminal law is thus 'adjectival', protecting goods, interests or rights that have been defined elsewhere, as pre-legal wrongs or in civil law, against certain kinds of serious and/or culpable interferences.[14] This is also linked to an account of the development of the law. Criminal law is understood as being founded on the protection of

[10] For discussion of this, see L Farmer, 'Criminal Wrongs in Historical Perspective' in Duff et al., *Boundaries*, n.1.

[11] See the critical discussion in Dubber, 'Between Public and Private', n.1, pp.206–11. See also I Leader-Elliott, 'A Critical Reading of RA Duff, *Answering for Crime*' (2010) 31 *Adelaide LR* 47 at pp.51–7.

[12] See US Model Penal Code ss.220.1–230.5. See also e.g. S Shute, 'Appropriation and the Law of Theft' 2002 *Crim LR* pp.445–58. See also S Gardner, 'Property and Theft' (1998) *Crim LR* 35 discussed Ch.7 at pp.222–24. See generally Dubber, 'Between Public and Private', n.1, pp.206–7.

[13] Cf the role of 'Rechtsgut' in German criminal law. For discussion see K Nuotio, 'Theories of Criminalization and the Limits of Criminal Law: A Legal Cultural Approach' in Duff et al., *Boundaries*, n.1, pp.244–52; MD Dubber, 'Theories of Crime and Punishment in German Criminal Law' (2006) 53 *Am J Comp Law* 679.

[14] The term 'adjectival' is taken from Bentham, *On the Principles and Morals of Legislation* (Oxford: Oxford UP, 1982). For discussion, see L Farmer, 'Reconstructing the English Codification Debate: the Criminal Law Commissioners 1833–45' (2000) 18 *Law & Hist Rev* 397 at pp.419–22.

individual rights, to which collective or welfare interests have been added. The problem from this perspective is to justify 'welfare' rights—and not infrequently the problem of over-criminalization is understood, at least in significant part, as a problem relating to those crimes which are not directly linked to individual rights.[15] As we shall see, the history of the law is considerably more complex than this; but more importantly, given the dubious historical accuracy of this account, it is best understood as a claim about the theoretical primacy of certain individual rights or interests. However, even from this perspective this approach is limited: it takes wrongs against individuals as fundamental and accordingly struggles to explain collective or welfare interests. Rights or interests which are created by law (as opposed to 'pre-legal' rights) may be seen as problematic;[16] and, perhaps most significantly, if the purpose of criminal law is primarily that of protecting private rights, there is little or no space for an account of the scope of criminal law that goes beyond this.

Where the aim of criminal law is discussed, it is generally seen in terms of the ends of punishment. In deterrence-based accounts, the aim of punishment is the reduction of socially harmful conduct. This means that there is only a contingent relation between the aim and the content of the law: the aim of harm prevention or reduction does not depend on the content of any particular harms, as notionally anything that is regarded by a society as harmful could be criminalized. A consequence of this position is thus that it is hard to specify anything distinctive about criminal law without considering further criteria about what might make criminal law an appropriate response to harm. In the absence of these criteria, it is just another instrument which might be deployed by the state for the prevention of harm. The picture is more complex with retributive accounts. Such accounts can generate strong reasons why we should only punish morally responsible actors (only culpable wrongdoing), and in certain cases (e.g. homicide or rape) they claim to identify wrongs that might uncontroversially be criminalized. However, beyond a narrow core retributive accounts can struggle to generate reasons why punishment is a justifiable response to a broader range of 'wrongs', or why some wrongs are appropriately addressed by the criminal law while others are not. The identification of the wrong thus needs to be supplemented by reasons, such as the degree of harm or the effectiveness of a particular mode of enforcement or definition, that have little to do with the aim of retribution as such. In each case, it is the further step—addressing the reasons why criminal law is the appropriate response—that is the central step in criminalization and whose theoretical significance requires proper acknowledgement. The key point here then is

[15] This also implicitly underpins the account of over-criminalization in Husak, *Overcriminalization*, n.5. See also AP Simester & A von Hirsch, *Crimes, Harms and Wrongs* (Oxford: Hart Publishing, 2011) Ch.1 where they make the claim that these kinds of individual wrongs are 'archetypal'—joining the sense of historical priority to that of being theoretically fundamental.

[16] Here I am referring to offences such as the failure to pay taxes, where the crime is the result only of the creation of a tax regime and cannot readily be linked to a private moral or legal right. See references at fn. 9 where these kind of 'mala prohibita' are discussed.

that while consideration of the ends of punishment might contribute to an explanation of the moral or political justification for the exercise of the criminal law, it radically under-determines the scope of the criminal law.[17]

This should lead us to ask whether the aims of criminal law can really be reduced to those of punishment. Writers such as Marshall and Duff have suggested that the relation between punishment and criminal law is at best historically and culturally contingent; that is to say that the aim of the criminal law is primarily to censure or condemn conduct of which the community disapproves and that this does not necessarily require punishment.[18] If we accept this argument, then it would imply that there is a public interest in resort to criminal law—either as an inherent quality of this type of law or as related to the practice of censure—which cannot be explained solely in terms of the punishment of an individual for a wrong.

This is an argument that has been addressed most fully by Duff, who seeks to identify the public interest in terms of the requirement that crimes be 'public wrongs'.[19] On his account, crimes should be understood as wrongs which concern us all as members of the community, and can thus be distinguished from private wrongs, which concern only those individuals directly involved (and so would be a matter only of private redress). For this kind of 'modest' legal moralism, the scope of the criminal law should not depend primarily on the 'wrongness' of conduct, but on the identification of those wrongs which properly count as public in the sense in which 'we are criminally responsible as citizens to our fellow citizens'.[20] There is therefore a need to begin with the public realm:

> A justification of criminalization will need to begin by specifying some value(s) that can be claimed to be public, as part of the polity's self-definition; show how the conduct in question violates that value or threatens the goods that it protects; and argue that that violation or threat is such as to require or demand a public condemnation.[21]

The importance of this account is that it seeks to go beyond narrow accounts of the criminal law as the protection of private interests, to identify a 'public' feature of the law based in the political values of a given community. But it is not clear that this goes far enough. First, it seems that many public values, or values which are part of the public realm, might equally well be protected by other forms of law. If, for example, tort law is understood as a form of redress

[17] See comments in Duff et al., 'Introduction' in Duff et al., *Boundaries*, n.1, pp.6–7. Cf. V Chiao, 'Punishment and Permissibility in the Criminal Law' (2013) 32 *Law & Phil* 729.

[18] SE Marshall & RA Duff, 'Criminalization and Sharing Wrongs' (1998) 11 *Can Jnl of Law and Jurisprudence* 7–22; cf. A von Hirsch, *Censure and Sanctions* (Oxford: Oxford UP, 1996) Chs2 & 3 arguing that censure is desert-oriented by nature: one is entitled to condemn only if one has reason to believe conduct is wrongful, and only to the degree of its wrongfulness. It is not clear to me that censure is a matter of degree, as this would suggest.

[19] See Duff, *Answering for Crime*, n.4, pp.6–7 and Chs.4 & 6; RA Duff & SE. Marshall, 'Public and Private Wrongs' in J Chalmers, F Leverick & L Farmer (eds), *Essays in Criminal Law in Honour of Sir Gerald Gordon* (Edinburgh: Edinburgh UP, 2010).

[20] Duff, *Answering for Crime*, n.4, p.142.

[21] Duff, *Answering for Crime*, n.4, p.143.

for wrongs, it is hard not to see why there is not also a form of public interest in ensuring that this redress takes place such that they are also public wrongs.[22] The answer to this might be that criminal law is a particular kind of public censure or condemnation. But while this might explain part of the function of the criminal law—identifying public wrongs and condemning individuals for their wrongful conduct—it does not help us to identify which wrongs might be criminal or how they might be defined in the criminal law.[23] In addition, it would be possible in principle, presumably, to justify the criminalization of an extensive range of conduct if the appropriate consensus can be produced. It is nonetheless arguable that some of these 'public wrongs' might be seen as inapt or inappropriate for criminalization: if, for instance, a political community were to adopt a repressive penal measure to punish minor public disorder; or if a community were to seek to criminalize conduct retrospectively. This suggests that, in addition to the putative political consensus, there are existing understandings of the criminal law and its appropriate uses, values, and ends that underlie or constrain debates about criminalization. The broader problem with this approach might be summed up in this way: it starts by trying to identify a specific quality of the wrong but in doing so it neglects, or does not fully develop, an account of the place of criminal law in modern society.

If we are to begin to develop such an account, one place that we can look is criminological approaches to criminalization that focus more on the social function of the criminal law. Here there are, broadly speaking, two kinds of approach. The first looks at the question of who is criminalized and how this process is exercised, seeing both over- and under-criminalization, in its analysis of the social function of law in practice.[24] Over-criminalization focuses on the criminalization of particular groups, communities, and locations. This has looked at the police practices of using stop and search powers against particular ethnic communities or groups defined by gender or age. It examines the use of powers, such as those under the anti-terrorism legislation, to police public order and so on. Or it looks at the intersections between, for example, housing or immigration policy and the criminal law to trace the increasing use of the criminal law in these areas.[25] Under-criminalization, by contrast, has focused on certain areas of social life, typically those connected with economic activity conducted by relatively powerful social groups, and argued that the 'social harm' caused by certain activities—typically in financial markets or business practices—matches or

[22] See A Lee, 'Public Wrongs and the Criminal Law' (2015) 9 *Crim Law & Phil* 155.

[23] See also Dubber here, criticizing the move to the publicness of wrongs as ignoring the 'lawness' of criminal law, n.1, p.206.

[24] See e.g. the discussion in C Pantazis, 'The Problem with Criminalisation' (2008) 74 *Criminal Justice Matters* pp.10–1. See also Muncie in the same issue (pp.13–14) tracing the roots of the analysis of criminalization within criminology. See generally, P Scraton, *Power, Conflict and Criminalisation* (London: Routledge, 2007).

[25] See e.g. A Aliverti, 'Making People Criminal: the Role of Criminal Law in Immigration Enforcement' (2012) 16 *Theoretical Criminology* pp.417–34; L Zedner, 'Security, the State, and the Citizen: the Changing Architecture of Crime Control' (2010) 13 *New Crim LR* pp.379–403.

exceeds the harm caused by more 'traditional' criminal activities, and that this is evidence of double standards in the recognition of the harms caused by, or censure of, certain activities.[26] 'Harm' is understood as a means of illustrating the symbolic equivalence of certain types of activities and as a potentially powerful argument in support of criminalization.

There are a number of important features of this kind of approach. The focus is not usually on legislation or the law-making process, but on how the law is used and enforced, or the use of police powers—even when this does not lead to prosecution.[27] This then produces a powerful empirical picture of state practices of criminalization (or of the social consequences of the failure to criminalize). This kind of approach is highly sensitive to questions of social exclusion and the exercise of social power. It looks at the groups or communities who are either criminalized or, conversely, neglected by the law, or the ways that criminal law supports these broader processes of social exclusion.[28] This allows the linking of questions of criminalization to broader trends in the use of the criminal law and their relation to social and economic developments in a way that is often absent from the perspective of more traditional normative approaches to criminalization. This points to the fact that the criminal law is often used instrumentally by the state or other socially or economically powerful groups to repress dissent or to bolster or protect their own economic position. A theory of criminalization must thus address the fact that conduct to be criminalized cannot always be identified independently of other legal, social, and institutional structures. The use of criminal law in these circumstances is about more than just the punishment of individual wrongs. Censure is a social process in which powerful social groups can and do use the symbolic value and power of the criminal law for certain self-interested purposes.

However, notwithstanding these strengths, there are problems with this approach in terms of thinking about criminalization more generally. This kind of approach can seem either too narrow or too broad in focus. Looking at particular instances or areas of the application of the criminal law might tell us little about the application or use of the criminal law in general: if certain communities are

[26] See e.g. P Hillyard et al., *Beyond Criminology. Taking Harm Seriously* (London: Pluto, 2004). See also essays by Pemberton, White, and Snider in 74 *CJM*. On the weaknesses of the social harm perspective, see Harcourt, 'The Collapse of the Harm Principle' n.4. Cf. A Ashworth & L Zedner, 'Preventive Orders: A Problem of Undercriminalization?' in Duff et al., *Boundaries*, n.1, Ch.3 arguing for an alternative understanding of under-criminalization as the use of preventive orders to avoid the procedural protections afforded by the criminal law. Discussed infra Ch.3 at pp.106–7.

[27] Cf. e.g. Simester & von Hirsch, *Crimes, Harms and Wrongs*, n.15, Ch.1 who define criminalization solely in terms of the legislative decision, suggesting that such an approach is 'uncontroversial'. For further discussion see RA Duff et al., 'Introduction. Towards a Theory of Criminalization' in RA Duff et al. (eds), *Criminalization. The Political Morality of the Criminal Law* (Oxford: Oxford UP, 2014) at pp.6–16.

[28] See e.g. J Young, *The Exclusive Society. Social Exclusion, Crime and Difference in Late Modernity* (London: Sage, 1999); L Wacquant, *Punishing the Poor. The Neo-Liberal Government of Social Insecurity* (Durham NC: Duke UP, 2009). See also P Squires & J Lea, *Criminalisation and Advanced Marginality: Critically Exploring the Work of Loïc Wacquant* (Bristol: The Policy Press, 2012).

criminalized through the use of stop and search powers, this does not necessarily tell us anything about the acceptance of norms of criminal law more generally, or about the attitudes of the criminalized community to those broader norms. Conversely, even where the criminal law can be characterized as representing a particular class interest, there is often evidence of a broader social acceptance of the norms of the criminal law.[29] As a result, the normative implications of this kind of analysis remain unclear.[30] There is, at best, a failure to develop a conceptual language that can bring together the normative and empirical dimensions of criminalization.[31] Overall, then, while the focus on social power and the uses of the criminal law is important, it can also be argued that the criminal law as a whole does not come clearly into focus.

The second kind of approach is focused on the social function or meaning of the criminal law more broadly. Here criminal law is seen as distinctive in terms of its social functions. Emile Durkheim, for example, argued that punishment had the particular social function of articulating and expressing forms of social disapproval for the breach of particular social norms, and that the form and degree of repressiveness of punishment would change according to the form of social solidarity. Thus the criminal law allowed for the continual process of social reintegration of communities through the identification and punishment of those who transgressed its norms.[32] Important as this is, though, it is necessary to distinguish between the aims and functions of the criminal law and those of punishment for, as penologists such as Garland have pointed out, criminal law and punishment are distinct social and cultural practices.[33] While for Garland this points to the need for sociologists to study punishment as a cultural practice in its own right, and not simply as an instrumental response to crime, the point might be reversed: the aims or social function of punishment are not necessarily the same as those of the criminal law. Thus rather than seeing criminal law as simply the obverse of punishment (or that the aims of criminal law flow from the aims of punishment), it is necessary to understand it as a distinct social practice. The function of punishment may be social reintegration, but it does not necessarily follow that this is the aim or function of the criminal law and it is accordingly important to study the culture and practices of the criminal law in its own right. This is not, of course, to claim that crime and punishment are unrelated, but merely that as a first step we

[29] Compare D Hay, 'Property, Authority and the Criminal Law' in D Hay et al., *Albion's Fatal Tree* (Harmondsworth: Penguin, 1975) with P King, *Crime, Justice and Discretion in England, 1740–1820* (Oxford: Oxford UP, 2000).

[30] For an attempt to engage with this issue, see A Millie, 'Value Judgments and Criminalization' (2011) 51 *BJ Criminol* pp.278–95.

[31] See N Lacey, 'Historicising Criminalisation: Conceptual and Empirical Issues' (2009) 72 *Mod LR* 936–60 at p.944.

[32] E Durkheim, *The Division of Labour in Society* (London: Macmillan, 1984), and 'Two Laws of Penal Evolution' (1973) 2 *Economy and Society* pp.285–308. See also discussion in D Garland, *Punishment and Modern Society* (Oxford: Clarendon, 1990) Chs.2 & 3.

[33] Garland, *Punishment* n.32, esp. pp.16–22: 'Like architecture or diet or clothing or table manners, punishment has an instrumental purpose, but also a cultural style and a historical tradition…' (p.19). See also D Garland & P Young, *The Power to Punish* (London: Heineman, 1983) Ch.1.

should be wary of assuming an equivalence between the aims or functions of the two practices. This is a point recognized implicitly by some Marxist analyses of criminal law, which point to the significance of the form and use of criminal law in protecting the interests of particular social classes or repressing others in certain historical periods.[34] These laws may be reinforced by penal sanctions, and the authority of the law may depend on the way that punishment is used, but the aims of the criminal law are not to punish but to support a particular kind of social structure. Such approaches have provided important accounts of how the legal form can be used to promote the interests of a certain class or why, say, property has been accorded particular significance by the criminal law in certain periods. The general point is that the scope or function of the criminal law at particular points in time might depend less on moral theory than the ability of social groups or classes to harness the power of the law. In short, an account of criminalization, and an understanding of the nature of particular wrongs and harms recognized in law, must be open to this particular combination of understanding how the law is used and enforced, the interests that it might serve, and the social functions that it might perform.

This brings us then to the question of how we might begin to integrate these insights in such a way as to retain sight of the distinctive social and legal character of criminal law. I shall argue in the next section that one way in which we might do this is through an understanding of law as an institutional normative order.

III. An Institutional Theory of Law

An institutional theory of law argues that law must be understood as a form of institutional normative order.[35] Law is not conceived of as a system of moral or social norms endowed with institutional existence; rather it is institutions that constitute legal norms. Thus, an understanding of law should not be based on an understanding of moral norms such as right and wrong, but on the norms that have become institutionalized in particular forms, agencies, and rules of law. Furthermore, an explanation of the institution requires an account of the relevant rules set out in the light of the point or end of that institution.[36]

[34] See EB Pashukanis, *Law and Marxism* (London: Pluto Press, 1977) Ch.7. See also D Hay, 'Property', n.29; A Norrie, *Crime, Reason and History. A Critical Introduction to Criminal Law* (3rd edn) (Cambridge: Cambridge UP, 2014).

[35] I shall develop my argument in this section primarily through an engagement with MacCormick's influential account: MacCormick, *Institutions*, n.2, pp.34–7 and 'Law as Institutional Fact' (1974) 90 *LQR* pp.102–29. See also the essays in M del Mar & Z Bankowski (eds), *Law as Institutional Normative Order* (Dartmouth: Ashgate, 2009). For other versions of institutional theory, see O Weinberger, *Law, Institution and Legal Politics* (Dordrecht: Kluwer, 1991) esp. pp.163–72 for a brief account of the history of institutional legal theory; H Ross, *Law as a Social Institution* (Oxford: Hart Publishing, 2001); M la Torre, *Law as Institution* (Dordrecht: Springer, 2010). Cf. N Luhmann, *Law as a Social System* (Oxford: Oxford UP, 2004).

[36] MacCormick, *Institutions*, n.2, pp.294–8; Weinberger, n.35, p.114, 158.

According to MacCormick, institutionalization of a social practice occurs whenever we encounter a 'two-tier' normative practice—that is, when there is not only the practice, but also more or less formal rules for ordering the practice.[37] What is important is not the 'pre-legal' practice, but the reflexive relationship between the two 'tiers' in which the institution is constituted. In the case of law, he thus seeks first to identify and explain how basic forms of obligation and duty arise between persons as social practice, and then how the process of institutionalization establishes particular powers and competences on the part of those articulating the norms and managing the institutional order.[38] The account thus proceeds from an investigation into the social quality of norms and how these are ordered and make interpersonal conduct or social life to some extent orderly, towards an explanation of how the norms are institutionalized and how the institutions then order and maintain the norms. While the formulation of law as an institution is deliberately broad, to include rules, institutional arrangements and competences, and practices and values, this account is also linked to a more schematic history of legal persons, rights, and things, and the development of modern forms of law, the modern state, and civil society. The point of this is to recognize that while law might be (and indeed has been) institutionalized in many different ways, the dominant form of institutionalization is through state law, and that it is accordingly necessary to acknowledge its central importance.[39]

A central idea is that of law as 'institutional fact': persons, acts, or events are to be understood as elements of an institutional normative order. Thus the existence of facts such as the ascription of legal personality or status, the recognition of the existence of a legal relationships, or the commission of a crime can only be understood in terms of the interpretation and application of the relevant legal norms. This entails not only knowledge of the law in a given system, but also of the values and ends to which the institutions were oriented. It is, for example, not possible to understand rules of contract or property, without also understanding them as rules directed towards certain ends in private law, which are part of system of rules—the law as a whole—that strives towards a basic coherence, and which is oriented towards the intrinsic ends of the enterprise of governance under law.[40] There are two dimensions to this claim. First, the resort to law or legal rules is purposive, both in the sense that law is understood as an instrument that can bring about socially desirable ends, and that, as one amongst a variety of means

[37] MacCormick, *Institutions,* n.2, Ch.2. While the existence of institutions is grounded in 'pre-legal' norms, this operates as an anthropological assumption about the conditions for social existence rather than providing the basis for the substance of particular moral or legal norms. Weinberger, n.35, for example denies the 'subsiduary [*sic*] validity of moral concepts as determinants for the law' (p.116).

[38] Cf. the distinction between primary and secondary rules in HLA Hart, *The Concept of Law* (Oxford: Clarendon, 1961).

[39] MacCormick, *Institutions*, n.2, pp.285–9.

[40] There is a striking affinity with the ideas of Fuller here in terms of the relation between legal form and the social purpose of law. See Lon L Fuller, *The Morality of Law* (revd edn) (New Haven: Yale UP, 1969). See also K Rundle, *Forms Liberate: Reclaiming the Jurisprudence of Lon L Fuller* (Oxford: Hart Publishing, 2012).

for addressing social problems in the modern state, the resort to law should be understood as a choice (even if this often appears to be unreflexive).[41] Thus, for example, even where the resort to law is for non-instrumental purposes, as in the classic liberal formulation that law is understood only as a framework for allowing individuals to pursue their own ends, the fact that law is adopted as the means of regulation is still purposive in the sense that the aim of protecting individual liberty within a structure of rules is the purpose which shapes and orients the institution of law. Second, the commitment to modern law as a means of bringing about certain social ends also entails a commitment to the forms and values of the institution of law. Thus, MacCormick argues that 'a coherent account of the character of any modern legal system [will] have to take seriously the very general values that are inherent in the character of the legal enterprise'.[42] These include the commitment to the rule of law, understood as the articulation of express and binding rules for the governance and adjudication of social conduct, and values such as legality. This commitment to what we might call the modality of law, however imperfectly realized in practice, both shapes and constrains the way that certain ends can be brought about and, arguably, also entails a commitment to a certain form of human agency.[43] In broad terms, the approach thus seeks to combine a positivist recognition that particular legal systems develop in distinctive ways, such that the content and mode of expression of legal norms may vary between legal systems, with the view that there are, notwithstanding this, certain features and values of modern law that are in some sense irreducible.[44]

Two further points should be noted. First, 'institutional facts' require to be interpreted in a basic hermeneutic that seeks always to reconstruct—whether from the position of a judge or an academic—the best possible understanding of rules and their place within the institution. This is a process that MacCormick describes as that of 'rational reconstruction'.[45] It is key to this claim that such reconstructions acknowledge both the systematicity of law—that the rules are conceived in terms of a system, and so should 'fit' in some way with other norms which are part of that system—and the values and ends to which the institution is oriented. This is a complex undertaking in which there is always a critical mediation between the rules, the consistency with other rules in the system, the principles of the particular system, and the values and ends of the institution of law more broadly conceived.[46] In addition, while recognizing certain irreducible

[41] On the conception of the modern state as a structure of rules and as a purposive entity, see M Oakeshott, *On Human Conduct* (Oxford: Oxford UP, 1975) pp.185–236 and pp.199–206.

[42] MacCormick, *Institutions,* n.2, p.294.

[43] See Rundle, n.41, Ch.1. See also Ch.6 at pp.166–71.

[44] See MacCormick, *Institutions*, n.2, pp.289–93, where he acknowledges the similarities to Luhmann's systems theory, in which each functionally differentiated social system is organized according to its own code. See Luhmann, *Law as a Social System*, n.35.

[45] MacCormick, *Institutions,* n.2, Ch.16. See also N MacCormick, 'Reconstruction after Deconstruction: A Response to CLS' (1990) 10 *Ox Jnl of Leg Stud* pp.539–58.

[46] MacCormick, *Institutions,* n.2, pp.290–8. See also Ch.5, pp.140–44.

features of law as a mode of governance, this approach does not seek to produce a stipulative definition of the nature or scope of law or of particular areas of law. Instead it acknowledges that this is continually in the process of being worked out within the institution. This points to a necessary element of temporality and change as the paradigm of the modern sovereign state is itself in the process of evolution. Second, while MacCormick contends that this process of interpretation and reconstruction cannot be value free—that is, that it must recognize both the values to which law is committed and the commitment to value that is entailed in the process of reconstruction—he is insistent on the separation of institutional from moral norms. This requires that when we are dealing with institutional legal facts we must recognize that, even where these are shaped by or seek to protect certain moral values, these must be understood primarily from the perspective of the institution of law. Moral values cannot be regarded as the source or foundation of law. MacCormick thus describes it as a 'post-positivist' theory of law in that it both denies a necessary connection between law and morals and recognizes that the modern institution of law is nonetheless committed to certain values.[47]

What does this mean for the criminal law? MacCormick gives only a brief and rather sketchy account of the criminal law, but this contains significant pointers as to how an argument about criminalization might be developed and so can be a useful point of departure for my argument.[48] His starting point follows from the argument above that law must be understood in a broadly purposive sense. He argues that the aim of the criminal law is to secure the conditions of civil society, understood in terms of facilitating relative peace and mutual trust between strangers:

> The collective sense of security and solidarity in a relatively peaceful society is likely to depend on a fairly high degree of confidence among law-abiding persons that those who do not abide by the law, engaging in violent or dishonest behaviour, will be effectively restrained.[49]

He suggests that in thinking about the conditions for a justifiable system of criminal law we should not begin from the requirement of a wrong (that punishment can only be justified when an individual has committed a wrong), such that securing civil peace is seen as a side effect of the imposition of justified punishment on individuals. Instead, this relation must be reversed: peace and civility should be seen as preconditions for justice, and the just imposition of punishment can only take place once institutions of law have been established.[50] This is an important

[47] MacCormick, *Institutions,* n.2, p.5.

[48] MacCormick, *Institutions,* n.2, Ch.12. See now also AE Bottoms, 'Civil Peace and Criminalization' in Duff et al., *Criminalization: The Political Morality of the Criminal Law* (Oxford: Oxford UP, 2014); N Lacey, 'Institutionalizing Responsibility' (2013) 4 *Jurisprudence* pp.1–19.

[49] MacCormick, *Institutions,* n.2, pp.207–8 going on to point out that it also requires confidence that wrongdoers will be tried and prosecuted fairly.

[50] MacCormick, *Institutions,* n.2, p.218.

shift in perspective. The aims of the criminal law are linked to the operation of an effective system of punishment, but they have conceptual priority and are broader in scope than simply the justification of punishment. Thus, while MacCormick recognizes a right to punish, this is understood as an institutional right which fits within and serves other broader aims or purposes of the criminal law, rather than being understood as the primary aim of the criminal law. This requires that we identify those other aims of the criminal law. Here MacCormick offers less guidance about the meaning of securing civil order, suggesting variously the ending of forms of private vengeance and bloodfeud or securing a state monopoly over the legitimate use of violence.[51] He goes on to argue that this sense of securing the civility of civil society is key to understanding the nature of criminal law as an institution for dealing with serious and wilful wrongdoing, as the civility of civil society is at least partly dependent on the existence of a fair and effective system of criminal law.[52] Security and civility are thus key themes running through his analysis. However he says little about what these terms mean, and so if we are to develop this perspective it will be necessary to analyse these concepts in greater depth.

MacCormick also insists on the claim that the criminal law operates within the broader framework of the institutional normative order that is state law. This, he argues, establishes limits to the criminal law both in terms of functional competence (establishing boundaries with areas of private or administrative law) and through the increasingly widespread application of values, such as the restraint of public actors, which have been developed in public law. Criminal law, on this view, may be expressive, or even constitutive, of the prevailing social morality adopted by the state—that is to say that it makes sense to conceive of criminal law as speaking in a moral voice, expressing community disapproval of conduct—but this moral voice is always mediated through the institutions of law.[53] This accordingly grounds the idea of public wrong in the aim of the institution and formulates it in a way which potentially has implications for the content of the criminal law.[54] Crucially, however, it starts from the claim that criminal law has some specific public institutional purpose which is more than, and distinct from, a right to punish or respond in some way to individual wrongs.

[51] MacCormick, *Institutions*, n.2, pp.207–9. This is discussed further below.

[52] There are, of course, a range of other institutions, both legal and non-legal, which also contribute to this general end. I shall discuss the sense in which securing civil order might be an aim specific to the criminal law below.

[53] 'Criminal law is always and inevitably expressive, or perhaps it is better to say constitutive, of a prevailing social morality adopted and enforced by the state' MacCormick, *Institutions*, n.2, p.211.

[54] MacCormick, *Institutions*, n.2, p.216. He also seeks to formulate this in terms which pull it away from a connection to something like the harm principle because the protection of peace or civility might include instances of criminalizing conduct where there is no clear harm (though recognizing that wrongful intention will be required).

IV. Criminal Law as an Institution

Notwithstanding these arguments, it is important to recognize that MacCormick's account of criminal law as an institution is undeveloped in certain key respects, and can at best be a starting point for development.[55] I want to take up three points here as a way of trying to build on these basic methodological foundations. These are: first, the appropriateness of the identification of securing civil order or the conditions of civil order as the aim of criminal law; second, the question of whether this offers an adequate foundation for identifying the distinctive character of criminal law; and lastly, I shall comment on how I see this kind of account feeding into normative theories of criminalization. I should also stress that my aim is less that of clarifying MacCormick's theory than to show how it might offer a basis on which I can develop a new kind of approach to thinking about criminalization.

A. Securing civil order

There is some confusion around the nature of the claim that the aim of the criminal law is to secure civil order. It appears in part as a threshold claim, drawing on Locke, about the need to establish peace in order to prevent private vengeance as a precondition for the development of legal institutions.[56] However, it can also be understood in more general terms as an aim of the institution of the modern criminal law, which can shape its content in some way. The first version of the claim would deny any specific organizing role to the idea of securing civil order or society, seeing it only as a basic condition for establishing institutions of law: once civil peace was established by the entering into of a social contract, then the criminal law would require an independent justification. This has led Ulväng to argue that the justification of the right to punish must in fact be central, for this becomes the operative aim of criminal law once civil order has been established.[57] I shall explain below why I think that there are good reasons for holding onto the second type of claim—that securing civil order is a general and continuing aim of the criminal law—but before doing so I want briefly to address this point. As I have already suggested, to reduce the aims of criminal law to those of punishment fundamentally underplays the extent to which criminal law might have other aims and functions, such as the articulation of norms which shape or guide conduct in modern society.[58] This is not to deny the need for the justification of

[55] For critical discussion of MacCormick on criminal law, see V Tadros, 'Institutions and Aims' and M Ulväng, 'Criminal Law and Public Peace' both in del Mar & Bankowski, *Law as Institutional Normative Order*, n.35. The points raised in these essays are also discussed in Bottoms, 'Civil Peace', n.48, pp.244–9.

[56] J. Locke, *Second Treatise on Government* (https://ebooks.adelaide.edu.au/l/locke/john/l81s/) Ch.2.

[57] Ulväng, 'Criminal Law and Public Peace', n.55, pp.133–6.

[58] This argument is developed in Chapter 2.

punishment: it is almost certainly the case that one of the means of securing civil order is through just rather than arbitrary punishment, justified through law—so that the ends and the means may combine in a way that acquires a force or weight of its own. But this is not a necessary relation—nor would it mean that this is the only aim of the criminal law.[59] This does not mean that the demands of justice with respect to punishment should be neglected, but that the justification of the right to punish should, at least in the modern criminal law, be seen as having emerged and been given shape with the development of the institution.[60]

A second set of concerns then relate to the question of what exactly it means to claim that the criminal law is pursuing this aim (of securing civil order). It has been pointed out that different parts of the criminal law might be regarded as pursuing different aims, that the law itself might pursue multiple aims, or that the aims of the legislator in respect of criminal law might be distinct from those who enforce the law and different again from the aims of criminal courts.[61] These arguments are important, and over the course of the book I will give due weight to the idea that parts of the criminal law are directed at different kinds of aims. However, the claim about securing civil order as an aim of the criminal law is of a different kind from these more immediate aims. It is deliberately pitched at a very general level, as an anthropological claim about human society, in order to introduce the idea that securing civil order, living under the governance of law, is an irreducibly social enterprise.[62] It also, however, introduces a normative orientation. Civil order is more than order. It is order of a particular kind, which must be defined and secured through law as a central element of its civility. And it is never completely secured, as it is not a state (such as the absence of war) but is a process. Thus it is less an aim in an instrumental sense, than a broader purposive orientation.[63] I do not mean by this to imply that criminal law is the only means of securing civil order, only that it is one means of doing so—and in modern Western states it has in fact been central to this enterprise. It is not intended to build in the more specific idea that criminal law is goal-oriented or consequentialist: it might be, and as I shall show in Chapter 3, for much of its modern history it has been oriented towards different kinds of specific aims. However, it is equally

[59] 'We do not live in society in order to condemn, though we may condemn in order to live': HLA Hart, *Punishment and Responsibility* (Oxford: Clarendon, 1968) p.172.

[60] In the modern criminal law, the requirement for just punishment has been institutionalized in some codes and human rights instruments, regulated by appeal courts and review commissions. The values and the demand for justice are important, but this should not obscure the fact that both the modern understanding of just punishment (proportional, certain, humane) and the particular form of its institutionalization are relatively recent, and followed on from the establishment of law.

[61] See e.g. discussion in HM Hart, 'The Aims of the Criminal Law' (1958) 23 *Law and Contemporary Problems* p.401. See also RA Duff, 'Responsibility, Citizenship and Criminal Law' in RA Duff & S Green, *Philosophical Foundations of Criminal Law* (Oxford: Oxford UP, 2011) p.125: 'It would be rash to posit a single determinate purpose or function as *the* purpose or function of criminal law.'

[62] See e.g. A Supiot, *Homo Juridicus. On the Anthropological Function of the La*w (London: Verso, 2007). See Ch.2 for further exploration of this idea.

[63] Cf. Fuller, *The Morality of Law*, n.40.

possible to conceive of a non-consequentialist account of criminal law that is nonetheless directed at the broader aim of securing civil order: to protect the rights of individuals under law is to secure a particular kind of civil order. Aims might also be different from functions both in the sense that the aim might differ from the function and that an institution like criminal law might perform a social function without there necessarily being any awareness or reflection on this. Durkheim's claim, for example, about the reintegrative function of criminal law discussed above, does not necessarily require any awareness of this function. Once this awareness exists, it might be possible to aim at making the function more effective, or aligning the aim with the function—and indeed Durkheim's sociology can be read as addressing the question of how to make the reintegrative function of the law more effective in modern society.[64]

This leads to the final set of concerns which cluster around the generality of the claim that criminal law aims at securing civil order and its relation to criminalization.[65] On the one hand, it can be argued that the aim of securing civil order is simply too thin or vague to contribute to any meaningful justification of why we might criminalize particular acts or omissions, or to explain why we might resort to criminal law rather than other forms of regulation.[66] On the other, it may be so broad as to be incapable of generating any limits to criminalization: almost any measure might be justified on the grounds that it contributes to securing civil order, and thus this can do no work in setting limits to the scope of the criminal law.[67] Thus, for example, if we talk about securing civil order this might mean anything from the establishment of the basic conditions of social life to the micro-management of civility in contemporary society.[68] However, rather than seeing this as a weakness, I am inclined to view it as a potential strength as it opens up a range of questions about how ideas of peace and civil order have shaped the criminal law, how criminal law as an institution has sought to secure these ends, and how the criminal law has interacted with other areas of law or forms of regulation. The generality of the claim is important as it is broad enough to allow us to group together the wide range of social practices that have been called criminal law in different historical periods. We are not restricted to looking primarily at wrongs against individuals, as the protection of other forms of common or collective good have been a substantial part of the criminal law and contributed to the securing of civil order.[69] It can also allow us to see how the aim of

[64] See e.g. Garland, *Punishment and Modern Society*, n.32, Chs.2 & 3. This, also, is the aim of restorative justice.

[65] A further question is whether we should see the aim of the criminal law as being fixed, or whether this also changes over time—and what this might mean for this theory. I do not address this here as I would argue that 'securing civil order' is a sufficiently broad way of describing the aim of the criminal law in the modern period.

[66] Or put in another way, securing civil order might be seen as an aim of law in general rather than being specific to the criminal law.

[67] See Ulväng, 'Criminal Law and Public Peace', n.55, pp.136–40. Cf. Dubber who regards this lack of limits as a characteristic of police power rather than the criminal law: MD Dubber, *The Police Power* (New York: Columbia UP, 2007).

[68] See, for example, A von Hirsch & A Simester (eds), *Incivilities* (Oxford: Hart Publishing, 2006).

[69] See Leader-Elliott, 'Critical Reading', n.11, pp.51–2.

securing civil order has been thematized or pursued in different historical periods, and the level of specificity with which it has been pursued.

In addition, it directs us to look at *how* these ends have been achieved and the role of law in securing civil order. Questions of values and justice are central, since to secure an end through law brings with it a commitment to certain broad values of generality, consistency, and justice. The approach must be to look at the particular ways that respect for values has been institutionalized—and how certain values have come to be seen as setting limits on the scope or form of the criminal law. For MacCormick, this is presented as a narrative of public institutions replacing private vengeance and the monopolization of force.[70] This is clearly an important step in the emergence of modern criminal law, but it does not exhaust the possible ways of thinking about the relation between law and civil order. The movement from private to public is not uni-directional: recent years have seen an increase in both public and private police; and moves towards increased public power might lead to increased regulation of the private domain.[71] But once again this potentially opens up questions about the relationship between private and public, as forms of law and as more general questions of the distribution of social and political space that need to be explored. This also brings us to the question of limits. Once again the question here is the priority given to the institution: it is not that values are not part of the law, but it is important to understand how they have developed. Thus we must address the question of how criminalization becomes formulated as an issue for criminal law theory, or how concerns about the limits of the law become institutionalized with the development of the modern criminal law.

Before leaving this point we should note one final way in which the question of aims is relevant to an understanding of criminalization: that the aims of the criminal law in general, or of particular areas of law, will shape understanding of the nature of particular wrongs and the way these are protected in law. The point can be made with a well-known example. It is, as I noted above, a common claim in criminal law theory that there are certain core wrongs, such as homicide or rape, which are recognized as such by all legal systems.[72] Even if we were to concede the general point—that homicide and rape are crimes in all legal systems at all times—it quickly becomes apparent that the way that these are criminalized is linked to the aims of the criminal law. Thus, although it appears that rape has always been treated as a serious crime, the meaning of rape, and what the criminal law has sought to achieve through its criminalization, has been very different in different periods and this shapes the scope of the crime—who is protected and

[70] Thus he is not seeking to answer the general question of 'why punish' but merely that of 'why states punish'.

[71] See e.g. R Matthews (ed.), *Privatizing Criminal Justice* (London: Sage, 1989); D Sklansky, 'Private Police and Democracy' (2006) 43 *Am Crim Law Rev.* 89; J Suk, 'Criminal Law Comes Home' (2006) 116 *Yale LJ* 2.

[72] See text at n.14. See also TB Lambert, 'Theft, Homicide and Crime in Late Anglo-Saxon Law' (2012) 214 *Past and Present* 1–41 who argues (at 8–9) that while homicide was a serious offence under Anglo-Saxon law, it was not regarded as a crime.

what they are protected against. It has been argued that the crime of rape in early medieval English law was an offence against sexual property—or the property of the father in the chastity (and hence marriageable value) of his daughter—and consequently the law distinguished between the rape of different types of women, treating the rape of a virgin as the most serious form of the crime.[73] By the eighteenth century, rape was seen as a crime of violence, with the consequence that non-consensual intercourse fell outwith the scope of the crime.[74] And in many jurisdictions, the crime of rape is now conceived of as an offence against sexual autonomy—the choice of the individual to decide when and with whom to have sexual intercourse.[75] This has the consequence of making consent (or its absence) the central element in the definition of the crime and broadening the definition of the *actus reus* (to include oral and anal penetration) as it is the wrong against sexual autonomy which is central, rather than the gender or status of the victim. The example is schematic but illustrates the central point that the wrong cannot be understood as an intrinsic quality of the conduct, but is linked to the aims of the criminal law which in turn shapes the scope of the legal protection.

B. The distinctiveness of criminal law

As noted above, a criticism of taking the aim of securing civil order as an aim of criminal law is that it is too general. Can it not be said that all forms of law are in some sense directed towards the end of securing civil order? If this is the case, then this account may be vulnerable to the same criticisms that I made of other theories in the first part of the paper: that it cannot identify anything that is distinctive about criminal law; or that in order to provide an account of the distinctiveness of criminal law it must fall back on something like an account of the ends of punishment, as the only distinctive feature of criminal law is the routine application of punishment. This is a serious criticism, and in addressing it we need to turn to the literature on the nature of crime and criminal law.

As an initial point, it is important to distinguish between two possible senses of the claim about being distinctive. The first is general, and the second is the more specific one of seeking to identify the positive characteristics that might be unique to the criminal law. Distinctiveness in the first sense takes the form of the claim that criminal law is not just adjectival, protecting rights that are defined

[73] See *Bracton on the Laws and Customs of England* (translated with revisions and notes by Samuel E Thorne) (Cambridge: Harvard UP, 1968) p.415: 'Punishment of this kind [castration] does not follow in the case of every woman, though she has been forcibly ravished, but some other punishment does follow, according as she is married or a widow living a respectable life, a nun or a matron, a recognised concubine or a prostitute plying her trade without discrimination of person.' This example and its implications is explored at greater length in Chapter 9.

[74] See W Blackstone, *Commentaries on the Law of England* (1769 edn) (Chicago: Chicago University Press, 1979) iv, p.201: Rape is the 'carnal knowledge of a woman forcibly and against her will'.

[75] See e.g. Scottish Law Commission, *Report on Rape and Other Sexual Offences* (Rept No 209) (London: HMSO, 2007) and Sexual Offences (Scotland) Act 2009.

elsewhere. It has a public function of its own, and it is also public law in a relevant sense. By this I mean that it is a means of protecting legally defined interests (rather than either private rights or moral wrongs).[76] Distinctiveness in this sense is intended not only to capture the difference between law and moral theory—in terms of the institutional dimension of any rules—but also to capture the way that the distinctive nature of criminal law is closely bound up with its purposive character.[77] This is thus to argue that if we wish to identify the distinctive character of criminal law, this cannot be done solely by looking at the nature or seriousness of legal norms, but must be done in terms of the institutional ends pursued by the criminal law as a whole.

In relation to the second sense, we should begin by noting that attempts to produce a definition of crime and criminal law have largely struggled to identify satisfactorily characteristics which are unique to the criminal law. We might, as a consequence, be wary of this attempt to identify unifying features or organizing principles, as it is not clear that this is a question capable of being answered in a straightforward way. Such attempts have routinely fallen into one of two traps. On the one hand, some definitions are seen as too broad and positivistic. The best known of these is perhaps Glanville Williams' claim that a crime is an act capable of being followed by criminal proceedings.[78] This has been criticized on the basis that while it might be descriptively accurate, it is circular and says nothing about what might make proceedings criminal, and so is of little normative value. On the other hand, some theories have sought to identify a characteristic of the criminal law, such as that it punishes serious moral wrongs, that might be the basis for conceptual identity.[79] A significant problem with these approaches is that by treating crime as an object which can exist independently of criminal law, unity might be achieved at the cost of sociological understanding.[80] Rather than focusing on the search for the single factor that is able to define the distinctive character of criminal law, it is better to note that there is instead a range of factors which might be capable of doing a certain amount of normative work in thinking about

[76] Cf. the idea of *Rechtsgut*, or legally protected interests in German criminal law. Criminal law is not about the protection against moral wrongs, but interests which have been defined in law. On the struggle to reconcile the descriptive and normative in this concept see MD Dubber, 'Theories of Crime', n.13.

[77] Cf. M Thorburn, 'Constitutionalism and the Limits of the Criminal Law' in RA Duff et al. (eds), *The Structures of the Criminal Law* (Oxford: Oxford UP, 2011) at pp.97–102 for a recent account which seeks to argue that the constitutional state establishes the framework for civil life and that criminal wrongs are those which attack the very idea of living together under law.

[78] G Williams, 'The Definition of Crime' (1955) 8 *Current Legal Problems* p.107. See Ch.3 at pp.95–6.

[79] See e.g. G Lamond, 'What is a Crime?' (2007) 27 *Ox Jnl of Leg Stud* pp.609–32.

[80] It can, of course, be argued that these are different kinds of question. The former is descriptive and analytical, and the latter is engaged in a philosophical attempt to identify principles or criteria which might assist in determining what might properly be criminal. However, they are closely related, and for reasons expressed in Section II above, I have reservations about approaches which seek to begin by identifying the character of wrongs without first acknowledging the role of law in shaping our understandings of those wrongs.

criminalization. The focus of the institutional theory is not necessarily to identify a single defining characteristic. Instead it is necessary to recognize that there are different kinds of norms in the criminal law and that the range of conduct regulated, the scope of wrongs that have been criminalized and so on, have changed over time. In doing this, however, we must recognize that there is not necessarily a single modern criminal law. There are different stages or periods of development and the current criminal law is a combination of different institutions, practices and so on from different periods.[81] Rather than producing an a priori definition of criminal law, the first task of the theorist should be to trace the range of possible factors and justifications and their changing relation to the justification of punishment. However, while this might produce a descriptively rich account of criminalization, it leaves open the question of how this would feed into a normative theory of criminalization.

C. Rethinking theoretical approaches to criminalization

In concluding this section, I want to address the question of how the approach set out here might contribute to normative theorizing about criminalization. My argument in this chapter has been that in thinking about criminalization we need to pay more attention to the institution of law, and specifically to the distinctive character or aims of the criminal law and their relation to questions of criminalization. In doing so, I am not suggesting that we should disregard central moral questions that have dominated writing about criminalization—wrongs, harm, punishment. However, I am arguing that neglect of the aims of the criminal law has led to certain odd features in the literature on criminalization, and further that it may offer a way of bridging the gap between this literature and important criminological writings on criminalization. A recognition of the distinctive institutional features of the criminal law has been absent from existing normative theories of criminalization, and the methodology outlined here is intended in the first instance to be a corrective to this neglect.[82] The purpose of a theory of criminalization is to come to terms with legal questions about the proper scope and limits of the criminal law. Moral theories have become an important resource in thinking critically about the limits and scope of criminal law, but should not necessarily be accorded priority.

Second, while it is clear that my approach is one that aims to present a descriptively richer account of the modern criminal law, we might ask whether this is likely to be theoretically useful. When building a theory, we might decide to picture criminal law in a certain way for strategic reasons, and provided that this is not too remote from 'reality', there are clear advantages to such selectivity in terms of reducing complexity—and moreover a description, however rich, is not

[81] See D Garland, *Culture of Control* (Oxford: Oxford UP, 2001) Ch.8.

[82] See D Brown, 'History's Challenge to Criminal Law Theory' (2009) 3 *Criminal Law and Philosophy* 271–87 which argues for greater attention to the institutional structure of criminal law.

a theory. But the question here is that of how we can be sure that in doing so we are taking the most relevant or salient features of the criminal law. It is clear that a certain kind of orthodoxy has developed within criminalization theory—about there being a core of moral wrongs, about the relationship between general part and particular crimes and about the rational character of the criminal law. But does it make sense to see criminal law as a form of 'rational coercion', appealing to a subject's responsible agency?[83] Can or should all forms of criminal law fit the model of moral condemnation? Are there core or paradigmatic crimes? Many criminological and sociological accounts of criminal law would question such assumptions and so the aim of beginning with this kind of descriptively rich account of the criminal law is to try and build up a more robust account of the relevant starting points for normative theory.

Finally, a concern that is addressed to positivist (or post-positivist) approaches, such as this, is that in defining the scope and aims of the law in terms of a description of field of the criminal law, we must accept criminal law's own account of its scope—a concern which can be seen to be linked to Tadros' claim that MacCormick's institutional theory, and his method of 'rational reconstruction', generally neglects the demands of justice.[84] It has become fashionable to describe normative theorizing in this area as 'rational reconstruction', an approach that aims not only to make the best sense of existing practices of the law, but also to reveal an underlying structure of moral and political values.[85] This kind of exercise might, in Tadros' sense, do no more than produce an elegant justification of an unjust system, papering over the cracks of irrationality and contradiction. Just as there may be little inherent value in producing a coherent account purely for the sake of coherency, there might be little value in an ideal theory which is remote from existing practices and institutions.[86] The argument here is that this kind of approach will be incapable of generating the necessary critical bite when discussing criminalization.

The reconstruction that is attempted here addresses this issue by clarifying our understanding of the potential and limits of normative theory. The initial step is to historicize the question: the aim is not to identify a theory of criminal law, but how theories of criminal law have been constructed, and the particular features of the law that were taken to be central to that theoretical self-understanding.

[83] Simester & von Hirsch, *Crimes, Harms and Wrongs*, n.15, p.6.

[84] Tadros, 'Institutions and Aims', n.55, pp.87–8.

[85] See e.g. RA Duff, *Answering for Crime*, n.4, pp.5–6; SP Green, *13 Ways to Steal a Bicycle. Theft Law in the Information Age* (Cambridge, MA: Harvard UP, 2012) p.70 ; CS Elliott & C de Than, 'The Case for Rational Reconstruction of Consent in Criminal Law' (2007) 70 *Mod LR* p.225.

[86] See the criticisms raised in Leader-Elliott, 'Critical Reading', n.11, pp.48–9. See also the discussion in E Melissaris, 'Theories of Crime and Punishment' in MD Dubber & T Hörnle, *Oxford Handbook of Criminal Law* (Oxford: Oxford UP, 2014) distinguishing between ideal, situated, and political constructivist theories of criminal law. Cf Bottoms' defence of MacCormick's rational reconstruction against Tadros' criticism: 'properly conducted…rational reconstruction aims to bring out into the open *all* aspects of the working of given institutions…' ('Civil Peace and Criminalization', n.48, p.245, my emphasis).

A theory of the criminal law will, to some degree, reflect its institutional form at a particular point in time, and we can understand criminal law theories as rational reconstructions (to a greater or lesser degree) of that institution. Thus, if we are looking at the institution of criminal law within the modern constitutional state, this should be done by exploring how the modern institution of criminal law developed—the habits, customs, theories, and practices of criminal law that have shaped the modern law.[87] This is more than just establishing the contingency of particular understandings of crime, or even wrongdoing, or even of particular institutional arrangements or practices—important as it is to be aware of these factors.[88] It is about the development of the criminal law as a distinct body of rules and of the reflexive understandings of the nature and purpose of the criminal law. This requires that we recognize the limitations of normative theory—precisely because criminal laws are institutional facts and as the institution evolves, so too does our understanding. However, it also refines the potential for a normative theory of criminal law by clarifying the relation between normative theory and the development of the law. The possibility of developing a normative theory of criminalization can only be enhanced by improving our understanding of the institution of modern criminal law and the role that theory plays within it.

That said, the risk here is the same as that run by any theoretical account of law: that of falling between irrelevance and apology. The answer to this lies in the critical space which is always opened between the institution and its values, and the process of reflecting on both the ideals and the practice in order to produce a critical understanding of the modern institution of the criminal law.

V. Conclusion

The focus in this chapter has been on methodological issues. I have reviewed the form of current debates around criminalization and identified what I see as weaknesses. These are the absence of a strong sense of the difference between criminal law and moral or political theory and the idea that in thinking about criminalization it is important to consider not only the nature of the interest to be protected, but also the aim of the criminal law in securing that interest. I have argued that one way of addressing these issues is through understanding criminal law as an institution, committed to the securing of civil order.

In Part II we will go on to look to develop this claim about criminal law as an institution in some detail by looking at the development of the modern criminal

[87] See also Lacey, 'Historicising Criminalization', n.31. See also S Skinner, 'Tainted Law? The Italian Penal Code, Fascism and Democracy' (2011) 7 *Intnl Jnl of Law in Context* 423 at p.434 arguing for the need to understand the 'associative identity' of law: its symbolic dimensions and its relation to larger social normative orders.

[88] See Farmer, 'Criminal Wrongs', n.10.

law, both in the specific historical sense of how the modern idea of criminal law has been instituted or made, and in the more general sense of the characteristic institutional features of the modern. But before doing so it is necessary in the next chapter to develop our understanding of how securing civil order can be seen as the aim of criminal law.

2

Securing Civil Order

I. Introduction

> We are not to expect that the laws of any country are to be framed as so many lessons of morality, to instruct the citizen how he may act the part of the virtuous man. Laws, whether civil or political, are expedients of policy to adjust the pretensions of parties, and to secure the peace of society.[1]

In this chapter I want to develop the argument that the aim of the criminal law can be understood as that of securing civil order. In doing so I want to move beyond the claim briefly canvassed in the last chapter that this means no more than that security or order is the minimum threshold for social life and to develop further the argument advanced there about the institutional character of criminal law. The claim that criminal law secures order usually takes one of two forms. It is either conceived of in negative terms—peace as opposed to war—or is understood as a baseline—order in the sense of the minimum protection of certain basic goods. The function of the idea of order in such arguments is to establish a basis for sovereignty, the moment of contract being the moment at which society passes from a pre-legal to a legal order. Civil order is thus a way of characterizing the fact of order rather than a term denoting anything specific about the nature of that order. Once civil order in this sense has been established, the nature of the order is taken as given, rather than being understood as an object that might itself be pursued through law or indeed as an object whose meaning is itself contested and the content of which may change over time. This kind of approach is familiar in political philosophy: linking different political theories to different possible conceptions of the criminal law as alternatives to, or varieties of, liberalism.[2] However, in this chapter I want to develop a different approach to understanding the relation between criminal law and civil order.[3]

[1] A Ferguson, *Principles of Moral and Political Science* (Edinburgh: W Creech, 1792) vol. II p.145.

[2] See e.g. P Pettit, 'Criminalization in Republican Theory' and S Dimock, 'Contractarian Criminal Law Theory and *Mala Prohibita* Offences' both in RA Duff et al., *Criminalization. The Political Morality of the Criminal Law* (Oxford: Oxford UP, 2014); A Ristroph, 'Hobbes on 'Diffidence' and the Criminal Law' in MD Dubber (ed.), *Foundational Texts in Criminal Law* (Oxford: Oxford UP, 2014). See also essays in RA Duff & SP Green (eds), *Philosophical Foundation of Criminal Law* (Oxford: Oxford UP, 2011) Part I.

[3] Thus a claim to be looking at criminal law in the liberal state should not be understood as a claim about criminal law and liberal thought, but at the form and functions of the criminal law

The chapter will address three overlapping themes, corresponding to different ways in which the term 'civil' is used, each of which has a descriptive and a normative dimension. The first of these is to examine the relation between law and civil order. As Oakeshott has pointed out, it can be difficult to identify the role of law, because the existence of social rules of all kinds makes it possible both to over- and under-estimate its importance.[4] It is thus necessary to begin by identifying the relevant features of civil order, before going on to look at the ways in which criminal law might contribute to the securing of that order. In doing this, we should note that security and civil order are not necessarily synonymous, although they are often treated as such. I will thus seek to distinguish, on the one hand, between security and civil order as objects or aims of the criminal law and, on the other, the use of criminal law as a means of securing civil order.

The second theme is to look at the understanding of the criminal law and the concept of civilization. In the modern period, it has become commonplace to claim that criminal law marks a distinction between civilization and barbarism. It might be argued that criminal law is all that prevents us from falling back into a state of nature, or that the criminal law can educate or train people into a civilized state, or even that the way that the criminal law is used is an index or measure of a state of civilization. These types of claim, and the contrast they rely on, are revealing about modern understandings of the relation between law and civil order and thus offer an important perspective on modern understandings of the development and function of the criminal law.[5] This also provides a way of understanding the relationship between the development of the criminal law and the civilizing process. Finally, I will look at the relation between criminal law and civility in the sense of understandings of rules of public and private conduct. The focus here will be on the regulation of relations between individuals, of standards of conduct and expectations of appropriate behaviour in public and private life. The aim is to show the links between the criminal law and the building of civil and political order, and also to look at the modality of law in contributing to understandings of civility. The commitment to legal regulation entails certain constraints and values which reflexively bind, however imperfectly, the state. The relation between criminal law and civility is thus not only a question of the substance of the law—what is regulated—but also a question of how it is regulated—why the criminal law is used and what this means for the self-understanding of a society. Overall, the focus is on expanding the account of the institutional character of criminal law introduced in the last chapter.

associated with the state forms which developed in the late eighteenth and early nineteenth centuries which can be characterized as liberal states.

[4] M Oakeshott, 'On the Civil Condition' in *On Human Conduct* (Oxford: Clarendon, 1975) p.181.

[5] I do not take the claims about civilization at face value, but am interested in the way that these are used as an index and what this then tells us about the understanding of the person making the claim.

II. Order, Social and Civil

> The most difficult feature of the civil condition to identify and get into place has been law. This is not because there was not law in abundance to be observed and to be observed in use, and not only because this law was an exceedingly ambiguous mixture of rules of all sorts, of moral precepts and of imperatives and directives which were not rules properly speaking and from which it has been a supremely difficult task to disentangle and distinguish the law (not the rules of law) appropriate to the civil condition.[6]

As a first step it is necessary to consider the relation between social and civil order. As I suggested above, a central issue here is that the concept of order itself is taken for granted as something that, once established, can safely be put aside as an issue of theoretical concern. However, if I am to make good on the claim that the aim of the criminal law should be understood in terms of securing civil order then it is necessary to set out a basic account of the terms in which we should understand the concept of civil order and the place of law within it.

Social theory generally recognizes different bases for social order—market, contract, community, state—and the priority given in different theories to one or other of these normally reflects different understandings of the individual, and has different implications for the roles of law and the state in terms of the objects to be protected and of the understanding of the 'proper' domain of the law.[7] While this can offer a useful analytical framework, I want to approach the issue here in a different way by looking at the historical and conceptual relations between different kinds of social and civil order and their relation to forms of the criminal law. It is thus both a theoretical and a descriptive exercise. The task, therefore is to outline, first, the conceptual relation between social order, civil order and the criminal law before moving to look at how the criminal law has in practice contributed to the securing of civil order.

I want to begin by drawing a distinction between social and civil order, the latter being distinguished by its character as a kind of institutional order. This, I shall argue, maps on to our understanding of the early historical origins of the criminal law, and also reinforces the claim made in the last chapter that the origin and aims of punishment can be seen as distinct from the origin and aims of the criminal law. I shall then go on to make two further points. The first is that our understanding of what makes civil order civil is not exhausted in the specification of certain a priori norms or conditions, but is itself linked to the continuing development of certain institutions. And second, that the question of how this

[6] Oakeshott, 'On the Civil Condition', n.4, p.181.

[7] See generally, D Wrong, *The Problem of Order. What Unites and Divides Society* (Cambridge MA: Harvard UP, 1994); M Hechter & C Horne, *Theories of Social Order. A Reader* (2nd edn) (Stanford: Stanford UP, 2009); M Lichbach & A Seligman, *Market and Community. The Basis of Social Order, Revolution and Relegitimation* (Univ. Park PA: Penn State UP, 2000).

order is secured—and thus of the role of criminal law—is related, at least in part, to the underlying conception of order. My aim then is to use this examination of the securing of civil order less as a means for reflecting on the basis of sovereignty than as means of demonstrating how this can be understood as an overarching aim of the modern criminal law.

The contrast between order and the absence of order, or *anomia*, is a distinction which underpins much modern political theory. According to Dahrendorf '*anomia* is a social condition in which the norms which govern people's behaviour have lost their validity'.[8] It is a state of extreme uncertainty or breakdown of social trust, in which no one knows what kind of behaviour to expect from others and there is no effective system of sanctioning. Conversely, he suggests that what is distinctive about human societies is that they operate according to a set of norms which make human behaviour predictable and which enable some degree of social trust in the sense of allowing us to cope with uncertainty over time.[9] On the conventional view, it is the establishment of order, the transition from the disorderly state of nature to order guaranteed by the power of the sovereign, that is seen as the fundamental condition of social life.[10] On this view, law and order are virtually synonymous: the foundation of law is the fundamental condition for the establishment of social order, as peace succeeds war. This also links law and security, with the insecurity of the state of nature being replaced by a collective security guaranteed by sovereign power. Law, security, and order are thus linked, with law seen as the guarantor of order, such that the absence of law would lead to insecurity or the complete breakdown of social order. It is the moment of transition from peace to war, from disorder to order, and from *anomia* to legal order, that is crucial to the definition of the sovereign order and the establishment of law. This moment, whether conceived as a social contract or the surrendering of natural liberty, is then the basis for the legitimation and limits of the sovereign order that it gives rise to; and it is accordingly this moment that has been the focus of much political theory.

However, the existence of social order, in the sense of the existence of settled norms of conduct, does not necessarily entail civil order in the specific sense of there being central legal or political institutions. What is essential to social order is that there be some mechanisms, whether operating in the form of negotiation or the exchange of gifts, which guarantee stability of social norms and consistency in

[8] R Dahrendorf, *Law and Order* (London: Stevens, 1985) p.24. He begins his account with a description of Berlin in 1945. Cf. the similar account in WO Weyrauch, 'The Experience of Lawlessness' (2007) 4 *New Crim LR* pp.415–40.

[9] Dahrendorf, *Law and Order*, n.8, p.24. On trust, see N Luhmann, *Trust and Power* (New York: Wiley, 1979); J-P Reemtsma, *Trust and Violence. An Essay on a Modern Relationship* (Princeton NJ: Princeton UP, 2012).

[10] Classically T. Hobbes, *Leviathan* (Harmondsworth: Penguin, 1968) Pt.II Ch.17; J. Locke, *Second Treatise on Government* (https://ebooks.adelaide.edu.au/l/locke/john/l81s/) Chs.7–9. See also J Dunn, 'Trust and Political Agency' in D Gambetta (ed.), *Trust. Making and Breaking Cooperative Relations* (Oxford: Basil Blackwell, 1988) pp.81–8 arguing that Locke's theory was based on the need for trust as mutual understanding and commitment, and of the need for a legitimate political authority as a means of ensuring this.

our behavioural expectations of others.[11] This implies a broad view of social order, which can include all societies where there are norms capable of guaranteeing predictable behaviour, even where there are not necessarily central legal institutions to enforce them. As anthropological studies of societies where the bloodfeud exists have shown, for example, this is in fact a process that is highly structured by norms, which may or may not be regarded as laws, which make conduct and outcomes highly predictable such that it makes sense to describe this as a form of social order.[12] Order requires security and a degree of social trust, but this can be secured through kinship ties and the existence of stable norms of conduct and so can be regarded as distinct from civil order secured through centralized sovereign institutions. On this account, then, social order in the absence of such institutions should be regarded as distinct from *anomia*, or the theoretical idea of the state of nature as extreme insecurity, and both should be regarded as distinct from civil order, where norms of conduct are guaranteed or enforced by central institutions through law.

Civil order can thus be understood as a particular kind of social order; it is not merely order as such.[13] It refers not only to the existence of norms and social relations guaranteeing stability of expectations, but also to a certain kind of institutional ordering in which the burden of guaranteeing social and normative order is taken on by centralized institutions, what Roberts has referred to as the 'aspiration to "govern"'.[14] The distinctive feature of civil order is thus the existence of legal institutions in the sense not only of the existence of norms of conduct but also as an apparatus of rule which can regulate social relations and settle disputes by adjudicating between norms.[15] This distinction between social and civil order is usually elided in classical political thought where order is understood as the absence of war, and typically the establishment of order and of political and legal institutions are seen as linked: it is precisely the establishment of a central authority which takes men out of the state of nature and guarantees the social order.[16] However, if the key distinction is not that between order and the absence of order or between peace and war, but that between social and civil order, it is necessary

[11] F Pirie, *The Anthropology of Law* (Oxford: Oxford UP, 2013) Ch.2; A Giddens, *The Constitution of Society* (Cambridge: Polity, 1984) pp.60–4 refers to the sense of 'ontological security' that humans require.

[12] See e.g. E Gellner, 'Trust, Cohesion and the Social Order' in Gambetta (ed.), *Trust*, n.10. See also M Gluckmann, 'The Peace in the Feud' (1955) 8 *Past & Present* pp.1–14.

[13] Cf. AE Bottoms, 'Civil Peace and Criminalization' in Duff et al., *Criminalization*, n.2, pp.237–43 treating civil peace and social order as synonymous.

[14] See S Roberts, 'After Government? On Representing Law without the State' (2005) 68 *Mod LR* 13. Also discussed in Pirie, *Anthropology*, n.11, pp.42–6 though she argues for a broader concept of law.

[15] See e.g. M Oakeshott, 'On the Civil Condition', n.4, p.141. Cf. N MacCormick, *Institutions of Law* (Oxford: Oxford UP, 2007) on the two tiers of normative structure.

[16] Hobbes, *Leviathan*, n.10. See M Oakeshott, *Hobbes on Civil Association* (Oxford: Basil Blackwell, 1975) Ch.1.

to focus more closely on the nature of civil order and of the institutions that have emerged to guarantee that order.[17]

Although this understanding of civil order points towards specifically modern institutions such as the nation state, it is worth looking briefly at debates about the earlier origins of modern criminal law as this can shed further light on the significance of this distinction.[18] Early European societies are understood to have been organized around the bloodfeud. The term bloodfeud refers to societies in which the response to the killing of a member of a family or social grouping was the use of, or threat of, retaliatory violence against either the assailant or another member of the assailant's group. As suggested above, these societies did not exist in a state of complete social disorder or *anomia*. In practice there were complex norms which circumscribed the range of possible victims or which allowed for composition to be paid in place of violence. What was thus distinctive about the operation of the bloodfeud was that it was a matter not of punishment but of negotiating order between individuals or groups of roughly equal social standing. This practice was transformed over a long period, running from the ninth to the fourteenth centuries, as centralized royal institutions outlawed both retaliatory violence and the payment of compensation, on pain of punishment (or outlawry). The introduction of punishment was thus based on a hierarchical relationship, between sovereign and subject, with crimes understood as breaches of a more general King's peace.

This has led to a reinterpretation of the relationship between bloodfeud and punishment. The origin of punishment is not seen as deriving from the logic of private revenge, but rather traces its origin to the establishment of sovereignty.[19] The conventional historiography traces a movement from revenge or feud to state justice as sovereign authorities gradually asserted a monopoly over legitimate violence and assimilated revenge within a network of state-sanctioned punishment practices.[20] On this view, the legitimation of a power to punish is linked historically and conceptually to the 'right' to revenge which pre-existed the establishment of the criminal law—and hence the justification of punishment is seen as the foundation for the legitimation of the criminal law.[21] The alternative view

[17] It should be stressed that this is not necessarily a matter of historical progression—from *anomia* to social to civil order, or from the pre-modern to the modern. The achievement of order is always capable of being reversed.

[18] See T Lambert, 'Theft, Homicide and Crime in Late Anglo-Saxon Law' (2012) 214 *Past & Present* pp.3–41; P Hyams, *Rancor and Reconciliation in Medieval England* (London and Ithaca: Cornell UP, 2003); G Halsall, *Violence and Society in the Early Medieval West* (Woodbridge: Boydell Press, 1998).

[19] The argument here draws on M Hildebrandt, 'Origins of the Criminal Law: Punitive Interventions before Sovereignty' in Dubber (ed.), *Foundational Texts*, n.2, pp.219–38. She traces this position to the work of Gustav Radbruch, 'The Origin of Criminal Law in the Status of the Unfree' also in Dubber (ed.), *Foundational Texts*, n.2, Appendix C.

[20] See JQ Whitman, 'At the Origins of Law and the State: Supervision of Violence, Mutilation of Bodies, or Setting of Prices' (1995-6) 71 *Chi-Kent L Rev.* pp.41–84 which traces the way that the connection between revenge and punishment was drawn in the German historiography of the criminal law. See also W Miller, *An Eye for an Eye* (New York: Cambridge UP, 2006) esp. Ch.2.

[21] This has then been characterized in an influential way as the state 'appropriating' the conflicts of private individuals, and used to argue for forms of community or private justice: N Christie,

argues, by contrast, that the establishment of sovereignty follows a different logic. Revenge was about making peace between social equals, and operated alongside systems of compensation, as both were understood as forms of repayment. The violation of the rules that established the king's peace, by contrast, was a violation of the obligation of fidelity owed to the king, and was met by punishment. Public punishment thus had its origins in royal authority, upholding an imposed order or norms established by the unilateral power of the sovereign.[22] Crucially, it follows from this that criminal law, as we know it, does not derive from private revenge, which was not 'appropriated' by the state, but was integral to the establishment of centralized institutions and civil order. It is, in its origins, a form of public law.[23]

This claim is important to my argument here in three respects. First, underlining a point made in the last chapter, criminal law is a distinct institution from revenge or negotiated 'private' order. On this account it emerges together with centralized 'state' institutions, rather than pre-existing them. Thus it is necessary to look at the emergence and justification of criminal law as a distinct public institution rather than as something that derives from a 'pre-legal' understanding of private revenge or retribution. Second, state punishment must be justified, but it must be justified as a form of state power. A theory of retribution might be central to this justification, but it cannot simply be 'read off', or equated to, moral ideas of private revenge or retaliation since punishment has its origins in public rather than private right. We should not confuse the form that the justification takes with what requires justifying. Finally, and most importantly, it ties the emergence of the institution of the criminal law to the idea of civil order in the specific sense in which I have been discussing it here. The development of the criminal law—indeed of our conception of law itself—is linked to the emergence of the state, or a body like the state, not only historically, but also as a matter of conceptual necessity. In this process the state realigns all other forms of authority within its jurisdiction, changing the conditions under which, and the mechanisms through which, trust and social order can be secured. This is achieved in part through the development of criminal law.

What then are the principal characteristics of the institution of criminal law? At this point, I shall identify four themes which will be developed from a number of different perspectives throughout the book.[24] The aim is not to produce a definition of criminal law: these characteristics are deliberately framed widely so as

'Conflicts as Property' (1977) 17 *Brit Jnl of Criminol* pp.1–15. This is discussed in V Halvorsen, 'Nils Christie: "Conflicts as Property"', in Dubber, *Foundational Texts*, n.2, pp.335–52.

[22] Hildebrandt thus argues that the state did not appropriate private revenge but in fact prohibited it ('Origins', n.19, p.223).

[23] It is interesting in the same connection to note that Lambert argues that homicide was not a crime in Anglo-Saxon law, in the sense that it was not a matter for the royal courts or law codes. Homicide was dealt with 'privately' by means of negotiation and compensation, see 'Theft, Homicide and Crime', n.18, pp.16–32.

[24] Drawing on the formulation in I Loader & N Walker, *Civilizing Security* (Cambridge: Cambridge UP, 2007) pp.26–7. Cf. S Roberts, 'After Government?', n.14, p.14 identifying six features necessary to any sustained attempt to institutionalize political power.

to capture general features of civil order and criminal law in modernity without committing to any particular normative understanding of the character and aims of criminal law.[25] It is the development and inter-relation of these characteristics which can then shed light on the question of civil order and how it has been secured by the criminal law.

First, there is the classic Weberian conception of the state as entailing a monopoly on the legitimate means of physical violence, both with respect to external conflicts and the internal maintenance of order.[26] This, as was argued above, should not be understood in terms of the appropriation of private remedies such as revenge and compensation, but as the establishment and codification of a new form of public rule based on a principle of hierarchy. Neither is it a static moment or condition; rather it is a process shaping forms of sociality and relations of trust.[27] The control of violence, however, is fundamental to the maintenance of civil order. Second, in the modern era law has been central to the process of marking the boundaries of the modern state and maintaining its sense of identity. In criminal law this is performed primarily, though not exclusively, through the regulation of jurisdiction: the process of determining who and what is subject to the law, or the realm and the limits of the criminal law.[28] Determining the proper scope of the criminal law must thus been understood as a question of jurisdiction in this wider sense of state-formation. Third, the rules of social order are fixed, or made increasingly formal, through a process of codification, systematizing, and establishing norms of conduct. This has allowed the criminal law to be used as a modality of rule in the modern state, a means of governing a population of individuals. This is not just a matter of establishing basic conditions of order, but of the use of law to achieve certain social ends. Importantly, the state does not rule in this way through the threat of punishment, but through the articulation of norms for the guidance of social conduct. And finally, as the rules of law are directed at individuals, the law has had to specify the conditions of personhood, designating the conditions under which individuals are deemed capable of responding to rules.[29] This has entailed a commitment to the rule of law and to individual liberty, as our understandings of law have come to shape the moral order of modernity. This is significant both in the sense that the state comes to be bound by its own violence-limiting and rule-defining conditions, and that the ideas of individual liberty and responsibility comes to acquire a particular weight as limits to state action.[30] None of these are necessary conditions of civil order, but rather reflect the particular form that it has taken in Western modernity. As we shall see, these can be combined with each other in various different ways, as

[25] Cf. C Taylor, *Modern Social Imaginaries* (Durham, NC: Duke UP, 2004).

[26] M Weber, 'Politics as Vocation' in H Gerth & CW Mills, *From Max Weber. Essays in Sociology* (London: Routledge, 1948) p.78; N Elias, *The Civilizing Process* (Oxford: Blackwell, 1994) pp.268–77.

[27] Reemtsma, *Trust and Violence*, n.9, esp. Ch.2.

[28] See Ch.4.

[29] C Thornhill, 'Guilt and the Origins of Modern Law' (2014) 43 *Economy & Society* 103.

[30] This is a new basis for legitimacy—but also an 'intensification of the burden of justification of political rule', Loader & Walker, *Civilizing Security*, n.24, p.35.

particular instantiations of the relationship between state, individual and society change over time.

Before I move on I want to draw attention to three further issues that arise here in terms of thinking about the relation between social and civil order.

First, my discussion up to this point has been focused on the idea of civil order conceived in terms of the development of state-like institutions, and, in particular, the 'law appropriate to the civil condition'.[31] It must, however, be acknowledged that law is not the only social institution that creates or manages civil order, so an important question becomes that of how the limits of law, and in particular criminal law, have been thought about, especially when the state order of criminal law runs up against other forms of social ordering, such as the market, kinship institutions such as families, or other social institutions such as the church or corporations, or indeed other jurisdictions. In social theory, the priority given to different institutions in explaining order usually reflects different understandings of the individual, and has different implications for the roles of law and the state.[32] This can be a useful heuristic device for understanding the relation between different forms of social ordering—and indeed this is the staple of many theoretical approaches to criminalization. Limits to criminal law are seen in terms of freely entered market transactions, the private sphere, individual autonomy, and so on, depending on the starting point in moral and political theory. However, the approach I want to take to these issues here is somewhat different.

It is clear that these 'limits' reflect a modern social imaginary, and that in earlier periods it would have been equally self-evident that the criminal law should or should not intervene in certain areas of social life—because they were seen as beyond the reach of law or subject to a different kind of order.[33] Even in modernity, ideas about the limits of law in the private sphere or the market rely on a negative sense of order: these spheres have their own order, and criminal law can be permitted to intervene only where this breaks down, or is not functioning properly. The 'proper' sphere of the criminal law is thus shaped by a combination of understandings about alternative spheres of social order and of when it is proper for the criminal law to intervene to reinforce or maintain that order. Thus, for example, the market might be seen as self-regulating and beyond the reach of the criminal law except in cases of egregious frauds; or alternatively, in a time of financial insecurity resort to criminal law can secure trust in financial transactions by underpinning the market as a whole.[34] This is to make the point that the limits to law cannot be worked out in terms of abstract conceptions of

[31] Oakeshott, 'On the Civil Condition', n.4, p.181.

[32] Taylor, *Modern Social Imaginaries,* n.25, Ch.1 identifies other forms of order as the economy, the public sphere, and democratic self-rule. Another limit is the private or intimate sphere.

[33] See, for example, Anglo-Saxon law, which treated many forms of homicide as non-criminal and a matter for private settlement: Lambert, 'Theft, Homicide and Crime' n.18. Alternatively consider the regulation of sexual conduct. See Ch.9.

[34] As in the contemporary criminalization of 'market abuse'. See E Herlin-Karnell, 'White-Collar Crime and European Financial Crises: Getting Tough on EU Market Abuse' (2012) 37 *European LR* 481.

markets or the private, and there are few, if any, absolute limits to law. This raises important historical questions. It is not merely that our modern understandings of order are historically contingent, but that we need to have a better understanding of how particular ideas of order have shaped both the development of, and our understandings of, the modern criminal law.[35] This requires that we ask how certain areas have been seen as limits (often because they are understood as having a natural quality of order), when there is still understood to be a residual role for the criminal law, and how these understandings have changed over time. Understanding of the normative question of the legitimate limits of legal intervention would greatly benefit from a more complete understanding of the subtle relations between these different forms of order.

Second, there is the question of the relation between criminal law and the police power. It has been argued, most influentially by Markus Dubber, that the police power, based on the patriarchal power of the householder over their household, is a mode of governance that not only lies at the origins of the modern criminal law, but that also continues to co-exist with other forms of state authority, notably a model of criminal law based on autonomy.[36] This comprises a descriptive and a normative claim about the scope, limits, and forms of legitimacy of the two forms of power. The descriptive claim is that the importance of the police power to modern government has been neglected; much state activity is better understood and characterized in terms of the police power. This power is a survival of the *patria potestas*, the power of the father, derived from the sovereign as head of the royal household and extended to the modern state as keeper of the peace. This leads Dubber to argue that, far from being obsolete, the police power is the basis for much of the contemporary criminal law. This is then linked to the normative claim that the police power and law are each marked by certain fundamental characteristics that mirror each other. While the police power is based on hierarchy between ruler and ruled, by its open-ended or discretionary character, by a concern with efficiency, and by a 'forward-looking' or preventive logic, the autonomy model of criminal law is marked by equality between individuals, legality, and a 'backward-looking' focus on punishment for past conduct as the basis for the legitimacy of state action.

This is an important position, a radical and illuminating corrective to much conventional thinking, which challenges many of the easy assumptions made in liberal political theory about the nature and limits of state power. However, it follows from my argument that limits to criminal law cannot be seen in absolute terms and that the question of the relation between law and police must be traced through specific historical contexts. I shall argue here that much of the traditional

[35] M Neocleous, *The Fabrication of Social Order. A Critical Theory of Police Power* (London: Pluto, 2000).

[36] MD Dubber, *The Police Power: Patriarchy and the Foundations of American Government* (New York: Columbia UP 2004). See also essays in MD Dubber & M Valverde (eds), *The New Police Science* (Stanford: Stanford UP, 2006), and MD Dubber & M Valverde (eds), *Police and the Liberal State* (Stanford: Stanford UP, 2008).

police power was juridified as the development of modern criminal law as a state institution transformed it. The contemporary police power is exercised by means of laws and is thus subject to the same constraints as any other rule-governed practice in the modern state.[37] It is the case that in certain areas of state action there is wide discretion and legal protections have been only imperfectly realized. But there is a difference between characterizing something as imperfectly regulated or constrained by law, and the suggestion that police power is a fundamental or irreducible form of government. There are residual references in English law to the police power as something outwith the scope of the formal criminal law—and it is clear that its significance is stronger in certain jurisdictions, particularly Canada and the US, where the distinction between national and local (state or provincial) jurisdiction is articulated at least partly in terms of the distinction. However, I shall argue that, at least in the development of English law, this vision of police as an alternative form of order seriously underplays the significance of prevention and deterrence as the logics which were understood to underpin the exercise of the modern criminal law, and the understandings of civil order that it sought to secure, and that it is more important to look at the range of relationships between criminal law, police, and civil order.

This is linked to the third issue, which is that of the relationship between criminal law and security.[38] Much recent work in this area begins from a Hobbesian contrast between peace and war, seeing security as a primary end of the state or viewing security as a collective good, the foundation on which individual interests can be pursued.[39] Security is seen as a distinct interest or good to be protected by the criminal law—perhaps, in Marx's formulation, 'the highest social concept of civil society'—which precedes and is a condition of both social order and individual liberty.[40] On this view, security, as a collective good, is always a potential threat to individual liberty and is something that must be tamed or civilized. However, I want to reverse this position here: rather than viewing security as a distinct object, the aim is to look at how civil order is secured by the criminal law. Thus, rather than seeing security as something which sits outside the law, as a necessary evil, the aim is to look at how the criminal law operates as a particular kind of security project.[41] In describing the project of securing civil order as a process, rather than taking security as a distinct object, I am taking my cue from Adam Smith who, in a well-known passage in his *Lectures on Jurisprudence*, delineated

[37] See L Farmer, 'The Jurisprudence of Security. The Police Power and the Criminal Law' in Dubber & Valverde (eds), *The New Police Science*, n.36, pp.145–67.

[38] See generally L Zedner, *Security* (London: Routledge, 2009); M Neocleous, *Critique of Security* (Edinburgh: Edinburgh UP, 2008). See also P Ramsay, *The Insecurity State* (Oxford: Oxford UP, 2012).

[39] See e.g. Loader & Walker, *Civilising Security*, n.24, p.7 describing security as a 'thick' public good.

[40] K Marx, 'On the Jewish Question' in D McLellan, *Karl Marx. Selected Writings* (2nd edn) (Oxford: Oxford UP) p.61

[41] M Valverde, 'Studying the Governance of Crime and Security: space, time and jurisdiction' (2014) 14 *Criminology & Criminal Justice* 382; L Farmer, 'Criminal Law as a Security Project' (2014) 14 *Criminology & Criminal Justice* 399.

the province of jurisprudence as 'the theory of the rules by which civil governments ought to be directed'.[42] He saw this as comprising four main objects: the maintenance of justice; the provision of police; the raising of revenue; and the establishment of arms. While these might all be understood as relating to security as an object (social security, financial security, national security), on his account these were rather ends to be secured through government, rather than preconditions of civil order. Smith himself saw security as more narrowly concerned with 'the prevention of all crimes and disturbances which may interrupt the intercourse or destroy the peace of the society by any violent attacks'.[43] The production of security, though, was not understood narrowly as a question of crime prevention, to be achieved solely by the passing of laws or increasing numbers of law enforcement officers, but was linked to the spread of commerce and prosperity and general questions of political economy. So civil order was continually continuously being produced by good government. It could consist in different things at different times and could be secured in different ways and through different institutions. The object of jurisprudence was thus the study of how civil order can be secured and maintained through law. And it is to the further development of the idea of civil order that we must now turn.

III. Civilization and Criminalization

An often overlooked feature of John Stuart Mill's famous statement of the 'harm principle' is that it refers to the 'civilised community': 'the only purpose for which power can be rightfully exercised against any member of a civilised community, against his will, is to prevent harm to others'.[44] Thus, for Mill, the operation of the harm principle is dependent, or at least conditional, on the existence of the civilized community. This raises the specific question of what Mill understood by this term, but it also, as we shall see, taps into a much broader issue of the relationship between criminal law and what has been called the civilizing process. Mill's distinction between civilized and uncivilized, between those who qualify for liberal government and those who do not, is based on a hierarchical view of society (and societies) and an understanding of the nature of progress. What is important here, then, is the relationship between concepts of civilization and modernity—specifically the idea that a modern society was civilized society—and the place of criminal law in the civilizing process.

A useful starting point for understanding the significance of the relation between civilization and criminalization is Mill's essay on civilization, published

[42] A Smith, *Lectures on Jurisprudence* (Oxford: Oxford UP, 1978) p.5. For further discussion of Smith and security see Neocleous, *Critique of Security*, n.38, pp.24–32.

[43] Smith, *Lectures*, n.42, p.331.

[44] *John Stuart Mill on Liberty and other Essays* (1859) (ed. John Gray) (Oxford: Oxford World Classics, 1991) p.14. See also J Hamburger, *John Stuart Mill on Liberty and Control* (Princeton: Princeton UP, 2001) Ch.1.

in 1836.[45] Mill argued that the term 'civilization' could be understood in a broad and a narrow sense. The broad sense was the way in which we might speak of one society as more perfect, as 'happier, nobler, wiser' than others, as in the civilization of ancient Greece or Rome.[46] This was civilization as an ideal. The narrow sense was comparative and relative: a society might be more or less civilized than another. The term could be used to distinguish a wealthy and populous nation from savages and barbarians, but in doing so could also recognize that the progression of civilization might be accompanied by new miseries or give rise to new kinds of vices.[47] Focusing on this latter sense, Mill argued that the degree of civilization could be measured by the degree of co-operation in a society: 'Wherever, therefore, we find human beings acting together for common purposes in large bodies, and enjoying the pleasures of social intercourse, we term them civilized'.[48] Savage society was violent and fragmented and power could be exercised in an arbitrary way. In a civilized society, security, which he understood as the protection of individual interests, would depend on the collective arrangement of society, rather than on individual strength or courage—indeed for Mill this was the measure of civilization.[49] This was because co-operation was something that was learned in the progress of civilization—the division of labour was, in his phrase, the 'great school of co-operation'. Civilization, moreover, brought about the diffusion of property and intelligence throughout society and taught self-control and compromise, the sacrifice of individual will to a superior purpose.[50] The operation of the 'harm principle' was thus linked to the division of labour and to the degree of social progress: the extent to which the harm principle might operate would depend on the degree of civilization; but it was also necessary to be aware that that same civilization might give rise to new vices or harms.[51]

The central features of Mill's account—the contrast with barbarism, and progress understood as the degree of social and political organization—connect his use of the idea of civilization to the history of the word more generally.[52] Older

[45] JS Mill, 'Civilization' (1836) 3 *London and Westminster Review*, pp.1–28. Mill's understanding of civilization is discussed in K Mantena, *Alibis of Empire* (Princeton: Princeton UP, 2010) pp.30–9. See also M Levin, *JS Mill on Civilization and Barbarism* (London: Routledge, 2004).

[46] Mill, 'Civilization', n.45, p.1.

[47] Mill, 'Civilization', n.45, p.1. See also 'The Spirit of the Age' (1831) *Examiner* (23rd Jan) 50–2: 'The present age is an age of transition', concluding that what was required was a transformation of institutions by the progressive part of mankind.

[48] Mill, 'Civilization', n.45, p.2.

[49] 'There is not a more accurate test of the progress of civilization than the progress of the power of co-operation'. Mill, 'Civilization', n.45, p.4.

[50] Mill, 'Civilization', n.45, p.4.

[51] 'Despotism is a legitimate mode of government in dealing with barbarians, provided the end be their improvement, and the means be justified in actually effecting that end'. JS Mill, *On Liberty*, n.44, p.14–5.

[52] L Febvre, '*Civilisation*: Evolution of a Word and a Group of Ideas' in P Burke (ed.), *A New Kind of History. From the Writings of Febvre* (London: Routledge & Kegan Paul, 1973) pp.219–57. See also B Bowden, *The Empire of Civilization* (Chicago: Chicago UP, 2009); Z Bauman, 'On the Origins of Civilisation. A Historical Note' (1985) 2 *Theory, Culture & Society* pp.7–14; M Neocleous, 'The Police of Civilization: The War on Terror as Civilizing Offensive' (2011) 5 *International Political Sociology* pp.144–59.

words like *civilité* or *politesse* had been used by the nobility to distinguish courtly or mannered behaviour from the ruder conduct of the lower orders, but the emergence of the term 'civilization' was linked to specific ideas about the development and malleability of society. (Indeed before the eighteenth century, the term referred only to the process of changing a legal case from a criminal into a civil action.[53]) This had three key dimensions. First, it was linked to an understanding of the degree of social development of a society: civilization as a form of progress relative to other lesser or less advanced forms of society. This was articulated in different ways, from the stadial theory of development of the Scottish Enlightenment to cruder distinctions between civilization and barbarism, but the core of the idea was the understanding of the present degree of civilization as the outcome of a historical progression or civilizing process.[54] This was linked to the second dimension which was a rational self-awareness, the expression of 'the self-consciousness of the West'.[55] The idea of civilization expressed a new kind of social awareness, which sought to understand not only the nature of society, but how societies could be remade or engineered. The concept of civilization (and related ideas) was used as an index of social development and as a way of judging the conduct of others and their fitness for regulation.[56] Civilization as a project thus had an 'inner tendency' to press for political action, informed by what Bauman has described as a new kind of legislative mentality based on the rational science of society.[57] Finally, it was linked to a particular kind of governing project, the act of civilizing. The idea of the malleability of society, as Bauman points out, was not in itself a new idea—it had previously been known as *police*. What was novel about the civilizing project was that it subsumed the idea of police within this new legislative mentality, making it into a new kind of government according to the principles of political economy.[58] Thus it was not just a matter of producing order or social organization, but organization according to certain 'civilized' standards.[59] State and law played a key role as 'rational laws were the first condition of a civilized society, shaped after the pattern dictated by reason and morality'.[60] Law was thus both an index and instrument of the civilizing process.[61]

[53] 'civilization, n.'. OED Online. June 2014. Oxford University Press. http://www.oed.com/view/Entry/33584?redirectedFrom=civilization (accessed June 17, 2014).

[54] An idea associated in particular with the work of Norbert Elias. See discussion below in relation to violence and the criminal law.

[55] Elias, *The Civilizing Process*, n.26, p.5. Cf. A Pagden, 'Only the civilized can know what it is to be civilized', quoted in Bowden, *Empire of Civilization*, n.52, p.43.

[56] There was a reciprocal relationship between political institutions and the character of a people, with the institutions requiring modification to suit the specific demands or needs of people in different stages of civilization: Mantena, *Alibis of Empire*, n.45, p.31.

[57] Bauman, 'Origins of Civilisation', n.52, p.9; Z Bauman, *Legislators and Interpreters* (Cambridge: Polity, 1987); Neocleous, 'Police of Civilization', n.52, p.151.

[58] Bauman, 'Origins of Civilisation', n.52, p.8. Cf. M Foucault, 'Governmentality' in J Faubion (ed.), *Essential Works of Michel Foucault*. Vol.3, *Power* (New York: New Press, 2000).

[59] Bowden, *Empire of Civilization*, n.52, p.30.

[60] Bauman, 'Origins of Civilisation', n.52, p.10.

[61] 'The general test of whether a nation was deemed civilized revolved around its degree of socio-political organization and capacity for self-government in accordance with accepted European standards. By the nineteenth century, a civilized state required (a) basic institutions of government

Viewing Mill's argument from this perspective shows the liberal project based on the harm principle in a new light. Political inclusion in the liberal project, as Mill conceived it, is based on a 'thicker' set of social credentials than is normally acknowledged.[62] Liberalism did not require just the minimum degree of security but also a broader assessment of the antecedent character of individuals and the collective organization of society according to its degree of civilization or development before it could be determined whether or not the extension of liberty was appropriate.[63] And we see further that this trope, of using a reference to the state of civilization as a measure of the criminal law, becomes a characteristic feature of modern discourses about criminal law.[64] Paternalism has thus always been as much of a social as a moral concept, resting on assumptions about class, race, and control. This had particular relevance in terms of the imperial project, where it justified despotism in the service of the civilizing burden of the imperial powers.[65] However, it was an argument that also justified domestic improvement, regulating and governing in different contexts where conduct or places were deemed barbaric or uncivilized, in a way that linked political freedom to character.[66]

This conception of the civilizing project does not necessarily entail the use of the criminal law but, as we shall see, the criminal law was in practice a key tool for the modern state in its project of civilizing society. A central factor in this process was the regulation of physical violence, something which has been explored in the work of Norbert Elias. Elias' distinctive contribution was to view this process in terms of the relation between the development of the modern state, and in particular its monopoly on violence, and the development of individual self-control.[67] Self-restraint is not seen by him as a natural attribute of persons, but as something that is inculcated in individuals in the development of the state and complex

and public bureaucracy, (b) the organizational capacity for self-defense, (c) a published legal code and adherence to the rule of law, and (d) recognition of international law and norms, including those on the conduct of war and diplomatic exchange. If a nation could meet these requirements, it was generally deemed to be a legitimate sovereign state entitled to full recognition as an international personality' (Bowden, *The Empire of Civilization*, n.52, p.16).

[62] Mantena, *Alibis of Empire*, n.45, p.35.

[63] Mill compared backward states of society to a state of childhood or non-age: *On Liberty*, n.44, p.14.

[64] E.g. Winston Churchill's much quoted 1910 statement: 'The mood and temper of the public with regard to the treatment of crime and criminals is one of the most unfailing tests of the civilization of any country'. Quoted in E Ruggles-Brise, *The English Prison System* (London: Macmillan, 1921) p.4.

[65] See Pirie, *Anthropology of Law*, n.11, Ch.2 pp.48–9; Mantena, *Alibis of Empire*, n.45, Ch.1.

[66] J Carter Wood, *Violence and Crime in Nineteenth Century England* (London: Routledge, 2004) Ch.2 maps the civilization/barbarism distinction onto ethnic and urban/rural divides, and also the control of interpersonal violence. See also M Valverde, '"Despotism" and Ethical Liberal Governance' (1996) 25 *Economy & Society* 357–72.

[67] Elias, *The Civilizing Process*, n.26, esp. pt.IV (Synopsis) and Postscript (1968) pp.449–83. On Elias generally see P Spierenberg, *Violence and Punishment* (Cambridge: Polity, 2013); R van Krieken, 'Violence, Self-Discipline and Modernity: Beyond the "Civilising Process"' (1989) 37 *Sociological Review* 193–218; D Garland, *Punishment and Modern Society* (Oxford: Oxford UP, 1990) Chs.10 & 11; L Ray, 'Mark of Cain: Shame, Desire and Violence' (2013) 16 *European Jnl. of Social Theory* 292–309.

modern societies. On the one hand, the growth of state power regulates the use of violence such that the only legitimate physical violence is that which is used by the state—whether dealing with internal or external threats. Internally, this creates what he calls 'pacified social spheres', areas of social life which are normally free of physical violence, or where there is an expectation that breaches of social order will be dealt with by the state or its representatives.[68] Crucially, though, this development is matched, or corresponds, to a different type of self-restraint, what he calls 'a more dispassionate self-control'.[69] As social roles become differentiated through the division of labour, individuals become increasingly dependent on others, requiring new methods of social co-ordination: 'as more and more people must attune their conduct to that of others, the web of actions must be organized more and more strictly and accurately'.[70] As a consequence, Elias argues, 'the individual is compelled to regulate his conduct in an increasingly... more even and more stable manner'.[71] The 'civilizing process', then, is directed towards the controlling of the desires and passions of individuals through a tightening of the controls imposed on individuals by society, and the attack on practices deemed to be immoral or uncivilized—often or usually led by cultural elites against practices of the lower orders.

This process is viewed in terms of general developments over the historical *longue durée*, and it is necessary at least to be wary about drawing simple conclusions about the influence of a specific institution (the criminal law) in a specific period. Elias discussed this process primarily in relation to pre-modern societies, notably the transformation from knightly warrior societies of the middle ages to pacified court societies of the sixteenth and seventeenth centuries.[72] Thus, he looks in particular at the development of social manners as ideas of chivalry or courtly behaviour moved from elite groups to the bourgeoisie. He is also wary about ascribing agency to particular classes or groups, describing the civilizing process as unplanned and unintended, and in fact says little about the role of institutions such as the law or police in this process.[73] However, the overall argument is consistent with the understanding of civilization outlined above, where civilization is understood in terms of a series of particular initiatives to improve or regulate social conduct in some way, or to secure particular forms of civil order. There are three themes in particular which will be explored throughout the book: the relationship between violence and trust in modernity; the relationship between criminal law and the development of self-control; and changing sensibilities around understandings of civility and sociability in public and private spaces. The first two will be discussed below, the last in the final section of this chapter.

[68] Elias, *Civilizing Process*, n.26, p.369.
[69] Elias, *Civilizing Process*, n.26, p.373.
[70] Elias, *Civilizing Process*, n.26, p.367.
[71] Elias, *Civilizing Process*, n.26, p.367.
[72] See examples in Elias, *Civilizing Process*, n.26, Pt.II on table manners, spitting, blowing one's nose, sexual conduct, etc.
[73] See e.g. *Civilizing Process*, n.26, p.366 and the long footnote 1. For criticism see van Krieken, 'Violence, Self-Discipline and Modernity', n.67, pp.208–14.

In understanding the relationship between violence and trust we must return to the question of the monopolization of violence by the state. There is clear historical evidence of a long-term decline in the use of interpersonal physical violence—if not in the use of state violence.[74] Primary evidence for this is seen in the decline in homicide rates, from between 20 and 40 per 100,000 of population in the late middle ages to less than 1 per 100,000 in the twentieth century.[75] Historians have also used available records to show that the incidence of assault declined over the same period, concluding that interpersonal conduct was becoming less confrontational and aggressive.[76] In addition to this, the number of public executions declines, as does the use of particularly cruel penal practices, a development which culminated in the shift from public forms of punishment towards the use of imprisonment.[77] This was, to be sure, an uneven process, proceeding in fits and starts over a period of several hundred years, but it was a move from a culture in which violence was accepted as a 'necessary, if not always optimal, way of maintaining order in any hierarchical relationship' to one where the private use of violence was frowned on, and where both individuals and the state regulated their own use of violence.[78]

The relationship between individual self-control and violence is expressed by Elias in the form of a trade-off:

> The individual is protected from sudden attack, the irruption of physical violence into his or her life. But at the same time he is himself forced to suppress in himself or herself any passionate impulse urging him or her to attack another physically.[79]

[74] See L Stone, 'Interpersonal Violence in English Society, 1300-1980' (1983) 101 *Past & Present* 22–33; J Sharpe, 'The History of Violence in England. Some Observations' (1985) 108 *Past & Present* 206–15; JS Cockburn, 'Patterns of Violence in English Society. Homicide in Kent 1560–1985' (1991) 130 *Past & Present* 70–106; M Eisner, 'Modernization, Self-Control and Lethal Violence. The Long-Term Dynamics of European Homicide Rates in Theoretical Perspective' (2001) 41 *Brit Jnl. Criminol.* 618–38. See also EA Johnson & EH Monkkonen (eds), *The Civilization of Crime. Violence in Town and Country Since the Middle Ages* (Urbana, Ill.: University of Illinois Press, 1996); KD Watson (ed.), *Assaulting the Past. Violence and Civilization in Historical Context* (Cambridge: Cambridge Scholars Press, 2007); P Spierenburg, *Violence and Punishment* (Cambridge: Polity, 2013). By contrast, genocides and industrialized warfare in which violence is used by the state are a marked feature of modernity.

[75] Eisner, 'Modernization' n.74, pp.628–30, with much of the decline being attributed to the decline in numbers of male-male fights resulting in fatal stabbings. Most western societies also record a marked increase in homicide rates from the 1960s onwards.

[76] J Beattie, *Crime and the Courts in England, 1660-1800* (Princeton: Princeton UP, 1986); P King, 'Punishing Assault: The Transformation of Attitudes in the English Courts' (1996) 27 *Jnl of Interdisciplinary Hist* 43–74; M Wiener, *Men of Blood. Violence, Manliness and Criminal Justice in Victorian England* (Cambridge: Cambridge UP, 2004) esp. Ch.1; VAC Gatrell, 'The Decline of Theft and Violence in Victorian and Edwardian England' in VAC Gatrell et al. (eds), *Crime and the Law* (London: Europa, 1980). See also Chs.8 & 9.

[77] The penitentiary 'exerted a hold on men's imaginations because it represented in microcosm the hierarchical, obedient, and godly social order, which they felt was coming apart around them.' M Ignatieff, *A Just Measure of Pain* (London: Macmillan, 1979) p.84; see also J Bender, *Imagining the Penitentiary. Fiction and the Architecture of Mind in Eighteenth Century England* (Chicago: University of Chicago Press, 1987).

[78] M Hunt, 'Wife Beating, Domesticity and Women's Independence in Eighteenth-Century London' (1992) 4 *Gender & History* 14.

[79] Elias, *The Civilizing Process*, n.26, p.370.

This process is viewed in psychoanalytic terms: the development of the individual super-ego capable of controlling aggressive impulses mirrors the function of the state at a societal level exerting a continuous pressure on individuals through its monopoly on violence.[80] He sees this occurring in different ways: the moderation of spontaneous emotion; the tempering of affects; the extension of mental space beyond the moment into the past and the future; the habit of connecting events in terms of chains of cause and effect.[81] These are in part the consequence of an increasing social interdependence which requires individuals to anticipate the consequences of their actions and the actions of others. This is not primarily achieved by means of direct threats, but by working on the self: encouraging self-reflection, the observation of self and others, and the development of an interior life.[82] Crucially, though, it is the individual that becomes the point of intervention, through forms of discipline that are directed at remaking the self.[83] This is mediated in a variety of ways including the law, which becomes a reason for action, articulating standards of conduct and associated reasoning processes. So we find this process tracked in the criminal law in the articulation of the mental element, the development of tests of foresight, and the restriction of defences.[84] This process also raises questions about the proper distribution and use of violence and how this can be regulated by law (where it was permitted, who is authorized to use violence, what levels of violence were permitted, and so on). The civilizing process is thus about creating the person who can be the subject of liberty as well as refining and re-articulating the scope of permissible and impermissible harms.

In modernity the use of violence is strictly regulated. The use of violence by the state must normally be instrumental rather than symbolic, indeed can only be legitimated in these terms.[85] Violence is a means of guaranteeing social relations rather than being expressive of them. The possibility and extent of its use is regulated by law. And the use of violence is further limited by a modern sensibility, shaped by normative understandings of the inviolability of the person, that regulates even the instrumental use of violence by the state.[86] There is an expectation of non-violence in our social relations, with the existence of the state monopoly on violence relieving us of the need to ask questions about the conduct

[80] Cf. S Freud, *Civilization and Its Discontents* (New York: Norton, 1962).

[81] Elias, *Civilizing Process*, n.26, p.370.

[82] See C Taylor, *Modern Social Imaginaries*, n.25, p.38. See also C Taylor, *Sources of the Self* (Cambridge: Harvard UP, 1989) where he identifies the characteristics of the modern idea of the self in terms of disengagement and inwardness, orientation to guiding ideas such as autonomy, self-responsibility and authenticity.

[83] M Foucault, *Discipline and Punish* (Harmondsworth: Penguin, 1977).

[84] See Ch.6.

[85] Thus, even retributive punishment must be for past conduct, and not simply vengeful. See Reemtsma, *Trust and Violence*, n.9, Chs.2 & 5. It is also striking that the recent development of international law is characterized by attempts to make forms of intra-state violence (war) and the use of genocide subject to legal regulation.

[86] E.g. prohibitions on the use of torture, the adoption of 'humane' forms of capital punishment, or the legal regulation of warfare.

of others.[87] That is to say that even though violence continues to occur, our normal expectation would be that it should not (and specifically that we should not be subject to violence or the threat of violence), and that the state would deal with any breaches of the law. What is key here is that in modern society this must be understood as linked to increasing social complexity and the division of labour: 'To trust in modernity is to trust in the stability of societal differentiation. It is to trust in the legal regulation of social relations and its enforcement by the state'.[88] This, of course, is an incomplete process: the state can never completely monopolize violence, and social trust is always potentially under threat, but the central question thus becomes that of how the criminal law can secure that social trust. Finally, while the decline in interpersonal violence is often understood as an index of increasing civilization, leading to animated debates about whether Elias was right or wrong, we can reverse this perspective. 'Civilization', understood in terms of a particular configuration of selfhood, violence, and law, is produced by the modernizing process, and our task is to understand the place of criminal law in this process.

IV. Civility

This leads into the final theme, which is the relationship between criminal law and civility. Civility as a theme is again deliberately broad, but is intended to allow us to approach questions of the content of the criminal law and how they are framed against wider, and changing, understandings of moral, political, and social order.

The idea of civility draws on Elias' analysis of changing social mores discussed above, but it also allows us to capture a broader set of ideas. In the words of an early modern historian, civility, or civil behaviour, is a 'technique for representation of personal virtue within a broader "civil" community'.[89] This articulates the idea that belonging or participation in a group relies on codes of social conduct, and that this in turn relies on modes of self-presentation.[90] However, there are two further dimensions to this. On the one hand, historians have pointed to the changed nature of this 'civil community' or society in modernity. Society in modernity is understood as an abstract system of common life, as opposed to more immediate forms of sociability, where individuals of equal status have

[87] 'The goal of the civilizing process is to make us all more susceptible to trauma by reducing the amount of it in our lives', Reemtsma, *Trust and Violence*, n.9, p.73.

[88] Reemtsma, *Trust and Violence*, n.9, p.90.

[89] A Bryson, *From Courtesy to Civility. Changing Codes of Conduct in Early Modern England* (Oxford: Oxford UP, 1998) p.277.

[90] Not necessarily of virtue, which is specific to the early modern context that Bryson discusses, but certainly of the absence of threat or making oneself 'disattendable'. The classic discussion of this in modern society is E Goffman, *The Presentation of Self in Everyday Life* (Harmondsworth: Penguin, 1959). See the discussion in JA Hall, *The Importance of Being Civil* (Princeton NJ: Princeton UP, 2013) Ch.6.

a series of social relationships with comparative strangers.[91] Where traditional forms of society were based on kinship and hierarchy, and criminal laws were mainly directed at protecting that hierarchy against threats, modern society is based on changed social geographies that raise different kinds of questions of order. In place of the household, modern society is organized around the city, the market, the workplace, the home and so on, each of which are themselves ordered in their own distinctive way. On the other hand, civility is understood in terms of changing norms of conduct, notably controlling one's body, adjusting one's conduct to accommodate others, an increased sensitivity to pain and suffering, and avoiding giving offence to others.[92] The focus is on the individual as the basis for social order and on making individuals who can live together with other individuals in complex modern societies. This shift is then reflected not only in the focus on individual conduct, but also in the fact that social wrongs are reconceived in terms of the harms or wrongs that are done to the interests of individuals.[93] While these forms of conduct primarily relate to manners and, as the quote from Adam Ferguson with which I began this chapter suggests, criminal laws may not be expected to make the virtuous citizen, we see here the emergence of the distinctions—private and public, harm, self-control, offence—which shape the modern criminal law.

We can see then how the idea of civility is central to an understanding of the content of the modern criminal law. This is not to be understood as a claim that the criminal law is concerned directly in the regulation of manners or social rules. This would be too simple, both because codes of social conduct or manners are 'more' than rules, in the sense of being habits or learned patterns of belonging, but also because such habits or customs are 'less' than rules, in that the criminal law is expected to deal only with the most serious forms of civil misconduct and is subject to different conditions of formality and institutionalization.[94] It is rather that modern codes of civility reflect the larger transformation of the understanding of the social, providing the categories in terms of which civility and incivility, order and disorder, are understood. Civil order in this sense is not just the absence of violence but, as the discussion in the last section suggests, requires reflection

[91] See MB Becker, *Civility and Society in Western Europe, 1300-1600* (Bloomington: Indiana UP, 1988) Ch.1, citing David Hume. This is a distinction that is central to modern social theory e.g. from status to contract (Maine), between mechanical and organic solidarity (Durkheim) or between *gemeinschaft* and *gesellschaft* (Tönnies) which captures the idea of movement from a fixed 'traditional' society to a more fluid and individualistic modern society.

[92] See J Carter Wood, *Violence and Crime*, n.66, Ch.1; K Halttunen, *Murder Most Foul. The Killer and the American Gothic Imagination* (Cambridge: Harvard UP, 1998) Ch.3; R McGowen, 'Cruel Inflictions and the Claims of Humanity in Early Nineteenth-Century England' in Watson (ed.), *Assaulting the Past*, n.74, pp.38–57.

[93] See e.g. A Ferguson, *An Essay on the History of Civil Society* (1767) (Edinburgh: Edinburgh UP, 1966) p.156: 'From whatever motive wrongs are committed, there are different particulars in which the injured may suffer. He may suffer in his goods, in his person, or in the freedom of his conduct'.

[94] See P Collett, 'The Rules of Social Conduct' in Collett (ed.), *Social Rules and Social Behaviour* (Oxford: Blackwell, 1977). Cf. N MacCormick, *Institutions of Law*, n.15, Ch.1 distinguishing between normative order and institutional normative order.

on a range of issues. These include the social distribution of violence, the means of regulation of property relations, the kinds of socially acceptable conduct, masculinity, the regulation of public and private space, and so on.[95] The precise relationship of the criminal law with civil order at any given time is then dependent on particular historical understandings of the appropriateness of certain areas for regulation by law and whether the use of the criminal law is seen as appropriate to specific forms of conduct—and even within the modern period we can see quite substantial variations in the scope of the criminal law as it has been used not just to build social order but also to protect the interests of certain classes or groups or in pursuit of other ends.

This brings us to the normative question of what the criminal law should regulate, or the 'proper' scope of the criminal law, for the emergence of this question—the question of criminalization—is fundamentally linked to the question of civility and the modern understanding of the social. To see this it is helpful to go back to the passage from Adam Smith that was discussed earlier, for in his analysis of the ends of civil government and the place of law we can see the space for a modern understanding of criminalization beginning to emerge.[96]

Smith argued that the 'first and chief design' of all civil governments was to 'preserve justice amongst the members of the state and prevent all incroachments on individualls in it, from others of the same society [sic]'.[97] In developing this argument he links civility to his account of civil society as a community of individuals pursuing multiple private interests ordered by manufacture, and commerce, and polite sociability.[98] Civil society is, though, a governed society in the sense that it has developed as a human institution (rather than as a natural state of affairs) in order to regulate economic progress in the form of the accumulation of property and the division of labour.[99] Civil society thus combines a theory of political economy and social cohesion and is, on this account, performing two roles: it explains the sources and legitimacy of political government as defending and regulating men's claims to life and property; and it provides the 'moral dimension of a modern world of economic transactions between benignly self-interested

[95] The control of 'incivilities' or offensive conduct has become a dominant theme of recent discourse on criminal law, but it is striking that this discussion is largely conducted without further analysis of the meaning of civility. See A von Hirsch & A Simester, *Incivilities. Regulating Offensive Behaviour* (Oxford: Hart Publishing, 2006).

[96] Supra at pp.47–8. This is not to claim that Smith is the originator of this kind of account, but that his account exemplifies this kind of account of modern society, and in terms which allow us to link up the themes of civil order, civilization, and civility discussed in this chapter.

[97] Smith, *Lectures on Jurisprudence*, n.42, p.7.

[98] It is thus both wider than the natural law conception of civil society as the political society (as opposed to the state of nature), and the later Hegelian conception which saw civil society as external to political institutions. This account of 'pre-Hegelian' civil society draws on F Oz-Salzberger, 'Civil Society in the Scottish Enlightenment' in S Kaviraj & S Khilnani (eds), *Civil Society. History and Possibilities* (Cambridge: Cambridge UP, 2001) pp.58–63.

[99] D Hume, *A Treatise of Human Nature* (Oxford: Oxford UP, 1978) p.541. Cf. Neocleous, *Fabrication*, n.35, Ch.2 stressing that Smith's account of the order of the market is not natural but 'fabricated' by the state (p.34).

individuals'.[100] Consistent with the analysis of civility above, it is the 'individual in society' which is seen as the source of order. By this I mean that although the individual is seen as the primary unit of analysis, it is recognized that the social individual is produced by government, rather than government resting on the natural or pre-social characteristics of individuals.[101] Individuals pursue their own interests and there would inevitably be clashes between the interests or desires of individuals and between individuals and social interests. The problem of civil order was that of accommodating the competing interests and providing redress where there had been breaches of the rights of another. The role of justice was to regulate these clashes through the principles governing the security of public and private relations between persons when a person was deprived of something that they had a right to or where they were done injury or hurt without a legitimate cause. The principle of justice was articulated through the figure of the impartial spectator as a way of placing yourself in the position of another individual.[102] This offered a unique and innovative way of institutionalizing the idea of accommodating the conduct of others.

In this brief summary of Smith's jurisprudence we can see how his subtle reordering of the categories of social thought has significant implications for thinking about the criminal law. The criminal law was to do justice, in the sense of protecting private interests but also reflecting a public good or utility which was the end or justification of civil government. The end of civil government was to preserve the security of rights, and civil institutions enable the redress of injuries and for that reason individuals will subordinate their own interests to the good of the whole.[103] Thus in the conflation of the individual and the social interest, civil order was to be secured through the securing of individual interests—even if the relation between the individual and the social interest is not further explored in any great detail. Second, the objects to be protected by the criminal law are reinterpreted as categories framed in terms of the interests of individuals—person, reputation, and estate—rather than the aim of protecting authority. These interests, and the ways that they could be injured, could then be broken down and analysed in a rational and systematic way. He thus set out the principal ways that a man might be injured—in his person, as a member of a family, and as a citizen or member of a state—before further breaking this down to consider the types of injury.[104] Thus, a man 'merely as a man' might be injured in his person, in his reputation, or in his estate, and the injury to his person might be either by killing, wounding or otherwise hurting his body or by restraining his liberty, which Smith considered included the right to free commerce.[105] These interests are calculable

[100] Oz-Salzberger, 'Civil Society', n.98, p.64.

[101] See Wrong, *The Problem of Order*, n.7, pp.88–9.

[102] Smith, *Lectures*, n.42, p.104; A Smith, *The Theory of Moral Sentiments* (1790) (London: Penguin, 2009) Pt.I. See discussion in J Bender, *Imagining the Penitentiary*, n.77, pp.218–29 linking the impartial spectator to the system of the panopticon. See Chapter 6.

[103] Smith, *Lectures*, n.42, p.402. See Neocleous, *Fabrication*, n.35, pp.41–4 on security.

[104] Smith, *Lectures*, n.42, p.7.

[105] Smith, *Lectures*, n.42, p.8. These were classified as 'natural rights' following Pufendorf. See pp.105–33 for a fuller discussion of crimes.

and susceptible to rational analysis, thus making both government and justice more predictable. We see the same process at work in Smith's analysis of punishment, where he argues that the amount of punishment should be derived from the individual interest that has been injured, in the 'concurrence of the impartial spectator with the resentment of the injured'.[106] This individualization was compared with the practices of barbarian societies. In barbarous or uncivilized societies punishment was merely for the preservation of the public peace but in developed commercial societies, the purpose of punishment was also to do justice which could be measured and proportionate.[107] There is one final important point that must be noted. The defence of civilized society by means of institutional justice brought with it a certain commitment to legal values or civil liberties. This is explicit in Adam Ferguson's history of civil society where he argues that 'the very restraints by which [the citizen] is hindered from the commission of crimes, are a part of his liberty. No person is free where any person is suffered to do wrong with impunity'.[108] Liberty in civil society was secured through law, setting limits on the powers of the magistrate and relying on written laws.

What we see in this idea of civility is the characteristic twofold formulation of the modern criminalization question. It is, on the one hand, a matter of formulating rules addressed to the individual in order to secure social interests in civil order; it is, on the other, a question of limiting the institution of law so as to secure a particular kind of civil order. What emerges from this reconstruction is the combination of individual and social interests: the individual interest in social order and the social interest in the individual life.[109] Criminalization, or the question of the proper scope of the criminal law, is thus framed as a question of the rational government of individuals and their interests in a commercial society with the end of securing civil order.

V. Conclusion

Each of the three sections in this chapter has developed a set of different but related ideas, challenging views which are taken for granted in much liberal thought, and seeking to integrate normative understandings with social theory in order to build up a richer picture of what is at stake in our understanding of criminalization. The first section explored the meaning of the term civil order and its specific linkage to the institution of law. The second looked at how criminalization, the role of the criminal law in securing civil order, is linked to understandings of civilization in

[106] Smith, *Lectures*, n.42, p.104. Indeed, he specifically argues against natural law theorists such as Grotius and Pufendorf that the aim of punishment is not the public good.

[107] Smith, *Lectures*, n.42, p.106.

[108] Ferguson, *History of Civil Society*, n.93, p.156. See generally Part III Sect.VI (Of civil liberty), though Ferguson concluded on the more pessimistic note that laws were of little value unless the people could also keep alive the spirit of liberty.

[109] See e.g. R Pound, 'The Future of the Criminal Law' (1921) 21 *Columbia LR* 7.

the specific modern sense of a governmental project. Then, finally, in the third section I looked at questions relating to the content of civil order, notably the idea of civility and the management of conduct in public space, and the place of criminal law in the construction of ideas of civil society and civil liberty. This has allowed me to trace the emergence of the conceptual framework within which criminalization has come to be understood, and to link this to underlying understandings of civil order and the criminal law. This thus performs a twofold function. On the one hand, it has sought to clarify the different meanings of civil order and how they might be linked in an account of the development of the criminal law, and thus develop the conceptual foundations for the analysis which follows. On the other, it has attempted to show how securing civil order as an aim of the criminal law is linked to the emergence of specifically modern understandings of civil order, the role of law and the formation of the question of criminalization. This, however, is merely a foundation or conceptual clarification—civil order has been conceived in different ways in modernity, as has the role of criminal law in securing this order and in terms of understanding its proper scope. What we have here is the identification of a backdrop against which the themes identified play out in different ways. The next step is to trace stages in the actual development of the criminal law and to see how they map on to these issues. As we do this we will see how different elements we have identified play a different role in the development of particular areas of the criminal law. The aim of the next part of the book is to begin to trace this process in more detail, showing how conceptions of civil order and the criminal law have changed over time.

Before I leave this chapter, I want to make one final remark. Civilization and criminalization are often seen as alternatives: a civil remedy is an alternative to criminalization; a civil order is an order without the need for criminal law. What I have attempted to show here is that civilization and criminalization, the civil and the criminal, are bound together historically, and arguably also conceptually, in much more complex ways.

PART II

GENERAL

3

The Emergence of Criminal Law

I. Introduction

> The law of England as a whole, or even the criminal law as a whole, can scarcely be said to have a history. There is no such series of continuous connected changes in the whole system as the use of the word 'history' implies. Each particular part of the law, however, has been the subject of such changes.[1]

This chapter moves away from the more abstract and theoretical discussion of the first two chapters to look in greater detail at the relationship between the criminal law and civil order in the period since the late eighteenth century. In doing this, I aim to show the changing scope of the different areas of social life that criminal law has been called on to regulate—and thus to show how the civil order that criminal law has been called upon to secure, and how it has sought to secure it, has changed over time. My aim is to show how the different dimensions of civil order explored in the last chapter can be used to open up analysis of the development of the modern criminal law, showing the different understandings of civil order that underlie the criminal law at different periods of time, and how have these shaped the understanding of the social function and aims of the criminal law. The broader aim of the chapter is to demonstrate that there is no single or simple concept of civil order which it is the aim of the criminal law to secure or produce. Even within the development of the broadly liberal modern state there are different forms and aims of criminal law and different understandings of civil order. The simple view of the criminal law as establishing only the threshold conditions for civil order either neglects substantial differences between different versions of civil order, or wilfully obscures these in order to promote one version above another.

The approach taken here is clearly at odds with James Fitzjames Stephen's suggestion that the criminal law as a whole can scarcely be said to have a history; indeed a central claim of the chapter is that it does have a history, though there is an important sense in which the history of the criminal law begins only in the modern period. Before that time there were individual crimes or wrongs, and rules

[1] JF Stephen, *History of the Criminal Law of England* (London: Macmillan, 1883) Vol. I p.6.

for their punishment, which have a rich and distinctive history of their own, but, as Stephen suggests, there was no separate understanding of the idea of criminal law as a unified and purposive body of rules—of criminal law as an institution—that could have its own history. Ironically in fact, given his disavowal, Stephen's magisterial *History of the Criminal Law* (1883) made an important contribution to the development of this modern understanding of the criminal law as a whole and of the distinctive elements which fell within its scope. My focus is thus on how the criminal law came to be thought about as a whole—and the history of that kind of thinking. The method of proceeding in this chapter is to identify four different moments in the development of the criminal law since the late eighteenth century and to analyse the characteristic features of the law at each of these moments. These are the late eighteenth century, the period in which I shall argue that a modern sense of criminal law articulated around public wrongs was formed; the mid-Victorian legislative state, in which criminal law was seen as an instrument for civilizing society; 'penal welfarism' which sought to combine social responsibility and individual liberty; and, finally, what I have described as contemporary 'neo-classical' accounts of criminal law which have sought to redefine the role of the criminal law in terms of a new retributivism. For each period I have taken one writer as representative—Sir William Blackstone, Sir James Fitzjames Stephen, Glanville Williams, and Andrew Ashworth—and have used their work as a point of access to an understanding of how these men and their contemporaries have thought about the criminal law. I have sought to place their work in context, showing both what was (and is) distinctive about their views, but also how their understandings of the criminal law can be seen as responding to and shaping underlying changes in the scope and function of the criminal law. It is not, of course, imagined that this will produce a complete account of the development of the modern criminal law; however, this kind of comparison makes it possible to map out broad and significant shifts in understandings of the aims and proper scope of the criminal law over the modern period.[2]

There are obvious limits to this kind of approach. It is necessarily schematic: the models are ideal types, general reconstructions of the social functions and aims of the criminal law at a particular point in time, and there may be questions as to the extent any given system of criminal law actually conformed to these models. It is also the case that the criminal law has developed by means of accretion and slow evolution, such that in any given historical period the law will be a palimpsest of different crimes, doctrines, or theoretical constructs which have developed in different periods, and we must accordingly be wary about reading the law in terms of a single or unifying purpose. However, we should also recognize that the converse might be true: a continuity in legal doctrine might obscure underlying changes in the social purpose or function of the law. Even as the function of the law changes,

[2] See N Lacey, 'Contingency, Coherence and Conceptualism: Reflection on the Encounter between "Critique" and the "Philosophy of the Criminal Law" in RA Duff (ed.), *Philosophy and the Criminal Law* (Cambridge: Cambridge UP, 1998) for a similar kind of approach.

certain doctrines or rules of law remain the same, so that at any moment the criminal law might best be characterized as a combination of different systems or aims. It will thus be the case that not necessarily every rule or doctrine will fit readily into the general understandings of the role or function of the criminal law that I identify.[3] Notwithstanding these reservations, I argue in this chapter that it is possible to identify certain central features of the criminal law at different periods in time. This can both illustrate the claim that the form and purpose of the criminal changes over time, and can be used to illustrate patterns in the development of the criminal law. This is important for the purpose of building up a general picture (or conceptual history) of the development of the criminal law. However, it is equally important as a corrective to certain common misapprehensions about the law: that the history of the criminal law is one of unbroken continuity; that there has been a progressive evolution towards a more refined conceptual structure; or that there is a settled core which is linked to an unchanged underlying conception of social order.[4] This account will then provide the foundation both for building up a more complex picture of the development of the institution of criminal law over the following three chapters, and for the account of the development of specific substantive areas of the criminal law in Part III. These subsequent chapters will both flesh out the general account, filling in omissions and dealing in greater detail with claims or doctrines that are passed over too quickly, and also show how the development of particular areas of the law conforms to—and departs from—the general pattern of development.

The analysis will start by looking at the changing scope of the criminal law at each moment—what was criminalized or decriminalized and why—as a way of building up a larger picture of how the general foundations of the criminal law as a unified and purposive body of rules were understood. It will then move on to look briefly at how the criminal law was classified in that period, identifying the features of the law that were taken as characteristic for each model and how these were understood to be related to the social role of the criminal law.[5] Most importantly, it will examine understandings of the relation between law and beliefs in the nature of civil or social order which underpin each of the models—what might be described as the social imaginary of the law at particular points in time.[6] This also allows us to look at how the question of criminalization—the proper scope of the criminal law—was understood at that time. The aim, then, is to trace the relations between understandings of the scope of the law and its social function and purpose so as to build up a fuller picture of the relationship between the scope and function of the criminal law.

[3] Cf. D Garland, *Cultures of Control* (Oxford: Oxford UP, 2001) Ch.2 describing the development of penal policy.

[4] Also for correcting the impression that development of criminal law is the working out of an internal logic. See e.g. KJM Smith, *Lawyers, Legislators and Theorists* (Oxford: Oxford UP, 1998).

[5] This question of classification will be addressed at greater length in Chapter 5 (Codification).

[6] See C Taylor, *Modern Social Imaginaries* (Durham NC: Duke UP, 2004) Ch.1.

II. Public Wrong

> The distinction of public wrongs from private, or crimes and misdemesnors from civil injuries, seems principally to consist in this: that private wrongs, or civil injuries, are an infringement or privation of the civil rights which belong to individuals, considered merely as individuals; public wrongs, or crimes and misdemesnors, are a breach and violation of the public rights and duties, due to the whole community, considered as a community, in its social aggregate capacity.[7]

William Blackstone occupies an important position in the modern criminal law for most common law systems. He was the first to provide a concise account of the law as a body of rules unified by a common aim and conceptual structure, that was capable of synthesizing traditional rules with a more recognizably modern approach.[8] This is exemplified by the above statement with which he signalled a clear break from older conceptions of the law of crimes. He made three key moves. First, he self-consciously moved away from forms of writing about crimes as Pleas of the Crown to a conception of the whole of the criminal law understood as comprising both crimes and misdemeanours.[9] He defined a crime as 'violation of a public law either forbidding or commanding it'.[10] Second, and linked to this, he produced a freestanding account of the substantive law as a body of rules divorced from procedural technicalities.[11] Third, this approach adopted a new taxonomy of crimes, articulated around the unifying concept of the public wrong. Private wrongs were committed against individuals, but public wrongs engaged public rights or duties owed to the community as a whole. These were overlapping concepts: 'besides the injury done to individuals, they [crimes] strike at the very being of society, which cannot possibly subsist where actions of this sort are suffered to escape with impunity'.[12] In serious injuries, the private wrong was 'swallowed up' in the public wrong but, Blackstone suggests, inferior crimes afforded room for private compensation.[13]

[7] W Blackstone, *Commentaries on the Law of England* (1st edn 1765–69) (Chicago: Chicago UP, 1979) iv, p.5.

[8] For general commentary, see D Lieberman, *The Province of Legislation Determined* (Cambridge: Cambridge UP, 1989); S Stern, 'Blackstone's Criminal Law: Common Law Harmonization and Legislative Reform (1769)' in MD Dubber (ed.), *Foundational Texts in Modern Criminal Law* (Oxford: Oxford UP, 2014).

[9] See D Lieberman, 'Blackstone and the Categories of English Jurisprudence' in N Landau (ed.), *Law, Crime and English Society, 1660–1830* (Cambridge: Cambridge UP, 2002).

[10] Blackstone, *Commentaries*, n.7, iv, p.5.

[11] FSC Milsom, 'The Nature of Blackstone's Achievement' (1981) 1 *Ox Jnl Leg Stud* 1–12.

[12] Blackstone, *Commentaries*, n.7, iv, p.5.

[13] Blackstone, *Commentaries*, n.7, iv, p.6. Though at the time Blackstone wrote it was still common to settle prosecutions for serious crimes such as assault and rape by the payment of private compensation. See Chs.8 & 9. His claim should thus be regarded as aspirational rather than as descriptive of the contemporary practice.

The law thus had a double aim: to provide redress to the injured party, but primarily 'to secure to the public the benefit of society.'[14]

Though apparently simple and straightforward, this formulation is rather more complex—notably in the tension between public and private, and between different understandings of the aims of the law—but it is precisely this complexity that is revealing of the changing understanding of the criminal law in the late eighteenth century.

A. The unity of the law

The eighteenth century was a period of substantial change in the development of the criminal law. Institutionally, it moved decisively away from organization around the protection of the King's peace and this had important consequences for the conception of the law as a distinctive body of rules.[15] Central to this development was the assumption by the common law courts of the jurisdiction of the prerogative courts—notably that of the Court of Star Chamber. Prior to its abolition in 1641, the Star Chamber had built up a substantial jurisdiction over a range of serious misdemeanours, including perjury, forgery, fraud, extortion, conspiracy and sedition. What was distinctive about these crimes was that they were crimes of 'cunning', as opposed to traditional common law treason and felonies, which were based on manifest disruptions of the peace by force and arms.[16] It was understood that wrongdoing was becoming more sophisticated, or could be committed in more sophisticated ways, and that these kind of crimes could pose an equal or greater threat to the King's peace.[17] With the abolition of the Star Chamber, these offences were largely absorbed within the jurisdiction of the common law courts as common law misdemeanours.[18] The common law courts then developed these doctrines and applied them in new ways. Thus the law of criminal conspiracy was applied to agreements which interfered with freedom of trade, and by the end of the eighteenth century was routinely being used against combinations of workmen.[19] And in the notorious case of *Sedley* in 1663, the Court of King's

[14] Blackstone, *Commentaries*, n.7, iv, p.7 He goes on: 'by preventing or punishing every breach and violation of those laws which the sovereign power has thought proper to establish for the government and tranquility of the whole'.

[15] This draws on H Berman, *Law and Revolution II. The Impact of the Protestant Reformations on the Western Legal Tradition* (Cambridge, Mass.: Harvard UP, 2003) Ch.10, although I characterize the shift in slightly different terms from Berman. On the King's Peace see FE Pollock & FW Maitland, *A History of English Law before the Time of Edward I* (2 vols.) (2nd edn 1898) (Cambridge: Cambridge UP, 1968). See also FE Pollock, 'The King's Peace' (1885) 1 *LQR* 37.

[16] See TG Barnes, 'The Making of the English Criminal Law (2). Star Chamber and the Sophistication of the Criminal Law' [1977] *Crim LR* 316.

[17] Ibid. p.317, suggesting that these were initially seen as wrongs because violence and disorder might ensue rather than some intrinsic quality of the conduct.

[18] W Holdsworth, *History of English Law* (3rd edn) (London: Methuen & Co, 1945), Vol. IV, pp.501–3.

[19] See Holdsworth, *History*, n.18, Vol. VIII, pp.378–84 and Vol. XI, pp.477–501. This was followed by legislation in 1799 and 1800 criminalizing combinations of workmen. See also Stephen, *History*, n.1, Vol. III, Ch.XXX at pp.202–27 (Offences relating to trade and labour).

Bench asserted that it was *custos morum*, or guardian of the morals, of the King's subjects and thus had power to take notice of and punish acts against public morals.[20] The eighteenth century, however, also saw the creation of a large number of new statutory felonies—the 'Bloody Code'—that have come to be seen as the defining characteristic of eighteenth century criminal law. These in part took on and extended jurisdiction over 'crimes of cunning' and morals offences that had been claimed by the common law courts; however, the growth in the number of penal statutes also reflected the growing power of the landed gentry and commercial interests: much of this legislation accordingly related to the protection of the property owned by these classes. While it is now accepted that the enforcement of the law was not as sanguinary as its early nineteenth-century critics implied, from the point of view of criminalization our interest lies in the fact of the development of the law by legislation and what the content of the legislation might tell us about the changing relation between criminal law and civil order.[21]

By the end of the eighteenth-century there were reckoned to be over 200 capital offences on the English statute book.[22] These penal statutes were often specific in nature, obtained by particular trade groups or groups of landowners, or applying to specific geographical localities. Notorious amongst these is the Waltham 'Black' Act of 1723, so-called because it was enacted in response to the conduct of poachers around Waltham forest in Essex, which made it a capital offence for any person armed with various weapons and with their face blackened to appear in any forest, chase or park where deer were normally kept. While the Act mainly aimed at criminalizing various forms of hunting deer or rabbits and fishing, it also criminalized a wide range of other actions from breaking ponds to damaging trees, cattle, setting fires, wounding and sending threatening letters.[23] There was also a series of statutes restricting the availability of benefit of clergy for various forms of larceny, ranging from theft from various physical locations (houses, shops, warehouses, ships, on the highways) to theft of different kinds of objects (cloth, sheep, horses, cattle, mail), goods over a particular

[20] *R v Sedley*, 1663 1 Sid. 168; (1664) 82 ER 1036. The judicial development of the criminal law is reviewed by Holdsworth, *History*, n.18, Vol. VIII, pp.301–7.

[21] On the enforcement of the criminal law in the eighteenth-century, see J Beattie, *Crime and the Courts in England 1660–1800* (Princeton NJ: Princeton UP, 1986); P King, *Crime, Justice and Discretion in England 1740–1820* (Oxford: Oxford UP, 2000); VAC Gatrell, *The Hanging Tree* (Oxford: Oxford UP, 1996).

[22] L Radzinowicz, *A History of English Criminal Law and its Administration* (5 Vols.) (London: Stevens, 1948–84) Vol. I, Ch.1. The claim is open to debate: it is not clear how many were new offences, as in many cases statutes removed the benefit of clergy from older offences (to get around the practice which had developed throughout the seventeenth century of allowing a convicted offender to escape capital punishment if they could show a degree of literacy), and statutes were not framed in general terms. See J Langbein, '*Albion*'s Fatal Flaws' (1983) 97 *Past & Present* pp.96–120 at 118.

[23] 9 Geo.I c.22. See EP Thompson, *Whigs and Hunters* (Harmondsworth: Penguin, 1977); Radzinowicz, *History*, n.22, Vol. I, Ch.2. He estimates that the statute created up to 200 new capital offences in itself (p.76).

value, or by particular types of persons (servants, clerks, or other employees).[24] As Beattie has commented, this new legislation was not enacted as part of any larger view of criminal law and its administration but in response to particular, even local, needs.[25] However, the formal severity of the law, in particular as it protected property, was part of a complex social system in which the criminal law was central to 'maintaining bonds of obedience and deference, in legitimizing the status quo, in constantly recreating the structure of authority which arose from property and in turn protected its interests.'[26] This order, as Hay has shown, was one in which property, and in particular land, was the foundation of social authority. The landed classes had access to Parliament and held local positions of social authority such as the office of Justice of the Peace—and the criminal law was manipulated, through the selective use of terror and mercy, to reinforce that authority.[27]

A different kind of understanding of the centrality of the relationship between property and social order is revealed in the law of forgery, the 'quintessential crime' of the eighteenth century. Its development was the result of a range of factors such as 'the increase of modern riches, the invention of paper, the many complex securities, the institution of national funds, and the rules of written evidence'.[28] In the early eighteenth century, statutes had made forgeries against some public institutions, notably the government and the Bank of England, into capital felonies, but most forgeries against private individuals or companies were misdemeanours, punished by the pillory.[29] This protection had been augmented in 1729 by an Act framed in more general terms, which made forgery of any kind of deed or promissory note that could be exchanged for money or goods a capital felony—that is to say protecting private instruments or financial transactions.[30] And by the end of the century statutes were routinely passed making forgery against specified public instruments and institutions a capital crime.[31] This resort to capital

[24] See discussion in Beattie, *Crime and the Courts*, n.21, pp.144–6. There is a survey of capital statutes in Radzinowicz, *History*, n.22, Vol. I, Appendix 1 (pp.632–40 for those related to larceny). See also infra Ch.7.

[25] Beattie, *Crime and the Courts*, n.21, p.145.

[26] D Hay, 'Property, Authority and the Criminal Law' in D Hay et al., *Albion's Fatal Tree* (London: Peregrine, 1977) p.25.

[27] Hay, ibid. See also Blackstone, *Commentaries*, n.7, iv, Ch.1 discussing the role of compassion and mercy in the criminal law.

[28] W Eden, *Principles of Penal Law* (3rd edn) (London: B White & T Cadell, 1775) pp.294–5. For a review of the extensive eighteenth century legislation, see R McGowen, "Making the 'Bloody Code"? Forgery Legislation in Eighteenth-Century England' in Landau, *Law, Crime and English Society*, n.9. He suggests (at 119) that this might be seen as the 'quintessential' crime of the long eighteenth century.

[29] See R McGowen, 'From Pillory to Gallows: The Punishment of Forgery in the Age of the Financial Revolution' (1999) 165 *Past & Present* 107–40. The pillory was seen as a shaming punishment, marking a person out as 'not fit to be trusted, but to be shunned and avoided by all creditable and honest men' (Sollom Emlyn, quoted in McGowen p.123).

[30] 2 Geo.II, c.25 (1729), made permanent by 9 Geo.II, c.18 (1736). McGowen argues that there were more, and more significant, prosecutions under this legislation than under the many statutes protecting public institutions and revenue, See McGowen, 'Making the Bloody Code', n.28, pp.135–6.

[31] There were estimated to be something in the order of 120 statutes dealing with forgery by the 1820s, containing around one third of the capital offences in the 'Bloody Code'. For sources and

punishment reflected the growing importance of credit to commercial life, public and private.[32] The increased significance of forgery in the criminal law had two dimensions, one concerning the peculiarities of the way that the system of credit operated, and the other concerning the role of credit more generally. Credit operated on the circulation of paper financial instruments of different kinds, which were used in place of money, guaranteed by the signature of those backing the debt. Their reliability depended on the reputation for trustworthiness or character of the guarantor, which was undermined when signatures or documents were forged—which is to say that the character of credit was primarily personal rather than systemic. Individuals had to build and sustain reputation and character over time, and the criminal law had traditionally been directed at specific types of conduct that undermined this sense of personal character.[33] However, the new legislation was increasingly directed at conduct which potentially undermined the system of commerce. The threat of forgery was seen as a 'public danger', not because it might lead to violence or unrest but because of the need to secure 'the integrity of social transactions necessary to sustain the life of the community'.[34] This new understanding of the systemic character of the threat led, by the end of the century, to the collapse of the distinction between forgeries against public and private instruments and the adoption of a more general definition. Thus, for Blackstone, forgery was defined in general terms as 'the fraudulent making or alteration of a writing to the prejudice of another man's right'.[35] This was indicative of the emergence of the new kind of civility identified by Adam Smith, based not so much on the preservation of traditional property but on securing transactions between relative strangers in the market. Civil government, Smith argued, had to secure the interests of individuals because '[w]hen contracts sustain action property can never be secure unless the forgeing (sic) of false ones be restrained.'[36]

commentary, see McGowen, 'Making the Bloody Code', n.28, p.119–21. For an illustrative list of statutes see Blackstone, *Commentaries*, n.7, Vol. IV, pp.246–7; EH East, *A Treatise of Pleas of the Crown* (2 vols.) (London: Butterworth & Cooke, 1803) where the chapter on forgery runs to over 160 pages.

32 See McGowen, 'Pillory to Gallows', n.29, pp.128–40 arguing that the resort to capital punishment was calculated and deliberate in this context. Forgery legislation was finally reformed in 1832 (2 & 3 Wm IV c.123), but the use of capital punishment for forgery was a key point in the debate over the reform of the Bloody Code.

33 D Andrew & R McGowan, *The Perreaus and Mrs Rudd. Forgery and Betrayal in Eighteenth Century London* (Berkely CA: Univ of California Press, 2001) p.141; M Finn, *The Character of Credit* (Cambridge: Cambridge UP, 2003) Pt.I.

34 McGowen, 'Pillory to Gallows', n.29, p.133. Elsewhere McGowen notes the 'concern for the vulnerability of a state whose strength seemed peculiarly dependent on the integrity of its system of finance' (McGowen, 'Making the Bloody Code', n.28, p.121).

35 Blackstone, *Commentaries*, n.7, iv, p.245. See also East, *Pleas of the Crown,* n.31, Vol. II, pp.852–3. On the traditional distinction, see W Hawkins, *A Treatise of the Pleas of the Crown* (London: J Walthoe, 1716) Vol. I, p.184.

36 A Smith, *Lectures on Jurisprudence* (Oxford: Oxford UP, 1978) p.483 although noting that forgeries connected with land were not capital because they were not so immediate and could be detected and remedied. Cf. Henry Fielding arguing that the impact of trade was to transform the 'commonalty' of England, requiring new systems of criminal prevention and detection: *An Enquiry into the Causes of the Late increase of Robbers* (2nd edn) (London: A Millar, 1751). On civility, see supra Ch.2 Section IV.

These developments had consequences for the way that the criminal law was conceived. As Blackstone recognized, it was now a unified jurisdiction, bringing together the diverse range of crimes that had previously been tried in different courts under a reasonably settled criminal procedure. However, the law had developed in a piecemeal way, in the courts and through legislation. The underlying difficulty, as Holdsworth commented, was that it struggled to escape its medieval foundations in feudal authority with, for example, the machinery of criminal justice remaining overwhelmingly local and based on personal relations.[37] For someone like Blackstone who was looking at the law as a whole, the challenge was that of articulating the conceptual language in which this could be done. This Blackstone sought in the idea of public wrong—the public rights and duties owed to the community—but the question is what did this mean, and how did it relate to other organizing concepts in the criminal law?

B. Public wrong

Traditionally, the main distinction in criminal law had been that between treason, felony, and misdemeanour. Felonies, broadly conceived, were common law offences against a feudal superior, that led to certain penal consequences: they were capital, led to the forfeiture of land or goods, and a person charged with a felony was not entitled to legal counsel.[38] Common law misdemeanours were lesser offences: indictable offences or offences subject to jury trial below the degree of felony (thus not including the large number of offences over which magistrates had an exclusive jurisdiction).[39] By the late eighteenth century this classification had been undermined in a number of ways: the development of serious common law misdemeanours; the creation of a large number of statutory felonies which might or might not be without benefit of clergy; and the gradual removal of the requirement of forfeiture. The consequence of this was, on the one hand, that there was no clear distinction in terms of degree of seriousness between felonies and misdemeanours, but on the other, it was unclear what, if anything, linked the various serious offences. These developments had to some extent been reflected in treatises written prior to Blackstone, even though these had not attempted to resolve these conceptual difficulties. Thus, Hawkins' *Treatise of the Pleas of the Crown* (1716) included, in spite of its name, a range of treasons, felonies, and serious misdemeanours, described as 'that part of the law which is peculiarly under the administration of the Chief Justice of England'.[40] Blackstone followed suit,

[37] Holdsworth, *History*, n.18, Vol. IV, p.531.

[38] Blackstone, *Commentaries*, n.7, iv, pp.94–8; A Amos, *Ruins of Time Exemplified in Sir Matthew Hale's History of the Pleas of the Crown* (London: V & R Stevens & GS Norton, 1856) p.46. See also T. Gallanis, 'Making Sense of Blackstone's Puzzle: Why Forbid Defense Counsel?' (2010) 53 *Studies in Law, Politics and Society* 35–57. Technically treason could also be regarded as a form of felony, though after 1696 it was dealt with under different procedural rules. See JH Langbein, *The Origins of the Adversary Criminal Trial* (Oxford: Oxford UP, 2005) Ch.2 on the Treason Trials Act 1696.

[39] Amos, *Ruins of Time*, n.38, p.46.

[40] Hawkins, *Pleas of the Crown*, n.35, Vol. I, Dedication.

though still falling short of a classification of crimes based on proportionate seriousness or guilt. He struggled with the distinction between treason, felony, and misdemeanour, but after a short discussion of the etymology and origins of the term declared that he would adopt the common legal usage, treating felony as a generic term denoting all capital crimes less than treason.[41] The effect was that felony lost any real force as an organizing concept.

One of the most distinctive aspects of Blackstone's categorization of the law was that he did so in terms of the interests to be protected.[42] He began with those crimes considered the most serious forms of public wrong, as crimes which might 'strike at the very being of society', and then moved to consider the protection of other interests in a descending order of seriousness.[43] The *Commentaries* thus began by looking at crimes against God and organized religion, before moving to crimes against the state (including crimes against justice, peace, trade, police, or economy). He then moved to consider crimes against the person, of which homicide took up the greatest space, before concluding with crimes against property, looking first at crimes against habitations before a separate chapter on crimes against private property.[44] While this has a certain logic, tracking his account of the sources of the law from divine to natural to municipal, it is only a register of seriousness at the level of the general categories. Thus, for example, if we look at the chapter on crimes against religion, we find that some eleven offences were considered ranging from apostasy, heresy, and witchcraft, to swearing and cursing, simony, sabbath-breaking, drunkenness, and lewdness.[45] Several of these had been crimes before the ecclesiastical courts, but were not enforced by the common law courts, several others were in practice obsolete. Those that were still enforced were, as Blackstone himself acknowledged, less crimes against religion than against the interest that the state, 'considered merely as a civil institution' had in in ensuring religious conduct as a means of 'humanis[ing] by the help of conversation and society the manners of the lower classes'.[46]

At the level of the general categories, his prioritizing of crimes against the state and public institutions suggests a more traditional understanding of public wrong in terms of the protection of the state, rather than a public interest in the protection of private interests. Treason was the paradigmatic crime because it broke the

[41] Blackstone, *Commentaries*, n.7, iv, p.98.

[42] This was even approved by his great critic, Jeremy Bentham. See *Fragment on Government* (1776), preface to the first edn pp.28–9: he has done 'as much as could reasonably be expected of a writer so circumstanced; and more and better than was ever done before by anyone'.

[43] Blackstone, *Commentaries*, n.7, iv, p.5. See Lieberman, 'Blackstone', n.9, pp.147–8. See also JW Cairns, 'John Millar's Lectures on Scots Criminal Law' (1988) 12 *Ox Jnl of Legal Stud* 364.

[44] Cf. D Hume, *Commentaries on the Law of Scotland Respecting Crimes* (4th edn) (Edinburgh: Bell & Bradfute, 1844). He adopts a broadly Blackstonian approach based on interests, though treating crimes against property first, as more serious—perhaps reflecting the belief in the link between property and social order.

[45] Blackstone, *Commentaries*, n.7, iv, Ch.4. See also East, *Pleas of the Crown*, n.31, Ch.1.

[46] Blackstone, *Commentaries*, n.7, iv, p.63.

bond of allegiance between sovereign and subject or feudal superior and inferior.[47] Priority was given to wrongs against the sovereign and public institutions; wrongs against individuals were subsumed within an account of the political obligation in which the protection of private rights was subordinate to the public interest. The duty of the king, as '*pater-familias* of the nation' was to 'protect the community, and each individual therein'; and conversely, 'the king, in whom centres the majesty of the whole community, is supposed by the law to be the person injured by every infraction of the public rights belonging to that community'.[48] Thus, injuries to individuals were public because they were violations of the law of nature, they included a breach of the public peace, and because 'by their example and evil tendency they threaten and endanger the subversion of all civil society'.[49] Criminal law was thus founded in this account of political obligation, and the idea of public wrong encapsulated the interest of the state in maintaining social order.[50]

One final categorization that must be noted here is that between criminal law and police, as some commentators have seen in this evidence of a path not taken, or an alternative approach to criminal law.[51] Blackstone is unusual amongst writers in the common law tradition for including a chapter on public economy and police within his account of the substantive law.[52] At one level this signifies his inclusive approach: various crimes were recognized by the law of England and must be included somewhere. Public police thus operates as a residual category which includes those crimes that do not seem to fit within the other categories of public justice: bigamy, Egyptians, common nuisances, idle and incorrigible rogues, sumptuary laws, gaming, and poaching. If there is a common theme it is, as he notes in relation to poaching, that the conduct prohibited in such crimes 'promotes idleness', taking people away from their 'proper employments and callings'.[53] Idleness was a vice that was seen as directly threatening social order and which was the target of campaigns for the reformation of social manners throughout the century.[54] He thus uses the term police in its traditional sense as relating

[47] Cf. Pollock & Maitland, *History*, n.15, pp.464–8 analysing felony in terms of the breach of the duty of allegiance. See also M Lockwood, 'From Treason to Homicide: Changing Conceptions of the Law of Petty Treason in Early Modern England' (2013) 34 *Jnl of Leg Hist* 31–49.

[48] Blackstone, *Commentaries*, n.7, iv, p.127 and p.2.

[49] Blackstone, *Commentaries*, n.7, iv, pp.176–7.

[50] Cf. the perceptive comments of Edwards in relation to the 'peace' in the antebellum American south: 'Although everyone had a place, coercion was essential to keep people in their places. The peace created a public order that extended to people and issues usually deemed private... they were only private to the extent that private meant they remained subordinated within the legal order'. LF Edwards, *The People and Their Peace* (Chapel Hill, NC: Univ of NC Press, 2009) p.95.

[51] See Garland, *The Culture of Control*, n.3, p.30. See also A Ashworth & L Zedner, *Preventive Justice* (Oxford: Oxford UP, 2013) Ch.2. See infra at pp.106–7.

[52] Blackstone, *Commentaries*, n.7, iv, ch.13.

[53] Blackstone, *Commentaries*, n.7, iv, p.175.

[54] On the movement for the reformation of social manners, see Beattie, *Crime and the Courts*, n.21, pp.594–600; MJD Roberts, *Making English Morals* (Cambridge: Cambridge UP, 2004) Ch.1. See also P Colquhoun, *A Treatise on the Police of the Metropolis* (7th edn) (London: Joseph Mawman,

to good order, but by including it within his account of the substantive law it is subsumed within his more general account of the function of the criminal law in securing civil order.[55]

C. The scope and purpose of the criminal law

It should be clear from this discussion that Blackstone's idea of public wrong did not entail any conception of limits on the power of the sovereign or the scope of the criminal law. For Blackstone 'peace is the very end and foundation of civil society' and the duty of the sovereign was to maintain that peace or restore order rather than protect individual rights.[56] However, he did go on to argue that criminal law 'should be founded upon principles that are permanent, uniform and universal; and always conformable to the dictates of truth and justice, the feelings of humanity, and the indelible rights of man'.[57] Criminal law, in other words, in its institutional form entailed a commitment to certain values, notably the recognition of certain basic civil liberties. As critics have noted, Blackstone's celebrations of the civil liberties of the Englishman—as protected by the law of *habeas corpus* and jury trial—were uncritical at best and clearly at odds with the reality of the enforcement of the law for the bulk of the population. However, as EP Thompson famously wrote, the idea of the rule of law had more than rhetorical force in late eighteenth-century England; there was a clear commitment to respect for the legal process but it was understood in terms of the rights of the (mainly propertied) individual to freedom from interference by officers of the despotic state.[58]

These ideas about civil liberties were of little consequence for the substance of the law—and how could it be otherwise when the conception of liberty was so clearly linked to the security of property as the foundation of social order. However, the question of limits arose for Blackstone in the area of punishment, where it drew on the developing idea of a science of legislation.[59] This had two dimensions: a critique of the disorder and inconsistency of statutory criminal law; and a link to the new Beccarian understanding of the social aims of punishment, and in particular the need for proportionality and restraint.

Like many others in late eighteenth-century England, Blackstone was damning about both the quality and the quantity of criminal legislation and in particular the 'multitude of sanguinary laws' that Parliament had created.[60] It had exercised

1806) for a more general contemporary discussion of the link between work, order and prosperity and the moral economy of labour.

[55] The same is true of his account of preventive offences (Ch.18) which summarizes powers to bind over and is again directed to securing the social bases of civil order by controlling idle or immoral conduct. For the connection to his account of punishment see discussion below.

[56] Blackstone, *Commentaries*, n.7, i, p.349.

[57] Blackstone, *Commentaries*, n.7, iv, p.3.

[58] Thompson, *Whigs and Hunters*, n.23, p.273. Cf. Ld Camden in *Entick v Carrington* (1765) 19 St Tr 1029 at 1066: 'the great end for which men entered into society, was to secure their property. That right is preserved sacred and incommunicable in all instances, where it has not been taken away or abridged by some public law for the good of the whole.'

[59] Lieberman, *Province of Legislation*, n.8, Ch.10.

[60] Blackstone, *Commentaries*, n.7, iv, p.17.

'too little care and attention in framing and passing new [laws]', imposing capital punishment upon crimes 'very different in their natures'.[61] One response to this was to be found in his injunction to legislators:

The enacting of penalties, to which the whole nation shall be subject, ought not to be left as a matter of indifference to the passions and interests of a few, who upon temporary motives may prefer or support such a bill; but be calmly and maturely considered by persons, who know what provisions the law has already made... who can from experience foresee the probable consequences... and who will judge without passion or prejudice how adequate they are to the evil.[62]

This was linked to a new approach to the question of punishment.[63] While his account of the power to punish began by grounding it in natural right, he quickly moved to an argument that in a state of society this right was transferred to a sovereign power.[64] This power to punish extended to all crimes, but he argued that the severity of punishment should be linked to the 'enormity or dangerous tendency' of the crime alone, rather than its frequency or the difficulty of prevention.[65] The limits to the power to punish were thus prudential and social, rather than founded in natural right, as the sovereign should only punish as much as was necessary to secure society. The aim of punishment was thus deterrence or prevention, the amending of the manners of a people, rather than atonement or expiation.[66] Citing Beccaria, he argued that prevention required certainty rather than severity.[67] The punishment of all crimes equally with death, he argued, showed a 'manifest defect either in the wisdom of the legislative, or the strength of the executive power', and rather than preventing crimes might actually increase their incidence. The answer was to be sought in an approach in which the legislature developed a scale of crimes, 'with a corresponding scale of punishments, descending from the greatest to the least'.[68] Deterrence required a new kind of

61 Blackstone, *Commentaries*, n.7, iv, p.4 and p.18.

62 Blackstone, *Commentaries*, n.7, iv, p.4. See also pp.16–7. Lieberman, *Province of Legislation*, n.8, Ch.10 argues that the Commentaries can be read as a manual for potential legislators, though this passage seems to be advocating a role for the judiciary.

63 See Stern, 'Blackstone's Criminal Law', n.8, p.70 arguing for his Beccarian reform agenda. See also Lieberman, *Province of Legislation*, n.8, pp.205–9. On Beccaria, see B Harcourt, 'Beccaria's *On Crimes and Punishments*: A Mirror on the History of the Foundations of Modern Criminal Law' in MD Dubber (ed.), *Foundational Texts*, n.8.

64 Blackstone, *Commentaries*, n.7, iv, pp.7–19. See also p.357, citing Beccaria: 'The right of punishing belongs not to any one individual in particular, but to the society in general, or the sovereign who represents that society'.

65 Ibid. p.9. Though his examples of severity mapped on to his account of criminal law, with treason or theft by a servant being identified as more serious forms of wrongdoing.

66 Blackstone, *Commentaries*, n.7, iv, p.11. Cf. Harcourt, 'Beccaria's *On Crimes and Punishments*', n.63, p.64.

67 Ibid. p.17. See Stern, 'Blackstone's Criminal Law', n.8: 'the capacity to control one's actions is sufficient to make human behavior legible according to the criminal law, so that properly crafted penalties... will produce the right incentives' (p.70).

68 Blackstone, *Commentaries*, n.7, iv, p.18. He continued '[B]ut, if that be too romantic an idea, yet at least a wise legislator will mark the principal divisions, and not assign penalties of the first degree to offences of an inferior rank'.

proportionality in which 'those [crimes] should be most severely punished, which are most destructive of public safety and happiness'.[69]

The significance of Blackstone's account lies in the fact that that we can see in it the beginnings of an articulation of the modern legislative mentality and its linkage, through his discussion of punishment, to the criminal law. Punishment is understood as an instrument for controlling behaviour, and the role of the legislator was to design a 'scale' of crimes and punishment that could secure that social order.[70] This account of punishment shared key features with other contemporary accounts. It was in tune with a developing humanitarian sensibility that deplored the overuse of capital punishment, but more importantly relied on a new understanding of civil order. William Eden's influential account of the *Principles of Penal Law* (1775), for example, was explicitly framed in terms of the progress of civilization: barbaric forms of punishment were rejected in favour of means that were more humane and civilized.[71] But civilized punishment was also civilizing, an instrument of social improvement by means of which the ruder classes could be educated in the ways of civilized conduct.[72] This linkage between a humanitarian sensibility and the legislative project drew on a new rationality of punishment, expressed through a new sense of proportionality as a measure of relative seriousness. This is captured in a passage from Patrick Colquhoun's *Treatise of the Police of the Metropolis* (1797):

> In offences which are considered by the legislature as merely personal and not of the class of public wrongs, the disproportion is extremely shocking. If, for instance, a personal assault is committed of the most cruel, aggravated, and violent nature, the offender is seldom punished in any other manner than by a fine and imprisonment, but if the delinquent steals from his neighbour secretly more than the value of twelve pence, the law dooms him to death.[73]

This is a critique of disproportion in punishment and an argument for reform: the law is criticized for brutality (that a thief is punished by capital punishment) and for disproportion (that an aggravated assault is scarcely punished at all, and certainly not capitally). However, it is implicit in any claim about disproportion that there is some other truer measure of proportion or a proper relation between things. For Colquhoun, as for Blackstone and Eden, the proper measure was public wrong in the sense of harm to the community.[74] The idea of harm in this

[69] Blackstone, *Commentaries*, n.7, iv, p.16.

[70] Significantly for Eden the discussion of punishment was the superstructure; the foundations of order were in his account of the criminal law (Eden, *Principles*, n.28, Ch.10).

[71] The first part of the *Principles* contrasts advice to legislators about principles of humane punishment with examples from both ancient history and contemporary law of punishments that he regarded as barbaric and inhumane.

[72] Eden, *Principles*, n.28, Chs.10, 24, & 26.

[73] Colquhoun, *Treatise on the Police of the Metropolis*, n.54, pp.30 & pp.35.

[74] Which would require that assaults cease being regarded as 'private' wrongs, capable of being settled between the parties or by a lesser form of punishment, and be seen in terms of their social harm. For Eden this was a change through which 'the public interest is recognized to be the great end of penal jurisdiction' (Eden, *Principles*, n.28, p.3). See also infra Ch.8.

sense becomes a measure of commensurability between different types of wrongful conduct, allowing them to be ranked in terms of seriousness. Finally, this was linked to an account of political freedom. For Colquhoun it is the 'triumph of liberty when the criminal laws proportion punishment to the particular nature of the offence', because ill-designed and inconsistently enforced laws would lead to uncertainty about the scope of the law and reduce the security of property.[75] The proper order of the criminal law would secure a broader order of civil liberty. The reform of the criminal law was thus linked to the foundations of social order.

Overall, Blackstone's attempt to produce an account of the criminal law grounded on public wrong was, at best, only partially successful. This was perhaps inevitable as he attempted 'a selective rationalization and adaptation of a messy and technical body of inherited materials'.[76] His account of the limits of the criminal law extended only to criminal statutes rather than the common law, and he did not resolve the tension between ideas of public wrong based on threat to the sovereign, and those based on new ideas of harm to individuals or the community. However, its importance lies in the fact that it drew on and showed how the new legislative mentality might be mapped onto the structures of the existing criminal law. This framework was to be taken forward as the legislative state developed in the nineteenth century.

III. The Legislative State

> The study of the criminal law might be made an instructive and interesting part of a liberal education, but, in order that this may be done, it must be viewed, not merely as a trade, but as an art founded on a science, the art of making wise laws, science of understanding and correctly classifying large departments of social conduct.[77]

In his *General View of the Criminal Law of England* (1863), Sir James Fitzjames Stephen set out a strikingly novel account of the criminal law. It set the development of the institutions of criminal law within a broader empiricist understanding of social order and analysed the rules of criminal law and punishment in terms of their moral and social significance. For Stephen, this linked the internal order of the criminal law to social order, not just of England but of empire, a combination of domestic and imperial governance. Above all, it recognized that the distinctive characteristics of nineteenth-century criminal law were shaped by the rise of the legislative state. Of course, penal legislation was not new, but the quality of, and motivation behind, the legislation was different. The aim was to be systematic and

[75] Colquhoun, *Treatise on the Police of the Metropolis*, n.54, p.30 (citing Montesquieu). See also Eden, *Principles*, n.28, Ch.24 (On the Composition and Promulgation of the Laws).

[76] Lieberman, *Province of Legislation*, n.8, p.140.

[77] JF Stephen, *A General View of the Criminal Law of England* (London: Macmillan, 1863) p.337. See also KJM Smith, *James Fitzjames Stephen* (Cambridge: Cambridge UP, 1988) Ch.3.

rational—the very qualities which were absent in the legislation that was seen to make up the 'Bloody Code'. More than this, though, the aim was to harness social science to law in order to manipulate human conduct. In the blunt formulation of Oliver Wendell Holmes, writing in 1881: 'the purpose of the criminal law is only to induce external conformity to rule'.[78] This then was a great civilizing initiative, an attempt to shape morals and social conduct on a grand scale as a new approach to criminal law and punishment, and it marked an important change in understandings of the question of criminalization.

A. The expansion of the criminal law

This was a period which saw a huge expansion of the criminal law. There were extensive reforms restricting the scope of punishment, particularly the removal of the death penalty from many offences and its replacement with imprisonment. However, the underlying offences were consolidated and rationalized, rather than abolished, and this gave rise to extensive codifying and consolidating projects. In addition to this, large numbers of new statutory offences were created in such diverse areas as education, licensing, Sunday trading, sale of poisons, copyright, child protection, and so on as more areas of social life were regulated. This expansion in the use of the criminal law also took place in relation to more established common law offences. The courts adapted the definitions of crimes such as theft, homicide, rape, and so on over the period, with the aim of regulating social conduct, expanding the scope of the crimes, and hence of criminal liability. There were areas in which the criminal law was no longer used, notably the decline in prosecutions for treason and sedition after 1832, and the decline in the number of prosecutions for forgery and coining offences, but in most cases these crimes remained part of the law.[79] This was matched by changes in the enforcement of the criminal law. Contemporary estimates suggested that the numbers of those prosecuted for indictable offences rose from around 20,000 in 1836 to 50,000 in 1896, and those prosecuted under summary jurisdiction from around 80,000 to nearly 500,000 over the same period.[80]

Notwithstanding (or perhaps because of) this overall expansion in the numbers of those prosecuted and punished, by the end of the century there was confidence that the crime problem was being addressed successfully, with the rise in prosecutions being taken as a measure of the moral health of society and the increased efficiency of the criminal justice system. Thus Pike concluded his two volume

[78] OW Holmes, *The Common Law* (Boston: Little, Brown & Co, 1881) p.49.

[79] See VAC Gatrell, 'The Decline of Theft and Violence in Victorian and Edwardian England' in VAC Gatrell et al. (eds), *Crime and the Law. The Social History of Crime in Western Europe since 1500* (London: Europa, 1980) pp.279–84 for a summary.

[80] See *Judicial Statistics*, England and Wales 1896 (C.8755) (London: HMSO, 1898) pp.18–31 comparing rates of crime and prosecution in 1836 and 1896 on the occasion of Queen Victoria's jubilee. The expansion of the number of summary prosecutions included the prosecution of some previously indictable offences, such as theft or assault in the summary courts.

history of crime and civilization in England with the claim that '[t]here never was in any nation of which we have a history, a time in which life and property were so secure as they are at present'.[81]

This confidence was in part brought about by the dramatic changes in the scope and the administration of the criminal law over the course of the nineteenth century. Of primary importance was the reduction in the number of offences subject to capital punishment, a development which marked the transition to a new understanding of criminal justice where punishment was to be certain, swift, humanitarian, effective, and according to law.[82] This was a process which began in the 1820s, as outrage came to a head over the extent and ineffectiveness of the 'Bloody Code'.[83] It was the start of a grand legislative initiative, comprising several major episodes of legislative reform, which was to continue for most of the century. While attention is inevitably drawn to the major codification initiatives of the 1830s and 1870s, of equal significance was the steady flow of legislation creating crimes in diverse areas of state activity that continued throughout the century.[84] This development was seen as a necessary consequence of the spread of commerce and wealth: 'Legislation, in fact, recognises a progressive increase in the numerical amount of crimes resulting from the development of civilisation; for every time that industry creates a new species of property, its possession is secured to the proprietor by a new guarantee of penal prohibition.'[85] These developments were accompanied by the widespread adoption of imprisonment as the primary form of punishment and the use of graduated forms of punishment. Organized policing was reconstituted, with the establishment of the Metropolitan Police Force in 1829 and the gradual development of professional police forces across the country, and the new police played an active role not just in detecting serious crime, but also in bringing disorderly or immoral conduct, which might have been tolerated in earlier years, before the courts.[86] Criminal procedure was transformed with, on the one hand, the formal introduction of defence counsel in felony trials in 1836, and, on the other, the rise and increasing formalization of summary jurisdiction, providing for the rapid trial of those charged with less serious offences.[87] The substantive criminal law of offences against the person, larceny, malicious damage,

[81] LO Pike, *A History of Crime in England* (2 vols) (London: Smith, Elder & Co., 1876) Vol. II, pp.480–1. It is notable that the subtitle of the book is 'illustrating the changes of the laws in the progress of civilization'. See also L Radzinowicz & R Hood, *History of English Criminal Law and Its Administration*. Vol.V *The Emergence of Penal Policy* (London: Stevens, 1986) Ch.5 ('The English Miracle').

[82] R McGowen, 'The Image of Justice and Reform of the Criminal Law in Early Nineteenth-Century England' (1983) 32 *Buffalo Law Rev* 89.

[83] For a summary see Radzinowicz, *History*, n.22, Vol. I, Part V.

[84] On codification see Ch.5.

[85] WC Taylor, 'Moral Economy of Large Towns. Crime and Punishment' (1839) 6 (July) *Bentley's Miscellany* p.481. He went on to argue that the number of crimes diminishes as a proportion ('the moral result of civilisation'). On Taylor's background and views on civilization see P Joyce, *The Rule of Freedom. Liberalism and the Modern City* (London: Verso, 2003) pp.63–4.

[86] For a summary, see M Wiener, *Reconstructing the Criminal* (Cambridge: Cambridge UP, 1990) Chs.2 & 3.

[87] On the Prisoners' Counsel Act 1836, see Langbein, *Origins*, n.35, Ch.5; DJA Cairns, *Advocacy and the Making of the Adversarial Criminal Trial, 1800–1865* (Oxford: Oxford UP, 1998); AN May,

forgery, coinage, and being an accessory was consolidated in legislation in 1861.[88] These developments were indicative of a more general transformation of the state and the understanding of the place of criminal law as both a tool of government and, increasingly, as a means of articulating democratic liberties. This period saw the emergence of a political system whose legitimacy was based on democracy.[89] Legislation had to secure popular support, and state actors and institutions were subject to new standards of legitimacy. This was also a modernization of governmental institutions. This entailed, on the one hand, the internal administration of the state as new bodies and bureaucracies were created, with law as an essential means of organizing and co-ordinating this bureaucracy; and, on the other, administration by the state as the scope of state action extended significantly.[90]

We can make some more general observations about the impact and significance of these changes in terms of the reconstruction of the province of legislation. First of all, crime and law were increasingly seen and understood in a national context.[91] The local structures of courts, policing, and punishment that had characterized criminal justice in the eighteenth century were gradually replaced by national institutions created under general legislation which laid down broad standards and regulatory frameworks. By the end of the century there were general statutes regulating policing and punishment, and legislation creating substantive crimes was framed in general terms. There were, of course, local differences in the implementation or enforcement of laws but, as a problem of government, crime and law were understood in national terms—as the recognition of these local differences as deviations from a national norm implies.[92] Second, central to this understanding of crime as a national problem was the development of criminal, or moral, statistics, as they were known.[93] These brought a recognition that 'the criminal records of almost every country prove that crimes are annually produced in very nearly the same number, the same order, and the same districts'.[94] The incidence

The Bar and the Old Bailey, 1750–1950 (Chapel Hill: Univ of NC Press, 2003). On the development of summary jurisdiction, see Gatrell, 'Decline of Theft and Violence', n.79, pp.273–9.

[88] See generally, CS Greaves, *The Criminal Law Consolidation and Amendments Acts of the 24 & 25 Vict.* (2nd edn) (London: Stevens & Hanes, 1862). See also Smith, *Lawyers, Legislators and Theorists*, n.4, pp.136–8.

[89] See discussion in N Lacey, 'What Constitutes Criminal Law?' in RA Duff et al. (eds), *The Constitution of the Criminal Law* (Oxford: Oxford UP, 2013) pp.21–5.

[90] L Farmer, 'Reconstructing the English Codification Debate: The Criminal Law Commissioners 1833–45' (2000) *18 Law & Hist Rev.* 405.

[91] C Emsley, *Crime and Society in England, 1750–1900* (3rd edn) (Harlow: Pearson, 2005) p.13. And of course in the imperial context, a measure of the degree of civilization—and hence the kind of criminal law that was required—was the state of development of the nation.

[92] For an example of local enforcement, see Judicial Statistics, *England and Wales 1896*, n.80, Introduction at pp.17–8, pointing out that a rise in prosecutions under the Sunday trading laws (to 3593) was almost entirely due to returns from Hull, and that rates of prosecution under the Vaccination Acts had been distorted by returns from Somerset and Gloucestershire.

[93] See Radzinowicz & Hood, *History*, n.81, Vol. V, Chs.3 & 4.

[94] Taylor, 'Moral Economy', n.85, p.476. Cf. Quetelet: 'Society contains within itself the seeds of all the crimes that are going to be committed. It is society which, in a sense, prepares them, and the offender is only the instrument which carries them out'. Cited in Radzinowicz & Hood, *History*, n.81, p.51.

of crime was understood as having its roots in social change, as industrialization and urbanization exposed people to vice and temptation. While there was disagreement over explanations of the precise causes of crime—poor education, drunkenness, poverty, idleness—there was a common understanding that paupers and criminals shared a 'cognate moral failing'.[95] Immoral behaviour was thus seen as a threat to social order: '[i]n apocalyptic language, moralists warned that persistent indulgence in immorality threatened to destroy institutions, such as the family and work, and shared values, such as honesty, decency, self-discipline, respect for the property and person of others, and diligence, upon which social stability and national survival supposedly depended'.[96] In short, the incidence of crime was seen as a measure of the moral character of the nation, both the index and the outcome of the progress of civilization.[97] Third, this was accompanied by the growing belief that the incidence of crime, like any other social phenomenon, could be affected by the proper type of legislative intervention.[98] Criminal law, in particular, could help build character, and inculcate the qualities of moral restraint and will necessary to a civilized society—a motivation that also informed the imperial mission in the second half of the nineteenth century. What is striking about this is that where previously it was particular crimes, or vices such as idleness, that had been seen as a threat to social order, crime was now described as an object, an aggregate social phenomenon that had an independent reality external to law and that law must respond to. Crimes were social harms caused by vices such as idleness and the role of the criminal law was to build character so that vices or temptations were resisted and the aggregate incidence of crime was reduced. In place of common law adjudication, and its piecemeal inductive development of principles, legislative science conceived the role of government as the 'detailed and continuous regulation of the human condition' according to empirical criteria.[99] Criminal law thus became a key tool for the legislator in responding to social problems. Finally, a consistent theme of writing about criminal law was the dismissal of retribution as an aim of punishment.[100] The aim of criminal

[95] VAC Gatrell, 'Crime, Authority and the Policeman-State' in FML Thompson (ed.), *The Cambridge Social History of Britain 1750–1950* (Cambridge: Cambridge UP, 1990) p.251.

[96] S Petrow, *Policing Morals* (Oxford: Oxford UP, 1994) p.3.

[97] See Pike, *History of Crime*, n.81, Vol. II, Ch.12. WD Morrison, *Crime and its Causes* (London: Swan Sonnenschein & Co, 1891) p.16 talks about the 'moral sentiments of a nation' and crime as an index of its condition. See also Wiener, *Reconstructing*, n.86, Ch.1; Gatrell, *Crime*, n.95, pp.249–57.

[98] 'The ordering of these returns is a measure of excellent use in furnishing *data* for the legislator to go to work upon. They will form altogether a kind of political barometer, by which the effect of every legislative operation relative to the subject may be indicated and made palpable.' Bentham, 'A View of the Hard Labour Bill' (1778) quoted in in Radzinowicz & Hood, *History*, n.81, p.92. See further discussion in LJ Hume, *Bentham and Bureaucracy* (Cambridge: Cambridge UP, 1981) Ch 5.

[99] JH Burns, *The Fabric of Felicity* (London: UCL, 1967) p.15. See also Farmer, 'Reconstructing', n.90, pp.409–10.

[100] See e.g. JS Mill, 'It is the business of the law to prevent wrongdoing and not simply to patch up the consequences of it when it has been committed' *Principles of Political Economy* in Collected Works, vol.3 (London: Routledge & Kegan Paul, 1991) p.908; Holmes, *The Common Law*, n.78, p.43.

law was prevention or deterrence, which was linked to legislation as the form of law: a 'systematic expression by the aid of general rules, by means of which the delinquent may be forewarned as well as punished, and by which the judgements of inferior criminal tribunals may be also guided.'[101]

These changes in the scope of the law posed significant challenges as criminal lawyers sought to define and classify the criminal law. On the one hand, it is common to find positivist definitions. Thus, in a characteristic formulation, for Stephen, 'a crime is an act of disobedience to a law forbidden under the pain of punishment'.[102] This conception was linked to the idea that if a wrong was a violation of a right, then the function of the criminal law was that of defending rights defined elsewhere in the law.[103] But while this was a useful formal definition, in practice it was recognized that it needed to be underpinned by an account of the meaning of crime as a moral or social phenomenon as a way of explaining which kinds of violation of rights were appropriately addressed by the criminal law. This problem of unity was also manifested as a problem of how the law should be articulated. The existing law was recognized by many to be 'a patchwork of law formed on inconsistent principles'.[104] The question though was how the criminal law might be organized in such a way as bring it into a conceptual and, therefore, legislative unity and to make it better suited to the managing of modern social relations.

B. Classification

> Most of the definitions of offences in the English law are of great antiquity; and having been adapted to times when it was more necessary to guard against force than fraud, have been found insufficient to meet the exigencies of a more civilized state of society, in which the means and opportunities, as well as the temptations, to commit fraudulent crimes have increased with advancing civilization.[105]

The problem for jurists was that the structure of the law was based on distinctions, such as that between treason, felony, and misdemeanour which reflected a view of social relations that was increasingly out of step with modern realities.[106] While

[101] Criminal Law Commissioners, *Seventh Report* (London: HMSO, 1843) p.9. See also e.g. E Cox, *Principles of Punishment* (London: Law Times, 1877) p.15.

[102] Stephen, *General View*, n.77, p.1, citing John Austin, *The Province of Jurisprudence Determined*, Lecture I; Pike, *History of Crime*, n.81, p.489: 'There has not, and never has been, any crime in any actions except those which a law declares to be criminal, or to which it assigns a punishment.'

[103] See Criminal Law Commissioners, *Fourth Report* (London: HMSO, 1839) p.xiii; Criminal Law Commissioners, *Seventh Report*, n.101, p.7.

[104] J. Austin, *Lectures on Jurisprudence* (5th edn, ed. R Campbell) (London: John Murray, 1885) Vol. II, p.1042.

[105] Criminal Law Commissioners, *Fourth Report*, n.103, p.xiv.

[106] WT Murphy, *The Oldest Social Science* (Oxford: Oxford UP, 1998) arguing that common law was a form of administration based on adjudication, by contrast with the modern legislative state. Cf. Amos, *Ruins of Time*, n.38, p.5: 'It was not until a century after his [Hale's] decease that Adam

Bentham had argued that the order of the common law should be swept away and replaced by a new natural arrangement of law based on utilitarianism, the more common approach was to try and find a way of reconciling traditional categorizations with modern scientific conceptual schemes.

One problem was that the classification of offences was still principally in terms of treasons, felonies, and misdemeanours, and that the problems encountered by Blackstone with these terms had, if anything, got worse. Andrew Amos described the classification as having been a 'rude contrivance' at the time of Hale that had now become a 'public nuisance'.[107] Few 'felonies' were capital after the reforms of the capital statutes in the 1820s and 1830s; the procedural distinction for the trial of felonies disappeared with the Prisoners Counsel Act 1836; and forfeiture of property as a consequence of conviction was unpopular with the courts and rarely used.[108] The problem, above all, was that the distinction corresponded to no clear measure of overall seriousness: 'In any new classification founded on proportionate guilt, many existing felonies and misdemeanors (sic) must change places'.[109] At the same time, crimes within each class comprised combinations of offences of different degrees of seriousness. For example, in their *Fourth Report* (1839), the Criminal Law Commissioners identified the characteristic feature of treason as the allegiance owed by the subject to the sovereign, and thus criticized diverse forms of constructive treason (such as counterfeiting or clipping coins, or rioting) as artificial because they were not consistent with this underlying principle.[110] The basis of the criticism was thus a focus on the underlying 'nature' of the offences, an approach which looked at the characteristics of conduct, and the interest protected by the law, and sought to develop new measures of classification and seriousness. The origins of this approach can be traced to Blackstone's categorization in terms of interests, but it was applied in a much more systematic way. Where Blackstone had based his account on public wrongs understood through the prism of the historical common law, the new approach sought to define interests in terms of 'the natural distribution of the class of actions to which it applies'.[111]

The most influential and systematic attempt to classify the criminal law in terms of interests was made by Jeremy Bentham. His aim was to combine a utilitarian ethics with the development of a systematic account of the law, which would distinguish between different crimes in terms of their degree of seriousness and thereby provide a basis for the identification of appropriate punishments.[112]

Smith founded political economy, a science which exhibits the fallacious basis of a large part of our ancient criminal law.'

[107] Amos, *Ruins of Time*, n.38, p.46. See also Criminal Law Commissioners, *Second Report* (London: HMSO, 1836) p.19.

[108] It was abolished by the Forfeiture Act 1870 (33 & 34 Vict. c.23). See, generally, Criminal Law Commissioners, *First Report* (London: HMSO, 1834) pp.31–2; Cox, *Principles*, n.101, pp.6–8.

[109] Amos, *Ruins of Time*, n.38, p.48. Although there was a reluctance to discard the terminology altogether: see Criminal Law Commissioners, *Fourth Report*, n.103, pp.ix-xii.

[110] *Fourth Report*, n.103, pp.ix–xi.

[111] Stephen, *History*, n.1, Vol. II, p.75.

[112] On Bentham and classification, see M Lobban, *The Common Law and English Jurisprudence* (Oxford: Oxford UP, 1991) Chs.5 & 6. See also HLA Hart, *Essays on Bentham: Jurisprudence and Political Theory* (Oxford: Clarendon, 1982).

This would enable the criminal law to be seen as a whole, with the interests to be protected by the law identified on the basis of the social ends that they served. He thus sought to sweep away what he saw as the illogical and unjustifiable categories of the common law, and while this resulted in moments of brilliant insight, the overall outcome was complex and over-elaborate.[113] The Criminal Law Commissioners, while influenced by Bentham, were more pragmatic, producing a systematic classification which married an adherence to older terminologies with a newly systematic ordering of the law. Their final Digest broke the criminal law into twenty-one separate classes of offences, beginning with treason and offences against public institutions, public peace and morals, and trade, before moving on to offences against the person and against private property.[114] Sir James Fitzjames Stephen in producing his *Digest,* similarly divided substantive offences into five large classes, again moving from offences against public institutions and authority to offences against the person and against property.[115] While there were differences between the particular schemes, this drive for classification had three common ends. First, it was a way of attempting to distinguish the criminal law from other areas of law. Private wrongs were to be distinguished from public ones, whether this was in terms of substantive and adjectival law, or the different kinds of interests represented.[116] Second, it was about the internal ordering of the law, distinguishing private and public crimes, identifying discrete interests, and then ordering and classifying crimes within these interests: 'every definition of a crime ought to distinguish it both from actions not criminal and from all other crimes'.[117] Public crimes were those against public institutions or officers, while private crimes were those against the interest of private persons or their property.[118] This saw the rejection of the idea that criminal law as a whole was aimed at the protection of the public peace, as this was recognized as a distinct and subsidiary interest relating only to public order.[119] Finally, it was aimed at marking out the degrees of seriousness of different offences, assessed in terms

[113] See *Introduction to the Principles and Morals of Legislation* (JH Burns & HLA Hart eds) (Oxford: Clarendon, 1982) Ch.XVI; Lieberman, *Province of Legislation*, n.8, p.263.

[114] See *Seventh Report*, n.101, pp.113–277.

[115] His five classes were: offences against public order, internal and external; abuses and obstructions of public authority; acts injurious to the public in general; offences against the person, conjugal and parental rights and the reputation of individuals; offences against rights of property and rights arising out of contract. See *A Digest of the Criminal Law* (1877) (4th edn) (London: Macmillan & Co, 1887). See also John Austin's plan for a code, in *Lectures,* n.104, p.1066.

[116] This was the approach of Bentham and the Criminal Law Commissioners, discussed in Farmer, *Reconstructing,* n.90, pp.418–22. Stephen distinguished between public and private interests, see Stephen, *General View*, n.77, pp.6–7.

[117] Stephen, *General View*, n.77, p.104.

[118] See e.g. Austin, *Lectures*, n.104, p.1066. Cf. Birnbaum's contemporaneous development of the idea of *rechtsgut*, although his route to this outcome was slightly different: 'Concerning the Need for a Right Violation in the Concept of Crime, having particular Regard to the Concept of an Affront to Honour' in Dubber (ed.), *Foundational Texts*, n.8, Appendix B.

[119] 'A large class of crimes may in strictness be denominated Offences against the Public Peace, as all forcible violations of the rights of person or property may without impropriety be comprehended under this division' (Criminal Law Commissioners, *Fifth Report* (London: HMSO, 1840) p.90) but going on to say that they will use it in a more restricted sense.

of the quality of the prohibited conduct and the motivation of the offender, so that punishments could be specified in advance for crimes: 'We have selected and prepared the definitions and rules contained in the Digest... that they may serve the technical purpose of distinguishing criminal wrongs from all others, as also the purpose of distinguishing the different degrees of liability'.[120]

This classification of offences led to one other significant innovation, which was the beginning of attempts to identify and specify rules of general application, which were distinct from the definitions of particular substantive offences. These included the classification of crimes (treason, felony, misdemeanour); of different types of punishment; rules as to who could or could not commit crimes or be criminally liable (capacity); and rules on parties to the commission of crime and inchoate liability. This was understood largely as a matter of organization, identifying rules of general application as a matter of convenience, rather than deriving from a more general commitment to principles of individual responsibility.[121] So far as these classifications were all directed at organizing and shaping the increased bulk of the criminal law it is now necessary to consider the understanding of crime and whether this revealed any 'natural' limits to the scope of the criminal law.

C. The scope and limits of the criminal law

> Thus, in criticising any set of definitions of crimes, two points require attention: the degree in which the definitions effect the intention of the legislator, and the degree in which the intention of the legislator consults the interest of the public... In our own time and country they form, substantially, one question, which may thus be expressed:—How ought definitions of crime to be framed with a view to the public benefits produced by the criminal law?[122]

In this statement Stephen sets up an understanding of the scope and limits of the criminal law (which is to say criminalization) in terms of two factors: first, the intention of the legislator, and second, the conventional and political limits on the criminal law. Before we turn to the question of limits, though, it is necessary to consider what he understood to be the public benefits of law.[123]

It is easy to read Stephen as being primarily concerned with revenge and retribution, reducing the aims of the criminal law to those of punishment. He made a number of aphoristic claims about punishment and revenge—notably the famous claim that 'criminal law stands to the passion of revenge in much the same relation as marriage to the sexual appetite'—which play up a crude moralism and

[120] *Seventh Report*, n.101, p.6. See also Farmer, 'Reconstructing', n.90, pp.416–7.
[121] For discussion of their understanding of criminal responsibility see Ch.6 at pp.175–81.
[122] Stephen, *General View*, n.77, p.98.
[123] Stephen, *General View*, n.77, Ch.IX is a discussion of legislation in general, and the respective roles of Parliament and the judiciary as legislators.

might be read as implying that the satisfying of emotional urges was the main object of the criminal law.[124] However, to see him in this way would be to overlook the way that his account of punishment is located within his account of the social role of criminal law. Though he used a language of revenge, terror, fear, intolerance and disgust, these were not presented as justifications for punishment, but as a description of what he saw as its social function—namely the recognition and inculcation of moral distinctions. This was consistent with a broader contemporary understanding of the aim of the criminal law as establishing 'a rule of civil conduct'.[125] Civil order, on this view, depended on discipline and self-control, and in particular the development of character as a form of moral restraint necessary to civilized society.[126] The social significance of the criminal law was as a medium for 'expressing and encouraging' the qualities of character as means of restraining barbaric or anti-social impulses.[127] Thus while it should be consistent with moral beliefs, as this would make it more legitimate and effective, the main function of criminal law was to restrain, rather than give rein to, impulse and emotion.

It followed from this that one of Stephen's aims was ensuring that the moral significance of law was better recognized. This had two dimensions. On the one hand, the law should be consistent with moral and social science, as the effectiveness of law was linked to its consistency with a broader understandings of moral order. Criminal laws would be ineffective if their foundation in this moral order was not recognized, and the aim of the legislator was to promote moral, as well as social, improvement.[128] On the other hand, there was the question of enforcement of morals—whether particular social vices should be criminalized because of their tendency to undermine civil order. While Stephen is well known for supporting the latter, his position is best understood in the context of the former. Thus, his claim that '[t]he object of promoting virtue and preventing vice must be admitted to be both a good one and one sufficiently intelligible for legislative purposes' makes sense because of his broader understanding of civil order and the role of law in securing that order.[129] This led him to distinguish between three different

[124] Stephen, *General View* n.77, p.99. For this view generally, see M DeGirolami, 'James Fitzjames Stephen: The Punishment Jurist' in Dubber (ed.), *Foundational Texts*, n.8, Ch.9. I am indebted to the perceptive reading of Stephen in S Collini, *Public Moralists. Political Thought and Intellectual Life in Britain 1850–1930* (Oxford: Clarendon, 1991) esp. pp.281–7.

[125] Criminal Law Commissioners, *Seventh Report*, n.101, p.4. The Commissioners described the great object of the criminal law as preventive: to deter men from violating the law; to recognize and inculcate moral distinction; to provide for public safety; and to define crimes and punishments with reasonable certainty (p.92).

[126] On the importance of character in nineteenth century political thought, see Collini, *Public Moralists*, n.124, Ch.3. Wiener, *Reconstructing*, n.86, Chs.1 & 2 discusses the importance of character to Victorian criminal law.

[127] Collini, *Public Moralists*, n.124, p.287. See Stephen, *General View*, n.77, p.233 where he describes the institution of English criminal law as 'a great practical school of truth, morality, and compassion'.

[128] Stephen, *History*, n.1, Vol. II, Ch.XVII; Radzinowicz & Hood, n.81, p.49.

[129] Stephen, *Liberty, Equality and Fraternity* (New York: Holt & Williams, 1873) p.146; 'The object of morally intolerant legislation... is to establish, to maintain, and to give power to that which the legislator regards as a good moral system or standard... [T]his object is good if and in so far as the system so established and maintained is good' (p.145).

classes of crime in terms of their relationship to morals: gross violations of plain moral duties; specific acts of disobedience to the legislator; and attacks on the authority of the legislator.[130] Of these, it was the first class only that had a clear and unambiguous relation to moral duties. The second class, he considered to be important, but the moral breach lay in the violation of an obligation established by the legislator for the public good, rather than the moral quality of the conduct itself. And the third class consisted mainly of what he had earlier termed 'public crimes', where the crime consisted in an attack on public institutions (from treason to the public peace). Here he argued that while any relation to morality was contingent, any government was entitled to 'punish with severity, and in an unqualified manner, every attack upon its existence or contempt of its authority, whether morally right or wrong'.[131]

This account of the benefits of law was significant in several ways. First, the terms of the discussion reflected an emerging distinction between what were now seen as the separate realms of law and morals, a distinction that was to become central to the criminalization question.[132] Second, the promulgation of the law should reflect moral distinctions where these were relevant; but if they were not, which would be the case with respect to the bulk of the criminal law, there was nonetheless a need for clarity and certainty—hence Stephen's support for codification.[133] Security depended to a significant extent on laws that were clearly expressed and properly enforced: predictability allowed individuals to manage themselves in complex modern societies. Third, while the law was directed at the 'self-distancing individual capable of disciplining his impulses and governing his life', the aims of the criminal law were generally understood in collective terms.[134] The 'public benefits' of criminal law for Stephen were in part to be derived from the moral role of law (where this was appropriate), but mainly from the existence of legal order as such, and its role in articulating clear rules to be followed irrespective of their particular content.[135] This, then, was a move away from the idea of public wrong articulated by Blackstone towards an order designed and guaranteed by the state. The collective interest in civil order was viewed as distinct from, and as a foundation for, individual goods: 'It is manifest that all specific laws for the security of persons of property would be unavailing, unless the due operation of such laws were protected by imposing efficient restraints on forcible violations of public order'.[136] And within this there was a move from seeing property as the

[130] Stephen, *General View*, n.77, pp.99–105; See also Stephen, *History*, n.1, Vol. II, pp.76–7.

[131] Stephen, *General View*, n.77, p.102. He also argued that punishment motivated by revenge was only appropriate in relation to the first class 'in which the acts forbidden by the law excite feelings of moral indignation' (p.99).

[132] See e.g. S Amos, *The Science of Law* (London: Kegan Paul, Trench, Trübner & Co, 1896) Ch.3.

[133] 'Every definition of a crime ought to distinguish it both from actions not criminal and from all other crimes.' (Stephen, *General View*, n.77, p.104.) See infra Chapter 5.

[134] Wiener, *Reconstructing*, n.86, p.47.

[135] Gatrell, 'Decline of Theft and Violence', n.79, p.254: 'order was a sufficient social value in terms of which the legitimacy of social policy might be assessed'.

[136] Criminal Law Commissioners, *Fifth Report*, n.119, p.90. Holmes, *The Common Law*, n.78, p.43: '[No] civilized government sacrifices the citizen more than it can help, but still sacrificing his will and his welfare to that of the rest.'

foundation of order to a concern with violence. Thus Edward Cox argued that 'It is even more necessary to repress by punishment crimes of violence [than crimes against property] because they are more noxious to the community by the terror and distrust they occasion, by their dangerous tendency to incite irregularly constructed minds to imitation and the dissolution of society itself that would result from any extensive following of the example.'[137]

This brings us to the question of how Stephen saw limits to the criminal law. In common with many of his contemporaries, Stephen saw no theoretical limits to the sovereignty of parliament and was sceptical of John Stuart Mill's attempt to frame such a limit in terms of a concept of liberty.[138] He did, however, concede that there were conventional limits. These fell into three classes. The first was the form of criminal law itself: 'The excessive harshness of criminal law is...a circumstance which very greatly narrows the range of its application. It is the *ratio ultima* of the majority against persons whom its application assumes to have renounced the common bonds that connect men together'.[139] In addition to this, resort to criminal law brought difficulties of enforcement and proof which led him to conclude that enforcement of vices through law would be generally inexpedient:

> Criminal law is...by far the most powerful and by far the roughest engine which society can use for any purpose...Before an act can be treated as a crime, it ought to be capable of distinct definition and of specific proof, and it ought also to be of such a nature that it is worthwhile to prevent it at the risk of inflicting great damage, direct and indirect, upon those who commit it. These conditions are seldom, if ever, fulfilled by mere vices.[140]

The second limiting factor was public opinion. Here, Stephen argued that legislation should be 'graduated to the existing level of morals in the time and country in which it is employed', and that the law cannot punish anything which common practice 'does not strenuously and unequivocally condemn'.[141] The nod to public opinion recognized the increased significance of democracy to the legitimacy of the law, but rather than presenting this as a licence for majority rule, Stephen regarded the law as a potential brake on public opinion, at the same time as he cautioned against the use of the criminal law in pursuit of ends which were not

[137] Cox, *Principles*, n.101, p.77. Elsewhere he argued that 'the foremost object of all legislation is security for *the person*. The security of property is second in importance to this' (p.93). See infra Ch.8 at pp.244–53.

[138] His book, *Liberty, Equality and Fraternity* (1873) was an extended response to Mill's essay 'On Liberty'. The dispute between Stephen and Mill is discussed in Smith, *James Fitzjames Stephen*, n.77, Ch.7.

[139] Stephen, *Liberty*, n.129, p.147.

[140] Ibid., pp.146–7; see also Cox, *Principles*, n.101, pp.5–6. He was careful to stress that these constraints were independent of any general considerations about liberty (ibid., p.137).

[141] Ibid., p.159. Cf. Holmes, *The Common Law*, n.78, p.41: 'The first requirement of a sound body of law is, that it should correspond with the actual feelings and demands of the community, whether right or wrong'.

supported by public opinion.[142] Finally, he argued that criminal law and public opinion should respect privacy. In terms which echoed those of Mill, he argued that 'there is a sphere, none the less real because it is impossible to define its limits, within which law and public opinion are intruders likely to do more harm than good'.[143] It is important to note these limits were not framed in terms of rights or civil liberties—and he took issue with Mill's argument that liberty was an interest against law. However, as Collini has pointed out, this disagreement was not based on an understanding of the nature or function of law as such, as a means of building character, but on the differences in their views of human nature and of the need to enforce the religious foundation of morals.[144]

Overall, Stephen's view of the criminal law reflected important features of the understanding of criminal law in the mid-nineteenth century. Criminal law was seen as a means of building civil order by laying down clear standards of conduct. However, while there was debate over the scope of the law, there was not yet anything like the criminalization debate in its modern form; although harm had been introduced as an idea by Mill, it was not yet reified as a concept. These were concerns that were to develop in the twentieth century.

IV. Penal Welfarism

> Civilized social thought regards the penal law as the ultimate weapon for diminishing the incidence of major injuries to individuals and institutions, with only such concessions to retaliatory passions as are practically necessary for the system to survive. In short, while invocation of a penal sanction necessarily depends on past behavior, the object is control of harmful conduct in the future. The legislative question therefore is: what past behavior has such rational relationship to the control of future conduct that it ought to be declared a crime?[145]

This framing of the 'legislative question' by Herbert Wechsler, the architect of the US Model Penal Code, captures a new kind of relationship between criminal law and civil order. This approach, which can be described as a form of penal welfarism, saw criminal law from a modern scientific perspective in which the criminal law was a dynamic instrument for dealing with social problems.[146] Crime was a manifestation of 'social danger' and a symptom of underlying social problems. These could be understood and addressed through a range of social interventions of which criminal law was only one possible response. The

[142] Reflecting the common elite fear of democracy, or legislative power being wielded by those who were insufficiently responsible to know how to use it. See e.g. JS Mill, 'The Spirit of the Age' (1831) *Examiner* (23rd Jan) 50–2.

[143] Stephen, *Liberty*, n.129, p.162.

[144] Collini, *Public Moralists*, n.124, p.286.

[145] H Wechsler, 'The Challenge of a Model Penal Code' (1952) 65 *Harv LR* 1097 p.1105.

[146] The term comes from David Garland, *Punishment and Welfare* (Aldershot: Gower, 1985). See also the summary in his *Cultures of Control*, n.3, Ch.2

core of penal welfarism is usually seen in the way it conceived of and dealt with the individual 'criminal'. Penal science studied the physical and psychological structure of each individual to assess the danger that they posed to society; and a correctional system proposed the treatment of each individual to address these causes.[147] Most of the work on penal welfarism has focused on the birth of criminology and has looked at changes to the criminal law mainly in the context of changes in sentencing and punishment. However, it also had a substantial impact on the criminal law, leading to sustained reflection on the form and scope of the criminal law in the post-war period. We will examine this here, looking primarily at the work of Glanville Williams, the leading English criminal lawyer in the 1950s and 1960s, in order to assess the impact of penal welfarism on understandings of the aims of the criminal law and understandings of criminalization.[148]

A. Characteristics of the criminal law

There were few major legislative initiatives in the first half of the twentieth century of a kind that would compare with the great Victorian legislation on criminal law. Indeed, until the post-second world war period there was little legislation solely on issues of substantive criminal law. In certain respects this is hardly surprising as war and the social impact of war meant that the defence of civilization was directed at external rather than internal threats. But in the early years of the century there were substantial legislative initiatives in areas of punishment, welfare, and criminal procedure which reflected the early growth of the welfare state. The impact of war and its aftermath, though, intensified the degree of regulation and raised questions about the role of the state.

As we have noted, by the end of the nineteenth century there had been a sustained decline in the incidence of crime, something attributed to 'the growing strength of educative and civilising influences'.[149] Serious crime as a social problem was linked to a smaller group of habitual criminals, and was understood to require a different kind of approach.[150] Criminals were described as degenerate,

[147] See A Lévitt, 'Some Societal Aspects of the Criminal Law' (1922) 13 *Jnl of the American Institute of Criminal Law and Criminology* p.92: 'The mental characteristics of the accused indicate the nature and extent of the peril he represents.'

[148] There are earlier important writings such as R Pound, 'The Future of the Criminal Law' (1921) 21 *Columbia LR* 1; *Criminal Justice in America* (New York: Henry Holt & Co, 1930).

[149] Judicial Statistics, *Part I.—Criminal statistics. Statistics relating to criminal proceedings, police, coroners, prisons, reformatory and industrial school and criminal lunatics for the year 1898* (Cd.123) (London: HMSO, 1900) p.14. See also Criminal Registrar for England 1901 (report for 1899) pp.36–7: 'We have witnessed a great change in manners: the substitution of words without blows for blows with or without words; an approximation in the manners of different classes; a decline in the spirit of lawlessness' (cited in Gatrell, 'Decline of Theft and Violence', n.79, p.241). See generally Radzinowicz & Hood, n.81, Ch.5.

[150] See Wiener, *Reconstructing*, n.86, Ch.9; D Garland, *Punishment and Welfare*, n.146; B Godfrey et al., *Serious Offenders. A Historical Study of Habitual Criminals* (Oxford: Oxford UP, 2010); Radzinowicz & Hood, n.81, Pt.IV.

socially inadequate, or moral imbeciles, and crime was seen as a form of social pathology.[151] If heredity and environment, rather than just bad character, were the causes of crime, a different response was required of the criminal law. The habitual criminal or recidivist would be targeted with specific institutional treatments, while the merely weak and socially unfortunate would be helped through the provision of social measures aimed at strengthening them and making them law-abiding members of society. These changes in the understanding of crime were reflected in legislation establishing new regimes for the punishment and treatment of offenders.[152] These established probation and supervision in the community for offenders who could demonstrate an intention to live an honest and orderly life.[153] The use of fines was authorized as an alternative to prison for less serious offences.[154] Alcoholics and those with mental illness could be sent to institutions which aimed to provide specialized treatment.[155] This approach was exemplified by the way that children were singled out in criminal justice policy as a group both requiring special protection or special treatment. There was extensive child welfare legislation from the late nineteenth century onwards, driven by philanthropic and moral reform bodies, which culminated in the passing of the Children Act 1908 regulating working conditions for children and protecting them from neglect and abuse, but also establishing juvenile courts and penal institutions as a concentration of effort on the young offender to 'strike at the source of crime'.[156] While the origin of many of these initiatives can be traced to legislation in the latter years of the nineteenth century, by the mid-twentieth century these had been consolidated into a new system for dealing with crime animated by the idea of 'preventive science'.[157]

There was, though, a paradox embedded in this approach, for while the aim of penal reformers was 'to limit by preventive measures the field of operation of Criminal Law', this was accompanied by an expansion of criminal law.[158] This was not only because, as Garland has argued, the introduction of systems such as probation created new forms of intervention and social control, but because the system of 'social hygiene' directed at improving social conditions—'better housing and lighting, the control of the Liquor Traffic, cheap food, fair wages, insurance'—in practice led to the creation of new criminal offences.[159] These were

[151] See e.g. the list of reports in Mannheim breaking down the problem of crime into penal institutions, criminal types, causes of crime, and so on. H Mannheim, *Social Aspects of Crime in England Between the Wars* (2nd edn) (London: George Allen & Unwin, 1950) pp.16–18.

[152] See e.g. Prevention of Crime Act 1908 Pt II on preventive detention. This was subsequently abolished, along with hard labour by the Criminal Justice Act 1948.

[153] Probation of Offenders Act 1907.

[154] Criminal Justice Administration Act 1914.

[155] Inebriates Act 1898; Mental Deficiency Act 1913.

[156] E Ruggles-Brise, *The English Prison System* (London: Macmillan, 1921) p.xx. G Behlmer, *Child Abuse and Moral Reform in England 1870–1908* (Stanford: Stanford UP, 1982). Appendix A lists 79 separate statutes on child welfare between 1870 and 1908. See also L Jackson, *Child Sexual Abuse in Victorian England* (London: Routledge, 2000). These provisions were further consolidated in legislation in 1932 and 1933, which brought the system under state control.

[157] See Ruggles-Brise, *English Prison System*, n.156, Preface.

[158] Sir Edward Ruggles-Brise, Address to International Penitentiary Congress 1910, quoted in Wiener, *Reconstructing*, n.86, p.374.

[159] Ruggles-Brise *English Prison System, op. cit.* n.156, p.xvi; Garland, *Punishment and Welfare*, n.146, Ch.8.

directed at different areas of social life, licensing certain socially useful activities, and the identification and amelioration of diverse social problems: the manufacture and sale of foodstuffs and other goods (including sale of drugs); employment and the regulation of the workplace; the licensing of certain economic activities; the prevention of cruelty to animals and so on.[160] The numbers of prosecutions for these kinds of offences increased hugely in the first half of the century, with prosecution for regulatory offences peaking during the two world wars—spurred by the recognition that the more intensive regulation introduced under wartime conditions might be extended in conditions of peace.[161] Many of these new offences adopted liability without need to prove fault, or strict liability as it came to be known. This was in part a result of the judicial approach of strict or 'literal' interpretation of the relevant statutory provisions, such that *mens rea* was not required unless expressly stated.[162] However, it was also believed to make the law more effective in achieving its ends, as the law was typically concerned with distributing the burden of avoiding the risk of harm by identifying the person or body that was responsible for performing certain duties or roles and criminalizing the failure to perform that role adequately.[163]

The prosecution of these offences was facilitated by the gradual professionalization of prosecution as the police and other specialized agencies took over the prosecution of crime. In these kinds of prosecutions, as with prosecutions for breaches of laws on education, retail, and so on, it was not necessary for there to be a victim or for a victim to appear in court, and this led to the spread of a more professional or technical understanding of crime as something that was dealt with by the police or other agencies.[164] There was also a substantial rise in the number of prosecutions for public order offences as the police sought to 'control public space and curb drunken disorder'.[165] In doing this, it has been suggested that the police saw themselves as acting on behalf of a notional community of the law-abiding, representing a particular kind of public interest and creating a certain

[160] B Godfrey, 'Changing Prosecution Practices and their Impact on Crime Figures in England and Wales, 1857-1940' (2008) 48 *Brit Jnl of Criminol* 171–89 at 182–3; C Emsley, '"Mother, what *did* Policemen Do when there weren't any Motors?" The Law, the Police and the Regulation of Motor Traffic in England, 1900–1939' (1993) 36 *Historical Journal* 357–81 at 360: 'In the second half of the century penal punishments were imposed to back up legislation on education, registration and vaccination; legislators saw failure to comply with the requirements of the state as the products of a defective conscience.'

[161] See Godfrey, 'Changing Prosecution Practices', n.160, p.183, giving figures for Crewe. See e.g. Ruggles-Brise, *English Prison System*, n.156, p.xvi on the achievements of social legislation during the war.

[162] The term was coined by FB Sayre, 'Public Welfare Offences' (1933) 33 *Columbia LR* 55–88; C Manchester, 'The Origins of Strict Criminal Liability' (1977) 6 *Anglo-American LR* 277.

[163] See Ch.6 at pp.185–7.

[164] Godfrey ('Changing Prosecution Practices', n.160) locates the change to police prosecution around the year 1880. See also Mannheim, *Social Aspect*, n.151, pp.55–61.

[165] Godfrey, 'Changing Prosecution Practices', n.160, p.174, though pointing to a surprising decline in prosecutions for assault.

kind of order.[166] This relationship between the police and order was exemplified in the development of the new area of road traffic offences.

Motor vehicles were first used on the roads in the early twentieth century, with car ownership and use expanding rapidly in the inter-war period.[167] They presented problems for the criminal law both in controlling speed and traffic and responding to the death and injuries caused by cars, and as a more direct issue of criminality—as the use of cars changed the way that other crimes were committed. By the middle years of the century there were over 200,000 fatal and non-fatal injuries on the roads every year in the UK, and the use of cars was linked to rises in the number of property crimes as criminals could travel to commit crimes, and cars themselves became the object of theft.[168] The coming of the 'motor age' thus gave rise to a new problem of civil order, or responding to 'carbarians'.[169] Individuals in cars were isolated from each other and had to find new ways of communicating with each other and with the police; mass-produced cars looked alike and could not easily be identified or traced; the volume and speed of cars raised issues of traffic and parking control; mobility presented a challenge to social order; and cars themselves (and their drivers) were a danger to life and limb. These were problems of external and internal control—regulating car ownership and use, but also creating norms of conduct for drivers and other road users.[170] The first Motor Car Act was passed in 1903 and was followed by further Acts in 1930 and 1934. These introduced, then removed and reintroduced, speed limits, brought in requirements for licensing and insurance of drivers and the identification of vehicles, and created offences of speeding and of dangerous, reckless, and careless driving.[171] The number of offences against these Acts rose rapidly as the police took on an active role in the enforcement of the new laws, setting speed

[166] Although commentators were keen to note that the police exercised a wide discretion and did not prosecute in every instance. See Mannheim, *Social Aspects*, n.151, pp.53–61. The courts were generally supportive of the police in this enterprise. See e.g. *R v Manley* [1933] 1KB 529 discussed infra.

[167] See generally Emsley, 'The Regulation of Motor Traffic', n.160; A Hunt, 'Police and the Regulation of Traffic. Policing as a Civilizing Process?' in Dubber & Valverde, *The New Police Science* (Stanford, 2007). See also S Seo, 'Antinomies and the Automobile: A New Approach to Criminal Justice Histories' (2013) 38 *Law & Social Inquiry* 1020–40 tracing the impact of automobiles on criminal procedure in the US.

[168] See Mannheim, *Social Aspects*, n.151, pp.115–8. See also figures in Emsley, 'The Regulation of Motor Traffic', n.160, p.359. The phenomenon of automobile theft is discussed in J Hall, *Theft, Law and Society* (2nd edn) (Indiana: Bobbs-Merrill, 1952) Ch.6.

[169] See N Elias, *The Civilizing Process* (Oxford: Blackwell, 1994) p.368. Emsley, 'The Regulation of Motor Traffic', n.160, p.374 notes that a misprint in *The Times* in 1930 gave rise to the terminology of the 'carbarians'—those who disregarded norms of civilized or respectable conduct.

[170] '[E]xternal control is founded on the assumption that every individual is himself or herself regulating his or her behaviour with the utmost exactitude in accordance with the necessities of this network. The chief danger that people here represent for others results from someone in this bustle losing their self-control. A constant and highly differentiated regulation of one's own behaviour is needed for individuals to steer their way through traffic'. (Elias, *Civilizing Process*, n.169, p.368).

[171] Motor Car Act 1903 (3 Edw.VII, c.36) introduced a speed limit of 20mph. The Road Traffic Act 1930 actually removed the speed limit for cars, but following a record number of fatalities it was reintroduced at 30mph by the Road Traffic Act 1934. In addition the Roads Act 1920 introduced the registration and taxing of vehicles.

traps and stopping those who were driving dangerously.[172] These Acts constructed road traffic as primarily a problem of order and safety, viewing motoring as a problem of traffic co-ordination and management, and the police were encouraged to take an active role in managing conduct to ensure the free movement of traffic in public places and respect for the law.[173] While criminal sanctions were used to reinforce these duties, the problem of criminalization was minimized to that of defining the distinction between the negligent and the reckless driver, so as to avoid the inadvertent criminalization of respectable members of the community.[174]

We can make some more general observations about the impact and significance of these changes on the criminal law. First, this was a broadly instrumental view of the law. Crime was understood as conduct which was socially harmful, and this shaped the way that the aim of the criminal law was understood.[175] The purpose of criminal law was harm reduction: responding to the conduct of the criminal and taking steps to prevent future occurrences of similar conduct.[176] But this differed from earlier approaches both in terms of how social harms were conceived and in the response to them. The idea of social harm was shaped by the widening role of the state. It was seen in collective terms, and the range of new social duties extended over a broader range of conduct than just the protection of central social institutions. However, an increase in the capacity of the state to do good, meant that the range of potential harms defined in the criminal law was expanded. Prevention was thus conceived in terms of an overall social programme which combined individualized treatment with social policy.[177] Second, the breadth of the law was seen as contributing to a reduction of the moral stigma attaching to breaches of the criminal law.[178] The role of the criminal law was seen as fundamentally linked to the work of a range of administrative agencies operating on the basis of specialized forms of knowledge in their own areas of competence.[179] However, by the post-war period, this was beginning to cause concern,

[172] See Emsley, 'The Regulation of Motor Traffic', n.160, p.359.

[173] This also led to initiatives such as the introduction of 'courtesy cops' in some areas of England in 1937 to teach better behaviour on the roads (Emsley, 'The Regulation of Motor Traffic', n.160, p.378. See also Hunt, 'Regulation of Traffic', n.167, p.175). The role of the police was contested as sections of the public complained about the officious and intrusive police.

[174] And thus, perhaps, allowing road traffic to be seen as a neutral problem of co-ordination. Important here is the creation of the separate offence of causing death by reckless or dangerous driving in 1956.

[175] G Williams, *Criminal Law. The General Part* (London: Stevens, 1953) p.17: '[c]riminal law is generally concerned to repress conduct hurtful to society.' Unless stated otherwise, references are to the first edition.

[176] Lévitt, *Societal Aspects*, n.147, p.90.

[177] 'The criminal law must analyze the social organization, determine how the criminal is related to and connected with this organization, and then devise the best means for protecting the organization from the danger with which the criminal threatens it.' Lévitt, *Societal Aspects*, n.147, p.90.

[178] See Wiener, *Reconstructing*, n.86, pp.262–4 arguing that the wider uses of the criminal law, the use of summary jurisdiction and lesser punishments took the moral stigma out of breaches of the criminal law.

[179] H Mannheim, *Criminal Justice and Social Reconstruction* (London: Kegan Paul, 1946) pp.196–7. See also Pound, 'Future of Criminal Law', n.148, p.1: 'the function of securing social

as commentators began to worry about the impact on the moral legitimacy of the criminal law. Third, the discourse linking criminality to character was replaced by an understanding of crime as caused by a combination of heredity and environment, as a form of individual and social pathology: 'Few diseases threaten civilization more persistently than the manifold forms of anti-social action that we call crimes'.[180] The response was a new kind of bio-politics, addressing social problems at the level of the population and individuals with an approach that was essentially therapeutic in character, adapted to the 'physio-psychological characteristics of the criminal'.[181]

These changes in the scope and function of the law had implications for the way that criminal law was conceived as a unified whole. Some scholars argued for an approach that would see criminal law as an element within a broader social science: criminal law together with criminology and criminal procedure, as part of a unified field of criminal science comprising law, criminal biology, and criminal sociology.[182] By contrast, Glanville Williams argued for a formal definition of crime based on linguistic philosophy and legal usage:

> A crime is an act capable of being followed by criminal proceedings having a criminal outcome, and a proceeding or its outcome is criminal if it has certain characteristics which mark it as criminal.[183]

This, he argued, was necessary precisely in order, to rescue the definition of crime from the 'unwelcome attentions' of criminologists and philosophers.[184]

B. Classification

While earlier jurists had, as we have seen, struggled to reconcile the changing scope of the evolving and modernizing criminal law with traditional classifications, criminal lawyers in this period showed a greater willingness to discard classifications and categories that were no longer useful and to think in a new way about the criminal law. The post-war period saw a renewal of interest in the

interests through punitive justice seems to be insensibly slipping away from courts and hence from law and...to be coming more and more into the hands of administrative agencies'.

180 Pound, 'Future of Criminal Law', n.148, p.15, going on to compare an unscientific approach to the 'faith of the Hindu'.

181 Lévitt, 'Societal Aspects', n.147, p.97, citing Lombroso, and also extensive references to contemporary psychology.

182 See essays in L Radzinowicz & JWC Turner, *The Modern Approach to Criminal Law* (London: Macmillan, 1945).

183 G Williams, 'The Definition of Crime' (1955) 8 *Current Legal Problems* 130. For a full discussion of his methodology, see G Williams, 'Language and the Law' (1945) 61 *LQR* pp.71–86, 179–95, 293–303, 384–406; Cf. HLA Hart, 'Definition and Theory in Jurisprudence' in *Essays in Jurisprudence and Philosophy* (Oxford: Clarendon, 1983) distinguishing between ordinary usage and ordinary legal usage. See further L Farmer, 'The Modest Ambition of Glanville Williams' in Dubber (ed.), *Foundational Texts*, n.8, ch.13.

184 Williams, 'Definition of Crime', n.183, p.130.

question of how the law should be organized—something that was also reflected in the revival of interest in codification on both sides of the Atlantic.[185]

This interest was reflected in Williams' writings. The question of the definition of crime was an important theme in writings on criminal law between 1900 and 1955, when Williams published his essay, as the growth and changing function of the criminal law had raised questions about its integrity.[186] Williams argued that any definition must reflect the contemporary legal reality. His approach was to look at decided cases which had addressed this question—many of which had arisen in relation to statutes such as the Police Acts, which had created offences to which the only penalty attached was a fine, thus raising the question of whether the penalty was criminal.[187] In these cases, the courts had recognized that the traditional categorization of crimes as 'public wrongs' or in terms of moral stigma could not help in determining the question, as they largely involved minor offences arising from particular regulatory provisions with no apparent reference to larger moral questions of right or wrong. The courts thus argued that 'proper' criminal offences could only be distinguished by reference to the practice of the criminal courts. The distinction between civil and criminal was sought in a characterization of the nature of the proceedings. The utility of the definition, according to Williams, lay in the fact that it was supported by legal authority, reproducing the legal distinctions that were familiar in the realms of jurisdiction, procedure and punishment, and could therefore offer practical assistance to lawyers.[188] Its significance, though, was broader. It was inclusive, covering the range of different kinds of criminal law; it had potential to unify the criminal law by identifying a common element; and, in contrast to social scientific approaches, it offered an account of the distinctiveness of the criminal law as a particular kind of institutional response to crime. The stress here then is on the modality of law—the consequences and constraints of the resort to criminal law.[189]

Williams addressed this question of the distinctiveness of the criminal law in a more systematic way in his book *Criminal Law: The General Part* first published

[185] The terms felony and misdemeanor were finally abolished in 1967: Criminal Law Act 1967 Pt.I. See Criminal Law Revision Committee, *Seventh Report. Felonies and Misdemeanours* (Cmnd.2659) (London: HMSO, 1965). On codification see Ch.5 infra.

[186] Two of the most important contributions were CS Kenny, *Outlines of Criminal Law* (Cambridge: Cambridge UP, 1902) Ch.1 and CK Allen, 'The Nature of a Crime' in *Legal Duties* (Oxford: Clarendon, 1931). This literature is reviewed in L Farmer, 'The Obsession with Definition: The Nature of Crime and Critical Legal Theory' (1996) 5 *Social & Leg Stud* pp.57–73.

[187] Kenny and Allen (ibid.) noted a number of other situations where the question of jurisdiction was raised, e.g., Appeals of Felony where the civil court was competent to inflict a capital punishment. There was also the question of whether an offender could be a competent witness in their own defence. This was not permitted in criminal trials until the passing of the Criminal Evidence Act 1898, which meant that the courts often had to consider whether proceedings were civil or criminal on these grounds.

[188] Williams, 'Definition of Crime', n.183, p.107. See also PJ Fitzgerald, 'A Concept of Crime' (1960) *Crim LR* pp.257–62.

[189] HM Hart, 'The Aims of the Criminal Law' (1958) 23 *Law and Contemporary Problems* 401–44: 'A complex of institutional ends must be served, in other words, as well as a complex of substantive social ends' (p. 402).

in 1953.[190] His approach to the general part of the criminal law was based on the simple idea of identifying those rules which were capable of applying to more than one crime.[191] This was necessary, he argued, in order to provide a systematic guide to the 'great proliferation of offences by the legislature', and to bring together the authorities on various points to ensure that the 'root principles are thrown into relief, and the attention of the practitioner is directed to relevant authorities'.[192] His aim was descriptive and practical: descriptive in the sense of identifying all those rules which were in fact of general application; and practical because this would have a utility for lawyers and thus the potential to limit judicial discretion. He thus combined the recognition of the diversity of criminal laws in the welfare state with the systematic attempt to organize and draw out the distinctive features of the criminal law as an institutional response to crime. This was approached in terms of three features. First, he sought to identify what he described as the underlying rationality of the law. He did not explicitly articulate what he meant by this term, but from his criticism of conflicting authorities and the lack of organization in the law, it is clear that he saw this in terms of consistency and coherency. Second, this rationality was identified in terms of underlying principles. These were understood inductively, in the common law sense, as emerging from case law, rather than as philosophical or political principles that might provide some sort of external constraint on, or structure for, the criminal law.[193] And third, a focus on general principles meant for him a focus on the question of *mens rea*: 'the chief problems of the general part pertain to the requirement of a criminal state of mind'.[194]

His method was to begin by specifying the legal meaning of *mens rea* as 'the mental element necessary for the particular crime' with a view to limiting judicial discretion, by identifying the central case, and thereby curbing what he saw as 'inflationary' tendencies in the law where confusion over statutory definitions of *mens rea*, and the policy issues raised in particular cases, had permitted judges to over-extend the application of the law.[195] Respect for the principle of *mens rea*, in Williams' view, should not be left to judicial interpretation or to the wording or social purpose of individual statutes—and whatever the social purpose it should not be permitted to override principle.[196] As a general principle and as a matter of 'fundamental criminal policy' the requirement of *mens rea* could be recognized

190 Williams, *Criminal Law,* n.175. In German criminal law theory the idea of the general part had emerged somewhat earlier in the work of Feuerbach. See T Hörnle, 'PJA von Feuerbach and his *Textbook of the Common Penal Law*' in Dubber (ed.), *Foundational Texts*, n.8, Ch.6. While Williams used the terminology of the general part, his approach owed little to German criminal law theory.

191 Williams, *Criminal Law*, n.175, Preface, p.v. 192 Ibid.

193 Lacey, 'Contingency, Coherence and Conceptualism', n.2, p.30 suggests that the appeal to principle was rhetorical rather than philosophical in tone. Cf. J Hall, *General Principles of Criminal Law* (2nd edn) (Bloomington IN: Bobbs Merrill, 1960) which adopted a more explicit 'normative-descriptive' approach to the identification of principles.

194 Williams, *Criminal Law*, n.175, p.1.

195 Williams, *Criminal Law*, n.175, p.29 and *Criminal Law: The General Part* (2nd edn) (London: Stevens & Sons, 1961) pp.54–6.

196 Williams, *Criminal Law*, p.270.

as always being present. The general part would accordingly serve the function of sparing the legislator from the requirement of specifying the particular presence or absence of a *mens rea* in any given statutory provision by identifying those principles which would apply to all criminal offences. The book thus aimed at the identification and classification of the central elements of the criminal law. With its focus on responsibility, the book offered a novel systematization, but there were limitations. Chapters were organized by topic, and while this followed a certain logic, with chapters on incitement, attempt, and conspiracy following each other, in other places this is less clear. Mental abnormality was followed by drunkenness, as both relating to proof of *mens rea*, but other defences were treated separately, and followed by chapters on status and persons. These were general rules, but in a descriptive sense, and there was no attempt to theorize further about classes or different kinds of rules.[197]

One final distinction that I want to note here is the identification of strict and vicarious responsibility as a separate class of offences because this demonstrates how the identification of a principle of *mens rea* could give shape to new concerns. While, as I noted above, there had been earlier cases and statutes which had imposed what might be regarded as strict or absolute liability, this had not been identified as a distinct legal category (and arguably could not be until responsibility was defined in more general terms).[198] From the 1930s onwards, legal commentators began to express concern about liability in statutory offences, although there was no settled terminology, and criticism often focused only on judicial interpretation in individual cases.[199] By the 1950s, though, this criticism had taken on a clearer focus, as collecting a range of diverse cases together allowed them to be seen in terms of more general analytical category.[200] This led some to argue that there should be a separate category of 'quasi-criminal law' so as to preserve the moral legitimacy of the criminal law.[201] Williams did not object to the inclusion of regulatory crimes in the criminal law, and was dismissive of writings which labelled such offences as not properly criminal or quasi-crimes;

[197] Cf. Hall, *General Principles*, n.193, who distinguished between principles and doctrines. He also includes a chapter on causation, which Williams did not.

[198] There is no mention in standard nineteenth century treatises such as JF Stephen, *Digest*, n.115 or WO Russell, *Treatise on Crimes and Misdemeanours* (3rd edn CS Greaves (ed.)) (London: Saunders & Benning, 1843). See also Chapter 6 at pp.185–7.

[199] RM Jackson, 'Absolute Prohibition in Statutory Offences' (1936-8) 6 *Camb LJ* 83–92; W Stallybrass, 'The Eclipse of Mens Rea' (1936) 52 *LQR* 60–67; CS Kenny, *Outlines of Criminal Law* (15th edn, GG Phillips ed.) (Cambridge: Cambridge University Press, 1936) pp.44–54. This tapped into a broader discussion in English language countries, see notably Sayre, 'Public Welfare Offenses' n.162. See Smith, *Lawyers, Legislators and Theorists*, n.4, pp.314–20 for discussion.

[200] *Criminal Law*, n.175, Chs.7 & 8. See also J Ll J Edwards, *Mens Rea in Statutory Offences* (London: Macmillan, 1955) p.247. See also D Ohana, 'Administrative Penalties in the *Rechtstaat*: On the Emergence of the *Ordnungswidrigkeit* Sanctioning System in Post-War Germany' (2014) 64 *UTLJ* 243–90.

[201] See P Devlin, *The Enforcement of Morals* (Oxford: Oxford UP, 1965) Ch.2. This is criticized in B Wootton, *Crime and the Criminal Law* (London: Stevens & Sons, 1963) Ch.2.

they clearly fell within his broad procedural definition of crime.[202] The problem as he saw it was where judicial interpretation of statutes led to the imposition of criminal liability on innocent persons or those who had not had the opportunity to act otherwise.[203] Such laws were likely to be ineffective, as those who were convicted had not knowingly permitted the breach of the norm in the first place. His argument, consequently, was that the criminal law would be more effective if it were to discriminate between culpable offenders—unscrupulous persons who were the real culprits—and innocent transgressors.[204] The categorization was thus in service of the broader aim of effective harm reduction.

C. Scope and limits of the criminal law

> The decision of the English law (is) that criminals be treated like game, only hunted under fixed rules and regulations, and not as vermin to be ruthlessly extirpated.[205]

For Williams, the general aim of the criminal law was the prevention of socially harmful conduct. However, this idea was in practice given substance by criminal policy. It is certainly clear that the idea of harm was not intended to be used in a limiting sense. Notwithstanding this, the *General Part* develops a subtle account of how institutional principles might limit the scope and application of the law. Some of these constraints, as I noted above, were to be derived from the more rigorous and consistent application of a principle of *mens rea*, made possible by the identification of the general rules. A more unusual contribution was his discussion of the principle of legality.

A curious feature of the *General Part* is that, in the middle of the book, following the long and detailed discussions of *actus reus* and *mens rea* and coming before the equally lengthy sections on inchoate offences and defences, there was a short chapter on the principle of legality.[206] The choice of subject matter was unusual as legality was not commonly discussed in the common law tradition and certainly

[202] *Criminal Law*, n.175, p.253 fn.54: 'this is objectionable because except in the absence of the requirement of mens rea there is no legal distinction between them and traditional crimes'. For the same reason he was highly critical of the distinction between *mala in se* and *mala prohibita*: see p.152 fn.2 & 'Definition of Crime', n.183, pp.118–9. See also JWC Turner, 'The Mental Element in Crimes at Common Law' in Radzinowicz & Turner, *The Modern Approach to Criminal Law* (Cambridge: Cambridge UP, 1948) pp.220–3.

[203] See *Criminal Law*, n.175, Ch.6 esp. pp.238–40.

[204] *Criminal Law*, n.175, p.269. He further contended that this was an abuse of the 'moral sentiments of the community', as branding those without moral fault as criminals would weaken respect for the law and the social condemnation of those who broke it. See also Hall, *General Principles*, n.193, Ch.10.

[205] Mannheim, *Social Aspects*, n.164, p.54, citing W Nott-Bower, *Fifty-two Years a Policeman* (1926).

[206] *Criminal Law*, n.175, Ch.12. The chapter begins (at p.434): 'After the general discussion of the *actus reus* and *mens rea* required in crime, it is convenient to consider certain fundamental requirements of form and promulgation…' Cf. Hall, *General Principles*, n.193, Ch.II viewing it as a fundamental principle.

not in books aimed primarily at practitioners.[207] This is also the only point in the book at which Williams explicitly framed the discussion in terms of continental sources, rather than domestic legal authority—the origin of the principle being traced to the French Revolution. This departure was necessary because, as he stated:

> It would be pleasant to be able to assert that the root principle underlying the administration of the criminal law is that of legality. Unfortunately…there is no unanimity about anything in criminal law: scarcely a single important principle but has been denied by some judicial decision or by some legislation. The principle of legality is a notable sufferer from this lack of agreement.[208]

The discussion of legality was in part an argument for the modernization of the form of the criminal law through codification, an initiative that Williams championed throughout his career.[209] He argued that a commitment to legality could improve the accessibility of the law: 'it is in the sphere of summary offences that the lack of adequate promulgation presses most hardly upon the ordinary citizen, for these do not reflect any obvious popular morality'.[210] This would mean ensuring that criminal offences, which on his view included all statutory and summary offences properly created by a democratic legislature as well as common law offences, were clearly defined and comprehensible. The principle of legality also required limitation of judicial discretion. He was particularly critical here of the decision in the 1933 case of *Manley*.[211] In this case, the court had convicted Manley of the novel crime of 'public mischief' for making false allegations to the police about the commission of a robbery, on the grounds that police time was wasted and innocent persons were brought under suspicion by the police investigation. In doing so, the court had claimed a power to be *custos morum*, or guardians of the morals, of the people.[212] This was criticized in part because the offence created was overly vague, but also because subsequent decisions had led to further confusion about the potential scope of this offence and the binding nature of the decision. His conclusion, that decisions relating to new questions of criminal policy should be left to Parliament, was thus consistent with the more general argument that legislation was the proper source of law.

The central feature of Williams' account is thus the commitment to legal values, and the constraints that they bring, as these had evolved with the institution—the

[207] See also the discussion in Mannheim, *Criminal Justice*, n.179, pp.203–18 linking legality to the developing administrative structure of the state. See, generally, MD Dubber, 'The Legality Principle in American and German Criminal Law: An Essay in Comparative Legal History' in G Martyn et al. (eds), *From the Judge's Arbitrium to the Legality Principle: Legislation as a Source of Law in Criminal Trials* (Berlin: Duncker & Humboldt, 2013).

[208] *Criminal Law*, n.175, p.434.

[209] Ibid., pp.441–5. See also infra Ch.5.

[210] Ibid., p.445, using the term summary offences in preference to 'public welfare' or 'petty offences' because it was the term used in the Magistrates' Courts Act 1952.

[211] [1933] 1 KB 529. For further contemporary discussion see W Stallybrass, 'Public Mischief' (1933) 49 *LQR* 183; RM Jackson, 'Common Law Misdemeanors' (1936–8) 6 *Camb LJ* 193.

[212] *Criminal Law*, n.175, pp.455–7. The power was originally claimed in *R v Sedley* 1663 1 Sid. 168; (1664) 82 ER 1036.

rules and regulations that framed the 'hunting' of the criminal in a civilized society.[213] Indeed, where he differs from Stephen is in the identification of the principle of *mens rea* as the source of legal values and the commitment to legality that followed from this. This was not motivated by an appeal to a political value of liberty, but by the aim of making the law more effective: if the law was adopted as the mode of regulation then it had to conform to certain principles which were specific to the institution of law. This was to be done by first specifying the legal meaning of *mens rea* as 'the mental element necessary for the particular crime' rather than starting from a theory of punishment.[214] He saw no point in punishment for its own sake: it should be linked to the impact that it might have on the intention of the actor, for anything else would be crude retaliation.[215] However, he was insistent that it followed from this that proof of *mens rea* was a necessary requirement for all offences in order that the aim of prevention could be achieved.[216] His commitment to individualism thus has to be read within an account of the social aims of the criminal law.[217] This was nowhere explicitly articulated in his work, but it is clear from what we have already seen that this law was primarily understood as a means of securing collective goods.

Such a view was not inconsistent with those of his contemporaries. In the immediate post-war period in which Williams was writing there was a widespread acceptance of the need to reconstruct and modernize social and political institutions, including the law. The fight against fascism had brought a new awareness of the importance of protecting individual liberty against the state, but this was accompanied by a commitment to addressing inequality and collective welfare.[218] If the criminal law was not seen as a means of bringing about social justice, it was at least recognized that many of the values protected by the criminal law were potentially unjust and that a commitment to reconstructing social and political institutions would require attention to the operation of legal institutions.[219] Reformers such as Mannheim argued that 'the function of the criminal law is no longer primarily to protect individual rights and interest, but at least

[213] See also *Criminal Law,* n.175, Ch.23 on the burden of proof. PJ Fitzgerald, *Criminal Law and Punishment* (Oxford: Clarendon, 1962) p.164: 'Important as it is to prevent crime, this is by no means the only aim of a civilized society, and in England the pursuit of this aim is subject to various limitations. In the first place... to prevent its use as an instrument of oppression'.

[214] *Criminal Law,* n.175, pp.28–30, because, as he pointed out, the theoretical justifications of punishment were not consistent with the legal understandings of *mens rea.*

[215] Though he was aware of the limits of deterrence, see e.g. Williams, *Criminal Law,* n.175, pp.98–100.

[216] Williams, *Criminal Law,* n.175, pp.30–2, referring approvingly to the definition of subjective recklessness in the US Model Penal Code s.2.02.

[217] See P Ramsay, 'The Responsible Subject as Citizen: Criminal Law, Democracy and the Welfare State' (2006) 69 *Mod LR* 29–58 linking responsibility in the criminal law to conceptions of citizenship in the welfare state.

[218] Notably in the Beveridge Report (1942). See e.g. HJ Laski, *Liberty and the Modern State* (London: Allen & Unwin, 1948); *Reflections on the Revolution of Our Time* (New York: Viking, 1943).

[219] Mannheim, *Criminal Justice,* n.179, Introduction and Ch.10 ('Re-Planning Criminal Justice'). Williams was a member of the Haldane Society of Socialist Lawyers and edited a volume called *The Reform of the Law* (London: Victor Gollancz, 1951).

as much to protect the rights and interests of the community at large,' and that this would entail large-scale preventive action which was largely administrative in character.[220] This should not interfere unnecessarily with the private lives of individuals, but at the same time the 'complexity of modern civilization' meant that there was recognition that some social and economic issues were too complex to be dealt with by the criminal law and the courts alone.[221] Responsibility on this view was social responsibility, something that took legal form, and was therefore subject to constraints such as the need to prove *mens rea*, but was shaped by broader political initiatives.[222] The role of the legislator was thus to elucidate 'standards of behavior which have to be observed, under existing social conditions, if social life is to be maintained'.[223] The force of law should rest on the citizen's sense of obligation; but the citizen should accept that the 'choice of means must be left to the State'.[224] The state, on this view, was both the guarantor and the provider of freedom: it should regulate social life in order to establish the conditions for individual freedom, but it should not do so in a way which breached its own commitment to individual liberty.

If Williams' account of the limits of the criminal law was framed from within the institution of law, it is important finally to note the development in the 1950s and 1960s of the debate over law and morals between Lord Devlin and HLA Hart.[225] This was to transform understandings of the criminalization question, hardening distinctions between law and morality and public and private, and reframing questions of criminalization, particularly as they related to sexual conduct, in terms of a relationship between law and morals. The immediate catalyst for the debate was the publication of the Wolfenden Report in 1957, which recommended decriminalization of homosexual conduct in private.[226] This was followed by the unsuccessful prosecution of the publishers of DH Lawrence's *Lady Chatterley's Lover* for obscenity in 1960, and then the case of *Shaw v DPP* in 1961 in which the House of Lords upheld a conviction for a conspiracy to corrupt

[220] Mannheim, *Criminal Justice*, n.179, pp.195–6. [221] Ibid., p.197.

[222] Hart, 'Aims of the Criminal Law', n.189, p.413: 'The inculcation of a sense of social responsibility throughout the society will be the dominant aim [of the legislator]' (and on p.417 he refers to it as training for responsible citizenship).

[223] Hart, 'Aims of the Criminal Law', n.189, p.418. He concluded by arguing that a statement of the purposes of the criminal law in these terms should be included in the draft MPC: 'To foster the development of personal capacity for responsible decision to the end that every individual may realize his potentialities as a participating and contributing member of his community' (at p.440).

[224] Devlin, *Enforcement of Morals*, n.201, p.30. Although for Devlin this obligation would be different for a law with moral content rather than a law aimed to secure a socially good end. The more important point here is the conception of citizenship which has much in common with the views of both Williams and Hart.

[225] HLA Hart, *Law, Liberty and Morality* (Oxford: Oxford UP, 1963); Devlin, *Enforcement of Morals*, n.201. Both books were based on talks or papers that had been published in the 1950s.

[226] *Report of the Committee on Homosexual Offences and Prostitution* (Cmnd.267) (London: HMSO, 1957). See infra Ch.9. The history of the debate is set out in Hart, *Law, Liberty and Morality*, n.225, Preface pp.vi–viii.

public morals on the grounds that the court was guardian of public morals.[227] The debate is not always easy to follow: they often seem to be speaking past each other, making different kinds of claims, and they seem to be in agreement on values such as respect for the importance of tolerance and privacy.[228] What was important, though, was what their arguments had in common. Although they differed in their conclusions, both saw law and morals as separate realms, and recognized that this was a consequence of the secularization of the state. The problem, in a secular age, was the nature of this relationship. Both saw the problem in broadly consequentialist terms as one of the harm caused by either permitting or prohibiting certain conduct. Both agreed that the criminal law should be used sparingly, but while Devlin's argument had echoes of Stephen's belief in the importance of the moral legitimacy of the criminal law, Hart's argument was more innovative. While he invoked the authority of Mill's harm principle, he actually nowhere sought to articulate or develop this in any systematic way—and in his examples, as Devlin points out, he adheres to an idea of social rather than individual harm.[229] The more important distinctions for Hart were, first, that between positive and critical morality, and second, between public and private. The first allowed him to argue that morality was a vantage point from which the criminal law could be criticized; the second was important for articulating a new standard for the limits to the criminal law. It is in these respects that Hart's comments were to provide a platform for the future development of the criminalization question.

Glanville Williams' *The General Part* was hugely influential, setting new standards for the systematic analysis of the criminal law, while also developing an, often implicit, account of how legal principles might act as an institutional constraint on the scope and application of the law in the social democratic state. It was thus radical and modernizing, even if it was presented in a form and idiom that was familiar—and thus, to some extent, reassuring—to the criminal lawyer. At its core lay a combination of ideas of social responsibility and individual liberty. These in themselves did not imply limits to the criminal law but the reformulation of the criminalization question by HLA Hart was to give rise to radical challenges to the role and functions of the criminal law.

V. A Neo-Classical Criminal Law

> The number of offences in English criminal law continues to grow year by year. Politicians, pressure groups, journalists and others often express

[227] *R v Penguin Books* [1961] Crim LR 176; *Shaw v DPP* [1962] AC 220. Williams criticized the decision in *Shaw* on the more limited grounds that it was a breach of the principle of legality: 'Conspiring to Corrupt' (1961) *The Listener* (Aug 24th) 275.

[228] While Hart was largely concerned with critical morality, Devlin was making a claim about the function of the relation between law and moral beliefs.

[229] Lacey suggests that it should be read as a 'principled liberal social policy, articulating a vision of a social democratic state.': *A Life of HLA Hart. The Nightmare and the Noble Dream* (Oxford: Oxford UP, 2004) p.259.

> themselves as if the creation of a new criminal offence is the natural, or the only appropriate, response to a particular event or series of events giving rise to social concern…There is little sense that the decision to introduce a new offence should only be made after certain conditions have been satisfied, little sense that making conduct criminal is a step of considerable social significance… [F]rom any principled viewpoint there are important issues—of how the criminal law ought to be shaped, of what its social significance should be, of when it should be used and when not—which are simply not being addressed in the majority of instances.[230]

These sentiments, eloquently expressed by Andrew Ashworth, capture an attitude that is characteristic amongst many contemporary criminal lawyers. In this literature there is a clear tendency to see the present in terms of novelty and excess—though in contrast to the modernizing attitudes that we have examined to date, where novelty was seen as a sign of progress or renewal, the typical attitude is that something has been lost, or that the development is to be regretted. This has led lawyers like Ashworth, one of the most distinguished and distinctive commentators on the contemporary criminal law, to try and articulate a new kind of approach based around the identification or restoration of a 'classical' idea of criminal law.[231]

A. Characteristics of the criminal law

It is widely recognized that recorded crime began to increase in the late 1970s, with particular increases in the areas of violent crime and in crimes against property; even with evidence of decreasing levels of crime since the mid-1990s, levels remain substantially higher than 50 years ago.[232] This increase, and the increased prominence of crime as a political issue, has shaped developments in recent years. There has been a change in the social role of criminal law and justice with the development of what has variously been described as 'law and order politics' or penal populism, as successive governments have competed to show themselves

[230] A Ashworth, 'Is the Criminal Law a Lost Cause?' (2000) 116 *LQR* 225.

[231] Although Ashworth has written extensively on criminal law, criminal procedure and sentencing, I am focusing my analysis here principally on three works. His inaugural lecture at Oxford (cited above); *Principles of Criminal Law* (Oxford: Clarendon, 1991) (Citations here are to the 7th edition (with J Horder)) (Oxford: Oxford UP, 2013); and (with L Zedner) *Preventive Justice* (Oxford: Oxford UP, 2014). The first is a neat summary, in slightly polemical form, of themes in his work; the other two have been influential and important. For more systematic discussion see the essays in L Zedner & J Roberts (eds), *Principles and Values in Criminal Law and Criminal Justice* (Oxford: Oxford UP, 2012) Pt.I.

[232] See summary in R Reiner, 'Citizenship, Crime, Criminalization. Marshalling a Social Democratic Perspective' (2010) 13 *New Crim LR* 241 at pp.252–6. See also M Maguire, 'Criminal Statistics and the Construction of Crime' in *Oxford Handbook of Criminology* (5th edn) (Oxford: Oxford UP, 2012) Ch.8; P Spierenburg, *A History of Murder* (Cambridge: Polity, 2008) p.210 pointing to rising rate of homicide and assault in the period since 1950.

ever more 'tough on crime'.[233] This has led in many Western countries to steady rises not only in the prison population, as prison has been presented as the only appropriate response to certain sorts of crime, but also in the number of people brought within the criminal justice system in a phenomenon described as 'net-widening'. We have also seen extensive use of the metaphor of 'war'—on drugs, on illegal immigration, on terrorism, and so on—which has led to the singling out of particular crimes or offenders, such as drugs, sex offenders, latterly terrorism, as requiring a special or exceptional kind of response. These changes have themselves been linked to more fundamental changes in the economic and social structure of society, with the decline of the welfare state and the global rise of neo-liberalism linked to the increased resort to criminal law as a way of managing marginalized communities.[234] This is summarized by Wacquant as the normalization of insecurity, based on the management of social inequality rather than its reduction, and reconceiving citizenship as based on contribution through work rather than an entitlement to support.[235]

In the substantive criminal law these developments have been linked to two related phenomena. First, there is so-called 'over-criminalization'.[236] This is the claim that there has been an increase in the overall number and rate of creation of new criminal offences, which results in unjust punishment as people are criminalized for conduct where there is no underlying wrong. Although there is dispute over numbers, and even ways of counting, the presumed growth in numbers of new offences is taken as evidence of an increased readiness on the part of governments to resort to the criminal law.[237] The growth of the criminal law is in part seen as a consequence of expansion into new areas, such the criminalization of forms of 'market abuse' or the recognition of new crimes against the environment. It is also seen as the outcome of more intensive criminalization of areas that are already covered by the criminal law, as new offences are created to recognize more specific forms of wrongdoing (such as extreme pornography, stalking or trafficking), or which simply sit alongside already existing crimes (such as assaulting

[233] For surveys see D Downes & R Morgan, 'Overtaking on the Left: The Politics of Law and Order in the "Big Society"' in *Oxford Handbook of Criminology op. cit.* n.232, Ch.9; R Reiner, *Law and Order. An Honest Citizen's Guide to Crime Control* (Cambridge: Polity, 2007).

[234] Though note N Lacey, *The Prisoners' Dilemma. Political Economy and Punishment in Modern Society* (Cambridge: Cambridge UP, 2008), which challenges the idea that these are the necessary consequences of neo-liberalism or late modernity.

[235] See L Wacquant, *Punishing the Poor* (London: Duke UP, 2009); See also his 'Marginality, Ethnicity and Penality: A Bourdieusian Perspective on Criminalization' in Duff et al., *Criminalization: The Political Morality of the Criminal Law* (Oxford: Oxford UP, 2014) Ch.10. He identifies a range of changes from reinventing penal and welfare bureaucracies, rendering the poor invisible or morally culpable; gutting welfare benefits and social insurance programmes to impose precarious wage labour as the new norm of citizenship; creating categories which can act as symbolic others. See also Garland, *Cultures of Control,* n.3, Ch.2.

[236] See notably D Husak, *Overcriminalization* (Oxford: Oxford UP, 2008) pp.33–45.

[237] For criticism of the empirical basis of the claim see J Chalmers & F Leverick, 'Tracking the Creation of Criminal Offences' 2013 *Crim LR* 543–60; J Chalmers & F Leverick, 'Quantifying Criminalization' in Duff et al. (eds), *Criminalization,* n.235, Ch.2. See also J Horder, 'Bureaucratic 'Criminal' Law. Too much of a Bad Thing?' in Duff et al., *Criminalization,* n.235, Ch.4.

emergency workers or forms of 'hate crime'). Resort to criminal law here is often a matter of 'labelling', or the recognition of specific, individualized wrongs. It manifests itself in different ways, from laws that have been passed in the name of individual or collective victims, as a kind of retrospective recognition and commitment to future victims, or as laws passed to protect putatively vulnerable groups.[238] Criminal law is a kind of politics of recognition, used as a way of demonstrating a commitment to the vulnerable or the insecure; and victimhood has a 'moral edge' which elevates the rights of the victim and the obligation to recognize these in law.[239] Over-criminalization has also been analysed in terms of the characteristics of newly created offences. Ashworth, looking at the year 1997, argues that the bulk of the new offences are regulatory, relating to specialized spheres of social or commercial activity. He also suggests that they are characterized by exceptional forms of liability—strict liability, omissions liability and reverse burdens of proof.[240] In another influential account of over-criminalization, Husak argues that the expansion of criminal law is not only a matter of quantity, but of the emergence of different forms of liability—overlapping offences, ancillary offences, and risk-prevention offences—that, by design or otherwise, criminalize a greater range of conduct.[241] At the core of both their arguments is the claim that these new forms of liability subvert or disturb settled principles of the criminal law in the name of expediency or political convenience.

The second way that these developments are seen as having an impact on the substantive criminal law is in the form of the 'preventive turn'.[242] This is a term which is used to describe what is seen as a decisive shift in the criminal justice system towards the use of a range of preventive measures, that is to say measures which are primarily directed at the prevention of future wrongdoing rather than punishment for past wrongdoing. This is tracked in terms of a number of related developments from diversion from the criminal process, through the use of fixed penalties and incentives to plead guilty, to the increasing use of control or supervision orders directed against individuals or groups of individuals identified as presenting a risk, and preventive aspects of public health and immigration law.[243] These developments go beyond issues of policing and enforcement to the substantive law where the preventive turn is seen in terms of the development of offences which have a 'heightened rationale' of prevention. Examples of these preventive offences are possession offences (of weapons or illegal drugs) where the conduct itself is not harmful, but is connected to other harms or socially damaging

[238] See MD Dubber, *Victims in the War Against Crime* (New York: NYU Press, 2002).

[239] H Boutellier, *The Safety Utopia* (Dordrecht: Kluwer, 2004) p.9.

[240] Ashworth, 'Lost Cause?' n.230, pp.228–9. See also Chalmers & Leverick, 'Quantifying Criminalization' n.237.

[241] See Husak, *Overcriminalization*, n.236, pp.33–45.

[242] See now Ashworth & Zedner, *Preventive Justice*, n.231, Chs.1 & 5; A Ashworth, L Zedner, & P Tomlin (eds), *Prevention and the Limits of the Criminal Law* (Oxford: Oxford UP, 2013); R Sullivan & I Dennis (eds), *Seeking Security. Pre-empting the Commission of Criminal Harms*, (Abingdon: Hart Publishing, 2012).

[243] Ashworth & Zedner, *Preventive Justice*, n.231, pp.2–5.

activities; substantive offences defined in inchoate mode (doing *x* with intent to cause *y*); so-called 'pre-inchoate' offences, which criminalize conduct which might be preparatory to the commission of future serious offences; and offences of risk-creation (conduct which creates risks either to a specified group of persons or to the public in general).[244] Thus we have seen the creation of new offences which criminalize preparing to commit certain crimes, or possessing information which might be used in the commission of a crime, the sexual grooming of children (consisting in communication with a child and travelling to meet them in any part of the world) and so on.[245] The kinds of interests which are to be protected by such measures are often those of the vulnerable (children, victims of domestic or sexual abuse, trafficked persons, and so on) against threats posed by dangerous persons or groups such as terrorists, paedophiles, sexual predators, or people traffickers. It is thus the relationship between the scale of the threat and the vulnerability of a particular class of victims that justifies the adoption of special measures. The analysis of preventive justice has also focused on the form of offences and their differences from traditional inchoate liability. The existence of inchoate offences—liability for attempted or incomplete crimes—has been justified on the basis of the need to prevent the immediate social danger posed by such conduct. The form of the new 'preventive' offences, however, extends liability beyond this to conduct which is not necessarily wrongful or harmful in itself, but which poses a (sometimes ill-defined) future threat to certain legally protected interests by criminalizing preparatory conduct or status.[246] Overall these are measures which seek to prevent possible, rather than probable, criminal conduct, conduct which unnerves or threatens the sense of security of others. The central issue here is seen as that of the control or management of uncertainty—the right to security from threat—and thus of the relationship between criminal law and security.[247]

These changes in the characteristics of the criminal law have been accompanied by changes in the way that criminal lawyers seek to define the criminal law, with Ashworth's approach again instructive. After looking at Glanville Williams' definition, he concludes that a descriptive definition is both impossible and undesirable as many offences which would meet its criteria for inclusion do not in his view properly fit within the criminal law as they are insufficiently general in application, have no requirement of culpability, or punish non-serious forms of wrongdoing. The way forward, he argues, is through a prescriptive definition,

[244] On possession offences see MD Dubber, 'Policing Possession. The War on Crime and the End of Criminal Law' (2001) 91 *Jnl of Crim Law & Criminol.* 829–996; A Ashworth, 'The Unfairness of Risk-Based Possession Offences' (2011) 5 *Crim Law & Phil.* 237–57. On preparatory offences see P Ramsay, 'Preparation Offences, security interests, political freedom' in RA Duff et al., *The Structures of the Criminal Law* (Oxford: Oxford UP, 2011). See, generally, Ashworth & Zedner, *Preventive Justice*, n.231, pp.96–102.

[245] See e.g., Terrorism Act 2000, s.12 (support for a prescribed organization), s.57 (possession of article for terrorist purposes), s.58 (possession of information); Terrorism Act, 2006 s.1 (encouragement of terrorism), s.5 (preparation of terrorist acts). Sexual Offences Act 2003, s.15 (meeting a child following sexual grooming).

[246] Ashworth & Zedner, *Preventive Justice*, n.231, pp.96–7.

[247] P Ramsay, *The Insecurity State* (Oxford: Oxford UP, 2012) Ch.10.

which would be 'more principled, conceptually more coherent, and constitutionally and politically more appropriate'.[248] He thus proposes a functional definition: '[p]erhaps the principal function of the criminal law is to censure persons for wrongdoing.'[249] The starting point is thus no longer the idea that a definition of criminal law should reflect or respond to the changing contours of 'crime' or the criminal law, but that it is first necessary to identify the features of the criminal law in order to define the scope of its application.[250]

B. Classification

In order to analyse the understanding of the criminal law that underpins this definition, it is necessary to look more closely at how Ashworth develops his argument. Key to his definition is the idea of censure, defined in terms of punishment: conviction plus the sentence of the court.[251] This is important in the first instance because the possibility of punishment should trigger the availability of procedural protections under Article 6 of the European Convention of Human Rights.[252] However, the idea of censure has a wider significance in the development of Ashworth's prescriptive definition of the criminal law, linking the justification of the criminal law to the justification of punishment. Following von Hirsch, censure is understood as an appropriate response to wrongdoing, a form of condemnation that is 'desert-oriented by nature'.[253] It is, moreover, argued that it is embedded in the relational structure of moral agency: it addresses the victim, or the person who has been wronged; the wrongdoers with an expectation of response or acknowledgement of their conduct; and the wider community providing reasons for desistance from such conduct.[254] This moral framework thus shapes the scope of the criminal law:

[248] Ashworth, 'Lost Cause?' n.230, p.225. This model has been described by Horder ('Bureaucratic Criminal Law') as the 'counter-reformation' model of the criminal law, though this is misleading as it implies an attempt to return to, or restore, something that was arguably never there in the first place.

[249] Ashworth, 'Lost Cause?' n.230, p.232.

[250] Note that his book is entitled *Principles of Criminal Law*, rather than of '*the*' criminal law, suggesting an appeal to a more abstract system rather than any specific system of rules. See also G Lamond, 'What is a Crime?' (2007) *27 Ox Jnl of Leg Stud* 609, who answers the question 'what is a crime?' by addressing the question 'what is criminal liability?', thus eliding the possible differences between the two.

[251] Ashworth, 'Lost Cause?' n.230, p.232.

[252] Together with the prosecution being brought by a public authority and having culpability requirements ('Lost Cause?' n.230, p.230 & pp.238–40). It is worth noting, though, that adoption of this test (penal sanctions as a measure of criminal proceedings) does not entail that we adopt the further conclusion (discussed below) that criminal law must be justified in terms of punishment.

[253] A von Hirsch, *Censure and Sanctions* (Oxford: Oxford UP, 1993) p.24. See also A von Hirsch & A Ashworth, *Proportionate Sentencing: Exploring the Principles* (Oxford: Oxford UP, 2005) Ch.2; AP Simester & A von Hirsch, *Crimes, Harms and Wrongs. On the Principles of Criminalisation* (Oxford: Hart Publishing, 2011) pp.10–14.

[254] Hence either to fail the victim by failing to censure, or to punish on instrumentalist grounds, would be 'to deny the status of the person as an agent capable of moral understanding' (*Censure and Sanctions*, p.11).

A primary justification for criminal law and sentencing is that offenders deserve punishment for their offences, and that it is therefore just to provide that serious wrongs culpably inflicted should lead to censure and sanctions by the State.[255]

The criminal law only has title to censure (punish) if there is reason to believe that the conduct was wrongful, and only to the degree of the wrongfulness (proportionality and seriousness). Wrongfulness requires not just harm (or the risk of harm) but also culpability.[256] Definitions of crimes must thus meet the minimum standards of being based on (serious) wrongful conduct that has been culpably inflicted. We can thus see what is prescriptive about this definition. The function of criminal law (censure) is seen in terms of justifying punishment; and punishment, broadly understood in terms of retribution, is appropriate only for serious culpable wrongdoing. It seeks to limit the potential sphere of the criminal law to forms of serious culpable wrongdoing, the punishment of which can be justified in retributive terms.[257] This thus responds to the disorder and fragmentation of the actual criminal law by positing a kind of ideal order in the criminal law.

This ideal order, based on the moral justification of punishment, has important consequences for the classification of the law. First, it places the idea of wrong or wrongdoing, understood in moral terms, at the core of the criminal law: if punishment is only justified for culpable wrongdoing it is then necessary to have an account of what constitutes a wrong. This is a move which locates criminal law theory within the field of moral and political philosophy.[258] There has consequently been a revival of interest in what, adopting the terminology of the Hart-Devlin debate, has been termed 'legal moralism'.[259] But where Devlin's moralism appealed to the parochial need to protect the existing moral institutions of society, whatever their specific content, and was the target of liberal critics, this version of legal moralism appeals to universal ethical standards, such that the account of moral wrongs is independent of law and, in theory at least, capable of acting as a constraint on it.[260] Criminal law is typically now discussed as being

[255] Ashworth & Horder, *Principles*, n.231, p.16.

[256] Ashworth, 'Lost Cause?' n.230, p.240; A von Hirsch & N Jareborg, 'Gauging Criminal Harm: A Living Standard Analysis' (1991) 11 *Ox Jnl of Leg Stud* 1. For further discussion of the centrality of culpability see infra Ch.6, Section III.4 ('The punishable subject').

[257] I should be clear that Ashworth is not arguing that the core of moral wrongdoing rests in a core of common law offences; he argues that this can provide a test for assessing seriousness according to the standards of a given community ('Lost Cause?' n.230, pp.243–5).

[258] This was famously signalled in the first line of GP Fletcher, *Rethinking Criminal Law* (Boston: Little, Brown & Co, 1978) p.xix: 'Criminal law is a species of moral and political philosophy'.

[259] It is notable that all five of the papers (plus comments) in a recent special issue on criminalization published in the journal *Criminal Law and Philosophy* (2014, vol.8 Issue 1) address the question of wrongs.

[260] See the discussion of varieties of legal moralism in RA Duff, 'Towards a Modest Legal Moralism' (2014) 8 *Crim Law & Phil* 217 at pp.218–24.

concerned with 'public wrongs', a characterization which has led to a revival of interest in the distinction between *mala in se* and *mala prohibita*.[261] This distinction was used in a restricted way by early modern lawyers as an argument for limiting the scope of the royal prerogative, before being restated in broader terms by Blackstone to designate a distinction between crimes punishable in a state of nature and crimes which were merely statutory prohibitions.[262] Although its role in Blackstone's account of the criminal law and punishment was largely rhetorical, it is now routinely cited in discussions of the characteristics of a legal wrong.[263] While precise usages vary, it is used as means of broadly distinguishing between 'real' and regulatory, or administrative, offences. *Mala in se* are wrongs which are 'prior to or independent of law'; these are serious wrongs, culpably inflicted, which are regarded as the 'core' of the criminal law.[264] *Mala prohibita* are seen as regulatory offences forming 'the major part of the criminal canon' but which, since they are not morally wrongful independently of the laws which create them, carry an additional burden of justification.[265]

This emphasis on retribution and culpability also plays out in terms of the conception of the general part. This is no longer conceived, as Williams saw it, in descriptive terms, as a collection of rules of general application, a demand for consistency across existing rules. It is instead seen as a looser collection of rules, doctrines and principles which do not necessarily apply to all offences, but which are of moral or normative significance.[266] These are capable of exercising prescriptive control over the content of the criminal law, establishing unity rather than uniformity.[267] As writers such as Fletcher and Moore have argued, the identification of the general part is determined by the function of the criminal law in attaining retributive justice—which is to say that offenders should be culpable.[268] A common starting point for accounts of the general part of the criminal law

[261] See e.g. Ashworth & Horder, *Principles*, n.231, pp.1–5; Lamond, 'What is a Crime?' n.250; Duff, 'Modest Legal Moralism' n.260. This is also discussed supra Ch.1 at pp.14–19.

[262] Anon, 'The Distinction between *Mala Prohibita* and *Mala in Se* in Criminal Law' (1930) 30 *Columbia LR* 74.

[263] Rhetorical because notwithstanding his use of natural law terminology, Blackstone's account of criminal law and punishment was in fact based on the authority of positive law. See supra at p.pp.71–4.

[264] Husak, *Overcriminalization*, n.236, p.105.

[265] Simester & von Hirsch, *Crimes, Harms and Wrongs*, n.253, p.24.

[266] See discussion in AP Simester & S Shute, 'On the General Part in Criminal Law' in Simester & Shute, *Criminal Law Theory: Doctrines of the General Part* (Oxford: Oxford UP, 2002). See also J Gardner, 'On the General Part of the Criminal Law' in A Duff, *Philosophy and the Criminal Law* (Cambridge: Cambridge UP, 1998).

[267] P Cane, 'The General/Special Distinction in Criminal Law, Tort Law and Legal Theory' (2007) 26 *Law & Phil* 465–500 at 476–81 argues that the general/special distinction commonly rests on one of three contrasts: generality and specificity; responsibility and wrongdoing; and principle and policy. The move in criminal law is away from the first, represented by Williams' approach, to the second and third.

[268] See M Moore, *Placing Blame* (Oxford: Oxford UP, 1997) p.30: 'Retributive justice demands that those [and only those] who deserve punishment get it'. See also Fletcher, *Rethinking*, n.285, Pt.II.

is thus that rules relating to *mens rea* or culpability should be central because (retributive) punishment cannot be justified in the absence of culpable wrongdoing. These rules of culpability should determine the form of liability, and even in certain cases, the content of crimes in the special part.[269] Thus, the argument that *mens rea* is a principle of culpability has been used to argue against the inclusion of offences based on negligence within the scope of the criminal law, and even more broadly to an argument for the recognition of 'civil offences' or 'administrative criminal law' as a separate area of law because offences of this type do not meet the criteria of culpability or seriousness for inclusion within the proper scope of the criminal law.[270] The same kind of move is arguably true of the idea of 'preventive' justice, where the sphere of preventive justice is identified as a distinct area—on the basis of its difference from 'normal' criminal law—and the problem is then characterized in terms of its failure to match the culpability requirements for 'normal' crimes.[271]

The final consequence of the definition is that it allows Ashworth to argue for the central role of legal principle. Culpability, and hence justified punishment, must be founded on certain core principles, which he argues should be respected by a liberal criminal law.[272] These principles are in part immanent to existing legal rules and practices, and are in part based on political or moral principles which may or may not be present in existing rules and practices but which are 'commended... on normative grounds'.[273] Thus, the moral principle that like cases should be treated alike is rearticulated as a principle of equal treatment: 'that those who commit wrongs of equivalent seriousness in relevantly similar circumstances should be subjected to censure of a similar magnitude.'[274] Likewise the principle of autonomy, which has its origins in liberal values of equal concern and respect, is defended on the grounds that it can protect the individual against the state and other collective interests, while also linking to more specific principles such as respect for human rights and that criminal law be used only as a last resort. However, these principles are also seen as a reflection of the modality of law, drawing in part on principles of common law, but also rearticulated through instruments such as the European Convention on Human Rights which give them a new, quasi-constitutional, form of expression and potentially greater weight.[275]

[269] See e.g. Husak's claim that doctrines of criminalization belong in the general part (the 'wrongfulness constraint'): *Overcriminalization*, n.236, pp.58–77.

[270] See e.g. AP Simester (ed.), *Appraising Strict Liability* (Oxford: Oxford UP, 2005) Preface and essays by Simester, Duff, and Spencer & Pedain.

[271] See Ashworth & Zedner, *Preventive Justice*, n.231, pp.112–3 on principled limits to preventive offences.

[272] See Ashworth & Horder, *Principles*, n.231, Ch.2.

[273] Ashworth & Horder, *Principles*, n.231, Preface. For two very different discussions of Ashworth on principles, see N Lacey, 'Principles, Policies and Politics of Criminal Law' and J Gardner, 'Ashworth on Principles' both in Zedner & Roberts, *Principles and Values*, n.231. See also A Halpin, *Definition in the Criminal Law* (Oxford: Hart Publishing, 2004) Ch.1.

[274] Ashworth, 'Lost Cause?' n.230, p.245. See also *Principles*, n.231, Ch.3 for more systematic discussion.

[275] See also *K* [2002] 1 AC 462 where the presumption in favour of *mens rea* was described by Lords Bingham and Steyn as a 'constitutional principle'.

Thus principles such as fair labelling, proportionality, non-retroactivity, maximum certainty and so on are seen both as having developed from within the legal institution itself, and as expressing core liberal moral and political values. These principles are not generally prescriptive, and Ashworth recognizes that there will be countervailing principles or policy considerations which courts and legislators will also have to take into account. They are, however, an important expression of central legal values. They create a burden of justification: if there is to be departure from the principle, the legislator carries the burden of justifying this departure. Principles on this account thus go beyond the immediate function of the internal coordination of rules of criminal law to act as a potential bulwark against legislative opportunism by constraining the scope of legislative action.[276] This definition of the criminal law thus places the question of criminalization at the centre of criminal law theory.

C. The scope and limits of the criminal law

This is perhaps where I would like to say least, for it takes us into the contemporary debates about criminalization that are the focus of this book more broadly. However, it is important to note the growth of interest in questions of criminalization and specifically the way that this can be seen as a response to the changes in the criminal law that were outlined above. What is broadly characteristic of contemporary discussions of criminalization is that questions of scope and limits are seen together. The question of the proper scope of the criminal law is understood in terms of limits; and the limits are defined by reference to the central or core idea of the criminal law.

Once again this is explicit in Ashworth's work, where the recognition of the centrality of questions of criminalization was marked by the inclusion of a chapter on the topic of criminalization from the earliest editions of his textbook—and there are features of his analysis that can be taken as characteristic of contemporary discussions.[277] He frames his discussion of criminalization in terms of a 'right not to be punished', which should be understood as placing the burden on the state to justify the decision to criminalize.[278] This right not be punished is based directly on the principle of individual autonomy—that individuals should be protected from official censure unless they are culpable—in the sense both that the wrong has been properly defined in the criminal law and that the individual has been found culpable under a proper criminal process.[279] This thus links the question of criminalization to a liberal democratic state or polity, in which laws are the outcome of a democratic process of law-making and the rights

[276] See Lacey, 'Principles, Policies and Politics', n.273, pp.32–3.

[277] Ashworth & Horder, *Principles*, n.231, Ch.2. From the 2nd edition (1995), though even in the first edition (1991) Chapter 2 was on the scope of the criminal law. Other textbooks now routinely include the topic.

[278] Ashworth & Horder, *Principles*, n.231, p.22; Husak, *Overcriminalization,* n.236, pp.92–103.

[279] Ashworth & Horder, *Principles*, n.231, p.24.

of individuals are protected under the rule of law. This is both permissive, in the sense that it recognizes that the particular content of the criminal law will be the outcome of political decisions about how to protect or distribute certain goods, but it is also subject to constraints in that the form of law in general (and of the criminal law in particular) will impose limits on what can be criminalized.[280] Culpability defines the core sense of 'crime', but is also seen as a limit, both in the case of an individual's right not to be punished if they are not culpable, but also, more generally, in the sense that crimes which are defined in such a way as to depart significantly from this 'core' sense of culpability are seen as illegitimate or 'perversions' of the criminal law.[281] The principle of individual autonomy also demands respect for a sphere within which individuals can develop their own life choices—engaging more traditional liberal ideas such as harm, sovereignty or dignity.[282] While Ashworth is reluctant to advance any single principle that would define the scope of the criminal law, he identifies three further limiting ideas.[283] These are respect for human rights, that criminal law should be a last resort, and that criminalization should not be used where the effect would be counter-productive. It is not clear that these would always be an argument against criminalization for Ashworth because he recognizes that there may in each case be countervailing considerations. Respect for human rights, for example, might lead to a demand that certain kinds of 'hate' speech might be criminalized to protect the rights of victims. The point is rather that these kind of requirements would clarify the nature of the burden of justification that lies on the state. Overall, following Jareborg, he characterizes this approach as 'defensive criminal law': criminal law should protect the individual against the potential abuse of state power, and if the criminal law cannot do good, then it should at least seek to minimize the harm that it done in its name.[284]

I want to look at one further characteristic feature of this approach to criminalization, the idea of fair labelling, which brings together the defensive concerns of those such as Ashworth with the new interest in the voice of the victim. The original idea was mooted by Ashworth, as representative labelling, in a paper published in 1981, and was taken up enthusiastically by Glanville Williams, who also suggested that the term 'fair labelling' might be more appropriate.[285] The original

[280] Ashworth & Horder, *Principles*, n.231, pp.23–7. See also RA Duff et al., 'Introduction' in Duff et al. (eds), *Criminalization. The Political Morality of the Criminal Law* (Oxford: Oxford UP, 2014) discussing the move to seeing criminalization as a question of political theory.

[281] See e.g. Ashworth & Zedner, *Preventive Justice, op. cit.* n.231, p.113–4; RA Duff, 'Perversions and Subversions of Criminal Law' in Duff et al., *Boundaries of the Criminal Law* (Oxford: Oxford UP, 2010). This is addressed further in Chapter 6.

[282] See J Feinberg, *Harm to Self* (Oxford: Oxford UP, 1986) Chs.17–19; A Ripstein, 'Beyond the Harm Principle' (2006) 34 *Philosophy and Public Affairs* 215–45; M Dan-Cohen, *Harmful Thoughts. Essays on Law, Self and Morality* (Princeton: Princeton UP, 2002) Ch.5.

[283] Ashworth & Horder, *Principles*, n.231, Ch.2.4.

[284] N Jareborg, 'What Kind of Criminal Law do we Want?' in A Snare, *Beware of Punishment. On the Utility and Futility of Criminal Law* (Oslo: Pax Forlag, 1995).

[285] A Ashworth, 'The Elasticity of Mens Rea' in CFH Tapper (ed.), *Crime, Proof and Punishment* (London: Butterworth, 1981); G Williams 'Convictions and Fair Labelling' (1983) 42 *Camb LJ* 85.

suggestion, that 'the label applied to an offence ought fairly [to] represent the offender's wrongdoing', was that the relevant fault element (intention, recklessness) should relate clearly to the *actus reus* of each crime, such that a conviction for a particular offence would convey the relevant information about the guilt of an offender.[286] The principle of fair labelling, as it is now known, reflects a much broader idea:

> that widely felt distinctions between kinds of offences and degrees of wrongdoing are respected and signalled by the law, and that offences are subdivided and labelled so as to represent the nature and magnitude of the law-breaking.[287]

The justification for this version of fair labelling broadly tracks von Hirsch's account of the structure of moral agency: fairness to the accused (fair punishment in accordance with retributive ideal); fairness to the victim in the recognition of the wrong that has been done to them; and the need for communication of the nature of wrongdoing within the criminal justice system and to the wider community.[288] This accordingly goes beyond questions of fault, to be seen as the legislative principle that it is necessary to distinguish between different kinds of wrong and label them in an appropriate way. Offences should thus be distinguished and labelled in a way that draws attention to, and communicates, the 'wrongness' of a particular course of action.[289] This is an intuitively attractive idea, appealing to ideas of clarity and certainty and to claims about the public nature and legitimacy of the criminal law—rooting the law in the ideal order in which citizens are addressed as moral agents, rather than the rather more messy reality. In practice, though, fair labelling is an expansive notion, particularly when it has been combined with victim-led demands for the recognition of certain wrongs that were noted above, where the moral weight of the victim's claim is used to present an unanswerable case for criminalization. And as we shall see in Part III, when combined with broad positive ideas of the interest to be protected by the criminal law, such as sexual autonomy, it is possible to recognize myriad ways that these interests and the rights of victims might be infringed, actually leading to an inflationary logic in the criminal law.

Andrew Ashworth has presented an elegant and lucid account of the criminal law. It places questions of criminalization at the centre of this account by linking questions of the proper nature and scope of the criminal law to questions of its limits—and responds directly to concerns about the over-reach or abuse of the criminal law. It is neo-classical in the sense that, in common with much contemporary theorizing, it links the justification of the criminal law to a classical retributive justification of individual punishment. It also places a heavy emphasis

[286] Ashworth, 'Elasticity', n.285, p.53.

[287] Ashworth & Horder, *Principles*, n.231, p.77. See also Simester & von Hirsch, *Crimes, Harms and Wrongs*, n.253, pp.202–8.

[288] See J Chalmers & F Leverick, 'Fair Labelling in Criminal Law' (2008) 71 *Mod LR* 217.

[289] Ashworth & Horder, *Principles*, n.231, p.77. See also V Tadros, 'Fair Labelling and Social Solidarity' in Zedner & Roberts, *Principles and Values*, n.231.

on the modality of law, in the form of human rights, principles and so on, to constrain the abuse of state power. This posits an ideal ordering of the criminal law, which maps on to an ideal political community. Together these are seen as providing potential resources for limiting the scope of the criminal law, even though in practice, as we have we seen, the development of these ideas has accompanied a large scale expansion in the use of the criminal law.

VI. Conclusion

This chapter has explored in some detail the relationship between an emergent understanding of criminal law, the development of the state, and underlying ideas about the nature of civil order. The aim has been to show how criminalization emerged as a matter of theoretical enquiry alongside the development of the modern criminal law, and how the formulation of the criminalization question at different moments was itself shaped by contemporary social concerns and understandings of the aims of the criminal law. As I acknowledged at the start of the chapter, the form taken—looking at different moments over a broad historical span, and taking the work of certain individuals as representative of those moments—necessarily means that the end result does not give a complete picture of the development of the criminal law, and was not intended to. Nonetheless, it has allowed me to point to changes in the way that aims of the criminal law have been understood, and I shall conclude this chapter by drawing out some initial and important conclusions.

It is important to begin by stressing that the argument presented here reinforces a claim that was made in Chapter 1. There is no evidence to suggest either that the criminal law was at any point based on more moral foundations, or organized around a core of moral wrongdoing, or that the use of punishment was justified in terms of retribution. The evidence, in fact, suggests the contrary. The foundations of modern criminal law as a distinct body of rules are to be seen in the attempt to combine laws which protected feudal order with an emerging civil order based on private ownership of property. In its origins, the criminal law, as a unified body of rules, had little 'moral' content—at least in the sense in which moral content was important either to shaping substantive content or legitimacy.[290] The criminal law was instead seen explicitly as a means for the building and maintenance of modern civil order. This becomes particularly clear if we consider the content of the law in relation to the aims as they were understood at different moments, for it also becomes apparent that the aims have always been oriented towards the maintenance of civil order, conceived in different ways, with the justification for the criminalization of certain conduct (and the assessment of its seriousness) understood in the light of these aims. The development of the modern criminal

[290] This claim is made with respect to the idea of criminal law as a body of rules. I shall look at claims about the moral content or origins of specific offences in Part III.

law cannot then be told as a story of decline or fall from an original form. Indeed we have seen the opposite: the understanding of criminal law as a system of rules has increasingly been understood to be possible only by understanding it in terms of a putative moral core. Whatever the normative arguments in support of this approach, these should not be confused with historical or anthropological claims about the nature of criminal law. Equally, it should be clear, the development of the law should not be understood in Whiggish terms, as a movement of progressive improvement, refinement, or liberalization. There have been important changes in terms of the development of the idea of criminal law as a system of rules, and in terms of the institutionalization of principles of legality, but we should be wary of reading these in terms of a straightforward progress, as the examples I have given suggest a more complex relation between the development and use of the criminal law and criminal law theory. In each of the periods examined, the form of the law can be linked to specific issues of civil order, to the form of the state, to ideas about individual agency, and so on. This should not be read as an invitation to relativism or moral vacuity; but, at this point, it is a caution against easy assumptions about either the moral purity of older law or the inherent superiority of our own understandings. It is also intended to begin the process of unpicking and challenging many of the normative assumptions which underpin normative theorizing about criminal law.

In more positive terms, this account has sought to show that the criminal law is purposive, and that this purpose has not historically been conceived of in terms of the purposes of punishment but as something distinct. What is striking across the different periods surveyed is that the criminal law is seen as articulating norms of a social or collective nature for advancing civil order and civilization and that the aim of the criminal law has been seen in these terms. This is not to suggest that the aims of punishment are not important, or even that they are not central to the legitimacy of the criminal law. It is, though, to claim that there is value in recovering an understanding of the aims of the criminal law that is not exclusively tied to the ends of punishment. The substantive aims of criminal law in this sense have been central to the development of the law and to understandings of the social functions of criminal law, and it is only recently that a narrower conception based on the aims of punishment has been adopted. There are, of course, significant differences in the way that order has been conceived and in the way that the function of criminal law has been articulated in relation to those aims, but what is important here is recognizing the broader point that we may develop a better understanding of criminalization if we understand the aims of the criminal law (or particular parts of it).

A second important theme of the chapter has been to trace the emergence of the 'criminalization question'. Here I have argued that this has only really emerged as a distinct question in the last fifty years. It was initially framed in narrow terms of the relationship between law and morals and the justifiability of criminalizing conduct solely on the grounds that it was contrary to moral beliefs. More recently, it has been framed in broader terms—what conduct should be criminalized—but the conception of criminal law in terms of which this has been addressed has been significantly narrowed. That said, a broader sense of criminalization—how criminal law was central to the making of civil order—can be seen to have underpinned the development of the modern criminal law. On this view, criminalization was not identified as a specific or distinct issue, but was seen as part of a wider set of fundamental questions about the nature of social and civil order and the role of government and the state in building that order. This should not be romanticized: the order that was constructed has been unequal, exploitative, patriarchal; the enforcement of the criminal law was unequal as one class (or nation) imposed their values on subordinate classes or countries in the name of civilization and order. However, this core sense, which places the criminal law at the core of institutional efforts to secure civil order and build civil society and understandings of citizenship, can and should be recovered.

As a final point we should note that the figures we have examined up to this point were in many respects exceptional. This is not only because of their intellectual standing, but also because their willingness to engage with larger questions, such as the social function or purposes of the criminal law, or to challenge the accepted systems of ordering or thinking about law, set them apart from their contemporaries. It is precisely this exceptionality that has allowed us, through their work, to gain insight into the development of criminal law theory. However, in order to develop the argument about the institutional dimension of criminal law, it is necessary in the next three chapters to go on to explore more specific institutional dimensions of the making of the modern idea of criminal law. In the first chapter, I identified certain key features of criminal law as an institutional normative order: that it has a certain aim or purpose, that it is authoritative in its field of application, and that it is a distinct system of knowledge and agency. In this chapter, we have looked at understandings of the aims of the criminal law, and in the next three chapters I am going to look at other features of the institutional development of the law. In Chapter 4 I will look at jurisdiction as the building of institutional authority and its relation to the scope of the criminal law. Then, in the two following chapters I turn to look at the criminal law as a system of knowledge and agency. Chapter 5 will look at the codification of criminal law, or how it was transformed into a systematic form of knowledge; and then Chapter 6 will look in more detail at agency, and specifically at the role that individual responsibility came to play as an organizing concept in the criminal law.

4

Jurisdiction

I. Introduction

> Of the *Territory* which the intended code is meant to embrace, and of the persons amenable to, and the crimes cognisable by, the Criminal Tribunals or Courts having jurisdiction therein.[1]

Jurisdiction, as Austin recognizes, is fundamental to the institution of the criminal law. In the modern law, it typically requires consideration of three elements: the identification of the territory within which the law applies; the specification of persons to whom the law applies; and rules concerning which crimes may be tried by which courts. Questions of jurisdiction thus inherently raise issues about the nature of legal authority, the scope and limits of the criminal law, showing how criminalization always has an institutional dimension.

This is not always recognized, jurisdiction often being viewed as either a purely technical matter—the competence or authority of particular courts to judge certain disputes—or as something linked pragmatically to the limits of enforcement of the law.[2] This linkage between jurisdiction and punishment has led to it being seen primarily in procedural terms. Indeed it is striking that the topic of jurisdiction is now rarely included in criminal law treatises, which tend to focus primarily on rules of substantive law; it is instead dealt with in specialized books dealing with criminal procedure. The topic of jurisdiction is regarded either as implicit, not needing to be discussed, or as procedural and technical and so not part of the formal architecture of the criminal law. There is some recognition of the relation between jurisdiction and the normative authority of the criminal law, particularly in the context of international criminal law, in recent writings which link jurisdiction and the justification of trial and punishment.[3] However, these works

[1] J Austin, 'Fragments of the Scheme of a Criminal Code' in R Campbell (ed.), *Lectures on Jurisprudence*, Vol. I (5th edn) (London: John Murray, 1885) p.1056.

[2] Country A might in theory legislate that their law extends to all the inhabitants/territory of country B, but in practice it is recognized that A would have difficulty bringing a national of B to trial in A for a crime, say of assault, committed in B against a resident of B—even if the conduct criminalized was similar in the laws of both countries. The problems would be even greater if A sought to criminalize conduct that was not criminal under the existing laws of country B.

[3] See RA Duff, 'Responsibility, Citizenship and Criminal Law' in RA Duff and SP Green (eds), *Philosophical Foundations of Criminal Law* (Oxford: Oxford UP, 2011) p.125; M Renzo, 'Responsibility and Answerability in the Criminal Law' in Duff et al., *The Constitution of Criminal*

have paid little attention up to now as to how this also impacts on criminalization, instead focusing on the question of the justifiability of punishment, and treating the content of the law as being linked to the preferences of one or other political or legal community.[4] However, as I have argued in the last two chapters, the question of the aims of the criminal law must be seen as distinct from that of the aims or justifiability of punishment. From this perspective, then, questions of jurisdiction and criminalization are fundamentally related—both concerning the question of what conduct falls within the scope of the criminal law of a particular court or country at a particular point in time. This is so both in the trivial sense of whether the law of a particular jurisdiction applies and can be enforced in the place where the conduct takes place at the time it took place, and in the broader sense in which questions of jurisdiction concern the power and authority of the criminal law. Indeed, it is questions of jurisdiction in this latter sense—the alleged loss of authority or legitimacy of the criminal law through its excessive and improper use—which lie at the heart of much of the recent literature on over-criminalization. However, in spite of the fact that criminal law has a body of rules which have been developed precisely to address the question of the extent and application of the criminal law, these have not been seen as relevant to a theory of criminalization.

Jurisdiction as a theme is potentially very broad. A theory of criminal jurisdiction can be defined, in literal terms, as a theory of the power to speak the criminal law.[5] This would include an account of legal authority and of the scope and the object of the law, or the regime of truth on which the application of the law is based. In an important sense jurisdiction is a pre-condition of the application of the law—of the nature and authority of legal rules—though it is rarely addressed as such.[6] However, the modern understanding of jurisdiction is much narrower and related to the spatial and temporal sphere of the application of the law, and the competencies of certain courts or bodies within this. It is these institutional dimensions, rather than more metaphysical conceptions of jurisdiction, that will be the focus of this chapter. My aim here is to trace the development of concepts of territory and persons in order to show that, far from being natural or self-evident in character, they are in fact closely connected to emergent ideas about civil order and the civilizing character of criminal law. This was manifest in the origins of criminal jurisdiction in the King's Peace, where the linkage between the extent of Royal jurisdiction and the kind of order that could be maintained was clear, but it is, as we shall see, no less true of the modern criminal law. Jurisdiction, in

Law (Oxford: Oxford UP, 2012); A Chehtman, *The Philosophical Foundations of Extraterritorial Punishment* (Oxford: Oxford UP, 2010).

4 Except where discussing so-called 'universal crimes' such as crimes against humanity, where it is more common to argue for universal jurisdiction. Cf. G Binder, 'Authority to Proscribe and Punish International Crimes' (2103) 63 *UTLJ* pp.278–309.

5 See M Foucault, 'Truth and Juridical Forms' in J Faubion (ed.), *Essential Works of Foucault. Vol. 3, Power* (New York: The New Press, 2000) p. 89.

6 Though see essays in S McVeigh (ed.), *Jurisprudence of Jurisdiction* (London: Routledge-Cavendish, 2007).

short, is central to the development of the aims and institutions of the modern criminal law.

The chapter is in three main sections. In the first, I discuss the institutional dimensions of jurisdiction in general terms, looking at the relation between jurisdiction and civil order, and at some of the basic distinctions which have shaped the emergence of modern ideas of criminal law jurisdiction. In the second section, I trace the outline of the development of the concept of territorial jurisdiction, looking at the means by which jurisdiction was extended from the governance of local community to nation states, and to its support for forms of imperial rule. In the third section, I reflect on these developments, looking in particular at how the meaning of territory has been linked to changing ideas of civil order and the changing aims of the criminal law, and looking at contemporary challenges to territorial conceptions of jurisdiction and their impact on questions of criminalization.

II. The Institution of Jurisdiction

In the modern law, jurisdiction is seen primarily as an institutional question—which is to say a question of how the criminal law organizes itself and its authority—what has been called the 'governance of legal governance'.[7] This can be described in Foucaultian terms as a matter of how law establishes a grid of intelligibility over certain practices—the means by which the institution of law orders itself so as to be able to read and regulate diverse social practices.[8] This has a number of different dimensions.[9] It is about the nature of legal authority, the sovereignty of law, or the claim to exercise a legitimate authority. This raises important metaphysical questions about the nature of law and legal authority.[10] However, institutionally, it is linked in the modern state to practical issues of the distribution of political and legal competences or the marking of the boundary between the political and the legal.[11] One central question is that of who (in the sense of which body) can legislate—whether the courts, for instance, are competent to develop the law. However, in different kinds of constitutional structures this might include the distribution of such legislative powers between federal and state or provincial

[7] M Valverde, 'Jurisdiction and Scale: Legal 'Technicalities' as Resources for Theory' (2009) 18 *Social & Legal Studies* pp.139–57 at 141.

[8] M Foucault, *The Birth of Biopolitics. Lectures at the College De France 1978–9* (London: Palgrave Macmillan, 2008) pp.252–3.

[9] Cf. the three dimensions identified in S McVeigh & S Dorsett, 'Questions of Jurisdiction' in McVeigh (ed.), *Jurisprudence*, n.6 pp. 4–5.

[10] See, for example, R Cover, 'Nomos and Narrative' (1983-4) 97 *Harvard LR* p.4; R Cover, 'Folktales of Justice: Tales of Jurisdiction' (1984-5) 14 *Cap UL Rev* p.179; C Douzinas, 'The Metaphysics of Jurisdiction' in McVeigh (ed.), *Jurisprudence*, n.6 pp.21–32.

[11] For an interesting examination of this question from the perspective of powers and responsibilities in a 'state of emergency' see M Hildebrandt, 'The Indeterminacy of an Emergency: Challenges to Criminal Jurisdiction in Constitutional Democracy' (2010) 4 *Crim. Law & Philos.* pp.161–81.

governments, and the way that these powers are characterized.[12] Second, there is a spatial dimension—the creation of different, contiguous, or overlapping legal spaces. This involves the drawing of jurisdictional boundaries, creating the territory or place of the law. These jurisdictional boundaries overlay or interact with other kinds of political, social, or even geographical spaces.[13] Jurisdictional rules establish external boundaries, or the limits of particular laws, but also distribute authorities or competences within a legal order. Third, it is also a matter of the creation of a certain kind of conceptual space for different areas of law, the drawing of boundaries between the rule of different bodies of law.[14] Thus, for example, it is to ask how criminal law came to be conceived of as a body of law, distinct from other areas of private or public law, and of how the relation between these areas is conceived. This links questions of jurisdiction to systems of knowledge in terms of the conception of the objects of different bodies of law (torts, contracts, medical) and the different aims and functions of these areas of law (distributive or corrective justice, regulation, and so on). Fourth, it is about binding persons to law—those who are protected and those who are bound by legal rules. This raises the question of who is a person at different points in time for the criminal law, in biological or political terms, and also the question of the limits of law: who is subject to a particular system of rules.[15] Finally, it is about the application of legal power in the sense of the establishment of different spheres of competence—specifically the competence of certain courts to adjudicate with respect to particular subject matter. This can be both a matter of internal ordering, the distribution of powers within a state, and of external relations between states or jurisdictions, often described in terms of conflicts of laws or the extraterritorial application of law.

In this chapter, I am principally concerned with the modern legal understanding of jurisdiction as the spatial and temporal sphere of the application of the law.[16] This kind of question can be looked at from the perspective of jurisdiction as designating the powers and organization of different courts—the courts of criminal jurisdiction. From this perspective, it can be seen as being related to

[12] See e.g. Canada where provincial government has competence to legislate in the area of criminal law, but federal authority is characterized in terms of police, order, and good government: British North America Act 1867 s.91. For discussion, see M Valverde, '"Peace, Order and Good Government": Policelike Powers in Postcolonial Perspective' in MD Dubber & M Valverde (eds), *The New Police Science* (Stanford: Stanford UP, 2006). See generally MD Dubber, *The Police Power* (New York: Columbia, 2004).

[13] RT Ford, 'Law's Territory (A History of Jurisdiction)' (1999) 97 *Michigan LR* pp.843–930 looking in particular at the link between cartography and jurisdiction. See also the essays in N Blomley, D Delaney, & RT Ford (eds), *The Legal Geographies Reader* (Oxford: Blackwell, 2001) esp. Pt II.

[14] See e.g. K. Veitch, *The Jurisdiction of Medical Law* (Dartmouth: Ashgate, 2007), which examines the creation of the novel field of medical law in terms of a theory of jurisdiction.

[15] N Naffine, *Law's Meaning of Life. Philosophy, Religion, Darwin and the Legal Person* (Oxford: Hart Publishing, 2009).

[16] See also MD Dubber, 'Criminal Jurisdiction and Conceptions of Penality in Comparative Perspective' (2013) 63 *UTLJ* pp.247–77 esp. pp.256–63. Aspects of the other questions, relating to the making of criminal law as a body of rules and the subjects of criminal law will be addressed in the next two chapters.

the process of state- and nation-building: how the legal authority is related to the monopoly of force within a given territory; and how competence or jurisdiction is ordered in a legal and bureaucratic form.[17] This links the criminal law to the process of state-building, the emergence of administrative powers and a centralized and hierarchical system of criminal courts. Developments such as the emergence of summary jurisdiction can provide an important perspective on the development of the criminal law.[18] However, this approach focuses more on the question of legal than civil order—how the legal order is organized and functions as a matter of the enforcement of the law. The question of the scope or limits of criminal jurisdiction, or the nature of civil order, is left unexamined except as a function of legal order. In this chapter, I want to examine categories of jurisdiction in common law systems as a way of opening up this question of the kind of order created. This is to ask about the kind of authority or community in the name of which the jurisdictional power is exercised. What is often seen as key here is the need to establish a linking point or nexus between the alleged criminal conduct and the state which claims or asserts jurisdiction over it.[19] Historically this link has been conceived in terms either of persons or territory—a distinction which is also then used to establish a claim of difference between common law and civilian systems of law.[20] Jurisdictional claims based on personhood are based on the nationality of either the offender (active) or victim (passive). This would thus assert that the jurisdiction of a particular state extended to the protection or prosecution of all citizens of that state wherever offences might have been committed. Territorial claims to jurisdiction, by contrast, are based on the place where the offence, or key elements of the offence, took place. Part of its attraction seems to rest in its very practicality and self-evidence, which is linked to the supposedly local origins of the common law in particular communities. However, as we shall see, in the development of criminal jurisdiction these ideas of territory and personality are exercised in the name of a particular kind of community or order the norms of which have been transgressed, so that it is necessary to supplement the analysis of jurisdiction with an understanding of civil order.

Before moving on, it is necessary to note one further distinction—that between ambit and venue as different dimensions of jurisdiction.[21] This can briefly be

[17] M Weber, *Economy and Society* (Berkeley: Univ. of California Press, 1978) pp.212–26; N Luhmann, *Law as a Social System* (Oxford: Oxford UP, 2004) pp.268, 276–8, 357–68.

[18] I have examined this in relation to the development of Scots criminal law in *Criminal Law, Tradition and Legal Order* (Cambridge: Cambridge UP, 1997) esp. Ch.3. This also looks at the relation between jurisdiction and the creation of an imagined space of legal nationhood.

[19] See e.g. I Cameron et al., *International Criminal Law from a Swedish Perspective* (Cambridge: Intersentia, 2011) p.53. See pp.53–7 for a more general review of principles of jurisdiction.

[20] See Dubber, 'Criminal Jurisdiction', n.16, pp.269–73.

[21] The distinction was drawn by Williams but has not always been used subsequently in a consistent manner. See G. Williams, 'Venue and the Ambit of Criminal Law' (1965) 81 *Law Quarterly Review* pp.276–88, 395–421, 518–38. There is a more recent work by M Hirst, *Jurisdiction and the Ambit of the Criminal Law* (Oxford: Oxford UP, 2003) Ch.1, which addresses this distinction and describes 'venue' as 'jurisdiction'.

summarized as follows. Questions of venue are understood to primarily concern the jurisdictional competence of a particular court. Can the court try either the particular defendant or the particular offence with which he or she is charged?[22] Questions of ambit concern the scope or extent of criminal laws. Venue is usually now addressed by provisions of criminal procedure which outline the jurisdiction of certain courts—thus in Scotland, the High Court of Justiciary has sole jurisdiction over the crimes of murder and rape, while other offences might be tried only in the summary courts. Equally, statutory provisions creating offences often specify the court or courts in which that offence might be tried. The question is made more complex, however, by provisions such as s.46(2) of the Supreme Court Act 1981, which assert the 'exclusive jurisdiction' of the English Crown Court 'in proceedings on indictment for offences wherever committed'.[23] While this might appear to extend the jurisdictional competence of the English courts to any offence committed anywhere in the world, it is understood in narrower terms as a 'venue' provision: that is, rather than asserting the universal jurisdiction of the Crown Court over all crimes, it merely asserts capacity to try such offences taking place outside England as would otherwise fall within the ambit of English criminal law.[24] Thus, even if it can be established that a court might be competent to try a certain offence (as under the Supreme Court Act), it is still necessary to establish that the offence falls within the 'geographical ambit' of English criminal law.[25] Questions of ambit concern the questions of substantive law: whether the offence definition applies to the conduct that is alleged to amount to that offence. These may arise in relation to questions of whether or not an offence has extra-territorial application—and these will then typically concern the geographical location of the crime or the nationality of the offender. However, as Hirst points out, as a matter of law, the *actus reus* of an offence will normally specify (either explicitly or implicitly) something about the circumstances in which the offence is committed.[26] Where these are implicit, the normal principle of the common law is that offences only apply within the territorial jurisdiction and over people within it; but there may also be statutory offences which specify location as an element of the offence.[27] However, as well as limitations, such provisions may also extend the ambit of the offence beyond the normal territorial area, such as by specifying that offences committed on British ships or aircraft, or by British soldiers while abroad, fall within the ambit of the law.[28] It is these questions of ambit, in particular, that raise issues of the scope of the criminal law.

[22] See Hirst, *Jurisdiction*, n.21, p.9.

[23] This re-enacts the Courts Act 1971 s 6.

[24] See Hirst, *Jurisdiction*, n.21, pp.10–12. See also *Treacy v DPP* [1971] AC 537 Lord Diplock p.559.

[25] See Hirst, *Jurisdiction*, n.21, p.11; Williams, 'Venue and Ambit', n.21, p.281.

[26] See Hirst, *Jurisdiction*, n.21, pp.2–9, giving the example of the traditional definition of murder as killing a person under the King's peace so that they die within a year and a day.

[27] E.g. certain types of fishing in particular rivers.

[28] Though it would also follow from this that if there were no provisions establishing venue that the crime could not be tried.

While it is clear that this distinction is somewhat artificial, the focus on ambit as a distinct matter is still a useful way of understanding how jurisdiction engages with the question of criminalization. This is in part a matter of description: if the concern is with the scope of the criminal law it is necessary to understand which offences comprise the criminal law of a given country and where they apply; or conversely, which law, of which countries, applies to people within a given geographical location. It is also a matter of theory, of the proper extent or scope of the criminal law. The concern here is with the ways in which the relation between jurisdiction and criminalization has been formulated in the common law, particularly the development of the paradigm of territorial jurisdiction up until the end of the nineteenth century, and of how the growth of what is known as extraterritorial jurisdiction has had an impact on this.

III. Territory

By the end of the nineteenth century, it was widely accepted that the principal basis of jurisdiction in common law systems was territoriality. The *locus classicus* for this position was the statement of Lord Halsbury that:

> All Crime is local. The jurisdiction over crime belongs to the country where the crime is committed, and, except over her own subjects, Her Majesty and the Imperial Legislature have no power whatsoever.[29]

In English law it was argued that there were no extraterritorial offences at common law, and that extraterritorial application depended on statutory extensions of the law.[30] In common law systems, this principle was linked historically to the local origins of the common law courts, and specifically the requirement of vicinage—that the jury should be summoned from the locality where the crime was committed because their decision was to be based on their own knowledge.[31] Crime was local disorder and should be dealt with by the local community or its representatives. As crime was gradually seen as a national problem, the scale of jurisdiction was generalized to the national level. Crime was a matter for the national courts, so conversely if a person from England murdered another in a different country that was a problem of order for that country and should not, in the normal course of events, concern English law. This position was also linked to considerations of practicality: it was the authority where the crime took place that normally had the principal interest in enforcing the law; and the local forum

[29] Ld Halsbury LC in *MacLeod v Att-Gen for New South Wales* [1891] AC 455 pp.458–9. The case concerned the prosecution of a man for bigamy where the alleged bigamous marriage had taken place in the US.

[30] See discussion in *The King v Casement* 1917 KB 98 p.123.

[31] See Hirst, *Jurisdiction*, n.21, Ch.2; Williams, 'Venue and Ambit', n.21, p.276. See also JF Stephen, *History of the Criminal Law* (London: Macmillan, 1883) Vol. I, Ch.IX, esp. pp.275–80 and Vol. II Ch.XVI.

was probably most convenient because the crime would be investigated and witnesses would be found there.

This position saw jurisdiction as principally a matter of venue: a practical question of bringing an offender before a court and ensuring that the court had jurisdiction to try the crime. In England, the primary unit of legal administration was originally the county and adjoining waters, with the Court of the Admiral having jurisdiction over offences committed in coastal waters and at sea.[32] This meant that even serious offences were to be tried in the county where the relevant acts were alleged to have occurred. However, this gave rise to considerable difficulties as situations arose in which the 'fact' of crime escaped the bounds of the local—such as where a person was wounded in one location but then died in another, or where a person stole goods in one county but was apprehended in another—where a defendant might fall between two different jurisdictions.[33] The response to these problems of 'venue' was twofold. One response came through the courts with the creation of legal fictions through which an act was held to have been committed again in different counties: thus thieves carrying stolen goods into a new county were considered to steal the goods again when they crossed into a new county. But even these rules were not without complication: as Hale noted, this fiction could not apply to a charge of robbery since the use of force was not a continuing act.[34]

The second kind of response was to provide for these situations by statute. This led to the development of a vast number of technical rules specifying the exact boundaries between counties, or where jurisdiction ended on the coast or rivers. Alternatively, there were statutes which created 'deeming' provisions—that an act which took place in one location was deemed to have taken place in another—to ensure that courts had jurisdiction, and rules on how to deal with offences that took place on these boundaries or where offenders were apprehended in a different location from where the crime had taken place.[35] The end result, though, was a system of considerable complexity, with Stephen, writing at the end of the nineteenth century, estimating that there were eighteen statutory exceptions to the general principle of local jurisdiction.[36]

[32] For a discussion of the county in jurisdiction in England and the US, see A Levitt, 'Jurisdiction over Crimes: I The Territorial Commission Theory' (1925) 16 *Journal of the American Institute of Criminal Law and Criminology* pp.316–59 at 324–37.

[33] See e.g. *Lacey's Case* (1582) 1 Leon 270 where the defendant was discharged because he had wounded his victim while at sea but the victim had not died until he was on the land. The assize had no jurisdiction to enquire about the blow, while the Court of the Admiral could take no cognizance of the death. This was remedied by statute in 1548 (2 & 3 Edw 6, c 24). A further statute (2 Geo 2, c 21) addressed this gap between admiralty and county jurisdiction. See now also Offences Against the Person Act 1861 s.10.

[34] M Hale, *The History of the Pleas of the Crown* (London: Payne, T, 1800) p.507.

[35] See e.g. Criminal Law Act 1826 (7 Geo IV c 64) s.12: 'That where any Felony or Misdemeanor shall be committed on the Boundary or Boundaries of Two or more Counties, or within the Distance of Five hundred Yards of any such Boundary or Boundaries, or shall be begun in one County and completed in another, every such Felony or Misdemeanor may be dealt with, inquired of, tried, determined, and punished in any of the said Counties, in the same Manner as if it had been actually and wholly committed therein.'

[36] Stephen, *History*, n.31, I at p.278.

These technicalities, and the recognition that counties were no longer the most practical unit of jurisdiction as urban centres grew up across county lines and people were generally more mobile with the coming of railways and systems of mass transport, led to proposals to change the basis of jurisdiction. Stephen's proposed remedy was a principle of convenience: 'all courts otherwise competent to try an offence should be competent to try it irrespectively of the place where it was committed, the place of trial being determined by the convenience of the court, the witnesses and the person accused.'[37] However, the solution which was eventually adopted in the Criminal Justice Act 1925 was more limited, establishing only that prosecutions could be brought in any county where an accused was apprehended or in custody by deeming the offence to have been committed there.[38] While this remedied some of the jurisdictional problems by replacing the mass of provisions by a single rule, the peculiarity of the provision was that it kept the underlying philosophy of venue alive by 'deeming' the offence to have been committed in that county.[39] This approach only ended with the Magistrates' Court Act 1952, which adopted a principle of convenience.[40] This was then extended by the Courts Act 1971 and the Supreme Court Act 1981, which created a unified Crown Court with jurisdiction over indictable offences committed anywhere in the world.[41] These provisions were essentially an administrative response, aimed at ensuring that there was universal jurisdictional competence, in particular for the lower courts, and that there was the legal means of bringing offenders to trial.

While these provisions dealt with questions of venue, problems of the ambit of the law could not be so easily remedied. These were also regarded as being governed by the principle of territoriality, but for this to apply it not only had to be determined where a crime had taken place, but also that there was a relation between the conduct and the norms of the broader community in whose name the law was enforced. By the late eighteenth century, this was, in most cases, straightforward: the territory was understood in geographical terms as the territorial nation state, and criminal law covered all acts which took place within the territory. A crime was a breach of the laws of England and this was accompanied by certain expectations about the norms of civilized conduct. There were, though, a substantial number of exceptions to the basic rule of territoriality, and looking at these exceptions allows us to see how this principle of community operated.[42]

[37] Ibid. A provision along these lines was accordingly contained in his Draft Code for 1879 (*Report of the Royal Commission Appointed to Consider the Law Relating to Indictable Offences* 1879 (London: HMSO) C.2345, s.504).

[38] s.11(1): A person charged with any indictable offence may be proceeded against, indicted, tried and punished in any county or place in which he was apprehended, or is in custody on a charge for the offence, or has appeared in answer to a summons lawfully issued charging the offence, as if the offence had been committed in that county or place, and the offence shall, for all purposes incidental to or consequential on the prosecution, trial or punishment thereof, be deemed to have been committed in that county or place.

[39] See Hirst, *Jurisdiction*, n.21, p.33.

[40] Ss.1 & 2. See discussion in Williams, 'Venue and Ambit', n.21, pp.280–2.

[41] 1971 Act s.6.

[42] See especially the very full discussion in Stephen, *History*, n.31, Ch.XVI.

These exceptions can be treated under two main headings: crimes committed at sea; and crimes committed on land abroad.

One of the oldest exceptions to the principle of territoriality was the admiralty jurisdiction, which covered crimes committed at sea.[43] Admiralty jurisdiction was transferred to the normal courts by the Admiralty Offences Act 1844, but the ambit of admiralty jurisdiction remained. This extended to British (but not foreign) ships at sea, and over inlets, bays, and rivers where ships could go, and to foreign ships within British territorial waters.[44] Furthermore, pirates were regarded in international law as enemies of the human race, and as such, foreign pirates fell under admiralty jurisdiction for offences committed at sea.[45] Jurisdiction was understood on the basis that offences on these ships or in these waters could be treated as though territorial: the Offences at Sea Act 1799 asserted jurisdiction over all offences on the high seas 'as if' they had been committed on the shore. It applied to all indictable offences committed on British ships even where these were committed by aliens; conversely this also meant that there was no jurisdiction over foreign vessels on the high seas outwith British territorial waters. Issues around admiralty jurisdiction became more complex as British ships took a role in policing the slave trade and piracy, with disputes arising over the exact status of certain captured ships.[46] Pirates or slave traders could be boarded with impunity, but if a foreign ship was not properly designated a slave trader then admiralty jurisdiction did not run.[47] The 'as if' of territory bound those deemed within it, and only them, to certain norms of civil conduct.

In relation to crimes committed on land, it was recognized that territorial jurisdiction might be extended where necessary to protect national security. One of the oldest extensions was the crime of treason, where jurisdiction was based on the duty of allegiance a subject owed to the sovereign, wherever the crime was committed.[48] The extraterritorial application of the law of treason can be traced to statutes of 1351 and 1543 making it an offence to be 'adherent to the King's enemies in his realm, giving to them aid and comfort in the realm, or elsewhere'.[49]

[43] Stephen, *History*, n.31, II, pp.16–58, especially at p.29 discussing *R v Keyn* ((1876–7) LR 2 Ex D 67). This led to the Territorial Waters Jurisdiction Act 1878 (40 & 41 Vict c.73). This same issue was later discussed in the case of the *SS Lotus (France v Turkey).* PCIJ Rep Series A No 1 (1927). For discussion see U Özsu, 'De-territorializing and Re-territorializing *Lotus*: Sovereignty and Systematicity as Dialectical Nation-Building in Early Republican Turkey' (2009) 22 *Leiden Jnl of Intnl Law* pp.29–49.

[44] Offences at Sea Act 1536; Williams, 'Venue and Ambit', n.21, pp.279–80, 285–7.

[45] Stephen, *History*, n.31, II, pp.27–9.

[46] See *R v Serva* 1845 1 Den 104; 169 ER 169 discussed further in L Farmer, 'Territorial Jurisdiction and Criminalization' (2013) 63 *UTLJ* p.225.

[47] On slavery, see Slave Trade Act 1824 (5 Geo IV, c 113) ss.2 & 9; Slave Trade Act 1843 s.1. See also discussion in *R v Serva*, n.46, pp.171–3.

[48] Williams, 'Venue and Ambit', n.21, p.396 quotes Sir Edward Coke from Calvin's Case 1608: 'ligeance cannot be circumscribed within the predicament of *ubi*'.

[49] This in part gave rise to problems of venue, but these were dealt with by the Treason Act 1543 (35 Hen VIII c.2), which provided that treason committed abroad should be triable by jury as if the treason had been committed in the county of trial. See also discussion in *King v Casement* 1917 KB 98 where the alleged acts had taken place abroad. See also Treason Felony Act 1848 s.3.

The nineteenth century then saw the creation of offences such as preparing to cause a serious explosion to take place within her Majesty's dominions, or accepting military service with a foreign state at war with another foreign state with whom Britain was at peace.[50] What these offences had in common was the recognition that a threat to the security of the UK or its laws could be posed even by someone who was acting outside the territory, and that jurisdiction could be asserted on the basis of the interest in state security. The situation was more complex with 'ordinary' crimes committed abroad, since these would not normally pose a threat to the British authorities or the security of the British state. There were, however, certain recognized categories of jurisdiction. Some of these track the reasons why a British subject might be abroad in some sort of 'official' capacity. Thus, it had historically been the position that there was jurisdiction over members of the armed forces and camp followers for crimes committed in foreign campaigns.[51] It was also recognized that officials in service of the British Crown abroad might under certain circumstances fall under the jurisdiction of the common law courts. These categories tracked the development of the British colonies and empire, initially asserting jurisdiction over senior officials such as governors, but later extending this to all public officials.[52] The clear justification for this was the moral authority claimed by Britain to police officials acting in its name and that such officials should neither be beyond the law nor fall between different jurisdictions.[53]

This form of personal jurisdiction was consolidated into a larger and more complex set of exceptions by the series of Foreign Jurisdiction Acts passed between 1843 and 1890.[54] These built on a form of consular jurisdiction, established by treaties and known as the Capitulations, under which in Muslim and non-Christian states (and in particular, the Ottoman Empire) British subjects would not necessarily be tried in the ordinary local courts but might, depending on local custom and usage, be tried under British law. These provisions were initially understood in protective terms—to shield British subjects from Ottoman 'barbarism'—but, by the time of the passing of the first Act in 1843, there was

[50] Explosive Substances Act 1883 s.3; Foreign Enlistment Act 1870 s.4.

[51] This was the jurisdiction of the Court of the Constable and Marshal. It lapsed in the 1600s, but was replaced by the jurisdiction of the courts martial (Williams, 'Venue and Ambit', n.21, p.279).

[52] See An Act to punish Governors of Plantations in this Kingdom for Crimes by them committed in the Plantations (1698 Wm III, c 12). This was the basis for the prosecution of Wall, former governor of Gorée, for the murder of a soldier by an illegal flogging: *R v Wall* (1802) St Tr 51. See Criminal Jurisdiction Act 1802 s.1, extending jurisdiction to all public officials. See R Jenkyns, *British Rule and Jurisdiction Beyond the Seas* (Oxford: Clarendon, 1902) Ch.VII. Stephen notes that the Government of British India claimed the power to legislate for public servants in native states both within and adjacent to British India (Stephen, *History*, n.31, II, p.12, fn 1) (but no authority is given in support of this claim).

[53] The general issue of the accountability of imperial power to law in Victorian Britain is discussed at length in RW Kostal, *A Jurisprudence of Power* (Oxford: Oxford UP, 2005) see esp. Ch.8.

[54] 6 & 7 Vict c 94 (1843); 29 & 30 Vict c.87 (1866); 38 & 39 Vict c 85 (1875); 41 & 42 Vict c 67 (1878); and 53 & 54 Vict c 37 (1890). These are discussed in Stephen, *History*, n.31, pp.58–61 and Jenkyns, *British Rule*, n.52. pp.142ff and Ch.VIII.

also a political concern that the British authorities had to take some responsibility for the disorderly conduct of their subjects in Ottoman territories and ensure that they were not shielded from the legal consequences of their actions.[55] The Act stated that where the Queen had power and jurisdiction outwith her dominions, established by 'treaty, capitulation, grant, usage, sufferance and other lawful means' such territories were to be treated 'as if' they had been conquered, thereby establishing the jurisdiction of British laws.[56] The effect was to enable British subjects in territories that were considered either uncivilized, or which were not under the protectorate of a foreign state, or a system of government that was considered civilized, to be punished for wrongs committed against British law. The subsequent Acts, and orders made under them, then extended these basic rules to cover diverse areas such as China, Japan, and Fiji. The central point is that British subjects all over the globe were to be protected from 'barbarous' indigenous laws, but were also expected to act in a civilized manner according to the standards established by British law.

The final form by which jurisdiction was extended over crimes committed on land was the straightforward use of statute, and these extensions tended to be in response to particular incidents or concerns about the spread of certain forms of criminality.[57] They fall into two classes: where jurisdiction over a crime committed outside Britain was straightforwardly claimed by the British legislature; or, alternatively, provisions covering participation in, or conspiracy to commit, a crime abroad, which treated the crime committed abroad as if it had been committed in England. The former type can be seen as more problematic, as it was recognized that any basis for jurisdiction might be tenuous where only the domestic laws of another state had been infringed. An example of this is the crime of murder. The power to try murder committed on land by a British subject can be traced back to an Act of 1541, and was re-enacted in various statutes up to the Offences Against the Person Act 1861.[58] This established a jurisdiction over murders committed in other states that might be resorted to if they were not prosecuted domestically.[59] The latter type of case is perhaps more straightforward, criminalizing that part of the crime which took place in England through the use of the fiction that the completed crime had taken place in England.[60] Prosecution could be justified on the grounds that the threat posed by someone who committed a crime abroad

[55] See the Memorandum by JR Hope-Scott, the draftsman of the Act on the problems of order caused by the ending of the Levant Company in 1825 (published as Appendix VI in Jenkyns, *British Rule,* n.52). See also CR Pennell, 'The Origins of the Foreign Jurisdiction Act and the extension of British sovereignty' (2010) 83 *Historical Research* pp.465–85.

[56] Preamble to 1843 Act.

[57] These are discussed in Part II of Williams' article (Williams, 'Venue and Ambit', n.21, pp.395–421). See also Stephen, *History*, n.31, pp.12–6.

[58] 33 Hen VIII.c.23, though this Act was primarily concerned with treason and it is not clear that it was intended to extend jurisdiction to all murders—though this is how it came to be interpreted. 1861 Act s.9. See discussion in Stephen, History, n.31, II, p.15 and Williams, Venue, n.21, pp.399–402.

[59] Though this power was rarely used. See Hirst, *Jurisdiction*, n.21, p.231 fn 96.

[60] Or in the case of a conspiracy that the crime was completed in England.

could potentially extend to domestic order. An example of this is the case of *R v Bernard*.[61] This was an attempted prosecution of a man who was involved in a plot on the life of Napoleon III, leading to a bomb being thrown at his carriage in Paris, which killed several people. There was uncertainty over whether or not this was a crime against English law and, at the trial, the defendant was acquitted—leading to complaints from the French. The legal position was subsequently settled with the passing of the Offences Against the Person Act 1861, which stated that persons who conspire in England to murder foreigners abroad or become accessories to murder or manslaughter committed abroad shall be treated as if the crime committed abroad had been committed in England.[62]

Extraterritorial jurisdiction over murder was also established in statutes such as the Murders Abroad Act 1817, which claimed an extended jurisdiction over homicides by treating them 'as if' committed at sea (and therefore subject to admiralty jurisdiction). This provided that:

> All murders and manslaughters committed or that shall be committed within any other islands, countries or places not within his Majesty's dominions, nor subject to any European state or power, nor within the territory of the United States of America, by the master or crew of any British ship or vessel... or by any person sailing therein or belonging thereto, or that shall have sailed in or belonged to and have quitted any British ship or vessel to live in any of the said islands countries or places... may be tried, adjudged and punished... in the same manner as if such offence or offences had been committed on the high seas.[63]

What is striking about this Act is that it extends the jurisdiction of the English law of homicide to so-called 'uncivilized territory' (i.e. that which is not controlled by Britain, other European powers or the United States).[64] The Act was passed as a particular response to outrages committed by sailors in the Pacific Islands—which seem to have been regarded as territory beyond the reach of law. Exceptions such as this were justified on the ground that:

> Every British subject, wherever he may be, continues to owe allegiance to the Crown... and that consequently if he does anything contrary to that allegiance or law is liable, if found within the jurisdiction of an English court, to be punished as if he had committed the offence within the dominions of the Crown.[65]

If these rules established the general ambit of the criminal law, there remained one final set of issues. Even if it was established that an offence fell within the ambit of the law, it was necessary, in the case of cross-frontier offences or offences at sea,

[61] 1858 1 F & F 240. Discussed in Stephen, *History*, n.31, II, p.13.

[62] (24 & 25 Vict c 100) ss 4 & 9. Lord Palmerston had introduced a Conspiracy to Murder Bill 1858 containing similar provisions in response to the immediate uproar.

[63] 57 Geo III c 53 s.1. Offenders were to be tried under the procedure established by the Offences at Sea Act 1806 (46 Geo III c.54).

[64] Williams, Venue, n.21, p.401. It is not based on nationality since jurisdiction extends not only to British nationals, but also those who travelled on British ships. The form, however, is analogous to that adopted in the Foreign Jurisdiction Acts (supra).

[65] Jenkyns, *British Rule*, n.52, pp.136–7.

to establish where the crime had actually taken place—and consequently whether the conduct was within the jurisdiction of the criminal law of a particular state. This generated a huge and complex jurisprudence around the question of whether the crime could be said to have been committed where it was initiated or where it was completed—or indeed in both places.[66] The former test was known as the subjective test, and the latter as the objective test—and their importance relates to developing theories of *mens rea*.[67] The English courts had historically taken the 'objective' view—that a crime was committed where it was completed. However, over the course of the nineteenth century there was growing interest in a subjective view—that the offence was committed where the offender's conduct took place—on the grounds that an offender who intended a certain outcome usually completed all that was in their power to complete in that territory and that it was within the power of the authorities in that place to prevent or control their actions.[68] It is interesting in this context to note that Stephen's draft code of 1879 recommended the adoption of a rule that:

> Every offence shall, for all the purposes of trial and punishment, be deemed to be committed at any place where any act is done or omitted, the doing or omission of which forms part of the offence, whether the person is at such place or not at the time of such act, omission or event.[69]

There have also been various presumptions or fictions which have been developed where a crime has been considered not to have extraterritorial effect in order to rule that it has been completed within a particular territory. Thus the Canadian Criminal Code criminalized extraterritorial bigamy by criminalizing those who left Canada with intent to commit bigamy, a rule which maintained the idea of territoriality by virtue of an emphasis on future intent.[70] And finally there have been rules developed that certain crimes are of a continuing nature and can thus be held to be committed in any jurisdiction in which they are partly committed.

This section has traced the series of extensions of the idea of territory from an immediate idea of locality and community justice to an extended idea of imperial territory, where the relation between space and law is conceived in terms of law's civilizing potential and the responsibility of the colonizer to carry a civilized law with them.

In the next section I shall discuss the meaning of territorial jurisdiction, with particular reference to its relation to the development of the concept of criminal

[66] See Hirst, *Jurisdiction*, n.21, Ch.4; Williams, 'Venue and Ambit', *Part III,* n.21, pp.518–38.

[67] Williams refers to them as the 'initiatory' and the 'terminatory' theories respectively; the courts have also used the distinction between conduct and result crimes: see *Treacy v DPP* [1971] AC 537.

[68] Note the clear parallels with subjective theories of attempts. See G Fletcher, *Rethinking Criminal Law* (Boston MA: Little, Brown & Co, 1978) Ch.1 on the emergence of subjective and objective tests of *mens rea* in relation to attempts.

[69] *Report of the Royal Commission Appointed to Consider the Law Relating to Indictable Offences* (London: HMSO, 1879) C.2345 s.4. See also Stephen, *History*, n.31, II, pp.10–2 discussing *R v Keyn* (1876).

[70] See discussion in Williams, 'Venue and Ambit', n.21, p.395 fn.45.

law. Before doing so, it is necessary to say a little more about territory and the extension of the criminal law. One point to note here is that it is not possible clearly to distinguish between territory and persons as a basis for jurisdiction because the understanding of territory has always included persons and it is the articulation of the relationship between territory and persons—or civil order—that is key. And this should not surprise once we recognize that jurisdiction cannot be reduced to the question of 'punishability' but is concerned with broader matters of 'governability'. It is also important to note the contrast between different visions of the civilized English criminal law. In the first, criminal law has a civilizing potential that spreads outwards from the metropolitan centre. This fits with early Victorian ideas of liberal imperialism, where the justification of the imperial mission was linked to liberal reform or the improvement of barbarous or uncivilized peoples.[71] In the second, the degree of civilization becomes a measure and law is applied differentially to civilized and barbarous peoples. Thus in the case of the Capitulations and the Ottoman Empire it was recognized that different standards, and different rules, applied, depending on the degree of civilization of the people. While British subjects were to be judged by what was understood to be a higher standard, because of Britain's place in the world, the broader aim of criminal law was to exert a form of control. The position, though, was clearly different between nations adjudged to be civilized, where jurisdiction was based on reciprocity between equal nations. This relied on an emergent sense of common understandings of wrongdoing—that certain conduct was criminal wherever it was committed or by the laws of any civilized nation—and that in these cases nations should assist each other in bringing offenders to trial because of the threat that they posed to order more generally.

IV. The Meaning of Territorial Jurisdiction

One of the most striking features of the development of the doctrine of territorial jurisdiction is that questions of jurisdiction have been dealt with on a piecemeal basis, responding to particular problems as they arose, with the result that the mass of provisions that developed in this area were (and remain) extremely technical and complex. There were various attempts to consolidate or clarify some of the rules over the course of the nineteenth century but there was little attempt to identify a clear or consistent basis for jurisdiction. Particular anomalies—say over venue or the extent of territorial waters—were addressed by legislative provision, but the underlying basis of the system was not addressed. Thus, while the normal account of the development of jurisdiction in the nineteenth century stresses the emergence of a new kind of hierarchical and systematic order at a nation-state level, stripping away the local and anachronistic and replacing it with

[71] On the distinction between different moral justifications of empire, see K Mantena, *Alibis of Empire* (Princeton: Princeton UP, 2010) Ch.1.

a new rational bureaucratic structure, it is clear that this is not the case in respect of rules defining the ambit of the criminal law. There is, nonetheless, a certain kind of underlying logic to its development, though grasping this requires that we understand territorial jurisdiction less in terms of ordered and rational principles and more as a form of paradigmatic reasoning connected to the development of the institution of criminal law. The idea of territorial jurisdiction is the central case and organizing idea, and other cases were either fitted in to this or treated as exceptions.

The key to understanding this logic is to grasp the idea of territory. Even in its origins territory is not a natural category, but was bound up with practices of administration and rule and ideas about the aims and authority of law. Territory does not begin as an already existing, empty space that requires mapping, as has been suggested in certain theories of jurisdiction, but is from the beginning a particular locality, that is to say a place with a history that is already bound up with the institution and application of law.[72] This is the significance of the claim, repeated in accounts of territorial jurisdiction, that its origins lie in vicinage and the local jury: territory on this account is thus inseparable from the institution of criminal law, and the place of jurisdiction is already a locus for a form of government.[73] And it also follows from this that the common law, as an idea of custom, has a temporal and legal primacy—captured in Lord Halsbury's claim that all crime was local, even though this was patently contradicted by the practices of empire in extending English law across the globe. The common law is always already there and statutory rules are accordingly viewed as having been superimposed on this underlying order, or as being capable of carrying it to new localities. If territory is thus the governing idea, the central ideas of territory have themselves been transformed in response to changes in social, political, and legal organization.

Central to the longevity of the idea of territorial jurisdiction has been the capacity of the courts and legislatures to expand the meaning of territory, assimilating even apparently personal forms of jurisdiction to territory or extending the rule of English law to remote places 'as if' they were England. This once again underlines the point that it is not to be understood as a natural but as a particular kind of legal space. This is clearest if we look at the form of legal reasoning in this area, the logic of jurisdictional reasoning. Central to the paradigm was the use of deeming provisions: that certain kinds of conduct were stated in statute to be treated 'as if' committed in England and thus within the jurisdiction of the English courts. While this kind of legal fiction might appear clumsy, it has long had a central place in the practice of the common law. Fictions were routinely used as a means of establishing the jurisdiction of the common law courts, averring that certain incidents had taken place in a particular locality where this was blatantly false.[74]

[72] See Ford, 'Law's Territory', n.13, pp.852–4 describing jurisdiction as the mapping of space.

[73] M Hildebrandt, 'Extraterritorial Jurisdiction to Enforce in Cyberspace?: Bodin, Schmitt, Grotius in Cyberspace' (2013) 63 *UTLJ* pp.196–224 at 204–10.

[74] For a full discussion of this, see D Klerman, 'Legal Fictions as Strategic Instruments' (2009) http://escholarship.org/uc/item/8zv9k24m [accessed 15 May 2015]; JH Baker, *The Law's Two Bodies: Some Evidential Problems in English Legal History* (Oxford: Oxford UP, 2001) Lecture 2.

While historians have struggled with this—how could litigants have accepted the manifest untruth of certain averments?—and fictions have been the subject of extensive theoretical critique from Bentham onwards, the significance of these kind of fictions was that they were a highly practical means of dealing with problems of jurisdiction. The deeming provision was a legal, not a factual, assertion and it was not based on a claim that there was some correspondence with an underlying natural reality (that the territory was in fact English or that the events alleged had in fact taken place in England). The fact that it was artificial did not mean that it was ineffective or imaginary.[75] Its significance ultimately depended on the capacity and effectiveness of the English courts in responding to certain problems.[76] The core justification was based on the ability of the legal order—be it local community, or nation state or empire—to try and to punish offenders in the name of that order and its shared values. This is what underlay the increasingly broad extensions of the idea.[77]

This allows us to understand the development of territorial jurisdiction through the kinds of justifications that were offered in support of its extended forms in terms consistent with the emergence of the modern idea of criminal law explored in the last chapter. The origins of jurisdiction lay in the power of the feudal superior, but the foundations of the legal concept of jurisdiction lie in the constitution of modern forms of sovereignty based on the 'institutional authority of an abstract sovereign'.[78] This public power to command depended in particular on the idea of a continuous legal authority through space and time, and the shift to a legislative conception of sovereignty. In jurisdictional terms, sovereign power was based on security—protecting territory from internal and external threats—and in the criminal law was concerned primarily with crimes committed within the territory because of the threat they posed to internal legal order. It is thus unsurprising that the initial extensions to the idea of national territory were made through the crime of treason, and offences which were considered as analogous to treason, extensions justified on the basis that these were necessary for the security of the British sovereign or institutions of state. The later extensions of jurisdiction, based on particular crimes, followed a different logic, namely that acts committed outside the territory could have harmful consequences for civil order or the legitimate interests of the state.[79] This preventive logic was behind the increasing importance of *mens rea*, which allowed the assertion of jurisdiction over an offender even if

[75] See LL Fuller, 'Legal Fictions' (1930) 25 *Ill L Rev* p.363 and p.390 arguing that fictions should not be criticized for their distance from reality but should be understood in terms of what they made possible. Cf. K Knop, R Michaels, & A Riles, 'From Multiculturalism to Technique: Feminism, Culture and the Conflict of Laws Style' (2012) 64 *Stanford LR* pp.645–8.

[76] Cf. Klerman, 'Legal Fictions', n.74, arguing that fictions in civil litigation were a way of evading appellate review.

[77] It is interesting to see this kind of justification being resurrected in recent debates about jurisdiction, though with insufficient attention to the institutional dimensions of criminal law: see Duff, 'Responsibility', n.3, on the role of the local community in calling offenders to account.

[78] Hildebrandt, 'Extraterritorial Jurisdiction', n.73, pp.208–9.

[79] See Levitt, *Jurisdiction over Crimes I*, n.32, pp.338–54 describing this as the territorial security theory of jurisdiction. This is often described as the 'protective principle'.

the harmful consequences occurred outwith the territory. In the case of crimes such as murder this could further be justified on the grounds that the laws of all civilized nations would criminalize this conduct, and that the problem was that of ensuring that wrongdoers should not be shielded from prosecution because they fell between different jurisdictions.[80] In other areas of law, crimes were seen as continuing acts, enabling jurisdiction to be asserted over those who threatened the stability of legal order. It is interesting to note that one of the principal nineteenth century extensions concerned the crime of bigamy, which was first made into an extraterritorial offence by section 22 the Offences Against the Person Act 1828, and was the subject of several leading cases on the extraterritorial ambit of the criminal law.[81] The questions that arose concerned cases where, for example, bigamy was committed under English law if a person celebrated a second marriage in a different country, or where a person who had been married elsewhere came to England and married again. While the cases concerned such arcane questions as whether marriage was a status or a ceremony ('celebrating marriage'), the jurisdictional issue was resolved on the basis of the need to protect the social institution of marriage. For Victorian lawyers, justification was also sought, as we have seen, in terms of empire and the assumed role of regulating British dominions and subjects across the globe. This was driven by a combination of expediency and belief in the rule of law that operates at a considerable distance from the original idea of local accountability, but could nonetheless be effective while empire survived.

If we can see that the expansion of extraterritorial jurisdiction has its origins in these kinds of justifications, much contemporary extraterritorial jurisdiction operates on a different basis, being more concerned with the threat posed by certain offenders or groups of offenders, than just the potentially harmful consequences of conduct.[82] This legislation takes different forms. One type is that jurisdiction follows an ever-expanding category of UK nationals, a group that now includes corporations, where acts are done abroad by employees who are not UK nationals.[83] In other cases, jurisdiction still relies on an increasingly tenuous link to territory: the Criminal Justice Act 1993 contains rules on jurisdiction over a range of property offences, and conspiracy to commit these offences, not only on the basis that a crime was planned, or originated in a particular place, but also where

[80] See Jenkyns, *British Rule*, n.52, p.13. M Wiener, *Men of Blood. Violence, Manliness and Criminal Justice in Victorian England* (Cambridge: Cambridge UP, 2004) pp.70–2 points out that this was also an important context for understanding the decision in the famous cannibalism case of *Dudley & Stephens* (1884).

[81] Later replaced by Offences Against the Person Act 1861 s.57. *MacLeod v Att Gen for NSW* [1891] AC 455; *R v Earl Russell* [1901] AC 446. See also Williams, 'Venue and Ambit', n.21, pp.402–8.

[82] 'It is based on the ideas that civilized nations are interconnected and inter-related; that what is harmful to one is likely to prove harmful to all the rest; that the important factor in criminal law is... that a human being existed who had exhibited tendencies which the history of civilization has shown to be harmful to other human beings', A Levitt, 'Jurisdiction over Crimes- II' (1926) 16 *Jnl of the American Institute of Criminal Law and Criminology* pp.495–518 at 496. See generally Hirst, *Jurisdiction*, n.21, Ch.5.

[83] Hirst, *Jurisdiction*, n.21, pp.203–8.

some communication relating to the offence took place in England and Wales.[84] In other instances jurisdiction is asserted on the basis that a state bears some moral responsibility for the conduct of its nationals abroad. The Sex Offenders Act 1997 asserts jurisdiction over sex crimes committed abroad by the nationals of any country provided first that the conduct was criminal under the laws both of the UK and where the conduct was committed, and that the person accused was either a British national or resident in the UK.[85] Finally, there are an increasing number of offences which are said to have a form of universal jurisdiction—that is to say that they are criminal under English law wherever they are committed. One recent example of this is UK anti-terrorism legislation, which criminalizes terrorist acts which take place outside the UK and which might be directed at the government of any other country.[86]

It is clear that changes in this area have been driven by the rise of forms of international crime in the wake of technological and economic development, and there is increasing concern with forms of cross-border or transnational crime, such as forms of trafficking (in drugs, illicit objects, or persons) and forms of financial crime.[87] It is certainly the case that the ease of movement of persons, property, and information create new opportunities for the commission of crime, but it is nonetheless worth reflecting on the logic behind the growing ambit of the criminal law. While this might appear in many cases to be simply a piling together of existing rules and justifications to ensure that nothing is excluded, it is arguable that something more significant can be discerned lying behind the developments, however incomplete at present.[88] First, there is a concern that in an interconnected world no 'truly' criminal conduct should be unjusticiable. This replaces a link to territory or the interests of particular states with the idea that all serious crimes are justiciable and that prosecution is merely a matter of convenience. This properly raises concerns about the legitimacy of trial and punishment, from the point of view of view of criminalization, but of greater significance is the idea of a global ambit of criminal law as an enclosed and governable legal space. Second, there is a recognition that this should not apply to all crimes, but only to those

[84] Criminal Justice Act 1993 Pt.I. see s.4(b). The conduct in question should be criminal under the law of the jurisdiction where the conduct takes place (s.6).

[85] Sex Offenders Act 1997 s.7. See discussion in Hirst, *Jurisdiction*, n.21, pp.268–71.

[86] Terrorism Act 2000 s.1(4). This was passed to comply with the provisions of UN Resolution No.1373. See KL Scheppele, 'The International Standardization of National Security Law' (2010) 4 *Journal of National Security Law and Policy* pp.437–5.

[87] Hirst, *Jurisdiction*, n.21, Ch.2. For a more extended discussion see M McGuire, *Hypercrime. The New Geometry of Harm* (London: Routledge-Cavendish, 2007).

[88] The themes discussed here are based on the tests set out in Home Office, *Review of Extraterritorial Jurisdiction, Steering Committee Report* (London: HMSO, 1996) para.2.21: (1) the offence is serious; (2) by virtue of the nature of the offence, witnesses and evidence are likely to be available within the United Kingdom; (3) there is international consensus as to the reprehensible nature of the crime and the need to take extraterritorial jurisdiction; (4) the vulnerability of the victim makes it particularly important that offences are prosecuted; (5) it is in the interests of the standing and reputation of the United Kingdom within the international community; and (6) there is a danger that such offences would not otherwise be justiciable. See discussion in Hirst, *Jurisdiction*, n.21, Ch.7.

that are considered more serious. In some instances, as we have seen, this applies a principle of double criminality—that the act was criminal both in the jurisdiction where committed and in the UK—but in other areas the claim to jurisdiction is based rather on a claim to international consensus about the morally reprehensible nature of the wrong. The universality of jurisdiction is thus linked to the universality of the wrong.[89] But while this is limiting in certain respects, as not all wrongs are sufficiently serious to meet this criteria, it actually reinforces the idea of gaplessness in relation to serious wrongs. Third, jurisdiction is claimed in the name of the vulnerability of certain victims or groups of victims and the need to extend the protection of the law to the vulnerable, wherever they are. This is linked to a logic of right—the rights of the victims must be protected. Finally, it is clear that the over-riding concern is with dangerous offenders, or the dangerous consequences of allowing serious offenders to escape with impunity.[90] Although the growth of jurisdiction is justified in the language of rights and the universality of wrongs, it serves the ends of prevention and security and leads to a growth of the criminal law.

This should lead us to view some developments in the area of universal jurisdiction with a degree of caution. Such jurisdiction may be justifiable in relation to a small number of genuinely international serious crimes, where states have a shared common interest in proscribing and prosecuting that conduct. Otherwise the tendency is expansionary and potentially riddled with problems, particularly where it goes beyond the claim to legislate or proscribe conduct to claims about enforceability and punishment. The question, for now, is not so much about the content of the wrongs as the logic of jurisdiction and criminalization, but we will need to return later to claims about the universalizability of moral wrongs as a proper basis for criminalization.

V. Conclusion

It is clear that, as I argued at the start of the chapter, jurisdiction in the sense of the ambit of the criminal law is central to the question of criminalization. This is so both in the sense that it is fundamental to an understanding of the scope of the criminal law, and also because it can assist in the explanation of the process of criminalization. An assertion of jurisdiction requires a claim that there is an order which has been breached by something which can be regarded as a crime, and that that order is entitled to respond to the breach in some way. It is arguable that this latter dimension is at least being recognized in recent debates in international law around international crimes or crimes against humanity and universal jurisdiction. Here there is a clear recognition of the relation between jurisdiction

[89] See e.g. C Ryngaert, *Jurisdiction in International Law* (Oxford: Oxford UP, 2008) p.101: 'the nature of the act in itself may confer jurisdiction on any state'.

[90] Ryngaert, *Jurisdiction*, n.89, p.107.

and the definition of the offence: the recognition of a crime against humanity invokes the existence of a community of humanity with shared norms and in whose name the law can act.[91] This, however, has not been recognized in the case of 'ordinary' crimes, where the ambit of the law has been regarded as a primarily technical question. The process of expansion of the law in the extraterritorial application of criminal offences is seen as a matter of the expediency or enforcement of the law and proceeds without comment in relation to the perception of particular threats—currently terrorism, child internet pornography, and sex tourism—continuing a pattern that, as I have shown, was established in the nineteenth century. While the proper response to this might be seen as the attempt to set jurisdiction on a more rational basis, the analysis developed here suggests that this can only be done by considering the relation to institutional purpose, the ends of particular areas of law and the types of space that are to be regulated.

I want to conclude with two further observations based on the argument here. First, it should now be clear that the question of the proper scope of the criminal law cannot be considered as an abstract issue relating to the qualities of certain conduct, without reference to the institution of the criminal law. The argument of this chapter has been that jurisdiction, in the sense of the ambit of the criminal law, opens an important perspective not only on how that institution has developed, but also on how the scope of the law is linked to certain institutional ends. It follows that the proper scope of the law, the question of the rightness or legitimacy of the use of the criminal law for certain purposes is inextricably linked to the purposes of the institution of criminal law in particular places. Second, I have shown that while there is a relationship between space and place and the scope of the criminal law, what is distinctive, though, about the emergence of the modern criminal law is the growing assertion of completeness and universality. This has an internal and an external dimension since the development of criminal law as a distinct and unified body of rules is linked to the organization and homogenization of space.[92] Externally, territorial jurisdiction has been concerned to ensure that it extends to all necessary places. Internally, much of the development of territorial jurisdiction was concerned with the closing of 'loopholes', seeking to ensure that the reach of the law was complete and without exceptions. The development of the institution of criminal law through jurisdiction is thus linked to codification, which we will examine in the next chapter.

[91] See MacMillan, 'Imagining the International: The Constitution of the International as a Site of Crime, Justice and Community' forthcoming *Soc & Leg Stud*.

[92] See Hirst, *Jurisdiction*, n.21, p.324: 'One cannot satisfactorily codify the general principles of English criminal law without considering where or to whom that system of law is to apply.'

hierarchy, tools which enable the users to distinguish between and order relevant practices. These encode expectations about social action, with the aim of controlling or managing uncertainty. This may be done in more or less formal ways—to the extent that norms are fully articulated or written down—but codification in this sense is foundational to the sense of law as a discrete social practice or institution.[5]

This, moreover, is a legal code so it is important to remember that the practices that are being codified are already rules of some sort: the code is a systematization of the norms used in the regulation of social conduct. However, the code must also, at least to some extent, present those norms in a way that is intelligible to ordinary citizens—though the question of the precise balance between legal systematicity, technicality, and intelligibility to non-lawyers will always be a matter of choice for any given codifier. Codification is thus primarily performing two functions. First, a code must render behaviour intelligible to law. Legal and social practices must be described and classified in terms of categories that will allow for the possibility of recognition and intervention.[6] Law must articulate an understanding of the social as a fit object for the governance of rules. The converse of this is also true, that a code should render the legal norms intelligible to those who are subject to them. It should be possible for the individual to order their own actions, by making judgments about what is or is not permissible under law. Second, a code must make the law intelligible to itself. It must ensure the reproducibility of prohibitions and sentences, making possible communication within the legal system—between different legal actors or institutions, or indeed between different rules or concepts.

By describing the process of codification in these terms, we can see that a number of further consequences ensue.[7] First, there is the establishment of normativity. The code is not identical to the custom or practice that it regulates; it must always be a representation.[8] The code in this sense is necessarily an evaluation, a symbolic representation of a social practice, which has an effect on the practice that it codifies by establishing standards, classifying and organizing. Second, this normativity applies not only to the conduct regulated, but to the norms themselves. The standards of the code can make the internal organization of the legal system more efficient, as the production of a written code makes for the possibility of revision and comparison between different rules or across different practices. This allows for the logical control of coherence, the replacement of diachronic by

[5] See discussion in Chapter 1 supra at pp.22–26. N MacCormick, *Institutions of Law* (Oxford: Oxford UP, 2007) Pt.1. On the idea of the coding of communication as constitutive of the legal system, see N Luhmann, *Law as a Social System* (Oxford: Oxford UP, 2004) pp.98–105.

[6] G Deleuze, *Foucault* (Minneapolis: University of Minnesota Press, 1986) p.32: 'Penal law concerns those aspects of criminal material that can be articulated: it is a system of language that classifies and translates offences and calculates sentences; a family of statements that is also a threshold.'

[7] See esp. Bourdieu, *Codification,* n.3, pp.80–1.

[8] P Goodrich, *Reading the Law. A Critical Introduction to Legal Method* (Oxford: Blackwell, 1986) p.27.

synchronic logic. In both of these respects, the practice of codification is reflexive, establishing the possibility (indeed the inevitability) of revisability against whatever internal and external measures are considered important. (Is the code internally consistent? Is it an accurate description of practice? Does the practice of adjudication measure up to the normative standards of the code? Is this an effective way of censuring behaviour?) It is thus important to note that the standards or norms of a code are not necessarily fixed—indeed they may be more or less flexible, and may even incorporate a mechanism that allows for revision of their own content. What is important is that they establish a measure or standard against which legal practice can judge itself. Third, any code in this sense also relies on a cognitive system or system of knowledge.[9] The requirement of system is inherent in the idea of codification: coding is a form of ordering and the success of any given code will depend on its intelligibility to those who are subject to, or use, the code. There must be an understanding, in general terms, of what lies within the field to be regulated and of the properties that the regulated objects and forms of conduct have in common. (This might include seeing general rules of liability as distinct from the definitions of particular crimes, or distinguishing between the elements of individual crimes.) The success of such schema, Douglas suggests, depends on analogy by which the formal structure of social relations can be found in the natural or supernatural world (e.g. a theory of human nature or natural rights) thus becoming endowed with a 'self-validating truth'.[10] System is also related to the issue of comprehensiveness. An extensive listing of rules would run the risk of being unmanageable, while too few rules, or rules of too great a degree of generality, would be difficult to apply. The question of system, then, is related to the degree of technicality of any given code. Of course, a system need not be complex,[11] but, in modern penal codes, system is understood as the need to present a clearly structured and consistent whole of legal rules and principles, promoting the internal coherence of the law.[12] Finally, the written code requires some sort of authorization, whether this means that the code be legitimated in the name of custom or community (common law), its internal coherence or formal rationality, by the status of its author, or its formal enactment by a political body, or by its effectiveness in bringing about a certain aim (such as reducing crime).[13] A code will not be authoritative, will not be accepted as a standard of conduct, unless those who are subject to the code recognize its authority. Thus, the success

[9] M Douglas, *How Institutions Think* (London: Routledge, 1987) Ch.4 on the cognitive processes that are at the foundations of social order. See also GC Bowker & SL Star, *Sorting Things Out. Classification and its Consequences* (London: MIT Press, 1999) Ch.2.

[10] Douglas, *Institutions*, n.9, p.48.

[11] E.g. alphabetical ordering as in the US Federal Code 1949.

[12] The presence of system is also usually understood as marking a difference from the mere collection or consolidation of existing laws. There is also a question here of the aesthetics of codification. Kelly points out that seventeenth century natural lawyers saw codes as a form of 'perfect jurisprudence' and Leibniz drew on Euclidean geometry. D Kelley, *The Human Measure. Social Thought in the Western Legal Tradition* (Cambridge, MA: Harvard UP, 1990) Ch.12.

[13] M Weber, *Economy and Society* (Berkeley: Univ. of California Press, 1978) Ch.III is the classic statement on the forms of legitimation.

or failure of a code will not depend on its coherence or rationality alone, but must also be assessed in terms of its (apparent) legitimacy or its success in coordinating values and functions.[14]

The question at issue, then, is never the purely abstract one of whether or not the law should be codified, but is always that of whether the law should be codified in a certain way, and thus whether or not the new code is in some way 'better' than already existing codifications. This, incidentally, also addresses one of the issues that surround many codification initiatives: whether the codification can simply restate the law without amendment or whether it necessarily involves legal change or reform.[15] This understanding of codification would imply that as a minimum, while substantive rules of law may simply be restated, there is necessarily a reclassification or reorganization at a conceptual level (either the form or the source of the law).[16] In the absence of this there is merely repetition. The issue is thus much more than the question of whether law should take the form of legislation as opposed to common law. The common law is already codified, and a conceptual reorganization, such as might be undertaken by treatise writers, would recodify the law.[17] These codifications have been achieved on the basis of a certain view of the functions of the law, understandings of efficiency and legitimacy, and according to a certain logic or system. New codes are normally a response to certain perceived failings: a lack of logical coherence, a failure in the normative structure; a failure of legitimacy (that it should be authorized in the name of Parliament or reason rather than that of the individual writer or custom); or indeed whether a recodification might simply make the law function better. The demand for codification will thus be expected to arise from actual or perceived shortcomings in the existing practice of co-ordination or legitimacy of the law.

If this clarifies the concept of codification generally, it is important to recognize that the question of codification has acquired a particular significance in modernity where the term refers to legislation of a particular kind: the production of a universal and complete body of rules which is intended to replace all pre-existing norms.[18] This understanding of legislation as the primary agent of legal change

[14] These are described by Niki Lacey as the functions of criminal law in co-ordinating knowledge and values. See 'In Search of the Responsible Subject: History, Philosophy and the Social Sciences in Criminal Law Theory' (2001) 64 *Mod LR* pp.350–71.

[15] Although the claim that a code is not changing the law is probably normally a matter of trying to make the code more acceptable politically. Cf. J Austin, *Lectures on Jurisprudence* (5th edn) (London: John Murray, 1885) II, 1026: 'Codification of existing law, and innovation upon the substance of existing law, are perfectly distinct; although a code may happen to be wholly or partially new in matter as well as in form.'

[16] And while this is the minimum, it is hard to conceive of codification which addresses issues of co-ordination which does not also require some changes to substantive rules to achieve greater consistency and coherence.

[17] See MD & A Fernandez (eds), *Law Books in Action,* n.2. For a slightly different analysis of 'non-legislative codifications' focusing on texts which identify themselves as 'codes' see N Jansen, *The Making of Legal Authority* (Oxford: Oxford UP, 2010) esp. Ch.2.

[18] Though the idea of a legal code stretches back to antiquity, the idea of a universal legislative code replacing all existing law is distinctively modern. The term codification was coined by Jeremy Bentham in the early nineteenth century, specifically because he sought to distinguish his project

is, as we have seen, closely connected to the development of the modern criminal law.[19] Given this significance, it will be necessary to look at the question of codification as legislation, but before doing so I want to examine how the modern criminal law has been codified in other forms of legal literature.

III. Legal Literature: Treatises and Textbooks

A. Treatises

There was an extensive literature on crimes and punishments in the early nineteenth century, with the range and variety of texts suggesting wide public interest in matters relating to crime and penal law.[20] However, while much of this literature spoke to a general concern that the law was complex and in need of organization, there was no settled understanding of criminal law as a distinct body of rules or of the best or most practical scheme for ordering the law.[21]

The dominant understanding was of criminal law as Pleas of the Crown, a view of the law shaped by Sir Matthew Hale's *History of the Pleas of the Crown*, which had been first published in 1736.[22] This dealt only with the most serious criminal offences—varieties of treason, homicide, and theft. These were discussed in a systematic way, treating issues relating to criminal capacity in a separate chapter and following a clear hierarchy of offences.[23] The book established a 'standard of orthodoxy',[24] going through four editions in the eighteenth century with later editors adding discussion of recent case law and statutes.[25] A work of similar standing and importance was Hawkins' *Treatise of Pleas of the Crown* (1716–21), which went through seven editions in the eighteenth century, with the last edition being

from other kinds of legislation in terms of the features identified below. See J Dinwiddy, *Bentham. Selected Writing of John Dinwiddy* (Stanford: Stanford UP, 2003) p.47.

19 See Ch.3.

20 For a fuller discussion see L Farmer, 'On Treatises and Textbooks. The Literature of the Criminal Law in Nineteenth-Century Britain' in Dubber & Fernandez, *Law Books in Action*, n.2, Ch.7.

21 See D Lieberman, 'Mapping Criminal Law: Blackstone and the Categories of English Jurisprudence' in N Landau (ed.), *Law, Crime and English Society 1660–1830* (Cambridge: Cambridge UP, 2002) pp.140–2.

22 M Hale, *The History of the Pleas of the Crown* (2 vols.) (London: Printed by E. Rider, 1800).

23 From treason to homicide, to grand and petit larceny, then other felonies. See Proemium for an explanation and plan of the work. This was stretching the original meaning of Pleas of the Crown as actions at common law in which the Crown formally appeared as the prosecutor. See also AWB Simpson, 'The Rise and Fall of the Legal Treatise: Legal Principles and the Forms of Legal Literature' (1981) 48 *Univ. of Chicago LR* 632–79 at p.640 on Hale.

24 A Amos, *Ruins of Time Exemplified in Sir Matthew Hale's History of the Pleas of the Crown* (London: V & R Stevens & GS Norton, 1856) p.1. He went on to describe Hale as a 'Pope of Criminal Law' (p.1) installed so as to exonerate the community from a multitude and diversity of opinions.

25 The last edition was published in 1800, with annotations on new statutes and cases 'appended at the bottoms of pages…like barnacles adhering to the bottoms of ships' (Amos, *Ruins of Time*, n.24, p.xxv).

published in 1824.[26] This largely followed the schema laid down by Hale, though with more extensive treatment of offences against religion and more detailed discussion of the substantive law.[27] The most direct successor to these works was East's *A Treatise of Pleas of the Crown* published in two volumes in 1803.[28] While East made a claim to innovation for his own work, the subject matter, Pleas of the Crown, and arrangement followed in the footsteps of Hale and Hawkins.[29] The first volume dealt with offences against religion, morality and the church; treason; offences against coin and bullion; homicide; assaults and maiming; rape and marriage; and sodomy. The second volume was largely concerned with offences against property (burglary, larceny, piracy, forgery, arson, and malicious mischief). It was thus broader in coverage than its predecessors, and, in drawing extensively on unpublished judicial notes, it provided the practitioner with access to recent case law.[30]

In addition to this literature dealing with serious crimes, there was a substantial literature aimed at the practising magistrate, which dealt largely with misdemeanours, recognized as penal, but not formally part of the law of crimes. The principal text in this area was Burn's *Justice of the Peace*, first published in 1755, which went through thirty editions by 1869 and which covered the full range of the law relating to civil and criminal matters to which a magistrate might have to refer.[31] It was organized alphabetically by subject, with cross-referencing where necessary. This kind of text was intended to be the sole or principal source of reference for Justices of the Peace, who might not have access to any other law books or reports, giving them access to a simple and up-to-date account of the law on any matter within their jurisdiction, and directing them in the exercise of their powers.[32]

This was largely a practical literature for a system in which the local lay courts were dominant, and in which the defence lawyer was, for the most part, absent from the criminal trial.[33] As this began to change in the early nineteenth century, there was a need for a literature of criminal law which could make it readily accessible to the emerging national criminal bar. It was in this context that the

[26] W Hawkins, *Treatise of Pleas of the Crown: Or a System of the Principal Matters Related to that Subject, Divided under the Proper Heads* (2 vols) (London: n.p. 1716–21). See also M Foster, *Crown Law* (3rd edn, ed. M Dodson) (London: E & R Brooke, 1762).

[27] Later editions became increasingly unwieldy, as annotations were added, with the fourth edition running to four volumes.

[28] EH East, *A Treatise of Pleas of the Crown* (2 vols) (London: Butterworths, 1803).

[29] East, *Treatise*, n.28, p.x.

[30] KJM Smith, *Lawyers, Legislators and Theorists* (Oxford: Oxford UP, 1998) pp.69–70 describes it as an 'up to date, fairly comprehensive, and accessible statement of the substantive law'. East used eleven sets of judicial notes: see Amos, *Ruins of Time*, n.24, p.5.

[31] See J Phillips, 'A Low Law Counter-Treatise? "Absentees" to "Wreck" in British North America's First Justice of the Peace Manual' in Dubber & Fernandez, *Law Books in Action*, n.2, Ch.10, for a discussion of these manuals and the 'low law' they covered. See also JA Conley, 'Doing it by the book: Justice of the Peace Manuals and English Law in Eighteenth-Century America' (1985) 6 *Jnl of Lg Hist* p.257.

[32] Farmer, 'Treatises and Textbooks', n.20, p.152.

[33] See J Langbein, *The Origins of the Adversary Criminal Trial* (Oxford: Oxford UP, 2005); DJA Cairns, *Advocacy and the Making of the Adversarial Criminal Trial* (Oxford: Oxford UP, 1999).

treatise emerged as the dominant form of legal writing, defining and organizing the field of criminal law over the course of the nineteenth century.[34] However, while Simpson has stressed the rationalizing and scientific aims of treatise writers, organizing their works around principles or the identification of an underlying conceptual structure, criminal law treatises were overwhelmingly practical in focus, written by practising lawyers and aimed at practitioners, and largely unconcerned with the matters of principle and structure.[35] Typical of these were Archbold's *Summary of the Law Relative to Pleading and Evidence in Criminal Cases* (1824) and Joseph Chitty's *Practical Treatise on the Criminal Law* (1816).[36] These books followed a similar schema, dealing first with rules of pleading and evidence generally, before dealing with these same topics in relation to particular crimes. Neither book offered much by way of conceptual or structural innovation, but they were comprehensive, practical, and accessible.[37]

A somewhat more systematic treatment, focused only on the substantive law can be found in WO Russell's *Treatise on Crimes and Misdemeanors* first published in two volumes in 1819.[38] What was novel about this book was that it covered crimes, rather than Pleas of the Crown: all indictable offences with the exception of treason, which was excluded on the grounds of space and because prosecutions were so infrequent, and a number of serious misdemeanours.[39] Russell's key innovation in organization was the method of grouping offences together under the broad heads of government, person and property, reflecting the practical importance of these categories of crime rather than the traditional schema of seriousness under the Pleas of the Crown.[40] There was a short treatment of criminal capacity

[34] See Simpson, 'Legal Treatise', n.23.

[35] See Simpson, 'Legal Treatise', n.23, p.664 on the backgrounds of treatise writers. See also W Cornish, 'Sources of Law' in W Cornish et al., *The Oxford History of the Laws of England* vol.XI *1820-1914 English Legal System* (Oxford: Oxford UP, 2010) pp.59–61.

[36] JF Archbold, *A Summary of the Law Relative to Pleading and Evidence in Criminal Cases: With Precedents of Indictments &c. and the Evidence Necessary to Support them* (London: Pheney, 1824); J Chitty, *A Practical Treatise on the Criminal Law, Comprising the Practice, Pleadings and Evidence which Occur in the Course of Criminal Prosecutions etc.* (4 vols.) (London: Butterworth & son, 1816). For biographical details see EI Carlyle, 'Archbold, John Frederick (1785–1870)', rev M Lobban, *Oxford Dictionary of National Biography* (Oxford, Oxford UP, 2004) [www.oxforddnb.com/view/article/614, accessed 2 October 2010]; M Lobban, 'Chitty, Joseph, the elder (1775–1841)', *Oxford Dictionary of National Biography* (Oxford, Oxford UP, 2004) [www.oxforddnb.com/view/article/5336, accessed 4 October 2010].

[37] See also T Starkie, *A Treatise on Criminal Pleading* (London: W Clarke & Sons, 1814), which covered similar ground to Archbold and Chitty.

[38] WO Russell, *A Treatise on Crimes and Indictable Misdemeanors* (London: J Butterworth, 1819). For biographical details see KJM Smith, 'Russell, Sir William Oldnall (c.1784–1833)', *Oxford Dictionary of National Biography* (Oxford: Oxford UP, 2004) [www.oxforddnb.com/view/article/24354, accessed 2 October 2010].

[39] See Russell, *Treatise*, n.38, Preface to 1st edn.

[40] It was divided into five books. Book I dealt with persons capable of committing crimes and principals and accessories (70 pp); Book II with offences against government, public peace, and public right (550 pp); Book III with offences against the persons of individuals (290 pp); Book IV with offences against public or private property (850 pp); and Book V dealt with offences which could affect the persons of individuals or property (principally, subornation of perjury and conspiracy) (100 pp). It is notable that Archbold dealt with crimes in the two broad categories of offences

and principals and accessories at the start of the book, but this was dwarfed by the lengthy sections on offences against government and property, cataloguing the vast compendia of early-nineteenth-century common law and legislation; the section on offences against individuals was short by comparison. The other key feature of the book was its extensive citation of recent case law, virtually without authorial comment, frequently drawing on unpublished judicial manuscripts. What was significant about this was that, in the absence of reliable case reporting, the *Treatise* actually became a source of case law. This sense of Russell's *Treatise* becoming, if not the source of the law, at least the main point of access to the sources of the law, is confirmed in a letter by Mr Justice Coleridge to the Lord Chancellor:

> At present, the student reads his Russell, or, it may be, East: he refers to Hale and Hawkins: he studies the Crown Cases Reserved which have been published since the last edition of Russell; and he easily keeps up, and notes in his Russell the two or three numbers which may come out in a year of the decisions of the Court of Criminal Appeal. This is no very laborious or expensive course.[41]

In the Preface to the third edition, for example, the editor commented that he had aimed to follow the system of Russell and in particular his method of citing case law so as to provide a clear view of the facts and the decision. He went on to say: 'Particular attention has been paid to this point, in order to render the work useful on occasions where a question suddenly arises in the course of a trial, or where there may not be the means of referring to the Reports from which the cases are taken.'[42] The work thus provided an invaluable resource for the practitioner: comprehensive and up-to-date, accurate and accessible, but without unnecessary discussion or commentary.

These treatises were extremely successful. Russell went through twelve editions in total, six of which were published in the nineteenth century.[43] Archbold went through a staggering twenty-one editions in the nineteenth century alone, and continues to be published today.[44] It is thus important to reflect on the qualities that contributed to this success. First of all, the law was conceived of primarily as a practical subject, and utility to the practitioner was the organizing principle both in terms of structure and substance. They had the 'quality of unity' that Simpson identified as the defining characteristic of the legal treatise.[45] This, however, was

against individuals and offences against government. Cf. Chitty who adhered to a more traditional schema (religion, state, public peace, and finally individuals).

[41] Cited in Amos, *Ruins of Time*, n.24, p.xxiv. See also A May, *The Bar and the Old Bailey* (Chapel Hill: The University of North Carolina Press, 2006) pp.77–8. On law reporting in the nineteenth century see P Polden, 'The Education of Lawyers' in W Cornish et al., *The Oxford History of the Laws of England* vol.XI *1820–1914 English Legal System* (Oxford: Oxford UP, 2010) pp.1211–22.

[42] Russell, *Treatise* (3rd edn, 1843) (ed. CS Greaves) Preface. Greaves, the editor of the 3rd and 4th editions, was also the main drafter of the criminal law consolidation Acts of 1861.

[43] The final edition being published in 1964.

[44] Simpson ('Legal Treatise', n.23, p.664) describes this as both the most successful of all the nineteenth-century treatises and 'possibly the worst of the lot'.

[45] Simpson, 'Legal Treatise', n.23, p.633.

less a matter of conceptual refinement or definition, than the broad positivist assumption that the criminal law was that which was dealt with by the criminal courts. In this there was a clear difference from both the approach of Blackstone, who sought a conceptual definition of crime in terms of public wrong, or earlier writers on Pleas of the Crown, who took a procedural feature as the defining characteristic of the law. This was still an approach which saw the field as the law of crimes, albeit more broadly conceived than Pleas of the Crown, rather than an idea of criminal law organized around a unifying principle or set of concepts. This stress on practice, however, did produce some interesting differences in scope, from their predecessors and from each other. The practical treatises could exclude unimportant offences such as treason, but in the interests of practical utility could also include misdemeanours where necessary. The different writers also struggled with the question of whether and how to include procedure.[46] Russell excluded procedure, except as relating to prosecution of particular crimes, but (from the second edition) included coverage of evidence; Chitty and Archbold were both framed wholly by procedure and saw the substantive law through procedural issues. On this view of law then, rules of substantive law could not be articulated wholly independently of their procedural context.

This approach reflected an important understanding of the criminal law in nineteenth-century England, one which was supported by the judiciary and used to defend the criminal law against proposed innovations such as the establishment of a Court of Criminal Appeal or the codification of the law.[47] What these initiatives shared was the idea they could, in different ways, contribute to the development of a settled and uniform criminal law by articulating substantive laws independently of particular cases or procedural contexts. Against this, the judiciary argued for the primacy of the jury trial as the 'focal point of the Victorian criminal justice system' and that reforms would risk undermining the independence of the jury or the finality of their decision.[48] While the law might be muddled and complex, the judiciary nonetheless retained their faith in it as a practical system, and in the ability of the jury trial to deliver clear public messages which would deter others from committing crime. The legitimacy of the system thus continued to be understood in terms of the expressive quality of the trial and the role of the jury in securing wider public support.[49] This was supported by the understanding of the criminal law being developed in the treatise. As the number of courts and cases increased with the rise of organized policing, and as lawyers 'entered' the criminal trial, there was a clear need for some sort of common understanding to replace the localized understandings that had given form

[46] Ibid., p.634 excludes from consideration those works whose structure is determined primarily by procedure.

[47] P Handler, 'The Court for Crown Cases Reserved, 1848-1908' (2011) 29 *Law & Hist Rev* p.259.

[48] Handler, 'Crown Cases Reserved', n.47, p.267. He goes on to argue that even after the Court of Crown Cases Reserved was established in 1848 judges 'consistently refused to stray beyond the specific facts of the case reserved to articulate anything approaching a general principle' (p.282).

[49] See e.g. JF Stephen, *A General View of the Criminal Law of England* (London: Macmillan, 1863) p.208; Handler, 'Crown Cases Reserved', n.47, pp.269–71.

to the criminal law up to that point. The importance of the treatise literature here was as a form of *de facto* codification of the criminal law, as a means of solving the co-ordination problems and ensuring that the law was applied according to the same standards and using the same authorities across the country. The publication of these texts and the availability of more systematic law reports, even if these were still fairly limited, allowed for the communication of knowledge about the criminal law in a reasonably standardized form. These works then played an important, and unacknowledged, role in synthesizing the criminal law and provided a means of transmitting knowledge about an increasingly formalized criminal law and procedure as they went through multiple editions in the course of the century. The achievement of the treatise, then, was the codification of practical knowledge, and of the idea of criminal law as a practical subject.

B. Textbooks

The literature of the criminal law began to change significantly over the course of the twentieth century. Of particular significance was the emergence of the textbook, written for students in the new university-based law degree. These courses created a demand for reasonably short, organized treatments of particular bodies of law with greater stress on principles and conceptual organization for didactic purposes.

Throughout the course of the nineteenth century legal education was primarily practice-based, with teaching at the university law schools largely moribund.[50] There were, however, many critics of this system and repeated attempts to put legal education on a more formal and systematic basis, both through the professional organizations and the universities.[51] This pressure began to bear fruit towards the end of the century as the older universities began to teach law courses—even if this was still piecemeal and dependent on the initiatives of individual professors and scholars. This new style of law teaching was aimed at building professional legitimacy through the conception of the discipline of law as a special kind of knowledge.[52] On this view law was more than just a practical vocation or an aggregation of authorities, but had a kind of internal coherence or underlying rationality which required a new kind of legal science to understand it.[53] This

[50] A law degree was not a pre-requisite of entering the profession. See generally Polden, 'Education', n.41, pp.1175–85; CW Brooks & M Lobban, 'Apprenticeship or Academy? The Idea of a Law University, 1830–1860' in JA Bush and A Wijffels (eds), *Learning the Law: Teaching and the Transmission of Law in England, 1150-1900* (London: Hambledon Press, 1999) pp.353–82; W Twining, *Blackstone's Tower. The English Law School* (London: Sweet & Maxwell, 1994) Ch.2 argues that university law teaching was mainly a post-war creation.

[51] Witnesses to the 1846 Select Committee on Legal Education criticized lack of scientific literature as compared with the continent: Polden, 'Education', n.41, p.1181. Law reports were seen as encouraging a memory-based system: Brooks & Lobban, 'Apprenticeship', n.50, pp.370–1.

[52] D Sugarman, 'Legal Theory, the Common Law Mind and the Making of the Textbook Tradition' in W Twining (ed.), *Legal Theory and Common Law* (Oxford: Blackwell, 1986).

[53] Sugarman, 'The Common Law Mind', n.52, pp.29–33, pp.44–6 also noting the influence of German legal science, in particular through the influence of John Austin, on English legal thought.

led to the emergence of a new kind of literature, the legal textbook. Textbooks in the UK took up and modified the treatise tradition, developing a scientific literature, written by academics for law students rather than practitioners, and often published by university presses rather than professional law publishers. The pragmatic aim of utility through comprehensiveness was replaced by a pedagogical simplification, which sought to identify principles and eventually present a more programmatic and conceptual understanding of the law.[54]

In criminal law the first work of this new type was CS Kenny's *Outlines of Criminal Law*, based on lectures that he gave at the University of Cambridge. First published in 1902, this had already gone through nine editions by 1918, and was to go through nineteen in total.[55] He also published one of the first casebooks for students on English criminal law.[56] Both the *Outlines* and the *Cases* had two important features, which drew on his experience of teaching law in a university: a focus on case law, and a clarity and accessibility in organization and style. In respect of the first, the important differences from the earlier treatises were a reduction in the number of cases cited, and a clearer focus on the principles they represented.[57] This focus on cases, though, also served to promote a view of the criminal law as being based around a core of common law principles.[58] However, in terms of organization and content, the book represented a clear shift from the earlier treatises. It retained a practical focus—Kenny presenting it as suitable either for law students or a Justice of the Peace—but it was more selective in coverage and contained more discussion of principle and, in particular, of questions of responsibility.[59] The book began with seven general chapters, two of which were explicitly about responsibility.[60] His discussion was framed in terms of a general principle that proof of a crime required both voluntary conduct and intention,

[54] See S Waddams, 'Nineteenth-Century Treatises on English Contract Law' in Dubber & Fernandez, *Law Books in Action*, n.2, Ch.6.

[55] CS Kenny, *Outlines of Criminal Law* (Cambridge: Cambridge UP, 1902). Kenny was Downing Professor of English Law at the University of Cambridge from 1907–1918. For biographical details, see AL Goodhart, 'Kenny, Courtney Stanhope (1847–1930)', rev Richard A Cosgrove, *Oxford Dictionary of National Biography* (Oxford, Oxford UP, 2004) [www.oxforddnb.com/view/article/34287, accessed 9 October 2010].

[56] CS Kenny, *A Selection of Cases Illustrative of Criminal Law* (Cambridge: Cambridge UP, 1901). See his generally appreciative discussion of Langdell's case method: 'The Case Method of Teaching Law' (1916) 16 *Journal of the Society of Comparative Legislation* pp.182–94.

[57] 'Elementary students who read the Reports under their own guidance are prone to reverse the true order of things, by attending to the names of cases rather than their facts, and to the facts rather than to the principles decided.' Kenny, *Selection*, n.56, Preface.

[58] Cf. Sugarman, '*The Common Law Mind'*, n.52, pp.34–5 noting the hostility of the textbook tradition to legislation as a source of law. Cf. the casebook method in the US: B Kimball, 'The Proliferation of Case Method Teaching in American Law Schools: Mr Langdell's "Emblematic Abomination" 1890–1915' (2006) 46 *Hist of Ed Quarterly* pp.192–247.

[59] Kenny, *Outlines*, n.55, p.vii. See also Smith, *Lawyers*, n.30, pp.189–90.

[60] These were on 'The Mental Element in Crime' and 'Exemptions from Liability'. The other general chapters were on the 'Characteristics of a Crime'; the 'Purpose of Criminal Punishment'; 'Inchoate Crimes'; 'Parties to Crime'; and the 'Classification of Crime'. It is also noteworthy that the chapter on punishment discussed retribution as an aim of punishment. See also Smith, *Lawyers*, n.30, pp.152–7 on precursors to Kenny, though these were principally general textbooks on jurisprudence.

while acknowledging that this general rule was subject to exceptions.[61] This was followed by a long section on the definitions of particular crimes (beginning with homicide and crimes against property), as well as shorter sections introducing criminal evidence and procedure. The *Outlines* then concluded with a brief discussion of contemporary developments in criminology. The book thus combined the case law focus of the treatise tradition with a more modern sense of legal and penological science.

A second important figure in this development was JWC Turner, also at the University of Cambridge, who from the 1930s onwards began to promote the idea of subjective fault, drawing on sources such as the reports of the Criminal Law Commissioners of 1833–45.[62] The vehicle that Turner adopted for his project was his new editions of the classic treatises of Russell in 1950 and Kenny in 1952, which were restructured and rewritten to include longer sections on subjective fault.[63] In an important shift of emphasis, he also wrote from a more avowedly 'censorial' perspective, criticizing authority where it did not accord with his account of the pre-established principles of fault. *Russell on Crimes* was rewritten so that it became a book about the substantive law, dramatically extending the first section on criminal liability and excluding discussion of evidence and procedure. Beyond this, it remained full in its treatment of specific offences, though there is no evidence of any attempt to apply the novel conceptual schema of liability outwith the law of homicide. Overall, though, there was a shift in tone from the book merely reporting authorities to discussing and analyzing them. This reflected the fact not only that law reporting was becoming more systematic, but also that the Court of Appeal, following its establishment in 1907 was now engaged in the more systematic discussion and review of substantive rules independently of their context in particular trials.

The most influential and important textbook of the postwar period was Smith & Hogan's *Criminal Law* (1965).[64] The first significant change that it made was in dealing only with the substantive criminal law, and even then by being selective and only focusing on the more 'important' crimes—beginning with homicide and offences against the person and proceeding through property offences to

[61] See Kenny, *Outlines*, n.55, Ch.3, pp.37–8.

[62] JWC Turner, 'The Mental Element in Crimes at Common Law' (1936) *Camb LJ* p.31 republished in L Radzinowicz and JWC Turner (eds), *The Modern Approach to Criminal Law* (London: Macmillan, 1945). See Smith, *Lawyers*, n.30, pp.297–304. See infra Ch.6 at pp.183–5 for analysis of his approach to subjective liability.

[63] He edited four editions of Kenny, with the last being produced in 1966, and two editions of Russell (1950 and 1958). See Smith, *Lawyers*, n.30, pp.301–4 describing Turner's 'conceptual colonisation' of Russell and Kenny. See also R Cross & A Jones, *An Introduction to Criminal Law* (London: Butterworths, 1948).

[64] JC Smith & B Hogan, *Criminal Law* (London: Butterworths, 1965). It is currently in its 13th edition. They also published a casebook: *Criminal Law: Cases and Materials* (London: Butterworth, 1975). Other books published around this time included PJ Fitzgerald, *Criminal Law and Punishment* (Oxford: Clarendon, 1962); G Williams, *Textbook on Criminal Law* (London: Steven & Sons, 1978). In Scotland GH Gordon, *The Criminal Law of Scotland* (Edinburgh: W Green & Son, 1967) is comparable in scope and ambition to Smith & Hogan.

offences against morals, public order, and state security. The criteria for selection were not explained, and while there was a chapter on road traffic offences suggesting a sense of practical importance, the emphasis was firmly on crimes against person and property.[65] The exclusion of evidence law was justified on the grounds that it was a 'worthy subject of academic study in its own right', while criminal procedure was just excluded without comment.[66] A second significant change in focus was signalled by the initial chapter on the general aims of the criminal law. Here they argued that the aims of the law were to be understood in terms of the aims or purposes of punishment: criminal law was not 'an end itself' for its object was conviction and sentence of offenders and that it must be justified in those terms.[67] Punishment, they argued, was then justified in terms of retribution (understood as a combination of vengeance and desert), the proportionality of punishment to the crime, and the protection of the public. This thus importantly frames an understanding of the criminal law in terms of the need for justification, even if this was only in the narrow terms of the justification of punishment. This also establishes the function of the book as more than merely exposition: the rules of criminal law must be justified, establishing the basis for a more critical engagement with the institution of criminal law. Third, the form of the book, was also strikingly different from previous works as, following the lead of Glanville Williams, the general principles were separated from the substantive law.[68] The first part of the book thus covered the elements of a crime, strict liability, modes of participation, defences, attempts, and inchoate crimes. This analytical framework was also carried through into more systematic analysis of individual crimes, formally distinguishing between the elements of *actus reus* and *mens rea*, with the focus on *mens rea* in particular leading the authors to identify and criticize a substantial number of 'anomalies' in the law. This was thus a systematic development of Williams' subjectivist project.[69] This was also one of the first books explicitly to analyse excusing and justifying conditions as general defences. Prior to this, circumstances such as mental abnormality, insanity, intoxication or duress were principally discussed in terms of their impact on *mens rea*, and rules on self defence or necessity were looked at only in the context of the law of homicide.[70] A final important feature of the book, which established its authority as it went through further editions, was the extensive and critical discussion of recent decisions of the Court of Appeal and the House of Lords.[71] While this was always respectful, it nonetheless did not hold back from delivering a damning verdict on

[65] The current (13th edition) is twice as long, but contains even less coverage of offences against the state.

[66] Smith & Hogan, *Criminal Law*, n.64, Preface.

[67] Ibid., p.3.

[68] The authors acknowledge their debt to Williams. Another important influence is J Hall, *General Principles of Criminal Law* (1947) (2nd edn Indianapolis: Bobbs Merrill, 1960).

[69] For discussion of Williams, see Chapter 3 pp.89–103.

[70] See Smith & Hogan, *Criminal Law*, n.64, Ch.8; Fitzgerald, *Criminal Law*, n.64, Ch.4.

[71] See notably the analysis of *DPP v Smith* [1961] AC 290, a case which was to become something of a *cause célèbre* for subjectivist analysis of *mens rea* at pp.183–94 of the first edition.

the state of the law where this was felt to be necessary. Overall this was a striking reversal in the relation between practitioner and academic text, as they argued that they had sought to make the book useful to practitioners, by including a more extensive citation of authorities than would otherwise have been necessary for students.[72]

Smith & Hogan established the template for a new kind of textbook literature that was systematic, analytical, and critical—and subsequent textbooks have not departed significantly from this model, even where the substantive focus or scope has been different. This codifies a new kind of understanding of the criminal law. Criminal law is understood as a systematic form of knowledge, unified around a certain understanding of general principles of criminal liability rather than practice. It is a body of substantive rules, articulated independently of context in procedure and the task for analysis is to understand the systemic quality of these rules. The law is presented as something that is developed and regulated by the decisions of appellate courts. Textbooks cover less of the scope of the substantive criminal law, partly for pedagogical reasons, but also because the focus is on crimes which illustrate or develop the principles of the law.[73] Completeness is thus conceived less in terms of thoroughness than as a contribution to a theoretical 'whole'. These 'paradigmatic crimes' have acquired a greater symbolic significance in the analysis of the law, while other crimes are analysed in terms of their 'fit' with this model. This has had implications for thinking about decriminalization, as certain areas—notably strict liability—are judged to be inconsistent with principle; it has also, as I shall argue in Part III, had consequences for criminalization. This is thus a critical literature, analysing and judging the law according to its systematic quality, but also in terms of whether the law is justified in terms of the aims of punishment. This is done in a more or less theoretical way in different books, but generally speaking there has been a focus on the philosophical justification of punishment, which has then been used to challenge the legitimacy of contemporary criminal law. In a final historical twist these new textbook writers and their works have been a major influence on the English codification initiatives of the late twentieth century in their attempts to establish the legitimacy of the criminal law on new foundations.

IV. Codes

As I noted above, the idea of codification in modern law is linked to legislation. Codification, as a form of legislation, is understood as central to the project of producing a rational and modern form of government: the idea of the code is the

[72] Smith & Hogan, *Criminal Law*, n.64, Preface.

[73] A notable illustration of this was the exclusion of the area of property crimes from the 1st edition of Clarkson & Keating because, in the view of the authors, there were no principles in this area of law. See *Criminal Law: Text and Materials* (1st edn) (London: Sweet & Maxwell, 1984) p.v.

expression of particular forms of legal rationalism. This also reflects two important transformations in understandings of the authority and legitimacy of law: that a sovereign people are the authors of the law, through the legislature; and a modern understanding of the rule of law, as general and binding even on its authors.[74] But if codification has been understood in this way as a vehicle for institutionalizing liberal beliefs about the rule of law and legality, the form of legislative codes is authoritarian, establishing mechanisms for the close and detailed regulation of individual and social bodies. While efforts to codify English criminal law in the form of legislation have been notoriously unsuccessful, the impact of codification initiatives on the development of the law has none the less been profound, and it is thus necessary to understand more about the types of codification.

A. Benthamite Codes

The modern concept of codification was decisively shaped by the work of Jeremy Bentham and his idea of the *pannomion*.[75] This was conceived as a complete body of law: 'a man need but open the book in order to inform himself what the aspect borne by the law bears to every imaginable act that can come within the possible sphere of human agency'.[76] This code was to be built on a science of legislation, which unified a theory of action, a theory of law, and a theory of punishment. This science began from the premise that the failures of the law could be attributed directly to the form of the common law. For Bentham, common law was not law, and could not be law, because it did not emanate from the sovereign but from judges; the law that was produced was arbitrary, in the sense that it was not clearly stated in advance; and it was stated in technical and obscure language.[77] Law for Bentham, by contrast, was legislation, imposed from outside, according to empirical criteria, that would also shape the institutions of government.[78] Although it might respect the existing common law, in terms of its content or arrangement, this was a matter of legislative policy and, in principle, the sovereign legislator could make law as they chose.[79] The *pannomion*,

[74] See JH Merryman, *The Civil Law Tradition* (2nd edn) (Stanford: Stanford UP, 1985) Ch.5; S Skinner, 'Tainted Law? The Italian Penal Code, Fascism and Democracy' (2011) 7 *Intnl Jnl of Law in Context* p.435.

[75] J Bentham, *An Introduction to the Principles and Morals of Legislation* (*IPML*)(1789) (ed. JH Burns & HLA Hart) (Oxford: Oxford UP, 1982) p.305. See generally D Lieberman, *The Province of Legislation Determined* (New York: Cambridge UP, 1989) Chs.11–13. For a broad survey of modern codification see G Weiss, 'The Enchantment of Codification in the Common Law World' (2000) 25 *Yale Jnl of Intnl Law* pp.435–532. See also L Farmer, 'Codification' in MD Dubber & T Hörnle (eds), *Oxford Handbook of Criminal Law* (Oxford: Oxford UP, 2014).

[76] J Bentham, *Of Laws in General* (ed. HLA Hart) (London: Athlone Press, 1970) p.246.

[77] His critique of the common law was most clearly articulated in *A Fragment on Government* (Cambridge: Cambridge UP, 1988).

[78] See Lieberman, *Province of Legislation*, n.75, pp.209–15, arguing that the foundations of a legislative science based on moral and social theory were laid by Eden and Romilly under the influence of Beccaria.

[79] The basis for this logically unified and exhaustive classification of law was laid down in *An Introduction to the Principles and Morals of Legislation* (first published in 1789) (n.75) and *Of Laws in General* (ed. HLA Hart) (London: Athlone Press, 1970), which remained unpublished during

then, would comprise both penal and civil law, and it would be exhaustive as it would be contained in an arrangement that comprised the rigorous division and classification of offences according to the principle of utility.[80] It would link his theory of punishment to the definition of offences: the 'parts or contents' of the legal system would become an 'object of arithmetic', and its 'lineaments and limits' an 'object of mensuration'.[81] His plan was nothing less than the definition and distribution of law as an aid to more effective government. This was captured in a striking image:

> On a map of the law executed upon such a plan there are no *terrae incognitae*, no blank spaces: nothing is at least omitted, nothing unprovided for: the vast and hitherto shapeless expanse of jurisprudence is collected and condensed into a compact sphere which the eye at a moment's warning can traverse in all imaginable directions.[82]

This was a new ideal of completeness in which system was elevated to an ordering principle.[83]

This was not based on an ideal of political liberty: individual freedom was less the core of the project than an incidental benefit, as the free individual would be constructed through regulation. Indeed, the resemblance between Bentham's vision of the science of legislation and his plan for the construction of a panopticon is not accidental.[84] The legislator, placed at the centre of the network of rules that govern the social, corresponds in location and symbolically to the gaze that animates his 'simple idea in Architecture', creating a new kind of legal order that corresponds to the institutions of police and discipline.[85] It is a striking feature of Bentham's proposal for the codification of the criminal law and the reform of punishment, and of those which followed his lead, that it did not explicitly raise the question of the limits of state power. Indeed, the issue of the restraint of political power was conspicuously absent from Bentham's discussion of the merits of systematizing the law. Codification was understood primarily as a means of improving the efficacy of existing governmental institutions. In his conception, legislation becomes the primary medium for the expression of the law, based on natural and universal principles, which should, in principle, extend over the entire realm of social life.[86] A complete catalogue of offences would lead to a complete understanding of everything that could be done by law, and crime became a social

his lifetime. The latter was a systematic attempt to define the nature of law and the relationships between penal and civil law.

[80] Bentham, *IPML,* n.75, Ch.XVI. See L Farmer, 'Reconstructing the English Codification Debate: the Criminal Law Commissioners 1833–45' (2000) 18 *Law & Hist Rev* 397; M Lobban, 'Theories of Law and Government' in W Cornish et al., *Oxford History of the Laws of England. Vol X 1820–1914 English Legal System* (Oxford: Oxford UP, 2010) Pt.1 Ch.IV.

[81] *IPML*, n.75, p.280.

[82] Bentham, *Of Laws in General*, n.76, p.246.

[83] And, of course, the paradox of Benthamite codification was that the aim of simplicity produced systems of daunting complexity.

[84] J Bentham, *The Panopticon Writings* (ed. M Bozovic) (London: Verso, 1995), esp. Bentham's preface and the introduction by Bozovic. On panopticism and modernity, see M Foucault, *Discipline and Punish: The Birth of the Prison* (Harmondsworth: Penguin, 1977).

[85] Bentham, *Panopticon Writings*, n.84, p.31. See also J-A Miller, 'Jeremy Bentham's Panoptic Device,' (1987) 41 *October* pp.3–29 at 14–16.

[86] Lieberman, *Province of Legislation*, n.75, Ch. 13 and Conclusion.

problem to be solved through the development of a penal policy. The reform of punishment and the criminal law was thus aimed at the renewal and extension of state power rather than its retrenchment.[87]

If the Benthamite version of the universal and complete code shaped the reception and development of the modern idea of codification in common law countries, it also became a serious obstacle to the success of any codification project, because of the procedural and political difficulties of producing and enacting a code on this scale. This was the fate of the first major English codification initiative of the nineteenth century.[88] Criminal Law Commissioners were appointed in 1833 and laboured for twelve years, producing eight reports which contained a digest of both the common law and statute law according to a broadly Benthamite plan. But the time taken meant that the government had changed and political support had dissipated by the time that draft was ready. The second major initiative led by Sir James Fitzjames Stephen between 1877 and 1880 met a similar fate, as the draft code was derailed by a combination of judicial opposition and the lack of parliamentary time.[89] At the same time, as we have noted, legislation was transforming the criminal law in the nineteenth century.[90] While these legislative changes are often understood as being second best to the more complete codifications that were on offer, the explanation is more complex. The combination of the reduction in the number of penal statutes in 1827 and the consolidation of the criminal law in 1861, however imperfect, restored the legitimacy of the criminal law, transforming punishment and reducing the complexity of the law. While the codifiers argued for the ever more complete and systematic codification of criminal law, the *de facto* codification of the criminal law by legal treatises was already addressing the same problems of complexity as the more ambitious political codification initiatives and resolving them in a different way. As long as the vision of the criminal law centred on the criminal trial retained its legitimacy, proposals for a legislative code could be resisted—and this was an understanding of the law that was not seriously challenged until well into the twentieth century.

The failure to legislate for a comprehensive criminal code in England in the nineteenth century can be contrasted with the comparative success of legislative initiatives in the imperial context.[91] While this can in part be explained in terms

[87] This is discussed at greater length in Farmer, 'Reconstructing', n.80, pp.417–25.

[88] On the membership and history of the commission, see Farmer, 'Reconstructing', n.80; KJM Smith, 'Criminal Law' in W Cornish et al., *Oxford History of the Laws of England* vol XIII (2010) Ch.6.

[89] See KJM Smith, *Sir James Fitzjames Stephen* (Cambridge: Cambridge UP, 1988) Ch.4. See also M Friedland, 'RS Wright's Model Criminal Code: A Forgotten Chapter in the History of the Criminal Law' (1981) 1 *Ox Jnl of Leg Stud* pp.307–46.

[90] See Ch.3 at pp.78–82.

[91] There is no systematic review of the spread of English criminal law through imperial codification projects. For the best general accounts, see B Wright, 'Renovate or Rebuild?' in n.2; B Wright, 'Criminal Law Codification and Imperial Projects. The Self-Governing Jurisdiction Codes of the 1890s' (2008) 12 *Legal History* pp.19–49; also Friedland, 'R.S. Wright's Model Code', n.89. For a general survey, not focused on criminal law, see ME Lang, *Codification in the British Empire and America* (Amsterdam: HJ Paris, 1924).

of the relative freedom from political obstacles to legislative enactment, it is also linked more fundamentally to the nature of the legislative project.[92] Codes were not only a tool for imperial governance, unifying diverse local laws and jurisdictions into the units of imperial administration, but they were also seen as a force for moral conquest, capable of lifting barbarous or backward peoples into metropolitan civilization. In the words of Thomas Macaulay: 'A code is almost the only blessing, perhaps is the only blessing, which absolute governments are better fitted to confer on a nation than popular governments.'[93]

Macaulay was appointed legal representative to the Governor General of India's Legislative Council in 1833, and in that role he initiated an ambitious plan to modernize the laws and colonial governance of India.[94] Central to this project was the drafting of a new penal code which would replace what he saw as the existing patchwork of Muslim, Hindu, and English laws and East India Company regulations. This would create uniformity and certainty in the law, and would apply equally to European and native subjects.[95] Macaulay's argument was that while the British Parliament was too riven by faction and too deferential to the judiciary to legislate a criminal code, this was not the case for India. Here Macaulay saw the prospects for British rule by an enlightened and paternal despotism. The codification of law could substitute for the checks on the common law that were provided by bench and bar in a domestic setting, while the content of the code offered the opportunity to introduce universal and civilized standards of conduct. His code was Benthamite in its foundations: it aimed to be simple, complete, and rational, organized along utilitarian principles, and it was to replace all existing systems of law (including the English common law). It aimed to limit judicial discretion, something which was attempted through the novel use of illustrations: hypothetical examples which followed on the statement of the rule in order to explain its scope.[96] These were in part aimed at making the law comprehensible to those who were to obey it. However, consistently with his Benthamite background, the illustrations were provided by the legislature, so that the lawmakers could more expressly articulate the meaning of the law. His code was presented to Parliament in 1837, but was not enacted until 1860 in the wake of the Sepoy Rebellion of

[92] On common law resistance to codification, see M Lobban, *The Common Law and English Jurisprudence* (Oxford: Oxford UP, 1991) Ch.7.

[93] TB Macaulay, 'Government of India' 10th July 1833 in *Macaulay: Prose and Poetry* (Cambridge MA: Harvard UP, 1970) p.675. Discussed in K Mantena, *Alibis of Empire* (Princeton: Princeton UP, 2010) Ch.3.

[94] See K Mantena, *Alibis of Empire*, n.93, Ch.3; B Wright, 'Macaulay's Indian Penal Code: Historical Context and Originating Principles' in W-C Chan et al., *Codification, Macaulay and the Indian Penal Code* (Dartmouth: Ashgate, 2011); S den Otter, '"A Legislating Empire": Victorian Political Theorists, Codes of Law, and Empire' in D Bell, *Victorian Visions of Global Order* (Cambridge: Cambridge UP, 2007); E Kolsky, 'Codification and the Rule of Colonial Difference: Criminal Procedure in British India' (2005) 23 *Law & Hist Rev* pp.631–83; S Kadish, 'Codifiers of the Criminal Law: Wechsler's Predecessors' in *Blame and Punishment. Essays in the Criminal Law* (London: Macmillan, 1987) pp.211–12.

[95] See TB Macaulay, 'Introductory Report upon the Indian Penal Code' in *Speeches and Poems* (New York: Riverside Press, 1867) pp.315–21.

[96] TB Macaulay, 'Introductory Report', n.95, pp.313–29.

1857.[97] Crucial to the adoption of the Code was the realization that the old system of government in India had broken down, and that a novel approach was required to reduce the reliance on military intervention and to make British rule more effective. Ironically, given its liberal and utilitarian character, the adoption of the Indian Penal Code (IPC) was seen as a necessary step in the new form of imperial rule, which aimed at the centralization of power and the introduction of new mechanisms of control and effective crime management based on developing understandings of the peculiarities of Indian culture.[98]

B. Contemporary codification

Following the collapse of Stephen's Code in 1880, there was little demand for codification in England until the issue was revived in the mid-twentieth century as part of the efforts to modernize the law in post-war welfare state. The immediate political impulse for this came from the modernizing Labour government of the 1960s which sought to adapt the law to modern conditions in a number of areas.[99] The codification project was thus initially conceived as a grand modernist initiative which would reform and update the substantive law in a clear, coherent, and accessible way, unifying legal form and penal policy. It ended, as we shall see, as a defensive move, updating segments of the law in a way which, while clarifying certain normative principles, seemed subservient to government demands for efficiency.

The postwar period saw extensive legislative revision of the criminal law, beginning with the Sexual Offences Act 1956 and the Homicide Act 1957 and continued with the Criminal Law Act 1967, the Theft Act 1968, the Criminal Damage Act 1971, and the Criminal Law Act 1977. Much of this legislation was based on the work of the Criminal Law Revision Committee and was aimed at updating and restating these areas, partly with a view to potential future codification.[100] More specific pressure to undertake a more complete codification came from academics such as Glanville Williams and JC Smith who argued for institutional

[97] See Wright, 'Macaulay's Indian Penal Code', n.94, pp.36–8 for discussion of the period between drafting and coming into force in 1862.

[98] See Mantena, *Alibis of Empire*, n.93, Ch.3 esp. pp.107–18; Kolsky, 'Codification', n.94. This process can be contrasted with the adoption of criminal codes in the 'self-governing' colonies of Canada, New Zealand, and Queensland, which Wright has argued were democratic in impulse and sought to make the rule of law more effective in culturally diverse frontier settings. See Wright, 'Criminal Law Codification and Imperial Projects. The Self-Governing Jurisdiction Codes of the 1890s' (2008) 12 *Legal History* pp.19–49.

[99] See the 1967 statement by the Home Secretary, Roy Jenkins, introducing the codification project, quoted in Law Commission, *Codification of the Criminal Law* (No.143) (London: HMSO, 1985) p.3. See generally G Williams, *The Reform of the Law* (London: Victor Gollancz, 1951). This was part of a trilogy: the second (G Gardiner & A Martin, *Law Reform NOW* (1963)) was instrumental in the establishment of the English Law Commission in 1965. See also P Archer & A Martin (eds), *More Law Reform Now* (Chichester: B. Rose Publishers, 1983).

[100] *Criminal Law Revision Committee Reports* (2 vols) (Abingdon: Professional Books, 1987). See G Williams, 'The Reform of the Criminal Law and of its Administration' (1957–8) 4 *J Soc'y Pub Tchrs.L* pp.217–30 arguing for the creation of a Criminal Law Committee.

mechanisms to review and update the law, simplifying the sources of the law, removing archaic religious influences and creating new offences where necessary for modern policies.[101] They, in turn, were drawing on the experience of the American Law Institute (ALI) and the creation of US Model Penal Code (MPC) (1962)—a code which linked modernization of the law to an explicit ideology of penal welfarism.[102] Codification of the criminal law was included in the programme of the newly created Law Commission in 1968—and remained there until it was finally abandoned in 2008. It strove—at least in its conception—for a Benthamite completeness including substantive law, procedure, and evidence.[103] However, as work on the code progressed it gradually moved away from an ambition to produce a complete code on these lines, to a focus only on the substantive criminal law. This in turn, moved from an approach which aimed at codifying the whole of the criminal law towards an approach which sought to codify particular sub-areas with a view to building these up into something more comprehensive.[104] The idea of completeness, then, or the proper content of a penal or criminal code, was gradually tempered by a kind of legislative pragmatism.

The aims of this codification project were generally expressed in terms of formal procedural values, rather than substantive aims of the criminal law or even punishment: comprehensibility, accessibility, consistency, and certainty.[105] These were linked to the principle of legality and the desirability of limiting judicial power, as well as to a broader idea that a code might 'synthesise the criminal law's conflicting aims of social protection and crime prevention with concern for legality and due process'.[106] However, by the time of the 1989 Law Commission Report these ambitious aims had contracted and the project was conceived in terms of co-ordination within the criminal justice system, and the possible savings in time and money, rather than benefits for the general public.[107] Codification

[101] G Williams, 'The Work of Criminal Law Reform' (1974–5) 13 *J Soc'y Pub Tchrs L* pp.183–98.

[102] See Williams, 'Reform', n.100, pp.218–9. The American Law Institute's Model Penal Code (MPC) was adopted in 1962 and covered sentencing and punishment as well as the substantive criminal law. See PH Robinson & MD Dubber, 'The American Model Penal Code: A Brief Overview' (2007) 10 *NCLR* p.319. See also H Wechsler, 'The Challenge of a Model Penal Code' (1952) 65 *Harvard LR* p.1097. The ALI produced a separate model code of criminal procedure in 1930.

[103] Roy Jenkins: 'A comprehensive criminal code should contain the following parts. It should provide a statement of general principles and their application; it should set out clearly the law relating to specific offences; it should contain a code of criminal procedure including a comprehensive statement of the law of criminal evidence and possibly a section on punishment' (n.99, p.3).

[104] The process is reviewed in A Ashworth & J Horder, *Principles of Criminal Law* (7th edn) (Oxford: Oxford UP, 2013) pp.45–7. The project was revived in *Criminal Justice. The Way Ahead* (Cm 5074) (London: HMSO, 2001) p.55, before its final abandonment was announced in 2008 (Law Commission, *Tenth Programme of Law Reform* (No. 311)).

[105] See Law Commission, *Codification of the Criminal Law* (No.143) (London: HMSO, 1985), pp.17–9; Law Commission, *A Criminal Code for England and Wales* (No.177) (London: HMSO, 1989) pp.5–8.

[106] Law Commission, No.177, p.5, citing ATH Smith, 'Codification of the Criminal Law (1): The Case for a Code' 1986 *Crim LR* 285 who was in turn citing Wechsler and the MPC.

[107] Law Commission, No.177, paras.2.5–2.7 & 2.10. In para.3.3 this is identified as the 'convenience of the users of the legislation', understood as criminal justice professionals. For comment see S Gardner and G de Búrca, 'The Codification of the Criminal Law' (1990) 10 *Ox Jnl. of Leg Stud* pp.559–71 at 563.

became an end in itself, rather than something which was linked to broader ideas about the social aims of the criminal law, which were not seen as something that needed to be articulated as part of this process.[108] The express aims—certainty, accessibility, and so on—were to be achieved by means of a particular system: the definition of a distinctive general part and the adoption of a particular analytical structure. General provisions would serve the aim of consistency by allowing individual offences to be defined using a common terminology and make possible the assessment of their relative seriousness.[109] The general part of the code defined principles of liability (rules relating to *mens rea*, causation, inchoate offences, complicity, etc.), so that the definition of each offence must look back to those general provisions. This also led to the adoption of a common offence structure, with the definition of each particular offence separated into distinct elements of *actus reus* and *mens rea*. For this reason, the writing of the general part was seen as the major part of the project as it would establish an exhaustive account of liability terms. The general part was thus to exert a strong definitional control over particular offences, and further aimed at standardizing judicial analysis by limiting the judge's powers to interpret the law.[110] The adoption of the general part also established a normative framework, in particular with the adoption of a subjective definition of *mens rea* expressing a particular kind of individualism and a particular understanding of the relationship between the individual and the state—even if the justification for the adoption of this understanding of *mens rea* was presented as a matter of logic (removing inconsistencies) rather than as a political choice.[111] This normative framework also exercised an implicit control over the substantive content of the code. This, for reasons of convenience, was understood as covering all indictable offences, to exclude minor or trivial offences or where the subject matter was not principally criminal—either because it was contained

[108] Cf. the MPC 1.02-(1). (1) The general purposes of the provisions governing the definition of offences are:

(a) to forbid and prevent conduct that unjustifiably and inexcusably inflicts or threatens substantial harm to individual or public interests;
(b) to subject to public control persons whose conduct indicates that they are disposed to commit crimes;
(c) to safeguard conduct that is without fault from condemnation as criminal;
(d) to give fair warning of the nature of the conduct declared to constitute an offence;
(e) to differentiate on reasonable grounds between serious and minor offences.

[109] Robinson & Dubber discuss the adoption of these measures by the US MPC, *The American Model*, n.102, p.330–6.

[110] Although, see Law Commission No.177 para.3.38 allowing that there may be instances in which judicial development of the law might be both permissible and desirable. Cf. I Leader-Elliott, 'Benthamite Reflections on Codification of the General Principles of Criminal Liability: Towards the Panopticon' (2006) 9 *Buffalo Crim LR* p.391 arguing that the primary audience for general principles of liability is the legislature because they will shape and constrain future legislation.

[111] See, for example, the discussion of Glanville Williams in N Lacey, 'Contingency, Coherence, and Conceptualism. Reflections on the encounter between "critique" and "the philosophy of the criminal law" in A Duff (ed.), *Philosophy and the Criminal Law* (1998) pp.29–36. See also S Gardner, 'Reiterating the Criminal Code' (1992) 55 *Mod LR* pp.839–47; and more generally, I. Dennis, 'The Critical Condition of Criminal Law' (1997) *Current Legal Problems* pp.213–49.

in legislation which was primarily regulatory, or where principles of criminal law had been expressly excluded by Parliament.[112] However, this led to some rather questionable exclusions, such as drug offences or serious road traffic offences. It was indicated that these were part of another regulatory scheme—a claim which overlooks the extent to which the same might be said of offences against property or the person.

In form, the draft codes look increasingly like textbooks—indeed the MPC was devised as a 'treatise on the major problems of the penal law' which might act as a model for future legislators rather than as a piece of legislation as such.[113] The content is the same: rules of substantive law, and increasingly only serious indictable offences. The aims are the same: consistency and accessibility and so on, conceived as ends in themselves. And the authors are in many cases the same as well. They share a similar conception of their audience: users of the criminal law as professionals or, in the case of textbooks, future professionals, rather than the general public. This, then, presents a shared, if rather restricted, view of the criminal law, legitimated as a form of professional knowledge.

V. Codification and Criminalization

The understanding of codification developed in this chapter allows us to see it in terms of the systematization of knowledge about the criminal law—new understandings that were to provide the resources for future initiatives in the systematizing of the law. We have thus been able to trace an extended conversation that took place over the course of the nineteenth century, and then in the second half of the century about the structure, system, and legitimacy of criminal law. The individuals involved were rarely only legislators or lawyers, but moved from codification commissions and law reform groups to the treatises and textbooks and the courts and back again. Draft codes were treatises, and treatises and textbooks codified the law. The boundaries between the different forms were porous—even if the political implications of legislative codification entailed a radically different view of the law and its legitimacy. This process of codification has established an understanding of the criminal law as a self-contained and rationally coherent system, organized according to internal principles. This is a view which has also had implications for understanding the nature and scope of the criminal law, as it has increasingly been seen in terms of substantive rules independent of procedure and sentencing, and as the application of these principles increasingly distinguishes between different classes or categories of offence.

The primary aim, though, of recent codification initiatives, both in textbooks and legislation, has been directed at the production of an increasingly sophisticated, coherent system of rules, directed at the co-ordination of understandings of

[112] Law Commission, No.143, para.2.10-13 and Appendix A; Law Commission, No.177, pt.3A.
[113] Wechsler, 'Challenge', n.102, p.1130.

criminal law for professional users of the system. As we shall see in the next chapter, understandings of the structure of the law, and its legitimacy, have increasingly been constructed in terms of a concept of individual responsibility linking the attribution of responsibility and the justification of punishment. This is clearly important, and can produce important benefits in terms of consistent application of the law and the equal treatment of offenders. However, I shall also argue that this view of the law has been cut off from a broader discussion of the aims or social function of the criminal law. Order has been secured through this codification, but it is a kind of internal ordering which serves the ends of lawyers and theorists, and has arguably been achieved at the cost of a connection to criminalization as a legislative project. The importance of the analysis of the history of legislative codes is that it both reconnects us to an understanding of the way that criminal law is connected to a governmental project, and that it has historically been more focused on questions of political legitimacy. In thinking about codification and criminalization, it is necessary to reconnect to these understandings of the law. This is a claim that I shall develop in the next chapter, which is focused on the role played by conceptions of responsibility both in the structuring and organization of the modern criminal law and as being central to the legitimization of the modern criminal law.

6

Responsibility

I. Introduction

For many—whether analysing the law from a conventional or a critical perspective—responsibility, and in particular individual responsibility, is foundational to the modern criminal law: it is treated as a concept that precedes and structures any theoretical account of the criminal law.[1] This focus on responsibility has been particularly marked in recent years, following the rise of retributive theories of punishment linking the justification of punishment, and hence the criminal law, to an account of moral responsibility. However, the focus on individual responsibility is not unique to such accounts, since consequentialist theories from Beccaria and Bentham onwards have argued that deterrence is most effective when directed at the rational, and thus responsible, individual. Either way, it is clear that an increasing recognition of the significance of responsibility is one of the principal features of the modern criminal law. The centrality of responsibility has a number of features. It is linked to a liberal view of criminal law, which sees the autonomous individual as the subject of the law; it is central to the justification of state punishment; and the law is understood as serving the overall end of protecting the liberty of the individual subject. In legal terms, this is articulated in the maxim *actus non facit reum nisi mens sit rea*, which underlies the distinction between conduct (*actus reus*) and a mental element (*mens rea*), which structures the modern criminal law.

The responsible individual is thus central to the modern normative imagination, shaping accounts of the rights and obligations that individuals owe to each other and understandings of the relationship between individuals and the state.[2] This centrality is normally understood as being linked to the structure of moral fault or a certain kind of liberal political subjectivity that precedes and limits law. In this chapter, however, I shall argue that responsibility should be understood

[1] See e.g. V Tadros, *Criminal Responsibility* (Oxford: Oxford UP, 2005); AW Norrie, *Crime, Reason and History. A Critical Introduction to Criminal Law* (3rd edn) (Cambridge: Cambridge UP, 2014).

[2] S Veitch, *Law and Irresponsibility. On the Legitimation of Human Suffering* (London: Routledge-Cavendish, 2007) p.35; C Taylor, *Modern Social Imaginaries* (Durham NC: Duke UP, 2004); N Lacey, 'Responsibility and Modernity in Criminal Law' (2001) 9 *Jnl of Political Philosophy* pp.249–76.

from an institutional perspective: the development of forms of responsibility has enabled the identification of particular subjects of law and has further been central to the development of ideas about the systematicity of the criminal law. The development of different forms of subjectivity has also been central to the articulation of ideas about civil order in terms of the relationships of subjects to themselves and others, the forms of permissible and impermissible conduct, and the consequences of the breach of criminal laws. This links understandings of responsibility to criminalization, but it does so in a way which challenges conventional understandings.

As we have seen, one of the commonplaces of contemporary criminal law theory is that responsibility can act as a constraint on criminalization through the operation of the principle of *mens rea*.[3] This operates, in part, at an individual level: all definitions of crimes should specify a mental element and a person cannot be found criminally liable unless they meet the *mens rea* criteria for the particular crime. Much of the contemporary debate is accordingly concerned with the characteristics of particular laws and the fairness of attributing liability to particular individuals or groups. In more general terms, though, it is argued that a principle of *mens rea* should constrain criminalization by helping to define the proper scope of the criminal law. Thus the principle of *mens rea*—that harmful wrongs or wrongful harms consist centrally in culpable conduct—is understood as an independent constraint on state power, a way of establishing the limits of permissible state action through criminal law. However, I will argue the opposite case: that responsibility, by defining the scope of that which is criminalized or what we are responsible for, has been central to the growth of the criminal law in the modern period. This requires that we think about responsibility as something which is not external to law, but which has shaped the substantive content of the criminal law, and has thus played a role in criminalization which goes far beyond the idea of constraint. This is to say that responsibility is not only a matter of answering to others for our conduct, for this understanding of liability or culpability is dependent on pre-existing expectations about the scope of our duties, roles or relations with respect to others, understandings which are centrally linked to understandings and expectations of civil order.

This is an approach that opens a different perspective on, and indeed allows for, a history of responsibility. It has been suggested that such a history is impossible, that the nature of responsibility, defined as holding an individual responsible for their conduct, is a universal principle.[4] Tadros has argued that theoretical accounts should focus on the fundamental features of agency, with changes in the practice of holding persons responsible, the proof of responsibility, or even the kinds of actions people could be responsible for, being of interest only to the extent that they can shed light on the question of what criminal responsibility

[3] See Chapter 3 at 108–15.

[4] Tadros, *Criminal Responsibility*, n.1, pp.5–8 taking issue with the argument in Lacey, 'Responsibility and Modernity', n.2.

ought to be. I am sceptical about the claim that the nature of responsibility is universal; if it were true, it could only be at such a level of generality as to be able to shed little light on the actual practices of holding people or things responsible.[5] It is, in any case, practically impossible to disentangle our ideas about the nature of responsibility from our practices of holding to account, or to imagine responsibility practices based on ideas of agency which are not centred on the relationship between mind and deed and the idea of moral fault.[6] However, by starting from the institutional form of responsibility in the modern criminal law, I want to show how certain responsibility practices have developed and shaped the institutional conceptions of responsibility in the criminal law.[7] The argument developed in this chapter thus presents a different view of responsibility, seeing it primarily as a legal artefact, the development of which is linked to the particular nature of civil order in modernity. It should also be added that this is why it is appropriate to address the topic of responsibility at this point in the book and not earlier. Having traced the development of the modern institution of criminal law, we can now see how ideas of responsibility developed within that institution, giving it a particular shape and identity. Responsibility in this sense is key to the modern law, but not because of any intrinsic connection between wrongdoing and responsibility and the justification of punishment, but because responsibility has become central to the modality or form of law, and thus to the way that civil order is secured. This does not exhaust the arguments which might be made about the significance of responsibility, and is not intended to; but it opens up a different kind of perspective on responsibility and its significance for understandings of criminalization.

The chapter is in three main sections. In the first section I will analyse responsibility as a legal institution. That is to say that I am not primarily interested in responsibility as a moral concept, but in how it is formulated as a legal concept as a way of designating subjects in the criminal law. I use the term responsibility in the most general sense here as a term which designates the characteristics of a legal subject. The second section is a long historical account of the development of specific doctrines of criminal law in particular periods. This traces the development of more specific concepts of fault and analyses how ideas of responsibility in different areas were brought together in a single idea of 'responsibility as liability' that could organize the distinction in the law between general and special parts and structure definitions of offences. Thus we can begin to see how responsibility began to shape the understanding of the proper structure and scope of the criminal law. Finally, I will argue that a broader, historically situated concept

[5] For a discussion of responsibility in ancient Greek thought, which radically rejects the idea of human agency, see R Calasso, *The Marriage of Cadmus and Harmony* (London: Vintage, 1994) pp.94–5 and L Siedentop, *Inventing the Individual. The Origins of Western Liberalism* (Harmondsworth: Penguin, 2014) esp. Chs.1-3.

[6] Veitch, *Law and Irresponsibility*, n.2, pp.39–41.

[7] See also N Lacey, 'Institutionalising Responsibility: Implications for Jurisprudence' (2013) 4 *Jurisprudence* pp.1–19 at p.6: 'Responsibility in law is shaped not only by that institutional framework but by the practical and normative tasks which it performs.'

of responsibility is necessary to reopen questions about the relationship between citizenship and criminalization.

II. Responsibility as a Legal Institution

> The ability to act or abstain from acting in a legally relevant sense is fundamental to legal order as a rational order of rational beings.[8]

I argued in Part I of this book that modern law is an institutional normative order that regulates the conduct of persons and the relations between them. As a normative order is for persons, it is necessary to understand how the concept of the person is institutionalized, for there is a clear link between the concept of legal personality and that of responsibility, understood as the capacities and expectations of legal persons, and what they can be held responsible for in law.[9]

In general terms legal institutions establish criteria of who counts as a person for the purposes of the law according to the order which they seek to secure. This can be more or less inclusive: disqualifying those such as slaves, women, or aliens who are seen as lesser classes or categories of person—or not persons at all—or including all humans as relevant persons under the rubric of human rights. And legal systems may have different degrees or categories of personhood for different purposes, distinguishing for example between those who can legally perform certain actions and those who are eligible for the protection of law but who are not qualified to act.[10] In principle, a legal system can lay down its own criteria of personhood, which may be more or less inclusive; the key point is the identification of the putative properties of the person who is subject to law. In practice, the criteria of personhood are shaped by cultural and political beliefs about the relevant properties of persons. In modernity, these have been increasingly framed in terms of beliefs about the natural capacities of humans and of their powers of reason, though there is considerable variation in how such broad cultural and philosophical beliefs are institutionalized in law.[11] As a form of normative order, law should be understood as articulating the properties of those capable of being ordered—in relation to the different ends or purposes of different areas of law.[12] The forms of legal personality might accordingly be different for different purposes in different

[8] N MacCormick, *Institutions of Law* (Oxford: Oxford UP, 2007), p.92.

[9] MacCormick, *Institutions*, n.8, p.78: 'what is ordered is the conduct of persons and the treatment they are to receive'.

[10] Children are an example of a class of persons who are protected by the law, but who may not legally perform certain actions, e.g., commit a crime, form a contract, or get married. Animals are protected by the law but may not perform legal actions. See infra. See also P Cane, *Responsibility in Law and Morality* (Abingdon: Hart Publishing, 2002) pp.40–1.

[11] For discussion of this see N Naffine, *Law's Meaning of Life. Philosophy, Religion, Darwin and the Legal Person* (Abingdon: Hart Publishing, 2009) esp. Chs.2–5.

[12] An important question then becomes that of the properties of the so-called 'natural' person, and why and how representing these properties as natural is significant to the self-understanding or legitimation of the law.

areas of law: children might be considered incapable of forming a contract yet be capable of committing crimes or vice versa; or forms of corporate personality, for example, might be recognized for the purposes of forming contracts or civil liability but not be seen as being capable of giving rise to criminal liability. In modern legal systems, persons are generally understood to be those who are capable of rational action and have interests and can suffer harm. This is to say that the person in modern law is not only subject *to* law, but also the subject *of* law: any account of the authority of law must thus take into account this institutional understanding of the autonomy of the individual person.

The different dimensions of legal personhood—those who may perform legal actions and those who are protected by the law—have been characterized as active and passive legal personality.[13] Active personality is, broadly speaking, understood in terms of the capacity to be guided by rules—to be the autonomous subject of law—a feature which is assumed in rules for the guidance of conduct; passive personality is aimed at preventing violations of protected persons or objects and their interests.[14] Capacities depend on features of the person that are treated as legally relevant at any given point in time or for particular purposes. These may be viewed as 'natural', such as age, sex, or mental competence; they may be based on institutional status such as citizenship, matrimonial status, or role (e.g. a licence holder); or they may be situational or dependent on particular circumstances (e.g. a duty of care arising from a person's prior conduct).[15] However, what is legally relevant will depend both on the scope of particular rules and on wider conceptions of civil order. Indeed, the recognition of a conception of the person based on common attributes of individuals was central to the development of the modern law, creating a reasonably static object of legal attribution and application which in turn allowed the articulation of norms capable of general application.[16] Active personality in the modern law is attributed to those who are deemed capable of making their actions conform to, or violate, norms of conduct—in short, to follow rules. This is to say that the institution of law posits that those to whom personality is attributed are those capable of acting in conformity to norms and being held responsible for breaches of those norms.[17] But presupposing the subject as a responsible agent in this way has further implications for the form or modality of law. Rules must take the form of general norms directed at, and capable of being

[13] MacCormick, *Institutions*, n.8, Ch.5. For a discussion of protected persons see Ch.8.

[14] There is no reason to think that passive personality (or the capacity to be wronged) need in criminal law apply only to humans and their immediate interests, or indeed to living entities or entities with self-awareness. It can and does apply equally to more abstract entities, such as the environment or the market, if 'identity' can be imputed to it in the sense of understanding it as a distinctive object which exists over time.

[15] This is not a claim that legal personality is fiction because that would imply that there is something 'real' against which it could be measured. It is rather that all forms of legal personality are fundamentally legal artefacts.

[16] C Thornhill, 'Guilt and the Origins of Modern Law' (2014) 43 *Economy & Society* pp.103–35; cf. also A Supiot, *The Spirit of Philadelphia* (London: Verso, 2012) Ch.8 on the historical origins and structure of responsibility.

[17] MacCormick, *Institutions*, n.8, p.89.

understood and followed by, persons deemed to possess the necessary capacities; and the attribution of responsibility for the breach of a norm should extend only to those who are recognized as possessing such capacities. Modern legal systems thus protect 'the means and liberties necessary to live well as a rational and reflective, project-centred agent', which is to say that a certain understanding of autonomy and social co-operation (or civil order) must be assumed to underlie the form of the modern law.[18]

The model of the legal person in modernity thus implies a certain kind of responsible agency: persons are capable of being guided by norms and may accordingly be answerable for their conduct when they breach those norms. Both active and passive aspects of personality imply 'the continuity of persons in time and some degree of actual or imputed consciousness of this'—that is to say a relation to self.[19] This is necessary both for an understanding of intentionality, or the capacity to plan action over time, and for a sense of self-identity. It is assumed that legal persons take decisions not only with respect to an awareness of rules, but also with respect to an overall 'life-plan' in terms of which they develop their interests and their sense of identity. These interests include not merely momentary gratification, protection from harm, or mechanical rule following, but also the capacity to develop those interests and their identity over time and in respect of other persons conceived of as pursuing similar interests. That this is the fundamental link between legal personhood, responsibility, and social order in modernity was recognized by Adam Smith in his account of the impartial spectator. This was an individual who is capable of imaginatively identifying with others (or a generalized other) while using the process of identification to generate impersonal norms for the regulation of their own conduct.[20] This used a juridical model of the responsible person as the basis for a general model of social order: internally, it is a mechanism by which the individual can regulate their own conduct through an imaginative identification with others; institutionally, it is a model of the reflective and responsible person that justifies the recognition of general legal norms of conduct and in its turn could justify the imposition of punishment.[21] This recognizes a central linkage between the idea of being responsible for oneself in relation to others, and in being capable of being held responsible (or answerable) to others for one's conduct.

[18] C Kutz, 'Responsibility' in JR Coleman et al., *The Oxford Handbook of Jurisprudence and Philosophy of Law* (Oxford: Oxford UP, 2004) p.567. Cf. L Fuller, *The Morality of Law* (Revised edn) (New Haven: Yale UP, 1969) pp.181–4. This is discussed in K Rundle, *Forms Liberate* (Oxford: Hart Publishing, 2012).

[19] MacCormick, *Institutions*, n.8, p.78. See also A Giddens, *Modernity and Self-Identity. Self and Society in the Late Modern Age* (Cambridge: Polity, 1991) Ch.2.

[20] A Smith, *The Theory of Moral Sentiments* (1790) (London: Penguin, 2009) Pt.I. For discussion see J Bender, *Imagining the Penitentiary. Fiction and the Architecture of Mind in Eighteenth-Century England* (Chicago: Chicago UP, 1987) p.223.

[21] Bender, *Imagining the Penitentiary*, p.221: 'Smith accounts psychologically for an emergent order based on guilt rather than shame and marked by the introjection of impersonal norms as character. In this new order, guilt is a permanent condition. It refers to the values of others, certainly, but rapidly takes on an independent life by generalizing and depersonalizing them.'

If we understand responsibility in this way then we can see criminal responsibility in particular as rooted in the practices of defining the scope of responsibilities and of holding to account by the legal institution.[22] The link between personhood and responsibility has primarily been recognized in relation to what has been called 'outcome' or 'historic' or retrospective responsibility, that is to say that we are responsible to others for our past conduct: '[This] is the counterpart and at the same time a constituent of our personal identity and character. We could not dispense with... responsibility without ceasing to be persons.'[23] Work on criminal responsibility has accordingly focused on the question of the conditions under which a person can be held to account for their conduct. However, it is important to note that active personality on this account includes both the idea of what has been described as 'prospective' responsibility—the imposition of obligations and duties on a person who is deemed capable of adapting their conduct to norms and planning their conduct over time—and that of 'retrospective' liability—being held responsible for past conduct (answerability or accountability).[24] Indeed, the latter to a great extent depends on the former: a person cannot be answerable to others for something unless there is some form of prospective responsibility in the sense of the existence of recognized norms of conduct.[25] These obligations may range from the general (do not kill, respect the person and property of others), to more specific duties, such as those which go along with understandings of parenthood or particular social roles such as being an officer of the law. An account of criminal responsibility must therefore be just as much concerned with the specification of roles and responsibilities in modern society as with the attribution of 'retrospective' responsibility.[26] It thus follows that what has to be justified is not only the imposition of punishment but the distribution of social responsibilities, explicitly linking responsibility and criminalization. It has been argued that the specification of responsibilities is beyond the scope of the criminal law—that the civil law is concerned with the identification of rights and duties and the criminal

[22] P Strawson, 'Freedom and Resentment' in J Fischer & M Ravizza, *Perspectives on Moral Responsibility* (Ithaca: Cornell UP, 1993); Kutz, 'Responsibility', n.18, pp.552–9.

[23] T Honoré, *Responsibility and Fault* (Abingdon: Hart Publishing, 1999) p.29. The terminology used in this area is confusing. The original typology is found in HLA Hart, *Punishment and Responsibility* (Oxford: Clarendon, 1968) Postscript, distinguishing between role, causal liability, and capacity responsibility. Subsequent accounts have adapted this, often using different terms. Here I am using the broad distinction between prospective and retrospective responsibility.

[24] Cane, *Responsibility,* n.10: 'The law is as much concerned with telling us how to behave as with holding us to account for the way we have behaved' (p.33). MacCormick, *Institutions,* n.8, p.91: '[W]hat is important here is the distinction which exists between capacity to be held liable and capacity to do that to which liability attaches.'

[25] It is precisely this relation that founds the principle of legality, with difficulties arising when the reactive mode is disjunctive with the prospective. See also infra.

[26] Cf. HM Hart, 'The Aims of the Criminal Law' (1958) 23 *Law and Contemporary Problems,* pp.401–41 recognizing that one of the aims of the criminal law is 'inculcating social responsibility' (at p.413). See also the important argument in Veitch, *Law and Irresponsibility,* n.2, pp.42–52 that legal conceptions of responsibility are organized according to narrow conceptions of proximity and foresight which distribute both responsibility and irresponsibility—or situations where responsibility is disaggregated in modern society.

law merely with specifying the principles of liability for breaches of those rights.[27] However, criminal law as a matter of fact routinely articulates responsibilities and duties, either explicitly or implicitly, even in areas where there are established regimes of rights in civil law. The failure to recognize this link in theories of criminalization leads to a significantly narrower view of the relevance of responsibility. This can be seen as a specific example of the limiting consequences of understanding the justification of the scope of the criminal law in terms of the justification of punishment, and I want to reconnect to this broader understanding of responsibilities through the idea of securing civil order.

One further general point here concerns the relationship with moral responsibility. It follows from what I have argued so far that responsibility is primarily a legal artefact. Thus, while this legal conception may be based on, or 'track', conceptions of moral responsibility, and conceptions of moral responsibility might help to refine legal doctrine, they are not 'foundational' in the sense of being pre-legal. It is the case, as we shall see, that, in the modern criminal law, legal responsibility (in the narrower sense of attribution or culpability) has come to be articulated by judges and theorists in a moral voice—that legal responsibility is conceived in some way as corresponding to moral responsibility—but this is a matter of historical development rather than conceptual necessity. For now I want to note two further aspects of this. First, the idea of fault has come to play a particular role in the specification of the distinctiveness of criminal law. This is sometimes expressed as the idea that criminal law deals with responsibility for acts and tort law for outcomes, or that criminal law should be concerned with more serious forms of fault or wrongdoing, or those wrongs deserving of punishment. The distinction is rarely so clear-cut (there are different standards of fault in both crime and tort, and attempts to distinguish between tort and crime are hard to sustain), but what it does capture is something about the way that conceptions of responsibility have come to be seen as in some way central to defining the scope of the criminal law. Second, responsibility is seen as central to the moral and political legitimacy of the criminal law. This has a number of different dimensions, which are all too often rolled up together in a single idea of responsibility, autonomy, or liberty: fairness in the definition of rules and responsibilities; fairness in the attribution of liability; fairness in the trial of an accused person; and fairness in punishment. But in fact, due process rules might respect liberty in the trial process but need not necessarily be related directly to responsibility in the sense of the definition of criminal law.[28] While these different dimensions cannot always be distinguished in practice, I want to focus on the first two elements as related to the institution of criminal law and to issues of criminalization. Here, as I have

[27] See J Bentham, *Introduction to the Principles and Morals of Legislation* (IPML) (ed. JH Burns & HLA Hart) (Oxford: Oxford UP, 1982) Concluding Note; Hart, *Punishment and Responsibility*, n.23, p.217.

[28] See TA Green, 'The Jury and Criminal Responsibility in Anglo-American History' (forthcoming) *Crim Law & Phil* (DOI 10.1007/s11572-013-9267-0) tracing separate and overlapping trajectories of political liberty, through the jury, and freewill.

noted above, the conception of the person, as addressee of law, also has implications in modernity for the modality of law in terms of treating them as an autonomous, reasoning person. One of the aims of the next section is thus to explore how this idea of the autonomous individual has been instantiated in criminal law and how this underpins the legitimacy of the modern criminal law.

III. Making Criminal Responsibility

> The notion of prevention through the medium of the mind, necessarily assumes mental ability adequate to restraint.[29]

The legal maxim that *actus non facit reum nisi mens sit rea*, understood as expressing the idea that the will is necessary to legal guilt, has been recognized by the criminal law since the medieval period, and was closely connected to Christian ideas about sin.[30] However, as Sir James Fitzjames Stephen pointed out, legal practice even in his day fell far short of recognising *mens rea* as a fundamental principle of criminal law.[31] The historical study of responsibility must accordingly examine the process by which specific doctrines (especially those around *mens rea*) were institutionalized in the criminal law in the form of particular rules establishing standards of conduct and conditions of liability for punishment. There has been a lot of recent work on the period since the late eighteenth century which has looked at such areas as the development of doctrines of liability, the movement from character to capacity and choice-based conceptions of responsibility, the treatment of mental abnormality and the relation between legal and medical conceptions of the person, and the relationship between changes in institutional practices, such as those of the criminal trial, and the development of conceptions of responsibility and so on.[32] My focus will be more limited. The general

[29] Criminal Law Commissioners, *Seventh Report*, p.22.

[30] F Pollock & FW Maitland, *History of English Law* (2nd edn) (Cambridge: Cambridge UP, 1889) II, 475 trace the phrase to St Augustine, and its first statement in law to the *Leges Henrici Primi* in relation to perjury. It is common to cite Coke's *Third Institute* fo.6 (on high treason) as authority for the maxim in English law: *The Selected Writings of Sir Edward Coke Vol. II Institutes* (ed. S Sheppard) (Indianapolis: Liberty Fund, 2003) p.961.

[31] JF Stephen, *History of the Criminal Law* (London: Macmillan, 1883) II pp.94–5. He went on to describe it as a *minim* rather than a *maxim*, because the exceptions and qualifications were more important than the rule.

[32] KJM Smith, *Lawyers, Legislators and Theorists* (Oxford: Oxford UP, 1998) is by far the most systematic in terms of looking at the development of particular fault concepts, though rather narrow in focus. For an account focused on the US see TA Green, *Freedom and Criminal Responsibility in American Legal Thought* (New York: Cambridge UP, 2014). In addition to works by Lacey already cited, see N Lacey, *Women, Crime and Character. From Moll Flanders to Tess of the d'Urbevilles* (Oxford: Oxford UP, 2008) and 'Psychologising Jekyll, Demonising Hyde: the strange case of criminal responsibility' (2010) 4 *Crim Law and Phil* p.109; M Wiener, *Reconstructing the Criminal* (Cambridge: Cambridge UP, 1990); L Rodensky, *The Crime in Mind. Criminal Responsibility and the Victorian Novel* (Oxford: Oxford UP, 2003); JP Eigen, *Unconscious Crime. Mental Absence and Criminal Responsibility in Victorian London* (Baltimore: Johns Hopkins UP, 2003); A Loughnan, *Manifest Madness* (Oxford: Oxford UP, 2012).

idea is to examine the incorporation of standards of conduct into the criminal law in relation to different areas of social life—as these were formulated in increasingly general terms. This must be understood not only in the context of doctrinal questions about responsibility, but also in terms of changing social roles and responsibilities and indeed conceptions of personhood.

A. Eighteenth-century conceptions of responsibility

While eighteenth-century writers on criminal law were quick to proclaim the liberty of the subject and defend the role of the criminal law in the preservation or securing of that liberty, this was understood in general terms of the role of law in protecting property and the individual against sovereign power rather than having any particular consequence for the proof of guilt. Malice was generally required for legal guilt in serious crimes, but in the ordinary case the proof of malice was presumed from the proof of an act. Responsibility, if it was discussed at all, was seen primarily in the context of explaining incapacity or exemptions from criminal punishment. The general structure of treatments of responsibility in eighteenth-century law was established by Hale.[33] He began his chapter on the incapacities of persons with a general statement about the capacities of the legal subject: 'Man is naturally endowed with these two great faculties, understanding and liberty of will, and therefore is a subject properly capable of a law properly so-called.'[34] Liberty or choice presupposed understanding, or 'to know the thing or action chosen by the will', so that if there were no understanding there could be no free act of the will—and consequently punishment would be ineffective.[35] But, he went on, general notions such as this were too vague for criminal law, so that law-givers instead focused on those persons or activities that were exempt from punishment because of incapacity or defect of the will. These incapacities were of three kinds: natural, accidental, and civil. The first was infancy or non-age; the second was principally madness or lunacy, but also included discussions of drunkenness, chance, and ignorance; and civil subjection was a discussion of forms of compulsion or necessity.[36] His discussion was, then, largely procedural in character, looking at a series of detailed questions about how persons falling into certain categories should be tried or punished, frequently with different rules for different kinds of crime. And it is also striking that discussion of such questions as self-defence or compulsion were seen as substantive rules of homicide rather than raising general questions of justification or excuse.[37]

[33] M Hale, *The History of the Pleas of the Crown* (London: Printed by E. Rider, 1800) Ch.II. See also W Blackstone, *Commentaries* (1769) (Chicago: Chicago UP, 1979) iv, Ch.2; W Eden, *Principles of Penal Law* (3rd edn) (London: B White & T Cadell, 1775) Ch.XI; WO Russell, *A Treatise on Crimes and Indictable Misdemeanors* (London: J Butterworth, 1819) Ch.1; D Hume, *Commentaries on the Law of Scotland Respecting Crimes* (4th edn ed. BR Bell) (Edinburgh: Bell & Bradfute, 1844) I, Ch.1. See the useful general discussion in S Stern, 'Blackstone's Criminal Law: Common Law Harmonization and Legislative Reform (1769)' in MD Dubber (ed.), *Foundational Texts in Modern Criminal Law* (Oxford: Oxford UP, 2014) pp.65–9.

[34] Hale, *Pleas of the Crown*, n.33, p.14. [35] Ibid., p.14. [36] Ibid., Chs.7–9.

[37] Ibid., e.g. Chapters 5 (on accidental deaths) and 8 (on compulsion or fear).

Blackstone's approach followed the same pattern, though framing the discussion in slightly more general terms. The main consideration, he stated, was the want or defect of will in certain circumstances.[38] He argued that to constitute a crime under human laws there must be 'first, a vitious will, and secondly an unlawful act consequent upon such vitious [*sic*] will, the presence of the will being necessary to render human actions either praiseworthy or culpable.[39] This recognized a more general distinction between act and mental state, for 'to make a complete crime under human laws, there must be both a will and an act'.[40] While this made possible a distinction between crime and sin, the former requiring an overt act while the latter did not, this was not understood as having more general implications for the proof of crime, a point underlined by Baron Hume in setting out the comparable position in Scots law:

> Now...those authorities are not to be understood in this sense, as if it were always necessary for the prosecutor to bring evidence of an intention to do the very thing that has been done, and to do it out of enmity to the individual who has been injured. In this more favourable sense to the prisoner, the maxim cannot be received into the law; for it would screen a great many offenders from the due punishment of their transgressions.[41]

Evidence of an overt act would in itself demonstrate malice, or the 'depravity of the will', unless the accused person could establish that they fell into one of the three categories in which the will did not join with the act. These were where there was a defect of understanding (idiocy, infancy, lunacy, intoxication); where there was understanding and will, but it was not exerted at the time of the action (chance or ignorance); or where the action was constrained by outward force and violence (compulsion or necessity).[42]

This emphasis on the conjunction of act and will allowed Blackstone to frame these categories in a more general way, but, in terms of substance, his treatment did not depart from that set out by Hale. The rules were broad categories of exclusion or exculpation, mainly directed at the fact-specific question of whether an accused person should suffer capital punishment or not, rather than attempting to elaborate any more nuanced understanding of fault.[43] Infancy and lunacy were treated together as species of a defect of understanding in relation to punishability. (Hale, indeed, formulated his test for lunacy in terms of whether the accused had the understanding of a fourteen year old child.[44]) Ignorance of fact might

[38] Blackstone, *Commentaries*, n.33, iv, p.20. See also Russell, *Treatise*, n.33, p.1: 'For without the consent of the will, human actions cannot be considered as culpable.'

[39] Blackstone, *Commentaries*, n.33, iv, p.21.

[40] Ibid.

[41] Hume, *Commentaries*, n.33, I, p.21. See also Eden, *Principles of Penal Law*, n.33, pp.85–7: 'Thus every criminal charge must be founded on some fact, with the evidence of which every trial should commence'.

[42] Blackstone, *Commentaries*, n.33, iv, pp.28–9 on husbands and wives.

[43] And indeed, as Lacey has pointed out, the criminal trial of this period was not capable of investigating such questions: 'Responsibility and Modernity', n.2, pp.256–61.

[44] These were not separated until Russell, who distinguished between infancy and being *non compos mentis* (*Treatise*, Ch.1). It is also surprising that Hale categorizes lunacy as a species of accident, rather than as something natural. Hale, *Pleas of the Crown*, n.33, p.30: 'The best measure that I can think of is this; such a person as labouring under melancholy distempers has yet ordinarily as

excuse a person intending to do a lawful act, but an error of law would not be a defence.[45] In the case of misfortune or chance, the strict rule was that a person would be excused from guilt if the mischief followed from the performance of a lawful act, but that lack of foresight was no excuse where a person was doing something unlawful.[46] There were signs of concern about the kinds of standards of conduct that might be expected of people with respect to certain activities. All the treatise writers gave the example of a workman throwing down rubble from the roof of a building and killing someone, as a means of illustrating the degree of caution or circumspection required in different circumstances: whether it should be murder, manslaughter or just misfortune would depend on whether a warning was given or not, or how crowded the street below was or might have been expected to be.[47] By the time of East, this had been generalized into a broader rule, which also extended to the case of neglecting to prevent a mischief which the person may, and ought to provide against: 'The criterion in such cases is to examine whether common social duty would, under the circumstances, have suggested a more circumspect conduct.'[48]

A further illustration can be seen in the category of 'civil subjection'. For Hale this was a broad category which primarily related to forms of compulsion arising from social circumstances or relationships such as sovereign and subject, master and servant, husband and wife, and the lawful authority of magistrates enforcing the law.[49] The largest part of the discussion was given over to the relation between husband and wife (or *femme couvert*). The wife acting under the coercion of the husband, if he were present, was excused in some felonies, though not serious ones such as murder or treason; and even if it appeared she was an equal partner she might, as a matter of practice, be excused capital punishment, as otherwise the husband might qualify for benefit of clergy while she could not.[50] There was limited discussion of other forms of compulsion or necessity, where Hale maintained

great understanding, as ordinarily a child of fourteen years hath, is such a person as may be guilty of treason or felony.' See also A Amos, *Ruins of Time Exemplified in Sir Matthew Hale's History of the Pleas of the Crown* (London: V & R Stevens & GS Norton, 1856) pp.34–6.

[45] Blackstone, *Commentaries*, n.33, iv, p.27; Hale, *Pleas of the Crown*, n.33, p.42; Russell, *Treatise*, n.33, p.20.

[46] Blackstone, *Commentaries*, n.33, iv, pp.26–7. See also pp.182–3 on homicide *per infortuniam*. Hale, *Pleas of the Crown*, n.33, Ch.5.

[47] See Hale, *Pleas of the Crown*, n.33, p.466; Blackstone, *Commentaries*, n.33, iv, pp.192–3; EH East, *A Treatise of Pleas of the Crown* (London: Butterworths, 1803) pp.262–71; Russell, *Treatise*, n.33, pp.535–6.

[48] East, *Treatise*, n.47, p.262. He also discusses the statement of Holt CJ in a case from 1704 in which a cart driver had run down a pedestrian, and notes the statutory provisions relating to deaths on passenger boats and stagecoaches (10 Geo.2 c.31 s.8; 28 Geo.II c.57). It was not, however, criminal for a person who was not a doctor to administer medicine to a patient where this resulted in death. The relevant cases are discussed in Smith, *Lawyers, Legislators and Theorists*, n.32, pp.87–92: 'What these relatively early decisions do not clearly establish is whether 'gross negligence' indicated the failure to achieve an objectively set standard of skill or whether... simply doing one's incompetent unskilled best was sufficient to escape liability' (pp.91–2).

[49] Hale, *Pleas of the Crown*, n.33, Chs.7 & 9. Both Hale and Blackstone discuss the position of the sovereign under this head, as being excused all crimes because of their incapacity to do wrong. See also Hale, *Pleas of the Crown*, n.33, p.43 & Blackstone, *Commentaries*, n.33, iv, pp.32–3.

[50] Hale, *Pleas of the Crown*, n.33, p.45; Blackstone, *Commentaries*, n.33, iv, pp.28–9.

that in time of peace it was never permissible either to take the life of others because of threats to one's own life, or to steal food in case of necessity because taking the laws into one's own hands in this way would threaten the ties of civil government.[51] The question of compulsion was formulated slightly more broadly by Russell as extending to all persons in subjection to the power of others. While this included much of the same content, there was slightly more emphasis on the circumstances of subjection, rather than status, and he characterized relationships, such as husband and wife, as private relationships which were subject to special rules, and thus separate from the general considerations.[52] Moreover, the tone of his discussion of the position of the wife is much more disapproving, characterizing the rule as merely a presumption of law and noting substantial exceptions and modifications to the general common law rule.[53]

Overall, there was a clear emphasis on the primacy of civil over natural order, with writers from Hale to Blackstone stressing the priority of rules of law or civil order over any natural sense of liberty. Blackstone began his discussion by stating as a general rule that no person shall be excused from punishment 'excepting such as are expressly defined and exempted by the laws themselves'.[54] The discussion corresponded with general features of law in this period. It only related to serious crimes, and was often about excusing from capital punishment. There was no general discussion of malice, which was discussed only in relation to murder and treason, and there was no settled terminology, with the writers using terms such as excuses, exemptions, and justification almost interchangeably. These rules about responsibility assumed the existence of general capacities to know and obey the law, and did not seek to specify these in any greater detail. There was an assumption about capacity, as a precondition of effective punishment.[55] However, this was largely framed in exculpatory terms—who was exempt from liability—rather than specifying how the individual was expected to govern themselves.

B. Responsibility and the nineteenth-century legislative state

The principal shift in the idea of responsibility over the course of the nineteenth century was the establishment of more explicit standards of conduct in relation to certain activities or roles—in line with the civilizing ambitions of the legislative state.[56] This can be seen in the articulation of a more inculpatory model, in which distinctions were drawn between different degrees or types of fault. However,

[51] Hale, *Pleas of the Crown*, n.33, p.54.

[52] Russell, *Treatise*, n.33, p.15.

[53] Russell, *Treatise*, n.33, pp.15–20.

[54] Blackstone, *Commentaries*, n.33, iv, p.20: also cited in Russell, *Treatise*, n.33, p.1.

[55] Punishing those who did not possess understanding and whose will would be ineffective: Hale, *Pleas of the Crown*, n.33, p.1.

[56] Analysis of Victorian concepts of criminal responsibility has focused on insanity and mental abnormality, or cases where the will is absent. I will not discuss this here for reasons of space. See JP Eigen, *Unconscious Crime*, n.32; Loughnan, *Manifest Madness*, n.32, Ch.5; Lacey, 'Psychologising Jekyll', n.32.

this was primarily done by developing the understanding of capacity, rather than through the articulation of a model of subjective liability.

The origins of the inculpatory model can be traced to Jeremy Bentham's theory of action. This distinguished between the act, the circumstances in which it was done, the intentionality of the act, and the consciousness that accompanied it.[57] It was worked out as a foundational part of his project of outlining the principles of legislation, since shaping human action required an understanding of its different elements. Specifically he argued that punishment for inadvertent or unforeseen consequences would be inefficacious because if a person were unaware of possible consequences, they could not take steps to avoid them.[58] What was especially novel in the context of responsibility was the working out of an analytical model of the relation between conduct and mental states. Writers like Bentham and Austin were expressly critical of moral concepts of fault such as malice, which they considered vague, and of the general concept of will as it had been used by criminal lawyers, because of its failure to distinguish between an act and its consequences.[59] This led to the development of the concept of intention as a way of linking actors to their conduct and its consequences—and as a means of understanding the degree of seriousness of the offence and its appropriate punishment. This new approach had three important characteristics. First, there was a separation between will, as a general condition, and ideas of *mens rea*, in the sense of a mental state relating specifically to degrees of guilt.[60] Acts could be voluntary or involuntary, according to whether or not they were willed, and involuntary acts should not give rise to criminal liability; but *mens rea* referred to specific states of mind with respect to an act and its consequences. Second, this gave rise to a distinction between action, the effects or consequences of action, and states of mind (*mens rea*). A state of mind might relate either directly to the act or to the consequences of the act, and thus had to be considered in relation both to acts and consequences: were the acts advertent or inadvertent, were the consequences desired, and so on. This created a matrix of possibilities, each of which could be weighed in terms of its consequences for liability.[61] Third, there was a recognition of degrees of fault. Intention was wider than malice, as it included consequences;

[57] Bentham, *IPML*, n.27, Ch.VII, paras.6–7; J Austin, *Lectures on Jurisprudence* (5th edn, ed. R Campbell) (London: John Murray, 1885) I, Chs.19–27. It is also clear that Austin was strongly influenced by German criminal law theory, and cites extensively from contemporary German sources. For a sample list, see *Lectures*, I, pp.ix–xiii. See discussion of Bentham and Austin in Smith, *Lawyers, Legislators and Theorists*, n.32, pp.30–41 and pp.122–7.

[58] Bentham, *IPML*, n.27, pp.161–2—as in forms of 'constructive liability' where liability for consequences flowed from the commission of an original unlawful act.

[59] According to Austin (*Lectures*, n.57, p.419), one could only will an act. It was not possible to will or intend consequences, only to desire them.

[60] This was reflected in the widespread discussion of the insanity defence, where an insane person was judged not to be acting voluntarily. For discussion of the test for insanity, see Eigen, *Unconscious Crime*, n.32.

[61] Act intended, consequences desired; act intended but consequences not desired (what Bentham termed oblique intention); consequences desired, but act not intended, and so on.

but, significantly, Austin went on to discuss negligence, heedlessness, and rashness as inadvertent forms of culpability.[62]

While the jurisprudential analysis of culpability developed under the influence of these ideas, the criminal law was slower to change.[63] The Criminal Law Commissioners made an attempt to incorporate some of these ideas in the criminal law, though their discussion was mainly framed in terms of reforming homicide law. Their Seventh Report, which contained a draft criminal code, set out some general provisions relating to responsibility founded on the principle that the object of the criminal law was the prevention of injury through deterrence, and thus that the aim was to make the law more effective rather than to respect liberty or moral agency. Any discussion of responsibility began, in their view, from an assumption about the general capacities of the person: that 'the party to be influenced by the penal law, possesses the power of electing to abstain from what is forbidden rather than suffering the consequences of offending'.[64] Their approach was thus founded on a distinction between capacity—those who possessed or lacked the power to respond to law—and intention—understood as the different ways in which individuals might be responsive to legal address.[65] The former, which included rules on insanity, intoxication, duress, children, and wives, covered situations where conduct was not voluntary by law because of the absence of will. Where conduct was voluntary it was analysed in terms of intention, which was understood as being central to both the correct legal definition of offences and to the proof of guilt in individual cases. Intention included 'every case of intentional or voluntary wrong, where the mind is actively at fault; and comprehends also all cases where the mind is, as it were, negatively or passively to blame, and where hurt or damage results from want of exercising sufficient caution'.[66] They thus distinguished between wilful and culpable injuries: the former were instances where the offender either directly intended a consequence or where they 'wilfully and knowingly incur the hazard of causing it'; the latter were aimed at protecting society against improvident rashness or negligence.[67]

A similar pattern can be seen in Stephen's analysis of responsibility later in the century.[68] Stephen argued that responsibility was a matter of positive law and the

[62] Austin, *Lectures*, n.57, I, Lecture XX: 'Absence of thought which one's duty would naturally suggest, is the main ingredient in each of the complex notions which are styled "negligence" and "heedlessness"' (p.440).

[63] See Smith, *Lawyers, Legislators and Theorists*, n.32, pp.127–59 for a discussion of the development of theories of responsibility and fault in the nineteenth century.

[64] Criminal Law Commissioners, *Seventh Report* (London: HMSO, 1843) p.17.

[65] They went on to argue (p.22) that this was not merely a moral distinction but one aimed at the protection of society. There was a third category of criminal agency, covering participation and conspiracy, which I do not discuss here.

[66] *Seventh Report*, n.64, p.22. It also covered 'failure in criminal purpose' or liability for attempted crimes.

[67] On wilful injuries, see *Seventh Report*, n.64, p.22–5, where the aim was to replace vague claims about evil character or constructive liability based on implied malice with a clearer legal test. They were also clear that rashness was a mental state with respect to consequences and not only a description of conduct. See also the discussion in Wiener, *Reconstructing the Criminal*, n.32, pp.62–4.

[68] See principally, JF Stephen, *General View of the Criminal Laws of England* (London: Macmillan, 1863) Ch.3 and *History*, n.31, II, Ch.18, though, strangely, the chapter does not address the history

effective administration of criminal justice rather than morality, and brusquely dismissed the idea that criminal responsibility might be concerned with such metaphysical questions as freedom of the will.[69] The criminal law was primarily directed at specifying the conditions of 'actual liability to legal punishment' in terms of specific crimes.[70] However, he identified six general conditions of criminal responsibility: age; that the act be voluntary or willed (i.e. not attended by compulsion); that it must be intentional (general intention and the specific intent for each crime); that it must be accompanied by knowledge (covering mistake of law and fact); that malice, fraud, or negligence may be relevant; and that each condition might be affected by the insanity of the offender.[71] This analysis thus distinguishes broadly between will and voluntariness, as conditions relating to conduct, and 'intentional' elements of the crime, understood as relating broadly to *mens rea*. There was far greater weight now on the intentional elements of the crime in terms of defining the degree of seriousness of an offence and of the culpability of the offender. Thus, while Stephen denied the possibility of defining *mens rea* in general terms, it was clear that this understanding of the general conditions of responsibility was the backdrop against which abnormal conduct could be measured and excused.[72]

In spite of this greater degree of conceptual sophistication, Stephen's view was subject to limits. He saw the effect of the requirement of malice as 'throw[ing] upon persons who commit acts of a particular class the burden of proving that they were not done under the circumstances contemplated by the legislature, but at the same time to permit them to give evidence to that effect'.[73] He defended the rule that every person should be presumed to intend the natural consequences of their actions, or what must have appeared to them at the time as a natural consequence of their conduct—notwithstanding that it appeared to conflict with more general claims about intention.[74] This he argued was little more than a rule of common sense, and a corrective against the temptation to confuse motive and

of responsibility at all. There is also a discussion along similar lines in his judgment in *Tolson* (1889) 16 Cox CC 629 at pp.643–49. See infra.

[69] Stephen, *General View*, n.68, p.82—it being an instance of these moral beliefs that a person should only be liable to punishment if they know that certain acts are prohibited and possess the power of abstaining from them (p.90). He also argued (p.83) that its retention gave the law a certain amount of flexibility in responding to new situations.

[70] Stephen, *History*, n.31, II, p.96.

[71] Stephen, *History*, n.31, II, p.97. His approach was also based on a kind psychological realism: that internal mental events occur in a certain order, seen as a 'substantially correct account of normal voluntary action' (*History*, II, p.101). He argued that every voluntary action comprised the following elements in the following order: 'knowledge, motive, choice, volition, intention; and thoughts, feelings and emotions adapted to execute the intention' (*History*, II, p.100).

[72] See Stephen, *General View*, n.68, p.75. Cf. 'The full definition of every crime contains expressly or by implication a proposition as to a state of mind' (*Tolson*, at p.645).

[73] Stephen, *General View*, n.68, p.83.

[74] See Stephen, *History*, II, n.31, pp.110–1. Cf. 'Every person must be deemed to intend the consequences which would naturally follow from his conduct…' (*A Digest of the Criminal Law*, Art.94, (4th edn) (London: Macmillan, 1887)—though note that this is offered as a rule relating to the law of treason, rather than as more general principle. See discussion in Smith, *Lawyers, Legislators and Theorists*, n.32, pp.166–71.

intention or to deny an immediate intention because of an ulterior intent.[75] This was in part an acknowledgement of the difficulties of proving intent, but it was also part of the broader project of establishing standards of conduct.[76] Individuals were presumed to possess certain capacities, including that of foresight, because this was consistent with the broader educative function of the law. The possession of a will, he argued, 'implies a power of attending to what is remote and of judging particular matters by general rules'.[77] Forms of strict and vicarious liability were introduced, and were endorsed by the courts on the grounds that people engaged in certain types of activities acted under duties towards the public and that statutes should be interpreted in such a way as to enforce these duties.[78] However, as Wiener has argued, 'high and expansive standards of personal liability—even strict liability—were... not alternatives to a standard of personal fault, but part of a moral agenda'.[79] This can also help to explain why writers such as Stephen viewed negligence as a state of mind, because they were not attempting to specify actual psychological facts which were capable of proof, but to specify the capacities which the responsible legal subject was presumed to be capable of exercising.[80] If an outcome could be prevented this could be seen as someone's responsibility, and criminal liability could arise if this was the result of neglect. The role of the law was thus to encourage careful or responsible behaviour by imposing liability in these cases.[81] The law increasingly recognized liability for unintentional omissions or crimes of neglect, where the mental element was the 'absence of due attention to the discharge of duties imposed by law'.[82]

The impact of this broad conception of capacities can be seen in the discussion in the celebrated cases, amongst others, of *Prince* and *Tolson*.[83] These both raised the question of the weight to be given to the knowledge or understanding of the

[75] See Stephen, *History, op. cit.,* n.31, II, p.111.

[76] Cf. Criminal Law Commissioners, *Seventh Report*, n.64, p.22 attempting to distinguish between matters of law and evidence. See L Farmer, 'Responsibility and the Proof of Guilt' in MD Dubber & L Farmer (eds), *Modern Histories of Crime and Punishment* (Stanford: Stanford UP, 2007). See also Rodensky, *The Crime in Mind*, n.32.

[77] Stephen, *History*, n.31, II, p.104.

[78] See the cases discussed in Smith, *Lawyers, Legislators and Theorists*, Ch.6; J Ll J Edwards, Mens Rea *in Statutory Offences* (London: Macmillan, 1955) esp. Chs.4 & 10. It is clear that there was no uniformity among judges, with cases often turning on the construction of the wording of particular statutes, or what judges saw as the justice or injustice of imposing liability in particular cases. It is also clear that some judges, such as Wright J, were trying to develop stronger arguments in favour of a presumption of *mens rea* (see e.g. *Sherras v de Rutzen* [1895] 1 QB 918).

[79] Wiener, *Reconstructing the Criminal*, n.32, p.48 and pp.81–2.

[80] Cf. Smith, *Lawyers, Legislators and Legal Theorists*, n.32, Pt.II which expresses puzzlement at the persistent characterization of negligence as a state of mind by nineteenth century theorists and lawyers.

[81] As Wiener points out (*Reconstructing the Criminal*, n.32, pp.74–83) these changes were matched by developments in the law of torts.

[82] Stephen, *History*, n.31, II, pp.113–4 and pp.122–3. He identifies the specific cases of railway servants, furious driving, and parents and children, where duties were specified by law. See also *Digest*, Ch.22 on forms of culpable negligence and duties for the preservation of life & Arts.264–6 on neglect of children and apprentices by parents and masters.

[83] Stephen, *History*, n.31, II, pp.116–8.

defendant at the time the conduct took place—or the meaning of the maxim *actus non facit reum nisi mens sit rea*.[84] The cases are often cited in support of the proposition that subjective *mens rea* is a necessary requirement for certain classes of offences, but are in fact more limited in what they established. The starting point in both cases was the recognition that in all cases *mens rea* was normally inferred from proof of the conduct, and so the issue was not whether the Crown had to prove knowledge, but on what grounds this presumption could be excluded.[85] It was accepted that, as a general principle, mistake of fact might exclude the presumption. The question in each case was then the narrow one of whether the particular statute was framed in such a way as to permit the defendant to defeat the normal rule that *mens rea* was inferred from the conduct.[86] The majority in *Prince* argued that it could, as the legislature was primarily concerned with establishing the rule that certain classes of person (i.e. seducers of young girls) should act at their peril.[87] In *Tolson*, by contrast, where it was clear that the sympathies of the majority of the court lay with the unwitting bigamist, it was argued that the remarriage of widows was not presumptively immoral, and thus that Parliament could not have intended that they should act at their peril. Two important points are to be noted. First, the question was framed as one of the presence or absence of moral transgression as a quality of the *act*, rather than the agency of the accused (seducers and abductors should act at their peril, the class of widows should not), and whether permitting mistake as an excuse would make a difference to the preventability of the wrong.[88] Second, it was strikingly argued in *Prince* (and affirmed in *Tolson*) that the approach of the court gave full scope to the doctrine of *mens rea*, because in each case the act was voluntary.[89] This accordingly suggests that rather than developing a subjective test of intention, the discussions were about defining the appropriate standards of conduct through an understanding of capacity.[90]

[84] *Prince* (1875) 2 LR 154; *Tolson* (1889) 23 QB 168; 16 Cox CC 629. Both were charges under the Offences Against the Person Act 1861: *Prince* concerned the abduction of a 15 year old girl (under s.55), where the defendant was said to have honest and reasonable grounds for believing her to be over 16; Tolson was charged with bigamy (under s.57) though she had reasonable grounds for believing that her first husband had in fact perished at sea.

[85] See especially the dissenting judgment of Brett J in *Prince* and the judgments of Hawkins J, Cave J, and Stephen J in *Tolson* which make these similarities clear. On the background to *Prince*, see L Bibbings, *Binding Men. Stories about Violence and Law in Late Victorian England* (London: Glasshouse, 2014) Ch.1.

[86] See e.g. Brett J in *Prince* at pp.169–70 cited by Stephen in *Tolson* at p.647. And again, all the judges appeared to accept that Parliament might exclude the presumption as to *mens rea*, if this were expressed in sufficiently clear terms.

[87] See also Stephen, *History*, n.31, II, p.117, also discussing the case of *Bishop* (1880) 5 QBD 259 on similar grounds.

[88] In *Prince* it was considered that permitting mistake might make the law less enforceable; in *Tolson* that it would make no difference.

[89] See Bramwell B in *Prince* at p.175: if he had believed he had the consent of the father, or that she was not in the possession of her father 'he would not know he was doing the *act* forbidden by the statute' (emphasis in original).

[90] However it is interesting here that the courts are in the process of assembling a body of case law covering a number of different issues into an argument about the strength of the principle of *actus non facit reum*. This was traced back specifically to a statement of Lord Kenyon in *Fowler v*

Overall this period saw the development of a more general account of responsibility, codifying the distinction between act and state of mind, will and intention, and different forms of intentionality. This could be articulated independently of particular crimes, but although culpability was beginning to be analysed in a more systematic way, it did not yet operate as an organizing principle at the level of the criminal law. As the Criminal Law Commissioners stated: 'It is not... necessary, and it would be highly inconvenient that the *mens rea* should actually enter into the definition of each individual crime...'[91] The individual who the law was addressed to was conceived as capable of reasoning, able to anticipate or foresee consequences, and to adjust his or her conduct according to certain stimuli.[92] This was not matched to the actual proof of subjective states of mind, but generally took the form of rules which laid down standards of conduct—reflecting the fact that trial procedure was not overly concerned with proving states of mind.[93] However, this more developed account of capacities grounded a broader range of responsibilities in criminal law, and contributed to the growth of the law in this period.[94]

C. The rise of subjective liability

The first half of the twentieth century saw an increasing refinement of the mental element in crime, as scholars and the courts developed the framework established during the nineteenth century. *Mens rea* was understood in Austinian terms as referring to intention and recklessness as distinct states of mind, defined in terms of knowledge and foresight; these were relevant both to the constitution of liability and the degree of culpability. This process was accompanied by a shift in the understanding of the significance of individual responsibility to the criminal law, signalled by claims, such as that of Glanville Williams, that the concepts of intention and recklessness 'hold the key to the understanding of a large part of criminal law'.[95] The aim, however, was not only the conceptual clarity that a general part

Padgett (1798) 101 ER 1103) and also began to draw a distinction between statutory and non-statutory offences and arguments about the morality/immorality of the conduct. This was also subtly changing the position of the courts vis-à-vis the legislature in suggesting that there were common law principles which might be read into statutes.

[91] Criminal Law Commissioners, *Seventh Report*, n.64, p.22.

[92] Stephen, *General View*, n.68, p.87: 'The general meaning of sanity is, that the person of whom it is predicated conducts himself in this normal manner, that he is acquainted with the circumstances by which he is surrounded, that he has objects in view in his actions, and that he regulates his conduct with reference to them and to the general considerations which affect matters of that class.'

[93] This reached its apogee in the robust formulation of Oliver Wendell Holmes who argued that the law must lay down objective standards of conduct: *The Common Law* (Boston: Little, Brown & Co, 1881) Lecture 2. See also Smith, *Lawyers, Legislators and Theorists*, n.32, pp.185–8.

[94] See also Wiener, *Reconstructing the Criminal*, n.32, p.54 pointing out that the criminal law in this period was not *laissez-faire* but interventionist. See pp.67–83 for a general review.

[95] G Williams, *Criminal Law. The General Part* (London: Stevens & Sons, 1953) p.29. Cf. JWC Turner, 'The Mental Element in Crimes at Common Law' in L Radzinowicz & JWC Turner, *The Modern Approach to Criminal Law* (London: Macmillan, 1948) at pp.206–8.

might bring, but also to link the criminal law to new conceptions of freedom in the welfare state.

This self-consciously modern approach to the mental element aimed finally to replace the moral language of fault in the common law with a descriptive concept of fault capable of matching legal definitions to certain legally 'provable' states of mind—in effect closing the gap between the presumed capacities of the legal subject and their actual psychological capacities.[96] Central to this process was the dismantling of the presumption that a person intended the natural consequences of their actions. Kenny, writing in 1902, stated the presumption in its nineteenth-century form, that 'in most cases the law regards the criminal act itself as sufficient *prima facie* proof of the presence of this *mens rea*'.[97] However, for Williams in 1955, this rule was at best to be regarded as an evidential presumption because the presumption in its original form 'contains a serious threat to any rational theory of intention'.[98] The proof of an act was distinct from proof of an intention, and while conduct might evidence intention, this would have to be judged by the standards of empirical proof rather than be assumed by means of the presumption.[99] Key to his argument was the claim that there was a distinction between a natural and an intended consequence. Natural consequences were things that happened, many of which could not be foreseen. Thus the scope of intended consequences was much narrower as not all natural consequences were necessarily intended. More importantly, he argued that a test of natural consequences was objective, destroying the possibility of a subjective definition of intention as well as any distinction between intention and negligence.[100] This theoretical critique went hand in hand with a number of important cases heard by the newly constituted Court of Criminal Appeal and the House of Lords which addressed the relationship between the subjective state of mind of the accused and the scope of the presumption.[101] Not all of the cases were decided in favour of subjectivity, but issues about foreseeability and fault and the relationship between them were discussed in an increasingly sophisticated way.

By far the most important of these cases was *Woolmington v DPP* (1935), which linked the question of proof of mental state to the presumption of innocence.[102]

[96] See e.g. Williams, *Criminal Law*, n.95, pp.79–80; Turner, *Mental Element,* n.95, p.199. See generally Farmer, 'Criminal Responsibility and the Proof of Guilt', n.76.

[97] *Outlines of Criminal Law* (1st edn) (Cambridge: Cambridge UP, 1902) p.41.

[98] Williams, *Criminal Law*, n.95, pp.77–81 at p.77. Cf. Turner, *Kenny's Outlines of Criminal Law* (19th edn) (Cambridge: Cambridge UP, 1966) pp.32–5 implying that the presumption had already been rejected in the nineteenth century and pp.460–1 discussing this as an evidential presumption.

[99] Both Williams (*Criminal Law*, n.95, p.80) and Turner ('Mental Element' n.95, p.200) cited WS Holdsworth, *History of English Law* (London: Methuen, 1903–72) Vol. II, p.374) in support of their argument: 'We must adopt an external standard in adjudicating upon the weight of evidence adduced to prove or disprove *mens rea*. That, of course, does not mean that the law bases criminal liability on non-compliance with an external standard. So to argue is to confuse the evidence for a proposition with the proposition proved by that evidence.'

[100] Williams, *Criminal Law*, n.95, p.78.

[101] See e.g. *Meade* [1909] 1 KB 895; *Ahlers* [1915] 1 KB 616 (CCA); *DPP v Beard* [1920] AC 479; *R v Steane* [1947] KB 997 (CCA). Cf *Cunningham* [1957] 2 QB 396 upholding a subjective test of recklessness.

[102] [1935] AC 462. The decision was affirmed in *DPP v Mancini* [1942] AC 1.

Woolmington, who had been charged with the murder of his wife, was convicted at trial on the basis of the established rule that if the Crown proved the fact of killing there was an inference of malice unless the accused could displace this. The House of Lords quashed the conviction, ruling that the burden of proof always rested on the prosecution—even in cases of accidental killing or where excuse was claimed—and that it was necessary to prove both the fact of killing and the intention of the accused. The traditional rule accordingly could not be understood as meaning that the burden of proof was on the accused to prove his innocence, but only as an evidential presumption.[103] Viscount Sankey's famous statement that 'throughout the web of the English Criminal Law one golden thread is always to be seen, that it is the duty of the prosecution to prove the prisoner's guilt' must thus be understood in terms of a shift in the understanding of what was entailed in proving guilt.[104] A precondition for the restatement of the presumption of innocence in these terms is that the idea of malice can be separated into distinct elements—the voluntary act and the more specific question of intention—and that the prosecution have to prove both beyond reasonable doubt.[105] Crucially, this novel linkage between criminal responsibility and criminal procedure is based on 'the perception of guilt as the central, all-encompassing, condition of criminal liability'.[106]

It is clear that this shift had some impact on the scope of criminal liability (and hence criminalization) as the increased burden on the prosecution made it harder for the Crown to prove intent in some cases. However, the wider impact was limited, applying mainly in murder cases and a limited number of other crimes where foresight of consequences was central to the proof of intent. It is better seen as redistributing, rather than restricting, liability as the limiting of proof of intention was accompanied by a growth in liability for reckless and even negligent conduct—for consequences that were or could have been foreseen—in areas such as manslaughter.[107] Liability for negligence was seen as particularly problematic: it seemed to rest on an objective standard and so was inconsistent with the idea of subjective liability; at the same time the function of criminal law was seen as that of specifying such objective standards of conduct. In an influential essay, Turner argued that the distinction between recklessness and negligence marked the boundary between civil and criminal law. Unlike liability in tort law, which was based on objective standards of conduct, liability in criminal law should require subjective awareness of the possible consequences of conduct. Negligence was the pursuit of a course of conduct without awareness of those consequences and, in the absence of subjective awareness or appreciation of a risk,

[103] See e.g. at p.475. See also Williams, *Criminal Law*, n.95, pp.703–6 referring to the common law rule as a 'heresy' that was extirpated from the law in *Woolmington*; Turner, *Kenny's Outlines*, n.98, pp.460–1.

[104] At p.481 (capitals in original).

[105] See G Fletcher, *Rethinking Criminal Law* (Boston MA: Little, Brown & Co, 1978) pp.537–8.

[106] Fletcher, *Rethinking*, n.105, p.537.

[107] See e.g. *R v Bateman* (1925) 19 Cr App R 8; *Andrews v DPP* [1937] AC 576. See infra Ch.8.

should not give rise to criminal liability because the person could not adjust their conduct.[108] Williams, by contrast, argued that while negligence was not properly a psychological state of mind, its use in the criminal law could nonetheless be justified.[109] Negligence, in his view, was 'a non-intentional failure to conform to the conduct of the reasonable man in respect of the consequence in question'.[110] It thus combined a subjective attitude with the objective assessment of normal conduct—with gross or criminal negligence being that which fell substantially below the standard of expected conduct.[111]

While Williams' defence of negligence did not go unchallenged, its interest lies in his combination of a commitment to subjective tests of liability with an account of the role of law in establishing standards of responsible conduct.[112] The key to his analysis was not starting from the question of the justifiability of negligence, but to start from a consideration of the activity to be regulated and the kind of rule that was appropriate to bring about the ends sought. In common law crimes, he argued that the test should normally be subjective, or based on advertence to risk; this required that the *mens rea* either be recklessness or, in the case of omissions or neglect of duty, an intentional or wilful neglect.[113] However, the appropriateness of negligence in statutory offences was more flexible. In certain areas legal regulations could prescribe exact and detailed rules of conduct (such as the use of speed limits or stop signs in road traffic) the deliberate breach of which would be crimes. This could thus concretize standards of conduct in specific offences.[114] In other areas he contended that law properly used broad standards, the departure from which could be regarded as negligence where it endangered others. Here he gave examples such as not neglecting children or driving without due care and attention, because there were many different ways to neglect children or to drive

[108] Turner, 'Mental Element', n.95, pp.207–11. Turner was also critical of constructive liability in homicide on the similar grounds that liability was based on objective standards or rules rather than subjective states of mind. For a further influential critique based on the ethical unjustifiability of punishing negligent conduct, see J Hall, *General Principles of Criminal Law* (2nd edn) (Bloomington, Ind.: Bobbs-Merrill, 1960) pp.133–41.

[109] Williams, *Criminal Law*, n.95, Ch.3 at p.88: 'Negligence is not by definition a state of mind, except in the negative feature of absence of intention.' See also G Williams, *The Mental Element in Crime* (Jerusalem: Magnes Press, 1965). Cf. Hart, *Punishment and Responsibility*, n.23, Ch.6, which criticized both Turner and Williams on the grounds that negligence was not a state of mind, and that liability could be justified where a person had the capacity to conform to the law but failed to do so.

[110] Williams, *Criminal Law*, n.95, p.86. He saw motor manslaughter as a particular problem, however, arguing that in crimes such as manslaughter there must be negligence as to the possibility of death and that it might be more appropriate to prosecute for lesser conduct crimes such as dangerous driving (p.93).

[111] Here he was careful to argue that, while this should take account of some circumstances or characteristics of the accused, it should not be collapsed into a completely subjective test. So it might depend on the skills of the individual, e.g. a doctor, but not on underlying personal characteristics e.g. irascibility or impulsiveness.

[112] This was not the only such defence: see Hart, *Punishment and Responsibility*, n.23, Ch.6 based on the capacities of the individual.

[113] On omissions, see Williams, *Criminal Law*, n.95, pp.40–1.

[114] As examples, he cited the Motor Vehicles (Construction and Use) Regulations 1947 and factory safety regulation (*Criminal Law*, n.95, p.87 at fn.11).

carelessly, and it would not be appropriate or possible to cast these into the form of specific detailed rules.[115] And finally, in instances where people in particular social positions had special duties, from doctors to seamen or railway signalmen, the culpable neglect of those duties could be justifiably criminalized because they were expected to be aware of the risks involved in the conduct of their activities. In all of these areas he argued that criminalization—and punishment—of negligent conduct could have a role in reinforcing prudential conduct.[116]

These debates around negligence were part of a broader debate that went on throughout this period about the place of individual responsibility within a modern system of criminal law.[117] The growth of legislation creating offences of strict or absolute liability was accompanied by a style of judicial interpretation which asserted that 'in construing a modern statute this presumption as to *mens rea* does not exist'.[118] This position was frequently justified on the grounds not only of the sovereignty of parliament, but also because for the courts to do otherwise would run the risk of defeating the social aims of the legislation. At least some judges and commentators sought to push back against this, criticizing the spread of strict liability on the grounds that it led to unjust practices.[119] The author of the first full-scale survey of the area in 1955 was forced to concede that there was no clear or coherent trend in the decisions, and that decisions were often motivated by little more than the courts finding ways of avoiding imposing liability on pragmatic grounds in order to avoid obvious cases of injustice.[120] By the end of the period, though, an understanding was emerging of strict liability as distinct and abnormal: its use might be justified in certain circumstances, but it should be seen as a departure from normal principles of subjective liability.[121] In his revisions of Kenny and Russell, Turner treated liability in statutory crimes as a distinct category, discussed separately from 'normal' common law principles

[115] E.g. Children and Young Persons Act 1933 s.1 prohibiting wilful neglect of a child under 16. In these areas, the use of codes of conduct, such as the Highway Code, was a way of establishing broad standards of proper conduct. See also Road Traffic Act 1930 s.45(4): failure to observe a provision of the Highway Code shall not in itself render a person subject to criminal proceedings, but such failure might be relied on in any criminal proceedings as tending to establish liability. See also Williams, *Criminal Law*, n.95, p.97, fn.13.

[116] Williams, *Criminal Law*, n.95, p.99. Cf. Hart, *Punishment and Responsibility*, n.23, pp.156–7 suggesting that legal sanction gives the actor additional reasons for acting.

[117] See e.g. Hart, *Punishment and Responsibility*, n.23, Chs.7 & 8.

[118] Kennedy LJ in *Hobbs v Winchester Corporation* [1910] 2KB 471 at 483. This was discussed at greater length in Chapter 3 supra pp.98–9.

[119] See e.g. decision of Wright J in *Sherras v de Rutzen* [1895] 1 QB 918; Ld Atkin in *Re Mahmood and Ispahani* [1921] 2KB at 73; Godard CJ in *Brend v Wood* (1946) 62 TLR 462. See also RM Jackson, 'Absolute Prohibition in Statutory Offences' (1936) 6 *Camb LJ* p.83. Smith, *Lawyers, Legislators and Theorists*, n.32, pp.314–21 is more sceptical about judicial attitudes in the inter-war period. As all the commentators acknowledge, the position was very uneven, often depending on the legislative history and interpretation of particular statutory provisions.

[120] J Ll Edwards, *Mens Rea in Statutory Offences* (London: Macmillan, 1955) Ch.11. See also Williams, *Criminal Law*, n.95, Chs.7 & 8.

[121] See e.g. Turner, *Kenny's Outlines*, n.98, pp.43–8, though he appears in places to have regarded the requirement of *mens rea* to have been satisfied by a voluntary act.

of liability—and by clear implication a departure from those principles.[122] This was built into a new and influential historical narrative of the development of criminal liability in which Turner argued that the origins of the law were in forms of what he called 'absolute' liability, and the course of development was towards the gradual recognition of subjective fault.[123] This allowed him to equate modern legislation creating offences of absolute liability with medieval law and thus to portray the use of objective standards in the criminal law as a regressive step. However, Edwards' analysis, by contrast, was based not on the unacceptability or illegitimacy of strict liability per se, but on the need to develop legal protections for the individual accused. In his words:

For too long the spirit has prevailed in which the general public interest is regarded as overriding any considerations designed to protect the accused. The time has come to redress the balance.[124]

A further threat to responsibility was seen as coming from the view that social protection required that offenders be treated in terms of their needs and the threat they posed to organized society rather than punished for criminal acts.[125] On this view *mens rea* was, at best, evidence of the threat posed by the offender and an aide to assessing necessary treatment rather than being a constitutive element of a crime.[126] A modern scientific criminal law would accordingly shed outmoded moral concepts and focus instead on ensuring that the 'appropriate steps [are] taken to prevent the occurrence of such actions'.[127] These ideas had an impact on criminal justice in the UK and beyond throughout the twentieth century, with the introduction of probation and indefinite detention, as well as measures which blurred the distinction between penal and welfare systems and between mental health and punishment.[128] These created a tension between the prospective and retrospective dimensions of responsibility as it was argued that ideas about liability or guilt interfered with the aims of treatment. While this is part of much wider debates, the criminal law response, even amongst progressive criminal lawyers, was organized around the continuing significance of the principle of *mens rea*. Williams, for example, conceded that penal measures should be directed at

[122] Turner, *Kenny's Outlines*, n.98, Ch.II.2; Turner, *Russell on Crime* (12th edn) (London: Stevens & Sons, 1964) I, Ch.3.

[123] Turner, *Mental Element*, n.9, pp.195–218; Turner, *Kenny's Outlines*, n.98, pp.7–15. See also W Stallybrass, 'The Eclipse of Mens Rea' (1936) 52 *LQR* p.57.

[124] Edwards, *Mens Rea*, n.120, p.258.

[125] The emblematic expression of this in the UK is B Wootton, *Crime and the Criminal Law. Reflections of a Magistrate and Social Scientist* (London: Steven & Sons, 1963).

[126] Wootton, *Crime and the Criminal Law, op. cit.* n.125, pp.52: '*mens rea* has, so to speak...*got into the wrong place*' (emphasis in original).

[127] Wootton, *Crime and the Criminal Law, op. cit.* n.125, p.54. She concluded; '[T]he contemporary extension of strict liability is not the nightmare that it is often made out to be, that it does not promise the decline and fall of the criminal law, and that it is, on the contrary, a sensible and indeed inevitable measure of adaptation to the requirements of the modern world'.

[128] See e.g. Criminal Justice Act 1948 ss.4 & 24 permitting forms of preventive detention and treatment. See also supra Ch.3 at pp.89–103.

making punishment more effective. In service of this aim, *mens rea* might properly be modified in order to recognize the special needs of juveniles or the mentally disordered, where the question of 'technical conviction for crime has lost much of its importance'.[129] He also supported the broadening of conceptions of mental abnormality to include the capacity to control one's conduct in addition to the traditional test of ability to distinguish right from wrong.[130] However, this was not done in order to collapse the concept of *mens rea*, but rather to reflect a contemporaneous psychological conception of subjective responsibility. Overall, he contended that to giving up the requirement of criminal responsibility should be resisted because it would lead to an abandonment of constitutional safeguards, and was inconsistent with the principles of a free society.[131] HLA Hart likewise stressed the values of fairness and individual liberty against moves to eliminate responsibility from the criminal law.[132]

The period of penal welfarism is often depicted as a time when doctrines of *mens rea* and responsibility were under threat, but in reality there was a marked consolidation of the centrality of subjective liability to the criminal law. Both Williams and Hart confidently identified the advance of the doctrine of *mens rea* as the 'hall-mark of a civilized legal system'.[133] However, this vision of civil order was based on an account of the criminal law that aimed to use *mens rea* both to establish standards of social responsibility in the pursuit of social goods and to inculcate standards of responsible conduct to protect against the 'intense selfishness of persons who, rather than deny themselves the satisfaction of their own immediate desires, expose another person to a risk'.[134] Responsibility was thus linked to political liberty in a complex way: social responsibilities specified by the state were recognized in the criminal law but the individual also required protection against state power.[135] This had two specific dimensions: shifting the burden of proof clearly onto the state; and developing a critique of objective standards of liability. However, while responsibility was seen as a way of limiting liability in individual cases, it was not seen as a principle which was capable of restricting the range of kinds of conduct that could be criminalized. It is thus not surprising that

[129] Williams, *Criminal Law*, n.95, p.30. See also Hart, *Punishment and Responsibility*, n.23, Ch.7 on the elimination of responsibility.

[130] There was partial recognition of this with the introduction of diminished responsibility in the Homicide Act 1957 s.2. For criticism see Wootton, *Crime and the Criminal Law*, n.125, Ch.3 and Appendix.

[131] See Williams, *Criminal Law*, n.95, pp.30–1 on proposals to abolish the *mens rea* requirement. Cf. Wootton, *Crime and the Criminal Law*, n.125, p.66 arguing that the concept of responsibility should wither away.

[132] Hart, *Punishment and Responsibility*, n.23, pp.181–5.

[133] Hart, *Punishment and Responsibility*, n.23, p.187; G Williams, *Textbook of Criminal Law* (London: Steven & Sons, 1983) p.70: 'Increasing insistence on this fault element was a mark of advancing civilization.'

[134] Turner, 'Mental Element', n.95, p.208.

[135] Turner, 'Mental Element', n.95, p.196: 'a rule which requires the mental processes of an accused person to be investigated is a rule which emphasizes the rights of the individual against the claims of the state'. See Green, *Freedom and Criminal Responsibility*, n.32, which characterizes this as a mid-century drift towards the idea that human freedom was necessary to the criminal law.

discussions of criminalization in this period did not raise the issue of responsibility as a limiting principle; or that the discussions of responsibility did not see criminalization as something that fell within their scope.

D. The punishable subject

In this final section I want to sketch some of the more recent changes in the scope of criminal responsibility. This will be done under two heads. First, I will look at the strengthening links between responsibility and theories of moral agency in criminal law and criminal law theory. This is directed at limiting the class of persons who can be found responsible and, in a more indirect way, argues that this can limit the scope of the criminal law. Second, I shall argue that this has gone hand in hand with a fundamental shift in the ways in which individuals are expected to be responsible for themselves and their relations with others. This is a move from social responsibility to identifying the conditions of individual punishability. However, I shall suggest that far from limiting the overall scope of the criminal law, these two trends have combined to further extend its range.

In broad terms there has been a consolidation of a subjective approach to the attribution of liability. This can be illustrated by three controversies that have dominated much of the discussion of responsibility in the criminal law over the last forty years. The first concerned the meaning of 'oblique intention' in murder: whether a person who intends to do one act (such as setting fire to a building to scare the occupants) can also be said to have an intention to kill if one of the occupants dies.[136] In a series of cases between 1975 and 1999, the House of Lords gradually narrowed the definition of intention holding that a result must be seen as a 'virtual certainty' before it could be regarded as intended.[137] The second concerned the scope of so-called *Caldwell* recklessness. In *Caldwell*, the House of Lords held that the test of recklessness should be objective: that the risk was obvious to a reasonable person.[138] The decision was much criticized for the unjust consequences of the application of an objective test in the case of those who were not, or could not have been, aware of a risk, as well as for the incoherence of having different (subjective and objective) tests of recklessness in different parts of the criminal law.[139] It was finally overturned in the case of *G*, which established a subjective test.[140] Lastly, there was the decision in *Morgan v DPP* (1975) in which

[136] Following *DPP v Smith* ([1961] AC 290). This was followed by the Criminal Justice Act 1967 s.8 which replaced the rule in *Smith* with a subjective test.

[137] *Hyam v DPP* [1975] AC 55; *Moloney* [1985] AC 905; *Nedrick* [1986] 83 Cr App R 267; *Hancock & Shankland* [1986] AC 455; *Woollin* [1999] AC 82. For discussion, see A Ashworth & J Horder, *Principles of Criminal Law* (7th edn) (Oxford: Oxford UP, 2013) pp.168–75 concluding that it is nonetheless still too flexible. For further discussion see N Lacey, 'A Clear Concept of Intention: Elusive or Illusory?' (1993) 56 *Mod LR* 621.

[138] [1982] AC 341, concerning the interpretation of the Criminal Damage Act 1971 s.1.

[139] [2003] UKHL 50. See *Elliott v C (A Minor)* (1983) 77 Cr App R 103. See discussion in A Halpin, *Definition in the Criminal Law* (Oxford: Hart Publishing, 2004) Ch.3.

[140] [2004] 1 AC 1034.

the House of Lords held that in a case of rape, an honest (subjective) but unreasonable belief in the consent of the complainant should lead to acquittal.[141] While this could be presented as a logical consequence of a commitment to subjective *mens rea*, it was attacked as a 'rapists' charter' because the commitment to subjectivism came at the cost of protecting victims of rape.[142]

The focus on these issues in the appellate courts and academic discussion has been criticized for its narrowness: objective tests have continued to be applied in the law and significant areas of the criminal law have bypassed these tests of liability altogether.[143] However, this has had little impact on the continuing effort to develop a coherent, systematic account of liability capable of general application across the criminal law. This has taken the form of the clarification of rules and principles, such as the articulation of the 'correspondence principle': that *mens rea* should correspond to each element of the *actus reus* (and that the two should coincide in time).[144] The 'fair labelling' principle has been used to argue that the label should describe the fault and not merely the outcome: it would be unfair to convict for offences where the label may not correspond to what the person intended or knowingly risked.[145] Particular emphasis has also been placed on the distinction between offences and defences, on the distinction between justification and excuse, and on efforts to distinguish formally between different types of defences. The targets of such criticisms have largely been familiar ones—strict liability, constructive liability, negligence, possession offences.[146] This has promoted a new kind of censorial jurisprudence, criticizing definitions or rules that do not conform to the ideal or seeking to show how such categories of liability might be made consistent with subjective tests.

Underlying this account of criminal liability is a new understanding of the idea that it is only morally justifiable to impose criminal liability on persons who are aware of what they are doing and for consequences which were intended or foreseen.[147] What is novel is that the theoretical basis for the subjective account has shifted, with more focus on the normative basis of responsibility than on its

[141] [1976] 1 AC 182. This rule was finally abolished by the Sexual Offences Act 2003 s.1. For further discussion see infra Ch.9 at pp.284–7.

[142] See also *B v DPP* [2000] AC 428 and *K* [2002] 2 AC 462 affirming the centrality of the presumption of *mens rea* in sexual offences analogous to *Prince*, though cf. *G* [2008] UKHL 37 upholding strict liability as to age in the offence of rape of child under 13.

[143] See especially Norrie, *Crime, Reason and History*, n.1, esp. Chs.3 & 4; N Lacey, 'The Resurgence of Character: Responsibility in the Context of Criminalization' in RA Duff & S Green (eds), *Philosophical Foundations of Criminal* Law (Oxford: Oxford UP, 2011); MD Dubber, 'Policing Possession: The War on Crime and the End of the Criminal Law' (2001) 91 *Jnl of Crim Law & Criminol* p.829.

[144] Ashworth & Horder, *Principles*, n.137, p.75; Tadros, *Criminal Responsibility*, pp.93–5. Cf. 'element analysis' in the US Model Penal Code. See PH Robinson & JA Grall, 'Element Analysis in Defining Criminal Liability: The Model Penal Code and Beyond' (1983) 35 *Stanford LR* 681.

[145] Ashworth & Horder, *Principles*, n.137, pp.77–9. Discussed supra Ch.3 at pp.113–4.

[146] AP Simester (ed.), *Appraising Strict Liability* (Oxford: Oxford UP, 2005).

[147] A Ashworth & J Horder, *Principles*, n.137, p.155.

psychological grounding.[148] This comes in different forms, variously stressing dimensions of character or capacity, Aristotelian or Kantian conceptions of the self, and so on, but we can see certain shared characteristics. These are, first, the idea of answerability: responsibility is identified etymologically and theoretically with practices of giving an account or being called to answer. It is relational, with weight being placed, for example, on the capacities of the person to answer or the standing of different institutions or persons to call to account.[149] Second, moral agency is treated as a fundamental or irreducible fact, with responsibility as a moral property of agents. Thus, while calling to account is a social practice, and might take different forms depending on the context, moral agency is a constant. It then follows that institutional practices of calling to account should respect, as best they are able, these qualities of agents.[150] Third, moral agency is linked to the conditions of punishability of a person. A moral agent deserves to be censured and punished, but only if they have culpably done wrong, and only to the extent of the wrongfulness.[151] Criminal law is thus understood as tracking, or giving institutional form to, the underlying moral structure of responsibility practices: the community or civic enterprise can respond to the commission of properly recognized public wrongs. Conduct which is judged wrongful should be censured or punished, and there is an obligation owed both to the wrongdoer and to the victim to respond to culpable wrongdoing.[152] This has led to the new interest in criminalization. These approaches postulate an intrinsic link between wrongfulness and responsibility, linking liability conditions to the question of the wrongfulness of conduct. The criminal law can contain only those (public) wrongs that merit the condemnation and punishment of the wrongdoer.[153] The punishable individual is thus both the source and the subject of the criminal law.

This increased emphasis on individual responsibility as punishability finds an inverse in the practices of 'responsibilization' which have been identified as a characteristic of neo-liberal forms of crime control.[154] The term is used to describe the political strategy whereby individuals or private entities are encouraged to see the prevention or reduction of social risks, such as crime, as an individual rather than a state responsibility.[155] This phenomenon was originally identified in relation to

[148] For a lucid discussion see Kutz, 'Responsibility', n.18.

[149] See RA Duff, 'Responsibility, Citizenship, and Criminal Law' in RA Duff & SP Green, *Philosophical Foundations,* n.143; J Gardner, 'The Mark of Responsibility' (2003) 23 *Ox Jnl of Leg Stud* p.157: 'being able to offer an account of oneself as a rational being' (at p.161).

[150] RA Duff, *Answering for Crime* (Oxford: Hart Publishing, 2007) p.47: 'Culpable responsibility *for* moral wrongdoing is responsibility *as* a moral agent' (emphasis in original).

[151] See e.g. A von Hirsch, *Censure and Sanctions* (Oxford: Oxford UP, 1994) p.24, discussed supra Chapter 3 at pp.108–12.

[152] RA Duff, 'Responsibility, Citizenship', n.149, p.140.

[153] RA Duff, 'Perversions and Subversions of the Criminal Law' in RA Duff et al. (eds), *The Boundaries of the Criminal Law* (Oxford: Oxford UP 2010) p.89.

[154] See D Garland, *The Culture of Control. Crime and Social Order in Contemporary Society* (Oxford: Oxford UP, 2001) pp.124–7; P O'Malley, 'Risk, Power and Crime Prevention' (1992) 21 *Economy & Society* 252. There are further examples of this trend in the substantive law in Chapters 7–9 infra.

[155] 'The recurring message of this approach is that the state alone is not, and cannot effectively be, responsible for preventing and controlling crime': D Garland, 'The Limits of the Sovereign State: Strategies of Crime Control in Contemporary Society' (1996) 36 *BJ Crim* 445 p.453.

crime prevention initiatives where people are expected or required to take responsibility for limiting or reducing opportunities for their own criminal victimization through 'target-hardening' or changing their own behaviour. The term has subsequently been used to describe a range of initiatives, which establish new, more demanding, responsibilities in criminal law. There has been the creation of new duties, such as to report or disclose specific forms of potential criminal activity. Recent statutes have created crimes of failure to report suspected money laundering, suspected financial offences related to terrorism, and information about terrorism and serious organized crime.[156] While these raise questions of the scope of civic obligations, it is worth noting that they are not inconsistent with subjective liability—the person who knows and intentionally withholds—and can readily be justified in the name of the potential victims of serious crime.[157] Second, there has been a growth in the number of offences which criminalize the creation of risk. The Serious Crimes Act 2007, for example, has replaced the common law of incitement with a group of new offences which criminalize encouraging or assisting crime.[158] More controversially, risk-based possession offences, such as the possession of offensive weapons, are justified in terms of the need to criminalize the creation of unjustified risks.[159] In these cases responsibility is conceived broadly in terms of being responsible for creating potentially dangerous situations, or for the future consequences of one's conduct.[160] The responsibility for order is passed to individuals. Finally, there are more complex structures of responsibility, particularly in instances of interpersonal relationships, where the issue is not only knowledge of consequences but the requirement to engage with the potential impact of conduct on the conduct of others. A paradigm instance of this is prosecutions for the reckless transmission of the HIV virus, where recklessness has been understood not just in terms of the magnitude of the risk of transmission, but as requiring the person who is HIV positive to disclose their status in order that the potential 'victim' is fully informed about the potential risks—irrespective of the willingness of that other person to consent to the risk.[161] In his important analysis of the 'insecurity

[156] Proceeds of Crime Act 2002 ss.330 & 331; Terrorism Act 2000 ss.19, 21A, & 38B; Criminal Justice and Licensing (S) Act 2010 s.31. See discussion in A Ashworth, 'Criminalising Omissions' in A Ashworth, *Positive Obligations in Criminal Law* (Oxford: Hart Publishing, 2013) pp.56–65; L Campbell, 'Organised Crime and the Criminal Justice and Licensing (Scotland) Act 2010' (2014) 18 *Edin LR* p.225.

[157] See e.g. Ashworth, 'Criminalising Omissions', n.156, p.62: 'the purpose of an offence of failure to report is to improve the protection of victims'.

[158] Serious Crime Act 2007 Pt.II esp. ss.44–6. See discussion in Ashworth & Horder, *Principles*, n.147, pp.476–84 where the offences are criticized for lack of specification of the terms 'encouragement' and 'assistance', but the general principle is supported.

[159] Controversial because much criticized. See Dubber, 'Policing Possession', n.143; A Ashworth, 'The Unfairness of Risk-Based Possession Offences' in *Positive Obligations*, n.156; Duff, 'Perversions and Subversions'; Simester & von Hirsch, *Crimes, Harms and Wrongs. On the Principles of Criminalisation* (Oxford: Hart Publishing, 2011) Ch.4. For a different view see V Tadros, ' Crimes and Security' (2008) 71 *Mod LR* p.940.

[160] Duff describes these as forms of implicit endangerment, *Answering for Crime*, n.150, Ch.7.

[161] *R v Dica* [2004] QB 1257; *Konzani* [2005] 2 Cr App R 13. For discussion see M Weait, *Intimacy and Responsibility. The Criminalisation of HIV Transmission* (London: Routledge-Cavendish, 2007) Ch.5.

state', Ramsay has characterized this broad shift in responsibilization practices in terms of a broader conception of 'vulnerable autonomy' which underlies a number of new powers in the criminal law. The person is vulnerable and requires reassurance against uncertainty; criminal responsibility in these cases extends to those 'failures to reassure' the potential victim which create a sense of insecurity.[162]

The significance of these developments lies in the interaction between moral and social responsibilities, the combination of the extension of social responsibilities and moralized forms of criminal liability.[163] Although the moralized conception of responsibility promises fairness to the individual (their 'punishability') and the potential limiting of the scope of the criminal law, it is arguable that this approach has at the same time afforded new possibilities for the extension of criminalization. The reshaping of the scope of social or civic responsibilities to prevent crimes has made individuals more responsible (or responsible for more), and criminal liability has been attached to the failure to fulfil these responsibilities. Clearly there is a tension here between these two trends. It may be, as Kutz has suggested, that the stress on concepts of responsibility is a reaction to loss of meaning, an attempt to anchor subjectivity in an increasingly complex world.[164] Alternatively, the more uncomfortable truth may simply be that this conception of responsibility has legitimized the extension of the criminal law. In the next section, I will discuss the implications of the historical account.

IV. Criminal Responsibility and Civil Order

In this chapter I have traced the gradual transformations in the content and significance of the concept of responsibility in the criminal law in the modern period. One key difference from existing historical accounts is that I have focused less on the questions of who is or is not a responsible person, or which characteristics of the person have taken on legal significance, and more on the question of how responsibility was conceived and distributed as a means of achieving the changing aims of the criminal law. That is to say, I have tried to open up a different kind of perspective by situating the concept of responsibility in an account of its functions. It is important to acknowledge that this is a schematic account: the shifts were sometimes incomplete, there have always been other modes of attributing liability, and I have of necessity had to be selective in my coverage of issues because the literature on questions of criminal responsibility is so vast. However,

162 P Ramsay, *The Insecurity State: Vulnerable Autonomy and the Right to Security in the Criminal Law* (Oxford: Oxford UP, 2012) Ch.5.

163 This is not to suggest that the same view of responsibility has not also been used to argue for a more minimalist view of the role of criminal law.

164 'The shift in contemporary moral and legal thinking...towards a deontology focusing on individual responsibility, manifests the central social and political dilemma of late modernity: reconciling individual meaning and autonomy with the increasingly consolidated social world.' Kutz, 'Responsibility', n.18, p.551.

some clear and important themes have emerged and in this section I want to draw out some of the implications of my account.

The central theme has been the recognition in the criminal law of a new kind of agency. As I argued in Chapter 2, the growth of the modern criminal law is fundamentally concerned with the question of securing civil order: the interaction of self-directed, autonomous individuals in a modern society. The individual is embedded in social relations and must attune their conduct to the conduct of others in an increasingly complex and interconnected society. The law is one of a range of external controls founded on the idea that the individual is him- or herself continuously regulating their own behaviour.[165] The criminal law's role in the management of social life is to curb passions and impulsive behaviour, stabilizing expectations about the conduct of others and helping to establish relations of trust. Civil order is not primarily about moral community, but about the co-ordination of complex modern societies composed of a range of entities or legal persons who are responsible in a range of different ways for their own conduct, for the wellbeing of others, and for the maintenance of social institutions. In substantive terms, this order has been secured by establishing rules for the conduct of social of life in an increasingly diverse range of activities—what we might call the establishment of *responsibilities*.[166] But this has also been accompanied by changes in the form of responsibility, with the law establishing a general framework of rules for how persons were expected to act and judging them according to these standards. In broad terms, this has developed over the period we have looked at from the elaboration of specific responsibilities in the context of particular relationships or activities, to the idea of the responsible individual as a general category and a subjectivity that extends across social life. The responsible individual foresees outcomes and measures probabilities, corresponding to longer and more complex social chains in which each act is now enmeshed.[167] In specific terms we see this in the shift from responsibility based on manifest culpability in the immediate physical context in which actions took place, to forms of agency which extend through time and space. The modern concepts of intention and recklessness are concerned with the future consequences of actions and the impact of conduct on persons beyond immediate spatio-temporal contexts. The legal person is constructed as a particular kind of risk-minimizing actor, one who takes precautions and who reflects on the possible impacts of their conduct. This model of agency, this continuous form of control, operates even in the absence of direct compulsion or punishment, as legal persons are expected to conduct themselves in a certain way. The story of the development of responsibility from this perspective

[165] N Elias, *The Civilizing Process* (Oxford: Blackwell, 1994) p.368.

[166] See discussion in Ch.3 supra. See also P Joyce, *The Morality of Freedom. Liberalism and the Modern City* (London: Verso, 2003).

[167] Something that is also capable of being reconstructed in courtroom procedures. See Lacey, 'Responsibility and Modernity', n.2, linking developments in the concept of responsibility to changes in the trial process.

is nothing less than the articulation of a generalized expectation of proper conduct for individuals in modern society.

A crucial issue here, as Norrie has recognized, is that of abstraction.[168] But while he has focused on abstraction from social life—the creation of a universal moral subject in law which was blind to the injustices and inequalities of social life—the process of abstraction is also an abstraction from the law relating to specific crimes. The focus here has been on the systematization of responsibility, or more specifically how a certain version of personal responsibility focused on foresight of consequences became the model for the systematization of the criminal law.[169] We have accordingly traced the development in the form of the law towards general rules, organized around a central conception of responsibility, which has then been taken as capable of defining the scope of criminal law. In this process there has been a standardization of terminology and tests, the recognition of a common conceptual structure.[170] We have seen this in the move from an idea of general *mens rea* and broad exculpatory conditions to a more refined conceptual schema or model that marks the distinction between capacity and knowledge or intention, different degrees of fault based on mental states, the state of knowledge necessary for different crimes, and so on. This same model has then been reflexively applied to the criminal law as a whole, as a general structure, enabling the identification of rules or areas of law, notably the marking out of strict liability, as impermissible or illegitimate forms of liability. There have undoubtedly been benefits from this process, but the narrow focus on form rather than function, with responsibility in the criminal law coming to be understood as primarily concerned with conditions of liability to punishment and not with the content of the criminal law, has led to the creation of certain theoretical blindspots.

The recognition of responsibility is central to the modality of law as a particular means of securing civil order: that is to say the resort to law as a form of government reinforces the civility of civil order. As a mode of governance, taking self-directing agents as the basic unit of social order requires certain features of law in the sense which distinguishes law from other modes of regulation, social control, or just plain coercion.[171] Modern law accordingly takes the form of rules of general application which assume the possibility of non-obedience, while at the same time binding the subject to the idea that obedience to the rules operates for

[168] See Norrie, *Crime, Reason and History*, n.1, Ch.2.

[169] 'Personal responsibility is not the only principle on which social relations could be (or are) organized, but it is the principle which is… "immanent" in the criminal law' (Cane, *Responsibility*, n.10, p.62). See Chapter 5 supra.

[170] There is also, as Loughnan has pointed out, an abstraction from place: responsibility is treated as a universal, moral concept which flattens temporal and geographical distinctions: 'Responsibility in Criminal Law' m/s pp.5–6. This is captured nicely in Fletcher's claim that there is a 'grammar' or 'deep structure' of criminal law that transcends particular systemic differences—and can found the authority of international or transnational jurisdiction. GP Fletcher, *The Grammar of Criminal Law. American, Comparative, and International* (Oxford: Oxford UP, 2007) Ch.1.

[171] A feature which was partially recognized by Max Weber is his distinction between domination and authority: *Economy and Society* (Berkeley CA: University of California Press, 1978) pp.212–6.

the benefit of all. This has been recognized in part through the formal attribution of certain capacities to the legal person. Modern law as a mode of governance assumes that the person is capable of understanding and responding to rules, that they can make their conduct conform to norms, that they have the capacity to act otherwise, that they are in control of their conduct.[172] These capacities can be codified in law in different ways—as general standards or as specific rules, as negativing the voluntariness of acts, as elements of *mens rea*, as defences—and the development of the modern law can be seen in terms of debates over which capacities (or non-capacities) should be recognized and how. However, these requirements have also had implications for the form of law, such as the requirement of legality. Being responsible in law for one's conduct formally requires the existence of some sort of prospective responsibility established in the form of pre-existing rules of general application—something now formally recognized as the principle of legality.[173] And this also has consequences for the legitimacy or authority of law, in particular in relation to particular practices of holding persons responsible. Holding a person responsible in law is done in the name of the state or the community, representing the generalized interest in law and in accordance with modern democratic beliefs in the authority of legal and political institutions.[174] Courts are expected not to assume the partisan position of the victim, but are at one remove from this, representing impartial justice. Even if the court speaks in a moral voice, it is not the naked expression of moral indignation, but gives particular shape to it in a way which links responsibility practices to emerging ideas of the fair trial.[175] These practices, by which law regulates itself, are a way in which civil order is conceived as a kind of moral community.

Notwithstanding this, it is also important to note the limits of responsibility, and in particular to underscore the link between the growth of this conception of individual responsibility and the expansion of the scope both of criminal liability and the criminal law. This is particularly apparent if we look at this in the longer historical view adopted in this chapter. Here we have seen that the more systematic account of criminal liability was developed primarily as means of criminalizing conduct on the basis of general standards, and this went hand in hand with an expansion in the scope of responsibilities. It is certainly true that in the second half of the twentieth century, the general concept of *mens rea* has been used as a basis for arguing for the limitation of liability, but this has focused on the fairness of attribution and punishment, rather than responsibility more generally. The limitation of this approach is that it displaces political questions of state power or criminal *justice*, onto questions of individual fairness. Although the critique of criminal liability has raised important questions, this should not blind us to the

[172] Hart, *Punishment and Responsibility*, n.23, Ch.9 esp. pp.227–30.

[173] ECHR Art.7. Although there remains considerable scope for argument over what amounts accessible and foreseeable general rules.

[174] A Supiot, *Homo Juridicus. On the Anthropological Function of Law* (London: Verso, 2007) Ch.1.

[175] Kutz, 'Responsibility', n.18, pp.570–1.

fact that the modern idea of the self-governing individual has underpinned and shaped the growth of the criminal law in the modern period, and continues to do so. While it may be no accident that the focus on criminal responsibility has come at a time when the expansion of the criminal law makes it harder to identify principles which might govern the scope of criminalization, it is not clear that a greater focus on principles of liability can be the answer.

V. Conclusion

This chapter has sought to reconstruct the development of normative theories of responsibility in the modern criminal law. In doing so, I have demonstrated how a particular conception of responsibility has become central to the making of the modern criminal law. This conception, largely focused on attribution, has been structured around a developing understanding of individual subjective fault. This in turn has been built on a particular conception of the legal person, and this has also been the basis for building conceptual coherency and the idea of system. It has also been central to the modality of law, requiring that rules have certain qualities and address legal persons in a particular way.

However, this account also requires that we rethink the relation between criminalization and responsibility. My argument here has shown that this is a close relationship, but not in the way that is often assumed. Much contemporary theorizing about criminalization is built on the concern with individual responsibility in the sense of liability and accordingly sees responsibility primarily as a means of limiting criminalization, either at an individual or institutional level, by focusing on the conditions under which liability is attributed. The narrative of development from this perspective sees responsibility as restricting criminalization as subjective liability develops. By contrast, I have shown here that responsibility must be understood in the much broader sense of establishing rules and standards of conduct, and that the development of modern law is one in which the increasing specification of liability has tracked the growth of prospective responsibilities in the criminal law. This is the fundamental link between responsibility and criminalization, and any attempt to limit or restrict criminalization needs to address this relationship.

It has been appropriate to finish this part of the book with a chapter on responsibility because it is clear that this has become a central concept in the process of seeing the criminal law as a unified and conceptually distinct body of rules. In the next part of the book we are going to leave aside consideration of the criminal law as a body of rules and look at specific areas of the criminal law. Rather than looking at responsibility in the abstract as a general concept, we will look at the shaping of particular responsibilities in particular areas of the law. We can talk in general terms about the development of self-restraint on the impulse to steal, or to violence, and sexual aggression, but the law in these areas has developed in diverse ways. We are rarely talking about a general restraint, but always a channelling, permitting some forms of conduct and criminalizing others. This is to say that what we are responsible for depends not only on general aims of the law but on the aims of particular areas. If, up to this point, we have been looking at the processes by which criminal law has been unified or drawn together, in the next part of the book we will look at different kinds of liability in different areas of the law. This will raise questions about the relation between the parts and whole, or the general and the particular, in terms of what has been described as a polycentric criminal law. It is not that there are not going to be some common principles of *mens rea*, and we have seen that this has been developed in increasingly generalizable form, but that the meaning of responsibility—what we are responsible for, and how that responsibility is supposed to be exercised—can be different in relation to different areas or objects. As we shall see, the importance of this argument for criminalization lies in recognizing that the weight, or bite, of different arguments about responsibility may well be different in different areas of the criminal law or in relation to different functions of the modern criminal law.

PART III

SPECIAL

7

Property

I. Introduction

The law of theft is the heart of the really *criminal* law[1]

For all that many would agree that the security of property, and hence theft, lies at the heart of the criminal law, property offences have had a complicated relationship with the rest of the criminal law. While they are of central practical importance, they have long been viewed as lacking a real intellectual coherence and as almost continually in need of reform. And while the security of property has been understood as central to the idea of both criminal law and civil order, property crimes, either singly or collectively, do not always fit within the structure of criminal law as it has developed over the modern period. As we shall see, the category of offences against property is not clearly organized around a single idea. It has never been clear whether it is about the protection of just private, as opposed to private and public, property; protecting all property or just certain forms of property; protecting ownership or possession; or indeed whether property is less foundational than some other concept such as dishonesty. One issue is that the definition of property in criminal law does not coherently track its definition in other areas of law. This raises the broad question of whether the criminal law should simply protect or sanction breaches of rights defined elsewhere (and, if so, which rights require criminal sanction, and which can simply be protected by civil remedies), or whether there is a distinct relationship between property and the criminal law that requires a definition of property that is specific to the criminal law. The aim of this chapter is to look at the way that the concept of property has been understood in property offences, and at what this tells us about the broader category of crimes against property. In doing this, I shall focus principally on the law of theft (known as larceny until 1968), partly for practical reasons, because a review of all property offences would require more than a single chapter, but also because in practice theft is often viewed as the

[1] Karl Lewellyn, from the Introduction to J Hall, *Theft, Law and Society* (1st edn) (Boston: Little Brown & Co., 1935) (All further citations to Hall are from the 2nd edn Indianapolis: Bobbs-Merrill, 1952).

central or 'paradigmatic' property offence, around which other offences are organized. However, I shall not look at theft in isolation but will show how developments in the law of theft have shaped broader understandings of the category of offences against property.

Our understanding of the development of property crime is dominated by George Fletcher's celebrated account of the 'metamorphosis of larceny': the movement from 'manifest' to 'subjective' liability.[2] This has achieved widespread acceptance amongst criminal law academics, fitting with broader interests in the emergence of subjective liability and its theoretical significance (discussed in the last chapter).[3] I shall argue here that his narrative distorts our understanding of the development of theft in so far as it privileges a certain model of property offences.[4] However, his account was also part of a bigger argument that there was a distinctive pattern of liability in theft offences and their development, and that this was distinct from forms of liability in other areas of the law—principally homicide and offences against the person. He suggested, on the basis of this, that it might be possible to think of criminal law in terms of a 'polycentric' model—the idea that there are different forms of liability in different parts of the law and that the general part, or accounts of the criminal law as a whole, should be sensitive to this diversity.[5] That said, he did not fully articulate what such an account of the criminal law might look like and, in this Part of the book, I want to look at 'polycentric' tendencies in the criminal law—patterns of criminalization which in different ways pull against, or raise questions about, the unifying tendencies in criminal law. In Part II of this book, I traced the processes by which the criminal law was made as a distinct and conceptually unified body of rules. This focused, amongst other things, on understandings of jurisdiction, codification, and responsibility in order to show how a unified conceptual structure was created—a certain way of understanding the nature and scope of the criminal law. Part of this understanding is the claim that the criminal law should protect certain individual interests—specifically those of individuals in property, the person, and sex. These are seen as fundamental to the modern criminal law, as interferences with these interests are serious wrongs against individuals; the protection of these interests is also seen as crucial to social order in the sense that

[2] G Fletcher, 'The Metamorphosis of Larceny' (1976) 89 *Harv LR* 469; *Rethinking Criminal Law* (Boston: Little, Brown & Co., 1978) Ch.2. Stuart Green, for example, in his recent systematic analysis of theft law largely follows Fletcher's historical account: *13 Ways to Steal a Bicycle. Theft Law in the Information Age* (Cambridge, MA: Harvard UP, 2012) Ch.1.

[3] There was a flurry of debate around the time of publication, most notably in Fletcher's exchange with Lloyd Weinreb, but otherwise little critical engagement. See L Weinreb, 'Manifest Criminality, Criminal Intent, and the "Metamorphosis of Larceny"' (1980) 90 *Yale LJ* 294; G Fletcher, 'Manifest Criminality, Criminal Intent and the Metamorphosis of Lloyd Weinreb' (1980) 90 *Yale LJ* 319. See also M Tigar, 'The Right of Property and the Law of Theft' (1984) 62 *Texas LR* 1443.

[4] See infra Section IV.

[5] Fletcher, *Rethinking*, n.2, p.389: 'There is no single mode of thinking that accounts for all crimes.'

the institution of criminal law is for the purpose of securing those individual goods in order that individuals might then develop their own interests as they choose. This kind of understanding thus places these interests, as the interests of individuals, at the core of the law. However, in this Part of the book, I want to look at these kinds of claims more closely, not taking the interest for granted, but to look at the way in which the interests have been identified and protected in law. This will show that there is no single or simple way of expressing an interest in property or the integrity of the person, but that the way these interests have been protected in law has been shaped by changing understandings of civil order. I will show how each area has had a distinctive pattern of criminalization and that the ways in which the interests have been seen as central to civil order have changed over time.

In starting this part of the book by looking at property, I am recognizing the link, seen as fundamental to many writers in the later eighteenth century, between property and civil order. As a first move, though, we need to broaden the argument. Fletcher looked only at patterns of *liability*, and only in relation to theft.[6] It is necessary to look at more than just the form of liability but also at the interest that is protected and what it is protected against (what kinds of property can be stolen, and what kind of interference with rights counts as stealing). In addition, we need to look beyond theft to consider other kinds of offences against property. I shall argue that to understand the development of this area of the law we must look at more than just the transformation in forms of liability, to see transformations in the conception of property and the kinds of social, political, and economic contexts in which property transactions take place.[7] This allows us to look for patterns of criminalization more generally and, thus, to raise questions about the nature of the link between property and civil order.

The chapter is in three main sections. In the first section, I shall look at the development of property offences in the period up to the passing of the Larceny Act 1916. Developments in this period can be seen broadly in terms of attempts to adjust property offences to fit within a traditional common law model based on the physical taking of moveable property. The second section will then look at debates about the reform and modernization of property offences as a result of the passing of the Theft Act 1968 and its aftermath, in particular the increasing importance of the concept of dishonesty. In the third section, I argue that the development of the criminal law—and developments in the contemporary law—are best understood in terms of changes in the underlying social functions of property and their link to trust and civil order.

[6] Fletcher has been criticized for the narrowness of his approach, and specifically the neglect of economic and social changes. See e.g. Tigar, 'The Right of Property', n.3, p.1444 comparing it with the work of Jerome Hall.

[7] Cf. Hall, *Theft, Law and Society,* n.1 where the aim was to look at how changes in the form of property necessitated reform of the law of theft.

II. Protecting Property

A. The metamorphosis of property offences

Blackstone's account of property offences was characteristic of discussions at the beginning of the modern period.[8] He dealt with offences against property in two chapters: offences against the habitations of individuals and offences against private property. The first comprised two main crimes, arson and burglary, both of which were seen as distinct offences against the right of habitation, the 'immunity of a man's house'. Arson was the 'malicious and wilful burning of the house or outhouses of another man', while burglary was breaking into a dwelling house in the night-time.[9] The chapter on offences against private property covered larceny, malicious mischief, and forgery. The greater part of the chapter was devoted to the discussion of larceny, the 'felonious taking, and carrying away, of the personal goods of another'.[10] This was divided into grand and petit larceny (the former being a capital felony), and between simple and mixed or compound larceny, where the taking was aggravated by some other circumstance, such as violence or taking from a house. The discussion of larceny included lengthy analysis of different forms of taking and of the kinds of property that could or could not be stolen. Malicious mischief was the damaging of private property done 'either out of a spirit of wanton cruelty, or black and diabolical revenge'.[11] Finally forgery was the 'fraudulent making or alteration of a writing to the prejudice of another man's right'.

While the general distinction was that between taking and damaging or destroying property, there are other significant features of this account. First, there is the distinction between habitations and other private property: the criminal law was not dealing with a general category of property, but with dwelling houses and the separate kinds of threat to them, on the one hand, and with other forms of property, on the other. And even this distinction was uneven since larceny could only be committed against moveable property, while malicious mischief could be committed against all forms of property. Second, these chapters did not include all offences related to property: offences relating to forms of public property (such as army stores), or to the coin, were classed as offences against the King's prerogative; the receiving of stolen goods was dealt with under the heading of principals and accessories; cheating and swindling of various kinds were seen as offences against public trade; and poaching was a matter of public economy and police.[12] Third, the overall structure rested on a

[8] W Blackstone, *Commentaries on the Law of England* (1769 edn) (Chicago: Chicago UP, 1979) IV, Chs.16 & 17; M Hale, *The History of the Pleas of the Crown* (London: Printed by E. Rider, 1800) Chs.43–9; W Eden, *Principles of Penal Law* (3rd edn) (London: B White & T Cadell, 1775) Ch.22.

[9] Blackstone, *Commentaries*, n.8, IV, p.221.

[10] Ibid., IV, p.230.

[11] Ibid., IV p.243. This was followed by long list of statutes criminalizing damage to particular kinds of property. It was not criminal at common law, but merely a civil trespass.

[12] Cf. WS Holdsworth, *A History of English Law* (London: Methuen, 1966) (Vol.4) pp.505–6 on the changing justifications for criminalization of poaching. It was initially criminalized on grounds

distinction between common law and statute. In each case there was a basic common law offence which had been supplemented by various statutory offences—to deal with new problems or gaps in the law—though problems with excessive punishment or over-technicality could then be attributed in large part to legislation.[13] Fourth, larceny was seen as central, with many other offences seen as subsidiary to, or deriving from, larceny. One of the principal issues was thus the scope of larceny and its relation to other offences.

The eighteenth-century law of larceny was organized around what Fletcher has described as the paradigm of manifest criminality.[14] This is captured in the idea that the felonious act should be an act of force or trespass, breaking the King's peace—paradigmatically the idea of a night-time burglary, breaking the security of the home. The main features of this paradigm were that the criminality was manifest in the act (breaking, taking), and that intent occupied a subsidiary position (i.e. it was assumed if the dangerous act were proven, and could operate largely as a means of providing an exculpatory account of why an otherwise criminal act might be innocent).[15] In the law of larceny, this was expressed in the requirement for a trespassory taking from the possession of the owner: the physical act of taking and carrying away of property (*amotio* or *asportatio*) that Baron Hume described as an act of 'profligacy or daring'.[16] Problems arose as the courts and legislature responded to changes in the forms and in the quantity of property in circulation.[17] Here, however, the focus on 'taking' gave rise to difficulties, particularly where the 'taking' appeared to be consensual, because it did not fit with the central idea of a trespass.[18] Certain cases were straightforward. If the consent was obtained by threats of force this was equivalent to trespass and was robbery.[19] Servants were deemed only to have the use and not the possession of the goods of

that it gave rise to disorder and that it interfered with a privilege of landowners; and only later because it caused the wanton destruction of game i.e. moving towards a property justification.

[13] As in the discussion of malicious mischief, where the discussion is almost entirely focused on statutory offences, *Commentaries*, n.8, iv, pp.242–5. Holdsworth, n.12, pp.242–5.

[14] Fletcher, *Rethinking*, n.2, pp.76–90, 115–8. JH Beale, 'Borderland of Larceny' (1892) 6 *Harvard LR* 244 argued that it required a breaking of the King's peace, an act *vi et armis*. See also TB Lambert, 'Theft, Homicide and Crime in Late Anglo-Saxon Law' (2012) 214 *Past & Present* 3.

[15] Fletcher, *Rethinking*, n.2, p.117: 'The issue of non-intent arises primarily as a challenge to the authenticity of appearances, rather than as a basis for inculpating the actor.' See BP Smith, 'The Presumption of Guilt and the English Law of Theft, 1750–1850' (2005) 23 *Law & Hist Rev* 133 at pp.137–48 for an account of the practical difficulties of prosecuting theft and the use of summary offences.

[16] D Hume, *Commentaries on the Law of Scotland Respecting Crimes* (4th edn) (Edinburgh: Bell & Bradfute, 1844) i, p.59.

[17] 'The increasing wealth of society during the later seventeenth and the eighteenth centuries, especially in the towns of Western Europe, not only created a greater abundance of items of value in each community—it also provided more favourable conditions for disposing of luxury goods: more mobility between town and country; more peddlers moving from place to place; more markets and fairs where goods could be stolen and resold almost immediately', B Lenman & G Parker, 'State, Community and Criminal Law' in VAC Gatrell et al. (eds), *Crime and the Law* (London: Europa, 1980) p.38.

[18] Cf. the discussion of crimes of cunning, Ch.3 supra at pp.67–71.

[19] See also 9 Geo.I c.22 (1722) s.1 (theft by coercion).

their master, and so a taking was a trespass.[20] Other cases—Fletcher's so-called 'enigmas of the common law'—which included 'theft by finding' and the taking of property by bailees, contractors, or hirers, were not so simple.[21] What these situations had in common was that the defendant had legitimately come into, or been given, possession of the property; but while there was no act of taking in the traditional sense, there was a breach of 'civil trust' raising the question of whether or not it should be regarded as a criminal rather than just a civil wrong.[22]

For much of the eighteenth century these cases were dealt with, either formally or informally, as private matters, but over the course of the eighteenth and nineteenth centuries an increasing range of these 'illegitimate' takings were criminalized, as the definition of the crime was extended and as the enforcement of the law increasingly came within the purview of the new police forces.[23] For the courts and legislature this was a matter of grappling with the limitations of a core definition of larceny that required a trespassory taking.[24] In *Pear* (1786) it was held that the hirer of a horse who had entered into the contract with the intention of taking and selling the horse could be convicted of larceny because the fact that the owner's consent had been obtained by trick meant that they retained 'constructive possession' of the horse.[25] In *Thurborn* (1848) it was held that a finder of lost property could be guilty of larceny if at the time of finding they were aware that the owner could be traced and the property returned.[26] In *Middleton* (1873) it was held that a man who had kept the additional money when he was erroneously handed an excess sum by a Post Office clerk could be guilty of larceny.[27] In *Ashwell* (1885) the Court for Crown Cases Reserved upheld the conviction for larceny of a man who had sought to borrow a small sum of money

[20] 21 Henry VIII c.7; Hale, *Pleas of the Crown*, I, n.8, p.506; EH East, *A Treatise of the Pleas of the Crown* (London: Butterworths, 1803) Vol. II, pp.564–8.

[21] See Fletcher, *Rethinking*, n.2, pp.59–76.

[22] Blackstone, *Commentaries*, n.8, iv, 230. These were often regarded as disputes properly to be dealt with by the civil courts.

[23] J Beattie, *Crime and the Courts in England 1660–1800* (Princeton: Princeton UP, 1986); P King, *Crime, Justice and Discretion in England 1740–1820* (Oxford: Oxford UP, 2000).

[24] This process can be dated back to at least the fifteenth century, but I shall focus here on the principal late eighteenth- and nineteenth-century cases. See generally G Ferris, 'The Origins of Larceny by a Trick and Constructive Possession' (1998) *Crim LR* 175–88; Hall, *Theft, Law and Society*, n.1, Pt. I; KJM Smith, 'Protecting Property from Dishonesty and Harm' in W Cornish et al., *The Oxford History of the Laws of England. Vol.XIII Fields of Development* (Oxford: Oxford UP, 2010). Up until 1837 this was also a matter of negotiating the question of the scope of capital larceny.

[25] *R v Pear* (1786) 1 Leach 409. This applied only to hires and not to goods obtained by a fraudulent contract, creating a problem of demarcation between the crime of larceny and the statutory crime of obtaining property by false pretences (30 Geo.II, c.24 (1757)); the latter was used where the 'thief' secured title to the property and not just possession.

[26] (1848) 1 Den CC 387; 169 ER 293 reversing Hale's view that the finder could not be guilty of larceny because the owner had already lost possession. See also *Merry v Green* (1841) 7 M. & W. 623, 151 E.R. 916. The Scottish case of *John Smith* (1838) 2 Swin 28 made a similar finding.

[27] (1873) LR 2 CCR 38. See also JWC Turner, 'Two Cases of Larceny' in L Radzinowicz & JWC Turner, *The Modern Approach to Criminal Law* (London: Macmillan, 1948). G Ferris, 'Larceny: Debating the "Boundless Region of Dishonesty"' in J Rowbotham & K Stevenson, *Criminal Conversations. Victorian Crimes, Social Panic, and Moral Outrage* (Columbus: Ohio State, 2005).

from an acquaintance, but who had mistakenly been handed a much larger sum which he had kept for himself.[28] In *Russett* (1892) it was held to be larceny where a man fraudulently induced the payment of a deposit for the sale of a horse.[29] In none of these cases was there a taking in the traditional sense; whether or not there was deemed to have been taking had come to depend on the nature of the possession and whether the conduct of the defendant was judged to be 'fraudulent' or dishonest. At the same time, in several instances where the courts had deemed a taking to be absent, legislation was passed to meet the particular situation. The holding in *R v Bazeley* (1799) that an employee who kept property received from a third party on behalf of his employer was not guilty of larceny led to the creation of the statutory offence of the dishonest retention of property, better known as embezzlement.[30] The decision in *R v Walsh* (1812) that a stockbroker who absconded with banknotes obtained by cashing a cheque written by his principal was not guilty of larceny led to a further legislative response criminalizing the same conduct.[31] Blackmail, or threatening to publish information in order to extort property, was made a crime in 1843, adding to earlier provisions which had criminalized demanding property by threats or menaces or accusing a person of having committed a crime.[32]

The upshot of these developments was that the requirement of taking was gradually weakened, increasingly becoming a purely formal requirement, with greater emphasis being placed on appropriation or conversion understood as covering various forms of possession or retention of property that were *de facto* innocent. But in the absence of a manifest act of taking much then depended on the 'fraudulent' character of the appropriation and the intention of the owner (*animo furandi*). This put greater weight on the subjective element of the crime, both in the sense of when the fraudulent intention was formed, thereby constituting the theft, and how this could be proved.[33] While the focus is normally on intent, or

[28] (1885) 16 QBD 190; (1885) 16 Cox CC 1. The ruling in this case, as Ferris points out, was controversial, and later cases declined to follow the apparent implication of the ruling that innocent receipt of property followed by fraudulent appropriation was larceny. Ferris, 'The Boundless Region of Dishonesty', n.27, pp.79–82. Cf. Fletcher, *Rethinking,* n.2, pp.109–10.

[29] [1892] 2 QB 312. See discussion in Beale, *'Borderland',* n.15.

[30] (1799) 2 Leach 835; 168 ER 517. This led to 39 Geo.III c.85 (1799) criminalizing embezzlement by any servant or clerk as a form of larceny. Prior to this there had been statutes criminalizing the conduct of Bank of England clerks (1742) and post office clerks (1765). See Hall, *Theft, Law and Society,* n.1, Ch.2.

[31] (1812) Russ & Ry 215; 168 ER 767. Leading to 52 Geo.III c.63 covering bankers, merchants, brokers, and agents of 'any description'. This was extended in 1857 to bailees generally (20 & 21 Vict. c.54) and again in 1868 to partners stealing or embezzling property held jointly (31 & 32 Vict. c.116). See JF Stephen, *History of the Criminal Law* (London: Macmillan, 1883) Vol. III, pp.151–9. See also discussion infra.

[32] 6 & 7 Vict. c.96 s.3 (Libel Act 1843). The sending of anonymous threatening letters had been criminalized by the Waltham Black Act 1723 (9 Geo I c.22). This was extended in 1827 (to menaces). On blackmail, see P Alldridge, 'Attempted Murder of the Soul: Blackmail, Privacy and Secrets' (1993) 13 *Ox Jnl Leg Stud.* 368 pp.371–3.

[33] Cf. JWC Turner, 'Middleton's Case and the Larceny Act 1916' (1939–41) 7 *Camb LJ* p.337: 'the intellectual aspect of the crime gained an ever increasing prominence at the expense of the physical aspect.' See Smith, 'Protecting Property', n.24, pp.380–4.

the state of mind of the accused, as an element of *mens rea*, the focus on mental states also included examination of the mental state of the owner and whether they had intended to part with possession. However, unlike the traditional law, where consent negated taking, now the owner's consent was necessary to prevent an appropriation being larceny.[34] The definition of larceny thus depended on both the intent of the defendant and that of the owner. This was an expansive definition of larceny that included fraud:

> If the possession of the money or goods said to have been stolen has been parted with, but the owner did not intend to part with the property in them, so that part of the transaction is incomplete, and the parting with the possession has been obtained by fraud,– that is larceny.[35]

The outcome was that the scope of larceny was expanded from being an offence against possession to being an offence against the right of possession.[36] This is to say that actual physical possession (or the taking from it) became less important than the right to possession which could extend over property that had been lost, entrusted or hired to others, and so on. The right to possession could continue in time and space if the owner were judged to have intended this. The protection of the law was thus extended to property that was in circulation or on public display; the physical object becomes an artefact of what was really being protected, that is to say the rights of ownership.[37]

This extended concept of possession also shaped the development of the offence of receiving stolen property.[38] From the mid-eighteenth century the argument developed that the incidence of property crime was encouraged by the existence of fences or receivers who allowed thieves to dispose of stolen property.[39] The answer to this was to discourage thieves by criminalizing receiving, so making it harder to dispose of stolen property. Receiving stolen property was just a misdemeanour at common law since it was only acting as an accessory after the fact to theft, and required that the thief be convicted. It was made a felony by a statute of 1692, but this provision was limited in its effect.[40] A number of further statutes were passed

[34] Ferris, 'Origins', n.24, p.182. This could also determine the status of apparently lost or abandoned property: had the owner intended that it be abandoned?

[35] Ld Coleridge CJ in *R v Russett* [1892] 2 QB 312 at p.314.

[36] Ferris, 'Origins', n.24, p.179.

[37] This became relevant, for instance, with the development of department stores, where goods were displayed and the public were expected to circulate and even handle the property of the shop owners. ES Abelson, *When Ladies Go A-Thieving. Middle Class Shoplifters in the Victorian Department Store* (Oxford: Oxford UP, 1989) links the rise of the department stores to changes in the personal freedom of middle class women and the emergence of shoplifting as a social problem.

[38] Hall, *Theft, Law and Society*, n.1, pp.52–8.

[39] See e.g. H Fielding, *An Enquiry into the Causes of the Late Increase of Robbers* (2nd edn) (London: A Millar, 1751); J Fielding, *A Plan for Preventing Robberies* (London: A Millar, 1755). P. Colquhoun, *A Treatise on the Police of the Metropolis* (7th edn) (London: J Mawman, 1806). This was also famously the subject matter of John Gay's *The Beggars Opera*, loosely dramatizing the exploits of renowned criminals such as Jonathan Wild and Stephen McDaniel.

[40] 3 & 4 Wm & Mary c.9 s.4 making it a felony. The weakness of this provision was that prosecution of the receiver depended on conviction of the thief. See East, *Pleas of the Crown*, n.20, pp.744–5.

during the eighteenth century to address shortcomings in the law, such that, at the time East wrote in 1803, the law on receiving stolen property comprised the common law, further general statutes remedying defects in the common law, and numerous statutes criminalizing the receiving of specific goods (by type) or taken from specific places.[41] This was finally made into a general offence of receiving stolen property in 1827.[42] The offence of receiving was interpreted by the courts as requiring actual or constructive possession—the concept of possession being extended to cover situations where, although a person was not in physical possession of the property, the offence could be completed if the circumstances indicated that they had 'accepted' them.[43] In this case, then, possession facilitated the enforcement of the law against receivers.

The traditional common law emphasis on taking also had implications for an understanding of the kinds of property that could be stolen.[44] The traditional idea was that property must be moveable—in the literal sense of being capable of being picked up and moved or taken. Land could not be stolen, and nor could things which were attached to that land; animals could not be stolen unless they were domesticated. Equally, forms of intangible personal property, such as stocks, bonds, bills and notes, deeds to land, and so on, could not be stolen. As Stephen commented, the law had developed in a society where there were very limited forms of personal property.[45] By the late eighteenth century, the basic common law rule had been supplemented by a complex of statutory rules protecting a range of different kinds of property, from *choses in action* (the right to recover a debt) to different kinds of plants and animals, to minerals or other goods produced by manufacturing processes, and things which were attached to buildings.[46] These laws contributed to much of the substance and complexity of the 'Bloody Code' and were directly aimed at protecting the interests of the propertied class in their homes and estates, as well as at the criminalization of traditional customary rights associated with the workplace.[47] This process continued in a similarly haphazard way throughout the nineteenth century, with the developing list of things that

41 East, *Pleas of the Crown*, n.20, pp.743–65.

42 7 & 8 Geo. IV c.29 ss.54 & 55. This was extended in 1861 to all property however obtained to reflect the broader definition of larceny: 24 & 25 Vict. c.96 ss.91–3 with the words 'extorting, obtaining or embezzling' added.

43 *R v Woodward* (1862) L & C 122.

44 See Hall, *Theft, Law and Society*, n.1, Ch.3. See also Smith, 'Protecting Property', n.24, pp.384–7, though focusing mainly on animals and poaching laws.

45 JF Stephen, *A General View of the Criminal Law of England* (London: Macmillan, 1863) pp.49–50 where he suggests personal property could be reduced to cattle, agricultural produce, household goods, and a limited amount of money in the form of coins.

46 See list in Blackstone, *Commentaries*, n.8, pp.232–6. For a review see Hall, *Theft, Law and Society*, n.1, p.89.

47 On the criminalization of customary workplace entitlements, see JP Locker & B Godfrey, 'Ontological Boundaries and Temporal Watersheds in the Development of White Collar Crime' (2006) 46 *Brit Jnl Criminol* 976; B Godfrey, 'Law, Factory Discipline and Theft: The Impact of the Factory on Workplace Appropriation in Mid- to Late-Nineteenth Century Yorkshire' (1999) 39 *Brit Jnl Criminol* 56. For a general survey see C Emsley, *Crime and Society in England 1750–1900* (3rd edn) (Harlow: Pearson, 2005) Ch.6.

might be stolen an index of commercial and technological development. Gas and electricity were both deemed to be things that could be stolen.[48] Criminal sanctions were provided for breach of copyright in literary works, artistic works, and sheet music.[49] And within the traditional definition of larceny, a weakening of the requirement that the property stolen have an intrinsic value led to the extension of the crime to things that were worthless in themselves, but had value to their owner: tickets, void cheques, discarded documents and so on.[50] These changes suggest that property was seen less as purely a 'thing' than either as a right in a thing, which should be protected irrespective of its value, or something which derived its value from use.

As I have already noted, the recognition of different forms of taking led to a greater focus on the motive and conduct of the taker in fraudulent or dishonest appropriations. This question of dishonesty was central to the further expansions of the law that followed the scandals about large-scale commercial fraud in the second half of the nineteenth century, a period described by contemporaries as 'the era of fraud and embezzlement'.[51] The immediate cause of this concern was the high profile frauds that emerged from the railway boom and from the collapse of savings banks in the 1840s and 1850s.[52] Speculators had encouraged investment in corrupt schemes, emboldened by the large profits on offer, and managers misappropriated funds to their own use or committed financial misdeeds to cover up mismanagement and maintain the confidence of investors. The scale of the frauds, and the potential threat to the security of property, was vastly greater than that posed by petty larcenies and was recognized as such by contemporaries—though in this case, the concern was less security in possession than confidence in the system of investment itself.[53] 'Fraudulent' crimes were an incident of social development: 'characteristic of a state less barbarous; they are divested of animosity on the part of the offender, of physical injury and physical alarm to the party defrauded'.[54] The problem, though, was that this was a

[48] *R v Firth* (1869) LR 1 CCR 172; Electric Lighting Act 1882 s.23 and later Larceny Act 1916 s.10.

[49] Copyright Act 1842 s.17; Fine Arts Act 1862 ss.6 & 8; Merchandise Marks Act 1887 (50 & 51 Vict. c.28) s.3; Musical Copyright Act 1906. See I Alexander, 'Criminalising Copyright. A Story of Publishers, Pirates and Pieces of Eight' (2007) 66 *Camb LJ* p.625.

[50] See CS Kenny, *Outlines of Criminal Law* (1st edn) (Cambridge: Cambridge UP, 1902) pp.202–3.

[51] AR Barrett (1895) quoted in Locker & Godfrey, 'Ontological Boundaries', n.47, p.980.

[52] For a contemporary account see DM Evans, *Facts, Failures and Frauds. Revelations, Financial, Mercantile, Criminal* (London: Groombridge & Sons, 1859). See generally, J Taylor, *Boardroom Scandal. The Criminalization of Company Fraud in Nineteenth Century Britain* (Oxford: Oxford UP, 2013); S Wilson, 'Law, Morality and Regulation: Victorian Experiences of Financial Crime' (2006) 46 *Brit Jnl Criminol* 1073–90; GR Searle, *Morality and the Market in Victorian Britain* (Oxford: Oxford UP, 1998) Ch.5.

[53] See for example, the character of Augustus Melmotte in Anthony Trollope's *The Way We Live Now* (London: Chapman and Hall, 1875) (1st edn). See E Cox, *The Principles of Punishment* (London: Law Times, 1877) Ch.6.

[54] Edwin Chadwick, *Report of the Royal Commission on the Constabulary Force* (1839), quoted in S Wilson, *The Origins of Modern Financial Crime* (London: Routledge, 2014) p.83.

non-manifest form of crime, committed by the class of respectable people, and raising difficult questions over what was or was not permissible business conduct.

The conditions had been fostered by longer-term changes in commercial practice, in particular the development of limited liability companies which traded shares on the stock exchange.[55] The growth of a widely expanded share market brought opportunities for investment and money making, but also brought new opportunities for fraud and deception. Joint stock companies created a distinction between investors and managers, but shareholders had a limited capacity to control directors—who could also use their status to inspire trust.[56] As a consequence there was a dispersal of financial trust relations: social bonds between employer and employee were more distant, and there were problems of social and financial accountability. This was a liberalized yet under-regulated economy and by the middle of the century Parliament was looking to use the criminal law to shore up these relations of trust.[57] However, the existing crime of embezzlement was ill-suited to these larger scale frauds, only applying to specific named classes of employees (clerks and servants and so on), and its enforcement was bedevilled with procedural problems.[58] Furthermore, individual victims commonly lacked the resources to prosecute company managers or financial speculators, and were in any case often involved in complex legal struggles to recover some of their money. As a consequence between 1850 and 1880 more concerted measures were taken to define and enforce laws against commercial fraud. This initially took the form of specific enactments, often in response to specific scandals, focusing on specified acts by promoters and management in order to protect investors. This process began with the Joint Stock Companies Act 1844, which established a new legal framework for the incorporation and regulation of companies.[59] Crucially this also created an offence of corporate fraud where a director or company officer falsified company documents with the intent to defraud the company or shareholders.[60] This was followed by the Fraudulent Trustees Act 1857, which was passed following the failure of the Royal British Bank in 1856.[61] This specifically criminalized larceny or embezzlement by a director, manager, or officer of the company (ss.5–6), the falsification of documents (s.7), and the dissemination of false statements (s.8).[62] Finally, the collapse of the City of Glasgow Bank in 1878, and the prompt response by the Scottish authorities in prosecuting the directors,

[55] Taylor, *Boardroom Scandal*, n.52, Ch.1; See generally Searle, *Morality and the Market*, n.52.

[56] Taylor, *Boardroom Scandal*, n.52, p.251.

[57] Wilson, *Law, Morality and Regulation*, n.52, p.1075.

[58] See Stephen, *History*, n.31, pp.151–9; Locker & Godfrey, 'Ontological Boundaries', n.47, p.988. The common law of conspiracy to defraud was frequently resorted to, as it was not necessary to prove specific acts.

[59] 7 & 8 Vict. c.110.

[60] s.31. See also 7 & 8 Vict. c.111 (The Winding Up Act) s.30. For discussion, see Taylor, *Boardroom Scandal*, n.52, pp.78–94 suggesting that there was still little inclination to enforce these provisions.

[61] 20 & 21 Vict c.54. See Taylor, *Boardroom Scandal*, n.52, Ch.5.

[62] Repealed and re-enacted in the 1861 Act ss.68, 75, & 88, increasing the maximum penalties for these offences. See also the Falsification of Accounts Act 1875 (38 & 39 Vict c.24).

was an important influence on the debates over the establishment of a public prosecutor.[63] This period thus saw the reconceptualization of commercial fraud as a public offence, rather than a private matter. Protecting investors against company directors and speculators was thus a matter not only the security of individual property but of public confidence in the market. The law, moreover, sought to foster norms of honesty and responsibility in business dealings, raising the expectations placed on company directors.

Finally, we should note the development of the law relating to the damage of property. As we saw at the start of this section, Blackstone separated out arson and malicious mischief, distinguishing the protection of dwelling houses from fire from damage to other forms of property by other means.[64] What is striking about this and other treatments from this period, such as East (1803), is that, although the treatment was lengthy, no clear basis was articulated for the crime. Damage to property was only a civil trespass at common law, so where the criminal law had been used it drew on connections with other crimes—riot or public disorder, or larceny, assaults or piracy.[65] Malicious mischiefs were identified in a long list of statutes criminalizing forms of destruction of, or damage to, property—a list which in great part reflected the specific kinds of property that were important in the eighteenth century. This included damage to trees and plants, to fences and enclosures, livestock, manufactures, highways and turnpikes, mines and engines, docks and ships, and so on.[66] These statutes were consolidated as part of Peel's reform of capital punishment in 1827, which repealed a large number of the older statutes, and again in 1861.[67] While the resultant law was still much criticized for its particularity, the character of the regime established by the 1861 Act differed in significant ways from the earlier law. The law was aimed at preventing malicious damage to property, and arson was merely one means of causing that damage.[68] There was also a changed understanding of property. There were some new forms which were now protected, such as railways (ss.35 & 36) and telegraphs (s.37). The definition of arson was extended to all kinds of buildings (ss.5 & 6), and could be committed where there was intent to defraud or to injure and not only destroy (s.59). And while the majority of the Act identified specific forms of property, a new general clause was inserted, extending the law to any property not hitherto identified.[69] This was necessary, in the words of the draftsman, CS Greaves, as a recognition of the fact that 'in the present times there are so many valuable instruments and machines daily invented, that it is impracticable to specify them

[63] Prosecution of Public Offences Act 1879 (42 & 43 Vict. c.22). Some prosecutions before this had been taken on by the Treasury Solicitor, who continued to conduct them after 1879.

[64] See also East, *Pleas of the Crown*, n.20, pp.1012–35.

[65] Ibid., pp.1035–103.

[66] Much of this is based on the Waltham Black Acts 1723. See EP Thompson, *Whigs and Hunters* (Harmondsworth: Penguin, 1977); D Hay et al., *Albion's Fatal Tree* (Harmondsworth: Penguin, 1975).

[67] 7 & 8 Geo.IV c.30; 24 & 25 Vict. c.97.

[68] Causing damage by explosions had been criminalized by 9 & 10 Vict. c.25 s.8.

[69] ss.51& 52: if the value of the property was over £5 it was a felony, and under £5, a misdemeanour. The 1827 Act had contained a similar provision (s.24) but had merely empowered the court to order restitution.

particularly in any Act'.[70] The courts also developed this broader understanding of property, criminalizing any conduct which interfered with ownership, however slight the damage—leading to extensive debates about what to do in the case where a person believed themselves to have a claim of right over the property.[71] The end result was a more overt protection of more different forms of property.

Overall, the model of offences against property that was developed over the course of the nineteenth century was 'larceny-centred': the crime of larceny as taking from possession provided the model in terms of which all kinds of appropriation of property were understood. The development of the law was consistent with Fletcher's account of the emergence of a model of subjective liability—where liability increasingly depended on proof of the mental state of the accused—but the picture is somewhat more complex. The scope of the criminal law was greatly increased, but not only through the expansion of the form of liability: the significance of possession was transformed, as were the concept of property, and the understanding of fraudulent taking. This involved a massive shift from seeing issues around property as civil wrongs, or matters of private dispute, to understanding them as criminal and of public concern. The system which was established was directed at the protection of a range of different kinds of property which posed different kinds of threat to social order: the consumption, use, and circulation of moveable property; the use and display of property in public spaces; and the security of property which was the subject of private commercial transactions.[72] The issue of how to respond to this transformation shaped attempts to codify the law of property offences in the nineteenth century.

B. Codifying offences against property

The reform of property offences dominated debates around the reform of the Bloody Code in the early part of the nineteenth century.[73] There was widespread unease about the use of capital punishment for forgery and grand larceny and the effectiveness of the patchwork of individual statutes making property crimes capital offences. Many of these problems were addressed by legislation which repealed

[70] CS Greaves, *The Criminal Law Consolidation and Amendment Acts* (2nd edn) (London: Stevens Sons & Haynes, 1862) p.249.

[71] *R v Day* (1844) JP 186; *R v Twose* (1879) 14 Cox 327. See also Smith, 'Protecting Property', n.24, p.389.

[72] This took place against the background of general decline in the incidence and prosecution of theft—so the problem was the orderliness of the law rather than social disorder. See VAC Gatrell, 'The Decline of Theft and Violence in Victorian and Edwardian England' in Gatrell et al. (eds), *Crime and the Law* (London: Europa, 1980) pp.301ff; C Emsley, *Crime and Society in England 1750–1900* (3rd edn) (Harlow: Longman, 2005) pp.157–8. Nine out of ten larcenies were transferred to summary jurisdiction between 1847 and 1879. This was coupled with a progressive mitigation of sentences: less transportation between 1830 and 1850; decline in the use of penal servitude between the 1850s and 1880s and a rise in the use of shorter prison sentences; and from the 1850s onwards an increasing use of fines and release on sureties.

[73] See discussion in Chapter 3 at pp.68–71.

the older statutes and reformed and restricted the use of capital punishment.[74] Notwithstanding this, offences against property were seen as requiring further codification—in part because of the continual emergence of new areas or problems as discussed above, but also because this area of the law in particular was seen as complex and technical. It was no surprise, for example, that in their first report the Criminal Law Commissioners 1833-45 took the law of theft as a means of illustrating general problems with common law development.[75] And ironically, notwithstanding the passing of major consolidation statutes in 1861 and in 1916, the demands for further reform continued unabated into the next century. In this section, I review this codification process, looking at the different classifying schema proposed over the course of the century and what these tell us about how the area of offences against property was understood.

East's *Pleas of the Crown* (1803) gave one of the most complete accounts of contemporary offences relating to property in the early nineteenth century, presenting the law in all its complexity. There was no explicit principle of organization, as different crimes were dealt with in eight separate chapters, which took up almost the entire second volume of his treatise.[76] There were broad distinctions between offences related to larceny (including burglary and robbery), forgery, and arson and malicious mischief, but he also included chapters on piracy, cheats, and falsely personating another. His major contribution, though, may have been his broad definition of larceny: 'the wrongful and fraudulent taking and carrying away by any person of the mere personal goods of another, from any place, with a felonious intent to convert them to his use, and make them his own property, with the consent of the owner.'[77] This potentially included all forms of criminal taking, and was routinely cited by later authors.

Later efforts, beginning with the Criminal Law Commissioners in 1834, took seriously the question of how the law might be codified or systematized in a way that made it responsive to the shifting nature of property in a modernizing commercial society.[78] They agreed with in many of the criticisms of the existing law—that it was technical, obscure, poorly expressed—and saw the draft code as an opportunity not only to clarify the language of the law but also to address

[74] The property-value-based distinction between 'grand' and 'petty' larceny was abolished in 1827 by 7 & 8 Geo. IV c.29, which further consolidated much of the law in this area. Certain forms of larceny from a dwelling house remained capital until 1834 (3 & 4 Will. 4, c. 44 (1833)).

[75] Criminal Law Commissioners, *First Report* (London: HMSO, 1834) pp.4–9, identifying the problems as the want of certain rules, discrepancies between definitions, uncertain application of legal terms, contradictory principles and authorities, isolated decisions, the adoption of subtle distinctions, and the constructive enlargement of the law. See also J Austin, *Lectures on Jurisprudence* (5th edn) (London: John Murray, 1885) II, pp.1042–4; A Amos, *Ruins of Time Exemplified in Sir Matthew Hale's History of the Pleas of the Crown* (London: V & R Stevens & GS Norton, 1856) Ch.VII.

[76] See also WO Russell, *Treatise on Crimes and Misdemeanours* (2nd edn) (London: J Butterworth, 1828) Vol.II Bk.4 which followed a similar pattern to East.

[77] East, *Pleas of the Crown*, n.20, p.553.

[78] They discussed theft in their *First Report* (1834) and again in their *Fourth Report* (London: HMSO, 1839), under the broader head of 'Criminal Violations of the Right of Property' pp.lxvii-xci. Burglary and Forgery were covered in their *Fifth Report* (1840).

more fundamental questions about the aims of the law. It should, they argued, be adequate to the needs of the nation, recognizing 'the necessity which grows with increasing wealth and commerce, for entrusting various agents and contractors with property to a large amount'.[79] However, the purpose of penal law in this area was not to protect against all frauds or lies but 'to guard the rights of property against frauds effected by means calculated to prevail over that degree of prudence and circumspection which every man is bound to exert for his own protection'.[80] There were thus clear limits in terms of prudence and self-management—being responsible, in other words—and those who were not vigilant in this way would have to fall back on the civil law for remedies. What is striking, though, is the increasing weight given to the idea of 'fraud', understood both as a quality of an appropriation and as a means of defining criminal intent. Traditional forms of larceny were characterized as fraudulent takings, where the criminal quality of the act was manifest, while in cases where the thief had possession it was the fraudulent intent of the appropriator that was crucial. The Commissioners' approach to specific offences thus fell back on common law distinctions between different modes of taking and whether it was an offence against possession or property.[81] They thus identified five classes of offence: wrongful removal (larceny); larceny by trick; obtaining by false pretences (where property is passed); cheats (fraudulent means other than false pretences); and embezzlement (or abuse of confidence).[82] While it may not be clear to us why it was necessary to distinguish between larceny and larceny by trick, or obtaining by false pretences and other cheats, the Commissioners none the less claimed by this means to have clarified the principled distinctions lying behind these categories and to have removed the artificial and constructive extensions of the law.

This process was taken a step further by Sir James Fitzjames Stephen in his codification initiatives towards the end of the century.[83] His aim was the codification of all offences against rights of property and arising from contract, a class of offences which brought together theft, receiving stolen property, forgery, coining offences, and actions by bankrupts and company directors. However, in most of these areas, his draft code did little more than consolidate the existing law. It was only in the area of larceny that there was more systematic analysis of the concept of property.[84] Property, he argued, was not a thing but 'a general name for a number of rights, or legal powers which may be exercised over things, each of which

[79] *Fourth Report* (1839) n.78, p.lxxviii. [80] Ibid., p.li.

[81] The section on malicious injuries to property was more or less a restatement of the 1827 Act. See *Fourth Report*, n.78, p.xlviii: 'the malicious destruction of property is an injury in respect of which a civil remedy to the proprietor may be deemed sufficient…'

[82] *Fourth Report* (1839) pp.l–li.

[83] See Stephen, *General View*, n.45, pp.125–44; Stephen, *History*, n.31, Chs.28, 29, 30; *A Digest of the Criminal Law*, (4th edn) (London: Macmillan, 1877) Pt.VI Offences Against Rights of Property and Rights Arising Out of Contract. See also *Report of the Royal Commission Appointed to Consider the Law Relating to Indictable Offences* (C-2345) (London: HMSO, 1879) pp.25–30 and Draft Code, Title VI, though the approach here was more pragmatic.

[84] See Stephen, *General View*, n.45, pp.127–30.

rights taken separately may be regarded as the property of the person who is entitled to it'.[85] This was essentially the idea that different kinds of rights may subsist in a single object, allowing different kinds of entitlements to different people at any given time. There might in addition be different factual circumstances or actual powers over things (possession, custody, or charge), which interacted with the rights.[86] The law of property offences should accordingly be directed at the protection of these different 'beneficial interests', not solely the right to possession, and should be capable of applying to all forms of property, real and personal.[87] Offences against property were thus misappropriations 'of the benefits derived by another from his proprietary rights over anything which is the subject of proprietary rights'.[88] These could in turn be classed as either fraudulent or 'mischievous' depending on whether they involved the taking or transfer of property or its destruction or injury. Stephen thus argued that it was possible to include all the recognized forms of 'misappropriation' (larceny, embezzlement, false pretences, and so on) within a single general offence of theft defined as:

> unlawfully, and with intent to defraud... to appropriate to the use of any person any property whatever, real or personal, in possession, or in action, so as to deprive any other person of the advantage of any beneficial interest at law, or in equity, which he may have therein.[89]

Central to this was the idea of fraudulent intent, understood as a requirement of the necessary intent at the time of the appropriation: a single idea of *mens rea* which could cover all misappropriations, making everything from breaches of trust to temporary deprivations criminal.[90] This broad definition was intended to ensure not only that the criminal law covered all fraudulent misappropriations of all kinds of property, but also that everything should be brought under the label of theft: a fraudulent breach of trust should be called a theft because, in Stephen's view, that was what it was.[91]

In the light of these discussions, the actual statutory consolidations of the law in this period were disappointingly unambitious.[92] The Consolidation Acts of 1861 were limited in scope, directed only at consolidating statute, not common, law.[93] The Larceny Act 1861 reproduced many of the problems of the criminal law. It contained no definition of larceny, and merely gathered together existing

[85] Stephen, *History*, n.31, III, p.122; Stephen, *General View*, n.45, pp.127–8.

[86] Stephen, *History*, n.31, III, p.123 setting out the principal forms of legal relation.

[87] Stephen, *History*, n.31, III, p.130.

[88] Stephen, *General View*, n.45, p.128.

[89] *General View*, n.45, p.129

[90] It was excluded only by a claim of right, either in property law or in contract: Stephen, *History*, n.31, p.142.

[91] Stephen, *History*, n.31, III, p.132: 'Some of the most cruel robberies ever committed have been committed by fraudulent trustees.'

[92] Though it should be noted that Stephen's Draft Code provided the model for the Canadian Criminal Code of 1892 and the Queensland Code in Australia. See D Brown, *The Genesis of the Canadian Criminal Code of 1892* (Toronto: Osgoode Hall Society, 1989).

[93] Four of the Acts related to property: Larceny (c.96), Malicious Damage (c.97), Forgery (c.98), and Coining (c.99).

provisions into a single statute.[94] The Larceny Act 1916 was more significant, bringing together the developments in common and statute law and reducing the 123 sections of the 1861 Act to a mere 50.[95] Most of the Act was, once again, a consolidation of existing statute law, which succeeded in retaining a remarkable level of specificity.[96] However, it also, for the first time, offered a statutory definition of larceny in section 1:

> A person steals who, without the consent of the owner, fraudulently and without a claim of right made in good faith, takes and carries away anything capable of being stolen with intent, at the time of such taking, permanently to deprive the owner thereof.

This is of note because it codifies the common law understanding of the offence at the turn of the century, systematically combining its various elements into a new form. This did not replace the common law, but by subtly reshaping the elements of the law it reflected changes in the scope and application of the law. Thus, while the broad definition would no doubt have looked familiar to East, the way the law had been understood had been transformed. We can see this if we look at the discussion of larceny in Kenny's *Outlines* (1903), which pre-dated the Act by some 10 years.[97] It is clear from this that the identification of general elements such as taking, carrying away, ownership, things capable of being stolen, without claim of right, and intent, has replaced specific rules. The discussion of intention referred primarily to the difference between temporary and permanent deprivation, but also implied a more general sense of intending to appropriate in a way which was inconsistent with the interests of the possessor.[98] The weight of the definition, though, was on what might be termed *actus reus* elements (without consent of the owner, claim of right) where the scope of the crime was shaped by understandings of the responsibilities which different people owed towards each other. Where East's discussion drew examples from the agricultural and manufacturing economy of the eighteenth century, Kenny referred to travel by railways, to banks and friendly societies and so on. There was still a discussion of taking and carrying away which referred, as was typical, to the absurdities and complexities of the common law rule, but the emphasis was on how recent cases had shaped the older rules, defining the responsibilities of servants, employees or indeed of citizens towards each other.[99]

[94] For a discussion of the history of the Acts and the method of proceeding, see CS Greaves, *Criminal Law Consolidation Acts*, n.70, Introduction. See Stephen, *History*, n.31, III, pp.146–60 for a systematic critique of the 1861 Act.

[95] 6 & 7 Geo.V c.50. There was also a Forgery Act 1913 (c.27) which contained a general definition of forgery in s.1.

[96] See for example ss.3–12 listing different classes of things that might be stolen or s.15 on larceny from ships or docks.

[97] CS Kenny, *Outlines of Criminal Law* (Cambridge: Cambridge UP, 1903) Ch.13.

[98] Kenny, *Outlines*, n.97, pp.214–8.

[99] See e.g. Kenny, *Outlines*, n.97, pp.183–92, discussing the responsibilities of railway employees, cab drivers, and shopkeepers as well as bailees, servants, and so on.

Overall we can see that these codifications sought to organize a range of offences in terms of their relation to a more general understanding of property, while keeping the traditional idea of theft as taking at the centre of the law. What was novel was the movement towards the identification of general elements, and in particular the stress on fraud and the intent to defraud as the unifying concept. This was thus pulling away from the traditional common law approach, and trying to unify through a more sophisticated institutional understanding of property not only as being about relations with things, but in terms of social relations and the responsibilities that individuals owed towards others in a modern society.

III. Modernization and Reform

Although the Larceny Act 1916 established a reasonably settled definition of theft, the demand for reform of the law of theft continued throughout the twentieth century.[100] Discussion of the law in the early part of the century took up the criticisms of the nineteenth century codifiers, arguing that the law continued to be technical and complex, and riddled with unnecessary distinctions.[101] It was typically acknowledged that the common law was generally responsive to novel forms of dishonest conduct when they came before the courts, but argued that proceeding, as the law did, on a case-by-case approach resulted in a law that was unsystematic and based on artificial or constructive rules. By the late 1950s this had coalesced into a view on the part of the judiciary and academics that there was a need for reform—indeed the law of theft was once again taken as the exemplar of the un-modernized state of the common law and of the need for codification.[102] The cause was taken up by the Criminal Law Revision Committee (CLRC) on its formation, leading to their *Eighth Report* (1966) which provided the basis for the Theft Act 1968.[103]

[100] Green, *13 Ways*, n.2, p.18, argues that the reform of the law in England and the US in the 1960s can be seen as a 'second metamorphosis'. This can be contrasted with Fletcher who sees the movement towards the Theft Act 1968 and the US Model Penal Code as part of a single thrust towards subjective liability. See Fletcher, *Rethinking*, n.2, Chs.1–3.

[101] See e.g. Turner, *Two Cases of Larceny*, n.27; JE Hall Williams, 'Reform of the Law of Larceny: An Urgent Task' (1958) 21 *Mod LR* 43; AL Goodhart, 'The Obsolescent Law of Larceny' (1959) 16 *Washington & Lee Law Rev.* 42; G Williams, 'Case Note: Walters v Lunt (1951)' (1952) 15 *Mod LR* 222. See also the minute discussions of inconsistencies between decided cases in JC Smith & B Hogan, *Criminal Law* (London: Butterworths, 1965) Ch.14 and JWC Turner, *Kenny's Outlines of Criminal Law* (19th edn) (Cambridge: Cambridge UP, 1966) Chs.13–20.

[102] See e.g. R Cross, 'Case Note: Moynes v Coopper' (1956) 72 *LQR* 183: '[Such cases] are a public scandal both because the courts are reluctantly compelled to allow dishonesty to go unpunished, and because of the serious waste of judicial time involved in the discussion of futile legal subtleties' (cited by Ld Goddard CJ in *Russell v Smith* [1958] 1 QB 27 p.31).

[103] Criminal Law Revision Committee, *Eighth Report. Theft and Related Offences* (Cmnd.2977) (London: HMSO, 1966). See generally Ch.5 supra at pp.158–9 on the CLRC. See paras.15–31 of the Report for a review of criticisms of the law. This was more or less contemporaneous with the development of the US Model Penal Code and reforms of Australian law, which consolidated theft offences in a similar way. For discussion, see Green, *13 Ways*, n.2, pp.20–36, though as Green points

This was followed by a Law Commission Report on offences of damage to property which led to the Criminal Damage Act 1971.[104]

The stated aim of the reformers was to identify the principles underlying the offences and to reconstruct the law in line with these principles.[105] The most important symbolic move was the abandonment of the traditional term 'larceny' for the more contemporary and colloquial term 'theft' which was to cover the different forms of taking under the common law. The basic definition of theft was set out in section 1 of the Theft Act 1968: 'A person is guilty of theft if he dishonestly appropriates property belonging to another with the intention of permanently depriving the owner of it'. Appropriation was defined as 'any assumption by a person of the rights of an owner' irrespective of how the person 'came by' the property.[106] In a similar vein, the Criminal Damage Act 1971 created a new offence of destroying or damaging the property of another, where the degree of seriousness was measured by whether this was done intentionally or recklessly.[107] What is striking about both Acts is that while they replaced the older law, they none the less retained strong traces of their common law origins. This can be seen in various ways, from the specificity of the provisions of the Theft Act defining property to the creation and retention of specific offences, even where these seemed to be covered by the more general provisions.[108] And it can also be seen in the curious insistence that 'dishonestly appropriates' meant no more than 'fraudulently converts'—though the interpretation of this phrase was to be developed in a different way in the case law.[109] The Acts, moreover, retained separate, if redefined, offences of burglary, blackmail, handling stolen goods, and arson.[110] This was modernizing legislation, but the form of the statutes suggests that it was hard to let go of the past. Notwithstanding this, it is arguable that the statutes enacted a changed understanding of property, reconceptualizing crimes in this area as 'assaults upon the single personal interest in holding private property'

out (p.37) it is curious that the Model Penal Code is not mentioned at all in the CLRC Report. See also I Elliott, 'Theft and Related Problems—England, Australia and the USA Compared' (1977) 26 *ICLQ* 110.

104 Law Commission, *Report on Offences of Damage to Property* (Rept. No.29) (London: HMSO, 1970).

105 CLRC, *Eighth Report*, paras.7–14. For a critical discussion, see S Roy, 'Law Reform and the Reform of the Law of Theft' (1967) 30 *Mod LR* 609.

106 s.3 seeing theft as a violation of ownership rather than possession. See CLRC, *Eighth Report*, para.33.

107 Criminal Damage Act 1971 s.1. The offence of arson was now simply defined as destroying or damaging any property by fire.

108 Property (s.4) included money and real and personal property including things in action and intangible property, but not services or land. There was further special provision for wild flowers, mushrooms, wild animals. Cf. Model Penal Code s.223.0(6): "Property' means anything of value'. The specific offences were removal of articles from places open to the public (s.11), taking motor vehicles (s.12), and abstracting electricity (s.13).

109 CLRC, *Eighth Report*, para.35: 'The effect will be as if fraudulent conversion were widened to include the whole of larceny and embezzlement'.

110 ss.8, 9, 21 & 22. The Act also included fraud offences, principally obtaining property by deception and false accounting (ss.15–17). These were revised in the Theft Act 1978 and then again in the Fraud Act 2006.

however this was accomplished.[111] That is to say that the kind of property, the type of interference with that property, or kind of relationship within which this occurred, was increasingly irrelevant to the definition of the crime.

The definition of theft under the Act has given rise to difficulties, specifically with respect to the central concept of the dishonest appropriation. The first set of problems arose where the appropriation seemed to have been with the consent of the owner.[112] The upshot of a series of cases involving institutions such as supermarkets, banks, bad cheques and so on, where consumers were passed or handled property or money with the consent of the owner, was a decision of the House of Lords in which it was held that appropriation could take place where there had been *any* interference with the rights of the owner, even if the owner had consented.[113] This broad interpretation was upheld in the more recent case of *Hinks*, where appropriation was held to include a freely made gift, creating the situation that there may be appropriation—and therefore theft—in situations where property had legally passed under the civil law.[114] This may be seen as a logical consequence of the removal of the requirement of taking, or that appropriation should be without the consent of the owner, but the effect is to make the offence more inchoate. There is no longer any need for an overt act of appropriation, just that the person do something inconsistent with the rights of the owner, even if this was something permitted or countenanced by owner.[115] The consequence is that more has come to depend on whether or not an appropriation is deemed dishonest by the courts.[116] The term 'dishonesty' was not defined in the Act, but is now principally understood as an independent fault element requiring a judgement of whether or not beliefs or attitudes would be regarded as dishonest by the standards of ordinary, decent people.[117] This is seen by some as having the potential to limit the broad definition of appropriation, such that criminal liability for an innocent appropriation might be avoided where the accused did not act dishonestly.[118] Yet while this may be so in certain individual cases, this is to disregard the

[111] Fletcher, *Rethinking*, n.2, p.35.

[112] For discussion of this point see the dissenting judgment of Lord Lowry in *Gomez* [1993] AC 442.

[113] That is to say that there is no requirement of adverse or wrongful interference: *Gomez* [1993] AC 442. See also *Lawrence* [1972] AC 626; *Dip Kaur* [1981] 2 All ER 430; *Morris* [1984] AC 320. For criticisms see AP Simester et al., *Criminal Law: Theory and Doctrine* (5th edn) (Oxford: Hart Publishing, 2013) pp.523–37.

[114] *Hinks* [2001] 2 AC 241 i.e. that the defendant was found guilty of stealing their own property, because of their dishonesty.

[115] E Melissaris, 'The Concept of Appropriation and the Offence of Theft' (2007) 70 *Mod LR* 582; A Ashworth & J Horder, *Principles of Criminal Law* (7th edn) (Oxford: Oxford UP, 2013) pp.373–81.

[116] Although there is a negative definition of dishonest appropriations in s.2 of the 1968 Act, it is likely that this was intended by the drafters to be a description of the quality of certain appropriations (i.e. part of the *actus reus* of the crime) rather than a distinct mental element.

[117] See *Feely* [1973] QB 530. There is a second (subjective) limb to this test, established in the case of *Ghosh* [1982] QB 1053, of whether the defendant believed their conduct to be honest according to the standards of ordinary people, but this is of little practical importance.

[118] Although noting that there may be difficulties with the assumption that there is a common belief or understanding. See Ashworth & Horder, *Principles*, n.115, pp.389–94.

extent to which the area as a whole is increasingly shaped by moves to criminalize dishonest conduct.

The definition of several offences now turns on the distinction between conduct which is ostensibly innocent and that which may be dishonest. Handling stolen goods or blackmail can thus in certain circumstances be distinguished from making a good deal or 'normal' economic bargaining only by the question of whether there was a dishonest or bad intention.[119] And in a similar vein, in the money laundering offences, which extend the idea of handling, the requirement that there be knowledge or suspicion that something is 'criminal property' relies on attitudes towards, or understandings of, licit or illicit dealings.[120] The increased stress on dishonesty has also facilitated moves towards the criminalization of temporary taking. According to the Theft Act, most forms of temporary taking or borrowing fall outwith the scope of theft: there must be an intention to deprive permanently.[121] The difficulty that this creates is that certain borrowings or temporary acquisitions may exhaust the value of an object, either to its owner (where an object has been acquired for a specific purpose) or in general (where the value of an object is time-limited e.g. a season ticket), but that these were not criminalized under the Act.[122] However, the widening of the requirement of appropriation to an interference with the rights of the owner means that there has been scope for criminalizing some temporary appropriations. While much of the discussion has focused on the value of the property, or its identity with that which was taken, such decisions arguably turn on the question of dishonesty, with the decided cases addressing the issue of whether the conduct manifested 'a dishonest acquisitive intention'.[123]

However, the greatest impact of this stress on dishonesty has been in the area of fraud and the reform of the deception offences created by the 1968 Act. In their original form they required that there be a pretence which deceived another and that property be transferred as a result of this.[124] This gave rise to problems in cases such as *Preddy* (1996), where the House of Lords held that no property was transferred under the Act in a fraudulent mortgage application.[125] While the decision itself turned on a narrow point about the definition of property under

[119] Elliott, 'Theft and Related Problems', n.103, pp.119–20: 'It is hardly a parody of the position adopted by the Theft Act 1968 to describe [the offence of blackmail] as prohibiting acquisitive threats if and only if the defendant considers them criminal.'

[120] Proceeds of Crime Act 2002 ss.327–9. See Ashworth & Horder, *Principles*, n.115, p.404.

[121] See Theft Act 1968 s.6. There are, of course, exceptions: see Simester et al., *Criminal Law*, n.113, pp.537–44. Cf. Scots law which has now changed the *mens rea* of theft to intention to deprive for any period of time: *Black v Carmichael* 1992 SCCR 709.

[122] See, for example, the complaints in G Williams, 'Temporary Appropriation Should be Theft' [1981] *Crim LR* 129–41.

[123] Ashworth & Horder, *Principles*, n.115, p.368. For cases see e.g. *Velumyl* [1989] Crim LR 299 (unauthorized borrowing of money from employer); *Marshall* [1998] 2 Cr App R 282 (re-selling London Underground tickets). For a general discussion of property in theft law see Green, *13 Ways*, n.2, Ch.4.

[124] Theft Act 1968 ss.15 & 16. For discussion, see CLRC, *Eighth Report*, pp.39–54.

[125] [1996] 3 WLR 255. An electronic payment between accounts was not property belonging to another.

the Theft Act, the broader concern was mortgage fraud or dishonest applications for credit. This led to the rapid passing of the Theft Amendment Act 1996, which criminalized the dishonest obtaining or retaining of credit.[126] This was in turn replaced by the Fraud Act 2006, which introduced a new general offence of fraud aimed at the 'growing menace of fraud'—understood both in quantitative terms of the actual or potential cost to the economy, but also as a response to developments in the area of property transfers and commercial transactions.[127] The new offence is framed in general terms to catch various sorts of dishonest conduct: making false representations, failing to disclose information, abusing a position of financial trust, or obtaining services.[128] It is organized around the idea of making false representations as a form of conduct, and knowingly and dishonestly misrepresenting the truth so as to make a gain or cause a loss. It thus does not require that property be transferred, or that there be any actual gain or loss, or indeed for anyone actually to have been deceived.[129] A leading commentator has thus pointed out that most cases will then turn on the judgement of whether or not such conduct is 'dishonest'.[130] While the Act does not go so far as to enact the mooted general offence of criminal deception, claiming to limit its scope by reference to certain situations and conduct or roles defined in the Act, the offences created are still broad in scope, covering everything from large scale commercial frauds, to cross-jurisdictional internet scams, to petty swindling. Moreover, as has been pointed out, these general provisions overlap with a range of existing provisions which criminalize dishonest conduct in relation to banking, by company directors, through financial services insider dealing and banking, cartel offences, and so on, where the aim is less the protection of property per se than securing confidence in the probity and stability of financial institutions and the market by preventing the manipulation or abuse of position.[131]

The outcome of this process has been a clear expansion of the criminal law, seen both in the widening of the scope of offences under the Theft Act 1968 and in the number and range of offences relating to the protection of different forms of property. It is also clear that there has been a shift in the form of the law, in the move towards offences defined in an inchoate mode, in the emphasis on conduct

[126] c.62 inserting new sections 15A,15B, and 24A in the 1968 Act.

[127] D Ormerod, 'The Fraud Act 2006—Criminalising Lying?' [2007] *Crim LR* 193 at p.195. The Law Commission, *Legislating the Criminal Code. Fraud and Deception* (Consultation Paper No.155) (London: HMSO, 1999) understood the problem in terms of the impact of technological advances, the financial cost to the country, and the loss of the reputation of the country as a good place to do business. See also Law Commission, *Fraud* (Rept. No.276) (Cmnd.5560) (London: HMSO, 2002). The common law offence of conspiracy to defraud was retained.

[128] Fraud Act 2006 (c.35) ss.2-4 & 11. See generally Ashworth & Horder, *Principles*, n.115, pp.405–11; Ormerod, 'Criminalising Lying', n.127.

[129] This is in part because in automated applications for credit or transfers of funds there is no person to be deceived, but it is also framed more widely to make the offence more inchoate. See V Tadros, 'Crime and Security' (2008) 71 *Mod LR* 940 at pp.952–4.

[130] Ormerod, 'Criminalising Lying', n.127, p.200: 'Given the breadth of definition of other key elements of the offences, dishonesty will be the principal determinant of criminal liability.'

[131] See Ashworth & Horder, *Principles*, n.115, pp.405–11; Ormerod, 'Criminalising Lying', n.127.

rather than outcomes, and in the growing importance of the concept of dishonesty. The area is now organized less around the idea of the actual harm to an owner by depriving them of their property, than around the risk of harm to the enjoyment or security of property interests posed by dishonest acquisitive conduct.[132] Indeed, these moves have been defended on the grounds of the tendency of the criminalized act to undermine the system of property rights by wrongful conduct.[133] In the next section, I will look at this claim more closely, but before doing so I want to note three further features of the emergent law. First, the criminal law is pulling away from definitions of property in the civil law. It is not always concerned with the precise nature of property rights or the formal legality of contracts but with the permissibility of modes of acquisition.[134] As a consequence, civil law does not necessarily define a boundary or limit to the scope of the criminal law, as conduct which is judged to be fraudulent or dishonest or exploitative runs the risk of falling foul of the criminal law irrespective of the status of the transaction in civil law. Second, the aims of the criminal law are no longer about protecting property as such, or protecting property rights as defined in the civil law; they are protecting the interests of the vulnerable against conduct which poses a threat to the security of property and the securing of confidence in institutions such as the market in which property is transferred. This is not necessarily driven by actual harm to actual victims, but by the risk of harm. The point here is not only that such conduct is inchoate—or even 'pre-inchoate'—it is that harms are conceived in relation to an abstract class of victims (the vulnerable) and to an abstract conception of a system of property rights.[135] Third, it is arguable this area is now shaped by a kind of 'public responsibility' consisting in the need to show respect for the property interests of others.[136] This is less a sense of subjective awareness of particular outcomes (and so differs in a strict sense from Fletcher's idea of subjective liability) than the responsibility not to act towards the property of others in a way which others (or the criminal law) would regard as dishonest or fraudulent or which might undermine trust in the security of property.

Overall this contributes to a sense that this area of the law is changing in a way which increasingly pulls it away from its eighteenth century roots, protecting different kinds of interests in different kinds of property. Indeed, the inexorable rise of the concept of dishonesty has led certain commentators to identify the area

[132] E Melissaris, 'Property Offences as Crimes of Injustice' (2012) 6 *Crim Law & Phil.* 149 at p.156. Cf. Fletcher, 'Metamorphosis', n.2, p.472: 'the end in sight is the criminalization of all cases of dishonest self-enrichment.'

[133] S Shute, 'Appropriation and the Law of Theft' [2002] *Crim LR* 445; AP Simester & GR Sullivan, 'On the Nature and Rationale of Property Offences' in RA Duff & SP Green, *Defining Crimes. Essays on the Special Part of the Criminal Law* (Oxford: Oxford UP, 2005).

[134] See S Gardner, 'Property and Theft' (1998) *Crim LR* 35.

[135] P Ramsay, *The Insecurity State* (Oxford: Oxford UP, 2012) pp.152–8. Cf. A Bogg & J Stanton-Ife, 'Protecting the Vulnerable: Legality, Harm and Theft' (2003) 23 *Leg Stud* 402.

[136] See Ashworth & Horder, *Principles*, n.115, p.369. Cf. Williams, 'Temporary Appropriation', n.122, p.138 arguing that criminalization might be justified in terms of its potential effect on public morality.

as that of 'crimes of dishonesty' rather than property.[137] Not only does this shift the focus of the law, but it also makes it potentially limitless as there is little or no reason why all dishonest contracts or business dealings should not be subject to the criminal law; and indeed that criminal law remedies may be available even where there is no possibility of a civil remedy. Recent accounts have therefore focused on trying to identify limits, to shape and rationalize criminalization by identifying the moral distinctions which underpin different types of interference and their importance in fair labelling terms.[138] This is an important development, but if we are to assess its significance we need to understand it in terms of a broader account of the relations between property and civil order.

IV. Property, Trust, and Civil Order

There are two dominant narratives of development of the law of offences against property. In the first, the main issue is modernization, understood as the need to avoid or remove technicalities from the law so as to develop a set of general rules appropriate to the needs of contemporary society. Indeed, we have seen that the one consistent feature of the law of property offences in the modern period is that it has always been viewed as in need of reform—even after it has been reformed. The law is viewed as complex, combining common law and statutory offences, and the aim of reform is always to create a simplified and more coherent system. Problems are attributed to existing reforms being incomplete or insufficiently systematic, or the inability of the law to keep pace with changes in the form of property or the inventiveness of criminals. The question for the reformers has always been that of identifying the interest (in possession, property, or something else) and ensuring that the law protected this interest in a technical and non-complex way.[139] The critique is organized around themes of generality, coherence and comprehensibility; and argument for reform is primarily a technical problem of co-ordination and effectiveness, as we saw, in particular, in the discussions which led up to the creation of the consolidated definition of theft (larceny) in the Theft Act 1968 and the US Model Penal Code.

The second narrative is more recent, having its origins in Fletcher's influential account, and sees the development of the contemporary law in terms of decline and the loss of meaning, as technical considerations are promoted at the expense

[137] Ashworth & Horder (*Principles*, n.115, Ch.9) for example have chapter on offences of dishonesty, which includes fraud and money laundering, but the book contains no discussion of criminal damage (except in the context of recklessness).

[138] See, most importantly, Green, *13 Ways*, n.2; and Green, *Lying, Cheating and Stealing: A Moral Theory of White Collar Crime* (Oxford: Oxford UP, 2006). See also Ashworth & Horder, *Principles*, n.115, pp.412–5.

[139] See, e.g., G Williams, *Textbook of Criminal Law* (2nd edn) (London: Stevens & Sons, 1983): 'The new offence of theft created by the Act was intended to be as free from technicality as human ingenuity could devise. Things have not worked out like that…Still, it is true that almost everyone whom common sense would regard as a thief is now a thief in law' (p.701).

of moral truths.[140] This narrative argues that, notwithstanding its undoubted complexity, the common law was a 'coherent system of legal thought' which captured important moral distinctions.[141] For Fletcher there are three fundamental distinctions, which corresponded to original common law crimes: taking from an involuntary victim (larceny); taking by a person who had been entrusted with possession of the goods of another (embezzlement or breach of trust); and taking from a victim who consents (fraud or false pretences).[142] The problems in the contemporary law, he argues, result from the failure to respect these distinctions. The reformers aimed at clarity and coherence through the identification of a single interest in property which could be harmed in various ways, but the cost was the loss of a system which recognized the significance of different types of interference with property.[143] One of his key insights is that different kinds of crime endanger property interests in different ways, and that the nature of harms is linked to the *relationships* in which they occur—thus that the harm in embezzlement is not just a matter of the value of the property that is taken, but the damage that this does to the relation of trust.[144] This approach thus shifts the focus from a property interest to the way that the interest is interfered with—and the consequences of that interference for specific relationships between people.

This recognition of the link between property and social relations is of vital significance: that is to say that the law in this area is not just about the protection of things, but also about our relations with things, our relations with others as mediated by these things, and thus in an important sense the question of who we are.[145] Important as this insight is, though, it is developed in a narrow way within the narrative of decline, in the form of the claim that there are a limited number of fundamental forms of wrongdoing that exist more or less independently of actual forms of property or changing social or commercial relations. However, it is not clear why we should take these crimes, and the social and moral distinctions that they articulate, as fundamental, rather than seeing them as merely reifying a set of distinctions which were peculiar to the criminal law at the end of the eighteenth century and the system of property relations that it sought to protect.[146] While

140 Fletcher, *Rethinking*, n.2, Chs.1–3: 'Something seems to have been lost in the modern reduction of theft offenses to parallel attacks on a single interest…' (p.31). See now also Green, *13 Ways*, n.2, Ch.1 ('Theft Law Adrift'): '[M]y argument is that the reformers followed the wrong path. In rewriting the law of theft they threw out the good with the bad…They replaced the common law of theft with a codified law divested of much of its moral content, inconsistent with community intuitions, and potentially unfair to prospective defendants' (p.9).

141 Fletcher, 'Metamorphosis', n.2, p.472; Green, *13 Ways*, n.2, p.13.

142 Fletcher, *Rethinking*, n.2, p.4; Green, *13 Ways*, n.2, pp.104–31.

143 Fletcher, *Rethinking*, n.2, pp.30–57.

144 Fletcher, 'Metamorphosis', n.2, p.474: 'An act of taking might endanger a range of interests other than wealth'. See also Green, *13 Ways*, n.2, p.46.

145 For discussion, see A Appadurai, 'Introduction: Commodities and the Politics of Value' in A Appadurai (ed.), *The Social Life of Things. Commodities in Cultural Perspective* (Cambridge: Cambridge UP, 1986) pp.3–63.

146 Fletcher, for example, seems puzzled by the fact that larceny is an ancient offence but that the recognition of embezzlement a relatively novel development in the common law: why should something so fundamental only have been recognized in the common law at this relatively late stage? (*Rethinking*, n.2, pp.4–10.)

moral concepts, such as breach of trust, may have a broad significance, helping to provide general categories in terms of which it is possible to understand social relations, focus on these moral categories does not explain patterns of legal development. It is not clear, for example, on this account why there was a systematic move towards the protection of relations of trust by the criminal, rather than the civil, law at the turn of the nineteenth century. Nor indeed can it explain developments such as the contemporary identification of dishonesty as a unifying concept in this area of law—another apparently moral category, but one which cuts across the distinctions identified by Fletcher—or the different significance of trust in other individuals and trust in institutions such as the market. The social significance of the moral distinctions and the form in which they are institutionalized in law can only be explained by reference to some further account of changes in forms of property and social and economic relations. Finally, while this account usefully directs our attention towards the interests of persons in property, and the function of the criminal law in securing social relations through the system of property rights, it tells us nothing, except in the most general terms, about the aims of the criminal law. We need to ask the further question of why certain property rights should be protected by criminal law (and not others) and why they should be protected in a certain way. In addressing these sort of questions it is more useful to return to the standard account of the modernization of the law. While it has been criticized for ignoring moral distinctions—or the social significance of property—its value may in fact lie in its recognition that the aims and content of the law may change as forms of property develop. In this section then I want to reframe these two narratives, and the insights that they offer, by looking at the relation between property, civil order, and criminalization.

We have seen that the eighteenth-century law was organized around the protection of land and the social authority of property owners. Blackstone's account of property offences is clear about the relation between property and social order, and the function of the criminal law in defending the system of property, but the world that he describes is very different from our own. Foremost is the protection of the home against sudden irruptions of violence and the threat of arson. Land was not protected directly by the law of theft because it did not need to be: the law of property provided an elaborate system for the protection of hereditary rights. Forcible incursions on the land of others, *vi et armis*, were manifest breaches of the King's peace and dealt with as such. However, the criminal law protected the things that were connected with land and gave it value—buildings, crops, game and so on—together with a growing list of manufactured items or commodities. These were tangible goods, physical items that could be moved, and the aim of the law was to keep them in their place. There was though, as I noted above, an increasing recognition of developments that placed this model under pressure. This was primarily expressed in terms of the critique of the severity of the law and the use of capital punishment, but if we look at the arguments more closely we can see that these also articulate a changing understanding of the relationship between property and civil order. The distinction between grand and petty larceny was historically expressed in monetary terms—theft of property of more than one shilling in value was capital. This formal definition had originally expressed a social distinction—that the law was directed at the protection of the interests of a particular social class as most people would not have possessed private property of great value. However, changes in the value and social distribution of property had outstripped the legal categorization of seriousness, and consequently conduct which posed little social threat was subject to capital punishment. The reformers thus argued that: '*Money, which in its nature is of fluctuating value, is in no case proper to be made the standard measure of criminality*'.[147] The seriousness of the crime, they maintained, should be measured by the conduct and the motivation of the thief; this was also a general measure which allowed for thinking about commensurability across different areas of the criminal law. This should not depend primarily on the value or even the type of the property but was a question of the threat that the conduct posed to civil order. This could also explain the application of the criminal law to breach of trust, as this was perceived to pose a new kind of threat.[148] As property owners were dealing with strangers, in commercial transactions and in growing cities, trust was no longer based solely on personal knowledge but was increasingly guaranteed by law. Overall we can see that the idea of property per se tells us little about the shape of the criminal law. What is revealing, however, is to look at the relations between the forms by which property was protected, the perceived threat to civil order, and the understanding of how the criminal law might reinforce that order by identifying threats and acting on the motivation of criminals.

By the end of the nineteenth century the law was very different in shape as the development of more general categories flattened some older distinctions and created new equivalences. There was an increasing emphasis on protecting rights in property of different kinds, rather than just the thing itself, which opened the path to a much more general account of offences against rights in property such as that envisaged by Stephen.[149] The function of the criminal law was to protect rights that existed in civil law, where the breach was sufficiently fraudulent to merit this protection—or, conversely, that the criminal law should protect the dealings of the reasonably prudent person.[150] It is clear from the complex regime of property offences that I have described, differentiating between multiple types of larceny, embezzlement and fraud reflects the fact that the concept of property itself was undergoing change. This was most marked in the recognition that a right in property was not exclusive of others, but that different kinds of rights and

[147] Eden, *Principles*, n.8, p.292 (emphasis in original). See further H Mannheim, *Criminal Justice and Social Reconstruction* (London: Kegan Paul, 1946) p.91.

[148] D Barrington, *Observations upon the Statutes* (2nd edn) (London: Bowyer & Nichols, 1766) pp.372–3. It is a 'point of infinite consequence to the public, as what are called breaches of trust do but too much increase, with the greater temptation, which daily arises from the increase of property and trade in this country, and which necessarily requires a confidence in men who have had but mean and illiberal educations, and often from thence an illiberal disposition.'

[149] See pp.215–6 supra.

[150] Criminal Law Commissioners, *Fourth Report* (1839) p.li.

powers subsisted in particular objects, and that these required different forms of protection. This is exemplified by the development of the joint stock company, where ownership and control were separated, and different kinds of rights and responsibilities were distributed between shareholders, managers, employees, and customers. The law was directed at protecting not only tangible goods manufactured or handled by employees, but also money and accounts handled by managers and even intangible rights in physical property that shareholders had, in all probability, never seen. Central to this new sense of property was that it was something that circulated, and that the regime of protection needed to extend in space and time: an owner retained possession and control over goods that were outwith their physical possession and could direct by their will the purposes for which they could be used. The aim of criminal law was thus extended to the securing of social relations and institutions, such as employment relations or the market, by means of which goods circulated.

This was linked to a shift in the boundaries between public and private. As capitalism expanded the circulation of private wealth was increasingly viewed as a public good, and so it was not surprising to see the expansion of criminal law into the formerly private realm of contracts and commercial relations. There was a public interest in protecting the reasonable person against harm in their contractual dealings because of the threat that fraud posed to the foundations of the financial system. There were other kinds of shift as well. New kinds of public spaces were emerging throughout the nineteenth century—from pleasure gardens and public parks, to theatres, music halls, and shops—which encouraged the public display of private wealth.[151] Such property, jewellery, clothes, and so on, were simultaneously more visible and more vulnerable to theft, but in this case the crime itself did not pose a threat to civil order but merely to the civilized enjoyment of those public places. There was thus a gap opening between different kinds of public interest in property. The rise of consumerism also reflected a transformation in the relation between property and the self, and between property and freedom. In particular, we see here the emergence of a new kind of psychological link between property and freedom in the emergence of the idea, central to the consumer society, that the possession and consumption of property is a form of freedom—even if, to be sure, this was not enjoyed equally by all classes of society. This freedom brought new opportunities for theft and new forms of deviance—also suggesting an alternative explanation for the emergence of the subjective paradigm in theft: if the emergence of consumer society entails the manufacturing of desire, so now the criminal law must be ever more closely engaged in the policing of those desires.[152] The law of larceny met these needs by 'lowering the

[151] Famously described by Thorstein Veblen in 1899 as conspicuous consumption. See also M Ogborn, *Spaces of Modernity. London's Geographies 1680-1780* (London: Guilford Press, 1998); P Joyce, *The Rule of Freedom* (London: Verso, 2003) esp. Chs.4 & 5.

[152] And new forms of pathological desire: Abelson, *When Ladies Go A-Thieving*, n.37, describes the emergence of the concept of kleptomania as a means of understanding and seeking to control the problem of shoplifting by women.

threshold of illegality and moving it earlier in time, [thus] provid[ing] new incentives for a more self-disciplined and foresightful behavior throughout society.'[153]

If these brief accounts demonstrate the ways that changes in social and economic relations have shaped the historical understandings of wrongdoing in the area of crimes against property, we must now turn to look at the contemporary law. As we have seen, recent developments have placed more emphasis on conduct, rather than outcomes, and on dishonesty as a defining characteristic of this area of the law. This has been accompanied by the movement away from the idea that criminal law aims to protect rights in property (as defined in the civil law) to the idea that the aim of the criminal law is to protect a system of property rights—even where this is inconsistent with a valid right in civil law. While it may be tempting to see this in terms of drift or a loss of moral bearings, this shift is arguably rooted in changes in the forms and function of property. The point can be illustrated by considering the example of so-called 'identity theft', or the fraudulent use of personal information to obtain credit. Of course, this is not formally theft at all, as neither information nor identity are property capable of being stolen under the current law, and so under UK law it is normally regarded as a form of fraud or deception.[154] However, what is significant about identity theft is less the question of whether it should be classed as a fraud or theft, but rather that in blurring these boundaries, it reveals something important about the contemporary law and how it is responding to changing problems in this area.

The important features of identity theft are that the person from whom the information is 'taken' may be unaware at the time, or until much later, that this has been done. Indeed, typically, this might be done through the obtaining of confidential information, such as addresses or passwords, from a third party—often through computer hacking or other kinds of automated programmes. Goods or services might then be 'fraudulently' obtained from another party, such as a retailer or credit provider, on the basis of certain markers of the original identity (date of birth, address, bank account details) which enable the construction of a new or duplicate 'transactional identity'.[155] However, if this is done through websites, the automated process means there is arguably no deception of individuals: information is entered in a system and, if it meets the relevant criteria, credit will be advanced.[156] Deception or dishonesty is thus a form of conduct—checking an online declaration or pressing a button marked 'I accept', rather than being linked to the outcome of deceiving someone. This presents a challenge to those who maintain that the moral content of the act is no different from other frauds in terms of the way it is done (deception) and the harm that it causes.[157] It is

[153] M Wiener, *Reconstructing the Criminal* (Oxford: Oxford UP, 1990) pp.68–9.

[154] Cf. US legislation: Identity Theft Assumption and Deterrence Act 1998. See generally Green, *13 Ways*, n.2, pp.240–5; D Marron, 'Alter Reality: Governing the Risk of Identity Theft' (2008) 48 *BJ Criminol* pp.20–38.

[155] See C Sullivan, 'Is Identity Theft Really Theft?' (2009) 23 *Intnl Rev of Law, Computers and Technology*, 77–87.

[156] See E Finch, 'What a Tangled Web We Weave: Identity Theft and the Internet' in Y Jewkes, *Dot.Coms. Crime, Deviance, and Identity on the Internet* (Cullompton: Willan, 2003).

[157] See Green, *13 Ways*, n.2, p.242; A Steel, 'Problematic and Unnecessary? Issues with the Use of the Theft Offence to Protect Intangible Property' (2008) 30 *Sydney Law Rev* 575.

notable that what is vulnerable here and in need of protection is not only the individual whose identity is used, but also the system of credit itself. Identity theft is a systemic risk stemming from the availability of automated credit and internet trading.[158] It is the vulnerabilities of the system that are being exploited, and as reported losses from identity theft increase in size, it is the system of credit that is being harmed.[159] There are, to be sure, individual victims as well, whose credit identity is used by others and who then face the burden of reconstructing that identity—and consumers are also expected to protect their own identity, and not make themselves vulnerable to exploitation.[160] However, the identity that must be protected is not a matter of who an individual really is as a person, but the protection of certain 'tokens' that are capable of identifying the person to the system as a creditworthy individual: that is, a person's identity as a consumer as inscribed in an individual's credit history—something which is itself generated by the system. In understanding the wrong, it is this relationship between the information and the capacity to consume that is central, rather than the cost of the goods or services obtained, or even the question of how the 'identity' is obtained in the first place. Thus, while it may be the case that the information that is taken is not property, and that identity also remains the possession of its original owner, what is in fact 'stolen' is a person's credit history and status as a form of 'transactional identity'.[161] Transactional identity is not a natural property or capacity but is created by, and does not exist independently of, the system that is producing it. The 'property' that is taken is thus not a thing, but a capacity: the capacity to transact as a member of consumer society; and if this is lost, the measure is not only the financial loss to the individual, but their potential access to a huge range of services from consumer credit and bank loans to communications and utilities, thereby creating a class of people who are not fully able to participate as citizens. The consumer is thus produced both as an object (the person who is the target of advertising and so on) and as a form of subjectivity in the consumer society.[162] The law here, then, is regulating the freedom to participate in the marketplace, to be a consumer.

[158] Marron, 'Alter Reality', n.154, p.23. Of course the market where this happens is no longer bounded by the sovereign state and this gives rise to additional problems in the enforcement and prosecution of crime.

[159] The US Bureau of Justice Statistics estimated the cost in the US in 2012 as over $24 billion, higher than other forms of property crime combined (http://www.bjs.gov/content/pub/press/vit12pr.cfm).

[160] It is instructive in this context to note the linkage to prevention through the regime of being a good consumer i.e. not to make oneself vulnerable, by taking relevant precautions to protect one's identity. See Marron, 'Alter Reality', n.154 for a discussion of how the risk is placed on the consumer.

[161] Sullivan, 'Identity Theft', n.155, pp.77–8 arguing that identity in this context should be seen as 'transactional', based on a set of systemic conditions regulating an individual's capacity to participate in certain activities.

[162] Z Bauman, *Consuming Life* (Cambridge: Polity, 2007) Ch.2. See, e.g., p.57: 'Members of the society of consumers are themselves consumer commodities'.

The point of this discussion is thus that the 'wrong' and the 'harm' in identity theft are categorically different from other property offences; they cannot be fitted into the three 'original' categories (larceny, embezzlement, fraud) precisely because the common elements that are taken to be fundamental to the law (property, appropriation, common moral understandings of wrongdoing) and the model of social relations that they assume are not themselves stable. The whole topology of traditional property offences was linked to certain forms of corporeal and moveable property and forms of face-to-face social interaction. These are not by any means irrelevant in the early twenty-first century—a burglary is still a burglary, taking things from others is still wrong—but their place within the criminal law is being altered as new kinds of interaction are made possible and the law seeks to protect or reinforce the establishment of trust in new contexts. As an alternative, it is sometimes argued that the best response would be to create a *sui generis* offence criminalizing the specific elements of identity theft: this would both respond to the particularity of the new conduct and maintain the unity of a more traditional understanding of property offences.[163] However, to follow this course would be to overlook the extent to which the developments I have traced here track a more significant transformation of the area of property offences—and that the value of the project of protecting a stable 'core' is at least questionable. The importance of the much quoted claim that the criminal law in this area is reinforcing the *system* of property rights is thus that it underlines the significance of systems such as credit to contemporary society. The criminalization of attitudes hostile to the system of property rights is a response to the removal of many transactions from this immediate face-to-face context. The rise of the conception of dishonesty as a unifying concept lends coherence to developments in this area. Criminal law establishes a system of public responsibility to guarantee systemic requirements of trust.

As we noted above, the system of criminal law that is created in response to these problems is expansive, and this has led recent commentators to suggest that it may be possible to identify limits or to shape the processes of criminalization by thinking systematically about property offences in terms of certain fundamental or underlying moral distinctions. In one of the most important and influential accounts, Green has argued for the need to identify the underlying wrongs so as to 'signal widely felt distinctions between kinds of offences and degree of wrongdoing'.[164] I do not wish to quibble with his specific prescriptions for designing a theft statute, which are measured and thoughtful and would surely in many jurisdictions lead to improvements in the quality of legislation. However, I have argued here that the scheme of moral distinctions which he sees underlying the law in this area is limited in its capacity to explain the contemporary law, precisely because in place of an adequate sociological account of property relations, and how the aims of law have developed in response to changes in this area,

[163] See e.g. Steel, 'Intangible Property', n.157.
[164] Green, *13 Ways*, n.2, p.271 (citing Ashworth). See also at pp. 35–6, 52–4, 271–2.

it falls back on a particular version of a 'moral' or pre-legal core which is in fact based on the typology of offences identified by Fletcher as the core of the common law in the late eighteenth century. There are important moral issues here, but these are surely better approached in the first instance by identifying the central features and aims of the contemporary criminal law and then asking whether the function of the law in supporting this particular system of property rights is or is not just.[165]

V. Conclusion

> Offences relating to property, that mainspring of industry on which depend the prosperity and happiness of a nation, have been subject to greater vicissitudes than those which relate to the person, owing to the altered circumstances of national wealth, and of the distribution of it among various classes of society.[166]

It is commonplace in discussions of offences against property to find vague references to social and economic changes and their impact on the law. This has contributed to the sense in which property offences are somewhat apart from other areas of law as rapid social and economic change continually reshapes both particular offences and the topology of the law more broadly. In spite of this process of change being a defining feature of this area of the law, there has been little reflection on the dynamics of change or on changing conceptions of property in the criminal law—and the most influential account of the development of the law has focused on changing paradigms of liability rather than looking at property more broadly. The result of this is that we have a narrow understanding of how the law has developed and of the factors driving that change. In this chapter I have tried to develop a different account that shows the relationship between the impact of social and economic change on the law, doctrinal developments, and the changing aims of the law of property offences. Viewed from this perspective, it is clear that the development of the law is less random or haphazard than is sometimes suggested by its critics. It is certainly the case that the law has developed in a piecemeal fashion, through case law and criminalizing statutes which respond to particular problems, but the fact that this is so should not be allowed to obscure the underlying patterns of criminalization. Here I have identified certain clear shifts which see the law moving away from the protection of specific forms of private property to the protection of rights in property, towards securing the public good in the increased circulation of different forms of property, and the need to

[165] Cf. Melissaris, 'Property Offences', n.132, p.163, who examines Green's arguments in terms of whether or not the moral conceptions are neutral or determined by a controversial conception of morality (whether they may reasonably be contested).

[166] Amos, *Ruins of Time*, n.75, p.176.

secure the social institutions (the market, banking, consumer credit, and so on) which depend on the circulation of these forms of property.

The identification of these patterns is crucial to understanding the nature of the law, as the framework for our normative thinking about criminalization does not always map onto the process of criminalization, and conversely (perhaps) our understanding of the historical processes of criminalization is at present insufficiently developed to contribute to such a normative theory. The account I have developed here raises important normative questions, such as the justifiability of the use of the criminal law as a backstop to systems of credit, and whether the focus on dishonest conduct as an organizing principle opens the door to an unduly expansive role for the criminal law. These are central questions for normative theory to address, but I would contend that it is better that it does so—and is more likely to develop effective principles which might limit the law—if it begins from a richer account of the phenomenon that it is seeking to regulate. The argument here develops some resources for beginning to address this task.

It has become clear, though, that while we can talk in general terms about offences relating to property, there is no consistent or stable conception of property—or indeed of any other principle—which lends coherence or unity to this area of the criminal law. The offences in this area have been grouped together under different headings of convenience over the last 200 years reflecting combinations variously of understandings of the things to be protected (from objects to contractual relations) to various modes of committing offences, to overarching moral concepts (dishonesty). Each of these accounts have struggled in various ways to include all offences relating to property or to introduce thematic coherence. I would thus argue that property offences is at best a descriptive rather than a normative category, and given that range of different kinds of interests and different relationships with things—and that these change so markedly over time—it is not even clear that as theorists we should try to capture these in terms of a single category. Overall, this lends support to the suggestion that not only that the criminal law may be polycentric, but even that there may be different principles within areas of the law such as property offences.

8

Person

I. Introduction

> The history of violence in modernity is the history of a changing meshwork of boundaries that limit violence both from without (the place of violence) and from within (the rules of violence).[1]

The law of offences against the person is one of the pillars of the modern criminal law. It was first recognized as a distinct area of the criminal law in the early part of the nineteenth century, and was then consolidated in the Offences Against the Person Act 1861, a statute which remains at the heart of the law today.[2] Yet the 1861 Act is complex and archaic, and reading it alone tells us very little about the contemporary law of offences against the person. It is also long, covering what to modern eyes appears as a broad and disparate range of offences from homicide to bigamy, sodomy and abduction, as well as forms of violence against the person.[3] Just the provisions on what we might loosely describe as assault and endangerment cover a wide variety of quite specific forms of conduct from neglecting servants to obstructing railway lines or assaults on seamen. Not only do modern lawyers in practice use only three sections of the Act—sections 18, 20, and 47—but the text of each of these sections has been amended and their interpretation is now the subject of its own substantial and complex body of case law. Nor is the complete law contained in the statute; this was never intended to be the case as the 1861 Act merely consolidated the existing statutory law. Thus the provisions of the Act exist alongside the common law of assault and battery, as well as numerous subsequent enactments that have created new offences. Given this complex set of old rules, new enactments, and case law there have been many attempts to reform the law of offences against the person, though none have as yet been successful.[4] However, one of the more surprising features of the law is that its supposed object—the person—is not only undefined, in the statute itself or in numerous commentaries,

[1] JP Reemtsma, *Trust and Violence. An Essay on a Modern Relationship* (Princeton: Princeton UP, 2012) p.105.

[2] 24 & 25 Vict. c.100.

[3] See Law Commission, *Reform of Offences Against the Person* (Consultation Paper No.217) (London: Stationery Office, 2014) Ch.2 for a comprehensive review of the provisions of the Act which are currently in use.

[4] For discussion see Law Commission, *Reform of Offences Against the Person*, n.3, Ch.5.

but is seemingly not regarded as a topic worth analysing. There are extensive discussions of injury, of harm caused, and of the structure of *mens rea*, but little direct discussion of the person as the interest which is to be protected by this area of the law.[5] This seems odd for, as we shall see in this chapter, the scope and structure of the criminal law in this area has been shaped by different understandings of the person and how the person should be protected. This chapter thus aims to reconstruct the missing person at the heart of the law.

The development of offences against the person must be understood in terms of the broader themes identified in Chapter 2, notably the 'civilizing offensive' against violence. It is now recognized that in the period from about 1750 to 1900 there was a shift in social attitudes towards interpersonal violence, which has been described as an 'intensification' of the longer civilizing offensive which began in the sixteenth century.[6] This had three dimensions: increased efforts to define and narrow the limits of legitimate violence; the linking of violence to social causes and effects; and the elaboration of a new 'mentality' of violence, or understandings of what constituted violence and its appropriate uses.[7] In practice, this meant the control and policing of violence, particularly in public places, and of the causes of violence, such as alcohol. The courts led the way in reshaping social attitudes towards the acceptability of violence, heightening the expectation that individuals control the urge to resort to violence. Forms of public and corporal punishment were restricted, and then abolished. Violence, in short, was not only to be the monopoly of the state, but was to be a last resort for both individuals and the state. However, as Wood has pointed out, this process involved more than a recognition and rejection of existing forms of violence; there was also the 'invention' of violence, as understandings of what constituted violence were reshaped.[8] Law was central to this process: codifying new understandings of violence, laying down expectations of proper conduct, and establishing the standards of self-control and foresight which were to be expected of civilized modern man. At the heart of this was a developing normative understanding of the inviolability of the person. This chapter thus aims to trace the development of ideas of the person in the context of this civilizing process.

The 1861 Act is an obvious focus for this analysis. While it has been much criticized, even from the moment of its passing, it has been at the centre of the law for over 150 years, and even contemporary attempts at reform take it as their starting point. However, the discussion is necessarily broader since the law on offences against the person extends beyond the 1861 Act, and my analysis must

[5] Cf. the discussion of persons as subjects of the law, or active personality, in Chapter 6.

[6] M Wiener, *Men of Blood. Violence, Manliness and Criminal Justice in Victorian England* (Cambridge: Cambridge UP, 2004) p.12; R McGowen, 'Cruel Inflictions and the Claims of Humanity in Early Nineteenth-Century England' in K Watson (ed.), *Assaulting the Past. Violence and Civilization in Historical Perspective* (Cambridge: Cambridge Scholars Publishing, 2007). See generally supra Ch.2, Section III.

[7] J Carter Wood, *Violence and Crime in Nineteenth Century England: The Shadow of Our Refinement* (London: Routledge, 2004) p.29.

[8] Wood, *Violence and Crime*, n.7, p.27.

also encompass wider changes in social attitudes to violence and civil order. This chapter will accordingly comprise three sections, each of which will look at a different stage in the development of offences against the person: first, the development of the 1861 Act, which was directed mainly at the protection of the body; second, the evolution of offences against the person after 1861, focusing particularly on attitudes to violence in the late nineteenth century; and, finally, at efforts to reform offences against the person in the period since 1970, in which the idea of the person has expanded to include the protection of personal autonomy. In each part, we will look at the scope of offences against the person in that period, and at how some of the principal crimes were defined. The aim of this chapter, then, is to trace patterns of criminalization in the area of offences against the person. This requires not only that we look at conceptions of the person in the law, but also at the meaning of violence and at measures of seriousness, that is to say the kinds of interference with the person that we regarded as sufficiently serious to warrant the use of the criminal law, and how seriousness was codified in the classification of offences.

Before going on we should note two other points about the scope of this chapter. First, the discussion will include some reference to homicide, though offences against the person as a category is normally understood more narrowly in contemporary law as comprising non-fatal offences against the person. It is arguably the case that homicide has developed according to its own particular logic, rather than as simply one offence—albeit the most serious one—in the larger category of offences against the person. For this reason, while I shall include brief reference to homicide in each period, this will be done for the light it can shed on the idea of the person and the broader civilizing process rather than as a more systematic attempt to explore the development of homicide in any great detail.[9] Second, I will not be looking here at rape and forms of indecent or sexual assault, which were characterized as crimes against the person throughout the nineteenth and into the twentieth century. The development of these crimes—and the emergence of the area of sexual offences—is the subject of the next chapter.

II. Towards the Offences Against the Person Act 1861

> The most extraordinary lenity of the English criminal law towards the most atrocious acts of personal violence forms a remarkable contrast to its extraordinary severity with regard to offences against property.[10]

[9] There are a great many discussions of the development of the law of homicide—which might in itself be seen as good reason for focusing on the broader area. For some studies focused on the nineteenth and twentieth centuries, see KJM Smith, 'Offences Against the Person' in W Cornish et al., *The Oxford History of the Laws of England. Vol.XIII 1820-1914 Fields of Development* (Oxford: Oxford UP, 2010) at pp.409–63; J Horder, *Homicide and the Politics of Law Reform* (Oxford: Oxford UP, 2012) Chs.1 & 2; L Farmer, *Criminal Law, Tradition and Legal Order* (Cambridge: Cambridge UP, 1997) Ch.5. For an excellent short account see G Binder, 'Offenses against the Person: Homicide' in MD Dubber & T Hörnle (eds), *The Oxford Handbook of Criminal Law* (Oxford: Oxford UP, 2014).

[10] JF Stephen, *History of the Criminal Law of England* (London: Macmillan, 1883), Vol. III, p.109.

As we saw have seen, one of the features of English law in the first half of the nineteenth century was the severity with which offences against property were treated, with the critique of the 'Bloody Code' directed at the use of capital punishment in respect of property crimes. From the late eighteenth century onwards, though, there was an increasing political and legal focus on crimes of violence against the person. This period thus saw the recognition in law of offences against the person as a serious form of crime.

As Beattie has argued, there was a high tolerance of violent behaviour in eighteenth century society. Violence, he suggests, was a common experience: in public, in the home, in workplaces.[11] It could be seen in popular culture in forms of recreation and sports, such as prize fighting, where the infliction of physical damage was central to the entertainment. Physical punishment was used in the domestic 'correction' of wives, children, and servants.[12] It was widely accepted that disagreements might be resolved by physical means and that such matters were private and should not engage the attention of the authorities. The use of flogging as a punishment was standard in the army and navy. And this was matched by judicial violence, in the hangings and floggings that were a routine part of criminal justice. Legally, assaults, batteries, and woundings were both a civil and a criminal wrong: the same incident might give rise to an action in civil law for compensation or damages and to a criminal action.[13] However, since prosecutions for all but the most serious offences were private, there was in practice a blurring of the categories of civil and criminal. Prosecutors who sought satisfaction for the wrong done to them would start a criminal prosecution with a view to securing compensation or an apology, effectively excluding the state from responding to the original violence.[14] There were accordingly relatively few prosecutions for simple assault, which was only a misdemeanour. Other forms of social violence could be prosecuted in different ways, such as riot, where the nature of the crime was seen in the threat to the social order rather than the injury to the individual. Not all commentators were happy with this state of affairs. Writing in 1769, Blackstone stressed the public dimension of assaults and the need for prosecution: 'as a breach to the king's peace, an affront to his government, and a

[11] J Beattie, *Crime and the Courts in England 1660–1800* (Princeton: Princeton UP, 1986) pp.74–5; GT Smith, 'Violent Crime and the Public Weal in England, 1700–1900' in R McMahon (ed.), *Crime, Law and Popular Culture in Europe, 1500–1900* (Cullompton: Willan, 2008) pp.190–218.

[12] M Hunt, 'Wife-Beating, Domesticity, and Women's Independence in Eighteenth Century London' (1992) 4 *Gender & History* 187.

[13] See e.g. W Blackstone, *Commentaries on the Laws of England* (1769 edn) (Chicago: Chicago UP, 1979) iv, 217.

[14] The action would conclude with the imposition of a nominal fine. See N Landau, 'Indictment for Fun and Profit: A Prosecutor's Reward at Eighteenth-Century Quarter Sessions' (1999) 17 *Law & Hist Rev* 507–36; Smith, 'Violent Crime', n.11, pp.200–9; DT Andrew, 'The London Press and Public Apologies in Eighteenth Century London' in N Landau (ed.), *Law, Crime and English Society 1660–1830* (Cambridge: Cambridge UP, 2002); D Gray, 'Settling Their Differences: The Nature of Assault and its Prosecution in the City of London in the Late Eighteenth and Early Nineteenth Centuries' in Watson (ed.), *Assaulting the Past*, n.2.

damage done to his subjects'. This meant, he argued, that 'prosecutions for assault are... too frequently commenced, rather for private lucre than for the great ends of public justice'.[15]

The shift towards seeing interpersonal violence as a public, rather than a private, concern began in the latter part of the eighteenth century as violence came to be understood as damaging to civil order.[16] This was not just a matter of the immediate social disorder, or breach of the King's peace, caused by fights or assaults. It rather began to be argued that violence potentially undermined the bases of social co-operation between individuals by injuring morals and crippling fellow feeling.[17] Likewise, legal violence, in the form of judicial punishment, was understood as exciting sympathy for the recipient of the punishment, rendering the law less effective.[18] Interpersonal violence, particularly where it happened in public, was seen as uncivilized and barbaric and not an appropriate standard of conduct for members of a modern commercial society. The emerging middle classes promoted a new humanitarian sensibility, a new standard of civility, through reforms to criminal law and punishment.[19] This led to a rise in the number of indictments for assault, and cases that were tried in criminal courts were increasingly likely to result in a sentence of imprisonment rather than a nominal fine.[20] The development of organized policing led to changes in the detection and apprehension of offenders—not least because it was often the police themselves who were breaking up fights. It also became increasingly common for the police, rather than victims to prosecute.[21] Where victims did prosecute, measures were taken to facilitate this by providing for payment of expenses to witnesses as well as prosecutors in prosecutions for more serious forms of assault, and after 1828 an increasing number of serious assaults could be tried under summary procedure.[22] The reform of capital

[15] Blackstone, *Commentaries*, n.13, iv, 217 & 356. See also W Eden, *Principles of Penal Law* (3rd edn) (London: B White & T Cadell, 1775) pp.257–8 for some critical remarks on the practice of settling cases.

[16] P King, 'Punishing Assault: The Transformation of Attitudes in the English Courts' (1996) 27 *Jnl of Interdisciplinary Hist* 43–74; Smith, 'Violent Crime', n.11, pp.204–9. For evidence of the decline of homicide, see J Sharpe, 'The History of Violence in England: Some Observations' (1985) 108 *Past & Present* 206; J Cockburn, 'Patterns of Violence in English Society: Homicide in Kent 1560–1985' (1991) 130 *Past & Present* 70; P Spierenburg, *A History of Murder. Personal Violence in Europe from the Middle Ages to the Present* (Cambridge: Polity, 2008).

[17] Changing social attitudes are discussed in McGowen, 'Cruel Inflictions', n.6; Wood, *Violence and Crime*, n.7 Chs.1 & 2; K Halttunen, *Murder Most Foul. The Killer and the American Gothic Imagination* (Cambridge, Mass.: Harvard UP, 1998) esp. Ch.3.

[18] McGowen, 'Cruel Inflictions', n.6, p.43 also pointing out that not all such efforts were successful. Note also the first statute criminalizing cruelty to animals in 1822: 3 Geo IV c.71.

[19] Reformers argued that human nature should be nurtured and civilized by more humane punishment, such as imprisonment. See Smith, 'Violent Crime', n.11, p.205; King, 'Punishing Assault', n.16, p.72.

[20] Smith also notes the use of recognizances to keep the peace: Smith, 'Violent Crime', n.11, pp.205–6. Generally see Wiener, *Men of Blood*, n.6, pp.10–22.

[21] D Hay & F Snyder, 'Using the Criminal Law, 1750–1850. Policing, Private Prosecution and the State' in D Hay & F Snyder (eds), *Policing and Prosecution in Britain 1750–1850* (Oxford: Clarendon, 1989) pp. 36–47.

[22] 7 Geo.IV c.64 (1826). See also Hay & Snyder, 'Using the Criminal Law', n.21, p.37 on the costs of prosecution. 9 Geo IV c.31 (1828) s.27 on summary punishments for assault.

laws that took place in the late 1820s and 1830s restricted capital punishment to homicide and treason, and made possible the more systematic and graduated punishment of different kinds of violence by imprisonment. Serious crimes of violence were punished with greater severity and summary jurisdiction over minor acts of violence was extended. As contemporaries recognized, these changes amounted not only to a redrawing of the boundaries between crime and tort, but also a transformation of the scope of the criminal law.[23]

It is possible to trace the influence of this transformation in the ways that offences against the person were defined. The law in the late eighteenth century was still largely organized around a conception of violence as something that breached the King's peace. Murder was the principal crime that might be committed against a private person, and it shaped the understanding of other offences against the person.[24] The broad definition of murder was unlawful killing with malice aforethought.[25] Central to the crime was the conception of killing as a form of manifest violence.[26] It ordinarily required a 'mortal stroke': a striking of the body of the victim and the infliction of a fatal wound or injury.[27] This could extend to other acts of violence that were culturally recognized as equivalent to violent assaults, such as starving, poisoning, suffocating, or imprisoning a person, where these could be seen as 'metaphoric extensions of the paradigmatic case of a mortal wound'.[28] Although murder required proof of malice, understood as the intent to kill, wound, or injure, this was generally presumed from the fact of killing:

> In every charge of Murder, *the Fact of Killing being first proved*, all the Circumstances of Accident, Necessity, or Infirmity are to be satisfactorily proved by the Prisoner, unless they arise out of the Evidence produced against him: for the Law presumeth the Fact to have been founded in Malice, until the Contrary appeareth.[29]

The fact of killing thus led to a presumption of malice, placing the onus on the accused to establish circumstances of excuse (such as provocation), accident, or self defence.[30] Manslaughter was limited to killings where there was provocation

[23] Wiener, *Men of Blood*, n.6, pp.15–6 and p.22 citing Burns' *Justices' Manual*. The extension of the jurisdiction of the Admiralty Courts over offences at sea in 1799 and the Murders Abroad Act 1817 (discussed in Ch.4 at pp.130–1) should also be seen as part of this move towards a diminished tolerance of violence.

[24] See Blackstone, *Commentaries*, n.13, Vol. IV, 205.

[25] M Hale, *The History of the Pleas of the Crown,* (London: Printed by E. Rider, 1800) Ch.33; W Hawkins, *Treatise of Pleas of the Crown* (London: n.p., 1716) Ch.31; M Foster, *Crown Law* (Oxford: Clarendon, 1762) Discourse 2.

[26] G Binder, 'The Act of Killing' in MD Dubber & L Farmer (eds), *Modern Histories of Crime and Punishment* (Stanford: Stanford UP, 2007).

[27] Hale, *Pleas of the Crown*, n.25, I, pp.425–32: 'giving a mortal stroke'.

[28] Binder, 'Act of Killing', p.91. See Hale, *Pleas of the Crown*, n.25, I, p.431 for a list of such acts.

[29] Foster, *Crown Law*, n.25, p.255 (emphasis in original).

[30] See Ch.6 at pp.172–4. G Fletcher, *Rethinking Criminal Law* (Boston: Little, Brown & Co, 1978) describes this as an exculpatory model of liability. See also P Handler, 'Intoxication and Criminal Responsibility in England, 1819–1920' (2013) 33 *Ox Jnl of Leg Stud*, 243 at p.248 on provocation.

or excessive self-defence, or where the commission of an unlawful act led to death.[31] Thus, although the difference between murder and manslaughter was notionally conceived of in terms of the presence or absence of malice, courts were primarily distinguishing between the categories of murder, manslaughter, and accidental death on the basis of conduct rather than mental states. The centrality of murder was also reflected in the fact that manslaughter was a misdemeanour, rather than a felony.[32]

The emphasis on manifest violence or disorder also shaped the way that the category of crimes against the persons of individuals was understood.[33] After homicide, the central crime was the felony of mayhem: cutting off, disabling, or weakening a man's members.[34] This initially included only disabling injuries, such as would render a man less able to fight, but was gradually extended by statute through the sixteenth and seventeenth centuries to include disfiguring offences, such as cutting off an ear or a nose.[35] This was supplemented by the common law misdemeanours of assault, battery, and wounding which, as we have seen, were normally treated as private wrongs, and punished only by fines.[36] Battery was defined as an injury done to another person in an 'angry, or revengeful, or rude and insolent manner'.[37] Blackstone described battery as 'the least touching of another', and then went on, in a passage much quoted by other writers, to state that 'the law cannot draw the line between different degrees of violence, and therefore totally prohibits the first and lowest stage of it: every man's person being sacred, and no other having a right to meddle with it, in any the slightest manner.'[38] However, it is important to note that this passage came in his treatment of private wrongs; for the purposes of criminal law, he required there to be an additional element of public wrong in the character of the attack or the circumstances in which it was made. It was thus not the 'sacredness' of the person, but the element of public wrong that engaged the criminal law. Assaults and batteries were thus largely private unless there was a characteristic of the attack (that it disturbed the peace, was made in anger, the status of the victim, or that it was unjustified) that made them public. This was further underlined by a series of statutory aggravations.[39] Most of these were distinct offences which were grouped with assaults,

[31] See e.g. Blackstone, *Commentaries*, n.13, iv, 192–3.

[32] It was normally tried at quarter or petty sessions, and punished by a fine.

[33] See generally Blackstone, *Commentaries*, n.13, iv, Ch.15 and iii, Ch.8; Eden, *Principles*, n.15, Ch.21; EH East, *A Treatise of Pleas of the Crown* (London: Butterworths, 1803) Vol. I, Ch.7 (mayhem or maiming), Ch.8 (Assaults), & Ch.9 (False imprisonment and kidnapping).

[34] Blackstone, *Commentaries*, n.13, iv, p.205; iii, p.121.

[35] 22 &23 Car II, c.1 (known as the Coventry Act). See discussion in Stephen, *History*, n.10, Vol. III, pp.112–3.

[36] See Blackstone, *Commentaries*, n.13, iii, 120–1.

[37] WO Russell, *A Treatise on Crimes and Misdemeanours* (3rd edn, ed. CS Greaves) (London: Saunders & Benning, 1843) p.751.

[38] Blackstone, *Commentaries*, n.13, iii, p.120. See e.g. Russell, *Treatise*, n.37, p.751 repeating the quote.

[39] East, *Treatise*, n.33, Ch.8 discusses an extended list of aggravations, including privy counsellors, members of parliament, revenue officers to prevent the free passage of grain, assaults in a church or the King's palace, and assault with intent to murder or rob. See also Russell, *Treatise*, n.37, pp.761–82; Blackstone, *Commentaries*, n.13, iv, p.219.

but their inclusion underlined the importance of the status of certain persons (such as judges, privy counsellors, or revenue officers) or places (churches or the King's palace) to the criminal law. The final feature of the law of assault was the recognition of situations where battery was justifiable or lawful: by a person in authority, such as a magistrate or law officer, the correction of children, scholars, and apprentices, and actions in self-defence.[40] Indeed, as in the case of homicide, much of the legal discussion related to the scope of these exceptions, in particular the delineation of the scope of lawful authority of those such as constables or magistrates, and can thus be understood as a form of public law. The larger category of crimes against the persons of individuals was then rounded out by the misdemeanours of false imprisonment and kidnapping understood as infringements of 'natural liberty' and the loss to the state of one of its members.[41]

The structure of offences against the person began to change in the early nineteenth century, moving from the focus on disruptions of the King's peace to defining offences in terms of standards of individual conduct. Legislation before this period had tended to be passed in response to particular cases or outrages without regard for developing a clear structure to the law.[42] However, a series of Acts, passed between 1803 and 1861, gradually led to a more systematic approach to the criminalization of some forms of serious interpersonal violence. Lord Ellenborough's Act 1803, described by Stephen as 'the first act approaching generality on this subject', provided the foundation for this new approach.[43] This Act made it a capital felony to 'wilfully, maliciously and unlawfully' shoot at, or stab or cut a person with intent to murder, rob, maim, disfigure or disable or do some grievous bodily harm if the court were satisfied that had death followed it would have amounted to murder.[44] While the Act was aimed at certain kinds of attempts to murder and forms of serious assault, it did not extend to all attempts to kill (e.g. if not using a weapon).[45] It was also initially interpreted restrictively by the courts—defining cutting and the intent to murder in narrow terms, probably so as to avoid the death penalty.[46] Notwithstanding this, there is evidence that more violent offences were charged under the Act and that they were punished more severely.[47] The 1803 Act was repealed and replaced by Lord

[40] See e.g. Blackstone, *Commentaries*, n.13, iii, p.120; Russell, *Treatise*, n.37, pp.755–8.

[41] Blackstone, *Commentaries*, n.13, iv, 218–9.

[42] Stephen, *History*, n.10, Vol. III, Ch.27 lists the Coventry Act and Waltham Black Acts and legislation on the setting of spring guns. See also Smith, 'Offences Against the Person', n.9, p.393.

[43] Stephen, *History*, n.10, Vol. III, p.113; 43 Geo.III c.58. 'The passage of this Act in retrospect seems a milestone in criminal justice, even if the actual disposition of cases shifted only slowly thereafter' (Wiener, *Men of Blood*, n.6, p.23). On the origins and operation of the Act see P Handler, 'The Law of Felonious Assault in England, 1803–61' (2007) 28 *Jnl of Leg Hist*, 183 at pp.188–90. He notes that it was used, but interpreted restrictively, by the courts.

[44] Section 1. The same section also criminalized administering poison with intent to murder and attempts to procure abortion.

[45] Liability for attempts at common law is usually traced to *Higgins* (1801) 2 East 5, 102 but was not developed until later in the century, and then only as a misdemeanour. On this see KJM Smith, *Lawyers, Legislators and Theorists* (Oxford: Oxford UP, 1998) pp.105–17.

[46] On the interpretation of the 1803 Act, see Handler, 'Felonious Assault', n.43, pp.189–95.

[47] See Wiener, *Men of Blood*, n.6, p.23 citing H Woolrych, *History and Results of the Present Capital Punishments in England* (London: Saunders & Benning, 1832) pp.127–35.

Lansdowne's Act 1828, one of Sir Robert Peel's reforms, which was aimed at limiting the use of the death penalty and thus making the enforcement of the law more effective.[48] It broadened the definition of violent offences by making attempts to murder by drowning, suffocating, or strangling capital, and introduced the word 'wound' ('stab, cut or wound') to make it clear that no weapon was required.[49] However, as attempted murder and serious assaults remained capital felonies, the provisions of this Act continued to be interpreted restrictively by the courts.[50] Further reforms, creating a greater range of offences and penalties, came with statutes passed in 1837 and 1851. The 1837 Act introduced a new division between offences: attempted murder which resulted in bodily harm remained a capital felony (s.2), but attempts to kill which did not result in harm and serious assaults were made non-capital (ss.3–5).[51] Lord Campbell's Act 1851 created a new misdemeanour of unlawful and malicious infliction of grievous bodily harm with or without a weapon punishable by up to three years imprisonment.[52] The overall effect was to expand the scope of liability for serious assaults, while also making it easier to convict of common assault if the specific circumstances under the provisions of the statute could not be proven.

The statutory law on offences against the person was consolidated in the Offences Against the Person Act 1861, which was the culmination of the approach that had been developed over the first half of the century.[53] The Act abolished the death penalty for all non-fatal assaults. It included provisions on a range of issues concerning the person, such as bigamy, child stealing and abortion, rape, abduction and 'unnatural offences' in addition to crimes of violence. The non-sexual offences of violence can be grouped into three broad categories. The first concerned homicide, and specifically the provisions on attempts to murder (ss.1–16); the second group concerned acts which endangered life or caused bodily harm (ss.17–35); and the third was various kinds of assault (ss.36–47). As a consolidation statute, the Act primarily brought together provisions from a range of other statutes. This meant that there was considerable specificity and detail. The provisions on assault, for example, specified assaults on various types of person (clergymen, magistrates, peace officers, or seamen). Likewise, the provisions on endangering life concerned different ways that this might be brought about

[48] 9 Geo.IV c.31. As part of Peel's reforms to capital punishment, it also repealed 57 statutes relating to violence, some dating back to the reign of Henry III. Section 2 abolished petty treason. This Act extended to Scotland, though the 1803 Act did not.

[49] Sections 11 & 12. See *R v Duffill* (1843) 1 Cox CC 49.

[50] Handler, 'Felonious Assault', n.43, p.195.

[51] 7 Wm.IV & 1 Vict c.85 (1837). The Act also allowed a prisoner to be charged with common assault at the same time as a more serious count, to diminish the likelihood of an acquittal (s.11). This Act was based on the Criminal Law Commissioners, *Second Report* (London: HMSO, 1836) but did not refer to any of their general remarks on *mens rea*. On this, see also L Radzinowicz, *A History of English Criminal Law and its Administration* (London: Steven & Sons, 1968) Vol. IV, pp.311–26.

[52] 14 & 15 Vict. c.19 s.4.

[53] 24 & 25 Vict c.100. See Handler, 'Felonious Assault', n.43; CS Greaves, *The Criminal Law Consolidation and Amendment Acts* (2nd edn) (London: VR Stevens, 1862); JE Davis, *The Criminal Law Consolidation Statutes* (London: Butterworths, 1861).

(choking, administering chloroform or poison, by gunpowder or spring guns) or the different circumstances where this might occur (on shipwrecks, obstructing railway lines, furious driving, neglecting servants, and exposing children). There were few general provisions. Sections 11–14 restated the range of provisions relating to attempted murder we have been tracing here, followed by a general provision in s.15 making any attempt to commit murder by means not otherwise specified in the Act a felony. Section 18 moved slightly away from the specificity of its previous incarnation by specifying that the wound or harm could be caused 'by any means whatsoever'. The distinction between grievous and actual bodily harm, in the endangering and the assault provisions, was not a general indicator of serious and less serious harms; indeed section 47, where the phrase assault occasioning actual bodily harm was used, which is treated by modern lawyers as a general provision, was one of a series of provisions relating to the trial and punishment of common law assault.[54] Equally, there was no clear or consistent identification of *mens rea* provisions. The most common terms used were 'unlawfully and maliciously' as general descriptions of the forms of conduct specified in each offence. The most striking formulation was that of performing some conduct with intent variously to murder, to commit another felony, or to maim or disfigure—a formulation which underlines the development of inchoate forms of liability.[55] The Act as a whole was thus a catalogue of different statutory provisions aimed at specific forms of more serious violent conduct. If it did not seek to create any clear hierarchy of offences, by bringing the various offences into relation with each other, it laid the groundwork for a more systematic understanding of this area.

If we look at the treatment of interpersonal violence by the criminal law in the period up to 1861 as a whole, we can draw some more general conclusions. The period can be characterized in terms of a shift from civil to criminal law as the primary means of responding to violence. Forms of interpersonal violence causing serious injury were singled out by legislation as serious wrongs against the individual short of homicide. Conceptually, the main shift was the introduction of inchoate liability (attempted murder or using violence with intent to commit another felony). This was less a form of preventive justice than a means of signalling social disapproval by characterizing and charging some assaults in a more serious form. Otherwise, the legislation was directed at certain forms of conduct rather than specifying forms of self-control or restraint through the *mens rea* element of the crime. The 1861 Act generally demonstrates a shift from seeing violence against the person as primarily a breach of public order, to conceiving the aim of the law in terms of protecting the persons of individuals. As we see from the breadth of the 1861 Act, the persons of individuals could be injured in various ways (bigamy, abduction, and so on), but the law was increasingly focusing on

[54] The phrase seems to mean no more than a common law battery resulting in physical injury. Terms such as wounding were used in some of the assault provisions. Equally while all of the assaults were misdemeanours, so too were some of the endangering offences—while others were felonies.

[55] Malice would thus be inferred from the conduct.

physical violence against individuals, such that protecting the person of the individual was seen as protecting their body against harm or the immediate infliction of violence.

III. The Evolution of Offences against the Person

> The definition of those offences against the person which fall short of the destruction of life ought to be an easy matter. The infliction of bodily injury like the infliction of death, takes its moral character almost entirely from the state of mind of the person inflicting it.[56]

There was a gradual decline in the prosecution of violence in the second half of the nineteenth century.[57] In spite of this, violence remained a matter of serious public concern, if now more focused on the policing of various forms of previously acceptable 'everyday' violence—particularly where this disturbed social order or threatened the stability of social institutions such as the family.[58] Campaigns against public fighting and 'wife beating' and other forms of brutal and 'uncivilized' conduct mark the changing boundaries between legitimate and illegitimate violence. The 1861 Act remained at the heart of the law, and though there were regular complaints about its lack of system, there were few calls to change it before the 1960s. Notwithstanding this, as we shall see, there was an evolution in understandings of violence and offences against the person, as the courts sought to use the few general provisions of the 1861 Act to create a more structured hierarchy of offences. However the law was also supplemented as particular classes of victims—notably women and children—were recognized as needing special forms of protection.

An excellent index to late Victorian understandings of the causes and appropriate legal response to violence is Edward Cox's *Principles of Punishment* (1877).[59] Cox was a Serjeant-at-Law and publisher of the popular journal, the *Law Times*, and he sought in the book to articulate how the criminal law should respond to certain types of crime and criminal. His discussion of crimes against the person

[56] JF Stephen, *A General View of the Criminal Laws of England* (London: Macmillan, 1863) pp.122–3.

[57] Seen as the English miracle, supra Chapter 3 at pp.90–1. On the gradual decline of violence between 1850 and 1914, see VAC Gatrell, 'The Decline of Theft and Violence in Victorian and Edwardian England' in Gatrell et al. (eds), *Crime and the Law* (London: Europa, 1980) pp.284–300.

[58] See the overview in S d'Cruze, 'Unguarded Passions: Violence, History and the Everyday' in S d'Cruze (ed.), *Everyday Violence in Britain, 1850–1950. Gender and Class* (Harlow: Pearson, 2000).

[59] E Cox, *Principles of Punishment as Applied in the Administration of the Law by Judges and Magistrates* (London: Law Times, 1877) Chs.11–13. For biographical information on Cox, see R Cocks, 'Cox, Edward William (1809–1879)', *Oxford Dictionary of National Biography* (Oxford: Oxford University Press, 2004) online edn, Oct 2009, http://www.oxforddnb.com.ezproxy.lib.gla.ac.uk/view/article/6522, accessed 14 June 2015.

was in three separate chapters—crimes of passion, crimes of violence, and crimes of cruelty and brutality—which cut across legal definitions and reflected a concern with the legal significance of different kinds of motivation and situation. Crimes of passion were crimes, ranging from murder to common assault, which were committed on impulse, without deliberation, and indicated 'the absence of that self-restraint which it is the duty of men to cultivate'.[60] This he saw as covering violence arising from quarrels and brawls, where individuals were angered or provoked. While these crimes could be serious, the aim of the law should be to teach to others the 'risk of indulging a passionate temper, or rather of not sufficiently laboring to keep it under restraint'.[61] Crimes of violence could cover the same range of offences, but the difference was that the infliction of violence was considered and deliberate, carried out from a pre-existing motive of 'jealousy, hatred or other malignity'.[62] Of particular concern here was the use of weapons or the use of violence in the pursuit of other crimes such as street robbery or lawlessness and brutality. These crimes, in Cox's view, were more wicked than other assaults and the punishment should reflect this by being exemplary, with the aim of deterring others from acting in a similar way.[63] Crimes of cruelty, finally, were motivated by the intention of inflicting pain, whether for motives of gain or just out of thoughtlessness, and committed against the weak such as wives, children, servants, 'imbeciles', and 'more than all, by human brutes upon animals'.[64] These cases fell into two classes: where there was deliberate cruelty, which the law should punish severely; and cases of culpable indifference or neglect, where the aim of the law should be to make an offender aware of their responsibilities to individuals or animals in their care.

These concerns—with passion, with brutality, and with cruelty—reflect the development and use of the criminal law in this period and its role in shaping both the boundaries of legitimate and illegitimate violence and rules for individual conduct. One central area of concern was the law of homicide, the reform of which was more or less constantly discussed throughout the late nineteenth and early twentieth centuries.[65] After 1861, murder was, to all intents and purposes, the only capital crime.[66] This led to extensive debate not only about the scope of murder, but also of capital murder—which killings were so serious as to

[60] Cox, *Principles*, n.59, p.77. He went on 'but the exercise of which is much more easily preached by those who have no fiery passions to bridle than observed by those unfortunately endowed by nature with strong emotions.'

[61] Cox, *Principles*, n.59, p.79. See also p.106.

[62] Cox, *Principles*, n.59, p.107.

[63] Flogging was a permitted and appropriate response following the 'garotting panic' of the early 1860s. See J Davis, 'The London Garotting Panic of 1862: A Moral Panic and the Creation of a Criminal Class in mid-Victorian England' in Gatrell et al. (eds), *Crime and the Law*, n.57, Ch.7.

[64] Cox, *Principles*, n.59, p.115.

[65] See Smith, 'Offences Against the Person', n.9, esp. at pp.409–63; L Radzinowicz & R Hood, *A History of English Criminal Law and its Administration.* Vol.5 *The Emergence of Penal Policy* (London: Stevens, 1986) Ch.20. See also J Flanders, *The Invention of Murder* (London: Harper Press, 2011).

[66] 24 & 25 Vict. c.100 ss.1–5. Treason also remained a capital crime, though it was rarely prosecuted.

merit capital punishment. This took the form of a discussion whether, on the one hand, reckless violence against others should fall within the scope of murder and, on the other, whether killings under the influence of extreme passions or other overpowering impulses should fall outside the scope of capital murder. Formally such questions were addressed in terms of the meaning of 'malice': was death an intended consequence of the violence? But the term malice was considered too broad, covering situations where juries (and courts) were reluctant to convict of murder—such as where there was an intention to injure only, where a person was killed in consequence of a wicked intention, where a person killed another in the course of committing a felony, however trivial, or where there was provocation by insulting words (not blows).[67] In practice these questions arose in specific contexts such as violent robberies or rapes, drunken brawling, or domestic violence and were determined by reference to informal standards, such as the degree of brutality of the assault.[68] At the same time, there was a growth in the number of prosecutions for manslaughter.[69] This was in part a matter of 'down-charging'—incidents that might formerly have been prosecuted as murder were instead charged as culpable homicide after the penalty for manslaughter was increased in 1828.[70] However, there was also growth in the number of prosecutions for negligently caused death arising from lawful activities—notably in areas such as manufacturing and railway transport.[71]

These changes in the prosecution of homicide raised questions about the boundaries between the legitimate and illegitimate resort to violence and I want to illustrate this further by looking at three particular areas where these boundaries were contested. The first is the regulation of semi-organized forms of public violence, particularly the use of 'fair' and consensual fights to settle disputes, and to a lesser extent prize fighting.[72] Historians have noted that such practices were widespread in the eighteenth and nineteenth centuries, with the resort to violence seen both as an appropriate means of settling disputes for those who did not have the resources to go to law, and as an expression of the values of manliness and English national character. For the upper classes, this took the form of the duel;

[67] See, e.g., the list of situations which might fall within the scope of 'general' malice in Radzinowcz & Hood, *History,* n.65, pp.662–3. See also Smith, 'Offences Against the Person', n.9, pp.410–20. Supra Ch.6, III.B for a discussion of malice and intention in nineteenth-century legal thought.

[68] See also the handling of discipline between masters and servants, army officers and soldiers, ships captains and sailors where there was a concerted attempt to civilize brutal disciplinary practices. Wiener, *Men of Blood*, n.6, Ch.2.

[69] Wiener, *Men of Blood*, n.6, pp.25–8: Judicial statistics for 1850 show 192 persons tried for manslaughter as opposed to 52 murder charges.

[70] (1822) 3 Geo.IV c.38 penalty raised from one year's imprisonment to three years, and the 1828 Act raised to transportation for life. This was re-enacted in the 1837 Act and the 1861 Act s.5.

[71] See Wiener, *Men of Blood*, n.6, pp.62; Smith, 'Offences Against the Person', n.9, pp.438–46.

[72] See generally Wood, *Violence and Crime,* n.7, Ch.4 describing these as 'masculine ritual fighting' at 75; Wiener, *Men of Blood*, n.6, Ch.2; C Conley, *The Unwritten Law. Criminal Justice in Victorian Kent* (Oxford: Oxford UP, 1991) Ch.2; J Archer, '"Men Behaving Badly?": Masculinity and the Uses of Violence' in d'Cruze (ed.), *Everyday Violence*, n.58, Ch.2; L Bibbings, *Binding Men. Stories about Violence and Law in Late Victorian England* (London: Glasshouse, 2014) Ch.2.

for lower classes, fist fights. In both cases there were accepted ritual codes of conduct, of how the fight should start and end and of the kinds of conduct that were, or were not, acceptable. However, this resort to violence was increasingly seen as inconsistent with ideals of civilized conduct, and the crowds that gathered to watch such bouts were seen as a threat to public order, such that over the course of the nineteenth century steps were taken to stamp the practice out.[73] The practice of duelling was largely eradicated by the 1840s, partly through the use of the new laws on attempted murder to prosecute participants, as well as by appealing to gentlemen to set an example for the lower orders.[74] Other forms of organized fighting continued throughout the century. In theory, such fights were outlawed. They were routinely broken up by the police, and participants (including spectators) could potentially be prosecuted for assault, affray, and even manslaughter if one of the combatants died.[75] The courts signalled disapproval of the practice by pressing for conviction, even if this was often followed by only minor or symbolic punishment.[76] In practice, there was a greater degree of toleration provided proceedings were deemed fair—only using fists, no foul blows (below the waist), no knives (or other 'foreign' practices), and no kicking.[77] The use of weapons or foul blows, by contrast, was taken as evidence of malice as it transgressed the boundaries of the 'fair' contest.[78] However, as the century progressed there was a greater tendency to see such fights as unprovoked and avoidable and to characterize any violence used as unlawful; that is to say that rather than being seen as crimes of passion or expressions of manliness, they were seen as brutal and uncivilized.[79] Evidence for this kind of hardening of judicial attitudes can be seen in cases such as *R v Coney and others* (1882).[80] Although the court in this case limited the application of the strict rule that mere presence at a fight could give rise to liability for assault, the judgments stressed the illegality of the contest, the disorderliness, and the harm such fights caused to the participants and their brutalizing impact on spectators. For Stephen J, 'the injuries given and received in prize-fights are injurious to the

[73] 'It is one of the first conditions of civilised society, not to mention Christianity or morality, that men should abstain from fighting out their quarrels and that they should be content to seek from the law the redress of any real injury they may suffer.' *The Times* 1875, quoted in Wiener, *Men of Blood*, n.6, pp.53–4.

[74] Wiener, *Men of Blood*, n.6, pp.43–6; J Horder, 'The Duel and the English Law of Homicide' (1992) 12 *Ox Jnl of Leg Stud* 419.

[75] *Murphy* (1833) 6 C & P 103. By contrast, deaths resulting from forms of lawful conduct, such as sports or exercises of strength or skill, would be treated as accidents: East, *Treatise*, n.33, Vol.I, 270.

[76] Wiener, *Men of Blood*, n.6, pp.49–50, 52–3.

[77] See Cox, *Principles*, n.59, pp.98–9 '[Use of a knife] has been always hitherto an un-English crime'. See also pp.87–8 (on kicking).

[78] The term 'maliciously' in ss.18 and 20 of the 1861 Act was held to include forms of recklessness (knowing that a certain outcome was likely) or where the harm done was of the general kind intended: *R v Pembliton* (1874) 2 CCR 119; *R v Latimer* (1886) 17 QBD 559; *R v Cunningham* [1957] 2 All ER 412.

[79] *Reports to the Secretary of State for the Home Department on the State of the Law Relating to Brutal Assaults* (C.1138) (London: HMSO, 1875).

[80] *R v Coney* (1882) 8 QBD 534. See Bibbings, *Binding Men*, n.72, Ch.2.

public', while Hawkins J talked of the tendency of such fights to 'rouse angry passions'.[81] It was made clear that consent was not a defence to forms of assault at common law or in the 1861 Act because assaults were always also a breach of the peace.[82] The public interest in preventing violence and disorder was thus central.

A second key area complicating the boundary between legitimate and illegitimate behaviour was the relationship between violence and alcohol.[83] In broad terms, while intoxication was never formally a defence to a criminal charge, and indeed was regarded by treatise writers as an aggravation, it had long been viewed as a mitigating factor in offences of violence, indicating variously a lack of premeditation, that it had made the defendant more excitable or open to provocation, or simply that he was unaware of what he was doing.[84] Attitudes towards alcohol changed in the middle of the nineteenth century as social statistics were used to establish an association between alcohol and crime.[85] This was further linked by the temperance movement to the absence of character and self-control, with even moderates such as John Stuart Mill recognizing this association: 'The making himself drunk in a person whom drunkenness excites to do harm to others, is a crime against others'.[86] Prosecutions for public drunkenness increased markedly in the latter half of the century, and the Licensing Act 1872 introduced restrictions on the sale of alcohol as well as a raft of new offences related to forms of drunken conduct.[87] This was accompanied by a change in the way that the courts dealt with drunken violence, especially where it was seen as revealing weakness of character or self-control and where it had led to unchecked brutality. In legal terms this led to a narrowing of mitigating circumstances and a refining of the concept of intention.[88] The reshaping of offences against the person had placed a new emphasis on proof of intent—to kill or do grievous bodily harm—and this required the courts to articulate the effect of drunkenness on intent.[89] In

[81] pp.549 & 554.

[82] See also JF Stephen, *A Digest of the Criminal Law* (4th edition) (London: Macmillan, 1887) Art.208; JWC Turner, *Kenny's Outlines of Criminal Law* (19th edn) (Cambridge: Cambridge UP, 1966) pp.208–10. Unless they took the authorized 'civilized' form of boxing under the Queensberry Rules.

[83] See P Handler, 'Intoxication', n.30, pp.243–62. Wiener, *Men of Blood*, n.6, Ch.5; A Loughnan, *Manifest Madness* (Oxford: Oxford UP, 2012) Ch.7.

[84] See D Rabin, 'Drunkenness and Responsibility for Crime in the Eighteenth Century' (2005) 44 *Jnl of Brit Stud* p.457.

[85] See the extensive literature cited in Radzinowicz & Hood, *History*, n.65, pp.61–4.

[86] Mill, 'On Liberty', in *On Liberty and other Essays* (ed. J Gray) (Oxford: Oxford UP, 1991) p.108. See, e.g., quote from Samuel Smiles, *Thrift* (1875) in M Wiener, *Reconstructing the Criminal. Culture, Law and Policy in England, 1830–1914* (Cambridge: Cambridge UP, 1990) p.79. See generally B Harrison, *Drink and the Victorians. The Temperance Question in England 1815–1872* (revd edn) (Keele: Keele UP, 1994).

[87] See M Wiener, *Reconstructing*, n.85, p.155; M Valverde, *Diseases of the Will. Alcohol and the Dilemmas of Freedom* (Cambridge: Cambridge UP, 1998) Chs.2 & 3.

[88] Smith, 'Violent Crime', n.11, p.197; Wiener, *Men of Blood*, n.6, pp. 176–200 & pp.269–70. At the same time chronic alcoholism was increasingly seen as excusing or diminishing responsibility: Handler, 'Intoxication', n.30, pp.258–61.

[89] Where there was a requirement of specific intent, rather than general intent. See Handler, 'Felonious Assault', n.43, p.202; Handler 'Intoxication', n.30, pp.250–4.

doing so, the courts relied on character and circumstance rather than attempting to investigate the actual state of mind of the accused. Brutality or the use of deadly weapons was taken as evidence of intent to inflict grievous bodily harm; drunken husbands, who assaulted or killed their wives, were treated more harshly than where there was no alcohol involved; drunken squabbles in pubs gave rise to less concern.[90] Drunken defendants were not necessarily liable for all harm that resulted from their conduct, but they were being held to higher standards of conduct.[91] The law was settled in the case of *DPP v Beard* (1920) in which it was held that evidence of intoxication might limit responsibility in cases involving specific intent where the defendant lacked the capacity to form the specific intent.[92]

The third area crucial to understanding the evolving boundaries between legitimate and illegitimate violence was that of cruelty and neglect, particularly in the context of violence against women and children. Wiener has noted the shift in ideals of masculinity and femininity in the first half of the nineteenth century, with women being seen as weak and fragile and in need of protection, and the ideal of manhood shifting towards ideals of non-violent respectable conduct and domesticity.[93] That the treatment of women was another measure of civilization is captured in the statement of James Mill that 'among rude people, the women are generally degraded, among civilized people they are exalted'.[94] The protection of women was thus a justification for measures to control uncivilized or barbarous male conduct at home and abroad. In the second half of the nineteenth century, this focused particularly on violence in the home or in intimate relationships: wife-beating and violence towards, and neglect of, children were increasingly seen as unacceptable forms of cruelty and neglect.[95] This was also driven by Victorian feminist demands for equal treatment: the protection of women's bodies and reform of the law of marriage to respect the independence and rights of women.[96] There was some ambivalence about the legal position: it was often

[90] Handler, 'Intoxication', n.30, p.252. This was consistent with the general approach to responsibility in this period.

[91] Wiener, *Men of Blood*, n.6, pp.287–8. Cf. Handler, 'Intoxication', n.30, p.254 who insists that this was not producing coherent outcomes as it was mediated through juror beliefs, which were harder to control.

[92] [1920] AC 479; i.e. it was a test of capacity rather than subjective intent. The courts also upheld the rule of constructive liability, that violent felonies resulting in death were murder. See further Chapter 6, IIIB.

[93] Wiener, *Men of Blood*, n.6, pp.29–39.

[94] Ibid., p.31.

[95] See generally ME Doggett, *Marriage, Wife-Beating and the Law in Victorian England* (London: Weidenfeld and Nicolson, 1992); AJ Hammerton, *Cruelty and Companionship. Conflict in Nineteenth-Century Married Life* (London: Routledge, 1992); S d'Cruze, *Crimes of Outrage. Sex, Violence and Victorian Working Women* (London: UCL Press, 1998) Ch.4; A Clark, 'Domesticity and the Problem of Wifebeating in Nineteenth-Century Britain: Working Class Culture, Law and Politics' in d'Cruze (ed.), *Everyday Violence*, n.58, pp.27–40; G Behlmer, *Child Abuse and Moral Reform in England, 1870-1908* (Stanford, CA: Stanford UP, 1982).

[96] JS Mill, 'The Subjection of Women' in *On Liberty*, n.86, pp.471–82; Frances Power Cobbe, 'Wife Torture in England' (1878) 32 *Contemporary Review* 55, which is widely credited with having led to the Matrimonial Causes Act 1878 allowing magistrates to grant an order of non-cohabitation to a woman whose husband had been convicted of an aggravated assault against her. See G Behlmer, 'Summary Justice and Working Class Marriage in England, 1870–1940' (1994) 12 *Law & Hist Rev* 229 at pp.241–2.

assumed that there was a customary power in law for a man to chastise his wife, though there was little legal authority in support of this, and many nineteenth century judges and commentators rejected the idea.[97] However, it was clearly recognized that the man had authority, or dominion, over women, children, and servants within the domestic sphere and that this extended to the use of physical violence.[98] Problems arose when this authority was misused, when excessive violence was used against women who were seen as helpless; conversely, if the husband was respectable and hard-working, the violence not 'brutal', or provoked by a disorderly, idle, or drunken wife, then this was less likely to be condemned.[99]

The first specific legislation on the protection of women and children came with the passing of an Act for the Better Protection of Aggravated Assaults upon Women and Children in 1853, which permitted summary trial of aggravated assaults on women or male children.[100] This was followed by further legislation in 1878, 1886, 1895, 1902, and 1914 aimed at ensuring that women could separate from a violent husband where he had been convicted of aggravated assault and there was fear of future injury.[101] This legislation was not always effective, and there is evidence that the courts used the law to try and force reconciliations between wives and violent husbands, but there was recognition that male violence towards women was a specific kind of problem.[102] By the end of the century this view had also been recognized in case law. In *R v Halliday* (1889), the term 'inflict' in s.20 of the 1861 Act was held to cover the situation where a man threatened his wife so that she jumped from a window and injured herself—that is to say it extended to cases where there was no direct infliction of force.[103] In *R v Jackson* (1891) Lord Halsbury dismissed the idea that a man might chastise his wife as without foundation and a 'quaint and absurd dicta' completely inconsistent with the standards of a 'civilized country'.[104] The child's entitlement to reasonable protection within the family did not emerge as a matter of 'pressing public concern' until slightly later, in the 1880s, with the formation of the Societies for

[97] See discussion in Wiener, *Men of Blood*, n.6, pp.172–6; Doggett, *Wife-Beating*, n.95, *passim*.

[98] Likewise, reasonable correction or chastisement of a child was permitted. See e.g. Stephen, *Digest*, n.82, Arts201 & 210; Kenny, *Outlines of Criminal Law* (Cambridge: Cambridge UP, 1902) p.154. It was even regarded as character forming. See J Rowbotham, '"Only when drunk": The Stereotyping of Violence in England, c.1850-1900' in d'Cruze (ed.), *Everyday Violence*, n.58, Ch.9.

[99] Cox, *Principles*, n.59, pp.99–105.

[100] 16 Vict. c.30. Re-enacted by Offences Against the Person Act 1861 (24 & 25 Vict. C.100) s.43. It also permitted prosecution by third parties if the woman was reluctant to prosecute. See Hammerton, *Cruelty and Companionship*, n.95, pp.27, 59–62; Behlmer, 'Summary Justice', n.96, pp.240–1.

[101] Matrimonial Causes Act 1878 (41 & 42 Vict. C.19); Married Women (Maintenance in Case of Desertion) Act 1886 (49 & 50 Vict. C.52); Summary Jurisdiction (Married Women) Act 1895 (58 & 59 Vict c.39); Licensing Act 1902 s.5 (2 Ed VII, c.28); Criminal Justice Administration Act 1914 (4 & 5 Geo V c.58 s.4).

[102] See Behlmer, 'Summary Justice', n.96, for an analysis of the working of these statutes in the first half of the twentieth century.

[103] *R v Taylor* (1869) LR 1 CCR 194; *Martin* (1881) 8 QBD 54; *R v Halliday* (1889) LT 701; *R v Coleman* (1920) 84 JP 112. Cf *Clarence* (1888) 22 QBD 23 where it was held that infliction required a battery and did not extend to infection with gonorrhoea.

[104] [1891] 1 QB 671 at p.678. See also Bibbings, *Binding Men*, n.72, Ch.5.

the Prevention of Cruelty to Children.[105] Once again, concerns about parental neglect and cruelty were framed in terms of a discourse of savagery and civilization: the ill treatment of children in England being compared to the slaughter of the innocents which created a moral imperative to act.[106] The solution was seen as legislation which formalized the responsibilities of parenthood and criminalized conduct which fell short of the expected standards. This duly followed with the Prevention of Cruelty Act 1889, better known as the 'Children's Charter', which criminalized any ill treatment or neglect of children likely to cause 'unnecessary suffering or injury to its health'.[107] This was amended in 1894 with the recognition that injury to health could include any 'mental derangement' or suffering that was caused, and again by the Children Act 1908 which further specified criminal harms against children.[108] The legislation was then consolidated again in the Children and Young Persons Act 1933, which embedded the criminal provisions in the regime of state sponsored child protection and treatment.[109] These developments established the idea that the state could intervene in the domestic sphere to protect women and children from cruelty and neglect, as the healthiness of the family as a civic question was linked to the healthiness of the state.[110]

Taken together these three areas show that while the 1861 Act could provide a basis for dealing with areas of social concern, it was also limited in so far as its categories did not reflect contemporary understandings of the social significance of violence. While the ambition of theorists was that the law should reflect a hierarchy of seriousness in the category of *mens rea*, descriptions of conduct in terms of brutality and cruelty gave substance in practice to the provisions of the Act. This was further underlined by the identification of offences directed at the protection of women and children, which supplemented the 1861 Act and undercut the ambition of creating general offences.

Before I move on, I want to note one last area of development, which sheds light on the emergence of a new preventive technique, aimed at limiting access to technologies of violence. This is the development of laws extending ideas of endangerment, such as legislation controlling the manufacture, sale and possession of weapons and explosives. There had been limited statutory provision on possession of weapons in the early nineteenth century, mainly relating to the activity of poaching, as well as a general provision under the Vagrancy Act 1824.[111]

[105] Behlmer, *Child Abuse*, n.95, p.12 & Ch.2.

[106] B Waugh & HE Manning, 'The Child of the English Savage' (1886) *Contemporary Review* (Jan) 687.

[107] 52 & 53 Vict. c.44, s.1. It also provided that child victims could be taken out of the custody of their parents or guardians in these cases, and regulated child employment. See Behlmer, *Child Abuse*, n.95, Ch.4.

[108] 57 & 58 Vict. c.41; Children Act 1908 (8 Edw VII, c.67) criminalizing, e.g. the sale of tobacco to children, or causing the death of a child by sleeping in the same bed intoxicated. It also provided for trial and punishment of juvenile offenders. See also Punishment of Incest Act 1908 (8 Edw.VII c.45).

[109] 23 Geo.V c.12. See also Children Act 1948.

[110] M Foucault, 'Governmentality' in *Selected Works*. Vol 3 *Power* (ed. J Faubion) (New York: Free Press, 2000).

[111] 5 Geo.IV c.83 s.4.

Beginning with the Gun Licence Act 1870 measures were introduced to restrict the sale and possession of firearms, explosives, and other offensive weapons as a way of preventing violence.[112] This culminated in the Prevention of Crime Act 1953, which was seen as 'a necessity dictated by the post-war wave of crimes of personal violence'.[113] This Act, which is still in force, prohibited the carrying of articles made, adapted, or carried for the purposes of causing injury to others, in public places.[114] This legislation sought to address violent crimes by establishing norms for public conduct—limiting access to weapons and restricting public possession and display.

Against this rich background, the treatment of offences against the person in the treatises and textbooks was disappointingly thin, mainly focusing on the 1861 Act and its interpretation. The dominant trope in treatises and textbooks throughout the period was to note how disorganized and unsystematic the statutory law was and then to explore ways of systematizing it. Writing in 1883, for example, Stephen commented that 'the history of our law upon personal injuries is certainly not creditable to the legislature, and the result at which we have at present arrived is extremely clumsy'.[115] His account was organized in terms of a basic distinction between fatal and non-fatal violence and then in terms of mental state—whether or not the infliction of harm was intentional. With respect to non-fatal violence he focused on analyzing conceptual difficulties with the core provisions of the 1861 Act, based on the new conceptual analysis of intention, and tried to systematize these into a hierarchy of offences expressed in general provisions. He thus criticized s.18 for creating 'twenty four separate offences as it forbids every combination of any one of four actions with any one of six intentions'.[116] In a notable innovation, in his Digest, he separated out general provisions applying to the law of offences against the person, such as actions of law officers, private defence, consent, and the kinds of actions that would be considered lawful—but this was not followed by other commentators.[117] Kenny's treatment of non-fatal offences against the person ('crimes springing from anger'), for example, followed the more general trend. He began by distinguishing between offences where actual bodily injury was occasioned and those where harms were not essential—a version of the common law distinction between assault and battery.[118] Otherwise the focus was on sections 18 and 20 of the 1861 Act (as felony and misdemeanour versions of similar offences) and the courts' interpretation of key terms such as

[112] 33 & 34 Vict. c.57; Explosive Substances Act 1883 (46 & 47 Vict. C.3), ss.2–4; Pistols Act 1903 (3 Edw.VII c.18); Firearms Acts 1920 (10 & 11 Geo.V c.43) and 1937 (1 Edw.VIII & I Geo. VI c.12) possessing firearms without a certificate and registration and licensing of persons, use of real or imitation firearms to resist arrest (s.23) possessing firearm with intent to endanger life or property (s.22); also Public Order Act 1936 s.4 (offensive weapon at a public meeting or procession).

[113] J Ll J Edwards, 'The Prevention of Crime Act 1953' (1953) 16 *Mod LR* 482 at p.484.

[114] S.1(4).

[115] Stephen, *History*, n.10, III, p.118. He went on: 'but I think its substance is greatly superior to the corresponding provisions of the French and German codes, besides being much more complete'.

[116] Stephen, *History*, n.10, III, p.117.

[117] Stephen, *Digest*, n.82, Ch.21.

[118] Kenny, *Outlines*, n.98, Ch.10. He began by noting the 'singularly fragmentary and unsystematic' nature of the law (p.145).

'wound', 'grievous bodily harm', and maliciously. This was followed by Turner in his edition of Kenny, though he did deal with general provisions on self defence, lawful force, and consent at the start of the chapter.[119] This did not substantially change with Smith and Hogan at the end of the period, though the inclusions of a section on firearms and offensive weapons reflected the increased prominence of endangerment provisions.[120]

In summary, the law of non-fatal offences against the person was increasingly organized around ss.18, 20, and 47, which were understood as creating a rough hierarchy of offences. At one level, this was a narrowing and a generalizing, as the myriad specific offences in the Act were less used. At the same time, the 1861 Act was supplemented by specific provisions on violence in marriage and cruelty and neglect, for example. There was increased recognition of endangering offences, including the new preventive offences, where conduct created situations of risk and of the need for the individual to be aware of the consequences of their conduct. The person now was understood specifically and significantly as the body of the individual, which might be injured or put at risk. Seriousness was assessed in terms of a combination of intent (mental state) and (to a lesser extent) degrees of harm, actual or grievous. The whole of the law, though, was interpreted through cultural understandings of violence (brutality, cruelty) or of conduct such as the use of weapons, as intent continued to be read off conduct. This concern with violent conduct rather than victims should be understood in the context of the broader aims of the law in this period, namely teaching internal restraint or civic virtues of self-discipline, control of the passions, raising expectations of personal responsibility and self-control in relation to violent conduct.[121] This was directed at pacifying the public sphere but also at protecting key social institutions such as the family.[122]

IV. Reforming Offences against the Person

In 1970 the Criminal Law Revision Committee (CLRC) was asked to review the law of offences against the person (including homicide), as part of the revived codification project, and it eventually reported on this in 1980.[123] This was then followed by Law Commission Reports in 1985, 1989, 1992, and 1993, each also part of the codification initiative, each of which considered reforms to the law of offences against the person.[124] A further Law Commission consultation paper on

[119] JWC Turner, *Kenny's Outlines,* n.82, Ch.8. The whole law of non-fatal offences against the person, including sexual offences, was dealt with in a mere 23 pages.

[120] JC Smith & B Hogan, *Criminal Law* (1st edn) (London: Butterworths, 1965). Strikingly, s.47 is not singled out, apparently being regarded as a provision concerning the punishment of certain common law assaults. See p.275.

[121] Wiener, *Men of Blood*, n.6, p.288.

[122] D'Cruze, 'Introduction' in d'Cruze (ed.), *Everyday Violence,* n.58, p.7.

[123] Criminal Law Revision Committee, *Fourteenth Report. Offences against the Person* (Cmnd 7844) (London: HMSO, 1980).

[124] Law Commission, *Codification of the Criminal Law* (No.143) (London: HMSO, 1985); Law Commission, *A Criminal Code for England and Wales* (No.177) (London: HMSO, 1989);

consent and offences against the person followed the decision in the case of *Brown*, in 1994.[125] There was then a Home Office Consultation Paper, which presented a draft statute based on the Law Commission proposals in 1998, before the publication in 2014 of the most recent Law Commission paper on this topic.[126] It can accordingly, and without exaggeration, be said that the period from 1970 to the present has been dominated by the (as yet unsuccessful) project of reforming of the law of offences against the person. However, I shall argue in this section that the narrow focus of the reformers on the 1861 Act and its structure has obscured a more important shift in the law. This is a transformation in the idea of the person, as reflected in the claim of Chalmers, in a recent overview, that offences against the person may be understood as 'protecting the individual's interest in physical integrity and personal autonomy'.[127] The 'person' protected by the law is no longer just the physical body but now extends to the protection of personal autonomy. This takes the aims of the law in an entirely new direction, and I explore this shift and its profound significance in the remainder of the chapter.

Violence continues to be a major social and political concern, despite the fact that the UK is experiencing a period of unprecedented security from 'everyday' violence. This 'crime drop' is captured in both recorded (officially acknowledged) and unrecorded (victim surveys) levels of crime, though it is recognized that there is likely to be underreporting of certain crimes, notably domestic and sexual violence and various forms of hate crime.[128] Violent conduct continues to be prosecuted mainly under sections 18, 20, and 47 of the 1861 Act, and the common law of assault. However, there have been important changes in the way that key concepts in the 1861 Act have been interpreted—variously described as 'wide [and] flexible' and 'imaginative'.[129] For example, in *Mowatt* (1968) it was held that

Law Commission, *Legislating the Criminal Code. Offences Against the Person and General Principles* (Consultation Paper No.122) (London: HMSO, 1992); Law Commission, *Legislating the Criminal Code. Offences Against the Person and General Principles* (Report No.218) (Cm 2370) (London: HMSO, 1993).

[125] *Brown* [1994] 1 AC 212 on consent to sado-masochistic practices; Law Commission, *Criminal Law. Consent and Offences against the Person* (No.134) (London: HMSO, 1994).

[126] Home Office, *Violence: Reforming the Offences Against the Person Act 1861* (London: Home Office, 1998); Law Commission, *Reform of Offences Against the Person. A Scoping Consultation Paper* (No.217) (London: Stationery Office, 2014).

[127] J Chalmers, 'Offences Against the Person' in MD Dubber & T Hörnle (eds), *The Oxford Handbook of Criminal Law* (Oxford: Oxford UP, 2014) p.728.

[128] http://www.ons.gov.uk/ons/dcp171776_394470.pdf . See also G Farrell et al., 'Explaining and Sustaining the Crime Drop: Clarifying the Role of Opportunity Related Theories' (2010) 12 *Crime Prevention and Community Safety* 24–41.

[129] N Lacey, C Wells, & O Quick, *Reconstructing Criminal Law* (4th edn) (Cambridge: Cambridge UP, 2010) p.234; J Herring, *Criminal Law. Text, Cases, Materials* (5th edn) (Oxford: Oxford UP, 2012) p.419. It should also be noted that the text of s.18 was amended by the Criminal Law Act 1967 Sched.3 Pt.III (deleting 'shoot at any Person, or, by drawing a Trigger or in any other Manner, attempt to discharge any Kind of loaded Arms at any Person, with Intent, in any of the Cases aforesaid, to maim, disfigure, or disable any Person...' See generally the discussion in M Weait, *Intimacy and Responsibility. The Criminalization of HIV Transmission* (London: Routledge-Cavendish, 2007) pp.89–96 and M Jefferson, 'Offences against the Person: Into the 21st Century' (2012) 76 *Jnl Crim Law* 472.

proof of recklessness under s.20 required merely recklessness as to the possibility of some harm, however minor. In *Wilson* (1984), the House of Lords held that there could be 'infliction' of grievous bodily harm under s.20 without the need for proof of a direct physical attack (battery); and in *Savage; Parmenter* (1992) that 'wound' does not require an assault.[130] In the case of *Ireland; Burstow* (1998), the defendant was found guilty of assault by making a series of silent phone calls which caused psychiatric injury to the victim.[131] There was no suggestion that the defendant was in the immediate physical proximity of the victim, but his conduct gave rise to the apprehension of immediate violence in the mind of the recipient of the calls. In *R v Dica* (2004) it was held that harm could include the transmission of a disease, over-ruling the nineteenth-century case of *Clarence* (1888).[132] This and other cases also raised the question of the kinds of risky or harmful activity that might be consented to, whether a person might consent at all to forms of assault (rather than the causing or risk of injury), and of the degree or extent of injury that might be consented to.[133] Taken together these (and other) decisions reflect changes in understandings of offences against the person. They can be committed against victims who are not in the immediate physical vicinity of their attacker, and can extend in time through the focus on the intended or risked effect of a person's conduct.[134] The fact that the offence can be constituted by the perception of the immediacy of the threat on the part of the person threatened means that there has been an extension of the idea of how harm is constituted: harm to the person includes the experience of the victim, and no longer requires physical injury of the body.[135] At the same time, the law in this area is coming up against arguments about the positive value of autonomy and choice, or the freedom to consent to certain forms of conduct. We are no longer content with the broad statements, common in the Victorian period, about whether or not certain conduct is morally valuable or in the public interest. The issues are reframed in terms of an individual freedom of a person to control their own body and to choose to undertake certain risks. Conduct hitherto viewed as violent might be reclassified as something else—sex, sport, or entertainment – which can be consented to. This might limit the scope of offences against the person, but it is also used to argue in support of criminalization where a person's capacity for self-determination is

[130] *Mowatt* [1968] 1 QB 421; *R v Wilson (Clarence)* [1984] AC 242; *R v Savage; R v Parmenter* [1992] 1 AC 699.

[131] *Ireland; Burstow* [1998] AC 147. See also *R v Constanza* [1997] 2 Cr App R 492; *R v Dhaliwal* [2006] EWCA Crim 1139.

[132] *R v Dica* [2004] QB 1257; *Konzani* [2005] 2 Cr App R 13. See Weait, *Intimacy and Responsibility*, n.129, Chs.2 & 3.

[133] *Brown* [1994] 1 AC 212; *R v Dica* [2004] QB 1257; *Konzani* [2005] 2 Cr App R 13. See the discussion and cases cited in A Ashworth & J Horder, *Principles of Criminal Law* (7th edn) (Oxford: Oxford UP, 2013) pp.320–8.

[134] Cf. Ashworth & Horder, *Principles*, n.133, p.319, describing this as a 'loosening' of the imminence requirement, and a 'gentle drift' to a crime that does not require immediacy in a strict sense—the terminology suggesting something mild and innocuous.

[135] P Ramsay, *The Insecurity State* (Oxford: Oxford UP, 2012) pp.158–9.

constrained by the intentional actions of another.[136] The upshot is that offences against the person are no longer seen exclusively as crimes of actual physical violence. There will still, in many instances, be violent conduct leading to bodily harm, but the law now also criminalizes forms of threatening conduct as well as non-consensual or unjustified causing of injury.[137]

The demand for the reform of the 1861 Act arises in part from a recognition that decisions, such as those noted above, are stretching the limits of the original offence definitions—but this is seen mainly as a symptom of the longer standing concern with the illogical structure of the Act.[138] The law reform bodies have argued consistently, from the first report in 1980 to the most recent, that the law is technical and complex: an incoherent and unprincipled group of offences based on obsolete legal concepts.[139] In its place it is argued that both common and statute law should be recodified to create fewer, more general, offences according to a set of clearly articulated principles. These should include that the law should establish a clear hierarchy of offences, that the offences should provide clear and accurate labels, and that 'fewer broader offences' are preferable to 'numerous specialized ones'.[140] The current proposals (2014) are a modification of the draft Act published by the Home Office in 1998, which in turn built upon the earlier work of the CLRC and the Law Commission (though focusing on non-fatal offences against the person only).[141] The aim is to create a clear hierarchy of seriousness articulated in terms of outcomes and mental state, sometimes described as a 'ladder' of ascending seriousness, which is then supplemented with a small number of additional named offences (e.g. assault on a police officer) and specified

136 E Schneider, 'The Violence of Privacy' in MA Fineman & R Mykitiuk (eds), *The Public Nature of Private Violence* (New York: Routledge, 1994).

137 Unless violence is very broadly conceived—as it was by the majority in *Brown* (supra n.125) who followed the older view of the law and saw engaging in sado-masochistic conduct purely as serious violence (cruelty), hence ruling out the possibility of consent. See S Cowan, 'Criminalising SM: Disavowing the Erotic, Instantiating Violence' in RA Duff et al. (eds), *The Structures of Criminal Law* (Oxford: Oxford UP, 2011) Ch.4.

138 This parallels the contemporaneous reform of the law of homicide, where the law was identified as a mess and reforms were aimed at grading and labelling offences according to a clearer hierarchy of seriousness. See Law Commission, *A New Homicide Act for England and Wales* (Consultation Paper No.217) (London: Stationery Office, 2005).

139 See Law Commission, *Reform of Offences against the Person* (2014), n.3, Ch.3 for a summary of the problems they identify. Note that this mirrors discussion in the main textbooks, which are generally supportive of the proposed reforms for similar reasons of clarity. See e.g. Ashworth & Horder, *Principles*, n.133, p.334 ('There is an overwhelming case for reform'); AP Simester et al., *Simester and Sullivan's Criminal Law. Theory and Doctrine* (5th edn) (Oxford: Hart Publishing, 2013) p.460 ('a significant advance'). See also N Fielding, *Courting Violence. Offences against the Person Cases in Court* (Oxford: Oxford UP, 2006) pp.209–12, arguing that the language of the 1861 Act causes practical difficulties because it is difficult to explain to juries.

140 Law Commission, *Reform of Offences against the Person* (2014), n.3 p.93.

141 Law Commission, *Reform of Offences against the Person* (2014), n.3 Ch.4 contains a summary of the previous reports. See also discussion in JC Smith, 'Offences against the Person: the Home Office Consultation Paper' [1998] *Crim LR* 317; CMV Clarkson, 'Law Commission Report on Offences against the Person and General Principles: (1) Violence and the Law Commission' [1994] *Crim LR* p.324.

aggravations.[142] The offences under the 1861 Act would accordingly be replaced by new offences of intentionally causing serious injury; recklessly causing serious injury; intentionally or recklessly causing injury; plus a combined 'assault' offence ('applying force to or causing an impact on the body of another, or causing the other to believe that this is imminent) which would replace the common law.[143] The approach has been challenged on the grounds of its 'moral vacuity', failing to capture the moral significance of how harms are committed.[144] However, its greater significance surely lies in the fact that its inclusive general terms ('causing', 'injury') create broad categories that would extend the scope of criminal conduct, while at the same time delivering on the promise of an orderly and conceptually coherent law.

There have been other changes in the law throughout this period which suggest broader changes in understanding and a widening of the scope of offences against the person in a way which is not addressed in the law reform reports.[145] Four related features of these changes mark out a shift in how the law conceives of the person. First, there is the recognition that particular kinds of wrongs arise in particular contexts. Of particular importance here is the increased recognition of the seriousness and distinctiveness of domestic violence, or intimate abuse.[146] Since the 1970s, feminist campaigners have argued that domestic violence, or violence against women in the private sphere, should be seen as a public wrong; that violence against women is an endemic problem; that the police are unwilling to get involved in domestic or private matters (between couples); and that there should be 'an end to all laws, assumptions and institutions which perpetuate male dominance and men's aggression towards women'.[147] They campaigned for criminalization of this violence, arguing that the existing criminal law should be enforced equally for all forms of violence, encouraging the reporting of the crime, pro-arrest policies, special courts, and the provision of refuges and support services to allow battered or abused women to leave violent relationships.[148] This

[142] Chalmers, 'Offenses Against the Person', n.127, p.728. Cf. the 'homicide ladder' discussed in V Tadros, 'The Homicide Ladder' (2006) 69 *Mod LR* p.601.

[143] The 2014 Consultation suggests modifications to the 1998 proposals, particularly in relation to the definition of mental injury and the exclusion of transmission of disease, in the light of developments in the law since 1998.

[144] See the influential critique in J Horder, 'Rethinking Non-Fatal Offences Against the Person' (1994) *Ox Jnl of Leg Stud* 335; J Gardner, 'Rationality and the Rule of Law in Offences Against the Person' (1994) 53 *Camb LJ* 502.

[145] There is limited recognition in Law Commission, *Reform of Offences Against the Person*, n.3, which discusses stalking and harassment and, at pp.125–7, the question of whether new specific offences of domestic violence should be created and/or included in the reforms.

[146] I am focusing here on violence against women, but many of the same arguments would apply to the 'discovery' of child abuse in the same period as a form of 'private' or intimate violence. For a critical discussion, see I Hacking, 'The Making and Molding of Child Abuse' (1991) 17 *Critical Inquiry* 253–88.

[147] From National Women's Liberation Conference Demand (1978) quoted in RE Dobash & RP Dobash, *Women, Violence and Social Change* (London: Routledge, 1992) p.25 and Ch.2. This also includes sexual violence, discussed in chapter 9 infra.

[148] This should not be taken as suggesting that criminalization was the only response, or the only appropriate response, as there have been many critics of the negative impact of the resort to criminalization. See generally C Hoyle, *Negotiating Domestic Violence. Police, Criminal Justice and Victims*

has sparked an important debate about how best to understand the nature of this kind of violence in order to determine the appropriate kind of legal response. While analysis initially focused on the private or domestic sphere, in order to argue about the public nature of private violence, the current focus is on the characteristics of this kind of violence and its impact on the autonomy of the victim.[149] What makes it distinctive is not that it happens in private or in the home, but that it takes place in an intimate relationship, where there would normally be an expectation of trust. Violence is also now more commonly referred to as abuse. This covers physical violence but also extends to forms of non-physical control and coercion such as emotional or financial abuse. This also responds to obligations under initiatives such as Convention on the Elimination of All Forms of Discrimination Against Women (CEDAW) by the United Nations (1979). Under General Recommendation 19, violence against women is defined as including 'acts that inflict physical, mental or sexual harm or suffering, threats of such acts, coercion and other deprivations of liberty' and the Convention imposes positive obligations on governments to take measures to address it because it deprives women of 'the equal enjoyment, exercise and knowledge of human rights and fundamental freedoms'. From this perspective, the distinctiveness of domestic abuse consists in the fact that it is conduct which is an attack on the conditions for the development of autonomy and personal integrity—that is to say that it is the context of the intimate relationship that gives this kind of violence its distinctive character.[150] This was recognized in the creation of a new offence of 'controlling or coercive behaviour in an intimate or family relationship' by the Serious Crime Act 2015.[151]

This is linked to a second change in which violence might consist in a larger course of conduct, as in the criminalization of stalking and harassment in the Protection from Harassment Act 1997.[152] Here harm is not produced by any single incident, which taken alone might appear to be quite innocuous. It is the

(Oxford: Oxford UP, 2000); S Walklate, 'What is to be done about Violence against Women? Gender, Violence, Cosmopolitanism and the Law' (2008) 48 *Brit Jnl of Criminol* 39–54.

149 E Stark, *Coercive Control* (Oxford: Oxford UP, 2007). See also V Tadros, 'The Distinctiveness of Domestic Abuse: A Freedom-Based Account' in RA Duff & S Green (eds), *Defining Crimes. Essays on the Special Part of Criminal Law* (Oxford: Oxford UP, 2005) Ch.6; MM Dempsey, *Prosecuting Domestic Violence. A Philosophical Analysis* (Oxford: Oxford UP, 2009) Ch.6.

150 See Home Office, *Information for Local Areas on the Change to the Definition of Domestic Violence and Abuse* (March 2013) with coercive control also extending to female genital mutilation and 'honour' crimes. See Tadros, 'Domestic Abuse', n.149, pp.125–31; Schneider, 'Violence of Privacy', n.136.

151 S.76. See also s.6 of the Act which extends the definition of child cruelty in the Children and Young Persons Act 1933 s.1 to physical and non-physical ill treatment. See also measures such as the Domestic Violence, Crime and Victims Act 2004 extending a range of protection and non-molestation orders to cohabiting and same sex couples.

152 Ss.2 & 4. See E Finch, 'Stalking: A Violent Crime or a Crime of Violence?' (2002) 41 *Howard Jnl of Crim Just.* pp.422–33. It is also worth noting that this is the paradigm form of anti-social behaviour justifying the imposition of an Anti-Social Behaviour Order under the Crime and Disorder Act 1998. See Ramsay, *Insecurity State*, n.135, Ch.1 and pp.54–7 where the two are compared.

cumulative effect of a series of connected incidents and the alarm or distress that this causes for the victim which is taken as the distinctive quality of the crime. Under the Act a course of conduct is defined as two or more incidents with a connection between them, where the person knew or ought to have known that it would amount to harassment of the other.[153] This model has also been adopted in the new 'controlling or coercive behaviour' offence under the Serious Crime Act 2015, where the offence is defined as 'repeated or continuous behaviour' that A knew or ought to have known would have a serious effect on B.[154] This thus reflects the contextual understanding of domestic abuse and is aimed at capturing forms of abuse, such as physical, sexual, mental and emotional, financial controlling behaviour, that is not covered by existing offences. This is also underpinned by justifications in terms of character, as those who engage in emotional abuse are viewed as manipulative or systematic abusers.[155]

This is in turn linked to the third change, which concerns the increasing recognition of the relevance of threats or threatening conduct. Certain kinds of threats have been criminal under English law for a long time, however the law has generally been framed in terms of a threat to do something else (commit a named crime) as a form of inchoate liability, rather than the impact of the threat itself.[156] However, in part following the decision in *Ireland; Burstow* (1998), where the silent phone calls were treated as a form of implicit threat, and also because a growing concern about the impact of so-called cyberbullying or trolling online, the issue of threats and bullying or abusive behaviour has become more prominent.[157] There is a recognition that, in certain circumstances, the threat is the attack and that words or messages might constitute assault, by putting the hearer in a state of fear or alarm.[158] The law is thus directed at conduct rather than outcomes, which further frees the commission of the offence from any requirement of spatial proximity as the person making the threat and the person threatened may be in distinct, geographically separate, physical locations.

[153] See ss.1 & 7 where harassment is defined. The courts have tended to interpret course of conduct and harassment quite loosely. See Herring, *Criminal Law*, n.129, pp.352–6.

[154] S.76(1) and (4) where serious effect is defined as either fear or violence or causing alarm or distress which would have an impact on B's day-to-day activities.

[155] See N Lacey, 'The Resurgence of Character: Responsibility in the Context of Criminalization' in RA Duff & SP Green (eds), *Philosophical Foundations of Criminal Law* (Oxford: Oxford UP, 2011) Ch.8.

[156] E.g. sending a letter threatening to kill under Offences Against the Person Act 1861 s.16. See, generally, P Alldridge, 'Threats Offences—A Case for Reform' [1994] *Crim LR* 176–86 for a list of threats offences.

[157] *Ireland; Burstow* [1998] AC 147. See also CPS Guidelines on Prosecuting Communications sent via social media (dated 19th December 2012) http://www.cps.gov.uk/consultations/social_media_consultation.pdf. See also N Geach & N Haralambous, 'Regulating Harassment—Is the Law Fit for the Social Networking Age?' (2009) 73 *Jnl of Crim Law* 241.

[158] See Alldridge, 'Threats Offences', n.156, p.483; See J Horder, 'Reconsidering Psychic Assault' [1998] *Crim LR* 392 at p.400: 'what should be regarded as morally significant about the *actus reus* of a psychic assault is that it is experienced as a threatening *confrontation* by the victim' (italics in original). See also Chalmers, 'Offenses against the Person', n.127, p.731.

Finally, we should note the protection of racial, religious, sexual, and gender identity in the recognition of 'hate crimes'.[159] Under the Crime and Disorder Act 1998, if the person charged with committing one of an identified range of offences demonstrates, or is proven to have been motivated by, hostility on the grounds of race or religion, that offence becomes an aggravated offence and is subject to a higher maximum sentence.[160] In addition, under the Criminal Justice Act 2003 enhanced sentencing provisions can be applied in any offence where an offender demonstrates or was motivated by hostility based on grounds of disability, sexual orientation, or transgender identity.[161] These aggravations make the conduct or motivation of the offender relevant in constituting a particular kind of harm. However, the recognition of these aggravations in law has much in common with the other features identified here. The harm is shaped by the pre-existing context—the recognition of the prior victimization or vulnerability of particular groups; the attitude of hostility or hatred as a form of conduct is criminalized; and it is measured by its actual or potential impact (the fear and anxiety created) on the victim, the community to which they belong, and (ultimately) on the standards of decency or civility of the wider community.[162]

Taken together these developments amount to nothing less than a transformation in the idea of the person. These expanded understandings of personal victimization reflect the growing importance of victim's own perception of threats and of their vulnerability in particular contexts. This extends the range of harms and the idea of violence to acts, and increasingly also courses of conduct, which create fear or anxiety. Personhood is understood as a kind of personal space in which an individual is able to exercise or develop their autonomy and sense of self.[163] This personal space is protected by the law not only against physical harm, but now also against threatening, intimidating, controlling or abusive conduct. While the idea of personal autonomy protected by the law is more abstract or idealized, concerning the capacity to make choices and develop one's identity, it is at the same time linked to more concrete understandings of persons located in particular contexts or relationships or with particular characteristics such as gender, race, or sexual identity. This shows that the law is not only protecting the person, in this extended sense,

[159] There is now a range of legislation on forms of 'hate crime'. For a review see Law Commission, *Hate Crime. Should the Current Offences be Extended?* (Cm.8865) (Report No.348) (London: Stationery Office, 2014). See also Equality Act 2010 securing legal status for these groups in civil law and recognizing a government duty to treat equally.

[160] Crime and Disorder Act 1998 ss.28–32. The offences are assault, Offences Against the Person Act 1861 ss.20 & 47, criminal damage, Protection from Harassment Act 1998, ss.2 & 4, and Public Order Act 1986 ss.4, 4A, and 5.

[161] Criminal Justice Act 2003 s.146.

[162] See Home Office, *Guide to Racially Aggravated Offences* (London: Home Office, 1998): 'it erodes the standards of decency of the wider community'. For a fuller discussion of justifications see J Stanton-Ife, 'Criminalising Conduct with special reference to potential offences of Stirring up Hatred against Disabled or Transgender Persons' (2013) (http://lawcommission.justice.gov.uk/docs/Hate_Crime_Theory-Paper_Dr-John-Stanton-Ife.pdf).

[163] D Cornell, *The Imaginary Domain: Abortion, Pornography and Sexual Harassment* (New York: Routledge, 1995). Cf. Gardner, 'Rationality and the Rule of Law', n.144, p.508: 'invasion by one person of another's body space'.

but the person in their relations with others, as the idea of abuse is the index of forms of legitimate and illegitimate conduct in relationships with others. The law is placing a particular weight on responsible conduct in relation to others by criminalizing conduct which the person knew, or ought to have known, would be experienced as abusive. This links to Ramsay's account of vulnerable autonomy and the failure to reassure in the criminal law.[164] Ramsay argues that recent developments institutionalize a 'right to security' for individuals based on an implicit principle of 'vulnerable autonomy'. The converse of this is the responsibility of others to reassure, or to be attentive to the needs of others for reassurance, and the imposition of liability for conduct which demonstrates hostility, hatred, or threats—and the criminalization of conduct which fails to meet these standards. This conception of personhood thus comes together with and facilitates a pressure for increased criminalization.

Overall, offences against the person have been substantially remade in the period since 1980 as the idea of the protection of personal autonomy has increasingly shaped the law. In certain cases this has led to arguments for restricting the scope of the criminal law, recognizing that consensual infringements of bodily autonomy should not be offences; but its greater impact has been to extend the scope of offences against the person, as conduct which limits or infringes personal autonomy has been criminalized. The recognition of rights leads to the recognition of new ways of infringing those rights, or new harms and wrongs, and the law increasingly criminalizes the conduct of those who present risks and protects those who feel threatened. That said, this change is not fully recognized in the formal law, where there is a bifurcation between the increasing generality and abstraction of the proposed reforms, alongside an increasing specificity of particular offences where law is pursuing more specific ends. In both cases, though, the movement is towards the expansion of law on the basis of the wider conception of personhood. This, indeed, might be described as a continuation of the civilizing offensive against violence, extending to the regulation of conduct in intimate relations, and reshaping ideas of civility in relation with others.

V. Conclusion

The development of the law of offences against the person shows the history of a changing meshwork of boundaries that have limited the permissibility of violence and the process by which understandings of self-control and responsible conduct towards others have been developed.[165] For Blackstone and his contemporaries, assaults and batteries were private unless there was something in the circumstances of the attack that made it a threat to public order. In the present day, there is a tendency to argue that all interferences with personal autonomy require a public

164 Ramsay, *Insecurity State*, n.135, esp. Ch.6.
165 See quote at n.1: Reemtsma, *Trust and Violence*, n.1, p.105.

recognition and remedy. There has thus been a dramatic transformation of the scope of offences against the person, as it now criminalizes not only physical violence but also a range of other forms of interference with, or unwarranted intrusions, on the person. The historical development of this area has been driven by a long term 'civilizing offensive'. This has not only restrained and limited violence, but it has also fundamentally reshaped our ideas of what constitutes violence. The law has moved from requiring a 'violent act'—physical violence causing harm to or endangering the body—to criminalizing acts of violence to others more broadly conceived.[166] An act of violence need not be violent in itself (an attack), but conduct which can be characterized as producing, or being capable of producing, violent effects on the persons of others. Hence we have more emphasis on terms like 'abuse'—concentrating on the use of another person or the failure to respect their integrity or personality. Conversely, some forms of injury to others which are regarded as non-violating, because consensual, can be regarded as outwith the scope of legal violence. This also has consequences for the form of liability, going beyond the central idea of direct interpersonal violence, with one person attacking or inflicting injury on a person who is in their immediate vicinity. Liability now extends to cover a range of other modes of causing harm to or interfering with another person. The significance of such provisions is that they impose liability for action at a distance, for actions that bring about consequences in a different place or at a later point in time.[167] Violence is not an objective quality of certain acts, but is reshaped by understandings of the context in which it takes place.

Fundamental to this has been a changed conception of the person, as our conception of what constitutes violence in this area depends on our understanding of the person, or what must be protected. Formally this is recognized in the designation of the category as offences against the person but, as I noted at the start of the chapter, the concept of the person, and its importance to shaping and understanding this area of the law, has been neglected. My account has demonstrated the different ways in which the person was conceived in the law. The conception of the person in the 1861 Act, which has been at the heart of the law for over 150 years, was that of the person as a body susceptible to injury, and it stands out for the lengthy and detailed enumeration of the different ways that injury might be inflicted on or caused to the body in an urbanizing and industrializing society. While the law still struggles to escape from under the long shadow of the 1861 Act, it is clear that a new conception of the person is emerging, encompassing the person in their relationships and their sense of identity or self—as illustrated through changing definitions of violence in fields like domestic abuse law and hate crime. This autonomy-based conception of the person changes the limits of the law in terms of what we should suffer or choose to suffer. The person might exercise their autonomy in consensual relationships, but the law is increasingly in tension with

[166] J Harris, *Violence and Responsibility* (London: Routledge & Kegan Paul, 1980) pp.13–16.

[167] See Chapter 6. See also Reemtsma, *Trust and Violence*, n.1, pp.150–3: 'The only violence we accept as legitimate is violence that prevents greater violence in the future'.

political conceptions of persons as vulnerable and in need of protection—and the duty on the state to intervene to protect the autonomy of the vulnerable. This underlines the fact that the person is not an abstract thing, a private good or interest that should be protected. The way that the idea of the person has been constructed in law always reflects some set of wider aims or beliefs about civil order in terms of acceptable conduct in relationships between individuals and between individuals and the state. In this chapter, I have traced the development of the law from the demand to refrain from socially disruptive violence to the positive requirement of protecting vulnerable individuals and groups. Civil order is thus no longer understood merely as freedom from violence, but in terms of a more general expectation of conduct from others. The person is thus not only the object of this area of law but is understood as a subject of law insofar as it extends to their relationships with others. This is something that we will explore further in the context of sexual conduct and relationships in the next chapter.

9

Sex

I. Introduction

The idea of sexual offences as a distinct area of the criminal law, organized around the protection of a distinct interest or wrong, is a surprisingly recent development in the criminal law. The term sexual offences was not used in any legislation in the UK until 1956 and, while occasionally used as a descriptive term in treatises, it was for a long time little more than a usage of convenience, a way of denoting a sub-category of offences against the person.[1] It was not until the 1970s that the idea of sexual offences began to change from being a descriptive grouping to something that reflected an underlying organizing principle. The term is now very widely used, as exemplified by the Sexual Offences Acts 2003 and 2009 (Scotland), and its use reflects a change in the understanding not only of the significance of sex crimes, but also in the way that they are understood as protecting an interest in sexual autonomy. While this transformation has led to some notable instances of decriminalization of consensual sexual conduct seen as inconsistent with this principle, it is arguable that the larger impact has been in terms of increased criminalization, as the recognition of this distinct interest has led to the identification of a growing range of ways that the interest can be interfered with or infringed.[2] The recognition of sexual offences as a category has thus transformed our understanding of this area of the criminal law, and must lead us to ask how it is that this term has emerged in this recent period, and what is included in (and excluded from) this newly recognized area. The central theme, then, of this chapter, is to trace how this interest has emerged

[1] The first use in a UK textbook was Smith & Hogan, *Criminal Law* (London: Butterworths, 1965). See also US Model Penal Code Art.213, though the usage is adopted without comment. See American Law Institute, *Model Penal Code and Commentaries. Part II Definition of Specific Crimes §§210.0 to 213.6* (Philadelphia, PA: American Law Institute, 1980).

[2] While the main focus here will be on the UK, there is evidence that this development has taken place on a much larger scale. See DJ Frank, BJ Camp, & SA Boutcher, 'Worldwide Trends in the Criminal Regulation of Sex, 1945–2005' (2010) 75 *American Sociological Review* 867–93. This paper identifies a similar pattern on a global scale over a shorter time period, attributing the change to a range of factors including increasing individualization and the decline of corporate bodies (society, the family, etc.) as victims.

and has been recognized in the law, and the consequences of this recognition for the criminal law.

It is true that criminal law has always regulated sexual conduct in some way. However, it has not always been the same kinds of conduct that have been regulated, or regulated in the same way, in every society, for the same ends. Indeed, even the most cursory historical survey suggests the existence of considerable diversity in the forms of regulation of sexual conduct by the criminal law. We should, accordingly, be wary of trans-historical claims that either the regulation of sex or particular sex crimes have always lain at the heart of the criminal law, for this is simply not the case.[3] Nor is it the case that any of those offences were regarded as 'sexual offences' in anything like the contemporary sense. As we shall see, it has not always been clear that crimes such as rape were seen as 'sexual' by the law in the way that we would understand the term (though clearly involving a 'sex act'); and laws regulating sexual conduct were often seen as religious or public order offences—or offences against the institution of marriage. What is thus remarkable is how quickly a distinct category of 'sexual offences' emerged in the second half of the twentieth century, bringing together under this rubric a range of pre-existing and newly created offences. If we are to understand the significance of this development, however, we cannot take the concept of 'sexual offences' as a starting point, as something that was always already there, waiting to be recognized or discovered. In order to understand this interest in sexual autonomy, it is necessary first to ask why and how certain behaviours have been grouped together under the rubric of sexual offences, the kinds of connection or thematic unity that makes this possible, and the consequences of this move for criminalization.

This will be done in three stages. First, I will review the diverse ways that crimes which had a sexual element were categorized in the law in the period prior to 1956. Here I will look in particular at rape, sodomy, and prostitution to see how these were categorized at different points in the development of the law.[4] Second, I will look at how a range of offences come to be grouped together to form the category 'sexual offences' after 1956 and how this category was understood. Third, I will look at how this category of sexual offences has changed, and is changing: what is included and what comes to be excluded; what kind of conduct is regulated; and the changing ends of sexual offences. The chapter will then conclude by reflecting on the process of categorization and its consequences for criminalization.

[3] See e.g. R Porter, 'Rape—Does it have a Historical Meaning?' in R Porter & S Tomaselli (eds), *Rape. An Historical and Cultural Enquiry* (Oxford: Blackwell, 1986) pp.216–36.

[4] Cf. V Munro, 'Sexual Autonomy' in MD Dubber & T Hörnle (eds), *Oxford Handbook of Criminal Law* (Oxford: Oxford UP, 2014) taking rape, prostitution and 'risky' sex as core areas for discussion of sexual autonomy in criminal law.

II. Before Sexual Offences

A. Rape, sodomy, prostitution in 1800

In Blackstone's *Commentaries*, published in 1769, there was no identification of a separate category of sexual offences. Many of the crimes that might putatively have been regarded as 'sexual' offences, in the sense that they related to sexual conduct in some way, were scattered across different sections of the book. The chapter on offences against the person of individuals covered forcible abduction and marriage, rape, and the 'crime against nature' (sodomy) alongside mayhem, assaults, batteries, wounding, false imprisonment, and kidnapping.[5] Lewdness was part of the chapters on offences against God and religion, while bigamy (and polygamy) were considered as offences against public health, police, or economy. What is striking about Blackstone's treatment is both that there are so few individual offences identified and that these are not accorded any particular weight or separate identity, notwithstanding that his work is usually seen as the first modern categorization of the criminal law.[6]

There is no consistent approach to categorization in other works from this period. Hawkins, for example, writing in 1716, dealt with rape and sodomy separately: sodomy was seen as a crime against religion (Ch.4) and rape was simply presented as the most serious statutory felony without further comment (Ch.41).[7] East's *Treatise of the Pleas of the Crown* (1803) had a chapter on 'Rape and the Carnal Knowledge of Female Children', which followed on from chapters on assaults and false imprisonment and was followed by chapters on forcible abduction and marriage, polygamy and bigamy, and clandestine and illegal marriages.[8] The volume then concluded with a brief chapter on sodomy, and while East pointed out that the evidence required for proof of the crime was the same as rape (i.e. carnal knowledge), he made no other connection between the two crimes. The Scots law treatises were similarly diverse. In Mackenzie's *Law and Customs of Scotland in Matters Criminal* (1678) there was no identification of a separate category of sexual offences. There was a separate chapter on rape, following the title on incest, sodomy, and bestiality, and followed by titles on adultery and bigamy,

[5] W Blackstone, *Commentaries on the Laws of England* (1769 edn) (Chicago: Chicago UP, 1979) iv, Ch.15 (a total of nine pages out of fifteen). Sodomy was defined as sexual intercourse between men, or by any person (male or female) with an animal.

[6] See notably J Bentham, *Fragment on Government* (1776) Preface to the First edn, pp. 28–9 where Blackstone's categorization of the law in terms of the distinct objects to be protected is singled out as his most distinctive contribution. See supra Ch.3 at p.72.

[7] W Hawkins, *Treatise of Pleas of the Crown: or a system of the principal matters related to that subject, divided under the proper heads* (2 vols) (London: n.p., 1716–21). Cf. M Hale, *Historia Placitorum Coronæ: The History of the Pleas of the Crown* (London: Printed by E. Rider, 1800), which divided crimes into common law and statutory felonies, and treated rape as a statutory felony (Ch.LVIII), followed by a chapter on abduction.

[8] EH East, *A Treatise of Pleas of the Crown* (2 vols) (London: Butterworths, 1803) Vol. I Ch.X.

suggesting an understanding of these crimes as moral or religious wrongs.[9] Hume's *Commentaries* (1797) had a separate chapter on rape, which followed on from other offences against the person, and also included a brief discussion of assault with intent to ravish and the corruption of the morals of female pupils and forcible abduction and marriage.[10] Later in the book there were chapters on incest, adultery, bigamy, and clandestine marriage and 'fornication, drunkenness and unnatural lusts', falling between chapters on breach of the peace and piracy.

The classifications in these books primarily reflect some of the different understandings of the purpose and scope of the law of rape in its development up to this point. Coke's definition of the crime as 'when a man hath carnal knowledge of a woman by force and against her will' was widely accepted, but this masked different interpretations of the scope and meaning of the crime.[11] Rape was a felony, and thus had more in common with other serious crimes, or Pleas of the Crown, than with lesser forms of sexual assault or immoral or lewd crimes. The association with forcible abduction and marriage could be traced to the idea that rape required a theft or taking of the woman, an association that lingered long after the law formally recognized, in 1487, that rape and abduction were separate crimes.[12] The early modern law protected virtue or chastity as a property of the unmarried woman, as a dimension of property or inheritance, that was damaged by rape, but which could also be restored if the woman subsequently married her attacker.[13] Hale, for example, discussed the situation in which a marriage which was voidable because of an initial rape might be ratified by the subsequent consent of the woman.[14] The association with property was also reflected in the fact that the law was more readily enforced where the victim was of higher social standing

[9] G Mackenzie, *Law and Customs of Scotland in Matters Criminal* (2nd edn) (Edinburgh: Andrew Anderson, 1678) Title XVI. I shall refer to Scots law in this chapter where it elucidates the development of the law as it followed a similar pattern. This was not the case with property offences or offences against the person, where English law was in statutory form and developed in a slightly different way.

[10] D Hume, *Commentaries on the Law of Scotland Respecting Crime* (4th edn) (Edinburgh: Bell & Bradfute, 1844) Vol.I; A Alison, *Principles of Criminal Law of Scotland* (Edinburgh: William Blackwood, 1832) follows the same pattern.

[11] E Coke, *Institutes*, 2 Inst 180; 3 Inst 60. Cf. Hale: 'Rape is the carnal knowledge of any woman above the age of ten years against her will' (Hale, *History*, n.7, p.627). Cf. Hume, *Commentaries*, n.10, i, 301: 'There must be carnal knowledge of the woman's person by penetration of her privy parts, or entry of her body.' Mackenzie was the only writer who did not reproduce a version of Coke's wording, rape being defined as 'the unjust oppressing of a woman, by a man, against the Kings peace' (Mackenzie, *Law and Customs*, n.9, p.164).

[12] 3 Hen.VII c.2 created the offence of forcible abduction and marriage for lucre. See F Pollock & FW Maitland, *History of English Law*, Vol. II, (2nd edn) (Cambridge: Cambridge UP, 1898) pp.490–1.

[13] *Bracton on the Laws and Customs of England* (translated with revisions and notes by Samuel E Thorne) (Cambridge: Harvard UP, 1968), Bk.III, c.28. The protection of the law was extended (notionally) to all women (i.e. not only virgins) by 1 Edw I c.13.

[14] Hale, *History*, n.7, pp.628–9. This also makes sense of Hale's notorious assertion that a wife could not be raped by her husband (p.628) as virtue had a different meaning in the context of marriage. That Hale offers no justification should probably be read as indicative that this point was self-evident to him and his contemporaries. See also discussion in C Herrup, *A House in Gross Disorder* (Oxford: Oxford UP, 1999) pp.151–2.

or had property, or a good family name to protect; in other cases the crime was hard to prove with women and servants regarded as unreliable witnesses.[15] There is evidence that the criminal process was used by those of lower social classes to obtain small amounts of compensation and a public recognition of the wrong that had been done to them, rather than to obtain a conviction.[16] Rape was a wrong inflicted on an individual, but its seriousness was measured in terms of its threat to property and family. The maintenance of social order required the infliction of punishment, but only in cases where the victim had not already acted to get compensation. Rape thus encompassed sexual behaviour, but its meaning was understood in terms of the institutions of property, marriage, and the family.[17]

By the late eighteenth century legal practice placed a greater stress on the degree of violence used and whether the will of the woman had been overcome, and this was increasingly reflected in discussions of the crime. For East, rape was characterized as a 'brutal and violent attack upon the honour and chastity of the weaker sex' and a violation of the 'quick sense of honour, the pride of virtue, which nature, to render the sex amiable, hath implanted in the female heart'.[18] While this makes clear the seriousness of the crime, the wrong is defined as consisting in an injury to the honour of the woman performed by sexual means. Violence was understood, by analogy with robbery, as something extraneous or additional to the sexual intercourse itself—though unlike in the case of robbery, the mere threat of violence was rarely enough to secure a conviction.[19] But the scope of the law was narrow. The age of consent at common law was ten, meaning that only very young girls were regarded as incapable of consenting.[20] However, crimes against girls

[15] On the enforcement of the law of rape in early modern England, see N Bashar, 'Rape in England between 1550 and 1700' in The London Feminist History Group (eds), *The Sexual Dynamics of History* (Pluto, 1983) Ch.2; G Walker, 'Rereading Rape and Sexual Violence in Early Modern England' (1998) 10 *Gender & History* 1–25; A. Clark, *Women's Silence, Men's Violence* (New York: Pandora, 1987).

[16] See AE Simpson, 'The "Blackmail Myth" and the Prosecution of Rape and its Attempt in 18th Century London: The Creation of a Legal Tradition' (1986) 77 *Jnl of Crim Law & Criminol* 101–50 at pp.116–9 for lengthy discussion of the survival of this practice into the eighteenth century. See also M Wiener, *Men of Blood. Violence, Manliness and Criminal Justice in Victorian England* (Cambridge: Cambridge UP, 2004) pp.86–7 discussing the later survival of this practice.

[17] Herrup, *House in Gross Disorder*, n.14, pp.37–8. See generally F Dabhoiwala, *The Origins of Sex. A History of the First Sexual Revolution* (London: Allen Lane, 2012) Ch.3.

[18] EH East, *Pleas of the Crown*, n.8, Vol. I, pp.436–7. This phrase is repeated verbatim in WO Russell, *A Treatise on Crimes and Indictable Misdemeanors* (2nd edition) (London: J Butterworth, 1826) p.560. See also Hume, *Commentaries*, n.7, I, p.301: 'Being a robbery of that in which a woman's honour, her place in society, and her estimation in her own eyes, depend; and being also, in the perpetration, necessarily accompanied with alarm and terror, beside actual violence to the person.' He went on: 'It is not as a lustful, but as a malicious and injurious act, that rape is the object of the vengeance of the law' (i, p.305).

[19] AE Simpson, 'Popular Perceptions of Rape as a Capital Crime in Eighteenth-Century England: The Press and the Trial of Francis Charteris in the Old Bailey, February 1730' (2004) 22 *Law & Hist. Rev* 27–70. Cf. Hume, *Commentaries*, n.10, pp. 302–3.

[20] See also 18 Eliz I, c.7 s.4. Intercourse with a girl between the ages of 10 and 12 was a misdemeanour only, irrespective of consent or its absence. Note that Hale, *History*, n.7, pp.630–1 suggested that as the age of consent for marriage was 12 it should also be rape if a girl was between the ages of 10 and 12. This view does not seem to have been followed by others. In Scots law, the age of consent was 12: Hume, *Commentaries*, n.10, i, p.303.

below the age of ten were especially hard to prove because children could not give evidence on oath.[21] As no violence was required to have sexual intercourse with an unconscious or insensible woman this was not regarded as falling within the scope of rape.[22] In addition, carnal knowledge was understood as requiring not only penetration, but also proof of emission of semen, making the crime extremely difficult to prove in practice.[23] The focus on honour and chastity also meant that there was a tension between extending the protection of the law to all women and recognizing limits in the case of the unchaste or those of 'easy' virtue, where there was no 'honour' to be lost. All the treatise writers discussed at some length the question of who may be raped, and though the developing consensus was that all women might be raped, there was considerable equivocation over how a prostitute or unchaste woman might demonstrate that, at the time of the attack, she had renounced her way of life.[24] Hume even went so far as to suggest that the degree of the injury might be less in the case of a woman who was unchaste, though this is followed by a long statement that the law must only be concerned with the unlawful act that has been done, and the violation of order, peace and security, rather than the precise degree of harm or distress suffered.[25] Thus, while the law was understood as being of broad application—applying to all women, including those who were unchaste, where the will of the woman had been overcome—in practice its scope was rather more limited.[26]

If the growing recognition of the significance of violence can explain why rape was coming to be seen as a species of offence against the person, this made it harder to see a possible relation with sodomy. Sodomy was a statutory felony, with its origins in ecclesiastical law, defined as carnal knowledge between two men, between human and animal or 'unnaturally' between a man and a woman.[27] It was linked to rape because it was constituted by 'carnal knowledge' and raised similar issues of evidence and proof. But, as with rape, while the definition required the performance of sexual acts it was not, in practice, wholly defined by them. It was

[21] AE Simpson, 'Vulnerability and the Age of Female Consent: Legal Innovation and its Effect on Prosecutions for Rape in Eighteenth-Century London' in GS Rousseau & R Porter (eds), *Sexual Underworlds of the Enlightenment* (Manchester: Manchester UP, 1987).

[22] All the treatise writers are clear that forms of assault falling outwith the scope of rape could be punished—if not capitally. However, procedurally, the lesser charges could not be brought at the same time, so, if a rape trial collapsed, the prosecutor/victim would face the burden of finding the resources to bring a new charge for the lesser offence. There is some evidence that prosecutors opted for lesser charges even where a rape took place, possibly in order to avoid this. See G Walker, 'Rape, Acquittal and Culpability in Popular Crime Reports in England, c.1670–1750' (2013) 220 *Past & Present* 115–42.

[23] *R v Hill* (1781) 1 East PC 439; *R v Parker* (1812) 1 Russell 560.

[24] Blackstone, *Commentaries*, n.5, iv, p.213; Alison, *Principles*, n.10, pp.214–5.

[25] Hume, *Commentaries*, n.5, i, p.304.

[26] See e.g. Hume, *Commentaries*, n.10, i, p.304 for the person of every woman is under the safeguard of law 'if she choose to abandon her vicious course of life'.

[27] 25 Hen VIII c.6 (1533–4) taking the jurisdiction over the crime away from ecclesiastical courts. See Pollock & Maitland, *History*, n.12, pp.556–7. It was capital for both parties, if of age, with capital punishment not formally repealed for this crime until 1861. See Herrup, *House in Gross Disorder*, n.14, pp.33–7 for a lucid discussion of the crime.

described as a crime against nature, and as a Plea of the Crown it fell within the class of crimes that were regarded as posing a serious threat to social order.[28] It was not prosecuted in any consistent way, which is perhaps not surprising where the parties were consenting, for the prosecution would normally be brought by the victim of the crime.[29] Herrup argues that when it was prosecuted in the seventeenth and eighteenth centuries this was usually because it was linked to some other threat posed by a particular individual or because it was seen as the manifestation of an underlying social disorder:

> The danger of the sodomite was not that the focus of his attention was a man, but that his desires had no focus; they ran in indiscriminate streams that undermined allegedly categorical boundaries between men and women, humans and animals, nobles and commoners.[30]

However, if sodomy could be understood in these terms as a crime against nature, this was conceptually distinct from the understanding of rape as a crime of violence.

To the extent that prostitution was regarded as criminal, it was in relation to public disorder. In the eighteenth century, prostitutes might be prosecuted for disorderly behaviour, and in London and other large towns watchmen patrolled the streets and were empowered to arrest 'nightwalkers' and other disorderly persons. However, these laws were only sporadically enforced and there seems to have been a general toleration of prostitution—except when it caused or attracted drunkenness or serious disorder.[31] The Vagrancy Act 1824 also criminalized solicitation by 'common prostitutes' in public places if done in a riotous or indecent manner—as well as forms of indecent exposure.[32] There was less tolerance of brothel keepers, who were not only seen as the principal beneficiaries of the commercial sex industry, but were also blamed for conduct such as the kidnapping and sexual exploitation of women and children and for the fact that other sorts of petty crime—theft, drunkenness, gambling—happened in the environs of bawdy houses or brothels.

[28] Blackstone, *Commentaries*, n.5, iv, p.215 describes it as 'the infamous *crime against nature*, committed with either man or beast' (emphasis in original). This was criticized in J Bentham, *On Sexual Irregularities* (Oxford: Oxford UP, 2014). For background, see L Crompton, 'Jeremy Bentham's Essay on Pederasty' (1978) 3:4 *Jnl of Homosexuality* 383–8; Dabhoiwala, *Origins*, n.17, pp.134–8.

[29] For some evidence of prosecution patterns during the seventeenth and eighteenth centuries see AD Harvey, 'Prosecutions for Sodomy in England at the Beginning of the Nineteenth Century' (1978) 21 *The Historical Journal* 939–48.

[30] Herrup, *House in Gross Disorder*, n.14, p.33. This explains the logic of conflating bestiality and sodomy in a category of buggery. It was against the order of nature, but the nature here was not heterosexuality 'it was organisation born of moderation'. See also T Hitchcock, *English Sexualities 1700-1800* (Palgrave: London, 1997) Ch.5.

[31] K Norberg, 'The Body of the Prostitute: Medieval to Modern' in S Toulalan & K Fisher (eds), *The Routledge History of Sex and the Body, 1500 to the Present* (London: Routledge, 2013) pp.401–3. See also Hitchcock, *English Sexualities*, n.30, Ch.7; R Trumbach, *Sex and the Gender Revolution* (Chicago: Chicago UP, 1998) Ch.4; AE Simpson, '"The Mouth of Strange Women is a Deep Pit": Male Guilt and Legal Attitudes Towards Prostitution in Georgian London' (1996) 4 *Journal of Criminal Justice and Popular Culture* 50–79.

[32] 5 Geo.IV c.83 ss.3 & 4.

The Disorderly Houses Act 1751 provided for rewards for those who denounced bawdy houses.[33] This Act, as the name suggests, was aimed at preventing the social disorder that might attend a brothel, and specifically identified the need to prevent thefts and robberies. It was thus aimed less at prostitution itself than at the associated disorder and crime. But in spite of the social disapproval, the offence was framed in terms that made successful prosecution difficult.[34]

Overall, we can see that although these three crimes were each understood in terms of the threat to social order, the kind of threat that each posed was very different. Rape was directed at the protection of women from violence; sodomy at acts which subverted a 'natural' order; and prostitution offences at conduct which led directly to public disorder. There were a few writers, such as Eden, who saw a connection between rape and sodomy in terms of them both being an abuse of passion, 'prejudicial to the well-being, morality, and safety of society'.[35] This was an understanding that was to become more prominent over the course of the nineteenth century.

B. Offences against the person and against morals 1800–1956

The categorizations in the treatises and legislation of the early Victorian period did not substantially depart from those established in the earlier treatises. Thus, Russell, in his influential treatise, discussed rape and sodomy as crimes against the person.[36] However, there were some subtle changes of emphasis. The chapter on rape singled out carnal knowledge of female children—reflecting, as we shall see, the growing interest in the protection of children.[37] This was followed by a chapter on forcible abduction, unlawful taking away of females, and clandestine marriages. While in certain respects this followed the traditional linking of rape, abduction and forcible marriage, Russell's treatment focuses more on the idea of the protection of female minors from sexual exploitation. There was brief mention of 'assault by indecent liberties with females' in the chapter on common assaults, but though this discusses cases where the verdict was assault with intent to ravish, no connection was drawn with the earlier discussion of rape.[38] There was brief mention of disorderly inns and bawdy houses, as well as lewdness and public indecency, in the chapter on public nuisance.[39] The Criminal Law Commissioners

[33] 25 Geo.II c.36, amended by 58 Geo.III c.70. Blackstone also states that bawdy houses could be prosecuted on indictment at common law: *Commentaries*, n.5, iv, 168. Discussed in Simpson, 'Male Guilt', n.31, pp.62–3.

[34] See AE Simpson, 'The Ordeal of St Sepulchre's: A Campaign against Organised Prostitution in Early Nineteenth Century London and the Emergence of Lower Middle-class Consciousness' (2006) 15 *Social & Leg Stud* 363; S Petrow, *Policing Morals* (Oxford: Oxford UP, 1994) pp.147–9.

[35] W Eden, *Principles of Penal Law* (3rd edn) (London: B White & T Cadell, 1775) p.259.

[36] Russell, *Treatise*, n.18, Bk.III, Chs.6–9. This pattern was followed in the 3rd edition, edited by CS Greaves (1843) and subsequent editions.

[37] Russell, *Treatise*, n.18, Bk.III, Ch.6 Pt 2.

[38] Russell, *Treatise*, n.18, I, pp.605–6. In spite of the growing importance of the crime of indecent assault both as an alternative charge to rape or for the prosecution of other sexual assaults, it is barely mentioned in either treatises or legislation in this period.

[39] Russell, *Treatise*, n.18, I, Bk.II, pp.298–9 and p.302. This part also contained a discussion of bigamy.

1833–45, by contrast, simply reproduced the existing law in this area with barely any comment and no innovation in either definition or arrangement. Articles 84–91 of their draft code covered rape, sexual intercourse with girls, and buggery within the broader category of offences against the person.[40] This structure was also broadly reproduced in the Offences Against the Person Act 1861, though with the insertion of bigamy between the sections on rape and abduction and those on procuring abortion and concealment of pregnancy.[41]

This can be contrasted with the categorization adopted by Stephen in his *Digest of the Criminal Law* at the end of the century.[42] Rape was still treated as an offence against the person, though in addition to the discussion of violence, there was now also recognition of situations in which the consent of the woman had been obtained by fraud (Ch.29). There was also discussion of offences involving sex with children.[43] This was followed by a new chapter on Crimes affecting Conjugal and Parental Rights (Ch.30) covering bigamy, irregular or clandestine marriage, forcible abduction, abduction of girls under 16, and stealing children. This placed greater emphasis on the protection of children, in the context of the rights of parents. The greater innovation was the recognition of a class of offences against morality as a species of 'Acts Injurious to the Public in General' (Pt. IV). This included sodomy, gross indecency between males, public indecency, obscene publications, and defilement of women and girls (procuring women for prostitution), and, more unexpectedly, preventing the burial of dead bodies.[44] A similar emphasis on morals can also be seen in the leading Scots law text of the period. Macdonald's *Practical Treatise* (1867) grouped rape and clandestine injury to women with offences against the person, while dealing with bigamy, incest, unnatural offences, and lewd indecent and libidinous practices later in the work.[45] Anderson's *Criminal Law* (1904) likewise distinguished between crimes affecting the public and crimes affecting persons. The latter included rape and clandestine injury to women, while the former, in a subsection entitled offences

[40] Law Commissioners, *Fourth Report* (London: HMSO, 1839) pp.45–6. This was followed by Articles on abduction, child stealing, and taking female children from the custody of their parents (Arts.92–5).

[41] Ss.48–55 on rape, abduction and defilement of women; s.57 bigamy; ss.58 & 59 abortion; s.60 concealing birth of child; ss.61 & 2 sodomy and unnatural offences; s.63 carnal knowledge defined—penetration not emission. This followed the 1828 Act 9 Geo.IV c.31.

[42] JF Stephen, *Digest of the Criminal Law* (4th edn) (London: Macmillan, 1887). This can be contrasted with his *History* where there is no discussion of the crimes of rape or abduction. He commented: 'Their history possesses no special interest and does not illustrate either our political or our social history.' (JF Stephen, *History of the Criminal Law of England* (London: Macmillan, 1883) Vol. III, p.118).

[43] Note that there was also a separate chapter (Ch.31) on offences against children.

[44] This same pattern was followed in his draft Criminal Code. Title IV Pt XIII is offences against morality and Title V Pt XX is rape, 'knowing children' and procuring abortion and Pt XXI crimes affecting conjugal and parental rights.

[45] JHA Macdonald, *A Practical Treatise on the Criminal Law of Scotland* (1st edn) (Edinburgh: William Paterson, 1867). Lewd practices were offences against children, corrupting individuals. He went on to argue that all behaviour which would corrupt public morals would also be criminal.

against religion, morality, and public economy, included sodomy, bestiality, lewd practices, dealing in obscene works, and immoral traffic (mainly prostitution, but also including sexual intercourse with children).[46] In JWC Turner's 11th edition of *Russell on Crime*, he took a reasonably novel approach in a chapter headed 'Rape and the Defilement or Corruption of Females', a class which allowed him to include with rape various forms of unlawful sexual intercourse and indecent assault, as well as prostitution. However, his broad understanding of the area was indicated by his definition of rape as an aggravated form of assault.[47] In order to understand these changes we need to look at developments in the law relating to rape, sodomy, and prostitution.

The growing understanding of rape as a crime against the person, and specifically against the person of a woman, reflected changes in the scope and enforcement of the law over the course of the nineteenth century.[48] The period from the late eighteenth to the end of the nineteenth century saw the law focused more clearly on extending protection against violent sexual conduct to a broader class of women and on making the prosecution of the crime more effective.[49] This was in part a consequence of broader changes in criminal justice, such as the reform of capital punishment and the presence of counsel in the criminal trial. Rape was a capital crime in England until 1841, but capital punishment was not used after 1836 as it was increasingly believed that juries would not convict in any but the most extreme cases.[50] An Act of 1837 facilitated the bringing of lesser charges, such as assault with intent to ravish or indecent assault, alongside rape making it easier to obtain alternative convictions.[51] The Offences Against the Person Act 1828 changed the definition of carnal knowledge so that only penetration and not emission of semen was required to constitute rape.[52]

[46] AM Anderson, *The Criminal Law of Scotland* (2nd edn) (Edinburgh: Bell & Bradfute, 1904).

[47] JWC Turner (ed.), *Russell on Crime* (11th edition) (London: Stevens & Sons, 1958) Ch.40, p.789. Abduction and sodomy were dealt with in the two following chapters. Cf. his 19th edition of Kenny's *Outlines of Criminal Law* (Cambridge: Cambridge UP, 1966) in which he retained Kenny's original chapter headings, but a section of the chapter was devoted to sexual offences including rape, indecent assault, abduction, incest, and sodomy (Ch.VII).

[48] Wiener, *Men of Blood*, n.16, p.76 and p.91. See generally G Walker, 'Sexual Violence and Rape, 1500–1750' and S d'Cruze, 'Sexual Violence since 1750' both in Toulalan & Fisher, *The Routledge History of Sex and the Body*, n.31.

[49] These changes are discussed at some length in M Wiener, *Men of Blood*, n.16, Ch.3. He suggests that conviction rates in the latter part of the century reached 60% of prosecutions.

[50] 4 & 5 Vict. c.56, substituting transportation for life. This mandatory penalty was itself abolished in 1845.

[51] 1 Vict. c.35 s.11; Administration of Justice Act 1851 s.29; 24 & 25 Vict. c.100 s.52 for statutory recognition of indecent assault. See discussion in Wiener, *Men of Blood*, n.16, pp.91–2; KJM Smith, 'Offences Against the Person' in W Cornish et al., *The Oxford History of the Laws of England.* Vol.XIII *1820–1914 Fields of Development* (Oxford: Oxford UP, 2010) pp.404–5; K Stevenson, 'Legal and Public Perceptions of Sexual Violence' in S d'Cruze (ed.), *Everyday Violence in Britain* (Harlow: Pearson, 2000) esp. pp.96–7.

[52] 9 Geo.IV c.31 s.18. In *R v Russell* (1831) the court held that the jury still had to be satisfied that emission had taken place. The point was finally settled in *R v Reekspear* (1832) 1 Mood 341, 186 ER 1296; *R v Cox* (1832) 5 Car & P, 172 ER 985. See also *R v Allen* (1839) 9 Car & P 31, 173 ER 727. For Scotland, see Alison, *Principles*, n.10, pp.209–10 citing the case of *Wm. Montgomerie* (1821) to suggest that Scots law was now also settled on this point.

Further changes came as the courts limited the admissibility of character evidence. It was held in the case of *R v Hodgson* that, while it was possible for the defence to bring general evidence of bad character or reputation, evidence of specific instances of sexual relations was not admissible.[53] Although this ruling was controversial and was contested throughout the rest of the century, it was evidence that the prior conduct or character of the victim was becoming less important where there was clear evidence of violence.[54]

The biggest shift came in a series of cases in which the courts explored the question of the meaning of force, gradually redefining the crime in terms of consent. Prior to 1845, the courts had been resistant to the idea that rape might be accomplished without force.[55] However, in *R v Camplin* (1845) the High Court upheld the conviction of a man for rape where he had got the victim, a thirteen-year-old girl, drunk, and had sex with her while she was unconscious.[56] The court held that actual force and actual resistance were not required for proof of rape, and that 'the rape was committed without the consent and against the will of the prosecutrix'.[57] This shift in the definition towards consent led to the inclusion within the definition of a range of situations where, in contractual terms, the consent had been vitiated in some way—coerced or fraudulently obtained. Later cases show the courts recognizing the possibility of lack of consent due to other causes—notably 'imbecility' and deception—culminating in the case of *R v Flattery* (1877) in which it was held that even though the victim had consented, fraud as to the nature of the act could vitiate consent.[58] This, though, was subject to important limitations. Free consent was understood in formal terms: if an unvitiated consent had been given, however obtained, then this would stand in law. In addition, the scope of impermissible fraud was limited

[53] (1811) Russell & Ryan 211. Moving towards the position that consent to sexual intercourse with another man was not evidence of consent in the instance charged. See Wiener, *Men of Blood*, n.16, pp.93–100.

[54] C Conley, 'Rape and Justice in Victorian England' (1986) 29 *Victorian Studies* 519–36.

[55] See *R v Jackson* (1822) R & R 487; *R v Saunders* (1838) 8 C & P 265 (impersonating husband); *R v Williams* (1838) 8 C&P 286; *R v Clarke* (1854) Dears CC 397. For a critical contemporary discussion of this line of authority see CS Greaves, 'Note on Rape', Appendix in H Taschereau, *The Criminal Statute Law of the Dominion of Canada* (Toronto: Carswell, 1888). Greaves complains that these cases are 'turning cases of seduction into rape' (p.1093).

[56] (1845) 169 ER 163.

[57] They went on: 'Your case, therefore, falls within the description of those cases in which force and violence constitute the crime, but in which fraud is held to supply the want in both.' Cf. *Chas Sweenie* (1858) 3 Irv 109 in Scotland where intercourse with a sleeping woman was held to be the lesser crime of clandestine injury to women. This might be explained by the fact that rape was, at least in theory if not in practice, a capital crime in Scotland until 1887 (also *Wm Fraser* 1847 Ark 280).

[58] (1877) 2 QBD 410. Though Cf. *Fletcher* (1859) Bell CC 63 in which it was held that consent produced by 'mere animal instinct' in a girl of weak intellect was enough to prevent it being a rape. See also Criminal Law Amendment Act 1885 s.4 (sexual intercourse by impersonating husband is rape); s.3(2) (procuring a woman by false pretences or representations to have unlawful sexual intercourse); s.5(2) carnal knowledge of idiot or imbecile girl or woman a misdemeanour. See F Mead & AH Bodkin, *The Criminal Law Amendment Act 1885* (London: Shaw & Sons, 1885) pp.31–8; Mental Deficiency Act 1913 s.56. See also Wiener, *Men of Blood*, n.16, pp.111–22 on this line of cases and esp. pp.120–1 on the provisions of the 1885 Act.

by understandings of 'normal' seduction—that is to say the kind of promises, inducements or deceptions that might be permitted by a man in the seduction of a woman. These limits were clearly articulated in the case of *Clarence*.[59] While the case was an appeal against a conviction under the Offences Against the Person Act 1861 for the transmission of gonorrhoea by a husband to his wife, the court took it as an opportunity to reflect on the nature of consent. Wills J expressed his concern that if the conviction were upheld:

> on the grounds of the difference between the thing consented to and the thing done, the principle will extend to many, perhaps most cases of seduction, and to other forms of illicit intercourse, including at least theoretically, the case of prostitution.[60]

This was echoed by James Fitzjames Stephen who worried that if the scope of fraud were extended beyond fraud as to the nature of the act or the identity of the person 'many seductions would be rapes, and so might acts of prostitution procured by fraud, as for instance by promises not intended to be filled.'[61]

The other major change in the law of rape related to the position of children, where a marked feature of later nineteenth-century law was the spread of legislation criminalizing forms of sexual conduct with minors.[62] Children were seen as vulnerable, and in criminal law this led, on the one hand, to the taking of special measures for the prosecution and punishment of juvenile delinquents, and, on the other, to the adoption of laws to protect innocent children against violence and sexual exploitation.[63]

Carnal knowledge of a girl under the age of 10 was a felony at common law, but the extent of the law was gradually increased through the criminalization of sexual intercourse with, or other kinds of indecent assault on, older children and by recognizing that boys as well as girls might be victims of sexual assault. The Offences Against the Person Act 1828 made carnal knowledge of a girl between the ages of 10 and 12 a non-capital misdemeanour.[64] The Offences Against the Person Act 1861 criminalized the attempted rape of, or indecent assault on, girls below the age of 12.[65] In 1875 this was extended again to girls under the age of

[59] (1888) 22 QBD 23. This is discussed in K Gleeson, 'Sex, Wives and Prostitutes: Debating Clarence' in J Rowbotham & K Stevenson, *Criminal Conversations. Victorian Crimes, Social Panic, and Moral Outrage* (Columbus, OH: Ohio State, 2005); L Bibbings, *Binding Men. Stories about Violence and Law in Late Victorian England* (London: Glasshouse, 2014) Ch.4.

[60] *Clarence* (1888) 22 QBD, p.50.

[61] Ibid., p.44. See also d'Cruze, 'Sexual Violence', n.48, p.449 on the role of the seduction narrative.

[62] See generally LA Jackson, *Child Sexual Abuse in Victorian England* (London: Routledge, 2000); G Behlmer, *Child Abuse and Moral Reform in England, 1870–1908* (Stanford: Stanford UP, 1982). On the age of consent see M Waites, *The Age of Consent. Young People, Sexuality and Citizenship* (London: Palgrave Macmillan, 2005) Chs.3 & 4.

[63] The law in this area was complex, and was also framed by the fact that a girl of 12 and a boy of 14 might validly marry. See Mead & Bodkin, *Criminal Law*, n.58, p.25. This was changed by the Marriage Act 1929, raising the age for children of both sexes to 16.

[64] 9 Geo.IV c.31 s.17. Re-enacted by the Offences Against the Person Act 1861 (24 & 25 Vict. c.100) s.51.

[65] S.52 as a misdemeanour.

13, and in 1880 to 13 for both boys and girls, additionally providing that consent could not be used as a defence in these cases.[66] The Criminal Law Amendment Act 1885 then consolidated the law in this area as carnal knowledge of a girl under the age of 13 was made a felony, and the rape or attempted rape of a girl between the ages of 13 and 16 was made a misdemeanour.[67] The Punishment of Incest Act 1908 criminalized carnal knowledge between persons within the prohibited degrees of consanguinity, an offence that in England had previously been within the exclusive jurisdiction of the Ecclesiastical Courts.[68] Finally the Criminal Law Amendment Act 1922 established that consent was not a defence to forms of non-penetrative sexual assault on boys and girls under the age of 16, thus establishing the legislative framework that governed this area for the rest of the twentieth century.[69]

This framework had a number of significant features. It was seen as an extension of the category of rape, with the new offences supplementing the common law crime, rather than replacing it. It was primarily directed towards the protection of girls rather than boys. Female children were understood to be more corruptible than boys, who were not initially deemed to require protection. This protection was primarily organized around the family, on the grounds that female children were in the protection of their father who would control who the girl could marry.[70] This was the basis for the linkage between the statutory rape and abduction offences in the Offences Against the Person Acts in 1828 and 1861.[71] This was clearly spelled out in the case of *R v Prince* (1875), which concerned the scope of the offence of taking a girl under 16 out of the possession of her parents, and Bramwell B defended the idea that the statutory provisions were clearly directed at the protection of girls of tender years who were under the protection

[66] Offences against the Person Act 1875 (38 & 39 Vict. c.34) s.4 'with or without' the consent of the girl reflecting the fact that there had been cases in which it had been alleged that girls as young as 6 had consented. Section 3 of this Act made carnal knowledge of a girl below the age of 12 a felony; Criminal Law Amendment Act 1880 (43 & 44 Vict c.45) s.2.

[67] Criminal Law Amendment Act 1885 (48 & 49 Vict. c.69) ss.4 & 5. Also providing that an offender under the age of 16 was subject to a lesser sentence, and that young girls did not have to give evidence on oath. Under the Act, the prosecution of the s.5 offence had to be commenced within 3 months; this was extended to 6 months in 1904, to 9 months in 1922, and finally to 12 months in 1928.

[68] Children, grand-children, siblings, and parents. Cf. Scotland, where this was criminal at common law. On the 1908 Act, see V Bailey & S Blackburn, 'The Punishment of Incest Act 1908. A Case Study of Law Creation' [1979] *Crim LR* p.708.

[69] Section 1 of the 1922 Act raised the age of consent to 16, amending the 1885 Act such that reasonable cause of belief that a girl was over 16 was not a defence unless the man was 23 or under. It had previously been held in *R v Banks* [1916] KB 621 that the man must have both reasonable cause and in fact believe that the girl was under the age of 16. In addition note that the Children Act 1908 allowed summary trial for indecent assaults on children under 16.

[70] They 'were designed to protect a guardian's right to control a girl's sexuality, rather than to prevent harm to the girl': D Gorham, '"The Maiden Tribute of Modern Babylon" Re-Examined: Child Prostitution and the Idea of Childhood in Late Victorian England' (1978) 21 *Victorian Studies* 353–79 at 363.

[71] 9 Geo.IV c.31 ss.19 & 20; 24 & 25 Vict. c.100 ss.53–5.

of their parents.[72] The political debates of this time began to frame questions of children and sex in terms of an age of consent, but this was understood in negative terms as the absence of agency on the part of the child, and their corresponding need for protection. This understanding was broadened somewhat in the latter part of the century as the social purity movement linked the question of the age of consent to child prostitution and sought to strengthen the protection of girls against moral corruption. This was based on a more general sense of sexual danger and moral corruption which required the protection of the innocent from the wickedness and lusts of those who would corrupt them.[73] This was extended as the criminalization of incest challenged the idea that the family was safe: fathers could be a source of moral danger as well as protection, and this required greater vigilance on the part of the state. The legislation thus established a high moral standard for all (rich or poor), and moral guardianship of those classes which could not control themselves.[74]

This theme of moral corruption was central to understanding the development of the criminal law in relation to sex between men and prostitution—where, in both cases, the Criminal Law Amendment Act 1885 was pivotal. The crime of sodomy had continued to be treated as an offence against the person throughout most of the nineteenth century. The biggest legislative changes concerned the penalty: it was made non-capital in 1861, though the last execution for the crime had taken place in 1835. The Offences Against the Person Act 1861 criminalized the attempt to commit sodomy and indecent assault on a man, apparently formalizing the practice of charging lesser forms of the felony as misdemeanours.[75] Consent was irrelevant in the construction of these offences, with the law based on straightforward prohibition, even if it was only irregularly enforced. However, this changed with the creation of the crime of gross indecency between men, in the provision known as Labouchère's amendment, in the 1885 Act.[76] While there is some dispute over the practical impact of this provision, what is clear is that it reflected a change in the understanding of the law. Gross indecency saw sex between men, in public or private, as a moral threat. The crime was a social manifestation of sexual disorder, the suppression of which, like other offences in the 1885 Act, was justified on the grounds of the need to prevent moral corruption.

Prostitution had continued to be regulated according to its potential for disorder, with the new police relying on the provisions of the Vagrancy Act 1824

[72] *R v Prince* 1875 CCR 2, 154 esp. Bramwell B. See also discussion of this case in Chapter 6 supra at pp.179–80.

[73] See generally J Walkowitz, *City of Dreadful Delight* (London: Virago, 1992); Gorham, 'The Maiden Tribute', n.70.

[74] See Gorham, 'The Maiden Tribute', n.70, p.370.

[75] Harvey, 'Prosecutions for Sodomy', n.29, p.941; Hitchcock, *English Sexualities*, n.30, pp.60–1. See *Boulton & Ors* (1871) 12 Cox 87, discussed in R Paley, 'Dragging the Law into Disrepute' in A Lewis et al., *Law in the City* (Dublin: Four Courts Press, 2007).

[76] For background on the amendment, including the suggestion that it was introduced as an extreme measure that could not be passed and which would require that the rest of the Bill be returned to Committee, see FB Smith, 'Labouchère's Amendment to the Criminal Law Amendment Bill' (1976) 17 *Historical Studies*, pp.165–73.

and other statutes, such as the Metropolitan Police Act 1839, which criminalized common prostitutes or nightwalkers who loitered in public places for the purposes of solicitation to the annoyance of the public.[77] Although these laws gave extensive powers to the police, in practice they were not effective, with distrust of the police often taking precedence over the criminalization of prostitutes.[78] Discourses around prostitution began to undergo a marked shift in the second half of the century as prostitution came to be seen as the 'great social evil'.[79] It had the potential to encourage sexual immorality in men, and the social purity movement attacked practices that encapsulated a double standard of sexual morality—allowing men sexual freedom while women were expected to remain chaste and virtuous. It was seen as a threat to social institutions, such as the family, both by encouraging sexual infidelity and by being a means by which venereal diseases might be transmitted to women—a heady combination of medical, social, and moral pollution. The linkage between prostitution and disease led initially to the passing of the Contagious Diseases Acts from 1864 onwards.[80] These Acts applied to specific garrison towns and ports and allowed the enforced medical inspection and treatment of women who were believed to be prostitutes. The Acts were highly contentious as they were used by the police against women of all classes and, after an extensive public campaign, were eventually repealed in 1886. However the campaign against the Acts had raised awareness of the working conditions of prostitutes more generally, with Josephine Butler, the leader of the campaign, specifically characterizing the condition of women as a form of slavery.[81] Her campaign argued that it was necessary to respect the rights of all women, while at the same time fighting for higher standards of sexual morality. If prostitutes were the victims of class and gender iniquities and exploitation this required a new kind of legal response.

Late Victorian anxiety then came to centre on organized prostitution as this was seen as where the worst forms of exploitation took place.[82] From the 1870s onwards there had been a number of exposés of child prostitution, leading to the establishment of a House of Lords Select Committee, which reported in 1882.[83] The efforts of reformers were given further impetus by WT Stead's famous

[77] 2 & 3 Vict. c.47 s.54(11). Extended to other areas by the Town Police Clauses Act 1847. See also Prevention of Crime Act 1871 s.11 (brothel keepers harbouring thieves).

[78] The police would use s.54(13) of the 1839 Act (using threatening words with intent to cause breach of the peace) to arrest women who were not known as common prostitutes. Generally see Petrow, *Policing Morals*, n.34, Ch.5.

[79] See J Walkowitz, *Prostitution and Victorian Society* (Cambridge: Cambridge UP, 1980) Ch.2.

[80] Extended in 1866 and 1869. See generally Walkowitz, *Prostitution*, n.79, Pts II & III; M Luddy, 'Prostitution from 1800' in S Toulalan & K Fisher (eds), *The Routledge History of Sex and the Body, 1500 to the Present* (London: Routledge, 2013) pp.414–19.

[81] See C Devereux, 'The 'Maiden Tribute' and the Rise of the White Slave in the Nineteenth Century: the making of an imperial construct' (2000) 26 *Victorian Review* pp.1–23 at 10–12.

[82] See also Prevention of Crime Act 1871 s.11 criminalizing brothel keepers who knowingly harboured thieves or received stolen property.

[83] See Report of the House of Lords Select Committee on the Law Relating to the Protection of Young Girls, (1882) (PP.1882.334). See Walkowitz, *Prostitution*, n.79, Epilogue.

exposure of the so-called 'white slave trade' in London—child prostitution and the abduction of English girls who were said to have been put to work in legal brothels in Belgium, Holland, and France.[84] The legal response, in the Criminal Law Amendment Act 1885 and subsequent legislation had two dimensions: criminalizing the procuring or sexual exploitation of women or girls; and criminalizing public solicitation those who ran brothels or profited from prostitution.[85]

It is clear that, in this period, there was an increasing legal recognition of crimes involving, or committed by means of, sex, but they were not understood as sexual crimes. The lack of any clear or coherent scheme partly reflects the piecemeal nature of development, but also reflects the fact that there was no clear or single sense of sexual conduct or of its danger. That these crimes were about something else—the person, marriage, morals, public order, and so on—is reflected in the different categorizations. There was no single sense of motivation, that something could be 'sexual'. Rape was talked about as motivated by 'lust', but its danger lay in the threat that the unregulated passion posed to morals and institutions—that is to say, social institutions—rather than individual harms.[86] In the work of Stephen and his successors, this did lead to a certain novelty of categorization, as offences against morals and marriage were identified as particular categories—and the idea of moral protection allowed reformers to see a linkage between child sexual abuse, prostitution, and gross indecency. This reflects a broader Victorian understanding of the civilizing role of morality, particularly sexual morality, in keeping the passions at bay.[87] The aim of law in this area was thus to protect passive and vulnerable women and children from male sexual urges; and the role of consent was that of demarcating the ever expanding categories of the vulnerable.

It is also clear that throughout the Victorian period, in particular, there was a reluctance to talk about certain offences, especially buggery or sodomy, for fear that it would encourage them. Stephen's definition of carnal knowledge, as

[84] On this, see WT Stead, *The Maiden Tribute of Modern Babylon. The Report of the Secret Commission* (ed. with Introduction by AE Simpson) (Lambertville: True Bill Press, 2007); Devereux, 'The Rise of the White Slave Trade', n.81; Gorham, 'The Maiden Tribute', n.70; Walkowitz, *City of Dreadful Delight,* n.73, Chs.3 & 4.

[85] Criminal Law Amendment Act 1885 esp. ss.2, 3, 7, 8, & 13; Vagrancy Act Amendment Act 1898; Criminal Law Amendment Act 1912. This also had specifically extraterritorial dimensions, extending to procuring women for prostitution whether 'within or without the Queen's dominions' (s.2). This was matched by the creation of international organizations for the suppression of trafficking, such as the International Bureau for the Suppression of Traffic in Persons, founded in 1899. See Gorham, 'The Maiden Tribute', n.70, pp.361–2; Petrow, *Policing Morals*, n.34, pp.158–76.

[86] See e.g. A Amos, *Ruins of Time Exemplified in Sir Matthew Hale's History of the Pleas of the Crown* (London: V & R Stevens & GS Norton, 1856) p.155; CS Kenny, *Outlines of Criminal Law* (Cambridge: Cambridge UP, 1902) also defines rape as a crime of violence 'springing from lust' (p.143).

[87] See e.g. JF Stephen, *Liberty, Equality, Fraternity* (New York: Holt & Williams, 1873): discussed supra Chapter 3. This is shaped by the view of male sexuality as active and female sexuality as passive, unless incited by males (or for prostitutes). See L Bland, *Banishing the Beast. Feminism, Sex and Morality* (London: Tauris, 2002); Walkowitz, *City of Dreadful Delight,* n.73.

'penetration to any the slightest degree of the organ alleged to have been carnally known by the male organ of generation', is an illustration of the lengths to which it was possible to go to avoid salacious language. The culmination of this can be seen in Kenny's *Outlines of Criminal Law* (1902) which, beyond noting the existence of crimes motivated by lust, omits discussion of the crime of rape altogether.[88] While this is probably due to the fact that it was based on lectures, and that sexual offences were deemed an unsuitable topic to discuss in front of a class of young men, it also underlines the point that crimes involving sex were not seen as central to an understanding of the criminal law. This is an understanding that was to change in the period after 1956.

III. Making Sexual Offences

A. The emergence of sexual offences

The decisive shift to the modern understanding of sexual offences came with the passing of the Sexual Offences Act 1956, the first use of the term to describe this area of the law.[89] This was a consolidation measure, bringing together into a single statute diverse provisions from a range of nineteenth-century statutes with some minor amendments, and passed virtually without debate. It was not a complete codification of the field, since the common law was left untouched where it was still relevant. The Act thus states in section 1 that rape is a felony, but contains no definition of the crime of rape. The term 'carnal knowledge' was replaced by the more modern 'sexual intercourse', though its meaning merely reflected the existing case law on 'carnal knowledge'.[90] The remainder of the Act was a restatement of a range of crimes: intercourse with minors, defectives, buggery and gross indecency, abduction, prostitution (with an emphasis on procuring) and living off the earnings of prostitutes.[91] There was at no point any indication of the meaning of sexual in this context and, as the language in many places was the language of the older statutes (immoral earnings etc.) and it contained provisions on abduction, it is hard to avoid the conclusion that the label 'sexual' was largely descriptive, referring if anything to an idea of sexual morality. However, this mundane reorganization set in train a more systematic re-conceptualization of the field.

It is striking that after 1956 the usage 'sexual offences' started to become more commonplace in treatises and academic works. The first book to have a separate chapter on sexual offences was the first edition of Smith & Hogan's *Criminal Law* (1965), though the usage of the term was apparently so unusual and worthy of

[88] He points the interested student to Stephen's *Digest*. Rape was not included in the English edition until Turner's editions in 1952 and 1966.

[89] A Sexual Offences Bill was introduced in the House of Lords in 1920, though considerably narrower in scope, as part of the discussions that led to the Criminal Law Amendment Act 1922.

[90] Sexual intercourse was defined in s.44 as penetration, not requiring emission of semen.

[91] Although note that the provisions on alternative verdicts in schedule 2 recognized, at least implicitly, the idea of some structure in this area.

remark that an asterisk after the title indicated that the term came from a study of sexual offences published in 1957.[92] In substance the coverage of the chapter broadly corresponded to the 1956 Act without further comment or discussion.[93] Glanville Williams' *Textbook of Criminal Law* more self-consciously modernized both the classification and treatment of the law.[94] Sexual offences were dealt with in Part II of the book on the protection of the person (following assault and preceding murder), but in a striking departure from conventional legal usage the chapter was called 'Sexual Aggression'. Williams began by distinguishing between different types of sexual offence:

> To speak of sexual offences as a class is somewhat misleading, since there are important differences of types. The two main groups are sexual aggression and breaches of sexual taboo.[95]

The distinction, in his view, was primarily founded in consent, with crimes in the first group consisting of 'injuries and affronts to a non-consenting victim'.[96] The chapter was concerned only with these crimes, thus leading him to exclude homosexual offences, forms of public indecency and 'morals' offences. His understanding of sexual aggression was informed by psychological literature on sex offenders, which was discussed extensively, considering the sexual motivation that might lie behind various forms of criminal conduct (from murder to insulting conduct) to argue that it was essential that 'sexual deviationists' (sic) receive special treatment at the sentencing stage. He also discussed psychoanalytical beliefs about women's rape fantasies in the context of a discussion on consent.[97] What is significant here is less his specific views than the adoption of an understanding of sexual motivation as the defining characteristic of the offences in this area of the law and the attempt to reshape the category in the light of this understanding.

[92] JC Smith & B Hogan, *Criminal Law* (London: Butterworths, 1965) Ch.12, citing L Radzinowicz, *Sexual Offences. A Report of the Cambridge Department of Criminal Science* (London: Macmillan, 1957). See infra.

[93] With the addition of public indecency. This corresponded to the understanding of 'sex crimes' in Radzinowicz, *Sexual Offenses,* n.92. For other books, see DW Elliott & JC Wood, *A Casebook on Criminal Law* (London: Sweet & Maxwell, 1963) Ch.10 (non-fatal offences against the person, including a section on sexual offences). Cf. PJ Fitzgerald, *Criminal Law and Punishment* (Oxford: Clarendon, 1962) Ch.2.6: immorality (including rape, unnatural offences and miscellaneous offences). For Scotland, see GH Gordon, *Criminal Law* (Edinburgh: W. Green & Son, 1967) with a separate section on sexual offences.

[94] G Williams, *Textbook on Criminal Law* (2nd edition) (London: Steven & Sons, 1983) Ch.10. Cf. T Honoré, *Sex Law* (London: Duckworth, 1976) for a comparable contemporary attempt to rethink legal categories in terms of a broader understanding of the meaning of sex.

[95] Williams, *Textbook*, n.94, p.227.

[96] Williams, *Textbook*, n.94, p.227. Abduction which had hitherto been classed as a sexual offence is dealt with in the preceding chapter on non-sexual injuries and threats.

[97] Williams, *Textbook*, n.94, pp.238–9 citing the work of Helen Deutsch and Paul Gebhard. This is further discussed by J Forrester, 'Rape, Seduction and Psychoanalysis' in Porter & Tomaselli, *Rape*, n.3, esp. pp.64–6 who criticizes Williams for sliding from recognizing the existence of rape fantasies to concluding that it is then possible to infer a woman's conscious consent in certain circumstances. For a discussion of Deutsch, see also J Bourke, *Rape. A History* (London: Virago, 2008).

These changes in usage reflect the fact that there had been a massive transformation in social and scientific understandings of sex in the early part of the twentieth century, and that these new ideas were beginning to shape legal understandings. A key development here was the emergence of a new interest in, or science of, sex at the end of the nineteenth century, which connected an account of sexual acts to an inner psychology or physiology—the recognition of which in its turn allowed for the possibility of acts being characterized as 'sexual' depending on their motivation. Foucault, in one of the most important analyses, viewed the science of sex as crystallizing around four themes: the hystericization of women's bodies; the supervision of children's sexual conduct; the stress on the importance of procreative sex for the social body; and the psychiatrization of perverse pleasure.[98] The new science of sexology stressed the importance and normality of sexual pleasure for both men and women, expressed in the Edwardian belief that intimate relations should be a free and equal partnership between men and women.[99] However it also recognized and sought to regulate or control forms of sexual perversion. Sexual conduct was categorized into normal and pathological forms, with an increased interest in, and regulation of, sexual deviancy. Sexual violence was distinguished from normal heterosexual behaviour by its inappropriate object choice, where children were the victims, or by the resort to extreme physical violence. In the area of criminal law this was reflected in developments in three different areas: the efforts to measure the incidence of sex offences; the idea of the sex offender and their treatment; and the recognition of the impact of sexual crimes on victims.

Although criminal statistics had been systematically collected since the 1840s, sexual offences had not been singled out as a distinct category. Rape was recorded as a crime against the person but information about other crimes involving sex was not disaggregated. Information was not routinely collected about the age or sex of victims, where this was not apparent from the crime definition, and few details were recorded for minor or summary offences. Beginning in the 1920s, there were moves to collect more, and more specific, information. The *Report of the Departmental Committee on Sexual Offences against Young Persons* (1925) contained a thorough discussion of these problems and recommended changes to the collection of criminal statistics to record the age and sex of victims and sentences imposed on offenders.[100] The 1957 *Cambridge Report on Sexual Offences* was the

[98] M Foucault, *The History of Sexuality*. I *The Will to Pleasure* (Harmondsworth: Penguin, 1978) pp.104–5. There is a huge literature on this. See e.g. J Weeks, *Sex, Politics and Society. The Regulation of Sexuality since 1800* (3rd edn) (London: Routledge, 2012); A Clark, *Desire: A History of European Sexuality* (London: Routledge, 2008) esp. Chs.8 & 9; S Toulalan & K Fisher (eds), *The Routledge History of Sex and the Body, 1500 to the Present* (London: Routledge, 2013). There is a useful discussion in H Cocks, 'Modernity and the Self in the History of Sexuality' (2006) 49 *Historical Journal* 1211–27.

[99] See e.g. discussions in Bland, *Banishing the Beast,* n.87.

[100] (London: HMSO, 1925) (CMD.2561) Ch.2 (Prevalence of Offences)—although many of these recommendations were not implemented. It also recommended changes to the trial of sexual offences against children. Many of these procedural changes were made in the Children and Young Persons Act 1933.

first systematic attempt to bring together the statistical evidence on different types of sexual offence, on the ways that they were committed, and on the characteristics of sexual offenders.[101] Studies carried out around this time noted rises in the incidence of sexual offences: the Cambridge Report finding an increase of 252 per cent in the number of indictable offences known to the police between 1937 and 1954, and noting that the actual number of offences was certainly higher.[102] These studies developed a distinct aetiology of the sex offender, assessing the seriousness of different types of crime in terms of the motivation of offenders, and linked this to the need to develop treatment regimes targeted at particular groups of offenders.[103] They also began to recognize the impact of sex offences, particularly on children, in terms of the trauma that it could cause and its interference with normal sexual development.[104]

The biggest legal changes came in the areas of sexual conduct between men and of prostitution, following the report of the Wolfenden Committee in 1957. The broad approach of the Committee was in line with that established in the late Victorian period—that the law in this area was to be seen in terms of the relation between law and morals—but they argued for a different legal regime on the basis of a changed understanding of the relation between public and private. Where the 1885 Act had been based on the idea that private conduct was a matter of public concern, this position was now reversed.[105] The Committee's view was that the function of the law was 'to preserve public order and decency, to protect the citizen from what is offensive or injurious, and to provide sufficient safeguards against exploitation and corruption of others'.[106] This meant that 'it was not the function of the law to intervene in the private lives of citizens' and they accordingly recommended the decriminalization of homosexual behaviour between consenting

[101] Radzinowicz, *Sexual Offences,* n.92. See also W Norwood East, *Society and the Criminal* (London: HMSO, 1949) Ch.7; W Norwood East, *Sexual Offenders* (London: Delisle, 1955); H Mannheim, *Social Aspects of Crime in England between Two Wars* (London: George Allen and Unwin, 1940) p.121; H Mannheim, 'Two Reports on Sex Offences' (1949) 12 *Mod LR* 488; JE Hall Williams, 'Sex Offenses: The British Experience' (1960) 25 *Law and Contemporary Problems* 334–60.

[102] Radzinowicz, *Sexual Offences*, n.92, p.5. See Pt I generally. See F Mort, *Capital Affairs. London and the Making of the Permissive Society* (New Haven: Yale UP, 2010) pp.43–4.

[103] See e.g. East, noting that the medical conception of sexual offences, based on the motivation of the offender, might be wider than the legal one, and that different crimes might be attended by different motivations: *Society and the Criminal*, p.94 and pp.107–21 for a typology (including the homosexual or invert, the sadist, fetishism and transvestism); Radzinowicz, *Sexual Offences*, n.92, Pt II (on offenders and their victims).

[104] *Departmental Committee on Sexual Offences* (1925) n.100, p.23 also pp.66ff. See Jackson, *Child Sexual Abuse*, n.62, Conclusion.

[105] The approach taken to public and private corresponded to that taken in the US MPC, although there it was influenced by the Kinsey Report, which does not seem to have been a significant influence on Wolfenden. For the influence of Kinsey on the MPC, see D Allyn, 'Private Acts/Public Policy: Alfred Kinsey, the American Law Institute and the Privatization of American Sexual Morality' (1996) 30 *Jnl of American Stud* 405–28. For the influence of Kinsey on Wolfenden see Mort, *Capital Affairs*, n.102, pp.1–3 and Ch.4.

[106] *Report of the Committee on Homosexual Offences and Prostitution* (Wolfenden Report) (Cmnd 247) (London: HMSO, 1957) pp.9–10.

adults in private.[107] The recommendation was controversial, but led eventually in 1967 to the decriminalization of sex in private between men over the age of 21.[108] Prostitution, by contrast, was seen in terms of public order or nuisance, and the Committee recommended changes to the law to remove the necessity of proving annoyance to individuals by solicitation.[109] The change of approach here, particularly in relation to homosexual conduct, is important in terms of the underlying schema. Although the Wolfenden Committee discussed scientific understandings of homosexuality, they did not directly base their recommendations on this—except in the negative sense that they took the absence of medical consensus as grounds for arguing for a more tolerant approach.[110] However, the approach translated the abstract distinction between the public domain of legally controlled activity and the private domain of personal morality into the physical terms of public and private spaces. Public sexual display or conduct was regulated by the criminal law; but conduct in private, including forms of private commercial sex which did not cause a nuisance, were beyond the law. This thus institutionalized a view of private morality that corresponded to understandings of middle class domesticity. Normal sex which took place in private, or private commercial sex, was not the concern of the law, but forms of sexual conduct which did not fit this model were subjected to ongoing regulation. Indeed, the recognition of diversity in the sphere of private freedom came at the cost of a more intense policing of the age of consent, public indecency, and prostitution.[111]

There was a growing recognition through the 1960s and 1970s that the law of sexual offences might require reform in particular in the light of decisions such as *DPP v Morgan* and of the conduct of rape trials more generally.[112] The main vehicle for considering this was the Criminal Law Revision Committee (CLRC)

[107] Wolfenden Report, n.106, p.10 and p.25.

[108] Sexual Offences Act 1967 s.1, subject to qualifications of privacy in s.1(2) (where more than two persons were present or in a public lavatory). On the political background to the introduction of the law see P Rock, *History of the Home Office* (forthcoming, London: Home Office). The law was not changed in Scotland until 1980: Criminal Justice (S) Act 1980 s.80.

[109] Street Offences Act 1959 s.1(1): 'It shall be an offence for a common prostitute to loiter or solicit in a street or public place for the purpose of prostitution.' The Street Offences Committee 1929 had earlier recommended abolition of existing laws on prostitution and their replacement with a single offence of importuning that applied to both sexes on the basis of a similar argument about the relationship between private morality and public nuisance. See S Slater, 'Lady Astor and the Ladies of the Night: The Home Office, the Metropolitan Police and the Politics of the Street Offences Committee, 1927–8' (2012) 30 *Law & Hist Rev* 533–73.

[110] Pp.11–7. Their view of homosexuality as a continuum corresponded to Kinsey, but they did not cite this.

[111] Cocks, 'Modernity and the Self', n.98, p.1224; J Scoular & V Munro, 'Harm, Vulnerability and Citizenship: Constitutional Concerns in the Criminalization of Contemporary Sex Work' in Duff et al., *The Constitution of the Criminal Law* (Oxford: Oxford UP, 2012) pp.34–5.

[112] [1976] AC 182. This was reviewed by the Heilbron Committee (1975) (Report of the Advisory Group on the Law of Rape, Cmnd 6352) and confirmed in the Sexual Offences (Amendment) Act 1976 s.1(1). See also B Hogan, 'On Modernising the Law of Sexual Offences' in P Glazebrook (ed.), *Reshaping the Criminal Law* (London: Stevens & Sons, 1978); DJ West, 'Thoughts on Sex Law Reform' in R Hood (ed.), *Crime, Criminology and Public Policy* (London: Heinemann, 1974). For a review of contemporary criticisms see J Temkin, *Rape and the Legal Process* (1st edn) (London: Sweet & Maxwell, 1987).

established in 1959.[113] The reform of sexual offences was considered by the CLRC in a systematic way in the late 1970s as part of its work on the codification project. It produced a consultation paper on sexual offences in 1980 and a final report in 1984.[114] Simultaneously with the reference to the CLRC, the Home Secretary established the Home Office Policy Advisory Committee on Sexual Offences, which reported on the age of consent in sexual offences in 1981, and provided information to the CLRC on the incidence of sexual offences, which was a foundation for some of their recommendations.[115] The CLRC took its lead from the position of the Wolfenden Committee that the criminal law should not intervene in the private lives of citizens or enforce any particular pattern of sexual conduct.[116] It also made two key classificatory moves: distinguishing between offences where the 'essence' was that the victim had not consented, and those where consent was immaterial to the definition of the offence; and seeking to remove existing provisions of the law which treated 'males' and 'females' differently.[117] However, while the CLRC showed an increased awareness of the position of the victim, and the criticisms that had been made by feminist campaigners of the conduct of rape trials and of lenient sentencing, they generally adhered to the established view of the law.[118] The wrong of sexual violence was understood in terms of the violation of the 'natural' integrity of the body. The general principle of non-intervention in private life underpinned their position that marital rape should not be criminalized, and they upheld the test of honest but unreasonable belief in consent established in the controversial case of *Morgan*—notwithstanding the criticism that there could give rise to situations where there was no liability even where a victim could be proven not to have consented.[119] However, there were limits to their understanding of conduct that could be consented to, particularly in relation to homosexual conduct in locations which did not correspond to a narrow definition of private.[120] Generally this was a more systematic approach, but the systematicity was in service of a view of codification as consistency and completeness: removing anomalies and filling loopholes to ensure a more complete coverage of the law.

Overall, there is evidence of a changing approach to sexual offences. There was recognition of their growing incidence and the idea that they represented a special

[113] See Home Office, *Penal Practice in Changing Society* (Cmnd. 645) (London: HMSO, 1959) para.15. Their first report was on *Indecency with Children* (Cmnd.835) (London: HMSO, 1959). The Indecency with Children Act 1960 criminalized any person committing an act of 'gross indecency' with a child, broadening the law of indecent assault.

[114] CLRC, *Working Paper on Sexual Offences* (London: HMSO, 1980); CLRC, *Fifteenth Report. Sexual Offences* (Cmnd 9213) (London: HMSO, 1984). The referral was made by the Home Secretary in July 1975 p.1. See also Howard League Working Party, *Unlawful Sex. Offences, Victims and Offenders in the Criminal Justice System of England and Wales* (London: Waterlow Publishing, 1985).

[115] See also Howard League Working Party, *Unlawful Sex,* n.114.

[116] CLRC, *15th Report*, n.114, para 1.5.

[117] CLRC, *15th Report*, n.114, para 1.6.

[118] They opposed, for example extending the definition of rape to other forms of penetration (paras. 2.45–2.47).

[119] On marital rape, see paras.2.64–2.70; on Morgan and the *mens rea* of rape, see paras 2.31–2.41.

[120] Part X. This was ostensibly gender neutral, directed at sex clubs and shows, but the discussion in this part is focused on homosexual sex and also singles out sex in public toilets.

sort of problem. This led to a rethinking of the idea of sexual offences as a field of law capable of being organized around principles of consent and protection of the vulnerable. This was underpinned by a scientific understanding of sexual motivation and that the sex offender (who was motivated by these abnormal desires) required a special form of response. However, the aim of the function of consent was to protect private life. These principles remained at the heart of subsequent attempts to modernize the law—though as we shall see they were articulated in different ways.

B. Reshaping sexual offences

The last 30 years have seen a transformation of the category of sexual offences. One index of this change is the number of Sexual Offences Acts passed since 1956, showing that the term has become commonplace: in 1967 (decriminalizing homosexual conduct in private);[121] in 1976 (clarifying the decision in *Morgan* and providing for changes in the trial of rape and sexual offences); in 1985 (criminalizing kerb crawling and persistent soliciting); in 1992 (on anonymity for victims in criminal trials); in 1993 (abolishing the presumption that a boy under fourteen is incapable of sexual intercourse); in 2000 (reducing the age of consent to homosexual sex to 16).[122] In addition the definition of rape was changed in England and Wales to include non-consensual anal intercourse with a man or a woman in 1994.[123] This legislative activity culminated in the Sexual Offences Act 2003 in England and Wales and the Sexual Offences (S) Act 2009 in Scotland, both of which abolished much of the pre-existing common law, redefined the core offences, and created a number of new offences.

Much of this legislation was aimed at making the prosecution of rape and other sexual offences more effective and less traumatic for the victim. Measures have been taken to reform police investigation and prosecution procedures so as to improve reporting of the crime and reduce attrition rates, as well as at protecting the victim in the courtroom through measures such as 'rape shield' legislation or provisions for anonymity of victims or measures to protect vulnerable witnesses.[124] The first 'rape shield' legislation was passed in 1976 and reformed in 1999. The courts were also sensitive to changing attitudes, recognizing marital rape in Scotland in 1989 and in England in 1992, and in Scotland rejecting the traditional common law definition which required force in favour of a definition

[121] The law was not changed in Scotland until the passing of the Criminal Justice (S) Act 1980 s.80.

[122] Sexual Offences (Amendment) Act 2000 s.1. See also Criminal Justice and Public Order Act 1994 s.145 and Criminal Law Consolidation (S) Act 1995 s.13, reducing the age of consent to 18.

[123] Criminal Justice and Public Order Act 1994 s.142.

[124] Sexual Offences Act 1976; Youth Justice and Criminal Evidence Act 1999 s.41. For a review see L Kelly, *Routes to Injustice: A Research Review on the Reporting, Investigation and Prosecution of Rape Cases* (London: CPSI, 2001); S Walklate, 'What is to be done about Violence against Women?' (2008) 48 *Brit Jnl Criminol* 39–5 at pp.44–7; for changes in Scotland, see M Burman, 'Evidencing Sexual Assault: Women in the Witness Box' (2009) 56 *Probation Journal* pp.1–20.

of the crime based on consent.[125] Finally, there have been important changes in the identification and tracking of sexual offenders, with the creation of the Sex Offenders Register in 1997 and sexual offences protection orders in 2003, which allow the courts to impose restrictions on individuals where they believe that person poses the risk of serious sexual harm to the community.[126]

The changed understanding of sexual offences that was driving these reforms can be seen by looking at the 2003 and 2009 Acts, which reformed and replaced the common law in each jurisdiction. Although there are slight differences in approach and emphasis, the Acts share a number of important characteristics. First, both Acts take a gender neutral approach to the law: although rape can only be committed by a man, most crimes are defined in such a way that both males and females can be victims. Second, the main offences are organized around the concept of consent, but, in an emphatic rejection of *Morgan*, the test is one of the reasonable belief of the accused in consent and the steps that they took to ascertain that belief.[127] Third, there are a growing number of offences.[128] The 2003 Act contains a range of child sexual offences which, in addition to sexual activity with a child, include causing a child to watch sex, sexual grooming of a child, and arranging and facilitating commission of a child sexual offence (ss.9–15). There are variants of these offences in relation to abuse of trust (ss.16–20) and persons with mental disorder (ss.30–33), plus offences relating to familial child sex, indecent photographs of children, and abuse of children through prostitution or pornography. And there are finally a number of further offences including trafficking for sexual exploitation, controlling prostitution, preparatory offences, sex with an adult relative, voyeurism, sexual exposure and sexual intercourse with animals or corpses and sex in a public toilet—not to mention extensive provisions on notification, risk of sexual harm orders, foreign travel orders, and so on. The 2009 Act is more limited in scope but still creates six new offences (sexual coercion; coercing a person to be present during sexual activity; coercing a person into looking at a sexual image; communicating indecently; sexual exposure; and voyeurism), all of which have variants with younger and older children. Fourth, there is a greatly increased level of specificity or detail in the definition of offences. This is shown both in the creation of numbers of distinct but related offences, as in the different

[125] *Stallard v HM Adv* 1989 SCCR 248; *R v R* [1992] 1 AC 599 following the Law Commission paper on *Rape within Marriage* 1990 (London: HMSO, 1990). *Lord Advocate's Ref (No.1 of 2001)* 2002 SLT 466.

[126] Sex Offenders Act 1997; Protection of Children and Prevention of Sexual Offences (S) Act 2005.

[127] Sexual Offences Act 2003 s.1(1); Sexual Offences (S) Act 2009 s.16. See J Temkin & A Ashworth, 'The Sexual Offences Act 2003: (1) Rape, Sexual Assaults and the Problems of Consent' [2004] *Crim LR* 328 at pp.340–2.

[128] J Spencer, 'The Sexual Offences Act 2003: (2) Child and Family Offences' [2004] *Crim LR* 347 at p.348: 'The new offences in the Sexual Offences Act 2003 are more numerous than those they replace—and extend, in many cases, the range of behaviour that is criminal. In broad terms, nothing that was previously criminal has ceased to be; much is made criminal that previously was not, and most of it is made more severely punishable.'

child sexual offences, and in the level of detail in the specification of elements of individual offences. Section 3(2) of the 2009 Act, for example, lists different forms of conduct that can amount to sexual assault: penetration, touching, other physical contact, ejaculating semen, or emitting urine or saliva. Finally, sexual motivation or the characterization of an activity as 'sexual' is made relevant to the definition of certain crimes. In the 2003 Act, for example, conduct amounts to voyeurism if it is 'for the purposes of sexual gratification' (s.67); and sexual penetration is relevant to, for example, sex with an adult relative (ss.64 & 65) and sexual penetration of a corpse (s.70).[129]

Notwithstanding the differences in content, the scope of sexual offences in both jurisdictions was understood in terms of certain underlying principles which made possible the organization of sexual offences as a unified field.[130] Central to this is the idea of consent understood as an interior state that expresses sexual desire or rejection. Consent is framed in positive terms, as not merely submission or acquiescence to the desires of another, but a negotiated interaction or agreement in which the needs and desires of both parties are expressed and respected.[131] This is articulated in terms of an ideal sexual relationship as a 'rich and fulfilling part of life', where consent is a means to the end of mutual pleasure.[132] Sex, it is argued, is a valued human activity such that the criminal law ought to protect our interest or right to pursue that end as we choose.[133] It thus follows that where a person has capacity to consent, but that consent to the conduct charged is absent, then a criminal wrong has been committed. However, this is strikingly framed in terms of human rights, as a principle of non-discrimination (supporting the decriminalization of homosexual conduct), and a right to private life (as a right to a more general sexual freedom).[134] This establishes sexual autonomy as a sphere in which women and men have the right to pursue a range of sexual options, free from fear of unwanted sexual encounters. From this perspective, the wrong of rape has come to be seen as the interference with sexual autonomy understood as, on the one hand, the protection of a sphere of intimacy and, on the other, the right

[129] See also the 2009 Act where forms of sexual assault, exposure, coercion, communicating indecently, and voyeurism are all 'for purposes of sexual gratification'. 'Sexual' is defined in s.78 of the Sexual Offences Act 2003 and s.49 of Sexual Offences (S) Act 2009 as what the reasonable person would consider to be sexual.

[130] The key documents in the framing of the 2003 Act were two Home Office Reports: *Setting the Boundaries* (London: HMSO, 2000) and *Protecting the Public* (London: HMSO, 2002). The Scottish approach is set out in Scottish Law Commission, *Report on Rape and Other Sexual Offences* (No.209) (Edinburgh: Stationery Office, 2007). For discussion, see N Lacey, 'Beset by Boundaries: The Home Office Review of Sex Offences' [2001] *Crim LR* 3; VE Munro, 'Dev'l-in Disguise? Harm, Privacy and the Sexual Offences Act 2003' in VE Munro & C Stychin (eds), *Sexuality and the Law. Feminist Engagements* (London: Glasshouse, 2007).

[131] See e.g. Scottish Law Commission, n.130, paras.2.23–25.

[132] *Setting the Boundaries*, n.130, para.1.1.3. See P Haag, *Consent. Sexual Rights and the Transformation of American Liberalism* (Cornell: Cornell UP, 1999).

[133] Scottish Law Commission, n.130, para.1.25: 'a person freely choosing to engage in sexual activity'; see *Setting the Boundaries*, n.130, paras.0.7 & 1.3.2.

[134] *Setting the Boundaries*, n.130, p.2 and section 1.2.

to choose with whom and when to have sexual intercourse.[135] However, as I shall argue below, this is a departure from Wolfenden in that the sphere of autonomy, or the private, is understood in conceptual rather than spatial terms.

The converse of this idea of sexual autonomy is the horror of abuse, exploitation, and victimhood: 'where sex occurs without consent, abusively or inappropriately it is harmful, unpleasant and degrading.'[136] The Home Office papers make clear the social damage and individual trauma that can follow when sexual autonomy is not respected. In the foreword to *Protecting the Public* there is a declaration from the Home Secretary that sexual crime 'destroys lives and communities and tears apart our most basic values'.[137] The language of *Setting the Boundaries* is framed in terms of protecting actual and potential victims and survivors of sexual abuse, seeing the law as part of a wider strategy to 'increase protection for children, vulnerable people and victims and to tackle violence against women'.[138] It thus followed that 'the criminal law should give special protection to persons [whose consent] to sexual activity is problematic'.[139] These fell into two categories: those who were incapable of consent because of age or mental disorder, and those who could consent but were in relations where they might be exploited. The first category is based around capacity to consent, largely restating existing understandings of offences based on age and mental disorder, though adding new offences such as grooming or facilitating in order to capture the particular forms of vulnerability through specific criminal labels.[140] The more radical departure was in the second category where ideas of breach of trust and exploitation were used in support of the criminalization of a range of conduct in relation to young adults, of care workers, in family situations and in relation to trafficking. The overall effect here is to expand the conception of the vulnerable.

The reform of the law is undoubtedly important in terms of removing forms of unjust discrimination and outdated moral attitudes from the law of sexual offences, and in giving expression to an idea of sexual autonomy that places sexual freedom and citizenship at the heart of the law. However, I want to draw attention to three further features of the new legal regime which follow from the way that sexual offences are now understood. First, this idea of 'sexual offences' is more inclusive. This is in part because the idea of sexual autonomy or positive consent sets a particularly high standard, and thereby extends the range of ways in which this autonomy might be infringed. This approach aims at a separation of sexual morality from judgement—not judging conduct in moral terms or privileging particular kinds of relationship (or judging lifestyles). However, what is also

[135] See the influential paper by J Gardner & S Shute, 'The Wrongness of Rape' in J Horder (ed.), *Oxford Essays in Jurisprudence. Fourth Series* (Oxford: Oxford UP, 2000). This was discussed in the Scottish Law Commission Report, n.130, at para.1.26.

[136] *Setting the Boundaries*, n.130, para.1.1.3.

[137] David Blunkett, *Protecting the Public*, n.130, p.5.

[138] *Setting the Boundaries*, n.130, para.1.1.1.

[139] Scottish Law Commission, n.130, para.2.6.

[140] Although the provisions on sexual activity between teenage children were heavily criticized. See e.g. Spencer, 'Child and Family Offences', n.128.

crucial here is that there is a redefinition of the idea of violence 'so that forms of power in sexual relationships—physical, emotional, psychological, intellectual or economic—can be thought of as violence by other means.'[141] This thus broadens the understanding of the forms of coercion that might vitiate consent—while at the same time leaving open the problems with the proof of consent (or its absence) that have bedevilled trials for rape and sexual assault.[142] Moreover, this understanding of autonomy, and its corollary protection, also means that some conduct which was previously criminalized on the grounds of being contrary to morals, can be reconceived in terms of exploitation. This is most notable in relation to prostitution, which is now increasingly understood in terms of the question of consent.[143] While arguments about autonomy and consent might seem to present an argument for decriminalization where a sex worker has chosen freely (where the market is working), it is in fact used to support more intense regulation of sex workers, who are seen as vulnerable and exploited: sex is not for the purpose of intimacy, and hence not fulfilling, and therefore the question of exploitation is present.[144] This is thus a redrawing of the ideas of public and private on which law was previously based: rather than being based on the home or ideas of physically private locations, private is that which is properly consensual, and those acts are of public concern which are deemed exploitative because they depart from the ideal model of consensual, mutually fulfilling, sex. What is especially controversial here is the wide understanding of what is exploitative, particularly in relation to the expanded idea of violence and to commercial sex. The state is not just protecting autonomy but is promoting it by regulating those kinds of relationships where it is presumptively absent. In the end, though, this is less a matter of undermining liberal ideals than re-articulating them around a different understanding of the private.[145]

Second, this approach is more systematic. At one level, this is a matter of filling gaps, imagining the various ways that autonomy might be infringed and legislating

[141] J. Suk, '"The Look in his Eyes": The Story of *Rusk* and Rape Reform' in D Coker & R Weisberg (eds), *Criminal Law Stories* (New York: Foundation Press, 2013) 171–211 at p.203. Cf. offences against the person, see Chapter 8 supra at pp.257–61.

[142] S Cowan, 'Freedom and Capacity to Make a Choice. A Feminist Analysis of Consent in the Criminal Law of Rape' in VE Munro & C Stychin (eds), *Sexuality and the Law. Feminist Engagements* (London: Glasshouse, 2007) p.68.

[143] L Kelly, M Coy, & R Davenport, *Shifting Sands. A Comparison of Prostitution Regimes* (2009) (http://www.turnofftheredlight.ie/wp-content/uploads/2011/02/Shifting_Sands_UK-HOMe-Office.pdf).

[144] Note e.g. the Policing and Crime Act 2009 s.14 making it a crime to have sex with a prostitute subjected to force—a real broadening of the way that consent is understood—and this allows a new link to develop between rape and prostitution where there is now seen to be a unifying principle (not sex directly, but autonomy). See also Munro & Scoular, 'Harm, Vulnerability and Citizenship', n.111. pp.43–8.

[145] See Munro, 'Dev'l-in Disguise?', n.130, p.3. Her argument proceeds on the basis that the approach laid out in *Setting the Boundaries* is non-interventionist, but as I have suggested here this is far from clear.

new offences.[146] It is also clear that the use of open-ended terms such as 'sexual gratification' or 'sexual' also leave space for criminalizing forms of conduct which are perhaps otherwise not explicitly captured in the legislation. However, the law is also systematic in the more fundamental sense that this is now underpinned by an infrastructure of regulation which records and monitors offences and offending. Criminal statistics now treat sexual crimes as a separate category.[147] These in turn are backed up by lists of sexual offences that trigger registration requirements or prevention orders.[148] The whole area of sexual offences is broken down and ordered into detailed hierarchies of offences.

Third, on this approach, sexual offences are more serious: 'Sex offences reach deeper into society than almost any other part of the criminal law'.[149] This is in part a factual claim about the social threat posed by certain kinds of sex offenders—paedophiles and serial abusers—but it is linked to the armoury of special measures developed to register, track, and control actual and potential offenders, which in fact reach deeper into society. Sex offenders on this view are not outsiders, but are enemies within—in institutions and communities—and require an extraordinary vigilance to be alert to the dangers that they pose. It is also a claim about the need to recognize the seriousness of, and the possible range of, harms done to victims—leading Lacey to suggest that harm here is a guiding rather than a limiting principle.[150] However, it is also a normative claim. The importance which is attached to sexual autonomy and sexual identity means that sexual offences are regarded as more serious. If sexuality is not only a form of sexual orientation, but is also linked to forms of personal identity or subjectivity and fulfilment then the protection of this in law becomes more important to the self-understanding of the community.[151] More is at stake in sexual offences than has previously been the case.

Developments in the area of sexual offences over the last twenty-five years show how the category has shifted from a descriptive to a normative category. At the level of definition this has been reflected in the increasing importance of consent as a definitional element of crimes in this area and the recognition of sexual autonomy as the central principle. This has made possible a more systematic understanding and redefinition of crimes in this area. More broadly, this has led to a shift in the purpose of the law in this area, from the regulation of violence and public disorder to a more specific—and more detailed—concern with protecting

[146] See e.g. the discussion of the offence of causing a person to engage in sexual activity or committing an offence with intent to commit a sexual offence in *Protecting the Public*, n.130, paras.46–7.

[147] In Scotland, until 1980–2, rape was still recorded as a crime against the person.

[148] See e.g. Sexual Offences Act 2003, Schedule 3. See discussion in S Shute, 'The Sexual Offences Act 2003: (4) New Civil Preventative Orders—Sexual Offences Prevention Orders; Foreign Travel Orders; Risk of Sexual Harm Orders' [2004] *Crim LR* p.417.

[149] *Setting the Boundaries*, n.130, para.1.1.3.

[150] Lacey, 'Beset by Boundaries', n.130, p.5.

[151] On sexuality and identity, see Foucault, *History of Sexuality*, n.98. See also HG Cocks, 'Approaches to the History of Sexuality since 1750' in S Toulalan & K Fisher (eds), *The Routledge History of Sex and the Body, 1500 to the Present* (London: Routledge, 2013).

sexual autonomy and protecting against exploitation. Making this point more starkly, it has been argued that the aim of the law on sexual offences has been reversed in the modern period: the older law aimed directly at limiting sexual freedom, or discouraging sexual intercourse outwith marriage; by contrast, the contemporary law aims to protect this right.[152] The significance of this transformation may easily be underestimated if we fail to recognize the novelty of the category, and in my concluding remarks I want to make some more general remarks about the significance of this conception of sexual offences.

IV. Conclusion

The development I have described in this chapter has been twofold. First, I have outlined the complex historical process in which this new category was created, systematizing a diverse range of crimes behind a new understanding of sex and its social significance. Second, I have argued that the modern category is organized around a particular view of sexuality and autonomy that both reflects, and has reflected on, the way that the sexual content of certain crimes has been thematized. This, I have argued, is not just descriptive but is an increasingly normative understanding of sexual offences, shaped by an understanding of sexual autonomy and the value of fulfilling sexual relationships that has had consequences for the increased criminalization of conduct in this area. This is important both for the process of criminalization in this area and for the way that we think about criminalization more generally. In this conclusion, I want to offer some further thoughts on these two points.

It is important to acknowledge that recognition of sexual autonomy has led to significant reforms in this area of the law—notably the decriminalization of homosexual sex and the increased recognition of forms of victimization and abuse. However, it has also had important consequences in terms of the more intensive criminalization of this field, and it is necessary to ask whether this is in some way linked to the recognition of the category of sexual offences itself. One way of understanding the development of the law would be to argue that women and the vulnerable have indeed been under-protected for too long, as the law was inadequate and was inadequately enforced.[153] The increased criminalization of exploitative sexual conduct, together with the recognition of sexual freedom, can thus be seen as a delayed recognition of the position of women through the gradual removal of impediments or obstacles to conviction of attackers, and through the creation of a non-discriminatory and fairer law. This can be seen as the working out of a liberal principle of sexual autonomy first identified by Mill (against

[152] See A Coughlin, 'Sex and Guilt' (1998) 84 *Virginia Law Rev* 1–46 at 7. Coughlin's point is stronger because she considers the law of rape in the context of the criminal prohibitions on adultery which existed in many jurisdictions.

[153] I am indebted to discussions with Ngaire Naffine on this point.

moralized understandings of proper sexual conduct), or a gradual convergence between the underlying wrong (the infringement of sexual autonomy) and the content of the law.[154] On this account, the modernization process is a civilizing process, where reform gradually (if imperfectly) reflects a modern sensibility about sex and its social significance. Criticisms can be made of the law on the grounds that the principle has been imperfectly realized—through clumsy drafting, the distortions wrought by populist fears of paedophiles, the return of moralism, and so on—but the fundamental correctness of the principle is not challenged. The recognition in the law of a category of sexual offences is the fulfilment of this process, identifying and recognizing the significance of these offences and making possible a more coherent and systematic approach, which has hitherto been absent from the law.

However, in this chapter I have set out a more complex account in which the development of the law cannot be seen in reformist terms as the gradual working out of an underlying principle (no matter how imperfectly enforced). Instead, I have shown that the development of the law must be seen in terms of the interests that the law sought to protect at different points in time and the contemporary understandings of the meaning and significance of sex. It follows that the development of concepts such as sexual autonomy must be seen in terms of particular understandings of sex and sexuality, and also that the development of the category is linked to wider institutions regulating sexual conduct. The apparent paradox that the liberalization of sexual conduct has led to a vast expansion in the number of sexual offences is not just a matter of accident, but must be understood in terms of the relationship between autonomy and state intervention. The recognition of autonomy requires increased levels of responsibility of individuals towards each other in sexual affairs; the state does not withdraw from these areas but the state of freedom is accompanied by more detailed specification of the appropriate standards of conduct and the regulation of those who either lack the capacity to consent or who have failed to meet the appropriate standards.

This, I think, has two further consequences. First, the question of criminalization of sexual offences is often approached in terms that suggest that questions as to the scope of the law can be answered solely by reference to clarifying the understanding of sexual autonomy. Sex, it is argued, is a valued human activity and so the criminal law ought to protect our interest or right to pursue that end as we choose. Criminal wrongs in this area are thus those that infringe or interfere with our capacity to realize that interest. However, in the history of criminalization of sexual offences outlined in this chapter, we see an example of the general point made in this book: the harms or wrongs of sexual offences cannot be defined in terms of abstract values such as autonomy alone—or even sexual autonomy—but must also be contextualized in terms of the aims of the law, the kind of civil order that the law is trying to achieve, and the institutional capacity that it possesses to

[154] E.g. 'At the most fundamental level a commitment to promoting and protecting citizens' autonomy lies at the heart of any liberal society': Munro, 'Sexual Autonomy', n.4, p.1.

produce that order. The criminal regulation of sex at different times in different communities has, I have shown, always depended on the social aims that criminal law has sought to pursue. This, of course, is no less true of contemporary ideas of sexual autonomy, even if they are presented as universal values or as interests rather than ends. Autonomy is given content by the purpose of the law; it is not only the interest that is to be protected, but also the aim of protection.

Second, interests such as sexual autonomy, and the categories of law which are organized around them, are often seen as natural, but it is important to understand not only that it is a social construction, but also how it has been constructed and the consequences of that way of viewing the law. The codification of sexual offences has brought with it a new drive for completeness, for further categorization and regulation. Internally, it becomes possible to imagine new kinds of wrong or new ways of committing existing wrongs. External demands for criminalization are framed in the new language of sexual autonomy, making their reception within the law easier to accomplish. Increased criminalization in the area of sexual offences is partly a product of the categorization itself, and its own expansive logic. This should give theorists pause for thought. It is an assumption of much writing about criminalization that thinking in terms of categories will not only bring clarity to the law, but also that an implicit consequence of this will be a decrease in criminalization as crimes that do not 'fit' are weeded out. My discussion here raises the possibility that this approach might have the opposite effect. Thinking in categories, at least in this area, has led to the identification of further crimes and to the expansion of the category since there is a tendency towards universalism: thinking of every possible instance of sexual wrong and every possible sphere of application. This suggests that a theory of criminalization needs to reflect not only on the content of the law but also on the kind of framework within which such theorizing is conducted and the consequence of adopting certain approaches—and indeed whether it is possible to think about sexual autonomy or sexual offences as an area in terms which do not produce such a strong demand for criminalization.[155]

[155] It is instructive to look at Bentham's approach. He distinguished between private offences, which included offences against the interests of private individuals, and the class of self-regarding offences (which caused no harm to others) which should not be criminal. Rape was classed as an offence against the person and reputation of the individual, and he noted lesser forms of assault where consent was not freely and fairly obtained (forcible seduction) or fairly obtained (seduction), or where there was simple 'lascivious injury'. This produces a more minimal category of sexual offences. J Bentham, *On Sexual Irregularities* (Oxford: OUP, 2014).

PART IV

CONCLUSION

10

Conclusion

Criminalization and Civil Order

> An effective and properly functioning system of criminal law and criminal justice is essential for that relative security of mutual expectations which is a condition of the civility of civil society. Criminal law becomes fully intelligible only from this perspective.[1]

This is a book about criminalization—about what and who should be treated as criminal under the law and the ways that this can be justified. However, I have approached this familiar question in an unfamiliar way. My aim has been to understand the criminal law as an institution, to look at how the criminal law has developed in the modern period and at the way that normative theoretical problems, such as criminalization, have been framed within that institution. In doing this, I have explored the emergence of the modern criminal law in such diverse areas as the eighteenth-century law of forgery, the nineteenth-century criminalization of wife-beating and child neglect, the emergence of road traffic law in the twentieth century, and the recent reform of sexual offences. And I have looked at areas, such as theories and practices of codification and the development of territorial jurisdiction, which are not normally seen as relevant to theories of criminalization. These, and the many other examples discussed throughout the book, demonstrate a different kind of approach to the question of the 'proper' scope of the criminal law, aimed at deepening our understanding of criminalization as a practice.

The substance of the law has changed quite dramatically, even over the modern period, in response to far-reaching social and economic transformations. The diverse, historical practices of criminalization explored in the book show criminalization as a social activity which is inherently defined by its specificity and contingency. The question of what it is proper or justifiable for the criminal law to regulate has not been determined by 'pre-legal' conceptions of the person or property or autonomy, or built up around a pre-existing core of moral wrongs; and this kind of model has only a limited capacity to explain contemporary practices. The development of the law has primarily been shaped by the need to respond

[1] N MacCormick, *Institutions of Law* (Oxford: Oxford UP, 2007) p.293.

to quite specific social problems of modernity: the invention of the car, the recognition of equal rights, the changing nature of property, and so on. Arguments about justification have rarely fallen into the neat theoretical categories of harms or wrongs, and have almost always been understood in terms of the protection of classes of victim or how certain types of conduct might be changed or prevented. This does not mean that the development of the criminal law has been completely random or opportunistic. We have seen clear patterns of criminalization, both in particular areas and in the development of the law as a whole. The making of new laws has been shaped by an understanding of what the criminal law is and how it should be used, a recognition that criminal law should be used sparingly and that the exercise of state power should be subject to constraints. The paradox of the modern criminal law is that despite being shaped by a liberal sensibility about the scope of state power and the desire to respect individual rights and liberties, it has expanded in scope, more or less continually, since the late eighteenth century.

Alongside this account of the making of the modern criminal law there has been a second one, which has traced the emergence of the 'criminalization question'. This has traced the emergence and development of a literature that has framed the question of the scope and limits of the criminal law as a problem of philosophical jurisprudence with the aim of producing a set of general principles of criminalization. To understand criminalization in these terms—identifying the 'object' of the criminal law—implies the prior existence of an understanding of the criminal law as a distinct body of rules with a defined area of application—'crime' as a conceptually unified group of serious offences—such that to criminalize something is to bring that activity within the scope of what it meant to be criminal. This is to say that it is only possible to have a theory of criminalization, or to see criminalization as a distinct question, once we already have a theory of the criminal law. The emergence of the criminalization question was thus linked to the emergence of criminal law. This, I have shown, was closely connected to the emergence of the modern legislative state in the late eighteenth century. The criminal law increasingly came to be seen as an instrument that the state could use to shape civil order; to criminalize was to signal disapproval or censure, but also to try to change conduct by laying down rules backed by the threat of criminal sanctions. As the criminal law developed in this way, theorists from Blackstone and Bentham onwards sought to classify and categorize the criminal law, to identify common features and characteristics of its rules, and explain how it could be effective in terms of the capacities of the legal person to respond to rules and punishment. There were few principled limits to the use of the criminal law, provided that it could be justified as effective.

This view of criminalization continues to shape the law, as legislatures routinely criminalize conduct that is seen as anti-social or undesirable in an effort to change the conduct of individuals or other legal persons. The precise terms in which issues are raised and in which the resort to criminal law is justified has shifted in response to changing demands on the law—recognizing the rights of victims or distinctive wrongs against them, upholding different forms or systems of property, or regulating systems of manufacturing or transport—but the view of the criminal law as an instrument of social change persists. What has changed in the late twentieth century is that theories of criminalization have been reimagined. It is now argued that criminal law is damaging society by intruding into private matters, limiting the autonomy of citizens, or punishing excessively where the law is ineffective in changing conduct. Criminalization is now understood in terms of excess and over-reach, and criminalization theory addresses the need to limit the legislative capacities of the state or establish constitutional constraints that might restrain legislation. Theorists argue for a more restricted understanding of the scope of the criminal law in which, if it is not going to do good, it should at least do no harm. In each case, whether criminalization is understood as doing good or limiting the harm done in the name of the criminal law, the criminalization question rests on an understanding of the 'proper' scope of the criminal law—the question being whether it is exceeding those limits or not. The question of the proper scope of the law is thus central, but I have shown in this book that this can only be understood in terms of an account of the development of the criminal law.

This is not simply to argue that criminal law scholarship should be more historically aware. Rather, by following the making of the criminal law, in the way that I have done, we can begin to see and to ground an account of the criminal law as a coherent whole. A central theme of my argument has been that the modern criminal law is shaped by the broad aim of securing civil order; or, in MacCormick's formulation, that the criminal law can only be made 'fully intelligible' by looking at it from the perspective of the aim of securing the *civility* of civil society. That is, one way of making the range or scope of the criminal law intelligible—at any given point in time or as a body of rules existing over time—is to understand how it has been directed at securing civil order. What links disparate rules on, say, forgery of documents, the sale of poisons, the regulation of jurisdiction overseas and so on, is a common sense that they belong to something which can be described as the 'criminal law'. What makes this intelligible as an idea is not only that the rules may share certain common properties (which is not always the case), or that the rules carry penal sanctions, but also that they are directed at securing civil order in some way.[2] Civil order in this sense is not primarily about moral community, but the co-ordination of complex modern societies composed of a range of entities or legal persons that are responsible, in a range of different ways, for their own conduct, for the wellbeing of others, and for the maintenance of social institutions. The problem of civil order has been seen as a problem of coordinating individuals and their interests, and the criminal law has been used to secure those interests by establishing measures for building and reinforcing trust between individuals.

In substantive terms, this order has been secured by establishing rules for the conduct of social of life in an increasingly diverse range of activities. This might take the forms of a response to actual or threatened disorder, or clarifying responsibilities in relation to potentially harmful conduct, or establishing rules

[2] This, it should be clear, is not a definition of either crime or criminal law. Nor is it intended to identify limits to the criminal law in terms of subject matter.

for coordinating complex social interactions. Thus the recognition of individual responsibility in the law was the counterpart of the elucidation of responsibilities for individual citizens. The protection of the person brought the expectation of higher standards of self-control and civilized conduct. And the spread of sexual freedom or citizenship was accompanied by the more intense regulation of exploitative sexual conduct. The way that the criminal law has secured trust has been different in relation to different social practices or interests, and it has changed over time, depending on changed understandings of those interests, of civility, and shifting perceptions of the legitimacy of certain forms of state intervention. However, looking at the criminal law in terms of securing civil order in complex modern societies can make its diverse practices intelligible – rather than focusing only on those parts of the law that 'fit' with a particular theoretical perspective. This, it should be clear, is not to take a naïve or one-sided view: the vision of civil order has often represented the views or interests of one class. It has involved the rejection of certain ways of life or customs that were viewed as 'barbarous'—and the criminal law itself has been used in ways that we might easily think of as distinctly 'uncivil'. Securing civil order is nonetheless, as I have shown, a frame through which we can make sense of the criminal law as a whole.

This brings us to a second way in which the idea of civil order can make the criminal law intelligible. This concerns the scope of criminal law, or how the question of the scope of the law has been understood by the criminal law itself. Where does the law apply? Who does it apply to? And what kind of conduct can be regulated? These kinds of question have been addressed in different ways. It is in part seen as a matter of jurisdiction. The law has claimed the authority to regulate particular spaces or persons or activities in the name of a certain political authority (a sovereign or political community) or in the name of certain values. I showed how the criminal law developed from ideas of local order to become a frame for conceptualizing crime as a national problem. Indeed, it became a central concern of an imperial order, which justified its rule over 'barbarous' peoples across the globe through its use of the civilizing medium of English law. Latterly, ideas of universal crimes, or conduct that should be wrong in any system of civilized law, have been folded into the scope of criminal law, attempting to legitimate claims that it is proper for the state, order, or international community to act in the name of humanity. It has been seen as a matter of responsibility as the criminal law has been addressed to persons who possess, or are deemed to possess, forms of responsible agency or the capacity to adjust their conduct to general rules, shaping the content of rules as the capacities of the person are specified in greater detail. And it has taken the form of the claim that there are certain kinds of conduct or interest the protection of which shapes the proper scope of the law. These have shifted over time as areas of social life that were regarded as beyond the legitimate scope of the criminal law because they were part of a private domain (as with family or intimate violence) or thought to be better regulated by civil law (such as market transactions) become taken for granted as areas of criminalization in other times.

The development of these different understandings of the scope of the law does not reflect an over-determined trajectory of progress—that we are gradually but inexorably moving towards the correct answer to this question. It is rather the case that understanding of what is or is not 'proper' at any given time will depend on understandings of what kind of regulation is necessary to civil order. This, I have shown, is particularly the case in relation to the protection of property, person, and sex. These are areas which are often seen as core areas of the criminal law, protecting fundamental liberal values where fundamental moral wrongs can be more easily identified. However, my account of the development of the law in each of these areas shows that the aims of the law have changed quite dramatically over the modern period, and that understandings of property, or the person, or sexual wrongs have shifted with our understandings of the meaning or social significance of private property or violence or sexual autonomy. The perception of what is harmful or wrongful conduct in any area will thus depend on the way in which particular social interests are seen to be related to the overall maintenance of civil order.

A third dimension of civil order concerns the civility of the criminal law itself. The criminal law not only has to secure trust between individuals, but also the trust of individuals in the order of law. This brings with it certain internal demands in terms of how citizens should be addressed and treated. Modern law takes the form of rules of general application which assume the possibility of non-obedience, while at the same time binding the subject to the idea that obedience to the rules operates for the benefit of all. Individuals are thus free to pursue their own interests without unjustified legal interference—placing a burden on the state to justify intrusions into those 'private' interests or the imposition of punishment for breach of the law. Once again, to be sure, it is important to acknowledge that this can be an incomplete process: claiming that the law respects these values is not the same as claiming that it always achieves or pursues this in a coherent or complete way. The criminal law has not protected all equally, and the enforcement of the law has often been partial and biased. However, a central element of the resort to law is that it takes the form of general rules and is subject to constraints of legality. The recognition of these rules means that the law itself can be called to account for departing from its own professed standards. This is not only a matter of internal coherence or order, but can also be judged in terms of the fairness of the enforcement or the practice of law. This helps us to make sense of the development of increasingly sophisticated rules for the attribution of liability, of principles, the institutionalization of review bodies, and so on. Criminal law thus secures civil order in a particular way. This, indeed, is what has shaped the understanding of criminalization in recent years: that the criminal law is departing from standards and principles, or that the form of rules has departed from the idea of general norms, or that the law is restricting the autonomy of individuals. The criminalization question is at least in part connected to this idea of civil order.

Finally, this understanding of civil order helps us to make sense of the modern criminal law as a kind of normative project. Civil order is normative in the sense that it operates as a kind of ideal for the law. The aim of the law is not that of securing order at any cost, but securing a *civil* order. This is more than order; it is order of a particular kind. The modern idea of criminal law is underpinned by understandings of the kind of society that we live in, the kind of values that are important, and how we ought to live together—what Taylor has called the 'modern social imaginary'.[3] This is normative in the sense that it frames understandings of what is permissible and indeed what is possible. Civil order is thus not any kind of order that exists, but an idea of civil order judged according to the ideas of other possible conceptions of civil order; and the role of criminal law in securing civil order can be judged according to other conceptions of how this might be done—by criminal law or other forms of social regulation. The idea of what constitutes a civil order is not fixed. Indeed, we have seen that the development of the law has been driven by debates about how the law might be better or more just. This has involved different ideas about permissible levels of violence, how individual autonomy or rights should be better respected, particular standards of civility in public or sexual conduct, and so on. This is not an attempt to give moral foundations to the law, by identifying pre-moral or fundamental wrongs, or identifying prescriptive principles, but it is normative in the sense that it recognizes that ideas about civil order can establish a kind of normative horizon for thinking critically about the criminal law.

My thesis that the aim of securing civil order is what makes the criminal law intelligible does not produce a definition of crime or criminal law, and it is not prescriptive. It does not offer neat solutions to normative questions. It cannot be used to answer the question of whether or not the use of the criminal law is appropriate, identify 'core' wrongs, or specify universal characteristics of criminal law. These are properly contested questions and cannot be resolved by a priori definitions of crime or law—however tempting that might be. However, in 'making intelligible' patterns of criminalization and the changing aims of the criminal law it gives us a rich picture of the development and functions of the law. I have shown that there are clear patterns in the development of the law, and in particular areas of the law, as understandings of civil order have changed and of the ideas and beliefs about law that have shaped these developments. The identification of these patterns is crucial to understanding the aims and functions of the modern criminal law, but the current framework for our normative thinking about criminalization does not always map onto this process of criminalization as it focuses on abstract and decontextualized ideas. This history thus cuts against the grain of many of the understandings that shape normative legal theory in its search for moral and philosophical foundations for the criminal law.

The problem with recent criminal law theory is a turning inwards to prescriptive definitions and a search for conceptual coherence. There is unease about the growth of the criminal law, but this has led many theorists to seek security in an ideal account of the law. The aims of criminal law are understood in terms of the aims of punishment, censure understood in narrow terms of individual retribution, and the content of the law is conceived in terms of a core of moral wrongs. While this approach produces a certain internal clarity and coherence, safe from

[3] C Taylor, *Modern Social Imaginaries* (Durham, NC: Duke UP, 2004).

the messy complexities of social life and change, it comes at the cost of an understanding of the diversity of norms and the complex institutional structure of the criminal law. I have tried to understand the aims of criminal law and criminalization more broadly, to see it as a form of public law and as a governmental project, and so to encourage the possibility of engagement with questions of politics and power. The aims of the criminal law are as much about distributing roles and responsibilities, laying down rules to guide the conduct of citizens as they are about justifying punishment. The fairness of these rules does not depend in the first instance on the aims of punishment but on such factors as how the rules have been made, whether the rules give fair opportunity of compliance to those to whom they are addressed, whether or not the criminal law is seen as an appropriate way of regulating the conduct in question, and whether they respect other civil rights. The punishment of those who break the rules must be fair, but this is only one dimension of the law and should not be focused on to the exclusion of all else. The substance of the law cannot be determined by a core of moral wrongs, as even in those areas which might be thought to be central (person, property, sex) to criminal regulation, wrongs are shaped by particular and emergent social problems and needs. Criminalization is a central issue—maybe the central issue—for criminal law and criminal law theory. It is proper that we debate the scope of the criminal law, but as I have shown here talking about criminalization requires a different sort of language and approach which reconnects with a more historical and political understanding of the practice and aims of the criminal law.

Bibliography

Abelson, ES (1989), *When Ladies Go A-Thieving. Middle Class Shoplifters in the Victorian Department Store* (Oxford: Oxford University Press).

Alexander, I (2007), 'Criminalising Copyright. A Story of Publishers, Pirates and Pieces of Eight' *Cambridge Law Journal*, 66: 625–56.

Alison, A (1832), *Principles of the Criminal Law of Scotland* (Edinburgh: William Blackwood).

Aliverti, A (2012), 'Making People Criminal: the Role of Criminal Law in Immigration Enforcement' *Theoretical Criminology*, 16: 417–34.

Alldridge, P (1993), 'Attempted Murder of the Soul: Blackmail, Privacy and Secrets' *Oxford Journal of Legal Studies*, 13: 368–87.

Alldridge, P (1998), 'Threats Offences—A Case for Reform' *Criminal Law Review*, 176–86.

Allen, CK (1931), 'The Nature of a Crime' in *Legal Duties, and Other Essays in Jurisprudence* (Oxford: Clarendon) pp.221–52.

Allyn, D (1996), 'Private Acts/Public Policy: Alfred Kinsey, the American Law Institute and the Privatization of American Sexual Morality' *Journal of American Studies*, 30: 405–28.

Amos, A (1856), *Ruins of Time Exemplified in Sir Matthew Hale's History of the Pleas of the Crown* (London: V & R Stevens & GS Norton).

Amos, S (1896), *The Science of Law* (London: Kegan Paul, Trench, Trübner & Co).

Anderson, AM (1904), *The Criminal Law of Scotland* (2nd edn) (Edinburgh: Bell & Bradfute).

Andrew, DT (2002), 'The London Press and Public Apologies in Eighteenth Century London' in N Landau (ed.), *Law, Crime and English Society 1660–1830* (Cambridge: Cambridge University Press) pp.208–29.

Andrew, DT & McGowan, R (2001), *The Perreaus and Mrs Rudd. Forgery and Betrayal in Eighteenth Century London* (Berkeley, CA : University of California Press).

Anon (1930), 'The Distinction between *Mala Prohibita* and *Mala in Se* in Criminal Law', *Columbia Law Review* 30: 74–86.

Appadurai, A (1986), 'Introduction: Commodities and the Politics of Value' in A Appadurai (ed.), *The Social Life of Things. Commodities in Cultural Perspective* (Cambridge: Cambridge University Press) pp.3–63.

Archbold, JF (1824), *A Summary of the Law Relative To Pleading and Evidence in Criminal Cases: With Precedents of Indictments &C. and the Evidence Necessary to Support them* (London: Pheney).

Archer, J (2000), '"Men Behaving Badly?": Masculinity and the Uses of Violence' in S d'Cruze, (ed.), *Everyday Violence in Britain. 1850–1950. Gender and Class* (London: Longman) pp.41–54.

Archer, P & Martin, A (eds) (1983), *More Law Reform Now* (Chichester: B. Rose Publishers).

Ashworth, A (1981), 'The Elasticity of Mens Rea' in CFH Tapper (ed.), *Crime, Proof and Punishment* (London: Butterworth).

Ashworth, A (2000), 'Is the Criminal Law a Lost Cause?', *Law Quarterly Review*, 116: 225–56.

Ashworth, A (2011), 'The Unfairness of Risk-Based Possession Offences' *Criminal Law and Philosophy*, 5: 237–57.

Ashworth, A (2013), 'Criminalising Omissions' in *Positive Obligations in Criminal Law* (Oxford: Hart Publishing) pp.31–80.

Ashworth, A & Horder, J (2013), *Principles of Criminal Law* (7th edn) (Oxford: Oxford University Press).

Ashworth, A, Zedner, L, & Tomlin, P (eds) (2013), *Prevention and the Limits of the Criminal Law* (Oxford: Oxford University Press).

Ashworth, A & Zedner, L (2010), 'Preventive Orders: A Problem of Undercriminalization?' in RA Duff, L Farmer, SE Marshall, M Renzo, & V Tadros (eds), *The Boundaries of the Criminal Law* (Oxford: Oxford University Press) pp.59–87.

Ashworth, A & Zedner, L (2014), *Preventive Justice* (Oxford: Oxford University Press).

Austin, J (1885), *Lectures on Jurisprudence* (2 vols) (5th edn, R Campbell ed.) (London: John Murray).

Bailey, V & Blackburn, S (1979), 'The Punishment of Incest Act 1908. A Case Study of Law Creation' *Criminal Law Review*, 708–18.

Baker, D (2011), *The Right Not to Be Criminalized* (Farnham: Ashgate).

Baker, JH (2001), *The Law's Two Bodies: Some Evidential Problems in English Legal History* (Oxford: Oxford University Press).

Barnes, TG (1977), 'The Making of the English Criminal Law (2). Star Chamber and the Sophistication of the Criminal Law' *Criminal Law Review*, 316.

Barrington, D (1766), *Observations upon the Statutes* (2nd edn) (London: Bowyer & Nichols).

Bashar, N (1983), 'Rape in England between 1550 and 1700' in The London Feminist History Group (eds), *The Sexual Dynamics of History* (London: Pluto) pp.28–42.

Bauman, Z (1985), 'On the Origins of Civilisation: A Historical Note' *Theory, Culture and Society*, 2: 7–14.

Bauman, Z (1987), *Legislators and Interpreters. On Modernity, Post-Modernity and Intellectuals* (Cambridge: Polity).

Bauman, Z (2007), *Consuming Life* (Cambridge: Polity).

Beale, JH (1892), 'Borderland of Larceny', *Harvard Law Review*, 6: 244–56.

Beattie, J (1986), *Crime and the Courts in England, 1660–1800* (Princeton, Princeton University Press).

Becker, MB (1988), *Civility and Society in Western Europe, 1300–1600* (Bloomington: Indiana University Press).

Behlmer, G (1982), *Child Abuse and Moral Reform in England, 1870–1908* (Stanford: Stanford University Press).

Behlmer, G (1994), 'Summary Justice and Working Class Marriage in England, 1870–1940' *Law and History Review*, 12: 229–75.

Bender, J (1987), *Imagining the Penitentiary. Fiction and the Architecture of Mind in Eighteenth-Century England* (Chicago: Chicago University Press).

Bentham, J (1838), *Principles of Penal Law* (J Bowring ed.), *Works*, Vol. 3 (Edinburgh: Wm Tait).

Bentham, J (1982), *Introduction to the Principles and Morals of Legislation* (JH Burns & HLA Hart eds) (Oxford: Oxford University Press).

Bentham, J (1970), *Of Laws in General* (ed. HLA Hart) (London: Athlone Press).

Bentham, J (1995), *The Panopticon Writings* (ed. M Bozovic) (London: Verso).

Bentham, J (2014), *On Sexual Irregularities* (Oxford: Oxford University Press).
Berman, H (2003), *Law and Revolution II. The Impact of the Protestant Reformations on the Western Legal Tradition* (Cambridge, Mass.: Harvard University Press).
Bibbings, L (2001), 'Human Rights and the Criminalization of Tradition: The Practices Formerly Known as "Female Circumcision"' in P Alldridge and C Brants (eds), *Personal Autonomy, the Private Sphere and the Criminal Law. A Comparative Study* (Oxford: Hart Publishing) pp.139–60.
Bibbings, L (2014), *Binding Men. Stories about Violence and Law in Late Victorian England* (London: Glasshouse).
Binder, G (2007), 'The Act of Killing' in MD Dubber & L Farmer (eds), *Modern Histories of Crime and Punishment* (Stanford: Stanford University Press) pp.88–114.
Binder, G (2013), 'Authority to Proscribe and Punish International Crimes' *University of Toronto Law Journal*, 63: 278–309.
Binder, G (2014), 'Offenses against the Person: Homicide' in MD Dubber & T Hörnle (eds), *The Oxford Handbook of Criminal Law* (Oxford: Oxford UP) pp.702–26.
Birnbaum, JMF (2012), 'Concerning the Need for a Right Violation in the Concept of Crime, having particular Regard to the Concept of an Affront to Honour' in MD Dubber (ed.), *Foundational Texts in Modern Criminal Law* (Oxford: Oxford University Press) pp.389–406.
Blackstone, W (1979), *Commentaries on the Laws of England* (4 vols) (1st edn, 1765–1769) (Chicago: Chicago University Press).
Bland, L (2002), *Banishing the Beast. Feminism, Sex and Morality* (London: Tauris).
Blomley, N, Delaney, D, & Ford, RT (eds) (2001), *The Legal Geographies Reader* (Oxford: Blackwell).
Bogg, A & Stanton-Ife, J (2003), 'Protecting the Vulnerable: Legality, Harm and Theft' *Legal Studies*, 23: 402–22.
Bottoms, AE (2014), 'Civil Peace and Criminalization' in RA Duff, L Farmer, SE Marshall, M Renzo, & V Tadros (eds), *Criminalization. The Political Morality of the Criminal Law* (Oxford: Oxford University Press) pp.232–69.
Bourdieu, P (1990), 'Codification' in *In Other Words. Essays Towards a Reflexive Sociology* (Cambridge: Polity) pp.76–86.
Bourke, J (2008), *Rape. A History* (London: Virago).
Boutellier, H (2004), *The Safety Utopia. Contemporary Discontent and Desire as to Crime and Punishment* (Dordrecht: Kluwer).
Bowden, B (2009), *The Empire of Civilization. The Evolution of an Imperial Idea* (Chicago: Chicago University Press).
Bowker, GC & Star, SL (1999), *Sorting Things Out. Classification and its Consequences* (London: MIT Press).
Bracton on the Laws and Customs of England (1968) (translated with revisions and notes by Samuel E Thorne) (Cambridge, Mass.: Harvard University Press).
Brooks, CW & Lobban, M (1999), 'Apprenticeship or Academy? The Idea of a Law University, 1830–1860' in JA Bush & A Wijffels (eds), *Learning the Law: Teaching and the Transmission of Law in England, 1150–1900* (London: Hambledon Press) pp.353–82.
Brown, D (1989), *The Genesis of the Canadian Criminal Code of 1892* (Toronto: Osgoode Hall Society).
Brown, D (2009), 'History's Challenge to Criminal Law Theory' *Criminal Law and Philosophy*, 3: 271–87.

Bryson, A (1998), *From Courtesy to Civility. Changing Codes of Conduct in Early Modern England* (Oxford: Oxford University Press).
Burman, M (2009), 'Evidencing Sexual Assault: Women in the Witness Box' *Probation Journal*, 56: 1–20.
Burns, JH (1967), *The Fabric of Felicity: The Legislator and the Human Condition* (London: UCL).
Cairns, DJA (2005), *Advocacy and the Making of the Adversarial Criminal Trial* (Oxford: Oxford University Press).
Cairns, JW (1988), 'John Millar's Lectures on Scots Criminal Law' *Oxford Journal of Legal Studies*, 12: 364–400.
Calasso, R (1994), *The Marriage of Cadmus and Harmony* (London: Vintage).
Cameron, I, Thunberg, M, Pale-Bartes, K, Wong, C, & Asp, P (2011), *International Criminal Law from a Swedish Perspective* (Cambridge: Intersentia).
Campbell, L (2014), 'Organised Crime and the Criminal Justice and Licensing (Scotland) Act 2010' *Edinburgh Law Review*, 18: 225–44.
Cane, P (2002), *Responsibility in Law and Morality* (Oxford: Hart Publishing).
Cane, P (2007), 'The General/Special Distinction in Criminal Law, Tort Law and Legal Theory' *Law and Philosophy*, 26: 465–500.
Carlyle, EI (2004), 'Archbold, John Frederick (1785–1870)', rev M Lobban in *Oxford Dictionary of National Biography* (Oxford: Oxford University Press) [www.oxforddnb.com/view/article/614, accessed 2 October 2010].
Chalmers, J (2014), 'Offences Against the Person' in MD Dubber & T Hörnle (eds), *The Oxford Handbook of Criminal Law* (Oxford: Oxford University Press) pp.727–46.
Chalmers, J & Leverick, F (2008), 'Fair Labelling in Criminal Law' *Modern Law Review* 71: 217–46.
Chalmers, J & Leverick, F (2013), 'Tracking the Creation of Criminal Offences' *Criminal Law Review*, 543–60.
Chalmers, J & Leverick, F (2014), 'Quantifying Criminalization' in RA Duff, L Farmer, SE Marshall, M Renzo, & V Tadros (eds), *Criminalization. The Political Morality of the Criminal Law* (Oxford: Oxford University Press) pp.54–79.
Chehtman, A (2010), *The Philosophical Foundations of Extraterritorial Punishment* (Oxford: Oxford University Press).
Chiao, V (2013), 'Punishment and Permissibility in the Criminal Law' *Law and Philosophy*, 32: 729–765.
Chitty, J (1816), *A Practical Treatise on the Criminal Law, Comprising the Practice, Pleadings and Evidence which Occur in the Course of Criminal Prosecutions etc.* (4 vols.) (London: Butterworth & Son).
Christie, N (1977), 'Conflicts as Property' *British Journal of Criminology*, 17: 1–15.
Clark, A (1987), *Women's Silence, Men's Violence: Sexual Assault in England 1770–1845* (New York: Pandora).
Clark, A (2000), 'Domesticity and the Problem of Wifebeating in Nineteenth-Century Britain: Working Class Culture, Law and Politics' in S d'Cruze, (ed.), *Everyday Violence in Britain. 1850–1950. Gender and Class* (Harlow: Pearson) pp.27–40.
Clark, A (2008), *Desire: A History of European Sexuality* (London: Routledge).
Clarkson, CMV & Keating, HM (1984), *Criminal Law: Text and Materials* (1st edn) (London: Sweet & Maxwell).
Clarkson, CMV (1994), 'Law Commission Report on Offences against the Person and General Principles: (1) Violence and the Law Commission' *Criminal Law Review*, 324–33.
Cobbe, FP (1878), 'Wife Torture in England' *Contemporary Review*, 32: 55–87.

Cockburn, JS (1991), 'Patterns of Violence in English Society: Homicide in Kent 1560–1985' *Past and Present*, 130: 70–106.

Cocks, HG (2006), 'Modernity and the Self in the History of Sexuality' *Historical Journal*, 49: 1211–27.

Cocks, HG (2013), 'Approaches to the History of Sexuality since 1750' in S Toulalan & K Fisher (eds), *The Routledge History of Sex and the Body, 1500 to the Present* (London: Routledge) pp.38–54.

Cocks, R (2004), 'Cox, Edward William (1809–1879)' in *Oxford Dictionary of National Biography* (Oxford: Oxford University Press) [http://www.oxforddnb.com.ezproxy.lib.gla.ac.uk/view/article/6522, accessed 14 June 2015].

Coke, E (2003), *The Selected Writings of Sir Edward Coke Vol. II Institutes* (S Sheppard ed.) (Indianapolis: Liberty Fund).

Collett, P (1977), 'The Rules of Social Conduct' in P Collett (ed.), *Social Rules and Social Behaviour* (Oxford: Blackwell) pp.1–27.

Collini, S (1991), *Public Moralists. Political Thought and Intellectual Life in Britain 1850–1930* (Oxford: Clarendon).

Colquhoun, P (1806), *A Treatise on the Police of the Metropolis* (7th edn) (London: Joseph Mawman).

Conley, C (1986), 'Rape and Justice in Victorian England' *Victorian Studies*, 29: 519–36.

Conley, C (1991), *The Unwritten Law. Criminal Justice in Victorian Kent* (Oxford: Oxford University Press).

Conley, JA (1985), 'Doing it by the Book: Justice of the Peace Manuals and English Law in Eighteenth-Century America' *Journal of Legal History*, 6: 257–98.

Cornell, D (1995), *The Imaginary Domain: Abortion, Pornography, and Sexual Harassment* (New York: Routledge).

Cornish, W (2010), 'Sources of Law' in W Cornish et al., *The Oxford History of the Laws of England Vol.XI 1820–1914 English Legal System* (Oxford: Oxford University Press) pp.41–71.

Coughlin, A (1998), 'Sex and Guilt' *Virginia Law Review*, 84, 1–46.

Cover, R (1983), 'Nomos and Narrative' *Harvard Law Review*, 97: 4–68.

Cover, R (1984), 'Folktales of Justice: Tales of Jurisdiction' *Capital University Law Review*, 14: 179–203.

Cowan, S (2007), 'Freedom and Capacity to Make a Choice. A Feminist Analysis of Consent in the Criminal Law of Rape' in VE Munro & CF Stychin (eds), *Sexuality and the Law. Feminist Engagements* (London: Glasshouse) pp.51–72.

Cowan, S (2011), 'Criminalising SM: Disavowing the Erotic, Instantiating Violence' in RA Duff, L Farmer, SE Marshall, M Renzo, & V Tadros (eds), *The Structures of Criminal Law* (Oxford: Oxford University Press) pp.59–84.

Cox, E (1877), *The Principles of Punishment as Applied in the Administration of the Law by Judges and Magistrates* (London: Law Times).

Criminal Law Commissioners (1834), *First Report* (London: HMSO).

Criminal Law Commissioners (1836), *Second Report* (London: HMSO).

Criminal Law Commissioners (1839), *Fourth Report* (London: HMSO).

Criminal Law Commissioners (1840), *Fifth Report* (London: HMSO).

Criminal Law Commissioners (1843), *Seventh Report* (London: HMSO).

Criminal Law Revision Committee (1959), *First Report. Indecency with Children* (Cmnd.835) (London: HMSO).

Criminal Law Revision Committee (1965), *Seventh Report. Felonies and Misdemeanours* (Cmnd.2659) (London: HMSO).

Criminal Law Revision Committee (1966), *Eighth Report. Theft and Related Offences* (Cmnd.2977) (London: HMSO).

Criminal Law Revision Committee (1980), *Fourteenth Report. Offences against the Person* (Cmnd.7844) (London: HMSO).

Criminal Law Revision Committee (1980), *Working Paper on Sexual Offences* (London: HMSO).

Criminal Law Revision Committee (1984), *Fifteenth Report. Sexual Offences* (Cmnd. 9213) (London: HMSO).

Crompton, L (1978), 'Jeremy Bentham's Essay on Pederasty' *Journal of Homosexuality*, 3: 383–405.

Cross, R & Jones, A (1948), *An Introduction to Criminal Law* (London: Butterworths).

Crown Prosecution Service Guidelines on Prosecuting Communications sent via social media (2012), http://www.cps.gov.uk/consultations/social_media_consultation.pdf (19 December 2012).

d'Cruze, S (1998), *Crimes of Outrage. Sex, Violence and Victorian Working Women* (London: University College London Press).

d'Cruze, S. (2000), 'Unguarded Passions: Violence, History and the Everyday' in S d'Cruze (ed.), *Everyday Violence in Britain. 1850–1950. Gender and Class* (Harlow: Pearson) pp.1–26.

d'Cruze, S. (2013), 'Sexual Violence since 1750' in S Toulalan & K Fisher (eds), *The Routledge History of Sex and the Body, 1500 to the Present* (London: Routledge) pp.444–60.

Dabhoiwala, F (2012), *The Origins of Sex. A History of the First Sexual Revolution* (London: Allen Lane).

Dahrendorf, R (1985) *Law and Order* (London: Stevens).

Dan-Cohen, M (2002), *Harmful Thoughts. Essays on Law, Self and Morality* (Princeton: Princeton University Press).

Davis, J (1980) 'The London Garotting Panic of 1862: A Moral Panic and the Creation of a Criminal Class in mid-Victorian England' in VAC Gatrell, B Lenman, & G Parker (eds), *Crime and the Law. The Social History of Crime in Western Europe since 1500* (London: Europa) pp.190–213.

Davis, JE (1861), *The Criminal Law Consolidation Statutes of 24 & 25 Victoria Chapters 94 to 100* (London: Butterworths).

DeGirolami, M (2012), 'James Fitzjames Stephen: The Punishment Jurist' in MD Dubber (ed.), *Foundational Texts in Modern Criminal Law* (Oxford: Oxford University Press) pp.183–98.

Deleuze, G (1986), *Foucault* (Minneapolis: University of Minnesota Press).

Dempsey, MM (2009), *Prosecuting Domestic Violence. A Philosophical Analysis* (Oxford: Oxford University Press).

Dennis, I (1997), 'The Critical Condition of Criminal Law' *Current Legal Problems*, 50: 213–49.

Devereux, C (2000), 'The "Maiden Tribute" and the Rise of the White Slave in the Nineteenth Century: The Making of an Imperial Construct' *Victorian Review*, 26: 1–23.

Devlin, P (1965), *The Enforcement of Morals* (Oxford: Oxford University Press).

Dimock, S (2014), 'Contractarian Criminal Law Theory and *Mala Prohibita* Offences' in RA Duff, L Farmer, SE Marshall, M Renzo, & V Tadros (eds), *Criminalization. The Political Morality of the Criminal Law* (Oxford: Oxford University Press).

Dinwiddy, J (2003), *Bentham. Selected Writings of John Dinwiddy* (Stanford: Stanford University Press).

Dobash, RE & Dobash, RP (1992), *Women, Violence and Social Change* (London: Routledge).

Doggett, ME (1992), *Marriage, Wife-Beating and the Law in Victorian England* (London: Weidenfeld and Nicolson).

Douglas, M (1987), *How Institutions Think* (London: Routledge).

Douzinas, C (2007), 'The Metaphysics of Jurisdiction' in S McVeigh (ed.), *Jurisprudence of Jurisdiction* (London: Routledge-Cavendish) pp. 21–32.

Downes, D & Morgan, R (2012), 'Overtaking on the Left: The Politics of Law and Order in the "Big Society"' in *Oxford Handbook of Criminology* (5th edn) (Oxford: Oxford University Press).

Dubber, MD (2001), 'Policing Possession: The War on Crime and the End of the Criminal Law' *Journal of Criminal Law and Criminology*, 91: 829–996.

Dubber, MD (2002), *Victims in the War Against Crime. The Use and Abuse of Victims' Rights* (New York: NYU Press).

Dubber, MD (2006), 'Theories of Crime and Punishment in German Criminal Law' *American Journal of Comparative Law*, 53: 679–707.

Dubber, MD (2007), *The Police Power. Patriarchy and the Foundations of American Government* (New York: Columbia University Press).

Dubber, MD (2010), 'Criminal Law between Public and Private Law' in RA Duff, L Farmer, SE Marshall, M Renzo, & V Tadros (eds), *The Boundaries of the Criminal Law* (Oxford: Oxford University Press) pp.191–213.

Dubber, MD (2013), 'Criminal Jurisdiction and Conceptions of Penality in Comparative Perspective' *University of Toronto Law Journal*, 63: 247–77.

Dubber, MD (2013), 'The Legality Principle in American and German Criminal Law: An Essay in Comparative Legal History' in G Martyn, A Musson, & H Pihlajamaki, (eds), *From the Judge's Arbitrium to the Legality Principle: Legislation as a Source of Law in Criminal Trials* (Berlin: Duncker & Humboldt) pp.365–86.

Dubber, MD & Valverde, M (eds) (2006), *The New Police Science. The Police Power in Domestic and International Governance* (Stanford: Stanford University Press).

Dubber, MD & Valverde, M (eds) (2008), *Police and the Liberal State* (Stanford: Stanford University Press).

Duff, RA (2007), *Answering for Crime. Responsibility and Liability in the Criminal Law* (Oxford: Hart Publishing).

Duff, RA (2010), 'Perversions and Subversions of the Criminal Law' in RA Duff, L Farmer, SE Marshall, M Renzo, & V Tadros (eds), *The Boundaries of the Criminal Law* (Oxford: Oxford University Press) pp.88–112.

Duff, RA (2011), 'Responsibility, Citizenship and Criminal Law' in RA Duff & SP Green (eds), *Philosophical Foundations of Criminal Law* (Oxford: Oxford University Press) pp.125–48.

Duff, RA (2014), 'Towards a Modest Legal Moralism' *Criminal Law and Philosophy*, 8: 217–235.

Duff, RA & Marshall, SE (2010), 'Public and Private Wrongs' in J Chalmers, F Leverick, & L Farmer (eds), *Essays in Criminal Law in Honour of Sir Gerald Gordon* (Edinburgh: Edinburgh University Press) pp.70–85.

Duff, RA, Farmer, L, Marshall, SE, Renzo, M, & Tadros, V (2010), 'Introduction: The Boundaries of the Criminal Law' in RA Duff, L Farmer, SE Marshall, M Renzo, &

V Tadros (eds), *The Boundaries of the Criminal Law* (Oxford: Oxford University Press) pp.1–26.

Duff, RA, Farmer, L, Marshall, SE, Renzo, M, & Tadros, V (2014), 'Introduction: Towards a Theory of Criminalization?' in RA Duff, L Farmer, SE Marshall, M Renzo, & V Tadros (eds), *Criminalization. The Political Morality of the Criminal Law.* (Oxford: Oxford University Press) pp.1–53.

Dunn, J (1988), 'Trust and Political Agency' in D Gambetta (ed.), *Trust. Making and Breaking Cooperative Relations* (Oxford: Basil Blackwell) pp.73–93.

Durkheim, E (1973), 'Two Laws of Penal Evolution' *Economy and Society,* 2: 285–308.

Durkheim, E (1984), *The Division of Labour in Society* (London: Macmillan).

East, EH (1803), *A Treatise of the Pleas of the Crown* (2 vols) (London: J Butterworth).

East, WN (1949), *Society and the Criminal* (London: HMSO).

East, WN (1955), *Sexual Offenders* (London: Delisle).

Eden, W (1775), *Principles of Penal Law* (3rd edn) (London: B White & T Cadell).

Edwards, J Ll J (1953), 'The Prevention of Crime Act 1953' *Modern Law Review,* 16: 482.

Edwards, J Ll J (1955), *Mens Rea in Statutory Offences* (London: Macmillan).

Edwards, LF (2009), *The People and Their Peace. Legal Culture and the Transformation of Inequality in the Post-Revolutionary South* (Chapel Hill, NC: University of NC Press).

Eigen, JP (2003), *Unconscious Crime. Mental Absence and Criminal Responsibility in Victorian London* (Baltimore: Johns Hopkins University Press).

Eisner, M (2001), 'Modernization, Self-Control and Lethal Violence. The Long-Term Dynamics of European Homicide Rates in Theoretical Perspective' *British Journal of Criminology*, 41: 618–38.

Elias, N (1994), *The Civilizing Process* (Oxford: Blackwell).

Elliott, CS & de Than, C (2007), 'The Case for Rational Reconstruction of Consent in Criminal Law' *Modern Law Review*, 70: 225–49.

Elliott, DW & Wood, JC (1963), *A Casebook on Criminal Law* (London: Sweet & Maxwell).

Elliott, I (1977), 'Theft and Related Problems—England, Australia and the USA Compared' *International and Comparative Law Quarterly,* 26: 110–49.

Emsley, C (1993), '"Mother, what did policemen do when there weren't any motors?" The Law, the Police and the Regulation of Motor Traffic in England, 1900–1939' *Historical Journal*, 36: 357–81.

Emsley, C (2005), *Crime and Society in England 1750–1900* (3rd edn) (Harlow: Pearson).

Evans, DM (1859), *Facts, Failures and Frauds. Revelations, Financial, Mercantile, Criminal* (London: Groombridge & Sons).

Farmer, L (1996), 'The Obsession with Definition: The Nature of Crime and Critical Legal Theory' *Social and Legal Studies*, 5: 57–73.

Farmer, L (1997), *Criminal Law, Tradition and Legal Order. Crime and the 'Genius' of Scots Law, 1747 to the Present* (Cambridge: Cambridge University Press).

Farmer, L (2000), 'Reconstructing the English Codification Debate: the Criminal Law Commissioners 1833–45' *Law and History Review*, 18: 397–425.

Farmer, L (2006), 'The Jurisprudence of Security. The Police Power and the Criminal Law' in MD Dubber & M Valverde (eds), *The New Police Science* (Stanford: Stanford University Press) pp.145–67.

Farmer, L (2007), 'Criminal Responsibility and the Proof of Guilt' in MD Dubber & L Farmer (eds), *Modern Histories of Crime and Punishment* (Stanford: Stanford University Press) pp.42–65.

Farmer, L (2010), 'Criminal Wrongs in Historical Perspective' in RA Duff, L Farmer, SE Marshall, M Renzo, & V Tadros (eds), *The Boundaries of the Criminal Law* (Oxford: Oxford University Press) pp.214–37.

Farmer, L (2012), 'On Treatises and Textbooks. The Literature of the Criminal Law in Nineteenth-Century Britain' in MD Dubber & A Fernandez (eds), *Law Books in Action. Essays on the Anglo-American Legal Treatise* (Abingdon: Hart Publishing) pp.145–64.

Farmer, L (2013), 'Territorial Jurisdiction and Criminalization' *University of Toronto Law Journal*, 63: 225–46.

Farmer, L (2014), 'Codification' in MD Dubber & T Hörnle (eds), *Oxford Handbook of Criminal Law* (Oxford: Oxford University Press) pp.379–99.

Farmer, L (2014), 'Criminal Law as a Security Project' *Criminology and Criminal Justice*, 14: 399–404.

Farmer, L (2014), 'The Modest Ambition of Glanville Williams' in MD Dubber (ed.), *Foundational Texts in Modern Criminal Law* (Oxford: Oxford University Press) pp.263–77.

Farrell, G, Tilley, N, Tseloni, A, & Mailley, J (2010), 'Explaining and Sustaining the Crime Drop: Clarifying the Role of Opportunity Related Theories' *Crime Prevention and Community Safety*, 12: 24–41.

Febvre, L (1973), 'Civilisation: Evolution of a Word and a Group of Ideas' in P Burke (ed.), *A New Kind of History. From the Writings of Febvre* (London: Routledge) pp.219–57.

Feinberg, J (1984), *Harm to Others. The Moral Limits of the Criminal Law*, Vol.1 (Oxford: Oxford University Press).

Feinberg, J (1985), *Offense to Others. The Moral Limits of the Criminal Law*, Vol.2 (Oxford: Oxford University Press).

Feinberg, J (1986), *Harm to Self. The Moral Limits of the Criminal Law*, Vol.3 (Oxford: Oxford University Press).

Feinberg, J (1988), *Harmless Wrongdoing. The Moral Limits of the Criminal Law*, Vol.4 (Oxford: Oxford University Press).

Ferguson, A (1767), *An Essay on the History of Civil Society* (Edinburgh: Edinburgh University Press).

Ferguson, A (1792), *Principles of Moral and Political Science* (Edinburgh: W Creech).

Ferris, G (1998), 'The Origins of Larceny by a Trick and Constructive Possession' *Criminal Law Review*, 175–88.

Ferris, G (2005), 'Larceny: Debating the "Boundless Region of Dishonesty"' in J Rowbotham & K Stevenson (eds), *Criminal Conversations. Victorian Crimes, Social Panic, and Moral Outrage* (Columbus: Ohio State) pp.70–86.

Fielding, H (1751), *An Enquiry into the Causes of the Late Increase of Robbers* (2nd edn) (London: A Millar).

Fielding, J (1755), *A Plan for Preventing Robberies* (London: A Millar).

Fielding, N (2006), *Courting Violence. Offences against the Person Cases in Court* (Oxford: Oxford University Press).

Finch, E (2002), 'Stalking: A Violent Crime or a Crime of Violence?' *Howard Journal of Criminal Justice*, 41: 422–33.

Finch, E (2003), 'What a Tangled Web We Weave: Identity Theft and the Internet' in Y Jewkes (ed.), *Dot.Cons. Crime, Deviance, and Identity on the Internet* (Cullompton: Willan) pp.86–104.

Finn, M (2003), *The Character of Credit. Personal Debt in English Culture, 1740–1914*, (Cambridge: Cambridge University Press).

Fitzgerald, PJ (1960), 'A Concept of Crimc' *Criminal Law Review*, 257–62.

Fitzgerald, PJ (1962), *Criminal Law and Punishment* (Oxford: Clarendon).
Flanders, J (2011), *The Invention of Murder. How the Victorians Revelled in Death and Detection and Created Modern Crime* (London: Harper Press).
Fletcher, GP (1976), 'The Metamorphosis of Larceny' *Harvard Law Review*, 89: 469–530.
Fletcher, GP (1978), *Rethinking Criminal Law* (Boston, MA: Little, Brown & Co).
Fletcher, GP (1980), 'Manifest Criminality, Criminal Intent and the Metamorphosis of Lloyd Weinreb' *Yale Law Journal*, 90: 319–48.
Fletcher, GP (2007), *The Grammar of Criminal Law. American, Comparative, and International* (Oxford: Oxford University Press).
Ford, RT (1999), 'Law's Territory (A History of Jurisdiction)' *Michigan Law Review*, 97: 843–930.
Forrester, J (1986), 'Rape, Seduction and Psychoanalysis' in R Porter & S Tomaselli (eds), *Rape. An Historical and Cultural Enquiry* (Oxford: Blackwell) pp.57–83.
Foster, M (1792), *Crown Law* (3rd edn, M Dodson ed.) (London: E & R Brooke).
Foucault, M (1977), *Discipline and Punish: The Birth of the Prison* (Harmondsworth: Penguin).
Foucault, M (1978), *The History of Sexuality.* I *The Will to Pleasure* (Harmondsworth: Penguin).
Foucault, M (2000), 'Governmentality' in J Faubion (ed.), *Essential Works of Michel Foucault.* Vol.3 *Power* (New York: The New Press) pp.201–22.
Foucault, M (2000), 'Truth and Juridical Forms' in J Faubion (ed.), *Essential Works of Foucault.* Vol.3 *Power* (New York: The New Press) pp.1–89.
Foucault, M (2008), *The Birth of Biopolitics. Lectures at the College De France 1978–9* (London: Palgrave Macmillan).
Frank, DJ, Camp, BJ, & Boutcher, SA (2010), 'Worldwide Trends in the Criminal Regulation of Sex, 1945–2005' *American Sociological Review*, 75: 867–93.
Freud, S (1962), *Civilization and Its Discontents* (New York: Norton).
Friedland, M (1981), 'RS Wright's Model Criminal Code: A Forgotten Chapter in the History of the Criminal Law' *Oxford Journal of Legal Studies*, 1: 307–46.
Fuller, LL (1930), 'Legal Fictions' *Illinois Law Review*, 25: 363–99.
Fuller, LL (1969), *The Morality of Law* (Revised Edition) (New Haven: Yale University Press).
Gallanis, TP (2010), 'Making Sense of Blackstone's Puzzle: Why Forbid Defense Counsel?' *Studies in Law, Politics and Society*, 53: 35–57.
Gardner, J (1994), 'Rationality and the Rule of Law in Offences Against the Person' *Cambridge Law Journal*, 53: 502–23.
Gardner, J (1998), 'On the General Part of the Criminal Law' in RA Duff (ed.), *Philosophy and the Criminal Law* (Cambridge: Cambridge University Press) pp.205–56.
Gardner, J (2003), 'The Mark of Responsibility' *Oxford Journal of Legal Studies*, 23: 157–71.
Gardner, J (2012), 'Ashworth on Principles' in L Zedner & JV Roberts (eds), *Principles and Values in Criminal Law and Criminal Justice. Essays in Honour of Andrew Ashworth* (Oxford: Oxford University Press) pp.3–18.
Gardner, J & Shute, S (2000), 'The Wrongness of Rape' in J Horder (ed.), *Oxford Essays in Jurisprudence. Fourth Series* (Oxford: Oxford University Press) pp.193–217.
Gardner, S (1992), 'Reiterating the Criminal Code' *Modern Law Review*, 55: 839–47.
Gardner, S (1998), 'Property and Theft' *Criminal Law Review*, 35–43.
Gardner, S & de Búrca, G (1990), 'The Codification of the Criminal Law' *Oxford Journal of Legal Studies*, 10: 559–71.
Garland, D (1985), *Punishment and Welfare. A History of Penal Strategies* (Aldershot: Gower).
Garland, D (1990), *Punishment and Modern Society* (Oxford: Clarendon).

Garland, D (1996), 'The Limits of the Sovereign State: Strategies of Crime Control in Contemporary Society' *British Journal of Criminology*, 36: 445–71.

Garland, D (2001), *The Culture of Control. Crime and Social Order in Contemporary Society* (Oxford: Oxford University Press).

Garland, D & Young, P (eds) (1983), *The Power to Punish. Contemporary Penality and Social Analysis* (London: Heinemann Educational Books).

Gatrell, VAC (1980), 'The Decline of Theft and Violence in Victorian and Edwardian England' in VAC Gatrell, B Lenman, & G Parker (eds), *Crime and the Law. The Social History of Crime in Western Europe since 1500* (London: Europa) pp.238–370.

Gatrell, VAC (1990), 'Crime, Authority and the Policeman-State' in FML Thompson (ed.), *The Cambridge Social History of Britain 1750–1950* (Cambridge: Cambridge University Press) Vol.III, pp. 243–310.

Gatrell, VAC (1996), *The Hanging Tree. Execution and the English People, 1770–1868* (Oxford: Oxford University Press).

Geach, N & Haralambous, N (2009), 'Regulating Harassment—Is the Law Fit for the Social Networking Age?' *Journal of Criminal Law*, 73: 241–57.

Gellner, E (1988), 'Trust, Cohesion and the Social Order' in D Gambetta (ed.), *Trust. Making and Breaking Cooperative Relations* (Oxford: Basil Blackwell) pp.142–57.

Giddens, A (1984), *The Constitution of Society. Outline of the Theory of Structuration* (Cambridge: Polity Press).

Giddens, A (1991), *Modernity and Self-Identity. Self and Society in the Late Modern Age* (Cambridge: Polity).

Gleeson, K (2005), 'Sex, Wives and Prostitutes: Debating Clarence' in J Rowbotham & K Stevenson (eds), *Criminal Conversations. Victorian Crimes, Social Panic, and Moral Outrage* (Columbus, OH: Ohio State) pp.215–31.

Gluckmann, M (1955), 'The Peace in the Feud' *Past and Present*, 8: 1–14.

Godfrey, B (1999), 'Law, Factory Discipline and Theft: The Impact of the Factory on Workplace Appropriation in Mid- to Late-Nineteenth Century Yorkshire' *British Journal of Criminology*, 39: 56–71.

Godfrey, B (2008), 'Changing Prosecution Practices and their Impact on Crime Figures in England and Wales, 1857–1940' *British Journal of Criminology*, 48: 171–89.

Godfrey, B, Cox, D, & Farrall, S (2010), *Serious Offenders. A Historical Study of Habitual Criminals* (Oxford: Oxford University Press).

Goffman, E (1959), *The Presentation of Self in Everyday Life* (Harmondsworth: Penguin).

Goodhart, AL (1959), 'The Obsolescent Law of Larceny' *Washington and Lee Law Review*, 16: 42–4.

Goodhart, AL (2004), 'Kenny, Courtney Stanhope (1847–1930)' (rev. Richard A Cosgrove) in *Oxford Dictionary of National Biography* (Oxford: Oxford University Press) [www.oxforddnb.com/view/article/34287, accessed 9 October 2010].

Goodrich, P (1986), *Reading the Law. A Critical Introduction to Legal Method* (Oxford: Blackwell).

Gordon, GH (1967), *The Criminal Law of Scotland* (Edinburgh: W Green & Son).

Gorham, D (1978), '"The Maiden Tribute of Modern Babylon" Re-Examined: Child Prostitution and the Idea of Childhood in Late Victorian England' *Victorian Studies*, 21: 353–79.

Gray, D (2007), 'Settling Their Differences: The Nature of Assault and its Prosecution in the City of London in the Late Eighteenth and Early Nineteenth Centuries' in K Watson (ed.), *Assaulting the Past: Violence and Civilization in Historical Context* (Cambridge: Cambridge Scholars Publishing) pp.141–59.

Greaves, CS (1862), *The Criminal Law Consolidation and Amendment Acts* (2nd edn) (London: Stevens Sons & Haynes).

Greaves, CS (1888), 'Note on Rape' in H Taschereau, *The Criminal Statute Law of the Dominion of Canada* (Toronto: Carswell) Appendix.

Green, SP (2006), *Lying, Cheating and Stealing: A Moral Theory of White Collar Crime* (Oxford: Oxford University Press).

Green, SP (2012), *13 Ways to Steal a Bicycle. Theft Law in the Information Age* (Cambridge, MA: Harvard University Press).

Green, TA (2014), *Freedom and Criminal Responsibility in American Legal Thought* (New York: Cambridge University Press).

Green, TA (2015), 'The Jury and Criminal Responsibility in Anglo-American History' *Criminal Law and Philosophy*, 9: 423–42.

Haag, P (1999), *Consent. Sexual Rights and the Transformation of American Liberalism* (Cornell: Cornell University Press).

Hacking, I (1991), 'The Making and Molding of Child Abuse' *Critical Inquiry*, 17: 253–88.

Hale, M (1800), *Historia Placitorum Coronæ: The History of the Pleas of the Crown, by Sir Matthew Hale. Published from the Original Manuscripts by Sollom Emlyn. With Additional Notes and References to Modern Cases Concerning the Pleas of the Crown. By George Wilson. A New Edition And an Abridgment of the Statutes Relating to Felonies Continued to the Present Time, with Notes and References, by Thomas Dogherty* (London: Printed by E. Rider, Little-Britain, for Payne, T, and Gardner, HL and Otridge, W and Brooke, R and Rider, J and Butterworth, J and Clarke, W and Pheney, R and Cuthell, J, and Walker, J and Bagster, J and Bickerstaff, R).

Hall Williams, JE (1958), 'Reform of the Law of Larceny: An Urgent Task' *Modern Law Review*, 21: 43–7.

Hall Williams, JE (1960), 'Sex Offenses: The British Experience' *Law and Contemporary Problems*, 25: 334–60.

Hall, J (1952), *Theft, Law and Society* (2nd edn) (1st edn 1935) (Indianapolis: Bobbs-Merrill).

Hall, J (1947) *General Principles of Criminal Law* (Bloomington, Indiana: Bobbs Merrill) (2nd edn 1960).

Hall, JA (2013), *The Importance of Being Civil. The Struggle for Political Decency* (Princeton, NJ: Princeton University Press).

Halpin, A (2004), *Definition in the Criminal Law* (Oxford: Hart Publishing).

Halsall, G (1998), *Violence and Society in the Early Medieval West* (Woodbridge: Boydell Press).

Halttunen, K (1998), *Murder Most Foul. The Killer and the American Gothic Imagination* (Cambridge, MA: Harvard University Press).

Halvorsen, V (2014), 'Nils Christie: "Conflicts as Property"' in MD Dubber (ed.), *Foundational Texts in Modern Criminal Law* (Oxford: Oxford University Press) pp.335–52.

Hamburger, J (2001), *John Stuart Mill on Liberty and Control* (Princeton: Princeton University Press).

Hammerton, AJ (1992), *Cruelty and Companionship. Conflict in Nineteenth-Century Married Life* (London: Routledge).

Handler, P (2007), 'The Law of Felonious Assault in England, 1803–61' *Journal of Legal History*, 28: 183–206.

Handler, P (2011), 'The Court for Crown Cases Reserved, 1848–1908' *Law and History Review*, 29: 259–88.

Handler, P (2013), 'Intoxication and Criminal Responsibility in England, 1819–1920' *Oxford Journal of Legal Studies*, 33: 243–62.

Harcourt, BE (1999), 'The Collapse of the Harm Principle' *Journal of Criminal Law and Criminology*, 90: 109–94.

Harcourt, BE (2014), 'Beccaria's *On Crimes and Punishments*: A Mirror on the History of the Foundations of Modern Criminal Law' in MD Dubber (ed.), *Foundational Texts in Modern Criminal Law* (Oxford: Oxford University Press) pp.39–60.

Harris, J (1980), *Violence and Responsibility* (London: Routledge & Kegan Paul).

Harrison, B (1994), *Drink and the Victorians. The Temperance Question in England 1815–1872* (revd edn) (Keele: Keele University Press).

Hart, HM (1958), 'The Aims of the Criminal Law' *Law and Contemporary Problems*, 23: 401–41.

Hart, HLA (1961), *The Concept of Law* (Oxford: Clarendon).

Hart, HLA (1963), *Law, Liberty and Morality* (Oxford: Oxford University Press).

Hart, HLA (1968), *Punishment and Responsibility* (Oxford: Clarendon).

Hart, HLA (1982), *Essays on Bentham: Jurisprudence and Political Theory* (Oxford: Clarendon).

Hart, HLA (1983), 'Definition and Theory in Jurisprudence' in *Essays in Jurisprudence and Philosophy* (Oxford: Clarendon).

Harvey, AD (1978), 'Prosecutions for Sodomy in England at the Beginning of the Nineteenth Century' *The Historical Journal*, 21: 939–48.

Hawkins, W (1716–21), *Treatise of Pleas of the Crown: or a system of the principal matters related to that subject, divided under the proper heads* (2 vols) (London: n.p.).

Hay, D (1975), 'Property, Authority and the Criminal Law' in D Hay, P Linebaugh, JC Rule, EP Thompson, & C Winslow (eds), *Albion's Fatal Tree. Crime and Society in Eighteenth-Century England* (London: Allen Lane) pp.17–63.

Hay, D, Linebaugh P, Rule, JC, Thompson, EP, & Winslow C (eds) (1975), *Albion's Fatal Tree. Crime and Society in Eighteenth-Century England* (London: Allen Lane).

Hay, D & Snyder, F (1989), 'Using the Criminal Law, 1750–1850. *Policing, Private Prosecution and the State' in D Hay & F Snyder (eds), Policing and Prosecution in Britain 1750–1850* (Oxford: Clarendon) pp.3–52.

Hechter, M & Horne, C (2009), *Theories of Social Order. A Reader* (2nd edn) (Stanford: Stanford University Press).

Heilbron Committee (1975), *Report of the Advisory Group on the Law of Rape* (Cmnd 6352).

Herlin-Karnell, E (2012), 'White-Collar Crime and European Financial Crises: Getting Tough on EU Market Abuse' *European Law Review*, 37: 481–94.

Herring, J (2012), *Criminal Law. Text, Cases and Materials* (5th edn) (Oxford: Oxford University Press).

Herrup, C (1999), *A House in Gross Disorder. Sex, Law and the Second Earl of Castlehaven* (Oxford: Oxford University Press).

Hildebrandt, M (2010), 'The Indeterminacy of an Emergency: Challenges to Criminal Jurisdiction in Constitutional Democracy' *Criminal Law and Philosophy*, 4: 161–81.

Hildebrandt, M (2013), 'Extraterritorial Jurisdiction to Enforce in Cyberspace? Bodin, Schmitt, Grotius in Cyberspace' *University of Toronto Law Journal*, 63: 196–224.

Hildebrandt, M (2014), 'Origins of the Criminal Law: Punitive Interventions before Sovereignty' in MD Dubber (ed.), *Foundational Texts in Modern Criminal Law* (Oxford: Oxford University Press) pp.219–38.

Hillyard, P, Pantazis, C, Tombs, S, & Gordon D (2004), *Beyond Criminology. Taking Harm Seriously* (London: Pluto Press).
von Hirsch, A & Jareborg, N (1991), 'Gauging Criminal Harm: A Living-Standard Approach' *Oxford Journal of Legal Studies,* 11: 1–38.
von Hirsch, A (1993), *Censure and Sanctions* (Oxford: Oxford University Press).
von Hirsch, A & Ashworth, A (2005), *Proportionate Sentencing: Exploring the Principles* (Oxford: Oxford University Press).
von Hirsch, A & Simester, AP (eds) (2006), *Incivilities. Regulating Offensive Behaviour* (Oxford: Hart Publishing).
Hirst, M (2003), *Jurisdiction and the Ambit of the Criminal Law* (Oxford: Oxford University Press).
Hitchcock, T (1997), *English Sexualities 1700–1800* (London: Palgrave).
Hobbes, T (1968), *Leviathan* (Penguin: Harmondsworth).
Hogan, B (1978), 'On Modernising the Law of Sexual Offences' in P Glazebrook (ed.), *Reshaping the Criminal Law* (London: Stevens & Sons).
Holdsworth, WS (1903–72), *History of English Law* (15 Vols) (London: Methuen).
Holmes, OW (1881), *The Common Law* (Boston: Little, Brown and Co).
Holmes, OW (1920), *Collected Legal Papers* (New York: Harcourt, Brace & Co.).
Home Office (1959), *Penal Practice in Changing Society* (Cmnd 645) (London: HMSO).
Home Office (1996), *Review of Extraterritorial Jurisdiction, Steering Committee Report* (London: HMSO).
Home Office (1998), *Violence: Reforming the Offences Against the Person Act 1861* (London: Home Office).
Home Office (1998), *Guide to Racially Aggravated Offences* (London: Home Office).
Home Office (2000), *Setting the Boundaries. Reforming the Law on Sex Offences* (London: HMSO).
Home Office (2002), *Protecting the Public. Strengthening Protection against Sex Offenders and Reforming the Law on Sexual Offences* (Cm.5668) (London: HMSO).
Home Office (2013), *Information for Local Areas on the change to the Definition of Domestic Violence and Abuse,* (March 2013) (https://www.gov.uk/government/uploads/system/uploads/attachment_data/file/142701/guide-on-definition-of-dv.pdf).
Honoré, T (1976), *Sex Law* (London: Duckworth).
Honoré, T (1999), *Responsibility and Fault* (Abingdon: Hart Publishing).
Horder, J (1992), 'The Duel and the English Law of Homicide' *Oxford Journal of Legal Studies,* 12: 419–30.
Horder, J (1994), 'Rethinking Non-Fatal Offences Against the Person' *Oxford Journal of Legal Studies,* 14: 335–51.
Horder, J (1998), 'Reconsidering Psychic Assault' *Criminal Law Review,* 392–403.
Horder, J (2012), *Homicide and the Politics of Law Reform* (Oxford: Oxford University Press).
Horder, J (2014), 'Bureaucratic "Criminal" Law. Too much of a Bad Thing?' in RA Duff, L Farmer, SE Marshall, M Renzo, & V Tadros (eds), *Criminalization. The Political Morality of the Criminal Law* (Oxford: Oxford University Press) pp.101–31.
Hörnle, T (2012), 'PJA von Feuerbach and his Textbook of the Common Penal Law' in MD Dubber (ed.), *Foundational Texts in Modern Criminal Law* (Oxford: Oxford University Press) pp.119–40.
Howard League Working Party (1985), *Unlawful Sex. Offences, Victims and Offenders in the Criminal Justice System of England and Wales* (London: Waterlow Publishing).

Hoyle, C (2000), *Negotiating Domestic Violence. Police, Criminal Justice and Victims* (Oxford: Oxford University Press).
Hume, D (1844), *Commentaries on the Law of Scotland Respecting Crimes* (4th edn, ed. BR Bell) (Edinburgh: Bell & Bradfute).
Hume, D (1978), *A Treatise of Human Nature* (Oxford: Oxford University Press).
Hume, LJ (1981), *Bentham and Bureaucracy* (Cambridge: Cambridge University Press).
Hunt, A (2006), 'Police and the Regulation of Traffic. Policing as a Civilizing Process?' in MD Dubber & M Valverde (eds), *The New Police Science* (Stanford: Stanford University Press) pp.168–84.
Hunt, M (1992), 'Wife Beating, Domesticity and Women's Independence in Eighteenth-Century London' *Gender and History*, 4: 10–33.
Husak, D (2008), *Overcriminalization. The Limits of the Criminal Law* (Oxford: Oxford University Press).
Hyams, P (2003), *Rancor and Reconciliation in Medieval England* (London and Ithaca: Cornell University Press).
Ignatieff, M (1979), *A Just Measure of Pain. The Penitentiary in the Industrial Revolution, 1750–1850* (London: Macmillan).
Jackson, LA (2000), *Child Sexual Abuse in Victorian England* (London: Routledge).
Jackson, RM (1936–8), 'Absolute Prohibition in Statutory Offences' *Cambridge Law Journal*, 6: 83–92.
Jackson, RM (1936–8), 'Common Law Misdemeanors' *Cambridge Law Journal*, 6: 193–201.
Jansen, N (2010), *The Making of Legal Authority. Non-Legislative Codifications in Historical and Comparative Perspective* (Oxford: Oxford University Press).
Jareborg, N (1995), 'What Kind of Criminal Law do We Want?' in A Snare, *Beware of Punishment. On the Utility and Futility of Criminal Law* (Oslo: Pax Forlag).
Jefferson, M (2012), 'Offences against the Person: Into the 21st Century' *Journal of Criminal Law*, 76: 472–92.
Jenkyns, R (1902), *British Rule and Jurisdiction Beyond the Seas* (Oxford: Clarendon).
Johnson, EA & Monkkonen EH (eds) (1996), *The Civilization of Crime. Violence in Town and Country Since the Middle Ages* (Urbana, Ill.: University of Illinois Press).
Joyce, P (2003), *The Rule of Freedom. Liberalism and the Modern City* (London: Verso).
Judicial Statistics (1898), *England and Wales 1896* (C.8755) (London: HMSO).
Kadish, S (1987), 'Codifiers of the Criminal Law: Wechsler's Predecessors' in *Blame and Punishment. Essays in the Criminal Law* (London: Macmillan).
Kelley, D (1990), *The Human Measure. Social Thought in the Western Legal Tradition* (Cambridge, MA: Harvard University Press).
Kelly, L (2001), *Routes to Injustice: A Research Review on the Reporting, Investigation and Prosecution of Rape Cases* (London: CPSI).
Kelly, L, Coy, M, & Davenport, R (2009), *Shifting Sands. A Comparison of Prostitution Regimes* (http://www.turnofftheredlight.ie/wp-content/uploads/2011/02/Shifting_Sands_UK-HOMe-Office.pdf).
Kenny, CS (1901), *A Selection of Cases Illustrative of Criminal Law* (Cambridge: Cambridge University Press).
Kenny, CS (1902), *Outlines of Criminal Law* (Cambridge: Cambridge University Press).
Kenny, CS (1916), 'The Case Method of Teaching Law' *Journal of the Society of Comparative Legislation*, 16: 182–94.
Kenny, CS (1936), *Outlines of Criminal Law* (15th edn, ed. GG Phillips) (Cambridge University Press).

Kimball, B (2006), 'The Proliferation of Case Method Teaching in American Law Schools: Mr Langdell's "Emblematic Abomination" 1890–1915' *History of Education Quarterly*, 46: 192–247.

King, P (1996), 'Punishing Assault: The Transformation of Attitudes in the English Courts' *Journal of Interdisciplinary History*, 27: 43–74.

King, P (2000), *Crime, Justice and Discretion in England, 1740–1820* (Oxford: Oxford University Press).

Klerman, D (2009), 'Legal Fictions as Strategic Instruments' [http://escholarship.org/uc/item/8zv9k24m, accessed 15 May 2015].

Knop, K, Michaels, R, & Riles, A (2012), 'From Multiculturalism to Technique: Feminism, Culture and the Conflict of Laws Style' *Stanford Law Review*, 64: 589–656.

Kolsky, E (2005), 'Codification and the Rule of Colonial Difference: Criminal Procedure in British India' *Law and History Review*, 23: 631–83.

Kostal, RW (2005), *A Jurisprudence of Power. Victorian Empire and the Rule of Law* (Oxford: Oxford University Press).

van Krieken, R (1989), 'Violence, Self-Discipline and Modernity: Beyond the "Civilizing Process"' *Sociological Review*, 37: 193–218.

Kutz, C (2004), 'Responsibility' in J Coleman, K Himma, & S Shapiro (eds), *The Oxford Handbook of Jurisprudence and Philosophy of Law* (Oxford: Oxford University Press) pp.549–87.

Lacey, N (1993), 'A Clear Concept of Intention: Elusive or Illusory?' *Modern Law Review*, 56: 621–42.

Lacey, N (1995), 'Contingency and Criminalization' in I Loveland (ed.), *Frontiers of Criminality* (London: Sweet & Maxwell) pp.1–27.

Lacey, N (1998), 'Contingency, Coherence and Conceptualism: Reflections on the Encounter between 'Critique' and the 'Philosophy of Criminal Law'' in RA Duff (ed.), *Philosophy and the Criminal Law* (Cambridge: Cambridge University Press) pp.9–59.

Lacey, N (2001), 'Beset by Boundaries: The Home Office Review of Sex Offences' *Criminal Law Review*, 3–14.

Lacey, N (2001), 'In Search of the Responsible Subject: History, Philosophy and the Social Sciences in Criminal Law Theory' *Modern Law Review*, 64: 350–71.

Lacey, N (2001), 'Responsibility and Modernity in Criminal Law' *Journal of Political Philosophy*, 9: 249–76.

Lacey, N (2004), *A Life of HLA Hart. The Nightmare and the Noble Dream* (Oxford: Oxford University Press).

Lacey, N (2008), *The Prisoners' Dilemma. Political Economy and Punishment in Modern Society* (Cambridge: Cambridge University Press).

Lacey, N (2008), *Women, Crime and Character. From Moll Flanders to Tess of the d'Urbevilles* (Oxford: Oxford University Press).

Lacey, N (2009), 'Historicising Criminalisation: Conceptual and Empirical Issues' *Modern Law Review*, 72: 936–60.

Lacey, N (2010), 'Psychologising Jekyll, Demonising Hyde: the strange case of criminal responsibility' *Criminal Law and Philosophy*, 4: 109–33.

Lacey, N (2011), 'The Resurgence of Character: Responsibility in the Context of Criminalization' in RA Duff & SP Green (eds), *Philosophical Foundations of Criminal* Law (Oxford: Oxford University Press) pp.151–78.

Lacey, N (2012), 'Principles, Policies, and Politics of Criminal Law' in L Zedner & J Roberts (eds), *Principles and Values in Criminal Law and Criminal Justice* (Oxford: Oxford University Press) pp.19–36.

Lacey, N (2013), 'Institutionalizing Responsibility' *Jurisprudence*, 4: 1–19.

Lacey, N (2013), 'What Constitutes Criminal Law?' in RA Duff, L Farmer, SE Marshall, M Renzo, & V Tadros (eds), *The Constitution of the Criminal Law* (Oxford: Oxford University Press) pp.12–29.

Lacey, N, Wells, C, & Quick, O (2010), *Reconstructing Criminal Law. Text and Materials* (4th edn, C Wells & O Quick) (Cambridge: Cambridge University Press).

Lambert, TB (2012), 'Theft, Homicide and Crime in Late Anglo–Saxon Law' *Past and Present*, 214: 3–43.

Lamond, G (2007), 'What is a Crime?' *Oxford Journal Of Legal Studies*, 27: 609–632.

Landau, N (1999), 'Indictment for Fun and Profit: A Prosecutor's Reward at Eighteenth-Century Quarter Sessions' *Law and History Review*, 17: 507–36.

Lang, ME (1924), *Codification in the British Empire and America* (Amsterdam: HJ Paris).

Langbein, J (1983), '*Albion's* Fatal Flaws' *Past and Present*, 27: 96–120.

Langbein, J (1999), *The Origins of the Adversary Criminal Trial* (Oxford: Oxford University Press).

Laski, HJ (1943), *Reflections on the Revolution of Our Time* (New York: Viking).

Laski, HJ (1948), *Liberty and the Modern State* (Revised edn) (London: Allen & Unwin).

Law Commission (1970), *Report on Offences of Damage to Property* (Rept. No.29) (London: HMSO).

Law Commission (1985), *Codification of the Criminal Law. A Report to the Law Commission* No.143 (HC.270) (London: HMSO).

Law Commission (1989), *A Criminal Code for England and Wales.* Vol. I *Report and Draft Criminal Code Bill* (No.177) (London: HMSO).

Law Commission (1992), *Legislating the Criminal Code. Offences Against the Person and General Principles* (Consultation Paper No.122) (London: HMSO).

Law Commission (1993), *Legislating the Criminal Code. Offences Against the Person and General Principles* (Report No.218) (Cm 2370) (London: HMSO).

Law Commission (1994), *Criminal Law. Consent and Offences against the Person* (Consultation Paper No.134) (London: HMSO).

Law Commission (1999), *Legislating the Criminal Code, Fraud and Deception* (Consultation Paper No.155) (London: HMSO).

Law Commission (2002), *Fraud* (Rept. No.276) (Cmnd.5560) (London: HMSO).

Law Commission (2005), *A New Homicide Act for England and Wales* (Consultation Paper No.217) (London: Stationery Office).

Law Commission (2008), *Tenth Programme of Law Reform* (No. 311) (London: HMSO).

Law Commission (2014), *Hate Crime. Should the Current Offences be Extended?* (Cm.8865) (Report No.348) (London: Stationery Office).

Law Commission (2014), *Reform of Offences Against the Person. A Scoping Consultation Paper* (No.217) (London: Stationery Office).

Leader-Elliott, I (2006), 'Benthamite Reflections on Codification of the General Principles of Criminal Liability: Towards the Panopticon' *Buffalo Criminal Law Review*, 9: 391–452.

Leader-Elliott, I (2010), 'A Critical Reading of RA Duff, *Answering for Crime*' *Adelaide Law Review*, 31: 47–78.

Lee, A (2015), 'Public Wrongs and the Criminal Law' *Criminal Law and Philosophy*, 9: 155–170.

Lenman B & Parker G (1980), 'The State, the Community and the Criminal Law in Early Modern Europe' in VAC Gatrell, B Lenman, & G Parker (eds), *Crime and the Law* (London: Europa) pp.11–48.

Levin, M (2004), *JS Mill on Civilization and Barbarism* (London: Routledge).
Lévitt, A (1922), 'Some Societal Aspects of the Criminal Law' *Journal of the American Institute of Criminal Law and Criminology*, 13: 90–104.
Lévitt, A (1925), 'Jurisdiction over Crimes: I The Territorial Commission Theory' *Journal of the American Institute of Criminal Law and Criminology*, 16: 316–59.
Lévitt, A (1926), 'Jurisdiction over Crimes- II' *Journal of the American Institute of Criminal Law and Criminology*, 16: 495–518.
Lichbach, M and Seligman, A (2000), *Market and Community. The Basis of Social Order, Revolution and Relegitimation* (University Park, PA: Pennsylvania State University Press).
Lieberman, D (1989), *The Province of Legislation Determined. Legal Theory in Eighteenth-Century Britain* (Cambridge: Cambridge University Press).
Lieberman, D (2002), 'Mapping Criminal Law: Blackstone and the Categories of English Jurisprudence' in N Landau (ed.), *Law, Crime and English Society, 1660–1830* (Cambridge: Cambridge University Press) pp.139–65.
Loader, I and Walker, N (2007), *Civilizing Security* (Cambridge: Cambridge University Press).
Lobban, M (1991), *The Common Law and English Jurisprudence, 1760–1850* (Oxford: Oxford University Press).
Lobban, M (2004), 'Chitty, Joseph, the elder (1775–1841)' in the *Oxford Dictionary of National Biography* (Oxford: Oxford University Press) [www.oxforddnb.com/view/article/5336, accessed 4 October 2010].
Lobban, M (2010), 'Theories of Law and Government' in W Cornish, JS Anderson, R Cocks, M Lobban, P Polden, & KJM Smith (eds), *Oxford History of the Laws of England*. Vol.X *1820–1914 English Legal System* (Oxford: Oxford University Press).
Locke J (1690), *Second Treatise on Government* (https://ebooks.adelaide.edu.au/l/locke/john/l81s/).
Locker, JP & Godfrey, B (2006), 'Ontological Boundaries and Temporal Watersheds in the Development of White Collar Crime' *British Journal of Criminology*, 46: 976–92.
Lockwood, M (2013), 'From Treason to Homicide: Changing Conceptions of the Law of Petty Treason in Early Modern England' *Journal of Legal History*, 34: 31–49.
Loughnan, A (2012), *Manifest Madness. Mental Incapacity in the Criminal Law* (Oxford: Oxford University Press).
Luddy, M (2013), 'Prostitution from 1800' in S Toulalan & K Fisher (eds), *The Routledge History of Sex and the Body, 1500 to the Present* (London: Routledge) pp.409–26.
Luhmann, N (1979), *Trust and Power* (New York: Wiley).
Luhmann, N (2004), *Law as A Social System* (Oxford: Oxford University Press).
MacCormick, N (1974), 'Law as Institutional Fact' *Law Quarterly Review*, 90: 102–29.
MacCormick, N (1990), 'Reconstruction after Deconstruction: A Response to CLS' *Oxford Journal of Legal Studies*, 10: 539–58.
MacCormick, N (2007), *Institutions of Law. An Essay in Legal Theory* (Oxford: Oxford University Press).
Macdonald, JHA (1867), *A Practical Treatise on the Criminal Law of Scotland* (Edinburgh: William Paterson).
McGowen, R (1983), 'The Image of Justice and Reform of the Criminal Law in Early Nineteenth-Century England' *Buffalo Law Review*, 32: 89–125.
McGowen, R (1999), 'From Pillory to Gallows: The Punishment of Forgery in the Age of the Financial Revolution' *Past and Present*, 165: 107–40.

McGowen, R (2002), 'Making the 'Bloody Code'? Forgery Legislation in Eighteenth-Century England' in N Landau (ed.) *Law, Crime and English Society 1660–1830* (Cambridge: Cambridge University Press) pp.117–38.

McGowen, R (2007), 'Cruel Inflictions and the Claims of Humanity in Early Nineteenth-Century England' in KD Watson (ed.), *Assaulting the Past. Violence and Civilization in Historical Context* (Cambridge: Cambridge Scholars Press) pp.38–57.

McGuire, M (2007), *Hypercrime. The New Geometry of Harm* (London: Routledge-Cavendish).

MacMillan, N (forthcoming 2016), 'Imagining the International: The Constitution of the International as a Site of Crime, Justice and Community' *Social and Leg Studies.*

McVeigh, S (ed.) (2007), *Jurisprudence of Jurisdiction* (London: Routledge-Cavendish).

McVeigh, S & Dorsett, S (2007), 'Questions of Jurisdiction' in S McVeigh (ed.), *Jurisprudence of Jurisdiction* (London: Routledge-Cavendish) pp.3–18.

Macaulay, TB (1867), 'Introductory Report upon the Indian Penal Code' in *Speeches and Poems* (New York: Riverside Press).

Macaulay, TB (1970), 'Government of India (10th July 1833)' in *Macaulay: Prose and Poetry* (Cambridge, Mass.: Harvard University Press).

Maguire, M (2012), 'Criminal Statistics and the Construction of Crime' in *Oxford Handbook of Criminology* (5th edn) (Oxford: Oxford University Press) Ch.8.

Manchester, C (1977), 'The Origins of Strict Criminal Liability' *Anglo-American Law Review*, 6: 277–83.

Mannheim, H (1946), *Criminal Justice and Social Reconstruction* (London: Kegan Paul).

Mannheim, H (1949), 'Two Reports on Sex Offences' *Modern Law Review*, 12: 488–93.

Mannheim, H (1950), *Social Aspects of Crime in England Between the Wars* (2nd edn) (London: George Allen & Unwin).

Mantena, K (2010), *Alibis of Empire. Henry Maine and the Ends of Liberal Imperialism* (Princeton: Princeton University Press).

Mar, M del & Bankowski, Z (eds) (2009), *Law as Institutional Normative Order* (Dartmouth: Ashgate).

Marron, D (2008), 'Alter Reality: Governing the Risk of Identity Theft' *British Journal of Criminology*, 48: 20–38.

Marshall, SE & Duff, RA (1998), 'Criminalization and Sharing Wrongs' *Canadian Journal of Law and Jurisprudence*, 11: 7–22.

Marx, K (2000), 'On the Jewish Question' in D McLellan (ed.), *Karl Marx. Selected Writings* (2nd edn) (Oxford: Oxford University Press) pp.46–70.

Matthews, R (ed.) (1989), *Privatizing Criminal Justice* (London: Sage).

May, AN (2006), *The Bar and the Old Bailey, 1750–1850* (Chapel Hill, NC:University of North Carolina Press).

Mead, F & Bodkin, AH (1885), *The Criminal Law Amendment Act 1885* (London, Shaw & Sons).

Melissaris, E (2007), 'The Concept of Appropriation and the Offence of Theft' *Modern Law Review*, 70: 581–97.

Melissaris, E (2012), 'Property Offences as Crimes of Injustice' *Criminal Law and Philosophy*, 6: 149–66.

Melissaris, E (2014), 'Theories of Crime and Punishment' in MD Dubber & T Hörnle (eds), *Oxford Handbook of Criminal Law* (Oxford: Oxford University Press) pp.355–78.

Merryman, JH (1985), *The Civil Law Tradition* (2nd edn) (Stanford: Stanford University Press).

Mill, JS (1836), 'Civilization' *London and Westminster Review*, 3: 1–28.

Mill, JS (1991), *On Liberty and other Essays* (ed John Gray) (Oxford: Oxford World Classics).

Mill, JS (1991), *Principles of Political Economy* in *Collected Works* Vol. 3. (London: Routledge & Kegan Paul).

Mill, JS (1991), 'The Subjection of Women' in *On Liberty and Other Essays* (ed. J Gray) (Oxford: Oxford University Press) pp.471–82.

Miller, J-A (1987), 'Jeremy Bentham's Panoptic Device' *October*, 41: 3–29.

Miller, W (2006), *An Eye for an Eye* (New York: Cambridge University Press).

Millie, A (2011), 'Value Judgments and Criminalization' *British Journal of Criminology* 51: 278–95.

Milsom, FSC (1981), 'The Nature of Blackstone's Achievement' *Oxford Journal of Legal Studies*, 1: 1–12.

Moore, M (1993), *Act and Crime* (Oxford: Oxford University Press).

Moore, M (1997), *Placing Blame* (Oxford: Oxford University Press).

Morrison, WD (1891), *Crime and its Causes* (London: Swan Sonnenschein & Co.).

Mort, F (2010), *Capital Affairs. London and the Making of the Permissive Society* (New Haven: Yale University Press).

Munro, VE (2007), 'Dev'l-in Disguise? Harm, Privacy and the Sexual Offences Act 2003' in VE Munro & CF Stychin (eds), *Sexuality and the Law. Feminist Engagements* (London: Glasshouse) pp.1–18.

Munro, VE (2014), 'Sexual Autonomy' in MD Dubber & T Hörnle (eds), *Oxford Handbook of Criminal Law* (Oxford: Oxford University Press) pp.747–67.

Murphy, WT (1998), *The Oldest Social Science. Configurations of Law and Modernity* (Oxford: Oxford University Press).

Naffine, N (2009), *Law's Meaning of Life. Philosophy, Religion, Darwin and the Legal Person* (Abingdon: Hart Publishing).

Neocleous, M (2000), *The Fabrication of Social Order. A Critical Theory of Police Power* (London: Pluto).

Neocleous, M (2008), *Critique of Security* (Edinburgh: Edinburgh University Press).

Neocleous, M. (2011), 'The Police of Civilization: The War on Terror as Civilizing Offensive' *International Political Sociology*, 5: 144–59.

Norberg, K (2013), 'The Body of the Prostitute: Medieval to Modern' in S Toulalan & K Fisher (eds), *The Routledge History of Sex and the Body, 1500 to the Present* (London: Routledge) pp.393–408.

Norrie, A (2014), *Crime, Reason and History. A Critical Introduction to Criminal Law*, (3rd edn) (Cambridge: Cambridge University Press).

Nuotio, K (2010), 'Theories of Criminalization and the Limits of Criminal Law: A Legal Cultural Approach' in RA Duff, L Farmer, SE Marshall, M Renzo, & V Tadros (eds), *The Boundaries of the Criminal Law* (Oxford: Oxford University Press) pp.238–62.

O'Malley, P (1992), 'Risk, Power and Crime Prevention' *Economy and Society*, 21: 252–75.

Oakeshott, M (1975), *Hobbes on Civil Association* (Oxford: Basil Blackwell).

Oakeshott, M (1975), *On Human Conduct* (Oxford: Oxford University Press).

Ogborn, M (1998), *Spaces of Modernity. London's Geographies 1680–1780* (London: Guilford Press).

Ohana, D (2014), 'Administrative Penalties in the Rechtstaat: On the Emergence of the *Ordnungswidrigkeit* Sanctioning System in Post-War Germany' *University of Toronto Law Journal*, 64: 243–90.

Ormerod, D (2007), 'The Fraud Act 2006—Criminalising Lying?' *Criminal Law Review*, 193–219.

Otter, S den (2007), '"A Legislating Empire": Victorian Political Theorists, Codes of Law, and Empire' in D Bell (ed.), *Victorian Visions of Global Order. Empire and Relations in Nineteenth-Century Political Thought* (Cambridge: Cambridge University Press) pp.89–112.

Oz-Salzberger, F (2001), 'Civil Society in the Scottish Enlightenment' in S Kaviraj & S Khilnani (eds), *Civil Society. History and Possibilities* (Cambridge: Cambridge University Press) pp.58–83.

Özsu, U (2009), 'De-territorializing and Re-territorializing *Lotus*: Sovereignty and Systematicity as Dialectical Nation-Building in Early Republican Turkey' *Leiden Journal of International Law*, 22: 29–49.

Paley, R (2007), 'Dragging the Law into Disrepute' in A Lewis, P Brand, & P Mitchell (eds), *Law in the City* (Dublin: Four Courts Press).

Pantazis, C (2008), 'The Problem with Criminalization' *Criminal Justice Matters*, 74: 10–12.

Pashukanis, EB (1977), *Law and Marxism* (London: Pluto Press).

Pennell, CR (2010), 'The Origins of the Foreign Jurisdiction Act and the Extension of British Sovereignty' *Historical Research*, 83: 465–85.

Petrow, S (1994), *Policing Morals. The Metropolitan Police and the Home Office, 1870–1914* (Oxford: Oxford University Press).

Pettit, P (2014), 'Criminalization in Republican Theory' in RA Duff, L Farmer, SE Marshall, M Renzo, & V Tadros (eds), *Criminalization. The Political Morality of the Criminal Law* (Oxford: Oxford University Press) pp.132–50.

Phillips, J (2012), 'A Low Law Counter-Treatise? "Absentees to" "Wreck" in British North America's First Justice of the Peace Manual' in MD Dubber & A Fernandez (eds), *Law Books in Action. Essays on the Anglo-American Legal Treatise* (Abingdon: Hart Publishing) pp.201–19.

Pike, LO (1876), *A History of Crime in England, illustrating the Changes of the Laws in the Progress of Civilisation* (2 vols.) (London: Smith, Elder & Co.).

Pirie, F (2013), *The Anthropology of Law* (Oxford: Oxford University Press).

Polden, P (2010), 'The Education of Lawyers' in W Cornish, JS Anderson, R Cocks, M Lobban, P Polden, & KJM Smith (eds), *Oxford History of the Laws of England.* Vol.X *1820–1914 English Legal System* (Oxford: Oxford University Press) pp.175–222.

Pollock, FE (1885), 'The King's Peace' *Law Quarterly Review*, 1: 37–50.

Pollock, F & Maitland, FW (1898), *The History of English Law before the Time of Edward I* (2 vols) (2nd edn) (Cambridge: Cambridge University Press).

Porter, R (1986), 'Rape—Does it have a historical meaning?' in R Porter & S Tomaselli (eds), *Rape. An Historical and Cultural Enquiry* (Oxford: Blackwell) pp.216–36.

Pound, R (1921), 'The Future of the Criminal Law' *Columbia Law Review*, 21: 1–16.

Pound, R (1930), *Criminal Justice in America* (New York: Henry Holt & Co).

Rabin, D (2005), 'Drunkenness and Responsibility for Crime in the Eighteenth Century' *Journal of British Studies*, 44: 457–77.

Radbruch, G (2014), 'The Origin of Criminal Law in the Status of the Unfree' in MD Dubber (ed.), *Foundational Texts in Modern Criminal Law* (Oxford: Oxford University Press) pp.407–14.

Radzinowicz, L (1948–84), *A History of English Criminal Law and its Administration* (5 Vols.) (London: Stevens).

Radzinowicz, L (1957), *Sexual Offences. A Report of the Cambridge Department of Criminal Science* (London: Macmillan).

Radzinowicz, L & Hood, R (1986), *A History of English Criminal Law and its Administration.* Vol V. *The Emergence of Penal Policy* (London: Steven & Sons).

Radzinowicz L & Turner, JWC (1945), *The Modern Approach to Criminal Law* (London: Macmillan).

Ramsay, P (2006), 'The Responsible Subject as Citizen: Criminal Law, Democracy and the Welfare State' *Modern Law Review*, 69: 29–58.

Ramsay, P (2011), 'Preparation Offences, Security Interests, Political Freedom' in RA Duff, L Farmer, SE Marshall, M Renzo, & V Tadros (eds), *The Structures of the Criminal Law* (Oxford: Oxford University Press) pp.203–28.

Ramsay, P (2012), *The Insecurity State. Vulnerable Autonomy and the Right to Security in the Criminal Law* (Oxford: Oxford University Press).

Ray, L (2013), 'Mark of Cain: Shame, Desire and Violence' *European Journal of Social Theory*, 16: 292–309.

Reemtsma, J-P (2012), *Trust and Violence. An Essay on a Modern Relationship* (Princeton, NJ: Princeton University Press).

Reiner, R (2007), *Law and Order. An Honest Citizen's Guide to Crime Control* (Cambridge: Polity).

Reiner, R (2010), 'Citizenship, Crime, Criminalization. Marshalling a Social Democratic Perspective' *New Criminal Law Review*, 13: 241–61.

Renzo, M (2011), 'Responsibility and Answerability in the Criminal Law' in RA Duff, L Farmer, SE Marshall, M Renzo, & V Tadros (eds), *The Structures of the Criminal Law* (Oxford: Oxford University Press) pp.209–36.

Reports to the Secretary of State for the Home Department on the State of the Law Relating to Brutal Assaults (1875), (C.1138) (London: HMSO).

Report of the Royal Commission appointed to consider the Law Relating to Indictable Offences (1879), (C.2345) (London: HMSO).

Report of the House of Lords Select Committee on the Law Relating to the Protection of Young Girls (1882) (London: HMSO).

Report of the Departmental Committee on Sexual Offences against Young Persons (1925), (Cmd.2561) (London: HMSO).

Report of the Committee on Homosexual Offences and Prostitution (1957), (Cmnd.267) (London: HMSO).

Ripstein, A (2006), 'Beyond the Harm Principle' *Philosophy and Public Affairs*, 34: 215–45.

Ristroph, A (2014), 'Hobbes on "Diffidence" and the Criminal Law' in MD Dubber (ed.), *Foundational Texts in Modern Criminal Law* (Oxford: Oxford University Press) pp.23–38.

Roberts, MJD (2004), *Making English Morals. Voluntary Association and Moral Reform in England, 1787–1886* (Cambridge: Cambridge University Press).

Roberts, S (2005), 'After Government?: On Representing Law without the State' *Modern Law Review*, 68: 1–24.

Robinson, PH & Grall, JA (1983), 'Element Analysis in Defining Criminal Liability: The Model Penal Code and Beyond' *Stanford Law Review*, 35: 681–762.

Robinson, PH & Dubber, MD (2007), 'The American Model Penal Code: A Brief Overview' *New Criminal Law Review*, 10: 319–41.

Rock, P (forthcoming), 'The Reform of Homosexual Offences' (Official History of the Home Office (London: HMSO))

Rodensky, L (2003), *The Crime in Mind. Criminal Responsibility and the Victorian Novel* (Oxford: Oxford University Press).

Ross, H (2001), *Law as a Social Institution* (Oxford: Hart Publishing).

Rowbotham, J (2000), '"Only When Drunk": The Stereotyping of Violence in England, c.1850–1900' in S d'Cruze (ed.), *Everyday Violence in Britain. 1850–1950. Gender and Class* (Harlow: Pearson) pp.155–69.
Roy, S (1967), 'Law Reform and the Reform of the Law of Theft' *Modern Law Review*, 30: 609–84.
Ruggles-Brise, E (1921), *The English Prison System* (London: Macmillan).
Rundle, K (2012), *Forms Liberate: Reclaiming the Jurisprudence of Lon L Fuller* (Oxford: Hart Publishing).
Russell, WO (1819), *A Treatise on Crimes and Indictable Misdemeanors* (London: J Butterworth).
Russell, WO (1826), *A Treatise on Crimes and Indictable Misdemeanors* (2nd edn) (London: J Butterworth).
Russell, WO (1843), *A Treatise on Crimes and Misdemeanours* (3rd edn, ed. CS Greaves) (London: Saunders & Benning).
Ryngaert, C (2008), *Jurisdiction in International Law* (Oxford: Oxford University Press).
Sayre, FB (1933), 'Public Welfare Offences' *Columbia Law Review*, 33: 55–88.
Scheppele, KL (2010), 'The International Standardization of National Security Law' *Journal of National Security Law and Policy*, 4: 437–53.
Schneider, E (1994), 'The Violence of Privacy' in MA Fineman & R Mykitiuk (eds), *The Public Nature of Private Violence* (New York: Routledge) pp.36–58.
Scottish Law Commission, *Report on Rape and Other Sexual Offences* (No.209) (2007) (Edinburgh: Stationery Office).
Scoular, J & Munro, V (2013), 'Harm, Vulnerability and Citizenship: Constitutional Concerns in the Criminalization of Contemporary Sex Work' in RA Duff, L Farmer, SE Marshall, M Renzo, & V Tadros (eds), *The Constitution of Criminal Law* (Oxford: Oxford University Press) pp.30–52.
Scraton, P (2007), *Power, Conflict and Criminalisation* (London: Routledge).
Searle, GR (1998), *Morality and the Market in Victorian Britain* (Oxford: Oxford University Press).
Seo, S (2013), 'Antinomies and the Automobile: A New Approach to Criminal Justice Histories' *Law and Social Inquiry*, 38: 1020–40.
Sharpe, J (1985), 'The History of Violence in England: Some Observations' *Past and Present*, 108: 206–15.
Shute, S (2002), 'Appropriation and the Law of Theft' *Criminal Law Review*, 445–58.
Shute, S (2004), 'The Sexual Offences Act 2003: (4) New Civil Preventative Orders—sexual offences prevention orders; foreign travel orders; risk of sexual harm orders' *Criminal Law Review*, 417–40.
Siedentop, L (2014), *Inventing the Individual. The Origins of Western Liberalism* (London: Penguin).
Simester, AP (ed.) (2005), *Appraising Strict Liability* (Oxford: Oxford University Press).
Simester, AP and von Hirsch, A (2011), *Crimes, Harms and Wrongs. On the Principles of Criminalisation* (Oxford: Hart Publishing).
Simester, AP & Shute, S (2002), 'On the General Part in Criminal Law' in AP Simester & S Shute (eds), *Criminal Law Theory: Doctrines of the General Part* (Oxford: Oxford University Press) pp.1–12.
Simester, AP, Spencer, JR, Sullivan, GR, & Virgo, GJ (2013), *Simester and Sullivan's Criminal Law. Theory and Doctrine* (5th edn) (Oxford: Hart Publishing).

Simester, AP & Sullivan, GR (2005), 'On the Nature and Rationale of Property Offences' in RA Duff & SP Green (eds), *Defining Crimes. Essays on the Special Part of the Criminal Law* (Oxford: Oxford University Press) pp.169–95.

Simpson, AE (1986), 'The "Blackmail Myth" and the Prosecution of Rape and its Attempt in 18th Century London: The Creation of a Legal Tradition' *Journal of Criminal Law and Criminology*, 77: 101–50.

Simpson, AE (1987), 'Vulnerability and the Age of Female Consent: Legal Innovation and its Effect on Prosecutions for Rape in Eighteenth-Century London' in GS Rousseau & R Porter (eds), *Sexual Underworlds of the Enlightenment* (Manchester: Manchester University Press) pp.185–201.

Simpson, AE (1996), '"The Mouth of Strange Women is a Deep Pit": Male Guilt and Legal Attitudes Towards Prostitution in Georgian London' *Journal of Criminal Justice and Popular Culture*, 4: 50–79.

Simpson, AE (2004), 'Popular Perceptions of Rape as a Capital Crime in Eighteenth-Century England: The Press and the Trial of Francis Charteris in the Old Bailey, February 1730' *Law and History Review*, 22: 27–70.

Simpson, AE (2006), 'The Ordeal of St Sepulchre's: A Campaign against Organised Prostitution in Early Nineteenth Century London and the Emergence of Lower Middle-class Consciousness' *Social and Legal Studies*, 15: 363–87.

Simpson, AWB (1981), 'The Rise and Fall of the Legal Treatise: Legal Principles and the Forms of Legal Literature' *University of Chicago Law Review*, 48: 632–79.

Skinner, S (2011), 'Tainted Law?: The Italian Penal Code, Fascism and Democracy' *International Journal of Law in Context*, 7: 423–46.

Sklansky, D (2006), 'Private Police and Democracy' *American Criminal Law Review*, 43: 89–105.

Slater, S (2012), 'Lady Astor and the Ladies of the Night: The Home Office, the Metropolitan Police and the Politics of the Street Offences Committee, 1927–8' *Law and History Review*, 30: 533–73.

Smith, A (1978), *Lectures on Jurisprudence* (ed R Meek, DD Raphael & P Stein) (Oxford: Oxford University Press).

Smith, A (2009), *The Theory of Moral Sentiments* (ed. RP Hanley) (London: Penguin).

Smith, ATH (1986), 'Codification of the Criminal Law (1): The Case for a Code' *Criminal Law Review*, 285–91.

Smith, BP (2005), 'The Presumption of Guilt and the English Law of Theft, 1750–1850' *Law and History Review*, 23: 133–71.

Smith, FB (1976), 'Labouchère's Amendment to the Criminal Law Amendment Bill' *Historical Studies*, 17: 165–73.

Smith, GT (2008), 'Violent Crime and the Public Weal in England, 1700–1900' in R McMahon (ed.), *Crime, Law and Popular Culture in Europe, 1500–1900* (Cullompton: Willan) pp.190–218.

Smith, JC (1998), 'Offences against the Person: the Home Office Consultation Paper' *Criminal Law Review*, 317–22.

Smith, JC & Hogan, B (1965), *Criminal Law* (London: Butterworths).

Smith, KJM (1988), *Sir James Fitzjames Stephen* (Cambridge: Cambridge University Press).

Smith, KJM (1998), *Lawyers, Legislators and Theorists. Developments in English Criminal Jurisprudence, 1800–1957* (Oxford: Oxford University Press).

Smith, KJM (2004), 'Russell, Sir William Oldnall (c.1784–1833)' in *Oxford Dictionary of National Biography* (Oxford: Oxford University Press) [www.oxforddnb.com/view/article/24354, accessed 2 October 2010].

Smith, KJM (2010), 'Offences Against the Person' in W Cornish, JS Anderson, R Cocks, M Lobban, P Polden, & KJM Smith (eds), *Oxford History of the Laws of England*. Vol. XIII *1820–1914 Fields of Development* (Oxford: Oxford University Press) pp.409–63.

Smith, KJM (2010), 'Protecting Property from Dishonesty and Harm' in W Cornish, JS Anderson, R Cocks, M Lobban, P Polden, & KJM Smith (eds), *Oxford History of the Laws of England*. Vol. XIII *Fields of Development* (Oxford: Oxford University Press) pp.375–91.

Spencer, J (2004), 'The Sexual Offences Act 2003: (2) Child and Family Offences' *Criminal Law Review*, 347–60.

Spierenburg, P (2008), *A History of Murder. Personal Violence in Europe from the Middle Ages to the Present* (Cambridge: Polity).

Spierenberg, P (2013), *Violence and Punishment. Civilizing the Body through Time* (Cambridge: Polity).

Squires. P & Lea, J (2012), *Criminalisation and Advanced Marginality: critically exploring the work of Loïc Wacquant* (Bristol: The Policy Press).

Stallybrass, W (1933), 'Public Mischief' *Law Quarterly Review*, 49: 183–91.

Stallybrass, W (1936), 'The Eclipse of Mens Rea' *Law Quarterly Review*, 52: 60–7.

Stanton-Ife, J (2013), 'Criminalising Conduct with Special Reference to Potential Offences of Stirring up Hatred against Disabled or Transgender Persons' (http://lawcommission.justice.gov.uk/docs/Hate_Crime_Theory-Paper_Dr-John-Stanton-Ife.pdf).

Stark, E (2007), *Coercive Control. How Men Entrap Women in Personal Life* (Oxford: Oxford University Press).

Starkie, T (1814), *A Treatise on Criminal Pleading* (London: W Clarke & Sons).

Stead, WT (2007), *The Maiden Tribute of Modern Babylon. The Report of the Secret Commission* (ed. with Introduction by AE Simpson) (Lambertville: True Bill Press).

Steel A (2008), 'Problematic and Unnecessary? Issues with the Use of the Theft Offence to Protect Intangible Property' *Sydney Law Rev*, 30: 575–614.

Stephen, JF (1863), *A General View of the Criminal Laws of England* (London: Macmillan).

Stephen, JF (1873), *Liberty, Equality and Fraternity* (New York: Holt & Williams).

Stephen, JF (1883), *History of the Criminal Law of England* (3 vols) (London: Macmillan).

Stephen, JF (1887), *A Digest of the Criminal Law* (4th edn) (London: Macmillan).

Stern, S (2014), 'Blackstone's Criminal Law: Common Law Harmonization and Legislative Reform (1769)' in MD Dubber (ed.), *Foundational Texts in Modern Criminal Law* (Oxford: Oxford University Press) pp.61–78.

Stevenson, K (2000), 'Legal and Public Perceptions of Sexual Violence' in S d'Cruze (ed.), *Everyday Violence in Britain. Gender and Class* (London: Longman) pp.89–103.

Stewart, H (2010), 'The Limits of the Harm Principle' *Criminal Law and Philosophy*, 4: 17–35.

Stone, L (1983), 'Interpersonal Violence in English Society, 1300–1980' *Past and Present*, 101: 22–33.

Strawson, P (1993), 'Freedom and Resentment' in J Fischer & M Ravizza (eds), *Perspectives on Moral Responsibility* (Ithaca: Cornell University Press) pp.45–66.

Sugarman, D (1986), 'Legal Theory, the Common Law Mind and the Making of the Textbook Tradition' in W Twining (ed.), *Legal Theory and Common Law* (Oxford: Blackwell) pp.26–62.

Suk, J (2006), 'Criminal Law Comes Home' *Yale Law Journal*, 116: 2–70.

Suk, J (2013), '"The Look in his Eyes": The Story of *Rusk* and Rape Reform' in D Coker & R Weisberg (eds), *Criminal Law Stories* (New York: Foundation Press) pp.171–211.

Sullivan, C (2009), 'Is Identity Theft Really Theft?' *International Review of Law, Computers and Technology*, 23: 77–87.

Sullivan, R & Dennis, I (eds) (2012), *Seeking Security. Pre-empting the Commission of Criminal Harms* (Oxford: Hart Publishing).

Supiot, A (2007), *Homo Juridicus. On the Anthropological Function of the Law* (London: Verso).

Supiot, A (2012), *The Spirit of Philadelphia* (London: Verso).

Tadros, V (2005), *Criminal Responsibility* (Oxford: Oxford University Press).

Tadros, V (2005), 'The Distinctiveness of Domestic Abuse: A Freedom-Based Account' in RA Duff & S Green (eds), *Defining Crimes. Essays on the Special Part of the Criminal Law* (Oxford: Oxford University Press) pp.119–42.

Tadros, V (2006), 'The Homicide Ladder' *Modern Law Review*, 69: 601–18.

Tadros, V (2008), 'Crime and Security' *Modern Law Review*, 71: 940–70.

Tadros, V (2009), 'Institutions and Aims' in M de Mar & Z Bankowski (eds), *Law as Institutional Normative Order* (Dartmouth: Ashgate) pp.83–102.

Tadros, V (2012), 'Fair Labelling and Social Solidarity' in L Zedner & JV Roberts (eds), *Principles and Values in Criminal Law and Criminal Justice* (Oxford: Oxford University Press) pp.67–80.

Taylor, C (1989), *Sources of the Self. The Making of the Modern Identity* (Cambridge. Mass.: Harvard University Press).

Taylor, C (2004), *Modern Social Imaginaries* (Durham, NC: Duke University Press).

Taylor, J (2013), *Boardroom Scandal. The Criminalization of Company Fraud in Nineteenth Century Britain* (Oxford: Oxford University Press).

Taylor, WC (1839), 'Moral Economy of Large Towns. Crime and Punishment' *Bentley's Miscellany*, 6: 476–82.

Temkin, J (1987), *Rape and the Legal Process* (London: Sweet & Maxwell).

Temkin, J & Ashworth, A (2004), 'The Sexual Offences Act 2003: (1) Rape, Sexual Assaults and the Problems of Consent' *Criminal Law Review*, 328–46.

Thompson, EP (1977), *Whigs and Hunters. The Origin of the Black Act* (Harmondsworth: Penguin).

Thorburn, M (2011), 'Constitutionalism and the Limits of the Criminal Law' in RA Duff, L Farmer, SE Marshall, M Renzo, & V Tadros (eds), *The Structures of the Criminal Law* (Oxford: Oxford University Press) pp.85–105.

Thornhill, C (2014), 'Guilt and the Origins of Modern Law' *Economy and Society*, 43: 103–35.

Tigar, M (1984), 'The Right of Property and the Law of Theft' *Texas Law Review*, 62: 1443–75.

La Torre, M (2010), *Law as Institution* (Dordrecht: Springer).

Toulalan, S & Fisher, K (eds) (2013), *The Routledge History of Sex and the Body, 1500 to the Present* (London: Routledge).

Trickett, W (1906), 'The Original Package Ineptitude' *Columbia Law Review* 6: 161–74.

Trumbach, R (1998), *Sex and the Gender Revolution. Heterosexuality and the Third Gender in Enlightenment London*, Vol.I. (Chicago: Chicago University Press).

Turner, JWC (1939–41), 'Middleton's Case and the Larceny Act 1916' *Cambridge Law Journal*, 7: 337–53.

Turner, JWC (1948), 'The Mental Element in Crimes at Common Law' in L Radzinowicz & JWC Turner (eds), *The Modern Approach to Criminal Law* (London: Macmillan) pp.195–261.

Turner, JWC (1948), 'Two Cases of Larceny' in L Radzinowicz & JWC Turner, *The Modern Approach to Criminal Law* (London: Macmillan) pp.356–89.

Turner, JWC (1958), *Russell on Crime* (11th edn) (London: Stevens & Sons).

Turner, JWC (1966), *Kenny's Outlines of Criminal Law* (19th edn) (Cambridge: Cambridge University Press).

Twining, W (1994), *Blackstone's Tower. The English Law School* (London: Sweet & Maxwell).

Ülvang, M (2009), 'Criminal Law and Public Peace' in M del Mar & Z Bankowski (eds), *Law as Institutional Normative Order* (Dartmouth: Ashgate) pp.131–44.

Valverde, M (1996), '"Despotism" and Ethical Liberal Governance' *Economy and Society*, 25: 357–72.

Valverde, M (1998), *Diseases of the Will. Alcohol and the Dilemmas of Freedom* (Cambridge: Cambridge University Press).

Valverde, M (2006), '"Peace, Order and Good Government": Policelike Powers in Postcolonial Perspective' in MD Dubber & M Valverde (eds), *The New Police Science* (Stanford: Stanford University Press) pp.73–106.

Valverde, M (2009), 'Jurisdiction and Scale: Legal "Technicalities" as Resources for Theory' *Social and Legal Studies*, 18: 139–57.

Valverde, M (2014), 'Studying the Governance of Crime and Security: Space, Time and Jurisdiction' *Criminology and Criminal Justice*, 14: 379–91.

Veitch, K (2007), *The Jurisdiction of Medical Law* (Dartmouth: Ashgate).

Veitch, S (2007), *Law and Irresponsibility. On the Legitimation of Human Suffering.* (London: Routledge-Cavendish).

Wacquant, L (2009), *Punishing the Poor. The Neo-Liberal Government of Social Insecurity* (Durham, NC: Duke University Press).

Wacquant, L (2014), 'Marginality, Ethnicity and Penality: A Bourdieusian Perspective on Criminalization' in RA Duff, L Farmer, SE Marshall, M Renzo, & V Tadros (eds), *Criminalization. The Political Morality of the Criminal Law* (Oxford: Oxford University Press) pp.270–90.

Waddams, S (2012), 'Nineteenth-Century Treatises on English Contract Law' in MD Dubber & A Fernandez (eds), *Law Books in Action. Essays on the Anglo-American Legal Treatise* (Oxford: Hart Publishing) pp.127–44.

Waites, M (2005), *The Age of Consent. Young People, Sexuality and Citizenship* (London: Palgrave Macmillan).

Walker, G (1998), 'Rereading Rape and Sexual Violence in Early Modern England' *Gender and History*, 10: 1–25.

Walker, G (2013), 'Rape, Acquittal and Culpability in Popular Crime Reports in England, c.1670–1750' *Past and Present*, 220: 115–42.

Walker, G (2013), 'Sexual Violence and Rape, 1500–1750' in S Toulalan & K Fisher (eds), *The Routledge History of Sex and the Body, 1500 to the Present* (London: Routledge) pp.429–43.

Walklate, S (2008), 'What is to be done about Violence against Women? Gender, Violence, Cosmopolitanism and the Law' *British Journal of Criminology*, 48: 39–54.

Walkowitz, J (1980), *Prostitution and Victorian Society* (Cambridge: Cambridge University Press).

Walkowitz, J (1992), *City of Dreadful Delight. Narratives of Sexual Danger in Late-Victorian London* (London: Virago).

Watson, KD (ed.) (2007), *Assaulting the Past. Violence and Civilization in Historical Context* (Cambridge: Cambridge Scholars Press).

Waugh, B & Manning, HE (1886), 'The Child of the English Savage' *Contemporary Review* (Jan) 687–700.

Weait, M (2007), *Intimacy and Responsibility. The Criminalisation of HIV Transmission* (London: Routledge-Cavendish).

Weber, M (1948), 'Politics as Vocation' in H Gerth & CW Mills (eds), *From Max Weber. Essays in Sociology* (London: Routledge) pp.77–128.

Weber, M (1978), *Economy and Society* (Berkeley, CA: University of California Press).

Wechsler, H (1952), 'The Challenge of a Model Penal Code' *Harvard Law Review*, 65: 1097–133.

Weeks, J (2012), *Sex, Politics and Society. The Regulation of Sexuality since 1800* (3rd edn) (London: Routledge).

Weinberger, O (1991), *Law, Institution and Legal Politics* (Dordrecht: Kluwer).

Weinreb, L (1980), 'Manifest Criminality, Criminal Intent, and the "Metamorphosis of Larceny"' *Yale Law Journal*, 90: 294–318.

Weiss, G (2000), 'The Enchantment of Codification in the Common Law World' *Yale Journal of International Law*, 25: 435–532.

West, DJ (1974), 'Thoughts on Sex Law Reform' in R Hood (ed.), *Crime, Criminology and Public Policy. Essays in Honour of Sir Leon Radzinowicz* (London: Heinemann).

Weyrauch, WO (2007), 'The Experience of Lawlessness' *New Criminal Law Review*, 4: 415–40.

Whitman, JQ (1995), 'At the Origins of Law and the State: Supervision of Violence, Mutilation of Bodies, or Setting of Prices' *Chicago-Kent Law Review*, 71: 41–84.

Wiener, M (1990), *Reconstructing the Criminal. Culture, Law and Policy in England, 1830–1914* (Cambridge: Cambridge University Press).

Wiener, M (2004), *Men of Blood. Violence, Manliness and Criminal Justice in Victorian England* (Cambridge: Cambridge University Press).

Williams, G (1945), 'Language and the Law' *Law Quarterly Review* 61: 71–86, 179–95, 293–303, 384–406.

Williams, G (ed.) (1951), *The Reform of the Law* (London: Victor Gollancz).

Williams, G (1952), 'Case Note: Walters v Lunt (1951)' *Modern Law Review*, 15: 222–3.

Williams, G (1953), *Criminal Law. The General Part* (2nd edn 1961) (London: Stevens and Sons).

Williams, G (1955), 'The Definition of Crime' *Current Legal Problems*, 8: 107–30.

Williams, G (1957–8), 'The Reform of the Criminal Law and of its Administration' *Journal of the Society of Public Teachers of Law*, 4: 217–30.

Williams, G (1961), 'Conspiring to Corrupt' *The Listener* (Aug 24th) 275.

Williams, G (1965), *The Mental Element in Crime* (Jerusalem: Magnes Press).

Williams, G (1965), 'Venue and the Ambit of Criminal Law' *Law Quarterly Review*, 81: 276–88, 395–421, 518–38.

Williams, G (1974–5), 'The Work of Criminal Law Reform' *Journal of the Society of Public Teachers of Law*, 13: 183–98.

Williams, G (1978), *Textbook on Criminal Law* (London: Steven & Sons) (2nd edn 1983).

Williams, G (1981), 'Temporary Appropriation Should be Theft' *Criminal Law Review*, 129–41.

Williams, G (1983), 'Convictions and Fair Labelling' *Cambridge Law Journal*, 42: 85–95.

Wilson, S (2006), 'Law, Morality and Regulation: Victorian Experiences of Financial Crime' *British Journal of Criminology*, 46: 1073–90.
Wilson, S (2014), *The Origins of Modern Financial Crime. Historical Foundations and Current Problems in Britain* (London: Routledge).
Wood, JC (2004), *Violence and Crime in Nineteenth Century England: The Shadow of Our Refinement* (London: Routledge).
Woolrych, H (1832), *History and Results of the Present Capital Punishments in England* (London: Saunders & Benning).
Wootton, B (1963), *Crime and the Criminal Law. Reflections of a Magistrate and Social Scientist* (London: Steven and Sons).
Wright, B (2008), 'Criminal Law, Codification and Imperial Projects. The Self-Governing Jurisdiction Codes of the 1890s' *Legal History*, 12: 19–49.
Wright, B (2011), 'Macaulay's Indian Penal Code: Historical Context and Originating Principles' in W-C Chan, B Wright, & S Yeo (eds), *Codification, Macaulay and the Indian Penal Code* (Dartmouth: Ashgate) pp.19–58.
Wright, B (2012), 'Renovate or Rebuild? Treatises, Digests and Criminal Law Codification' in MD Dubber & A Fernandez (eds), *Law Books in Action. Essays on the Anglo-American Legal Treatise* (Oxford: Hart Publishing) pp.181–201.
Wrong, D (1994), *The Problem of Order. What Unites and Divides Society* (Cambridge, Mass.: Harvard University Press).
Young, J (1999), *The Exclusive Society. Social Exclusion, Crime and Difference in Late Modernity* (London: Sage).
Zedner, L & Roberts, JV (2012), *Principles and Values in Criminal Law and Criminal Justice. Essays in Honour of Andrew Ashworth* (Oxford: Oxford University Press).
Zedner, L (2009), *Security* (London: Routledge).
Zedner, L (2010), 'Security, the State, and the Citizen: the Changing Architecture of Crime Control' *New Criminal Law Review*, 13: 379–403.

Index